GREENLAND

GREENLAND
SEA

BARENTS
SEA

KARA
SEA

NORWEGIAN
SEA

ICELAND

NORWAY
SWEDEN
FINLAND

UNION OF SOVIET SOCIALIST REPUBLICS

UNITED
KINGDOM DENMARK
IRELAND   NETH. W. E. POLAND
           GERMANY
           BELG.   CZECHOSLOVAKIA
                            HUNGARY
FRANCE AUSTRIA   ROMANIA
SWITZ.   YUGOSLAVIA
MONACO   BULGARIA
                ITALY   ALBANIA
PORTUGAL SPAIN   SYRIA
                   GREECE TURKEY   LEBANON
        MALTA

NORTH

ATLANTIC

BERMUDA

CYPRUS
ISRAEL

AFGHANISTAN

CHINA

MOROCCO TUNISIA
                      IRAQ   IRAN
                 JORDAN KUWAIT PAKISTAN
ALGERIA LIBYA EGYPT   QATAR
                      SAUDI
                      ARABIA

NEPAL
BHUTAN

OCEAN

HAMAS

WESTERN
SAHARA

UN.
ARAB
EMIRATES

INDIA

BANGLADESH
BURMA

HAITI DOMINICAN
       REPUBLIC
PUERTO VIRGIN ISLANDS
RICO   WEST INDIES
        TRINIDAD
        TOBAGO
ENEZUELA   GUYANA
                 SURINAM
MBIA   FR.
             GUIANA

MAURITANIA

MALI   NIGER   CHAD
                        SUDAN

YEMEN

OMAN

SO.
YEMEN

SENEGAL
GAMBIA
GUINEA BISSAU
GUINEA
SIERRA LEONE
LIBERIA
IVORY COAST
GHANA
TOGO
BENIN
CAMEROON
EQUAT.
GUINEA
GABON

UPPER
VOLTA

NIGERIA

CENTRAL
AFRICAN
REPUBLIC

ETHIOPIA

SRI
LANKA

CONGO

ZAIRE

UGANDA
KENYA

SOMALIA

RWANDA
BURUNDI

SEYCHELLES

BRAZIL

TANZANIA

INDIAN

BOLIVIA

ANGOLA

MALAWI

ZAMBIA

ZIMBABWE

MOZAMBIQUE

MADAGASCAR

OCEAN

MAURITIUS

PARAGUAY

SOUTH-WEST
AFRICA
(NAMIBIA)

BOTSWANA

SWAZILAND

SOUTH   LESOTHO
AFRICA

SOUTH

URUGUAY

ATLANTIC

CHILE
ARGENTINA

OCEAN

THE HUMAN MOSAIC

THE HUMAN MOSAIC

A Thematic Introduction to Cultural Geography

Third Edition

Terry G. Jordan

North Texas State University

Lester Rowntree

San José State University

HARPER & ROW, PUBLISHERS, New York
Cambridge, Philadelphia, San Francisco,
London, Mexico City, São Paulo, Sydney

1817

Sponsoring Editor: *Kathy Robinson*
Project Editor: *Cynthia L. Indriso*
Designer: *Frances Torbert Tilley*
Production Manager: *Willie Lane*
Photo Researcher: *Mira Schachne*
Compositor: *Black Dot, Inc.*
Printer and Binder: *The Murray Printing Company*
Art Studio: *J&R Art Services, Inc.*
Color Photo: *The town of Thera on the island of Santorini.*
  Photo by Terry G. Jordan, 1971.

THE HUMAN MOSAIC: A Thematic Introduction to Cultural Geography, Third Edition

Library of Congress Cataloging in Publication Data

Jordan, Terry G.
  The human mosaic.

  Includes bibliographies and index.
    1. Anthropo-geography. 2. Ethnology. I. Rowntree,
Lester, 1938-   . II. Title.
GF41.J67   1982   900   81-6968
ISBN 0-06-043461-9   AACR2

Acknowledgments and Credits

We gratefully acknowledge the use of the following photographs:

Chapter 1
German Information Center, pp. 3, 4; Culver Pictures, p. 5 (right); Myers/Afrique, p. 7; Luthy/de Wys, p. 8; Swedish Institute, p. 15; USDA, p. 20; de Wys, p. 23; American Airlines, p. 24 (right).

Chapter 2
Don Briggs/UNICEF, Danish Information Office, p. 32; Culver Pictures, p. 38 (left); David Margurian/UNICEF, p. 40; United Nations/ILO, p. 41; National Library of Ireland, p. 47; National Film Board of Canada, p. 48; Public Health Service, p. 59; B. C. McLean, p. 62 (bottom right).

Chapter 3
Philip Jon Bailey/Jeroboam, p. 68; Nets/Editorial Photocolor Archives, p. 71; Japan National Tourist Organization, p. 73; Novosti/Sovfoto, p. 75; USDA, p. 77; Holton/UNICEF, p. 79; Bettmann Archives, p. 92; U.S. Forest Service, p. 102.

Chapter 4
Peter Martens/Nancy Palmer Agency, p. 106; Swiss National Tourist Office, p. 108; NASA, p. 115; Henriques/Magnum, p. 119 (top); The National Archives, p. 131 (bottom); © Timothy Eagan, 1981/Woodfin Camp, Moore McCormack Lines/Monkmeyer, p. 134; USDA, p. 135.

Chapter 5
Rapho/Photo Researchers, p. 144; VIVA, p. 152 (bottom); Capa/Magnum, p. 153.

Chapter 6
© Bob Davis, 1979/Woodfin Camp, p. 167; Leonard von Matt/Rapho/Photo Researchers, p. 171; Vincent/AAA, p. 173; Franck/VIVA, p. 175; Dorha Raynor, de Wys, p. 182 (top); David Kennedy/Contact/de Wys, p. 194; Elliott Erwitt/Magnum, p. 195 (right); Wide World, p. 197; E. Ragazzini/FAO, p. 198 (top left).

Chapter 7
Strickler/Monkmeyer, p. 204; photo courtesy of Pennsylvania Dutch Tourist Bureau, p. 205; Wyatt/Philadelphia Museum of Art, Bettmann Archives, p. 208 (top); Beckwith, p. 209 (top); Earl Palmer/Monkmeyer, pp. 219, 223 (top); Carlson/Stock, Boston, p. 224; E. Pierson/FAO, p. 228 (top left).

Chapter 8
Hester and John Bonnell/de Wys, p. 239; de Wys, p. 243; Nancy Palmer Agency, p. 245; Beckwith, p. 248; © Watriss-Baldwin, 1980/Woodfin Camp, p. 250; Mimi Forsyth/Monkmeyer, p. 253; de Wys, p. 254; UPI, p. 255; Hulstein/de Wys, p. 258; de Wys, Van der wall/de Wys, p. 262; Bodin/Stock, Boston, p. 263.

Chapter 9
© Kroll/Taurus, p. 277.

Chapter 10
Manchester Public Library, p. 301; UPI, Paul Conklin/Monkmeyer, Fujihira/Monkmeyer, p. 303; Fritz Henle/Monkmeyer, p. 314; Rosenthal/de Wys, p. 317; Linares/Monkmeyer, p. 321; Michael Hardy/Woodfin Camp, p. 324 (bottom); Snark International, p. 327; Nancy Palmer Agency, p. 330 (middle); United Nations,

Contents

4 Political Patterns   106

5 The Babel of Languages   139

6 Religious Realms   167

7 The Geography of Folk Culture   204

8 The Geography of Popular Culture   239

9 Ethnic Geography   267

Preface

The Human Mosaic, Third Edition is intended as the basic text for a college-level, introductory course of one semester or one quarter in cultural or human geography. It is an outgrowth of a decade of our own experience in teaching cultural geography to college freshmen. We found that beginning students learned best when provided with a precise framework. They need to know, at any given time in the course, exactly how the material they are studying relates to the geographical whole. Most introductory textbooks, we felt, lacked such a framework. *The Human Mosaic* is structured around five themes: culture region, cultural diffusion, cultural ecology, cultural integration, and cultural landscape. These five themes are introduced and explained in the first chapter and serve as the framework for the topical chapters that follow. The student, at every point in *The Human Mosaic,* is able to relate to one of the five themes.

We do not claim to have invented this structure. Its roots run deep in cultural geography, as deep as Carl O. Sauer's "The Morphology of Landscape," August Meitzen's classic work on European settlement forms, Eduard Hahn's publications on agricultural origins and dispersals, and George Perkins Marsh's nineteenth-century writings on environmental modification. Much inspiration was derived from the innovative *Readings in Cultural Geography,* written in 1962 by Philip L. Wagner and Marvin W. Mikesell.

Nor do we propose that our framework is the only one possible. We can say, however, that in our own classroom experience we have found this approach highly successful. The enthusiastic reception enjoyed by the two previous editions of *The Human Mosaic* led us to believe that our thematic approach to cultural geography is educationally sound. Our culture region theme appeals to the student's natural human curiosity about the differences between places. The dynamic aspect of culture, particularly relevant to an age of incessant and rapid change, is conveyed through the theme of cultural diffusion. Students acquire an appreciation for how cultural traits spread—or don't spread—from place to place. The topics employed to illustrate the concepts of diffusion include many that the college student can quickly relate to: country-western music, football, and migration. Cultural ecology, also highly relevant in our age, is addressed to the complicated relationship between culture and the physical environment. Cultural integration permits the student to view culture as an interrelated whole, in which one facet acts upon and is acted upon by other facets. Lastly, the theme of cultural landscape heightens student awareness to visible expressions of different cultures. These five themes are applied to a variety of geographical topics: demography, agriculture, the city, religion, language, ethnicity, politics, industry, folklife, and popular culture.

The book offers a variety of special learning devices to motivate and assist the student. These include:

(1) A glossary at the end of each chapter, giving the student precise definitions of terms and concepts.
(2) Boxes scattered through each chapter, elaborating on concepts, presenting illustrative examples or case studies, and introducing famous geographic personalities who contributed to the rise of our discipline. Each box is interspersed with the text at an appropriate place.
(3) Extensive lists of suggested readings at the end of each chapter, of special value to superior students who may wish to probe more deeply into cultural geography on their own.
(4) Figure captions written to stimulate thinking; many captions ask questions intended to elicit a geographic response or to heighten geographic awareness. Illustrations are included for their instructional value rather than as mere decoration.

To assist the professor, Michael J. Libbee has prepared a totally new Instructor's Manual to accompany the third edition. It contains classroom exercises, elaborates on key points, contains audiovisual references for complementing films and slides, and suggests test questions that best examine textual concepts.

Combining a thematic approach with a wide variety of topics and learning devices, we believe, produces a disciplined approach to an inherently interesting and important subject. We are confident that the beginning student will develop an appreciation and understanding of our academic discipline from *The Human Mosaic.*

This third edition represents a modest revision of the award-winning second edition of 1979. Our goals in the revision have been to correct errors of fact, interpretation, or omission; to incorporate some suggestions for improvement made by numerous users of the second edition; to update statistical data; and to include findings contained in recently-published geographical research. Many maps have been revised, and some forty-odd new maps, sketches, and photographs appear in the third edition.

No textbook is written single-handedly (or even "double-handedly"). In particular, an introductory text covering a wide range of topics must draw heavily upon the research and help of others. We have not hesitated in the various chapters to mention by name a great many geographers whose work we drew upon. We apologize for any misinterpretations or oversimplifications of their findings that may have crept in due to our own error or to the limited space available. Numerous geographers have contributed advice, comments, ideas, and assistance as this book moved from outline to draft to first, second, and now third edition.

Special thanks go to: James P. Allen, California State University, Northridge; John Alwin, Montana State University; George Aspbury,

Illinois State University; John A. Carthew, Pierce College; Robert Christopherson, American River College; Richard D. Dastyck, Fullerton College; Larry Ford, San Diego State University; Sam B. Hilliard, Louisiana State University; Rex Honey, University of Iowa; Fred B. Kniffen, Louisiana State University; Ann Larimore, University of Michigan, Ann Arbor; George Lewis, Boston University; Michael Libbee, University of Oklahoma, Norman; Bonnie Loyd, *Landscape* Magazine; Risa Palm, University of Colorado; John Ressler, Central Washington University; John F. Rooney, Jr., Oklahoma State University; Christopher L. Salter, U.C.L.A.; James Scott, Western Washington University; James B. Sellers, Douglas College; Joseph Velikonja, University of Washington; Howard Vogel, Shoreline Community College; Philip L. Wagner, Simon Fraser University; and Wilbur Zelinsky, Pennsylvania State University. Of course, the authors remain fully responsible for any errors found within the text.

Our thanks, too, go to various members, past and present, of the staff at Harper & Row whose encouragement, skills, and suggestions have created a special working environment and to whom we express our deepest gratitude.

Terry G. Jordan
Lester Rowntree

The Nature of Cultural Geography

1

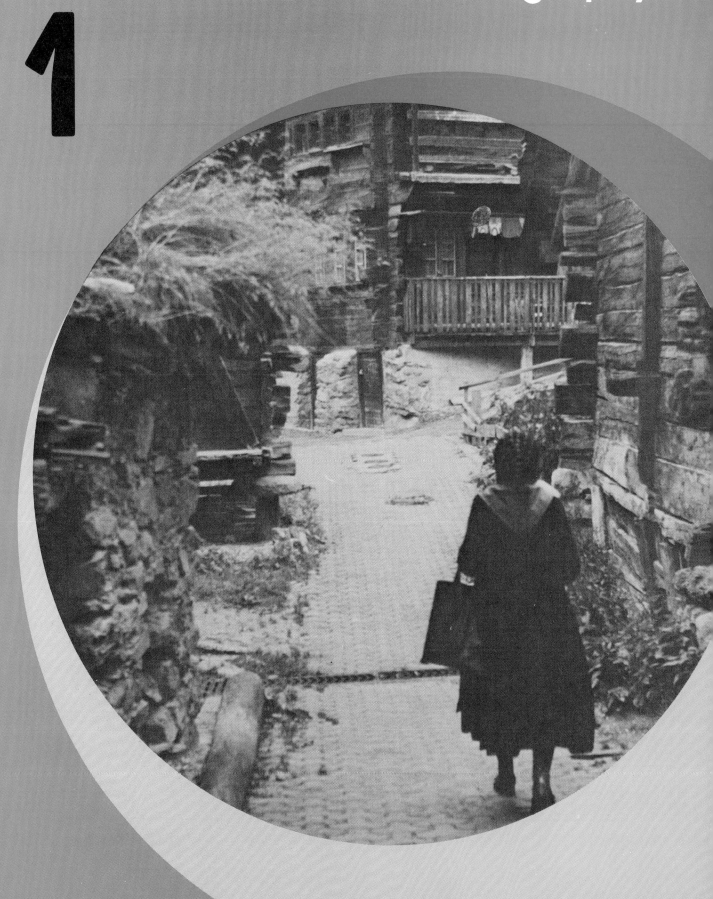

◄ *Chapter-opening photo:* A Swiss village in Canton Valais.

Humans are, by nature, geographers. Children create carefully mapped kingdoms in tiny spaces—a small room, a single backyard, a neighborhood (see box, "Sizing Up the World"). As we grow, our concepts of spatial relationships change constantly, gaining a partially magical quality. And always beyond what we have explored lies the unknown, the mysterious lands that we move into at our own peril and that we often populate with our fears and dreams. The academic discipline of geography is basically the product of human nature, of humans' ancient and insatiable curiosity about lands other than their own.

In time this natural curiosity was strengthened by the practical motives of traders and empire builders, who wanted information about the world for the purposes of commerce and conquest. It is not surprising, then, that "geography" first arose among the ancient Greeks and Romans, the former the greatest traders of their time and the latter the builders of one of the greatest empires in world history.

Initially, Greek and Roman geographers were most interested in practical knowledge. They cataloged factual information on locations, places, and products. But they were not content merely to chart and describe the known world. These ancient geographers soon began to ask questions about why cultures and environments differ from place to place. By the end of the Roman era, geographers had developed theories about the earth's roundness, latitudinal climate zones, environmental influences on humans and people's role in modifying the earth.

SIZING UP THE WORLD: THE MAPS CHILDREN DRAW

"In the Mission Hill area of Boston, . . . Florence Ladd asked a number of black children to draw a map of their area, and then she tape-recorded her conversation with them. On Dave's map, the Mission Hill project is where the white children live, and he has drawn it as the largest, completely blank area on his map. From his taped conversation it is clear that he is physically afraid of the area and has never ventured near it. On his map the white residential area is literally *terra incognita*, while all the detail on the map is immediately around his home and school on the other side of Parker Street.

Ernest also puts in Parker Street dividing his area from the white Mission [Hill] project, and uses about a quarter of his sheet of paper to emphasize, quite unconsciously, the width of this psychological barrier. Both of these boys going to the local neighborhood schools have never ventured across this barrier to the unknown area beyond."

From Peter Gould and Rodney White, Mental Maps *(Baltimore: Penguin, 1974), pp. 31–33. Maps from F. Ladd, "A Note on 'The World Across the Street'," Harvard School of Education Association Bulletin, 12 (1967), 47–48.*

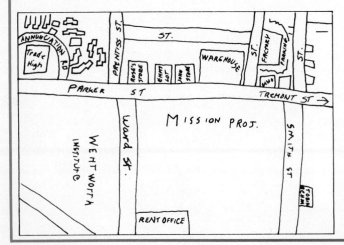

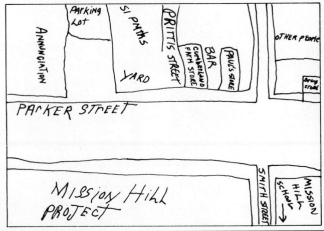

During Europe's Dark Ages, a newly expanding Arab empire took over academic geography. Muslim Arab scholars, following in the wake of trade and conquest as their Greek and Roman predecessors did, further expanded geographical knowledge. These Arab geographers were great travelers, ranging from China to Spain in search of new knowledge. Although they tended to be even more practical than the Greeks and Romans, they did not entirely ignore the theoretical side of learning. For example, Arab geographers proposed theories about the evolution of mountain ranges.

With the European cultural reawakening known as the Renaissance and the beginning of the Age of Discovery, the center of geographical learning shifted to Europe. The modern scientific study of geography arose in Germany during the seventeenth, eighteenth, and nineteenth centuries, at the same time that European power was slowly spreading over much of the globe. In the 1700s, the German philosopher and geographer Immanuel Kant (see biographical sketch) defined **geography** as the study of spatial patterns—that is, the differences and similarities between one place and another. Kant compared geography and history, because he recognized that both disciplines thrive on variations. Just as geographers emphasize the differences between areas, so historians emphasize the difference between periods of time. If every year were identical—and the same events occurred over and over again—no academic study of history would be needed. In the same way, if every place on earth were identical, we would not need geography. Fortunately, plenty of differences exist to provide ample fuel for both fields.

Let us extend Kant's comparison. When geographers consider the differences and similarities between places, or when historians study different points in time, they want to understand what they see. Historians compare two periods and try to find reasons for the change or lack of change from one period to the other. Geographers study spatial patterns in the same way. They first find out exactly what the variation between the areas is by describing differences and similarities as precisely as possible. Then they try to interpret the data and to decide what forces made these two areas different or alike. This process merely reflects the basic human curiosity that makes us all geographers. No one needs special training to wonder why things are where they are, and that is the geographer's key question. That question comes to us naturally in our everyday lives. Historians ask the questions What? When? and Why? Geographers ask What? Where? and Why? In both disciplines, Why? is the all-important question, because it leads to interpretations. This type of scientific, analytical geographic research was begun in the nineteenth century by the German geographers Alexander von Humboldt and Carl Ritter (see biographical sketches). As a result, they are generally recognized as the fathers of modern geography.

Another similarity between geographers and historians is the way they subdivide their disciplines. Historians divide time into manageable sections called periods: the Napoleonic period, the Civil War period, the Elizabethan period, and so on. The geographic equivalent of the period is the *region*, a subdivision of the earth. Examples of regional geography are the geography of Europe, of Latin America, or of California. Both periods and regions are characterized by certain unifying traits that justify picking them out of time and space.

Another way of dividing subject matter common to both geography and history is the *topical* or *systematic* method. Using this method, the

IMMANUEL KANT   1724-1804

Kant is best known as a philosopher, but he taught a course in physical geography between 1756 and 1798 at the University of Königsberg in East Prussia. Königsberg, today called Kaliningrad, was on the far edge of the Prussian state, much as Alaska is on the far edge of the United States. Kant brought international attention to this provincial German town and university. He organized geography into such categories as mathematical, "theological," commercial, political, and "moral" (an account of differing customs of peoples). In addition, he developed the distinction between geography and history described in the text. Kant defined geography as the study of spatial variations.

geographer or the historian singles out a certain topic rather than a period or region. A geographer might choose to study political geography, urban geography, or agricultural geography; a historian might select military history, agricultural history, or economic history. Within geography, the two principal topical divisions are physical and cultural geography. Each of these is, in turn, separated into smaller topical divisions. In this book, we use mainly a topical approach to cultural geography. However, as the "culture region" theme discussed later in this chapter indicates, the regional approach is not ignored.

Also like history, geography belongs as much to the humanities as to the social sciences. The humanistic branches of learning are those having mainly a cultural character, and many geographers regard themselves primarily as humanists. It is no accident that Immanuel Kant was both a philosopher and a geographer. The social sciences, by contrast, deal with the institutions and functions of human society. Cultural geographers with social science inclinations are concerned with the spatial functioning of society, humanistic cultural geographers with the spatial characteristics and interworkings of cultures. Both are necessary to the continued advancement of cultural geography; both help produce the distinctively geographic way of looking at, understanding, and appreciating the human world. Both approaches seek to know What? and Where? Both are analytical and seek the answer to Why? It is our aim in this textbook to teach you to see the human world through the geographer's eyes. If we succeed, you will have a new perspective of the world, a useful one, we believe. Analysis and answer-seeking are important, and we will show you how geographers solve problems. But equally important is the geographer's perspective of the world, a unique perspective that we regard as essential for any truly educated person.

What Is Cultural Geography?

The term **cultural geography** implies an emphasis on human cultures rather than on the physical environment they live in. To understand the scope of cultural geography, we must first agree on what the word **culture** means. Social scientists and humanists have suggested many definitions of culture, some broad and some narrow. Furthermore, even within some disciplines not all scholars agree on a common definition. For our purposes, we will define culture as a total way of life held in common by a group of people. Learned similarities in speech, behavior, ideology, livelihood, technology, value system, and society bind people together in a culture. Cultural geography, then, is the study of spatial variations among cultural groups and the spatial functioning of society. It focuses on describing and analyzing the ways language, religion, economy, government, and other cultural phenomena vary or remain constant from one place to another. Because cultures are formed by groups of people, the cultural geographer is necessarily concerned with humans in the aggregate. However, you should not make the mistake of assuming that the individual person is culturally unimportant or powerless. A culture, after all, is not an organism or an irresistible force compelling its members to behave in a certain way. At the most basic level, culture is simply people interacting with one other. An individual is therefore potentially able to modify the culture he or she shares with others. Partly for this reason, change is an ever-present cultural phenomenon.

ALEXANDER VON HUMBOLDT
1769-1859

Humboldt, a world-famous German scientist, traveled widely and wrote extensively on geographical topics. In 1797, with the permission of the Spanish crown, he sailed to South America. For the next five years, he explored from Mexico to the Andes. Later, at the age of sixty, he accepted an invitation from the czar of Russia to explore mineral resources. He traveled by carriage through Siberia, carefully recording and describing the landscape. His interests were in physical geography—the study of climate, terrain, and vegetation—but Humboldt's writings reveal his belief that humans are part of the ecological system. His main contribution to geography was his attention to cause-and-effect relationships. Most geographies of earlier times merely compiled facts. When Humboldt tried to explain spatial patterns of certain physical phenomena, he found geography useful. Because he brought the prestige and methods of science to geography, he is considered one of the founders of modern geography. Humboldt never held a university position, but he was widely respected as a scholar. His single most important geographical publication was *Cosmos*, a five-volume work.

Anthropologists, historians, and sociologists share geographers' fascination with culture. Geographers' attention to cultures overlaps that of many of these other social scientists and humanists. Even so, it is still possible to discern a focus of concern that sets geographers apart from other students of culture. This focus is cultural geographers' concern with the ways cultures and societies vary and function *spatially* (see Figure 1-1). Geographers are trained to observe spatial patterns of all kinds, both human and environmental. Therefore, they are particularly well qualified to describe and interpret spatial variations in culture. Geographers recognize that any differences and similarities in cultures are the result of complex forces. As a result, they can rarely find easy explanations for the questions raised by spatial patterns in culture.

The complexity of the forces that affect culture can be illustrated by an example drawn from agricultural geography: the distribution of wheat cultivation in the world. Looking at the map in Figure 1-2, you can see important wheat cultivation in Australia but not Africa; the United States but not Brazil; China but not Southeast Asia. Why does this spatial pattern exist? Partly because of environmental factors such as climate, terrain, and soils. Some regions have always been too dry for wheat cultivation, others too steep or infertile. Indeed, there is a strong correlation between wheat cultivation and midlatitude climates, level terrain, and good soil. Still, do not place too much importance on such physical factors. People

CARL RITTER   1779-1859

Ritter, a longtime and close associate of Alexander von Humboldt, was a professor of geography at the University of Berlin beginning in 1820. He began his career as a tutor for a wealthy family in Frankfurt. In these comfortable surroundings, he was able to meet other intellectuals and study geography. During the long period he taught in Berlin, his work influenced the thinking of many people, including military leaders. In contrast to Humboldt, his chief concern was cultural geography, the geography of humans. He sought to bring the rigor of science to the study of human geography and believed that laws of human spatial behavior could be discovered. His first book discussed Africa, then a little-known continent, but he is best known for the massive work entitled *Die Erdkunde (Geography)*, which appeared in nineteen volumes between 1822 and his death. Ritter is widely regarded as a cofounder, with Humboldt, of the academic discipline of geography.

FIGURE 1–1
Geographers seek to learn how and why cultures differ, or are similar, from one place to another. Often those differences and similarities have a visual expression. In what ways are these two structures—one a rural Lutheran church in the treeless tundra of Iceland and the other a Greek Orthodox chapel amidst the olive groves of Crete —alike and different?

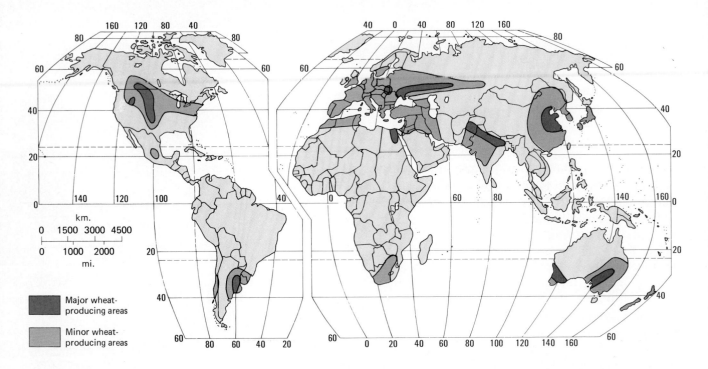

FIGURE 1-2

This map shows areas of wheat production in the world. These culture regions are based on a single trait—the presence of wheat in the agricultural system.

can now modify the effects of climate through irrigation, the use of hothouses, or the development of new, specialized strains of wheat. They can conquer slopes through terracing, and they can make infertile soils productive through fertilization. For example, farmers in mountainous parts of Greece wrest an annual harvest of wheat from tiny, terraced plots where soil has been trapped behind hand-built stone retaining walls. Even in the United States, environmental factors alone cannot explain the curious fact that major wheat cultivation is concentrated in the semiarid Great Plains, some distance from states such as Ohio and Illinois, where the climate for wheat is better.

The cultural geographer knows that wheat has to survive in a cultural as well as physical environment. Agricultural patterns cannot be explained by the characteristics of the land and climate alone. Many factors complicate the distribution of wheat, including people's tastes, desires, and traditions. Food preferences and taboos, often backed by religious beliefs, strongly influence the choice of crops to plant. Some cultural groups, such as the Poles, prefer dark bread made from rye flour. Other groups, particularly American Indians, would rather eat breads made from corn. Obviously, wheat will not "thrive" in such cultural environments. But where wheat bread is preferred, people are willing to put great efforts into overcoming hostile physical surroundings. They have even created new strains of wheat, thereby decreasing the environment's influence on wheat distribution. Economics also enters the picture. Wheat cultivation can be encouraged or discouraged by tariffs like those that protect the wheat farmers of Germany and other Common Market countries from competition with more efficient American and Canadian producers. In addition, wheat farming is a less profitable use of the land than dairying or fattening livestock. For this reason, wheat is sometimes not grown in the most suitable regions, such as the American Midwest.

This is by no means a complete list of the forces that affect wheat distribution. But it should be clear that the map of wheat reflects the pushing and pulling of many factors. The distribution of all cultural elements, not only the distribution of wheat, is a result of the constant interplay of **push-and-pull factors**.

Themes in Cultural Geography

Our study of cultures will be organized around five concepts or themes. These are **culture region, cultural diffusion, cultural ecology, cultural integration,** and **cultural landscape**. These themes will be stressed throughout the book, giving structure to each chapter. They represent only one of many possible ways to study cultural geography and not all cultural geographers employ them. However, we find them to be useful devices for teaching the concepts of cultural geography.

The theme of culture region

If, as is often said, one picture is worth a thousand words, then a well-prepared map is worth at least ten thousand words to the geographer. No description in words can rival the descriptive force of maps. Maps are valuable tools particularly because they portray spatial patterns in culture. Geographers can use maps to see cultural differences and similarities at a glance. The more complex the distribution of cultural traits under study, the more valuable the map. There are two major types of culture regions: formal and functional. To these we might add a third type, the vernacular or perceptual region.

Formal culture regions. A **formal culture region** can be defined as an area inhabited by people who have one or more cultural traits in common. (see Figure 1-3). You cannot go into the street and find a formal culture region. Yet there is nothing mysterious about it. Geographers find the formal culture region useful for grouping people with similar cultural traits. It is a tool geographers can use to describe spatial differences in culture. For example, a German-language culture region can be drawn on a

FIGURE 1–3
The Masai people of Kenya have developed distinctive ritual dances, one of which is pictured here. The cultural geographer could devise a single-trait formal culture region by plotting on a map the African villages where this particular type of dance is performed.

map of languages, and it would include the area where German is spoken. Or a wheat-farming culture region could describe the parts of the world where wheat is a major crop.

The examples of German speech and wheat cultivation represent the concept of formal region at its simplest level. Each is based on a single cultural trait. More commonly, culture regions depend on multiple related traits (see Figure 1-4). Thus an Eskimo culture region might depend on language, religion, type of economy, type of social organization, and typical form of dwellings. The Eskimo culture region would reflect the spatial distribution of these five Eskimo cultural traits. Districts where all five of these traits are present would be part of the culture region.

Another example of a multitrait culture region is shown by the traditional cultures that took root in the eastern United States in colonial times. Figure 1-5 shows three major American culture regions: New England, Middle Atlantic, and Lower Southern. Each culture region is, in turn, divided into subcultures. These divisions are based on each region's economy, dialect, religion, and ethnic-racial population. Each culture has a nucleus, where it first took shape and later spread to occupy a larger area.

The nucleus of New England was settled almost exclusively by colonists from England, whose agricultural technology was poorly suited to such cold, infertile lands. Marginal success in farming caused many colonists to turn to fishing, trading, manufacturing, and lumbering as occupations. In its early stage, New England was a theocracy, controlled by Puritan leaders.

In contrast to New England, the Middle Atlantic region's culture embraced a great variety of ethnic groups. English, Scotch-Irish, Germans, Swedes, and other European groups met and mingled here, importing rich and diverse agricultural heritages into a fertile land. The middle-class family farm was instituted here. Quakers, Lutherans, German and Dutch

FIGURE 1–4
In this market in Morocco, various facets of a multitrait formal culture region are apparent. Agricultural products, marketing, architecture, and clothing all contribute to the region's identity.

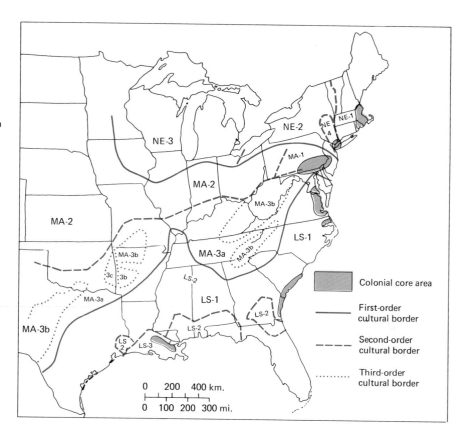

NE = New England culture
  1. Nuclear New England
  2. Zone of primary New England expansion
  3. Zone of secondary New England expansion with heavy overlay of 19th-century Europeans
  4. New York Dutch-German with New England overlay

MA = Middle Atlantic culture
  1. Nuclear Middle Atlantic
  2. Lower Midwest with overlay of 19th-century Europeans
  3. Upper South
    a. Middle-class lowland farmers
    b. Mountaineer Southerners
    c. Oklahoma Indians

LS = Lower Southern culture
  1. Plantation aristocracy
  2. Piney Woods poor whites
  3. Louisiana French

Colonial core area

First-order cultural border

Second-order cultural border

Third-order cultural border

FIGURE 1–5

Traditional rural culture regions of the eastern and central United States are based largely on dialect, traditional economy, generic place-names, national origin, and race. What other traits might contribute to the distinctiveness of your own culture region?

Reformed, Presbyterians, Mennonites, and various other Protestant sects were represented. Here was America's first "melting pot." The result was a farming culture that shaped the face of the rural United States from then on.

In the Lower South, British, French, and African traits were combined in a plantation system of agriculture. Large estates, specializing in subtropical cash crops and depending on a large body of slave laborers, gave rise to a landed aristocracy that quickly assumed political control of the plantation colonies.

As each of these three cultures expanded westward, the diversities of the eastern seaboard were transplanted to the interior. In this way, many present-day patterns of economy, dialect, and religion were established throughout the country.

Formal culture regions are the geographer's somewhat arbitrary creations. No two cultural traits have the same distribution and the territorial extent of a culture region depends on what defining traits are used (see box, "No Two Cultural Phenomena Have the Same Spatial Distribution"). For example, Greeks and Turks differ in language and religion. Culture regions defined on the basis of speech and religious faith would separate these two groups. However, Greeks and Turks hold many other cultural traits in common. This is partly because of the long Turkish rule of Greece and the lengthy coexistence of Greeks and Turks in Asia Minor. Both groups are monotheistic, worshipping a single god. In both groups, male supremacy and patriarchal families are the rule. Certain folk foods, such as shish kebab, are enjoyed in common. Whether Greeks and Turks are placed in the same formal culture region or in different ones depends entirely on how the geographer chooses to define the culture region. That

NO TWO CULTURAL PHENOMENA HAVE THE SAME SPATIAL DISTRIBUTION

No matter how closely related two elements of culture seem to be, close investigation always shows that they do not exactly cover the same area. This is true regardless of what degree of detail is involved. Thus, just as the map of languages does not duplicate the distribution of religions, governments, or economies, so also no two words or pronunciations within a single dialect or language cover precisely the same area.

What does this mean to the cultural geographer in practical terms? First, it means that every feature and detail of culture is unique to an area and that the explanation for each spatial variation is different in some degree from those for all other cultural phenomena. Second, it means that culture changes continually through an area, that every inhabited place on the earth has a unique combination of cultural features, differing from every other place in one or more respects.

Does this cultural uniqueness of each place prevent geographers from seeking explanatory theories? Does it doom them to explaining each distribution separately? The answer must be no. The fact that no two hills or rocks, no two planets or stars, no two trees or flowers are identical has not prevented geologists, astronomers, and botanists from formulating theories based on generalizations. They often make explanations through the use of models.

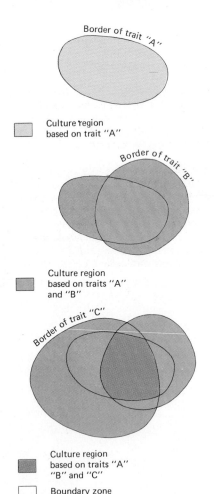

Culture region based on trait "A"

Culture region based on traits "A" and "B"

Culture region based on traits "A" "B" and "C"

Boundary zone

FIGURE 1–6
Hypothetical formal culture regions based on one, two, and three traits. Notice that no two traits have the same spatial distribution. Thus with each additional trait, the core of the region grows smaller and the boundary zone broader.

choice in turn depends on the specific purpose of research that the culture region is designed to serve. Thus an infinite number of formal culture regions can be created. It is unlikely that any two geographers would use exactly the same distinguishing criteria.

Often cultural geographers attempt to delimit culture regions based on the totality of traits displayed by a culture. The term **culture area**, derived from anthropology, is sometimes used for such regions. Because of the greater complexity of traits involved, culture areas are typically even more arbitrarily delimited than are formal regions based on fewer characteristics. Often they are based more on the geographer's intuition, derived from intimate knowledge of an area, than on carefully marshaled facts.

By definition, the geographer who identifies a formal culture region must locate cultural borders. Because cultures are fluid, such boundaries are rarely sharp, even if only a single culture trait is being mapped. For this reason, geographers often speak of cultural border zones rather than lines. Naturally, these zones broaden with each additional cultural trait that is considered, because no two traits have the same spatial distribution. Most formal culture regions have a core where the defining traits are strongest. Away from that core, the defining traits gradually weaken and disappear, as is shown in Figure 1-6. Where sharply defined formal culture borders exist, they usually correspond to physical barriers or closed political boundaries that separate different cultural groups. But in most cases, cultures blend gradually into one another through boundary zones. Cultural borders, whether zones or lines, often survive long after the forces that created them have vanished, as occurred in central Europe (see Figure 1-7).

Functional culture regions. A **functional culture region** is quite different from a formal culture region. The hallmark of the formal type is cultural homogeneity, and the formal culture region is abstract rather than concrete. By contrast, the functional culture region is generally not culturally homogeneous. Instead, it is an area that has been organized to function politically, socially, or economically. A city, an independent state, a precinct, a church diocese or parish, a trade area, a farm, and a Federal Reserve Bank district are all examples of functional regions. Functional culture regions have **nodes,** or central points where the functions are coordinated and directed. Examples of such nodes are city

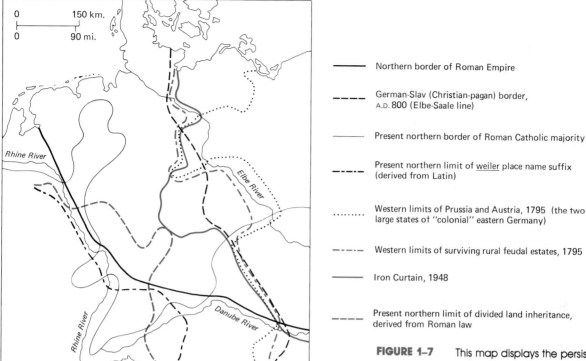

— Northern border of Roman Empire

- - - German-Slav (Christian-pagan) border,
A.D. 800 (Elbe-Saale line)

—— Present northern border of Roman Catholic majority

-·-·- Present northern limit of weiler place name suffix
(derived from Latin)

········ Western limits of Prussia and Austria, 1795 (the two
large states of "colonial" eastern Germany)

-·-·- Western limits of surviving rural feudal estates, 1795

—— Iron Curtain, 1948

- - - Present northern limit of divided land inheritance,
derived from Roman law

FIGURE 1–7 This map displays the persistence of a cultural border in central Europe. Since Roman times, an east-west cultural division has characterized central Europe. This ancient cultural divide has taken many forms—political, legal, religious, social, economic, and place-names. It has persisted in spite of repeated German attempts to unify central Europe. (Derived in part from Werner B. Cahnman, "Frontiers Between East and West in Europe," *Geographical Review*, 39, 1949, 605–624.)

halls, national capitals, precinct voting places, parish churches, factories, farmsteads, and banks.

Some functional regions have clearly defined borders and are concrete units. A farm is a functional region that includes all land owned or leased by the farmer (see box, "Culture Regions in a Microcosm"). Its operation is

CULTURE REGIONS IN A MICROCOSM

Imagine a valley filled with farms. Each farm consists of a strip of land reaching from the center of the valley up to the adjacent ridge crest (see map). Farmsteads are at the front of the farms, along a road that bisects the valley. On each farm, the slope of the land becomes steeper as we go away from the road. On the most level land, at the front of each farm, wheat is raised, and with the steadily increasing slope toward the rear of each farm, we encounter vineyards, then pastures, and finally, on the steepest slopes at the rear of the farm, forest. Thus each farm in the valley consists of wheat fields, vineyards, pastures, and woodland with increasing distance from the road. Each of these types of land use occupies a continuous strip running lengthwise through the valley.

In this situation, both formal and functional culture regions are present. Each farm constitutes a functional region, and the strips of wheat, vineyards, pasture, and woodland are each formal culture regions, defined by the homogeneity of land use.

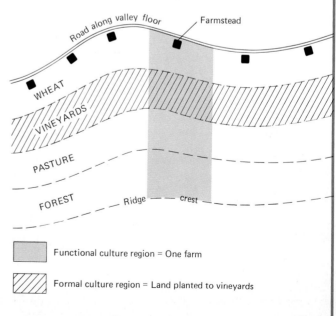

Functional culture region = One farm

Formal culture region = Land planted to vineyards

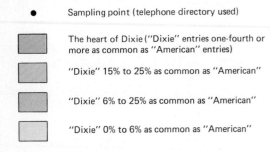

- Sampling point (telephone directory used)

The heart of Dixie ("Dixie" entries one-fourth or more as common as "American" entries)

"Dixie" 15% to 25% as common as "American"

"Dixie" 6% to 25% as common as "American"

"Dixie" 0% to 6% as common as "American"

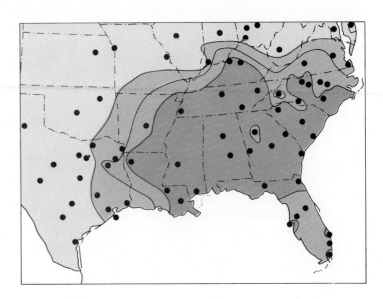

FIGURE 1–8

Dixie: A Vernacular Region. "Dixie" is a more restrictive regional term than is "South," and it is loaded with historical and cultural connotations. The territorial extent of "Dixie" was determined by counting the number of times it appeared in telephone directories as part of the name of business establishments. The total for each city was then divided by the entries for "American," to adjust for the different population sizes of the cities, producing the numbers on the map. The higher the number, the more common the use of "Dixie." Make a count of regional terms in your telephone directory. Does the place where you live lie within a vernacular region such as Dixie? (After John Shelton Reed, "The Heart of Dixie: An Essay in Folk Geography," *Social Forces*, 54 (1976), 932, with modifications for Texas.)

directed by the farmer, who has organized the land to function as a distinct spatial unit. The node is the farmstead, which contains the home of the farmer and various structures essential to farming, such as barns, implement sheds, and silos. The borders of this functional region will probably be clearly marked by fences, hedges, or walls. Similarly, each state in the United States is a functional region, coordinated and directed from the state capital and extending government control over a fixed area with clearly defined borders.

It is misleading to think all functional culture regions have fixed, precise borders. It is better to imagine these borders in terms of increasing or diminishing flows of energy out of or into nodes. On a map, this motion might be represented by directional arrows rather than boundary lines— as a network, not a territory. A good example is a daily newspaper's trade area. The node for the paper would be the plant where it is produced. Every morning, trucks move out of the plant to distribute the paper throughout the city. But the newspaper may also have a sales area extending into the city's suburbs, local bedroom communities, nearby towns, and rural areas. There its sales area overlaps the sales territories of competing newspapers published in other cities. Its sales area will therefore gradually peter out. It would be futile to try to define borders for such a process. How would you draw a sales area boundary for the *New York Times*? Its Sunday edition is sold in some quantity even in California, thousands of miles from its node.

The sales areas for manufactured goods present similar problems. Every time you buy a soft drink or a bottle of beer, you are a part of a dynamic functional culture region. Which bottle you choose depends on the region you are in. Is your area a nationwide, multistate, or purely local functional network? Some beer manufacturers have gone nationwide in their marketing, establishing branch breweries in various parts of the country. Schlitz, Budweiser, and Pabst are in this category. Others, such as Coors, have traditionally confined sales activity to selected large multistate regions. Still others, such as Lone Star of Texas, are marketed largely within a single state. Finally, some beers are sold only in small, local areas, as Pittsburgh's Iron City beer is. Each beer has a unique market area—a functional region—and these often completely overlap one another. The node for each beer's functional area is the brewery.

Vernacular culture regions. Some geographers recognize a third type of culture region, the **vernacular** or **perceptual**. This is a region perceived to exist by its inhabitants, as evidenced by the widespread acceptance and use of a regional name. The map, Figure 1-8, reveals one such popular region in the United States, "Dixie," and the photograph, Figure 1-9, shows a visible expression of that region. Some vernacular regions are based on physical environmental features, while others find their basis in economic, political, historical, or promotional aspects. Vernacular regions, like other culture regions, generally lack sharp borders, and the inhabitants of any given area may claim residence in more than one such region. These perceived regions are often created by publicity campaigns, and their use in the communications media have a lot to do with acceptance by the local population.

Vernacular culture regions, as you can see, are rather different from the functional or formal types. They often lack the organization necessary for functional regions, though often they are centered on a single urban node, and they frequently do not display the cultural homogeneity that characterizes formal regions. They are a type unto themselves, a type rooted in the popular or folk culture. Geographers are devoting increasing attention to vernacular culture regions, as we will see in Chapter 8.

FIGURE 1-9

Notice the "Heart of Dixie" symbol on this Alabama state license plate.

The theme of cultural diffusion

The culture regions of the world, regardless of type or method of delimiting, evolved through communication and contact among people. In other words, they are the product of **cultural diffusion**, the spatial spread of ideas, innovations, and attitudes. As Figure 1-10 shows, each element of culture originates in one or more places and then spreads. Some innovations occur only once, and therefore geographers can some-

FIGURE 1-10

Types of cultural diffusion are presented here. These diagrams are merely suggestive; in reality, spatial diffusion is far more complex.

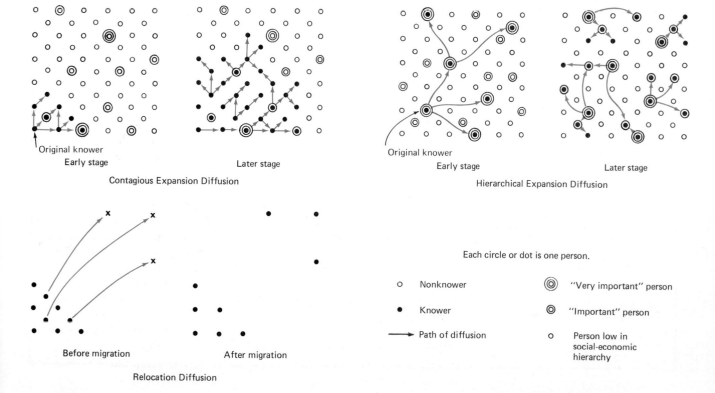

Original knower

Early stage

Later stage

Contagious Expansion Diffusion

Original knower

Early stage

Later stage

Hierarchical Expansion Diffusion

Before migration

After migration

Relocation Diffusion

Each circle or dot is one person.

o   Nonknower

•   Knower

→   Path of diffusion

◎   "Very important" person

◉   "Important" person

o   Person low in social-economic hierarchy

times trace a cultural element back to a single place of origin. In other cases, **independent invention** occurs. The same or very similar innovation is independently developed at different places by different peoples. The study of cultural diffusion—the origin and spread of ideas and innovations throughout an area—is a very important theme in cultural geography. Through the study of diffusion, the cultural geographer can begin to understand how spatial patterns in culture evolved.

Any culture is the product of almost countless innovations that spread from their points of origin to cover a wider area. Some of these innovations occurred thousands of years ago, others very recently. Some spread widely (see box, "Cultural Diffusion: A 100 Percent American"), while others remained confined to their area of origin. Geographers, drawing upon the research of Torsten Hägerstrand (see biographical sketch), recognize several different kinds of diffusion. Two important types are **expansion diffusion** and **relocation diffusion**. In expansion diffusion, ideas spread throughout a population, from area to area, in a snowballing process, so that the total number of knowers and the area of occurrence become ever greater. Relocation diffusion occurs when individuals or groups with a particular idea move bodily from one location to another, thereby spreading the innovation to their new homeland. Religions are frequently spread this way. An example is the migration of Christianity with European settlers who came to America. Indeed, the entire process of European-based colonialism, lasting from about 1500 to 1950, constituted perhaps the most important occurrence of relocation diffusion in all of history.

Expansion diffusion can be further divided into subtypes called **stimulus diffusion, hierarchical diffusion**, and **contagious diffusion**. In hierarchical diffusion, ideas leapfrog from one important person to another or from one urban center to another, temporarily bypassing other persons or rural territory. We can see hierarchical diffusion at work in everyday life by observing the acceptance of new modes of dress or hairstyles. By contrast, contagious diffusion involves the general spread of ideas, without regard to hierarchies, in the manner of a contagious disease.

CULTURAL DIFFUSION: A 100 PERCENT AMERICAN

"Our solid American citizen awakens in a bed built on a pattern that originated in the Near East but that was modified in Northern Europe before it was transmitted to America. He throws back covers made from cotton, domesticated in India, or linen, domesticated in the Near East, or silk, the use of which was discovered in China. All of these materials have been spun and woven by processes invented in the Near East. He slips into his moccasins, invented by the Indians of the Eastern woodlands, and goes to the bathroom, whose fixtures are a mixture of European and American inventions, both of recent date. He takes off his pajamas, a garment invented in India, and washes with soap, invented by the ancient Gauls. He then shaves—a masochistic rite that seems to have been derived from either Sumer or ancient Egypt.

". . . On his way to breakfast, he stops to buy a paper, paying for it with coins, an ancient Lydian invention. At the restaurant, a whole new series of borrowed elements confronts him. His plate is made of a form of pottery invented in China. His knife is of steel, an alloy first made in southern India; his fork, a medieval Italian invention; and his spoon, a derivative of a Roman original.

". . . When our friend has finished eating, . . . he reads the news of the day, imprinted in characters invented by the ancient Semites upon a material invented in China by a process invented in Germany. As he absorbs the accounts of foreign trouble, he will, if he is a good, conservative citizen, thank a Hebrew deity in an Indo-European language that he is 100 percent American."

From Ralph Linton, The Study of Man. *Copyright © 1936, renewed 1964, by Prentice-Hall, Englewood Cliffs, New Jersey.*

Sometimes a specific trait is rejected, but the underlying idea is accepted. This is stimulus diffusion. For example, it is generally believed that early Siberian cultures domesticated reindeer only after exposure to the domesticated cattle and horses raised by cultures to their south. The Siberians had no use for these domesticated animals; however, the idea of domesticated herds was appealing, so they applied the concept to their homeland and began domesticating reindeer.

If you throw a rock into a pond and watch the spreading ripples, you can see them become gradually weaker as they move away from the point of impact. In the same way, the acceptance of a cultural innovation decreases with distance. An innovation will be accepted most in the areas closest to where it originates. This concept can be called distance decay. Time decay is also a factor: It takes increasing time for innovations to spread outward. Because acceptance decreases with distance, acceptance also decreases with time. This is what geographers mean by **time-distance decay**.

In addition to the "natural" weakening or decay of an innovation through time and distance, barriers tend to retard its spread. **Absorbing barriers** completely halt the diffusion, allowing no further progress. For example, television was for decades prevented from entering the Republic of South Africa because the government there objected to it. The border of the Republic thus served as an absorbing barrier to the spread of television. More commonly, barriers are **permeable**, allowing part of the innovation wave to diffuse through but acting to weaken and retard the continued spread. For example, when a school board objects to long hair on boys, the principal of a high school may set a limit on hair length for male students. This length will likely be longer than the haircuts before the "long hair" innovation, but it will be shorter than the length of the new hairstyle. In this way, the principal and school board act as a permeable barrier to a cultural innovation.

Barriers may be either cultural—in the form of social or governmental taboos and restrictions—or environmental. The old joke about selling refrigerators to Eskimos as the ultimate test of a salesperson's ability reveals the environmental barrier that can be encountered by innovations. Indeed, the cultural geographer is much concerned with the physical environment, as we will see in the following section on cultural ecology.

Acceptance of innovations at any given point in space can be depicted with an S-shaped curve that includes three distinct stages. The first stage sees acceptance taking place at a steady, yet slow, rate, perhaps because the innovation has not yet caught on, the benefits have not been adequately demonstrated, or the trait is not physically available. But then during the second state, there is rapid growth in acceptance—the trait will spread widely, as with a fashion style or dance fad. Often diffusion on a microscale will exhibit what is called the **neighborhood effect**, which means simply that acceptance is usually most rapid in small clusters around an initial adopter. Think of a fad that first appeared in your neighborhood one day; then a few days later it seemed that everyone on the block was doing the same thing. Direct exposure to an innovation is the best advertisement. The third stage of growth shows a slower rate than the second, perhaps because the fad is passing, or because an area is already saturated with the innnovation.

Some other cultural geographers, most notably James M. Blaut, have criticized the Hägerstrandian concept of diffusion. They regard it as too narrow and mechanical, since it does not give enough emphasis to

TORSTEN HÄGERSTRAND   1916-

A native and resident of Sweden, Hägerstrand is professor of geography at the University of Lund, where he received a doctorate in 1953. His doctoral research was on innovation diffusion, and his findings were published in 1953. His work on diffusion is significant because it is based on models and statistical techniques. As a result, it has been the basis for many theories and has elevated cultural geographers' research on diffusion to a higher, more scientific level. Sweden, and particularly Lund, has become a major center of innovative work in cultural geography.

cultural variables. As a result, wrote Professor Blaut, "serious difficulties arise whenever efforts are made to generalize the . . . Hägerstrand theory or to apply it in realms and epochs which are culturally distant from the modern Western world." Nondiffusion—the failure of innovations to spread—is more prevalent than diffusion, a condition Hägerstrand's system cannot successfully accommodate. Furthermore, Blaut argued, the Hägerstrand concept lacks explanatory power.

The theme of cultural ecology

Cultural geographers look on people and nature as being completely interacting. Cultures do not exist in a vacuum. Each human group and the way of life they have developed occupy a piece of the physical earth. Cultures, as you might expect, interact with the environment, and it is necessary for the cultural geographer to study this reciprocal interaction in order to understand spatial variations in culture. This study is called **cultural ecology**. The word **ecology**, as used here, refers to the two-way relationship between an organism and its physical environment. It comes from two ancient Greek words. *Oikos* means "house," or "habitat"; *logia* means "words," or "teachings." Thus the Greek *oikologia* could be rendered "teachings about the habitat." Cultural ecology, then, is the study of the cause-and-effect interplay between cultures and the physical environment. A **physical environment** is understood to include climate, terrain, soil, natural vegetation, wildlife, and other aspects of the physical surroundings.

A closely related term is **human ecology**. The basic difference is that cultural ecology implies the study of interaction between physical environment and people as culture-bearing animals, whereas in human ecology, human populations are studied in their physical environments in much the same manner as noncultural animal populations. Some regard human ecology as more oriented to the study of people as instruments of environmental modification. In reality, however, the two terms are often used interchangeably by geographers. Another frequently used word is **ecosystem**. By this, we seek to describe the functioning ecological system in which biological and cultural *homo sapiens* live and interact with the physical environment. In sum, we may define cultural ecology as the study of (1) environmental influence on culture and (2) the impact of people, acting through their culture, on the ecosystem. Cultural ecology, then, implies a "two-way street," with people and the environment exerting influence on one another.

The theme of cultural ecology is the meeting ground of cultural and physical geographers and has traditionally provided a focal point for the academic discipline of geography. In fact, some geographers have proposed that geography *is* cultural ecology. They argue that study of the intricate relationships between people and their physical environments constitutes a valid academic discipline. While few accept this narrow definition of geography, most will agree that an appreciation of the complex people-environment relationship is a necessary undertaking for concerned citizens of the late twentieth century. Through the years, cultural geographers have developed various perspectives on the spatial interaction between humans and the land. In a broad sense, four schools of thought have developed: environmental determinism, possibilism, environmental perception, and humans as modifiers of the earth.

Environmental determinism. During the first quarter of the twentieth century, many English-speaking geographers adhered to the doctrine of

environmental determinism. These geographers believed that the physical environment—especially the climate and terrain—was the active force in shaping cultures, that humankind was essentially a passive product of the physical surroundings. According to the logic of the determinist, humans were clay to be molded by nature. Similar physical environments were likely to produce similar cultures. In effect, environmental determinists view cultural ecology as a "one-way street."

There are many examples of determinist beliefs. Determinists believed that peoples of the mountains were predestined by the rugged terrain to be simple, backward, conservative, unimaginative, and freedom loving. Dwellers of the desert were likely to believe in one god, but to live under the rule of tyrants. Temperate climates produced inventiveness, industriousness, and democracy, whereas coastlands pitted with fjords produced great navigators and fishermen. Environmental determinists had a handy explanation for England's preeminent position in the world at that time: the surrounding waters demanded seamanship, and an optimum climate produced genius for government and a work ethic.

From the perspective of the late twentieth century, we can see that the determinists overemphasized the role of environment in human affairs. This does not imply that environmental influence is inconsequential or that the cultural geographer should not study such influence. Rather, it suggests that the physical environment is only one of many forces affecting human culture and rarely the sole determinant of human behavior and beliefs.

Possibilism. Since the 1930s, environmental determinism has fallen from favor among cultural geographers. **Possibilism** has taken its place. Possibilists do not ignore the influence of the physical environment. They realize that the imprint of nature shows in many cultures. However, possibilists stress that cultural heritage is at least as important as the physical environment in affecting human behavior (see box, "The Facts Are Incontestable").

"THE FACTS ARE INCONTESTABLE": AN ENVIRONMENTAL DETERMINIST'S VIEW OF CREATIVE GENIUS

"The absence of artistic and poetic development in Switzerland and the Alpine lands [may be ascribed] to the overwhelming aspect of nature there, its majestic sublimity which paralyzes the mind. . . . This position [is reinforced] by the fact that . . . the lower mountains and hill country of Swabia, Franconia and Thuringia, where nature is gentler, stimulating, appealing, and not overpowering, have produced many poets and artists. The facts are incontestable. They reappear in France in the geographical distribution of the awards made by the Paris Salon of 1896. Judged by these awards, the [people of the] rough highlands . . . are singularly lacking in artistic instinct, while art flourishes in all the river lowlands of France. . . . French men of letters, by the distribution of their birthplaces, are essentially products of fluvial valleys and plains, rarely of upland and mountain."

From Ellen Churchill Semple, Influences of Geographic Environment. Copyright 1911 by Holt, Rinehart and Winston. Copyright © 1939 by Carolyn W. Keene.

A POSSIBILIST REACHES A DIFFERENT CONCLUSION

"All [European] patent offices report the Swiss as the foremost inventors. . . . A partial list of books published in different countries showed Switzerland to be far ahead of any other country in this sphere. . . .

"The Swiss themselves attribute much importance in the growth of their industries to the religious persecutions in neighboring countries in the sixteenth and seventeenth centuries—persecutions which drove thousands of intelligent men . . . into Switzerland. The revocation of the Edict of Nantes . . . in 1685 is credited with driving sixty thousand Huguenots from France into Switzerland. They founded the silk industry of Zurich and Bern. It was a Huguenot who founded the watch business at Geneva. . . . Spanish persecution in the Low Countries and Swiss neutrality during the Thirty Years' War added to the human resources of Switzerland."

From Mark Jefferson, "The Geographic Distribution of Inventiveness," Geographical Review, 19 (1929), 660–661.

According to possibilists, people, rather than their environment, are the primary architects of culture. Possibilists claim that any physical environment offers a number of possible ways for a culture to develop. How people use and inhabit an area depends on the choices they make among the possibilities offered by the environment. These choices are guided by cultural heritage. Possibilists, then, see the physical environment as offering opportunities and limitations; people make choices among these in order to satisfy their needs. In short, local traits of culture and economy are the products of culturally based decisions made within the limits of possibilities offered by the environment. The higher the technological level of a culture, the greater the number of possibilities and the weaker the influences of the physical environment.

This possibilist view is nicely expressed in the concept of **cultural adaptation**—the nongenetic, long-term adjustment of people, through their culture, to the physical environment and to changes in the environment. The adjustments vary from one culture to another, underlining the importance of culture in producing spatial patterns.

Environmental perception. Each person has mental images of the physical environment, and within a cultural group these perceived images are largely shared. To describe such mental images, cultural geographers use the term **environmental perception**. Whereas the possibilist sees humankind as having a choice of different possibilities in a given physical setting, the environmental perceptionist declares that the choices people make will depend more on what they perceive the environment to be than on the actual character of the land (see box, "Buffalo No Bigger than

---

BUFFALO NO BIGGER THAN INSECTS: THE PYGMY AND THE RAIN FOREST

The sun is a network of flickering lights dotting the ground, not a bright disk moving across the sky. The stars are not visible at night. The seasons hardly vary. The chief landmark of the area is no landmark at all—no distant rise of ground, no special tree standing out against the sky, nothing. Sound is supreme. In hunting, game is merely heard until it appears yards away from the hunter. The clearest idea of the supernatural that the inhabitants of this land have is not God, not a visual land to which the dead depart, but a sound: the "Beautiful Song of a Bird."

Although this may seem like science fiction, it is in fact the world of the Ba Mbuti pygmies, who live in the Congo rain forest. As an environment, the rain forest is all-enveloping and naturally affects every aspect of pygmy life, even the way they see. Living underneath a thick, almost impenetrable canopy of branches and leaves, hemmed in on all sides by lush, green foliage, the pygmies never have the experience of seeing anything from a distance. As a result, their sense of perspective is severely curtailed.

Can you imagine what it would be like to step out of that all-sustaining world for the first time? Kenge, a pygmy of the Ba Mbuti tribe, actually had the experience. The anthropologist Colin Turnbull took him to an area of open grasslands. A flock of buffalo grazed several miles away, far below where they were standing. Familiar with the size of buffalo in the forest, Kenge could make no sense of these tiny dots in front of him. He asked Turnbull, "What insects are those?" "When I told Kenge that the insects were buffalo," Turnbull wrote, "he roared with laughter and told me not to tell such stupid lies." When Turnbull tried to explain how far away they actually were, Kenge "began scraping mud off his arms and legs, no longer interested in such fantasies."

Later, as the men approached the herd in a car, Kenge became frightened. He could see the animals growing bigger and bigger and feared that a magic trick was being played on him. In fact, his eye/brain had never learned something we take for granted: the ability to correct for changes in the size of the retinal image when looking at an object, so that the image remains relatively the same size as the object moves closer or farther away. Bewildered by distance, the lack of trees, and the sharpness of relief, Kenge's brain was making wrong guesses based on inadequate experience. Used to the environment of the rain forest, Kenge, for a moment at least, found the world a less stable and predictable place.

Insects"). Perception, in turn, is colored by the teachings of culture. The perceptionist maintains that people cannot perceive their environment with exact accuracy and that decisions are therefore based on distortions of reality. To understand why a cultural group developed as it did in its physical environment, geographers must know not only what the environment is like, but also what the members of the culture think it is like.

Some of the most productive research done by environmental perceptionists has been on the topic of natural hazards, such as floods and droughts. Different cultural groups react to the same hazards in varied ways. Some reason that natural disasters are unavoidable acts of the gods; others seek to cope with environmental hazards by placating the gods; and still others place responsibility for preventing calamities on the government. In Western cultures, people tend to regard hazards and disasters as natural phenomena that they can manipulate and control through technology.

The perceptionists' ideas are particularly striking when applied to migrations. They have found that people migrating from one environment to another usually imagine their old and new homelands to be environmentally more similar than is actually the case. For example, American farmers migrating from the humid eastern regions of the United States onto the semiarid Great Plains consistently overestimated the rainfall of their new homeland. Accustomed by the experience of many generations to living and farming in moist climates, they were initially unable to perceive the realities of their new climatic setting. They made decisions based on their experience and had to learn by trial and error that the realities of the Great Plains climate were not what they imagined (see Chapters 3 and 9).

Different cultures, surveying their environment, treat the natural resources around them quite differently. What to one cultural group is a major resource may be completely worthless or even a nuisance to another. To hunters and gatherers, the principal resources of an area may be wild berries, game animals, and flint deposits from which weapons can be fashioned. An agricultural group in the same environment may regard level land, fertile soils, and reliable sources of water as their most valuable resources. An industrial society may cherish the oil, coal, and other minerals buried beneath the land. In this way, people of three cultures perceive the resources of the same environment in different ways.

Humans as modifiers of the earth. Some cultural geographers, observing the changes people have wrought in their physical environment, have chosen to study humans as modifiers of the earth. This exposes yet another facet of cultural ecology. In a sense, this human-as-modifier theme is the opposite of environmental determinism. Whereas the determinists proclaim that nature molds humankind, those cultural geographers who study the human impact on the land emphasize that humans also mold nature (see box, "The Final Touches?").

Even in ancient times, perceptive observers realized that people influenced their environment, and this theme often appears in the great literature of the Western world. The scholars of classical Greece recorded the observation that humankind is a modifier of its habitat. Plato, commenting on the soil erosion around Athens around 400 B.C., lamented that the once fertile district has been stripped of its soil so that "what now remains compared to what formerly existed is like the skeleton of a sick man, all the fat and soft earth having wasted away, and only the bare framework of the land being left" (see Figure 1-11).

THE FINAL TOUCHES?

As it crosses an area of the Mediterranean Sea south of Italy, an American ocean-exploring vessel, *Atlantis II*, sights several thousand "lumps" of tar on every square mile of the sea's surface, the result of oil humans have spilled into the ocean. A man-made "dead sea" of sewage floats off the coast of New York City. Pesticides used on African land are detected in the Caribbean Sea, many thousands of miles away. A scientific report suggests that pollution from man-made nuclear wastes is gradually seeping into the oceans and polluting the human food chain. The report suggests that, in the future, people eating fish may become increasingly prone to cancer.

Industrial societies have normally treated the oceans as a giant garbage dump, a bottomless pit for their wastes. As a disposal system, offshore waters have the advantage of being both cheap and relatively invisible. "Out of sight, out of mind" might be the industrial credo in dealing with the waters that cover three-fourths of the earth's surface. As a result, the oceans have been the receptacle of raw sewage, factory waste products, giant oil spills, cyanides, mercury compounds, pesticides, and numerous other man-made poisons.

Unfortunately for humankind, the oceans—a giant hundred-million-year-old ecosystem—have developed an incredibly effective system of circulation. What starts out in one spot is hardly likely to remain there. In addition, the oceans are a complex life system, so large that the harm done to them takes a long while to get back to humans. Consequently, the effects of industrial pollution are not only presently incalculable, but also hardly likely to be noticed until major damage has already been done. For instance, polychlorinated biphenyls (PCBs) are an industrial product similar chemically to DDT. They appear to have been accumulating in the oceans for twenty years without anyone noticing them. Their presence in global waters was discovered quite by accident. The toxic effect of PCBs on marine wildlife and the birds and mammals that feed on marine life has already been significant. Similarly, oil wastes spilled purposely or accidentally in the oceans have hurt or killed countless thousands of diving birds.

The diving bird seems biologically a long way away from humankind. However, Jacques Cousteau, the scientist who has spent a lifetime at underwater exploration, claims that "life in the sea has diminished by 40 percent in the last twenty years." Whether Cousteau has overestimated or not, today the ocean's food resources account for over 15 percent of humankind's protein intake. Thus, what affects birds now will undoubtedly affect human populations later on. It might, then, be worth asking: Is humankind making its final modifications on earth?

Adapted from Harry Rothman, Murderous Providence *(Indianapolis: Bobbs-Merrill, 1972), pp. 218–247, Reprinted by permission of A. D. Peters & Co., Ltd.*

FIGURE 1–11
Human modification of the earth includes such severe soil erosion as on this farm in Kentucky. The erosion could have been caused by poor farming methods, overgrazing the cattle, or other careless abuses to the land.

In more recent times, cultural geographers began to concentrate on the human role in changing the face of the earth long before North Americans gained their present level of ecological consciousness. They found, not surprisingly, that different groups have widely different outlooks on humankind's role in changing the earth. Some, such as those rooted in the Judeo-Christian tradition, tend to regard environmental modification as divinely approved, viewing humans as God's helpers in completing the task of creation. North Americans particularly have viewed humans as creatures apart from, and often at war with, nature. Some other groups are much more cautious, taking care not to offend the forces of nature. To many of these latter groups, humans are part of nature, meant to be in harmony with their environment.

The theme of cultural integration

The relationship between people and the land, the theme of cultural ecology, lies at the heart of traditional geography. However, the explanation of human spatial variations requires consideration of a whole range of cultural factors. The cultural geographer recognizes that all facets of culture are spatially intertwined, or **integrated.** In short, cultures are complex wholes rather than series of unrelated traits. They are integrated units in which all parts fit together causally. The theme of cultural integration reflects the geographer's awareness that the immediate causes of some cultural phenomena are other cultural phenomena. It is impossible to understand the distribution of one facet of culture without studying the spatial variations in the other facets of that culture in order to see how they are interrelated and integrated with one another.

For example, religious belief has the potential to influence a group's voting behavior, diet, shopping patterns, type of employment, and social standing. Traditional Hinduism, the religion of India, segregated people into social classes called *castes* and specified what forms of livelihood were appropriate for each. The Church of Jesus Christ of Latter Day Saints forbids the consumption of alcoholic beverages, tobacco, and certain other products, thereby influencing both the diet and shopping patterns of its members. There are countless other ways in which one facet of a culture influences other facets. The cultural integration theme allows the geographer to see how these intracultural causal forces help determine spatial variations.

Indeed, it is through the theme of cultural integration that geographers have made strides in developing theories to help explain spatial variations of culture. Ironically, to get at the ways a culture is integrated and why it is integrated the way it is, geographers have generally gone through a stripping-down process, separating cultural causal factors. Geographers are aware that, in the real world, so many causal factors are involved in any problem that confusion may result. So they have employed a simpler way of testing how a culture works. It is called **model building**. Unlike physical scientists, scholars studying cultures are unable to achieve laboratory conditions, where certain causal forces can be isolated from those forces surrounding them. To simulate a laboratory, social scientists imagine model situations in which they can observe certain isolated forces. For example, the nineteenth-century scholar Johann Heinrich von Thünen created a model consisting of a single country isolated from all others. Physically, he envisioned it as a flat plain surrounding a central city. He declared the soils and climate uniform throughout the country and assumed that all persons living a given distance from the city could transport goods to it in equal time and at equal rates. Von Thünen's purpose in creating this model of an isolated country was to study the effect of transportation costs and increased distance from the market on agricultural land use. The result was a theory that could then be applied to more complex real situations. His model is still recognized as valid and helpful by today's geographers (see Chapter 3). The task of building models and formulating theories goes on with increased vigor in modern cultural geography. In the following chapters, you will be introduced to some of the models that geographers have built. Hägerstrand's concept of diffusion, discussed earlier, provides another example of a model.

However, a number of cultural geographers have gone about the job of explaining cultural variations without attempting to apply their findings to situations other than the one they are studying. These scholars, who perhaps form the majority of cultural geographers, tend to regard geography as an **idiographic science**, one that deals with phenomena that are never identical and therefore not susceptible to the type of generalization required for formulating theories. The theorists, on the other hand, believe that geography is a **nomothetic**, or law-giving, science and that the chief purpose of geographical scholarship should be the discovery of universal principles. Many geographers value both of these approaches and feel that each has a contribution to make. We will become acquainted with both approaches in this text.

The danger inherent in cultural integration and model building is that it will lead the geographer to **cultural determinism**. Advocates of this extreme viewpoint, developed in reaction to the earlier environmental determinism, maintain that the physical environment is inconsequential as an influence on culture. Any facet of a culture, they would argue, is shaped entirely by other facets of culture. Cultural integration, for them, offers all the answers for spatial variations. People and culture are the active forces; nature is passive and easily conquered. You should be as wary of cultural determinism as of environmental determinism.

The theme of cultural landscape

The **cultural landscape** is the artificial landscape that cultural groups create in inhabiting the earth. Cultures have shaped their own landscapes out of the raw materials provided by the earth. Every inhabited area has a cultural landscape, fashioned from the natural landscape, and each uniquely reflects the culture that created it (see Figure 1-12). Landscape mirrors culture, and the cultural geographer can learn much about a group of people by carefully observing the landscape. Indeed, so important is this visual record of cultures that some cultural geographers regard landscape study as the core of geographical concern, geography's central interest.

Why is such importance attached to the cultural landscape? Perhaps part of the answer is that it visually reflects the most basic strivings of humankind: for shelter, food, clothing, and entertainment. The cultural landscape also reflects different attitudes concerning modification of the earth by people. In addition, the landscape contains valuable evidence about the origin, spread, and development of cultures. It is this potential for interpretive analysis that most attracts the geographer to study the landscape. Properly studied, this visible evidence can teach the observer much about the aspects of culture that are invisible, about a past long forgotten by the present inhabitants, and about the choices made and changes wrought by a people. Although we may not notice it in our daily

FIGURE 1-12
Rice on the lower slopes of the Sierra
Madre, island of Luzon, Philippines.

lives, the cultural landscape constantly changes across both space and time. The unraveling of its mysteries has occupied the attention of many of the foremost cultural geographers.

The content of the cultural landscape is both varied and complex. Most geographical studies have focused on three principal aspects of this landscape: settlement patterns, land-division patterns, and architecture. In the study of settlement patterns, cultural geographers describe and explain spatial variations in the arrangement of the buildings, roads and other features that people construct while inhabiting an area. Land-division patterns reveal the way people have divided the land for economic and social uses. Such patterns vary a great deal from place to place. They range from huge corporate-owned farming complexes to small family operated farms composed of tens or even hundreds of separate tiny parcels of land; from the fenced, privately owned home lots of American suburbs to the city's public squares. Perhaps the best way to glimpse settlement and land-division patterns is through an airplane window. Looking down, you can see the multicolored abstract patterns of planted fields, as vivid as any modern painting, and the regular checkerboard or chaotic tangle of urban streets.

Perhaps no other aspect of the human landscape is as readily visible from ground level as the architectural style of a culture. In North American culture, contrasting building styles cannot help catching the eye: modest white New England churches and giant urban cathedrals; hand-hewn barns and geodesic domes; New York City's rocket-shaped Empire State Building, a monument to the doctrine of progress; the last of the little red schoolhouses and the new windowless schoolbuildings of the urban areas. This architecture provides a vivid record of the resident culture. For this reason, cultural geographers have traditionally devoted considerable attention to such structures.

We can distinguish two basic types of architecture in the cultural

FIGURE 1-13
The Swiss log structure is an example of folk architecture. It stands in sharp contrast to the professional architecture of the New York skyline.

landscape, as Figure 1-13 shows: folk architecture (see Chapter 7) and professional architecture. Folk architecture includes all buildings erected without professional architectural help. The styles and methods used to build them are derived from the folk culture rather than from drawing boards and schools of architecture. The resultant structures are monuments to traditional practices and skills. Folk houses are often faithful copies of dwellings built in the same style for perhaps thousands of years. The works of professional architects and draftsmen also reflect their culture, although on a different level of technology. The professionally designed skyscraper or the mass-produced mobile home are as revealing of the North American material culture and way of life as the Brazilian Indian farmer's thatched hut is of that culture.

The Cultural Geographical Past

We must now discard Kant's neat division of geography and history. The spatial distribution of cultural features is the result of changes through time, so cultural geographers have traditionally been concerned with areal patterns as they evolved through time. Cultural landscapes are often the products of centuries of human action. Ecological decisions made by humans are rooted in their past interactions with the environment, and cultural diffusion by its very nature depends on the passage of time. In short, if the cultural geographer hopes to understand and explain spatial similarities and variations in culture, she or he must adopt an historical perspective and delve into the past for answers. Truly, culture is time-conditioned and cannot profitably be studied devoid of its temporal dimension.

The cultural landscape illustrates this point. Much of what meets the eye in that landscape comes from vanished causal forces and circumstances. To see this, all you have to do is stroll through any large American city. Like the ancient cities that archeologists sometimes discover—built one on top of the other over thousands of years—American cities, too, are really layered by time, cities inside cities inside cities. The modern office buildings of two decades ago are already being covered over by new steel and glass giants. The buildings they had once replaced are often still standing, although perhaps less noticed today. Even the use of buildings changes over time. New York City's Academy of Music, in the 1890s an elegant meeting place for high society, still exists. Today, however, it shows Spanish-language films to Puerto Rican immigrants who inhabit the now run-down neighborhood. In some other areas of the world, geographers must often delve thousands of years into the past to explain elements in the cultural landscape. Cultural geographers are interested in determining when and especially where cultural artifacts, practices, and beliefs originated.

The cultural landscape theme is a valuable tool for examining the sequence of settlement by different groups in an area, for usually each group leaves some sort of visible reminders of their presence that show up in the landscape. This concept of **sequent occupance**—or the sequence of settlement—is an important part of the cultural-historical method. For example, in California, it is still possible today to pick out traces of past cultures in the landscape. Grassland and forest vegetation show the effects of prehistoric Indian burning; Spanish roads and missions still appear in the countryside, as do the land-division lines from the Mexican rancho period. Reminders of the early American period are everywhere, from Eucalyptus trees covering parts of the state to the mine tailings and dredging deposits of the Gold Rush days. All of these parts of the cultural landscape tell us something about how past cultures interacted with their environment.

If cultural geographers study spatial patterns through time, why are they geographers rather than historians? The answer is that their first concern is always spatial; they study changes through time mainly because that study helps them understand spatial patterns.

Conclusion

The interests of cultural geographers are, as we have seen, quite diverse. It might seem to you, confronted by the various themes, viewpoints, and methodologies described in this chapter, that cultural geographers are running off in all directions, that they lack unity of purpose. What does a geographer studying folk architecture have in common with a colleague studying the human role in shaping the earth? What interests do an environmental perceptionist and a student of cultural diffusion share? Why do scholars with such apparently different interests belong in the same academic discipline? Why are they all geographers?

The answer is that, regardless of the particular topic the cultural geographer studies, he or she necessarily touches on several or all of the five themes we have mentioned. The themes are all closely related segments of a whole. Spatial patterns in culture, as revealed by maps of culture regions, are reflected in the cultural landscape, require an ecological interpretation, imply cultural diffusion, and suggest cultural integration.

As an example of how the various themes of cultural geography overlap and intertwine, let us look at a specific example from the realm of folk architecture—the American log house. Once found widely on the American frontier, many log cabins can still be found in the mountains of the South and West. They are obviously part of the cultural landscape, and their spatial distribution constitutes a formal culture region that can be mapped. In addition, geographers studying such houses need to employ the other themes of cultural geography to gain a complete understanding. They can use the concept of cultural diffusion to learn when and by what routes these techniques diffused and what barriers retarded their diffusion. In this particular case, the geographer would be led back to the history of the Neolithic period in central and northern Europe and, later, to the early Swedish and German colonies in the Delaware Valley. Further, the cultural geographer would need an ecological interpretation of the log house. How does the environment influence the log cabin? Is the form of the house related to types of trees? How do houses built of pine differ from those built of oak? Does the use of logs for houses decline as the forest become thinned out? Do log houses differ from one climatic zone to another? Finally, the cultural geographer wants to know how the use of log houses is integrated with other facets of the culture. Did changes in the economy and standard of living lead people to reject log houses? Did changes in technology lead to more elaborate houses? Are American political images linked to log cabins?

Thus the geographer interested in folk housing is firmly bound by the total fabric of cultural geography, unable to segregate a particular topic such as log houses from the geographic whole. In this way, culture region, cultural landscape, cultural integration, cultural ecology, and cultural diffusion are interwoven. Geography's focus on spatial pattern, together with five interrelated themes, distinguishes the cultural geographer from other students of culture.

Glossary

Absorbing barrier   one that completely halts diffusion of innovations and blocks the spread of cultural elements.

Contagious diffusion   a type of expansion diffusion; the spread of cultural innovation by person-to-person contact, moving wavelike through an area and population without regard to social status.

Cultural adaptation   nongenetic adjustment of culture to physical environment and environmental change.

Cultural determinism   the viewpoint that the immediate causes of all cultural phenomena are other cultural phenomena.

Cultural diffusion   the spread of elements of culture from the point of origin over an area.

Cultural ecology   the study of the complex, intricate relationships between the physical environment and people as culture-bearing animals.

Cultural geography   the description and explanation of spatial patterns in human culture.

Cultural integration   the relationship of different elements within a culture.

Cultural landscape   the man-made landscape; the visible human imprint on the land.

Culture   a total way of life held in common by a group of people, including such learned features as speech, ideology, behavior, livelihood, technology, and government.

Culture area   a composite formal culture region based on cultures, on the totality of cultural traits.

...gion an area or region occupied by people who ...nething in common culturally; a spatial unit that ... politically, socially, or economically as a ...ntity.

... study of the relationship between an organ- ...physical environment.

... functioning ecological system in which ... cultural *homo sapiens* live in and interact ...ical environment.

...eterminism the school of thought based ...hat cultures are, directly or indirectly, ...physical environment, that cultures are ...cal surroundings.

En... ...ception the school of thought based ...ultural attitudes shape perception of ...using people of different cultures to ...undings differently and to make ...a result.

Expansi... ...e spread of innovations within an area in... ...ocess, so that the total number of knower... ...er and the area of occurrence enlarges.

Formal cult... ...gion inhabited by people who have one ... ...traits in common.

Functional cu... ...egion or area that functions as a unit po... ...or economically.

Geography the ...al patterns, of differences and similaritie... ...e to another in environ-ment and cultu...

Hierarchical diffu... ...f expansion diffusion; innovations sprea... ...ortant person to anoth-er or from one u... ...another, temporarily bypassing persons ...ance and rural areas.

Human ecology the ...elationship between biological *homo sa...* ...physical environ-ment, with particul... ...eople as agents of environmental chang...

Idiographic science o... ...the study of phe-nomena that are nev... ...therefore do not lend themselves to t... ...of explanatory laws.

Independent invention cultural innovations that are developed in two or more locations by persons or groups working independently.

Model an abstraction, an imaginary situation, proposed by geographers to simulate laboratory conditions so that they may isolate certain causal forces for detailed study.

Neighborhood effect the rapid acceptance of an innovation in a small area or cluster around an initial adopter.

Node in a functional culture region, a central point where functions are coordinated and directed.

Nomothetic science a law-giving science.

Permeable barrier one that permits some aspects of an innovation to diffuse through but weakens and retards continued spread; an innovation can be modified in passing through a permeable barrier.

Physical environment includes all aspects of the natural physical surroundings, such as climate, terrain, soils, vegetation, and wildlife.

Possibilism the school of thought based on the belief that humans, rather than the physical environment, are the primary active force; that any environment offers a number of different possible ways for a culture to develop; and that the choices among these possibilities are guided by cultural heritage.

Push-and-pull factors unfavorable, repelling conditions and favorable, attractive conditions that interact to affect cultural distributions.

Relocation diffusion the spread of an innovation or other element of culture that occurs with the bodily relocation (migration) of an individual or group that has the idea.

Sequent occupance a sequence of settlements, implying distinct occupance phases.

Stimulus diffusion when a specific trait fails to diffuse but the underlying idea or concept is accepted.

Time-distance decay the decrease in acceptance of a cultural innovation with increasing time and distance from its origin.

Topical geography the division of geographical subject matter into topics, such as agricultural geography, rather than into regions.

Vernacular culture region a perceptual region; one perceived to exist by its inhabitants.

Suggested Readings

James M. Blaut. "Two Views of Diffusion," *Annals, Association of American Geographers*, 67 (1977), 343–349.

Karl W. Butzer. "Adaptation to Global Environmental Change," *Professional Geographer*, 32 (1980), 269–278.

James D. Clarkson. "Ecology and Spatial Analysis," *Annals, Association of American Georgraphers*, 60 (1970), 700–716.

James S. Duncan, "The Superorganic in American Cultural Geography," *Annals, Association of American Geographers*, 70 (1980), 181–198.

S. R. Eyre and G. R. J. Jones. *Geography as Human Ecology*. London: Edward Arnold, 1966.

Raymond D. Gastil. *Cultural Regions of the United States*. Seattle: University of Washington Press, 1975.

Derek, Gregory. *Ideology, Science and Human Geography*. New York: St. Martin's Press, 1978.

Charles F. Gritzner, Jr. "The Scope of Cultural Geography," *Journal of Geography*, 65 (January 1966), 4–11.

Larry Grossman. "Man-Environment Relationships in Anthropology and Geography," *Annals, Association of American Geographers*, 67 (1977), 126–144.

Human Ecology: An Interdisciplinary Journal. Published by the Plenum Press, New York and London. Provides a forum for papers concerned with the complex and varied systems of interaction between people and their environment. Volume I was published in 1972.

The Journal of Cultural Geography. The only English-language journal devoted exclusively to cultural geography. Published semiannually by the Department of Geography, Bowling Green State University, Ohio. Volume 1 was published in 1980.

Journal of Regional Cultures. Published by the Popular Culture Association, Bowling Green State University, Ohio. Volume I was published in 1981.

Landscape. Published at Berkeley, California, and edited by Blair Boyd. An interdisciplinary journal devoted to the cultural landscape. Cultural Geographers regularly contribute articles. Volume I was published in 1951.

David Lowenthal and Martyn J. Bowden. *Geographies of the Mind*. New York: Oxford University Press, 1976.

James R. McDonald. "The Region: Its Conception, Design and Limitations," *Annals, Association of American Geographers*, 56 (1966), 516–528.

D. W. Meinig (ed.). *The Interpretation of Ordinary Landscapes: Geographical Essays*. New York: Oxford University Press, 1979.

Robert D. Mitchell. "The Formation of Early American Cultural Regions: An Interpretation," in James Gibson (ed.), *European Settlement and Development in North America: Essays on Geographical Change in Honour and Memory of Andrew Hill Clark*. Toronto: University of Toronto Press, 1978.

W. B. Morgan and R. P. Moss. "Geography and Ecology: The Concept of the Community and Its Relation to Environment," *Annals, Association of American Geographers*, 55 (1965) 339–350.

Howard J. Nelson. "The Spread of an Artificial Landscape over Southern California," *Annals, Association of American Geographers*, 49:3, part 2 (1959), 80–99.

Richard Peet (ed.). *Radical Geography: Alternative Viewpoints on Contemporary Social Forces*. Chicago: Maaroufa Press, 1977.

Progress in Human Geography. A quarterly journal providing authoritative and critical appraisal of developments and trends in the discipline. It aims to report on and stimulate research and progress in both traditional and new aspects of human geography. Volume 1 was published in 1977.

G. W. S. Robinson. "The Geographic Region: Form and Function," *Scottish Geographical Magazine*, 69 (1953), 49–58.

John F. Rooney, Jr., Wilbur Zelinsky, Dean R. Louder, et al. (eds.). *This Remarkable Continent: An Atlas of North American Society and Culture*. College Station: Texas A & M University Press, 1981. The first work of its kind, this atlas contains over 400 maps illustrating the cultural geography of the United States and Canada, and is an indispensable reference for students of North American human geography.

Lester B. Rowntree and Margaret W. Conkey. "Symbolism and the Cultural Landscape," *Annals, Association of American Geographers*, 70 (1980), 459–474.

Thomas F. Saarinen. *Perception of Environment*. Resource Paper No. 5. Washington, D. C.: Association of American Geographers, Commission on College Geography, 1969.

Christopher L. Salter. *The Cultural Landscape*. Belmont, California: Duxbury Press, 1971.

Carl O. Sauer. "Morphology of Landscape," *University of California Publications in Geography*, 2 (1925), 19–54.

David M. Smith. *Patterns in Human Geography: An Introduction to Numerical Methods*. New York: Crane, Russak & Co., 1975.

William L. Thomas, Jr. (ed.). *Man's Role in Changing the Face of the Earth*. Chicago: University of Chicago Press, 1956.

Yi-fu Tuan. "Humanistic Geography," *Annals, Association of American Geographers*, 66 (1976), 266–276.

Yi-fu Tuan. *Man and Nature*. Resource Paper No. 10. Washington, D.C.: Association of American Geographers, Commission on College Geography, 1971.

Philip L. Wagner. "Cultural Landscapes and Regions: Aspects of Communication," in *Man and Cultural Heritage*, ed. by H. J. Walker and W. G. Haag, vol. 5 of *Geoscience and Man*. Baton Rouge: School of Geoscience, Louisiana State University, 1974, pp. 133–142.

Philip L. Wagner. "The Themes of Cultural Geography Rethought," *Yearbook of the Association of Pacific Coast Geographers*, 37 (1975), 7–14.

Philip L. Wagner and Marvin W. Mikesell. *Readings in Cultural Geography*. Chicago: University of Chicago Press, 1962, pp. 1–24.

Wilbur Zelinsky. *The Cultural Geography of the United States*. Englewood Cliffs, N.J.: Prentice-Hall, 1973.

People on the Land

2

Today, *overpopulation* is a word constantly on the tips of our tongues. It leaps forward as a ready explanation for many different irritating or frightening problems. You go to Yellowstone Park, and the ranger says you should have reserved your campsite last winter—overpopulation. You hear your neighbors arguing all night through the badly insulated walls of your apartment building—overpopulation. Population words bombard us constantly: the population crisis, the population bomb, the population explosion, zero population growth. People are compared to fast-breeding rats; the United Nations informs us that approximately four and one-half billion humans are alive on the earth. Overpopulation seems to hang over us all like a specter (see box, "Is the World Really Overpopulated?").

IS THE WORLD REALLY OVERPOPULATED?

Have you ever dreamed that every spot you visited was swarming with humans—elbow to elbow, jostling, pushing, touching, talking, shouting, complaining? The geographer William Bunge may have had such a dream, because one day he decided to figure out mathematically just how crowded the world really is. His results were startling. He took the earth's present estimated human population of 4 billion and awarded each of them only four square feet of space to stand in. His calculations:

"Four billion standing in four square feet each would need sixteen billion square feet. The square root of sixteen billion is approximately one hundred and thirty thousand, so a square one hundred and thirty thousand feet on a side should contain the whole world's population. Dividing this distance by the number of feet in a mile (5,280) shows that the total population of the world could stand in a loose crowd in a square only twenty-five miles on each side. This is about the size of an average American county."

From William W. Bunge, "The Geography of Human Survival." Reproduced by permission from the Annals of the Association of American Geographers, Volume 63, 1973, p. 288.

Would it surprise you, then, to learn that if people were evenly distributed over the earth's land surface, the resulting **population density** would be only about fifty-five people per square mile (twenty-one per square kilometer)? Of course, this is hardly the case, as all of you who live in less than one fifty-fifth of a square mile of personal space know. In fact, anyone who has traveled from a large city to a small town realizes that humankind has distributed itself most unevenly over the earth's surface. Variations in population density range from zero in the uninhabited expanses of Antarctica to an average of 77,000 people living in each square mile of space (30,000 people per square kilometer) on the island of Manhattan (see Figure 2-1).

Population geographers study these variations in density of people and the closely related "population explosion." So important is population distribution that some geographers even regard it as "the essential geographical expression," a worthy focus for the entire academic discipline. Most cultural geographers would at least agree that the uneven spatial distribution of people is a vitally important phenomenon. It provides us an appropriate point of departure for our study of cultural geography.

Population geographers also devote attention to the spatial variation of certain qualities or kinds of people. They are interested in the differences from one place to another in demographic characteristics such as birth rates, death rates, sex ratios, age groups, marriage, divorce, and human mobility (see Figure 2-1a). **Demography** is the name given to the statistical study of human population. In sum, the population geographer seeks to

◀ *Chapter-opening photo:* A large crowd in Djakarta, on the densely populated island of Java, Indonesia.

describe, explain, and measure the significance of spatial differences in the number and kind of people.

All these topics will receive our attention in this chapter. Our study of population geography will make use of the five themes outlined in Chapter 1. Accordingly, this chapter will delimit demographic regions, consider cultural diffusion as it relates to population, probe the ecology of population, investigate the ways population characteristics are integrated with other cultural patterns, and view the settlement landscapes produced by differing densities and distributions of people.

Demographic Regions

The culture regions devised by population geographers can be called **demographic regions**. They are very helpful in describing spatial variations in population density, growth, and characteristics. In this way, population geographers learn how humankind is distributed over the earth's surface and how other demographic traits differ from place to place.

Population density regions

There are many ways to view spatial variations in population density. If we study the distribution of people by continents, we find that 76 percent of the human race live in Eurasia. The continent of North America is home to almost 9 percent of all people; Africa, to nearly 10 percent; South America, to 5 percent; and Australia and the Pacific islands, to less than one-half of 1 percent. If we consider population distribution by political units, we find that approximately 22 percent of all humans reside in the People's Republic of China; 15 percent in India; 6½ percent in the Soviet Union; and 5½ percent in the United States.

We can also divide population density into categories such as: (1)

FIGURE 2–1

The world's population is spread unevenly over the earth's surface. In Lima, Peru, some residents crowd into a hillside slum near the modern downtown. They might not suspect that a country as empty as Greenland exists. How would you describe the population density in your home area?

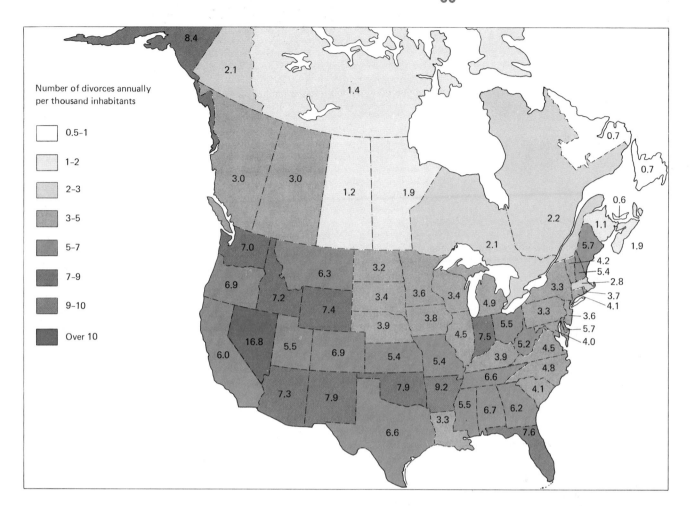

FIGURE 2–1a

Divorces per thousand inhabitants, by state, province, and territory in the United States and Canada in the mid-1970s. The U.S. data are for 1978, the Canadian for 1975. What might account for the higher divorce rate in the South and West? Why does only one state in the United States have a rate lower than the highest rate for a Canadian province? (Sources: National Center for Health Statistics, August, 1980; and *Canada Year Book 1978–79*.)

densely settled areas, which have 250 or more persons per square mile (100 or more per square kilometer); (2) moderately settled areas, with 60 to 250 persons per square mile (25 to 100 per square kilometer); (3) thinly settled areas, inhabited by 2 to 60 persons per square mile (1 to 25 per square kilometer); and (4) largely unpopulated areas, with fewer than 2 persons per square mile (fewer than 1 per square kilometer). These categories represent demographic regions based on the single trait of population density.

As Figure 2-2 shows, a fragmented crescent of dense settlement stretches along the western, southern, and eastern edge of the huge Eurasian continent. Two-thirds of the human race is concentrated in this crescent which stretches through the southern half of Japan, the plains and hills of eastern China, the monsoon coasts and great Ganges River plain of India, to the industrial districts of Europe. Outside of Eurasia, only scattered districts are densely settled. These include the most highly industrialized parts of the United States and the irrigated farmlands along the lower Nile River in Africa.

Despite our image of global overpopulation, sparsely settled regions are much more extensive than heavily settled ones and appear on every continent. Thin settlements dot the northern sections of Eurasia and North America, the interior of South America, and most of Australia. Another major zone of sparse population reaches through North Africa and Arabia into the heart of Eurasia.

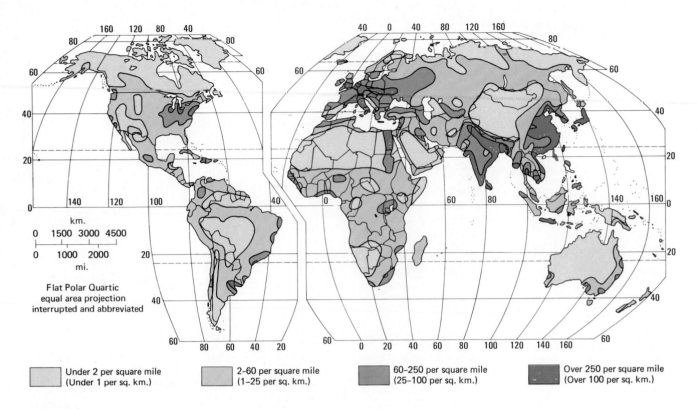

Under 2 per square mile (Under 1 per sq. km.)	2–60 per square mile (1–25 per sq. km.)	60–250 per square mile (25–100 per sq. km.)	Over 250 per square mile (Over 100 per sq. km.)

FIGURE 2–2

This map shows population density in the world. Despite our concern with overpopulation, large areas of the world are thinly settled. Within the densely settled zones, some areas, such as the United States, consume large amounts of the world's resources and maintain a high standard of living. Meanwhile, other areas with similar densities are unable to provide enough food for the population.

It is important to recognize that population density is a relative concept. Although it allows us to view the distribution of people, it does not tell us anything about standard of living, overpopulation, or underpopulation. Some of the most densely populated areas in the world have the highest standards of living—and even suffer from labor shortages. For example, this has been true of the major industrial areas of West Germany and the Netherlands. In certain other cases, regions designated as "thinly settled" may actually be severely overpopulated marginal agricultural lands. Although 1000 persons per square mile (400 per square kilometer) is a "dense" population for a farming area, it is "sparse" for an industrial district.

Density is also a static concept. It does not allow us to see the changes that constantly occur. It does not indicate the pronounced regional differences in birth rate, death rate, and population growth. Nor does density indicate migration. Therefore, in order to underscore the dynamic aspects of population, we will next explore culture regions based on birth and death rates.

Patterns of natality

No less than population density, **birth rates**, the number of births in a year per 1000 people, vary greatly from one area to another, as Figure 2-3 shows. In many ways, the map of birth rates does not correspond to the map of population density. Some densely populated areas, such as western Europe and Japan, have very low birth rates. Some sparsely settled regions, such as Arabia and interior Africa, have very high birth rates. In general, high birth rates are concentrated in a belt through the lower latitudes, especially the tropics and subtropics. As a rule, midlatitude and high-latitude countries presently have low birth rates.

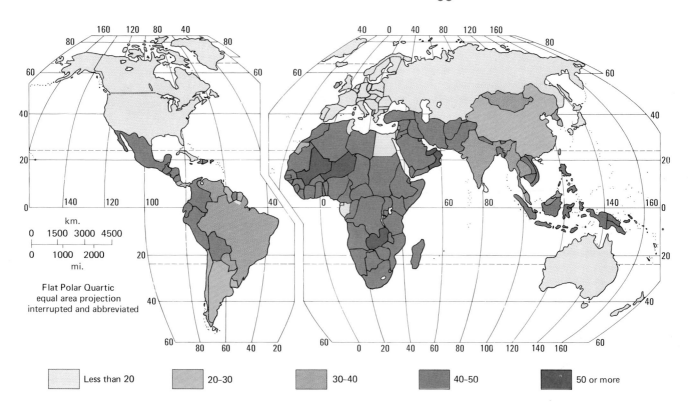

Less than 20	20–30	30–40	40–50	50 or more

Viewed economically, birth rates tend to be highest in countries that are less industrialized and urbanized, those of the so-called underdeveloped world. By contrast, the main manufacturing countries, where most people live in cities, generally have low or very low birth rates. Indeed, population geographers recognize birth rates as one of the best single socioeconomic variables for distinguishing between "developed" and "underdeveloped" countries.

Another perspective for looking at birth rates is cultural heritage. It seems that the lowest birth rates are usually found in European countries and lands peopled by European emigrants, such as the United States, Canada, Argentina, and Australia. However, the low birth rates now typical of Europeans and their overseas kin are relatively recent, coinciding with urbanization and industrialization. Population maps of the nineteenth rather than the twentieth century would show quite a different picture. Giant waves of emigration around the turn of the century drew millions of "excess" Europeans out of their own countries to settle distant areas of the earth. Yet this massive surge of colonial migration did little to hold down population growth. Europe's population rose from 194 million in 1840 to 463 million in 1930, approximately double the rate for the world as a whole. It has been estimated that, between 1750 and 1930, the number of Caucasians increased 5.4 times; Asians, only 2.3 times; and blacks, less than 2 times. Today, the process has been reversed. The children of the European birth-rate "explosion" can now watch the populations of non-European countries increase at an accelerated pace.

Patterns of mortality

The global pattern of **death rates**, the number of deaths in a year per 1000 people, is quite similar to that of birth rates, but there are also some

FIGURE 2–3

The annual birth rate per thousand population (about 1975) is shown for each country. The countries of the world tend to have either high or low birth rates, with few occupying the middle ground. In general, the highest birth rates are in the most impoverished, rural countries. The lowest rates are in urbanized, industrialized nations. (Source: United Nations, *Demographic Yearbook,* 1977, 283–287.)

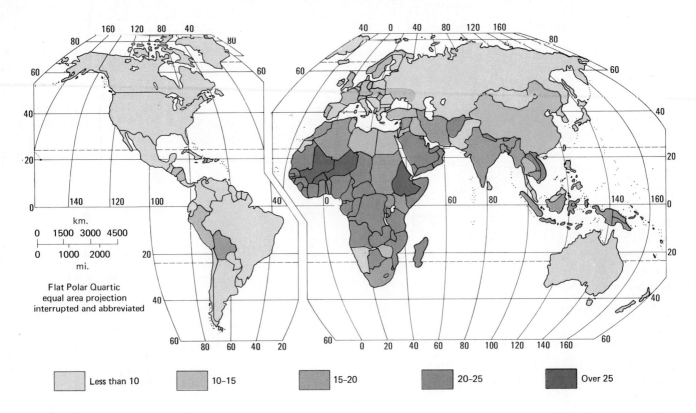

Less than 10	10–15	15–20	20–25	Over 25

FIGURE 2–4

The annual death rate per thousand (about 1975) is shown for each country. (Source: United Nations, *Demographic Yearbook,* 1977, 362–366.)

TABLE 2-1 The World Population Growth

Year	World Population
40,000 B.C.	1,500,000
8,000 B.C.	10,000,000
Birth of Christ	200,000,000
1000	275,000,000
1300	380,000,000
1500	450,000,000
1650	500,000,000
1750	700,000,000
1800	910,000,000
1850	1,100,000,000
1900	1,600,000,000
1950	2,500,000,000
1960	3,000,000,000
1965	3,200,000,000
1970	3,610,000,000
1975	4,000,000,000
1980	4,400,000,000

notable differences. As Figure 2-4 shows, the most striking feature of the death-rate map is the concentration of high figures in tropical Africa. This is the worst area in the world for serious diseases. On the other hand, urban and industrial nations have low death rates, just as they have low birth rates. But low death rates are also found in such countries as Thailand, Turkey, and Ecuador, where urbanization and industrialization are not well developed and where birth rates are moderate or high.

Many factors contribute to the death rate—from suicide to disease, from starvation to traffic accidents. But the greatest reshaper of the global death-rate map has been Western medical technology. In the twentieth century, this technology, in one form or another, has reached almost every part of the world. It was carried by colonial governments, missionaries, and other agencies. The net result has been greatly lowered death rates, even in areas such as tropical Africa, where the rate is still comparatively high.

The population explosion

The spatial contrasts in population density, birth rates, and death rates, when considered together, underscore the dynamic aspect of population. They provide the background for a discussion of the **population explosion**. On a global scale, we can easily describe the population crisis. The number of people in the world has been increasing geometrically, doubling in shorter and shorter periods of time. Table 2-1 shows the progression. The overall effect of even a few population doublings is startling. An example of a geometric progression is the legend of the king who was willing to grant any wish to the person who could supply a grain of wheat for the first square of his chessboard, two grains for the second square, four for the third and so on. To win, the candidate would have had

---

2000 YEARS OF POPULATION GROWTH REDUCED TO A SINGLE DAY

We can better visualize the frightening rate of population increase by reducing the 2000-year span since the birth of Christ to a single day, with midnight as the Nativity and the following midnight as the year 2000. We begin this day with a population of 200 million. The population on this scale does not double until 7:48 P.M., nearly twenty hours later. The next doubling of the world population occurs at 10:12 P.M., again at 11:00, and at 11:36, which we can consider as the year 1965. Before "midnight," or the year 2000, the population will double again.

---

to present a cache of wheat many times larger than today's worldwide wheat crop to cover all sixty-four squares.

The same phenomenon seems to apply to population growth. Humans have actually reproduced themselves at an extraordinarily modest rate throughout history—about 0.02 additional persons per 1000 per year. Since A.D. 1, the population has doubled about once every 500 years. At present, about 75 million more people come into the world each year than go out of it. The time span between doublings of the world population has grown progressively shorter and now stands at about thirty-five years (see box, "2000 Years of Population Growth Reduced to a Single Day").

For the most part, this population explosion did not come to light until the twentieth century. Nevertheless, some scholars foresaw long ago that an ever-increasing population would eventually present difficulties. As early as the 1600s, Sir William Petty, an Englishman who pioneered the science of statistics, predicted that an overpopulation crisis would develop one thousand years in the future. According to Petty, in the year 2600 there would be one person for each three acres of land. Then, in the 1700s, the Prussian army chaplain Johann Süssmilch estimated the world population at 1 billion, a reasonably accurate figure. He believed that God was steadily reducing the average human life span to accommodate the steadily increasing number of people. Süssmilch reached this conclusion by comparing the life expectancy for people of his own day with the 969-year life span attributed to Methuselah in the Old Testament.

The most famous early-day observer of population growth was an English clergyman. In 1798, Thomas Malthus published *An Essay on the Principles of Population* (see biographical sketch). Malthus believed that the human ability to multiply far exceeds our ability to increase food production (see box, "Excerpts from the Writings of Thomas Malthus). Consequently, Malthus maintained, "a strong and constantly operating check on population" will necessarily act as a natural control on numbers. Malthus felt that famine and war are inevitable because they curb population growth (see Figure 2-5). Today, almost two centuries after Malthus penned his warnings, his basic argument is still accepted in many quarters.

At the present rate of increase, the world population would, within a relatively few centuries, reach a level where each person had only one square foot (less than one-tenth of a square meter) of land area. Obviously, conditions could never become this crowded. It would be impossible to feed and house such a dense clustering of people. Indeed, some population scholars tend to see the extraordinary rise in human fertility rates at the present time as something of an historic oddity. They expect the world population to level out, perhaps early in the twenty-first century, at somewhere between 8 and 15 billion people. Some feel that this number

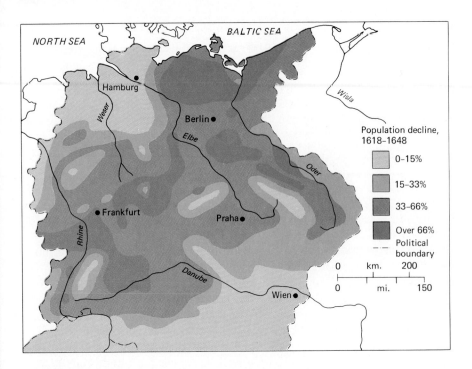

FIGURE 2-5

War as a device for population control in central Europe, 1618 to 1648. Thomas Malthus regarded war as inevitable, since it was necessary to help control population growth. He would understand this map, which reveals how effective war can be in destroying people. The Thirty Years' War, with its attendant killing, starvation, and disease, drastically reduced the population in some central European provinces, leaving few districts untouched. Population density was greatly altered. (After *Westermanns Grosser Atlas zur Weltgeschichte*, Braunschweig: Georg Westermann, 1956, p. 107.)

THOMAS R. MALTHUS   1766-1834

Born in the shire of Surrey, England, Malthus studied theology at Cambridge and became an ordained minister. While still a minister, he began writing his essay on population. Gradually, writing and lecturing became his major interest. In 1805, he was appointed a professor of modern history and political economy at Haileybury College, a position he held until his death. Long before most scholars were concerned with overpopulation, Malthus warned of it. His famous *Essay on the Principles of Population* was published in 1798. Marx, Darwin, and many others read and commented on his work. Malthus rejected most artificial birth control techniques as theologically unacceptable, approving only delayed marriage and moral restraint. He believed in the inevitability of warfare, famine, and disease. In recent decades, his ideas have received renewed attention as the world approaches a population crisis.

of people still does not exceed the earth's resources. Others, alarmed by the present rate of increase and convinced that the earth cannot support more people without an ecological catastrophe, argue for **zero population growth**. Each couple, they feel, should merely "replace" themselves by having only two children.

A global perspective on the population explosion is useful, but it does not provide a complete picture by itself. We also need a regional and local perspective. The term *population explosion* is generally applied to underdeveloped countries with a large difference between birth and death rates. Yet many countries in this category, such as Brazil, are not overpopulated. Others may be reaching the point where additional population will spell disaster. However, we must also take into account regional variations in forms of livelihood. Would an additional 500 million people overpopulate India? Very likely it would if India remains an agrarian land; perhaps not if India were to become industrialized. Certainly Tokyo and New York City now contain more people per square mile than most areas of India.

At the same time, we should realize that the seriousness of the population problem varies with the way resources are used. We might well argue that 1 million more persons in agrarian India or China are less serious globally than 100,000 more in urban and industrial America. On the average, each American consumes more than ten times as much food, energy, and other resources as each rural Asian. As demographers Ronald Freedman and Bernard Berelson have suggested, overpopulation "is not

EXCERPTS FROM THE WRITINGS OF THOMAS MALTHUS

"I think I may fairly make two postulata.

"First, that food is necessary to the existence of man.

"Secondly, that the passion between the sexes is necessary, and will remain nearly in its present state.

". . . Assuming, then, my postulata as granted, I say, that the power of population is indefinitely greater than the power in the earth to produce subsistence for man.

"Population, when unchecked, increases in a geometrical ratio. Subsistence only increases in an arithmetical ratio. A slight acquaintance with numbers will show the immensity of the first power in comparison of the second.

"By that law of our nature which makes food necessary to the life of Man, the effects of these two unequal powers must be kept equal.

"This implies a strong and constantly operating check on population. . . ."

From Thomas Malthus, An Essay on the Principles of Population (London, 1798), chap. 1.

the problem of countries such as India but the problem of countries such as the U.S.; the solution calls not for fewer babies there but for less consumption here."

Facing the population crisis. How will the population explosion be controlled? We know that the continued growth of human numbers must end sometime. But are war, famine, and disease the only answers? Are there viable alternatives to the fearsome "natural" controls envisioned by Malthus? The answer to these questions may well differ from one culture to another. And even to attempt to answer these questions, we must look at the experiences of the industrialized areas of the world in "solving" their population problems.

Starting in the eighteenth century, a number of European countries began to undergo what population geographers now call the **demographic transformation**. In other words, they underwent certain changes in birth and death rates that seem to accompany the movement from a rural, agrarian society to a primarily urban and industrial one. In preindustrial societies, birth and death rates are both normally high, leading to almost no population growth. With the coming of the industrial era, such medical discoveries as inoculations with cowpox serum to prevent smallpox, improvements in diet, and other factors set the stage for the drastic drop in death rates. Human life expectancy in the industrialized countries soared from an average of thirty-five years in the eighteenth century to seventy years or more at present. The result in Europe was a population explosion as fertility outran mortality. Eventually, after a lag, a decline in the birth rate followed the decline in the death rate, as is shown in Figure 2-6.

FIGURE 2-6

The demographic transformation as a graph. The "transformation" occurs in several steps, as the industrialization of a country progresses. Initially, the death rate declines rapidly, causing a population explosion as the gap between the number of births and deaths widens. Then the birth rate begins a sharp decline. The transformation ends when both birth and death rates have reached low levels.

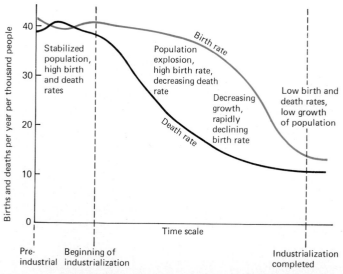

Today, from Japan to the United States, industrialized, technologically advanced nations have achieved an almost universally low fertility rate. This universal change is even more remarkable because it has been accomplished in countries with quite different cultures and with quite different "birth-control" strategies. At present, low growth rates and low birth rates exist throughout the industrialized world.

It is tempting, but not necessarily accurate, to credit this universal lowering of the birth rate to the discovery of modern birth control methods—the pill, intrauterine devices, vasectomies—and to the legalization of abortion. But it should be pointed out that, although many industrialized countries had previously experienced a remarkable population explosion, birth rates were lower in the 1930s than they are today. The main methods of achieving this lowered rate—intercourse without ejaculation, celibacy, **infanticide**, the use of abortifacients, and later marriages—were known for centuries. What this implies is that lowering a population's birth rate is a cultural, not a technical, problem. In other words, the birth rate declines when people decide that it is personally beneficial to have a smaller family, not when they are convinced of the dangers of overpopulation (see Figure 2-7). The fact is that in an urban, industrial society, children lose much of their economic significance to the family. Thus, having fewer of them can be a benefit. Even so, Western population scientists, politicians, and others are today approaching the global population problem as a matter of technology. They are offering the rest of the world mainly technological solutions rather than cultural ones. They are ignoring the cultural geography of population.

The Western technological "solutions." Western technological and scientific innovations, in no small measure, caused the population explosion. Their principal effect was to lower death rates without lowering birth rates. This same technological civilization, centered in Europe and America, has now produced techniques and devices for birth control. Western experts in a variety of academic fields have offered many

FIGURE 2–7
In many areas, large families represent economic security to parents. This family in rural Paraguay belongs to a culture that discourages birth control for both economic and religious reasons. Although it may be difficult to provide food and clothing for the infants, the children are soon old enough to work and contribute to the family income.

FIGURE 2–8
The government of India sponsors an extensive program of family planning. Until the population growth rate subsides, the country cannot hope to cope with its economic problems. Throughout the country, birth-control clinics educate men and women and provide medical assistance. How is family planning education handled in this country?

proposals for controlling population growth. These proposals fall into several categories.

Some of the experts' suggestions involve voluntary fertility control. They propose to provide free contraceptive devices, remove all remaining legal restrictions on abortion, encourage vasectomies, and develop improved contraceptive devices (see Figure 2-8). Many of these proposals are familiar to us because they are already being used. In addition, much research is in progress to improve voluntary birth-control methods and to discover new ones.

A second category of possible ways to control population includes various proposals for incentive programs. For example, taxes could be raised as each child is born to a family, with the lowest tax rate reserved for childless couples. Monetary rewards for voluntary sterilization could be offered, and the government could guarantee old-age care to people with no children. Parents might be required to pay a set amount of tax for the birth of each child, beginning with the third-born.

In a third category are proposed laws aimed at changing basic traditions. The law could be changed to encourage more women to go to work. Another law could dissolve the family as a social institution by removing children from their parents at birth and allowing the state to rear and educate all offspring. Special legal recognition could be given to the childless marriage. For instance, laws could be changed to make it easier for childless couples to obtain divorces.

A fourth category of proposals involves involuntary fertility control. Oral contraceptives could be added to water supplies and to staple foods such as bread. Or they could be sprayed from airplanes with the method now used for pesticides. Governments could demand that anyone wanting to have children apply for a license, and they could require abortions for all illegal pregnancies. Children could be temporarily sterilized at puberty, and adults could be forcibly sterilized after producing two surviving children.

Most of these proposals are feasible only in industrially advanced, urbanized nations with well-developed technologies and relatively efficient central governments. Even there, many are unworkable. Most could succeed only among literate, educated, relatively prosperous peoples. As we have already seen, such peoples have, in the main, already significantly lowered their birth rates. In effect, most Western proposals for population control are applicable only in industrial cultures, those that have already "spontaneously" adopted birth control.

Solutions in the underdeveloped world. Looking at Figure 2-9, you can see that exploding populations are found mainly in economically underdeveloped countries. Many of these agrarian lands can hardly afford the rapid increase in population. Yet their populations are not responsive to Western birth-control solutions, even though Western methods of death control were gratefully accepted.

From the viewpoint of the United States in the 1980s, it is hard to understand how the "scientific" solutions of Western scholars can be rejected. The problem of overpopulation seems so clear and "rational." However, what is rational and scientific to an urban scholar may appear to be little short of lunacy to an Asian peasant. For a peasant in India, children may appear the only way out of a life of poverty and an old age of solitary begging. An urban society puts large sums of money into the formal education of its children and forbids child labor, making children a financial burden (as any parent who has financed a college education for a son or daughter knows all too well). In a rural society, the costs of raising and educating a child are minimal and grow smaller the more children there are in a family. The advantages are enormous. The children can work from an early age, replace otherwise expensive hired laborers in the fields, and provide a form of support for the parents in old age. To suggest

FIGURE 2-9
The annual natural increase of population (about 1974) is a product of the birth and death rates. The lowest rates of increase are found in major industrial countries. The most rapid increase is taking place in Latin America, North Africa, and southwestern Asia. In 1800, the map of natural increase differed considerably from the contemporary one. At that time, how did population growth in the United States and Europe compare to the rest of the world? (Source: United Nations, *Demographic Yearbook,* 1977, 151–155.)

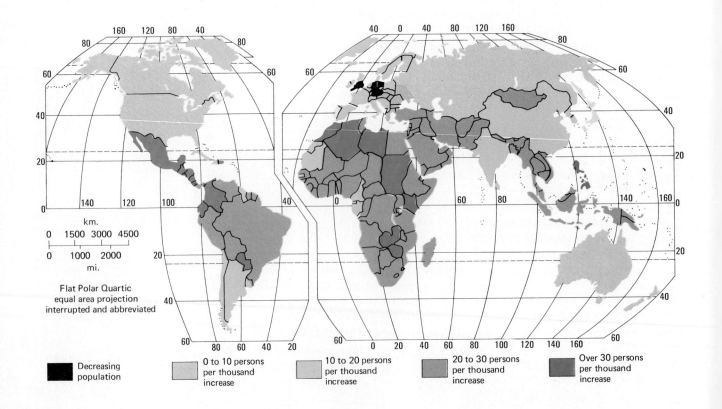

WHY BIRTH CONTROL FAILED IN MANUPUR

"'[They] were trying to convince me in 1960 that I shouldn't have any more sons,' commented Thaman Singh, water carrier in Manupur village, part of India's Punjab state. 'Now, you see, I have six sons and two daughters and I sit at home in leisure. They are grown up and they bring me money. One even works outside the village as a laborer. [They] told me I was a poor man and couldn't support a large family. Now, you see, because of my large family, I am a rich man. . . . Time has proven me right.'

"Thaman Singh, along with the rest of Manupur's villagers, was the subject of a multiyear birth control project sponsored by Harvard University, the Rockefeller Foundation, and the Indian government. The project attempted to get Manupur's villagers to adopt modern birth control methods, and voluntarily limit family size. Often, the villagers politely accepted the birth control tablets offered by the study's field workers. 'But they were so nice, you know,' commented one villager. 'And they came from distant lands to be with us. Couldn't we even do this much for them? Just take a few tablets?' However, many never actually used the foam tablets. In fact, the villagers considered the whole project bizarre, and were constantly looking for 'the clue' to what the project workers were really doing. In the end, the project failed to dent the area's birth rate. Project workers attributed this to peasant illiteracy, ignorance, or prejudice. The villagers, particularly the poor farmers and tenant farmers of Manupur who resisted the project most strongly, looked on the matter quite differently.

"'A rich man invests in his machines. We must invest in our children. It's that simple,' said Manupur blacksmith Hakika Singh. The arithmetic of land and labor makes this easy to understand. With a tractor, three people can work about fifty acres. Without a tractor, the same land would take fourteen people year around and twenty at sowing, weeding, and harvesting time. Hakika Singh, like other Manupur villagers, is aware that people are not stuck in poverty because they have large families. Rather they have large families because they are poor, and desperate to change that situation. Sons and daughters in Manupur cost little to raise, replace far more expensive hired laborers in a farmer's fields, can emigrate to other areas or even the city to get jobs augmenting the family's overall income, and support the parents in old age. As one villager put it: 'Without sons, there is no living off the land. The more sons you have, the less labor you need to hire and the more savings you can have'."

to an Indian villager that he or she practice birth control without also suggesting a method for attacking the root of the high birth rate—the structure of peasant poverty, tenancy, and insecurity—is to offer less than nothing (see box, "Why Birth Control Failed in Manupur").

In this respect, the experience of China may prove valuable. The government there has attempted to guarantee old-age security to its population regardless of the children produced by each set of parents. If we may judge from the recent information from the People's Republic, it seems likely that the old-age security provided by the government, coupled with a well-publicized birth-control campaign and an effort to encourage later marriages among youth, has significantly reduced the growth rate of the Chinese population. This birth-control program has progressed largely without the technology of the West.

Age and sex distributions

Some countries have overwhelmingly young populations, with close to half of their people under fifteen years of age. Mexico is such a country, as are many other nations of Latin America, Africa, and tropical Asia. Others, generally the countries that industrialized early, have a great preponderance of people in the over-twenty/under-sixty age bracket.

A very useful graphic device for depicting such national age character-

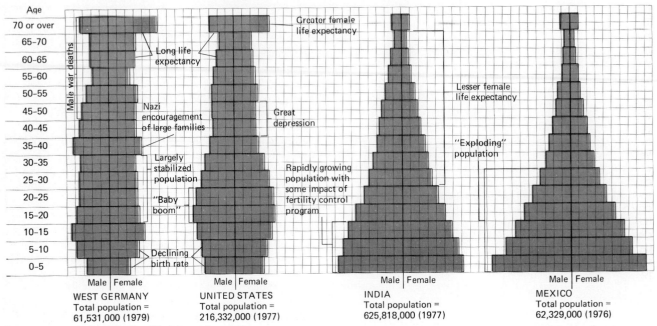

Age

70 or over	
65–70	
60–65	
55–60	
50–55	
45–50	
40–45	
35–40	
30–35	
25–30	
20–25	
15–20	
10–15	
5–10	
0–5	

WEST GERMANY: Male war deaths, Long life expectancy, Nazi encouragement of large families, Largely stabilized population, "Baby boom", Declining birth rate

UNITED STATES: Greater female life expectancy, Great depression

INDIA: Rapidly growing population with some impact of fertility control program

MEXICO: Lesser female life expectancy, "Exploding" population

Male | Female
WEST GERMANY
Total population =
61,531,000 (1979)

Male | Female
UNITED STATES
Total population =
216,332,000 (1977)

Male | Female
INDIA
Total population =
625,818,000 (1977)

Male | Female
MEXICO
Total population =
62,329,000 (1976)

Each unit on the horizontal scale = 1% of the total population

FIGURE 2–10

Population pyramids for the United States, West Germany, Mexico, and India are shown. West Germany's "pyramid" looks more like a precariously balanced pillar, an indication that its population is approaching stability. Mexico, by contrast, displays the classic stepped pyramid of an exploding population. The American pyramid reveals recent sharp declines in the birth rate. The modest progress of birth control in India can also be seen. (Source: United Nations, *Demographic Yearbook*, 1977, 200–213.)

istics is the **population pyramid**. (Figure 2-10 compares four pyramids.) Careful study of such pyramids not only reveals the past progress of birth control, but also allows geographers to predict future population trends. Youth-weighted pyramids, broad at the base, suggest the extremely rapid growth typical of the population explosion. Those excessively narrow at the base represent countries approaching population stability. Population pyramids also allow a graphic portrayal of **sex ratios**.

Similar age and sex contrasts are also apparent within individual countries. For example, rural populations in the United States are usually older than those in urban areas. Indeed, the flight of young people to the cities has left some rural counties in the United States with populations forty-five years or older in median age. Some warm areas of the United States have even become retirement havens for the elderly, so that parts of Arizona and Florida have populations far above average in age (see Figure 2-11). Communities such as Sun City near Phoenix, Arizona, actually legally restrict residence to the elderly. In Great Britain, the elderly are concentrated in the coastal areas, causing the map of persons over sixty years of age to resemble a hollow shell (see Figure 2-12).

Sex ratios also vary by region sometimes. "Frontier" areas typically have far more males than females, as is evident in parts of Alaska and northern Canada. In Alaska, 56 percent of the population sixteen years of age or older are male, according to the 1970 census. By contrast, 47 percent are male in Mississippi, where many young men have left for other places. The same is true of many economically depressed rural areas and agrarian nations. For instance, many prime-age males have emigrated from Spain and Portugal. They reside for most of the year in industrialized countries such as France and West Germany, often leaving their families behind. Similarly, in the African nation of Malawi, according to the 1978 United Nations *Demographic Yearbook*, the attraction of jobs in the cities has made the urban population 53 percent male. Only 46.5 percent of rural people are men.

FIGURE 2–11
This map shows the median age of Florida's population in 1970. "Median" age means that half of the population is older and half is younger than the median figure. American culture is perhaps unique in the degree to which it has segregated elderly people. In some other cultures, such as that of India, elderly people commonly reside in the homes of their children and grandchildren. In Florida, the range in median age is from about 23 years in some northwestern and interior countries to over 58 in the major retirement district of the lower Gulf coast. What socioeconomic impact might such an uneven age distribution have? What effect would it have on the distribution of hospitals, the density and specialties of physicians, the products sold in pharmacies, the school systems, and recreational facilities? (Source: 1970 U.S. Census of Population.)

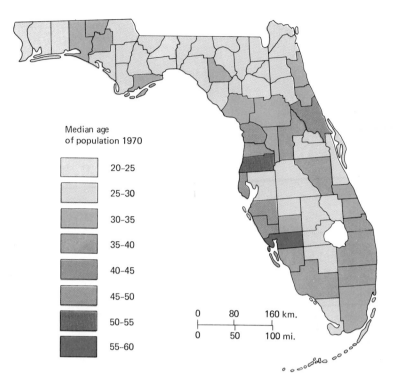

Median age
of population 1970

	20–25
	25–30
	30–35
	35–40
	40–45
	45–50
	50–55
	55–60

    Thus human population varies spatially in density, as well as in rates and proportions of birth, death, age, and sex. All these variations have been shown through the device of demographic regions. Now let us turn to the other themes of cultural geography. Through them, we will learn more about population characteristics and perhaps find some explanations for these sometimes striking spatial distributions.

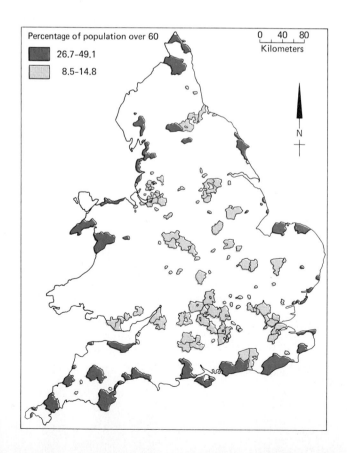

Percentage of population over 60

	26.7–49.1
	8.5–14.8

FIGURE 2–12
Distribution of the elderly in England and Wales, 1971. Why do elderly people form a larger part of the population in the coastal regions than in the interior? Does the seaside environment encourage longevity; have the elderly migrated to the shore; or have younger people moved away from the sea? (After C. M. Law and A. M. Warnes, "The Changing Geography of the Elderly in England and Wales," *Transactions, Institute of British Geographers,* New Series 1 (1976), 461.)

Diffusion in Population Geography

In population geography, cultural diffusion operates on many levels. Migration of people is perhaps the most basic type of cultural diffusion. Geographers, with their concern for spatial processes, have a natural interest in the movement of population. The territorial redistribution of people is therefore a major concern of population geographers.

Migration

Humankind has never been tied to one locale. Although our species probably evolved in tropical Africa, we have proven remarkably adaptable to new and different physical environments. We have made ourselves at home in all but the most inhospitable climates, shunning only such places as ice-sheathed Antarctica and the shifting sands of Arabia's "Empty Quarter." Even there, temporary migrants frequently come to stay for a while. Our permanent habitat extends from the edge of the ice sheets to the seashores, from desert valleys a thousand feet (310 meters) below sea level to mountain slopes 16,000 feet (4900 meters) or more up. This far-flung distribution is the product of migration.

Migration takes place when people decide that it is preferable to move rather than to stay, when the difficulties of moving seem more than offset by the expected rewards. Migration is relocation diffusion, though the decision to migrate can spread by means of expansion diffusion. For more detail on these processes, see Chapter 9.

Every migration, from the ancient dispersal out of Africa to the present-day movement toward urban areas, is governed by a host of push-and-pull factors. These act to make the old home unattractive or unlivable and the new home attractive or at least an alternative. As we will learn in our discussion of cultural ecology, migration is often influenced by people's perceptions, however inaccurate, of lands available for settlement. Perhaps the most important factor prompting migration throughout the thousands of years of human existence is economic. More often than not, migrating people are seeking greater prosperity than they have known.

In the nineteenth century, more than 50 million European emigrants, seeking better lives outside their native lands, changed the racial character of much of the earth. By 1970, about one-half of all Caucasians did not live in the European homelands of the ancestors. In our time, this flow has been reversed. For example, Sweden, long a country of emigration, became a host to immigrants after 1930. Between about 1950 and 1970, about 20 million people migrated into eleven New World and European industrial nations from the more agrarian areas of the world. They, like their emigrating European predecessors, were looking for jobs, better wages, and a new and more secure economic life (see Figure 2-13).

One of the greatest mass movements presently under way is the migration of southern Europeans from Spain, Portugal, southern Italy, Greece, and Yugoslavia to the industrial districts of western and central Europe. Although supposedly temporary, this migration has already resulted in the diffusion of many southern cultural traits to the north. A similar migration, involving many illegal aliens, is bringing hundreds of thousands of Mexican, Central American, and Caribbean people into the United States each year.

FIGURE 2–13
One of the massive migrations to the United States was the influx of Irish. Many people fled from the famines in Ireland during the last century. the immigrants had images of America as a land of wealth and opportunity that encouraged them to attempt the long trip. Who are the modern immigrants to North America, and what are their images of their new homeland?

International migration often occurs because a country has a negative image in the minds of some of its people. Foreign lands seem more attractive to them. Great Britain, for many years a goal of emigrants, especially from Ireland, now loses about 60,000 of its people per year. Many British emigrants are attracted to Australia and New Zealand. These Southern Hemisphere nations have, respectively, 110,000 and 17,000 more immigrants than emigrants each year. Britishers are attracted to Australia and New Zealand because these countries are British in culture yet seem to lack many of the economic and social problems that plague Great Britain. Whether deserved or not, Australia and New Zealand are perceived as something of an earthly paradise by much of the British middle class, an image promoted by publicity offices throughout Britain.

People in the United States have traditionally been mobile. From the country's beginnings, Americans have been a migrating people. The nation has "tilted west," with most migration occurring from east to west. The spectacular growth of California, especially in this century, is the culmination of the westward movement. By contrast, black migration in the United States has flowed mainly from south to north as rural blacks were attracted to large northern cities. In fact, throughout the past century or more, there has been a general movement of Americans from rural to urban areas, although recent censuses suggest that this migration to cities may be ending. Also, both the south to north movement of American black people and the east to west shift of whites seem to have ended, being replaced by a north to south migration of both races to the "Sunbelt" states. A similar farm-to-city migration can be detected in a large majority of the world's countries.

While human migration may be the most fundamental type of diffusion, there are other population phenomena that may profitably be studied through the concept of cultural diffusion. For example, we can apply the principles of diffusion to some of the proposed methods of population control that were discussed earlier.

Diffusion of population control

How can we determine which, if any, of the proposals for population control are likely to succeed? Cultural geographers can best approach this question by using the theme of cultural diffusion and, in particular, the concept of absorbing and permeable barriers. After all, most methods of population control are simply cultural innovations. Different barriers to those innovations are present in different cultures.

For example, adding contraceptives to the water supply is impractical in countries such as India, where water is hand-drawn from millions of separate wells rather than tapped from central water-purification systems. Similarly, it is impossible to raise the taxes of people living in abject poverty, because they simply do not have the money. In fact, many of the population-control proposals outlined earlier in this chapter—such as involuntary fertility control—require huge bureaucracies. In countries such as India, where existing bureaucracies are already terribly inefficient and ineffective, many measures would be hard to oversee. Moreover, democracy is well-rooted in India, and it is unlikely that any government other than dictatorship would be able to institute unpopular birth-control schemes.

Birth-control programs can also run into social barriers. In India, the cultural preference for large numbers of children is so deeply entrenched that a woman has traditionally been considered immoral if she dies without having mothered at least one son and inadequate if she mothers only a small family. Children provide old-age security, and a son must perform certain rituals at the death of his father. In some other cultures, particularly in Latin America, large numbers of children prove the husband's virility.

Organized religions often block the control of population growth. For instance, the Roman Catholic Church opposes modern methods of artificial birth control, including abortion (Figure 2-14). This opposition is based partly on the belief that such controls constitute a human disruption of the divine order. Partly as a result, many areas of strong Catholicism have high birth rates. In studying Northern Ireland, for example,

FIGURE 2–14
Religion can play a major role in determining family size. In some Roman Catholic areas, large families are admired. What is the acceptable family size among your friends? How are their views affected by religion, politics and economy?

geographer P.A. Compton found that "significant disparities exist between Roman Catholics and Protestants," to the extent that continuation
of current birth-rate patterns would produce a Catholic majority there at
some time in the first half of the twenty-first century. Some sects
encourage large families as means of expanding their membership.

International rivalries and nationalist feelings sometimes affect population growth. The leaders of a country may not encourage birth control for
fear that their population will become smaller than that of a hostile
neighbor country. They look at each newborn child as a future soldier, a
defender of the homeland. Similarly, in some diplomatic quarters power
and influence in international affairs are seen as linked to the size of
population. China's diplomatic victories, in particular its displacement of
Nationalist China (Taiwan) in the United Nations, are related to its huge
population. Diplomats were repeatedly reminded that "you can't ignore a
quarter of the human race," a reference to China's 800 million people. The
same problem often arises within countries where two or more ethnic
groups compete for influence. For example, some black leaders in the
United States view birth control as a scheme devised by white people to
reduce the size of the black population. They refer to birth control as
"genocide."

Even within areas as small as western Europe, geographers have found
major regional contrasts in attitudes toward population growth. In France,
the revolution of 1789 reduced Roman Catholic influence and gave
individuals more of a chance to advance economically and socially on the
basis of their native ability. Partly as a result of these developments, the
birth rate in nineteenth-century France declined rapidly. However, neighboring countries, such as Germany, Italy, and the United Kingdom, did
not experience the same decline. Consequently, the French population
did not keep pace numerically with that in nearby lands (see Figure 2-15).

Table 2-2 compares the populations of five countries from 1720 to 1977.
France, the most populous of these countries in 1800, was the least
populous of the four European countries included in the table in 1977.
During this same period, millions of Germans, Britishers, and Italians
emigrated overseas, whereas relatively few French left their homeland. At
the same time, the French Canadians of Québec, whose ancestors had left
France long before, still favored large families. Consequently, the 10,000
people who settled in Québec between 1608 and 1750 multiplied into
today's population of over 6 million. This number does not include many
French Canadians who migrated from Canada to New England and other
areas. In order to promote population growth in the colony, the Québec

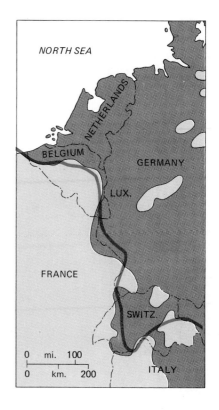

Birthrate 25.0 per 1000 and under

Birthrate 25.0 per 1000 and over

Germanic/Romance language border

International borders

FIGURE 2-15
Birth-rate pattern in western Europe,
1910. Notice how the birth-rate border
paralleled the linguistic rather than the
political boundary. French-speaking
people in France, southern Belgium,
western Switzerland, and northwestern
Italy, together with their
Romance-language kinsmen, the
Romanish-speaking people of eastern
Switzerland, were reproducing at a
lower rate than their German-speaking
neighbors. What cultural factors might
have helped produce this contrast?
(Adapted from Terry G. Jordan, *The
European Culture Area: A Systematic
Geography*, New York: Harper & Row,
1973, p. 73.)

**TABLE 2-2 Population Growth in France, French Canada, Germany, Italy,
and the United Kingdom (Population in millions)**

Country	1720	1800	1850	1900	1930	1977	Increase from 1720 to 1977
France	19	27	36	38	42	53	179%
Québec	0.02	0.2	0.9	1.7	2.8	6.3	3140%
Germany	14	25	35	56	64	78*	457%
Italy	13	18	23	32	41	56	331%
United Kingdom	7	11	27	37	46	56	700%

* East and West Germany together.

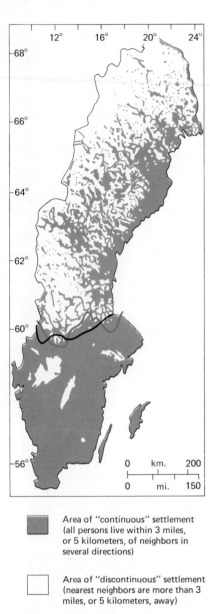

Area of "continuous" settlement (all persons live within 3 miles, or 5 kilometers, of neighbors in several directions)

Area of "discontinuous" settlement (nearest neighbors are more than 3 miles, or 5 kilometers, away)

Southern border of subarctic climate and infertile soils

Northern border of main zone of "continuous" settlement

Discontinuous
—————
Continuous

Settlement
boundary

FIGURE 2-16
Environment and population distribution in Sweden. The northern boundary of the thickly settled area corresponds closely to the southern limit of the bitterly cold subarctic climate and the infertile, acidic soils of the coniferous forests. (Adapted from Kirk H. Stone, "Swedish Fringes of Settlement," *Annals, Association of American Geographers,* 52 (1962), 379.)

government at times supported this enthusiasm for parenthood by offering tax deductions for large families.

The contrasts between densely settled regions and uninhabited wastelands, between countries with exploding populations and those in which the numbers have stabilized, between highly mobile and stay-put populations, provide spatial variations for the population geographer to analyze. Cultural diffusion has suggested some reasons for these variations. The themes of cultural ecology and cultural integration will suggest others.

Population Ecology

If you could live anywhere in the world, what physical setting would you choose? Would you pick a place that is different from or similar to where you live now? What aspects of the environment would you consider in making your decision? Geographers have discovered that a variety of environmental factors influence people's choices of where to settle. They have also observed that people naturally look at the physical features of their environment through the lenses provided by their own particular culture. A person's choice of where to live, necessarily influenced by culture, will in turn have some impact on the environment. Naturally, then, when considering population distribution, we should ask how environmental influence, perception, and modification are involved. In other words, we must think in terms of a "population ecology."

Environmental Influence

As a general rule, population tends to be densest where the terrain is level, the climate mild and humid, the soil fertile, mineral resources abundant, and the sea accessible. Conversely, population tends to thin out with increasing elevation, dryness, coldness, ruggedness of terrain, and distance from the coast (see Figure 2-16).

Climatic factors strongly affect where people settle. Most of the sparsely populated zones in the world have, in some respect, "defective" climates, from the human viewpoint. The thinly peopled northern edge of Eurasia and North America is excessively cold, and the belt from North Africa into the heart of Eurasia matches the major desert zones of the Old World. Humans remain creatures of the humid and subhumid tropics, subtropics, and midlatitudes. People have not fared well in excessively cold or dry areas. Small populations of Eskimos, Lapps, and other peoples do live in some of the supposedly "uninhabitable" areas of the earth, but these areas simply cannot support large populations of humans. Perhaps, as a species, we have not fully forgotten the climatic features of sub-Saharan Africa, where we began. In avoiding cold places, we may reveal even today the tropical origin of our species.

Humankind's preference for lower elevations holds especially true for the middle and higher latitudes. Indeed, most mountain ranges in those latitudes stand out as regions of sparse population (see Figure 2-17). By contrast, inhabitants of the tropics often prefer to live at higher elevations, typically concentrating in dense clusters in mountain valleys and basins. By doing so, they escape the humid, hot climate of the tropical lowlands. For example, in tropical portions of South America, more people live in the Andes Mountains than in the nearby Amazon lowlands. And the capital cities of many tropical and subtropical nations lie in mountain areas above about 3000 feet (900 meters) in elevation.

Our tendency to settle on or near the seacoast is also quite striking. If you look again at Figure 2-2, you can see that the continents of Eurasia, Australia, and South America resemble hollow shells, with the majority of the population clustered around the rim of each continent. In Australia, half the total population lives in just five port cities, and most of the remainder is spread out over nearby coastal areas. This preference for living by the sea can be partly explained by the trade and fishing opportunities the sea offers. At the same time, continental interiors tend to be regions of climatic extremes. For example, Australians speak of the "dead heart" of their continent, an interior land of excessive dryness and heat.

People are also attracted to those places where fresh water is available. In desert regions, population clusters reflect the location of scattered oases and occasional rivers, such as the Nile, that rise from sources outside the desert. Figure 2-18 shows this settlement pattern.

Still another environmental factor that affects population distribution is disease. In the Mediterranean region, especially in Italy, thickly settled, agriculturally productive coastal lands were virtually depopulated by the spread of malaria after Roman times. Only in recent times, as malaria was eradicated by modern scientific methods, were these districts reclaimed and repopulated. Other diseases attack valuable domestic animals, depriving people of food and clothing resources. Such diseases have an indirect but profound effect on population density. For example, in parts of East Africa, livestock are attacked by a form of sleeping sickness. This particular disease is almost invariably fatal to cattle but not to humans. The people in this part of East Africa depend heavily on cattle. Cattle provide food, are symbols of wealth, and serve a semireligious function in some tribes. Thus, the spread of a disease fatal to cattle has caused entire tribes to migrate away from infested areas, leaving them unpopulated. Figure 2-19 charts the movements of African peoples in response to this disease.

Environmental perception and population distribution

The most telling geographical commentary on a place is made when people perceive it as a suitable home and choose to live there. Perception of the physical environment plays a role in this choice. Different cultural groups often "see" the same physical environment in different ways. These varied responses to a single environment may influence the distribution of people. A good example of this appears in that part of the European Alps shared by German- and Italian-speaking people. The mountain ridges in that area—near the point where Switzerland, Italy, and Austria join—run in an east-west direction, so that each ridge has a sunny, south-facing slope and a shady, north-facing side. Good sun exposure originally led both groups to settle on south-facing slopes. Nevertheless, they differ markedly in the way they have populated their respective slopes. German-speaking people, who rely on dairy farming, established permanent settlements some 650 feet (200 meters) higher on the shady slopes than the settlements of Italians, who are culturally tied to warmth-loving crops, on the sunny slopes. This example demonstrated contrasting cultural attitudes toward land use and differing perceptions of the best use for one type of physical environment.

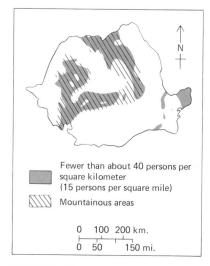

Fewer than about 40 persons per square kilometer (15 persons per square mile)

Mountainous areas

0   100   200 km.

0   50   150 mi.

FIGURE 2-17
This map presents population distribution in Romania, based on population data for the early 1960s. Environmental features, such as mountain ranges, may discourage settlement. In Romania, the mountainous areas are also the areas of sparse settlement. In what ways might mountains in midlatitude areas repel population?

FIGURE 2-18
Environmental factors—in this case, water in the midst of the desert—mold population distribution. These scattered clusters of people are in the Sahara of North Africa, but the pattern is typical of many arid regions. Dot clusters indicate the presence of oases. Imagine how the economy differs in the areas of sparse and dense population. (After Paul F. Mattingly and Elsa Schmidt, "The Maghreb: Population Density." Map Supplement No. 15, *Annals, Association of American Geographers*, 61 (1971).)

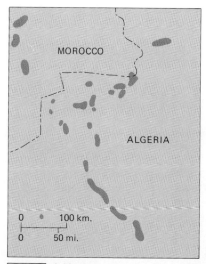

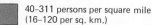

0-39 persons per square mile (0-15 per sq. km.)

40-311 persons per square mile (16-120 per sq. km.)

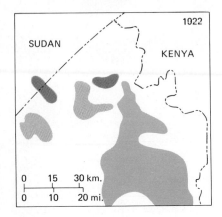

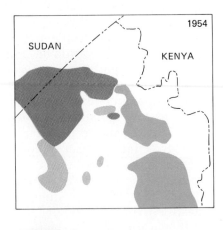

 Napore and Nyangeya tribes

------- International borders

 Dodos tribe

Areas infested with livestock trypanosomiasis (sleeping sickness)

FIGURE 2-19

Disease is an environmental factor that influences settlement. The effect is apparent in this example in northeastern Uganda, East Africa. Note in particular the changing distribution of the Napore and Nyangeya groups based on the spread and eradication of sleeping sickness. (Adapted from Walter Deshler, "Livestock Trypanosomiasis and Human Settlement in Northeastern Uganda," *Geographical Review*, 50 (1960), 549.)

Sometimes, the same cultural group changes its perception of an environment through time, with a resulting redistribution of its population. The coal fields of western Europe provide a good case in point. Before the industrial age, many coal-rich areas—such as southern Wales, the lands between the headwaters of the Oder and Vistula rivers in Poland, and the Midlands of England—were only sparsely or moderately settled. However, the development of steam-powered engines and the increased use of coke in the iron-smelting process created a tremendous demand for coal. Industries grew up near the European coal fields, and people flocked to these areas to take advantage of the new jobs. In other words, once a technological development had given a new cultural value to coal, many sparsely populated areas containing that resource acquired heavy concentrations of people.

How people view their environment often plays a key role in determining their voluntary migration and, consequently, the population density of an area. For a variety of reasons, migrants develop positive or negative perceptions of possible new homelands. Any one person will view some regions as highly desirable and others as less livable. When a person has a negative view of his or her home area and a positive view of one or more other regions, then that person is a prime candidate for migration. That is, people have in their minds what can be called **mental maps** that lay out various places to live in terms of their perceived attractiveness. The mental map in Figure 2-20 is a composite of the individual perceptions of Texas-born middle-class white college students attending North Texas State University. It suggests that relatively few of these students will migrate from Texas. The mental image of their native state is overwhelmingly positive. Those who do migrate will probably choose the West Coast, the Rocky Mountains, or Florida as a new home. The map also suggests that north Texans identify more closely with the West than with the South.

Recent studies indicate that much of the interregional migration in the United States is prompted by a desire for pleasant climate and other desirable physical environmental traits, such as beautiful scenery. Surveys of immigrants to Arizona revealed that its sunny, warm climate is a major reason for migration. Attractive environment was seen as the dominant factor in the growth of the population and economy of Florida in a study covering the 1939-1954 period. Another study ranked desirable

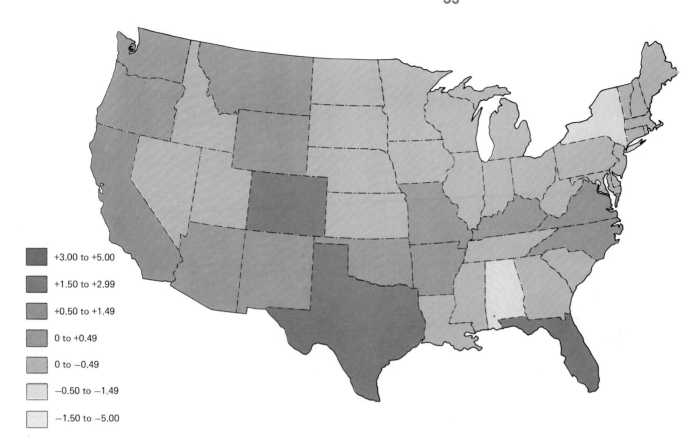

+3.00 to +5.00

+1.50 to +2.99

+0.50 to +1.49

0 to +0.49

0 to −0.49

−0.50 to −1.49

−1.50 to −5.00

FIGURE 2–20
The mental map of native Texans, 1974, is shown here. A large sample of Texas-born students attending North Texas State University was asked to list the five states they would most like to live in and the five they would least like to live in, ranking them on a scale of +5 to −5. Results indicate that the white middle-class students have an overwhelmingly positive perception of their native state and are unlikely to emigrate elsewhere. Compare this map to your own mental map of the United States.

environmental traits in the following order as stimulants for American migration: (1) mild winter climate and mountainous terrain, (2) a diverse natural vegetation that includes forests and a mild summer climate with low humidity, (3) the presence of lakes and rivers, and (4) nearness to the seacoast. Similarly, migrating New Zealanders are drawn to mild climate coastal districts, and many Britishers prefer the south and southwest coast, where the climate is not so rainy and cloudy as elsewhere in Britain. Different age and cultural groups often display different preferences, but all are influenced by their perceptions of the physical environment in making decisions about migration.

Many elements go into shaping a mental map. Misinformation is at least as important as accurate impressions, because a person will often form strong images of an area without ever visiting it. Many Europeans, particularly in the nineteenth century, were urged to leave their homelands by land speculators who depicted the United States as a second paradise, a new land whose golden streets flowed with milk and honey. Present-day land developers often create distorted, overly favorable environmental images in order to sell their lots.

Population density and environmental alteration

In most areas where population is dense, people have radically altered their environment. In fact, it stands to reason that if large numbers of people inhabit a region, the environment cannot remain the same. Naturally, then, the degree to which humans modify their environment often reflects the population density of their area (see box, "The Valley of the Ashes").

THE VALLEY OF THE ASHES

The environmental impact of huge urban agglomerations is considerable. "Out of sight, out of mind" may reduce this impact for many of us, but even as early as the 1920s a leading American novelist was repelled by what he saw on Long Island, near New York City.

"About half-way between West Egg and New York [City] the motor road hastily joins the railroad and runs beside it for a quarter of a mile, so as to shrink away from a certain desolate area of land. This is a valley of ashes—a fantastic farm where ashes grow like wheat into ridges and hills and grotesque gardens. . . . Occasionally a line of grey cars crawls along an invisible track, gives out a ghastly creak, and comes to rest, and immediately ash-grey men swarm up with leaden spades and stir up an impenetrable cloud, which screens their obscure operations from your sight. . . . The valley of ashes is bounded on one side by a small foul river, and, when the drawbridge is up to let barges through, the passengers on waiting trains can stare at the dismal scene for as long as half an hour."

From F. Scott Fitzgerald, The Great Gatsby.

We are now facing a worldwide ecological crisis, having modified our environment so massively that we threaten the continued existence of humankind and many other species. Many experts concerned with the spreading destruction of the human habitat feel that the population explosion and the ecological crisis are closely related. They believe that attempts to restore the balance of nature will not succeed until we halt population growth, although they recognize that other causes are at work in ecological crises.

The changes in the vegetation of western and central Europe since medieval times demonstrate how a region's population density can have a long-term effect on the environment. During the Middle Ages, farmers cleared vast forests from the plains and valleys of western and central Europe. In time, these fertile agricultural districts became densely populated. Interspersed among these lowlands were small areas of forested hills and low mountains, which the medieval farmers found unsuitable for agriculture and spared from the ax. As a result, surviving woodlands were so often limited to the hilly areas in Europe that the term *forest* is frequently used simply to describe areas of rough terrain, as in Germany's famous Black Forest. Whenever population was on the decline, particularly in times of warfare and plague, these surviving forests expanded, spilling onto the lowland plains. The spread of the forests that accompanied the Hundred Years' War, a conflict between England and France lasting from 1337 to 1453, can be linked to the numerous deaths caused by the war. In fact, surviving peasants coined the saying that "the forests came back to France with the English." Similarly, now that many twentieth-century American farmers have abandoned the countryside, woodlands in many parts of the eastern United States have expanded into what were formerly farmlands.

Although population density can affect an area's environment, these environmental modifications can, in turn, affect the area's population density. For instance, in a place where human activity has severely damaged the land in some way, some or all of the inhabitants may abandon the area. Some evidence suggests that the Sahara has steadily expanded since Roman times because domestic sheep and goats have overgrazed the short-grass steppes that border the desert. In the same way, a crust of mineralized "hardpan" has developed on the land's surface as a result of badly planned irrigation projects in some desert regions. This, in turn, has caused a decline in the population of these regions. In urban areas, the pollution and noise of a car-oriented industrial society have helped cause large numbers of city dwellers to migrate to suburban areas in the last two decades.

It would be misleading to say that the worldwide ecology crisis is strictly a function of overpopulation. It might be more accurate to call it a crisis of consumption. A relatively small percentage of the world's population controls much of the world's industrial technology and absorbs a gargantuan percentage of the world's productive capacity each year. For example, Americans, who make up less than 6 percent of humankind, account for about 40 percent of the world's resources consumed each year. Thus a child born in the United States has more of an impact on the global environment than one born in India or China.

Cultural Integration and Population Patterns

Population patterns are closely tied to both the physical environment and numerous facets of culture. The theme of cultural integration allows us to look at some of these relationships among culture, population density, migration, and population growth. For example, you might find it difficult, at first glance, to imagine how density of settlement can be related to the laws of a country. Indeed, inheritance laws, food preferences, politics, differing attitudes toward migration, and many other cultural features all can influence the pattern of population distribution (see Figure 2-21).

FIGURE 2-21
Inheritance systems and land fragmentation in the West German province of Hessen, 1955. In the southern and western parts of Hessen, the tradition, dating to Roman times, was to divide the farms among the various heirs. As a result, the farms there became ever smaller over the centuries, with excessive fragmentation of the holdings. What impact would this have on population density and agricultural prosperity? Northern and eastern Hessen, by contrast, clung to the ancient Germanic custom of primogeniture, by which the farm passes intact to the eldest son. (Adapted from E. Ehlers, "Land Consolidation and Farm Resettlement in the Federal Republic of Germany," in Robert C. Eidt, et al. (eds.), *Man, Culture, and Settlement: Festschrift to Prof. R. L. Singh,* New Delhi and Ludhiana, India: Kalyani Publishers, 1977, p. 124.)

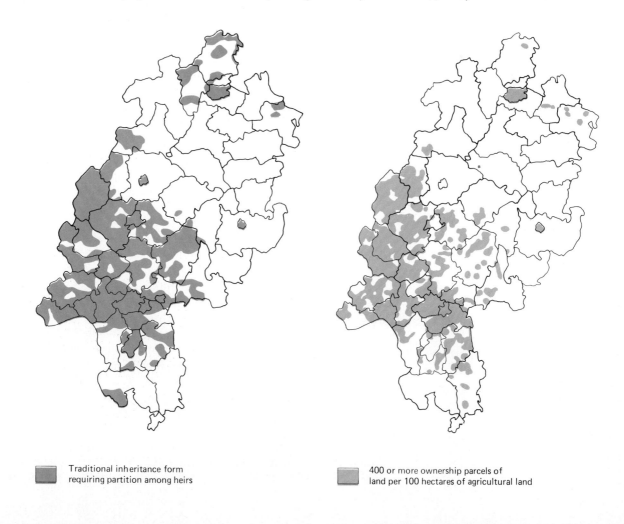

Traditional inheritance form requiring partition among heirs

400 or more ownership parcels of land per 100 hectares of agricultural land

CULTURE AND POPULATION

A study of the Tenetehara and the Tapirapé, two Tupi-speaking Indian tribes of central Brazil, shows the range of population choices available to different cultures within the same physical and material environment. Before European contact, both tribes inhabited similar tropical forest areas, had the same level of technology, and were horticulturists who depended on hunting, fishing, and wild fruits to supplement their diets. Yet the Tapirapé population was, by choice, relatively small and stable, whereas the Tenetehara population of perhaps 2000 was at least twice as large and probably expanding.

Among the Tenetehara, there was little effort to limit family size. Men took pride in the number of children they fathered. Women, eager to bear children, would leave a husband whom they considered sterile. There seem to have been few cultural values in the tribe that would discourage large families.

The Tapirapé, however, had an explicit idea of maximum family size. When asked why their families were no larger, they would say, "The children would be hungry." In Tapirapé society, this meant "hungry for meat," which was sometimes scarce—but no scarcer than for the more numerous Teneteharas. In other words, Tapirapé population controls were based not on possible starvation levels, but on a specific desire for a larger quantity of meat in their diets. Other cultural factors also played a role in the Tapirapé decision. As a result, the tribe set limits on how many children a woman should have (no more than three living and no more than two of the same sex). To keep their society within its desired limits, they practiced infanticide, the killing of newborn infants.

The arrival of the Europeans in Brazil highlighted each tribe's population choice. The Teneteharas' first contacts with Europeans in the seventeenth century were violent. Slavery, massacres, war, and epidemics decimated tribal ranks. Yet by 1945, after 300 years of contact with Europeans, their population still numbered 2000. In 1947 the Tapirapés, after less than forty years of contact—mainly with European diseases—numbered no more than one hundred. Their society was in shambles; their social organization ruined. Unlike the Tenetehara, their age-old population policies worked against them in this new situation. Culturally unable to replenish themselves fast enough, they were on the road to extinction.

Adapted from Charles Wagley, "Cultural Influences on Population: A Comparison of Two Tupi Tribes," in Daniel R. Gross (ed.), Peoples and Cultures of Native South America. (Garden City, N.Y.: Doubleday, 1973), pp. 145–156. Reprinted by permission.

Cultural factors

Many of the things that influence the distribution of people are basic characteristics of a group's culture (see box, "Culture and Population"). For example, we must understand the rice preference of people living in Southeast Asia before we can try to interpret the dense concentrations of people in Southeast Asian rural areas. The population in the humid lands of tropical and subtropical Asia expanded as this highly prolific grain was domesticated and widely adopted. Some of the highest rural densities in the world are now in this area. Environmentally similar rural zones elsewhere in the world, where rice is not the staple of the inhabitants' diet, never developed such great densities. Similarly, the introduction of the potato into Ireland in the 1700s allowed a great increase in rural population. The potato yielded much more food per acre than did traditional Irish crops. Failure of the potato harvests in the 1840s greatly reduced the Irish population, both through mass starvation and emigration.

Cultural groups also differ in their tendency to migrate. Religious ties bind some groups to their traditional homeland. Sometimes travel outside the sanctified bounds of the motherland is considered immoral. For example, religious restrictions have kept many Chinese in their native land. The Navaho Indians of the American Southwest practice the custom of burying the umbilical cord in the floor of the hogan (house) at birth. Psychologically, this seems to strengthen the Navaho attachment to the home and retard migration. Other religious cultures place no stigma on emigration. In fact, some groups consider migration a way of life. The

Irish, unwilling to accept the rural poverty of their native land, have proved so prone to migration that the population of Ireland today is only about half the total of 1840.

Migration tendencies can also differ between the sexes, for cultural reasons. In some parts of rural India, particularly the north and west, marriage is typically between persons from different villages. Since it is traditional in those parts of India for the woman to move into the household of her husband, females are much more likely to migrate than are males. As Figure 2-22 shows, a fifth or fewer of all married women in northern and western India live in the village of their birth; and in many districts their marriage migration has taken them eighteen miles or more from their original home, a considerable distance in a society with few automobiles. In south and east India and in Kashmir in the far north, by contrast, females are much less likely to marry outside their village. Cultural differences lie at the root of these contrasts. In some parts of south India, for example, matrilineal societies, those that trace lineage primarily through the mother, encourage females to remain close to their place of birth. Even in patrilineal south Indian communities, a preference for marriage within the village prevails, so that marriage migration is uncommon. The net result is to reduce cultural diffusion between villages in southern India.

Culture can also condition a people to accept or reject crowding. Studies have been made to determine the dimensions of **personal space**, the amount of space that individuals feel "belongs" to them as they move about their everyday business. Personal space seems to vary from one cultural group to another. For example, when Americans talk with each other, they typically stand farther apart than, say, Italians do. The large personal space demanded by the American may well come from a heritage of sparse settlement. Early pioneers reportedly felt uncomfortable when they first saw smoke from the chimneys of neighboring cabins. Perhaps

FIGURE 2–22

Female marriage migration in rural India. Major differences in the tendency of women to migrate for the purpose of marriage and in the distance of migration can be seen from one part of India to another. What might some of the cultural causes of this spatial pattern be? (Maps by M. J. Libbee, in Libbee and D. E. Sopher, "Marriage Migration in Rural India," in Kosinski and Prothero, *People on the Move*, pp. 352, 354.)

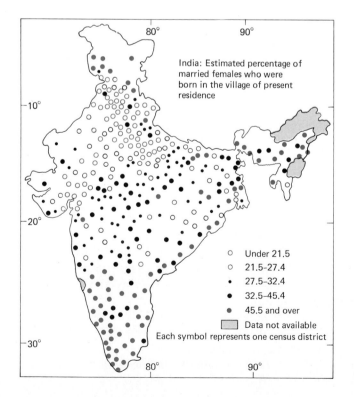

India: Estimated percentage of married females who were born in the village of present residence

○ Under 21.5
○ 21.5–27.4
· 27.5–32.4
● 32.5–45.4
● 45.5 and over
▭ Data not available
Each symbol represents one census district

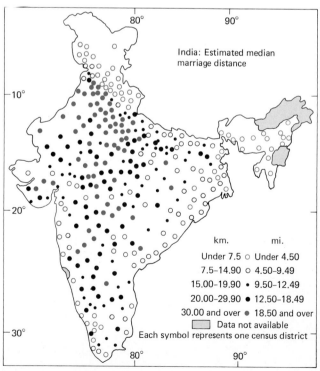

India: Estimated median marriage distance

km. mi.
Under 7.5 ○ Under 4.50
7.5–14.90 ○ 4.50–9.49
15.00–19.90 · 9.50–12.49
20.00–29.90 ● 12.50–18.49
30.00 and over ● 18.50 and over
▭ Data not available
Each symbol represents one census district

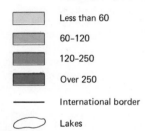

Persons per square mile

Less than 60

60–120

120–250

Over 250

——— International border

Lakes

FIGURE 2-23

Population density along the Haiti–Dominican Republic boundary on the island of Hispaniola. Migration across this frontier has been restricted, causing the political boundary to become also a demographic border. (Adapted from John P. Augelli, "Nationalization of Dominican Borderlands," *Geographical Review,* 70 (1980), 32.)

this is why American cities sprawl across large areas, with huge suburbs dominated by separate houses surrounded by private yards. Most European cities are compact, and their residential areas consist largely of row houses or apartments. Perhaps as more and more Americans accept apartment living, our need for personal space will decline.

Political and economic factors

The pattern of population distribution often arises from actions of governments or world economic conditions. For instance, nations have expelled cultural groups for thousands of years. The Romans dispersed the Jews from Palestine. However, twentieth-century governments certainly take the laurels in this category. One estimate of worldwide population displacements between 1913 and 1968 comes to an extraordinary 71 million people, many millions higher than the voluntary European emigration to the New World the century before.

During the World War II, Nazi Germany directed the forced migration of millions of people. After the war, partly in retribution, nearly all the German-speaking people of western Czechoslovakia and eastern Germany, perhaps 12 million of them, were forcibly expelled from their ancestral homelands. Many districts were left virtually unpopulated. Only slowly did Czechs, Slovaks, Poles, and Russians resettle these regions. Expulsions were carried out by the governments of Poland, Czechoslovakia, and the Soviet Union when German territory was annexed by these countries after the war. The leaders responsible for the forced expulsions felt that the German-speaking people would not be loyal citizens. Even today, some of these areas have lower population densities than they did in 1945.

For centuries, forced mass migration, motivated by either economic or political forces, has been a potent factor in the growth and decline of populations. It has been estimated that 9.6 million slaves, almost all from Africa, were imported into slave-using areas of the Old and New Worlds between 1451 and 1870. Up to one-fourth of the Africans died on the way, so more than 11 million Africans were actually enslaved during that period. For the population geographer, the most startling result of this mass forced migration was probably that by 1930 more than a fifth of all blacks did not live in Africa.

Governments can also restrict voluntary migration. The two independent nations of Haiti and the Dominican Republic share the tropical Caribbean island of Hispaniola in the West Indies. Haiti, which supports over 500 persons per square mile (over 190 per square kilometer), is more than twice as densely settled as the Dominican Republic, which has only 238 persons per square mile (90 per square kilometer) (see Figure 2-23). Government restrictions make migration from Haiti to the Dominican Republic difficult and thus help produce the different population densities. If Hispaniola were one nation, its population would probably be much more evenly distributed over the island.

Every culture has a set of laws to maintain order within the society, and these laws can affect population density. In most cases, these bodies of law include regulations about inheritance. In Europe, the legal code derived from Roman Law requires that all heirs of a deceased person divide land and other property equally among themselves. Germanic law, on the other hand, favors the custom of primogeniture, or inheritance of all land and property by the first-born son. In areas where divided inheritance is the tradition, farms fragment as the generations pass, causing rural population density to increase. Where primogeniture is the rule, on the other hand, emigration by landless sons retards the growth of population. It is not surprising, then, that the most severe rural overpopulation in Germany during the mid-nineteenth century was in the southern lands along the Rhine River and its tributaries. In that area, the custom of primogeniture had not overcome the tradition of divided inheritance that the Romans had implanted over 1500 years earlier.

Economic factors are often the reason that cultural groups embark on migrations. Hundreds of thousands of impoverished men from southern China came to the western coast of the United States in the nineteenth century (see Figure 2-24). They sought support for their families still in China. While sending money back to China, many of them stayed on, restricted to ghettos in San Francisco and other West Coast cities. Economic conditions often influence population density in other profound ways. Indeed, the process of industrialization over the past 150 years has caused the greatest voluntary relocation of people in world history. Within industrial nations, people have fled from rural areas to cluster in manufacturing regions. Commercialized agriculture has also attracted people in a similar way. For example, the Indonesian island of Java is one of the most densely settled rural areas in the world, with a population density greater than that of other large islands nearby. This concentration of people on Java results partly from the efforts of the Dutch, who ruled Indonesia until 1949, to concentrate tropical plantations there. Employment opportunities offered by these plantations drew people from the surrounding islands to Java. Consequently, Java's population expanded.

The Population Landscape: Settlement Patterns

The distribution of people is clearly reflected in the cultural landscape. Differing densities and degrees of clustering of population are revealed by maps showing the distribution of dwellings. We can illustrate these cultural landscape contrasts by using the example of rural settlement types. Farm people differ greatly from one culture to another, one place to

FIGURE 2-24
Many Chinese men migrated to California to make money for their families at home. Chinese laborers built railroads, panned for gold, and did farm labor. They played an essential part in the development of the American West. This group waits to go through customs on Angel Island in San Francisco Bay in 1924.

another, in how they situate their dwellings. The range from tightly clustered villages on the one extreme to fully dispersed farmsteads on the other is shown in Figure 2-25.

Clustered rural settlement: the farm village

In many parts of the world, farming people group themselves together in clustered settlements called **farm villages**. These settlements vary in size from a few dozen inhabitants to as many as 25,000 in large agrarian settlements called **agro-towns**. Contained in the village lot itself are the farmer's house, barn, sheds, pens, and sometimes the garden, collectively called the **farmstead**. The fields, pastures, and meadows lie out in the country beyond the limits of the village, and there are no dwellings in the surrounding farmland. The farmers must journey out from the village each day to work the land.

FIGURE 2-25
The way individual farmers choose to locate their farmsteads leads to a general settlement pattern on the land. In some areas, farmsteads are scattered and isolated. In areas where farmsteads are grouped, there are several possible patterns of clustering.

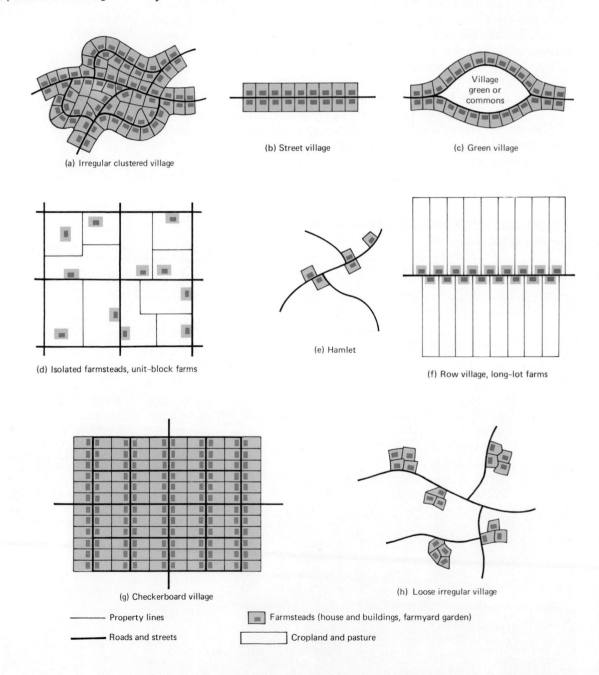

(a) Irregular clustered village

(b) Street village

(c) Green village

Village green or commons

(d) Isolated farmsteads, unit-block farms

(e) Hamlet

(f) Row village, long-lot farms

(g) Checkerboard village

(h) Loose irregular village

——— Property lines

■ Farmsteads (house and buildings, farmyard garden)

▬▬▬ Roads and streets

☐ Cropland and pasture

OVERLOOKING A VILLAGE IN INDIA

"On the steep ascent of the first range of hills bordering the southern edge of the great Ganges Valley in the Indian state of Madhya Pradesh, we ask our hired driver to stop the car, overlooking a tightly clustered farm village in the plain below. The village, tucked up against the foot of the hill, is open to our view from above. We look down upon a disorderly jumble of tile-roofed, mud-walled farmsteads, each consisting of single-story buildings grouped protectively around a central courtyard. So compact is the settlement that it is difficult to tell where one farmstead leaves off and the neighboring ones begin. Rounded mounds of threshed rice straw rise from many courtyards, and an occasional shade tree conceals parts of the village from our view. From the narrow dusty lanes and tiny courtyards, a rich variety of village noises drifts up to us on our god-like perch—the noises of animals and people going about their daily routines, noises unchanged for thousands of years. Off into the hazy distance stretch tan fields, another reminder that it is December, a month of gathering. Near the village are bright green rectangles of vegetables, irrigated and lush in the subtropical winter sun. Here is simplicity, continuity, attachment to place.

The twentieth century returns abruptly and disagreeably with the noise of a loaded truck rumbling along the narrow asphalt highway skirting one side of the village, gearing down for the steep slope ahead. Like proper citizens of the new age, we return to the hired automobile and continue our journey."

From the travel journal of Terry G. Jordan, 1975.

Farm villages are the most common form of settlement in much of Europe; in many parts of Latin America; in the densely settled farming regions of Asia, including much of India, China, and Japan; and among the sedentary farming peoples of Africa and the Middle East (see box, "Overlooking a Village in India"). These compact villages come in many forms, as Figure 2-25 shows. Most are irregular clusterings—a maze of winding, narrow streets and a jumble of farmsteads (Figure 2-26). Such irregular clustered farm villages developed spontaneously over the centuries, without any orderly plan to direct their growth. They are found in lands as diverse as China, India, and western Europe. Other types of farm village are very regular in their layout and reveal the imprint of planned design. The **street village** is the simplest of these planned types and consists of tightly clustered farmsteads lined up along either side of a single, central street, producing an elongated settlement. Street villages are particularly common in Slavic eastern Europe, including much of Russia. Another type, known as the **green village**, is characterized by farmsteads grouped in an orderly fashion around a central open place, or green, which forms a village commons. Green villages occur through most of the plains areas of northern and northwestern Europe, including England, and English immigrants laid out some such villages in colonial New England. Also very regular in layout is the **checkerboard village**, based on a gridiron pattern of streets meeting at right angles. Mormon farm villages in Utah are often of this type, as are some rural settlements in southeastern Europe.

Why do people who live in farm villages tend to huddle together in this way? In the past, a nucleus-type community filled many of the needs of rural people (see box, "Notes from a French Village"). Traditionally, the countryside was unsafe, threatened by roving bands of outlaws and raiders. Farmers could better defend themselves against such dangers by grouping together in villages. In many parts of the world, the populations of villages have grown larger during periods of insecurity and have shrunk again when peace was restored. Many farm villages occupy the most easily defended sites in their vicinity. These are referred to as strong-point settlements.

In addition to defense, the quality of the environment helps determine

FIGURE 2-26
Different rural settlement types are revealed in the accompanying photo montage. An unplanned irregularly clustered farm village in western Europe, a type found widely in the Old World, contrasts sharply with the regular layout of an East German street village. Both differ from the green village of African cattle herders in Uganda, with its circular houses clustered around a communal cattle pen. Typically American is this isolated farmstead on the Great Plains of North Dakota. What form of rural settlement dominates in your region? How did that form come to be established?

NOTES FROM A FRENCH VILLAGE

"*Where* do the people live who care for all this splendid farming country? We see them working in the fields, these superb wheat-fields, or harvesting the oats, but you can drive your car for mile after mile and never see a human habitation. . . . The people who till the fields all live in the villages. If you inhabit such a settlement you hear every morning, very, very early, the slow heavy tread of the big farmhorses and the rumble of the huge two-wheeled carts going out to work. . . .

"Of course this arrangement whereby country folk all live in villages turns inside out and upside down most of those conditions which seem to us inevitable accompaniments of country life; for instance, the isolation and loneliness of the women and children.

"There is no isolation possible here, when, to shake hands with the woman of the next farm, you have only to lean out of your front window and have her lean out of hers, when your children go to get water from the fountain along with all the other children of the region, when you are less than five minutes walk from church and the grocery store, when your children can wait till the school-bell is ringing before snatching up their books to go to school. . . . And if one of the children breaks his arm, or if a horse has the colic, or your chimney gets on fire, you do not suffer the anguished isolation of American country life. The whole town swarms in to help you in a twinkling of an eye. . . ."

From Dorothy Canfield, Home Fires in France *(New York, 1918). Copyright 1918 by Holt, Rinehart and Winston. Copyright 1945 by Dorothy Canfield Fisher. Reprinted by permission of Holt, Rinehart and Winston, Publishers.*

whether people settle in villages. In deserts and in limestone areas where the ground absorbs moisture quickly, farmsteads huddle together at the few sources of water. Such wet-point settlements tend to cluster around oases or deep wells. Conversely, a superabundance of water—in marshes, swamps, and areas subject to flood—prompts people to settle together on available dry points of higher elevation.

Various communal ties bind villagers strongly together. Groups of farmers linked to one another by blood relationships, religious customs, communal landownership, or other similar bonds are likely to form clustered villages. Mormon farm villages in the United States provide an excellent example of the clustering force of religion. In addition, nearly all the numerous utopian experiments in rural America—including the communes that have recently sprung up—have formed around a nucleus. Communal or state ownership of the land—as in China, the Soviet Union, and parts of Israel—has encouraged the formation of some larger farm villages and agro-towns.

The people who settle in these tightly knit villages generally depend on crops for their livelihood. Farming requires less land than raising livestock does. Thus a farming economy permits villagers to live close together without having to travel an undue distance from farmstead to field. For this reason, villages are very common in areas of paddy rice farming and plantation agriculture but normally absent in dairy and ranch zones, where dwellings are generally scattered over the land. Exceptions are the irregular clustered villages of African cattle herders, one of which is shown in the accompanying photo montage.

Dispersed rural settlement: the isolated farmstead

In many other parts of the world, the rural population lives in dispersed, isolated farmsteads, often a mile or more from their nearest neighbors. These dispersed rural settlements grew up mainly in Anglo-America, Australia, New Zealand, and South Africa; that is, in the lands colonized by emigrating Europeans. But even in areas dominated by village settlements—such as Japan, Europe, and parts of India—isolated farmsteads do appear.

The conditions encouraging dispersed settlement are precisely the opposite of those favoring village development. These include (1) peace and security in the countryside, removing the need for defense; (2) colonization by individual pioneer families rather than by socially cohesive groups; (3) agricultural private enterprise, as opposed to some form of communalism; (4) unit-block farms, in which all land belonging to a farmer is in one block rather than fragmented into many parcels, as is typical in most farm villages (see Chapter 3); (5) rural economies dominated by livestock raising; and (6) well-drained land where water is readily available.

We have seen that clustered rural settlements developed over centuries and were molded by cultural necessities—some of which have since disappeared. On the other hand, most dispersed farmsteads originated rather recently. They date primarily from the colonization of new farmland in the last two or three centuries. During the same period, dispersed farmsteads replaced villages in some older settled areas. In Scandinavia, for example, governments abolished fragmented holdings and thereby promoted the dispersal of the rural population in the late 1700s and early 1800s. Sweden and Denmark, for example, deliberately encouraged the movement of farmers from villages to isolated farmsteads because such a migration reduced the amount of travel between home and field, thereby increasing efficiency. Farm families abruptly torn away from the social life of villages in this way often have difficulty adjusting to their isolated dwellings. A study in Italy, where some dispersal has occurred in recent times, revealed that mental depression was more common among such relocated rural persons.

Semiclustered rural settlement

Some forms of rural settlement are neither clustered nor dispersed. Instead, they share characteristics of both. These may best be referred to as semiclustered settlements.

The most common type of semiclustered settlement is the **hamlet**, which consists of a small number of farmsteads grouped loosely together. As in farm villages, the hamlet farmsteads lie in settlement nuclei separate from the cropland. But the hamlet differs from the farm village because it is smaller and less compact. Farmsteads are not so tightly clustered as are the dwellings within villages. In such semiclustered settlements, there are from three or four up to as many as fifteen or twenty houses.

We might best look at hamlets as "stunted" villages, whose growth has been hindered for some reason. Geographers often relate the failure of hamlets to grow into villages to the low potential productivity of the areas where the hamlets are. In many countries, hamlets have developed most frequently in poorer hill districts. This is true in parts of western Europe, India, the Philippines, and Vietnam.

Occasionally, several clusters of farmsteads lie close to one another, sharing a common name and administration. These constitute what amounts to a **loose irregular village**. The individual clusters in such a group are often linked to various clans or religious groups. These loose villages are especially typical of the Balkan region of southeastern Europe. They also appear in parts of Malaya, Bengal, southern Japan, and India. Loose irregular villages involve a deliberate segregation of rural people, either voluntary or involuntary. In India, farmers of the "untouchable"

CONCLUSION
65

caste are occasionally segregated from other people by means of loose irregular villages.

The **row village** is a third common type of semiclustered settlement. In this settlement pattern, a line of farmsteads is spaced at intervals along a road, a river, or a canal. A group of farmsteads along a transportation artery suggests the clustering typical of a true village, but the houses of a row village fall in a loose chain that often extends for many miles. The individual farmsteads that make up a row village are spaced farther apart than those in a street village and do not abut one another. Row villages are common in the hills and marshlands of central and northwestern Europe; along the waterways in French-settled portions of North America, especially Québec and Louisiana; and in southern Brazil and adjacent parts of Argentina.

Conclusion

In our brief study of population geography, we have seen that humankind is unevenly distributed across the earth. Despite the pressures of the population explosion, vast areas of the earth remain empty. Spatial variations also exist for birth rates, death rates, rates of population growth, age groups, and sex ratios.

Human beings have traditionally been mobile. This human diffusion, or migration, has been part of the human experience from the time of our earliest emergence as a biological species, and mobility remains part of our way of life today. Although our ancestors migrated to find more abundant game animals, better soil to till, or freedom on a new frontier, we migrate to go to school, to find jobs, and to enjoy the amenities of life. Particularly in the United States, mobility has become part of the fabric of life, and the average American family moves every few years. The principles of cultural diffusion are useful in analyzing human migration. They also help explain the spread of birth-control innovations. Although birth control is increasingly important to slow the multiplication of people on our planet, many cultural barriers still delay its diffusion.

By adopting the viewpoint of cultural ecology, we have seen how the environment influences the distribution of people and sometimes helps guide migrations. Whatever the real environment, each person has a perception of it—a mental map on which some areas are viewed as desirable and others as undesirable. Migration is guided, in part, by such mental images of the environment, however distorted they might be. Humans are clearly part of a dynamic ecological system. They migrate to new areas, alter the environment, and readjust their perception to the changed environment.

Cultural integration is the device used to suggest ways that population distribution and mobility are linked to such elements of culture as legal systems, food preferences, migration taboos, international political disputes, and economic opportunity. Cultural attitudes, we know, can encourage people to be mobile or to stay in one place; they can encourage people to accept crowding or to feel uncomfortable without plenty of room for their personal space. Governments can also encourage or restrict movements of people, force migration or prohibit it. Cultural attitudes, governments, and religion can all help to promote birth control or encourage large families. In many ways, then, spatial variations in population traits are enmeshed in the fabric of culture. The understanding of any aspect of demography demands an investigation of many aspects of human culture.

How people distribute themselves across the earth's surface is expressed visibly in the cultural landscape. Using the example of the rural settlement landscape, we have seen how different cultures have developed their own distinctive forms, each of which reflects a unique distribution of population on the local level. Some are scattered, and others are clustered.

In these ways, our five themes have been applied to the study of population geography. In the remaining chapters, you will learn how we can apply them to a variety of other topics.

Glossary

Agro-town a very large clustered rural settlement, consisting of many thousands of people who are employed in agriculture.

Birth rate number of births in one year per thousand persons in the population.

Checkerboard village a farm village composed of farmsteads lined up along a gridiron pattern of streets meeting at right angles.

Death rate number of deaths in one year per thousand persons in the population.

Demographic region a culture region based on characteristics of demography.

Demographic transformation a change in population growth that occurs when a nation moves from a rural, agricultural society with high birth and death rates to an urban, industrial society in which death rates decline first and birth rates decline later.

Demography the statistical study of population size, composition, distribution, and change.

Farmstead the heart of a farm, containing the house, barn, sheds, and livestock pens.

Farm village a clustered rural settlement of moderate size, inhabited by people who are engaged in farming.

Green village a farm village built around a communal open area, or green.

Hamlet a small, loosely clustered group of farmsteads, smaller and less compact than a farm village.

Infanticide the killing of newborn children, often for purposes of population control.

Loose irregular village a type of semiclustered rural settlement consisting of several small clusters separated from one another.

Mental map a map of the world or any part of it, including positive or negative images of different areas, as perceived in the mind of an individual person.

Personal space the amount of space that individuals feel "belongs" to them as they move about their everyday business.

Population density the number of people in an area of land, usually expressed as people per square mile or people per square kilometer.

Population explosion the rapid, accelerating increase in world population since about 1650 and especially since 1900.

Population geography the study of spatial differences in the distribution, density, and demographic types of people.

Population pyramid a bar graph used to show the age and sex composition of a population.

Row village a type of semiclustered rural settlement composed of farmsteads lined up at regular, spaced intervals along a road, river, or canal; differing from a street village in that the farmsteads are spaced farther apart and do not abut one another.

Sex ratio the numerical ratio of males to females in a population.

Street village a farm village composed of tightly clustered farmsteads lined up along either side of a single, central street.

Zero population growth an effort to create a stabilized population by having an average of two children per couple; if practiced over three or four generations, the number of deaths comes to equal the number of births; sometimes abbreviated ZPG.

Suggested Readings

Jacqueline Beaujeu-Garnier. *Geography of Population*, S. H. Beaver (trans.). 2nd ed., London: Longmans, 1978.

Ian Burton and Robert W. Kates. "The Floodplain and the Seashore: A Comparative Analysis of Hazard-Zone Occupance," *Geographical Review*, 54 (1964), 366–385.

John I. Clarke. *Population Geography*, 2nd ed. Elmsford, N.Y.: Pergamon Press, 1972.

John I. Clarke, *Population Geography and the Developing Countries*. Elmsford, N.Y.: Pergamon Press, 1971.

John I. Clarke. "Population Geography," *Progress in Human Geography*, 1 (1977), 136–141; 2 (1978), 163–169.

P. A. Compton. "Religious Affiliation and Demographic Variability in Northern Ireland," *Transactions, Institute of British Geographers*, N.S. 1 (1976), 433–452.

George J. Demko, Harold M. Rose, and George A. Schnell (eds.). *Population Geography: A Reader*. New York: McGraw-Hill, 1970.

Ronald Freedman and Bernard Berelson. "The Human Population," *Scientific American* (September 1974), 30–39.

Alice Garnett. "Insolation, Topography, and Settlement in the Alps," *Geographical Review*, 25 (1935), 601–617.

David J. M. Hooson. "The Distribution of Population as the Essential Geographical Expression," *The Canadian Geographer*, 4:17 (November 1960), 10–20.

R. J. Johnston. "Population Distributions and the Essentials of Human Geography," *South African Geographical Journal*, 58 (1976), 93–106.

Leszek A. Kosínski. *The Population of Europe: A Geographical Perspective.* Harlow, England: Longman, 1970.

Leszek A. Kosínski and R. Mansell Prothero (eds.). *People on the Move: Studies on Internal Migration*. London: Methuen & Co., 1975.

Gary L. Peters and Robert P. Larkin. *Population Geography: Problems, Concepts, and Prospects*. Dubuque, Iowa: Kendall-Hunt, 1979.

Brian K. Roberts. *Rural Settlement in Britain*. Hamden, Conn.: Archon Books, 1977.

L. Dudley Stamp. *The Geography of Life and Death*. Ithaca, N.Y.: Cornell University Press, 1964.

Kirk H. Stone. "Geographical Aspects of the Limits to Growth Concepts," *Professional Geographer*, 28 (1976), 336–340.

Larry M. Svart. "Environmental Preference Migration: A Review," *Geographical Review*, 66 (1976), 314–330.

Glenn T. Trewartha. *A Geography of Population*. New York: Wiley, 1969.

Glenn T. Trewartha. *The Less Developed Realm: A Geography of Its Population*. New York: Wiley, 1972.

Harald Uhlig and Cay Lienau (eds.). *Rural Settlement, Basic Material for the Terminology of the Agricultural Landscape*, Vol. II. Giessen, West Germany: Lenz Verlag, 1972.

Paul E. White and Robert Woods (eds.). *Geographical Impact of Migration*. London, New York: Longman, 1980.

Robert Woods. *Population Analysis in Geography*. New York: Longman, 1979.

Edward A. Wrigley. *Population and History*. New York: McGraw-Hill, 1969.

Wilbur Zelinsky, Leszek A. Kosínski, and R. Mansell Prothero (eds.). *Geography and a Crowding World*. New York: Oxford University Press, 1970.

The Agricultural World

3

Most of us know very little about farming. The only peanuts, pineapples, and potatoes we see are on supermarket shelves. The brisket and bacon we get comes wrapped in cellophane with a price stamped on it. If we live in a city or a suburb, our relationship to the land may not extend much beyond the lawn in front of the house or the vegetable garden in the backyard. Today, less than 5 percent of all Americans are farmers. Farming is increasingly a corporate activity. Farms, more and more, are factories in the countryside, covering giant tracts of land and using expensive machinery to do much of the work. The family farm, once a basic ingredient in the American economy, is less and less evident.

Americans are now urbanized. Yet the large majority of people on the earth spend their waking hours tending the land on which they live. As late as World War I, the majority of Americans lived in rural areas and engaged in rural occupations. Now most Americans would have to stretch their imaginations to understand the problems and pleasures of a close relationship with the land. We can easily forget that the food surplus produced through agriculture is the base upon which our urban, industrial world rests. Without farming, there would be no cities or universities.

Agriculture is tilling crops and herding animals to produce many of the necessities of life, especially food, drink, and fibers. As the main activity of humankind throughout much of history, it is of particular interest to the geographer. Over thousands of years, agricultural pursuits became highly diverse regionally, and cultivators and herders altered the environment on a massive scale. The cultural landscape over much of the earth's surface became largely agricultural. The themes of culture region, diffusion, ecology, integration, and landscape are thus highly relevant to the study of agriculture.

Agricultural Regions

The practice of raising plants and animals has spread to most parts of the world. Cultures living in differing environments adopted and developed new farming methods, creating numerous spatial variations in agriculture. Agricultural geographers attempt to highlight these regional contrasts by using the culture region concept, in particular, formal **agricultural regions.** Figure 3-1, which shows these agricultural regions, should be referred to as we discuss each type.

Shifting cultivation

The native peoples of remote tropical lowlands and hills in the Americas, Africa, Southeast Asia, and Indonesia practice an agricultural system known as **shifting cultivation.** Essentially, this is a land rotation system. Farmers, using machetes or other bladed instruments, chop away the undergrowth from small patches of land. They then kill the trees by cutting off a strip of bark completely around the trunk. After the dead vegetation has dried out, the farmers set it on fire to clear it from the land (see Figure 3-2). These clearing techniques have given shifting cultivation the name of "slash-and-burn" agriculture. Working with digging sticks or hoes, the farmers then plant a variety of crops in the clearings. These crops vary from the corn, beans, bananas, and manioc of American Indians to the yams and nonirrigated rice grown by hill tribes in Southeast

◄ *Chapter-opening photo:* A farmer in Mali, western Africa.

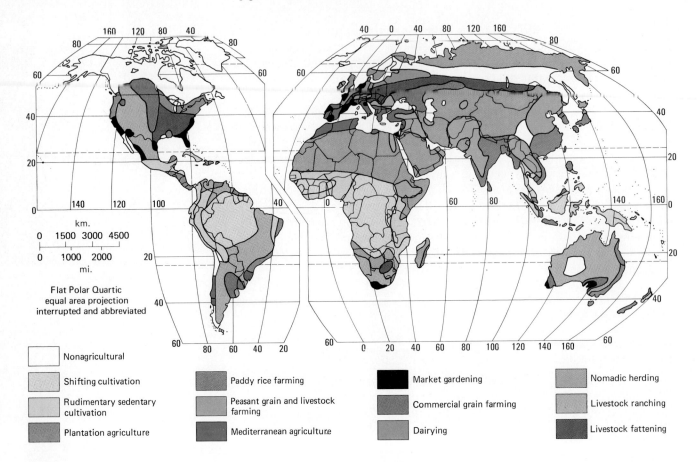

FIGURE 3–1
Major agricultural regions of the world.

Asia. Different crops are typically planted together in the same clearing, a practice called **intertillage**. This allows taller, stronger crops to shelter lower, more fragile ones from the tropical downpours and reveals the rich lore and learning acquired by shifting cultivators over many centuries. Relatively little tending of the plants is necessary until harvest time, and no fertilizer is applied to the fields. Farmers repeat the planting and harvesting cycle in the same clearings for perhaps four or five years, until the soil has lost much of its fertility. Then these areas are abandoned, and the farmers prepare new clearings to replace them. The abandoned fields lie unused for ten or twenty years before farmers clear and cultivate them again. Shifting cultivation is one form of **subsistence agriculture**—farming to supply the minimum food to survive, with none produced for market.

Farm animals play a very small role in shifting cultivation. Farmers keep few if any livestock, often relying on hunting and fishing for much of their food supply. The technologies of cultures that practice shifting cultivation may seem crude and poorly developed, but they have proved efficient for the people who practice them. For instance, it has been estimated that slash-and-burn farming returns more calories of food for the calories spent on cultivation than does modern mechanized agriculture (see box, "Is Shifting Cultivation Productive?").

Rudimentary sedentary cultivation

Another traditional form of tropical agriculture is **rudimentary sedentary cultivation.** Farmers use this system mainly in the highlands and moun-

FIGURE 3-2
An Indian in the Amazon Basin of Brazil is preparing a field for new cultivation by cutting and burning the forest cover. Although slash-and-burn agriculture appears to be disorganized and primitive, it is actually a carefully planned system of crop combinations and field rotation.

tain valleys of the tropics, as well as in some river plains. Rudimentary sedentary cultivation differs from shifting cultivation in numerous ways. Fields are fixed and permanent. Farmers keep more livestock, and they rely more heavily on farming, instead of hunting or fishing, for their food supply. Although many shifting cultivators are women, rudimentary sedentary farmers are generally men. Population densities are greater as a result of the more intensive farming, and the cultures of the sedentary cultivators are often more complex and elaborate than those found among shifting cultivators. In America, for example, descendants of the highly advanced Inca and Aztec Indians of the Andean and Mexican highlands

IS SHIFTING CULTIVATION PRODUCTIVE?

The Kuikuru tribe of Brazil is probably a typical group of slash-and-burn cultivators. They have lived in the same spot for the last ninety years. In the early 1950s, when they were visited by scholarly observers, the 145 Kuikuru people lived in a single village consisting of nine large, well-built thatched houses. Almost all their agricultural work is done by men. Within the four-mile radius of the village a Kuikuru man is willing to walk to work. There are perhaps 13,500 cultivatable acres of unused forest land. At any given moment, the Kuikuru have under cultivation only about 95 acres. So unused land is plentiful.

Manioc, a high-yield, reliable crop, is the main pillar of the Kuikuru diet. Other domesticated plants, including maize, make up only about 5 percent or less of their diet; fishing accounts for 10 to 15 percent; and hunting accounts for less than 1 percent. Though slash-and-burn or shifting agriculture has often been considered unproductive, the average Kuikuru garden produces four or five tons of manioc tubers per acre per year. In fact, computations show that the Kuikuru consume, after all crop losses to insects and animals, over 2 million calories per acre per year.

From our point of view, perhaps the most surprising thing about Kuikuru agriculture is that, for the population that it supports, it is an economy of abundance, not mere subsistence. It was reported, for instance, that a family losing several hundred pounds of manioc flour in a fire did not even bother to borrow from neighbors. The woman of the family simply dug up and processed new, unused tubers. The event was in no way considered a disaster.

Just as surprising is the small amount of effort that goes into slash-and-burn cultivation. A Kuikuru man spends only about 2 hours a day on his garden. Another 1½ hours goes to fishing. The rest of his time is spent dancing, wrestling, in various other forms of entertainment, or just relaxing. If he were to devote just an extra half hour a day to manioc growing, he could easily produce a substantial manioc surplus. However, in Kuikuru society, no reason for such extra activity presently exists.

Source: Robert L. Carneiro, "Slash-and-Burn Cultivation among the Kuikuru and Its Implications for Cultural Development in the Amazon Basin," in Daniel R. Gross (ed.), Peoples and Cultures of Native South America. (New York: Doubleday, 1973), pp. 98–123. Reprinted by permission.

practice rudimentary sedentary cultivation. The farming techniques in this system occasionally do not involve even such basic tools as the plow. Major crops raised by sedentary cultivators include white potatoes, corn, wheat, and barley in South America, while sorghums and millet are more common in Africa. Sheep, llamas, and alpacas are the main livestock in the American areas, while African farmers keep cattle, donkeys, and sheep.

Plantation agriculture

In certain tropical areas, Europeans and Americans desiring to supply themselves with tropical crops have imposed a commercial agricultural system on the two native types of subsistence agriculture that we have just discussed. This system is called **plantation** agriculture. A plantation is a large landholding devoted to the specialized production of one tropical or subtropical crop raised for market. Such a system relies on large amounts of hand labor. Most workers live right on the plantation, where a rigid social and economic segregation of labor and management produces a two-class society of the wealthy and the poor. Traditionally, as in the southern United States, many plantation owners relied on slaves to provide the needed labor. Today, because of the capital investment necessary, corporations or governments are usually the owners of plantations.

Most plantations are located on or near the seacoast, in order to be close to the shipping lanes that carry their produce to nontropical lands such as Europe, the United States, and Japan. Scholars believe that the plantation system originated in the 1400s on Portuguese-owned islands off the coast of tropical west Africa. The greatest concentration of plantations is now located in the American tropics.

The plantation provided the base for European (and later American) economic expansion into Asia, Africa, and Latin America. As such, it played havoc with the traditional agricultural economies of those areas. It particularly promoted the production of nonessential crops for the luxury diet of Europeans and Americans: sugar cane, bananas, coffee, coconuts, spices, tea, cacao, and tobacco. Similarly, Western textile factories required cotton, sisal, jute, hemp, and other fiber crops from the plantation areas. Profits from these plantations were usually "exported" along with the crops themselves to Europe and North America, impoverishing the colonial lands where plantations were located.

Owners in each plantation district in the tropical zone tend to specialize in one particular crop. Coffee and tea, for instance, grow in the tropical highlands, with coffee dominating the upland plantations of tropical America and tea confined mainly to the hill slopes of India and Sri Lanka. Today, coffee is the economic lifeblood of about forty underdeveloped countries. Sugar cane and bananas are the major lowland plantation crops of tropical America. In most cases, plantation workers at least partially process the crop before sending it to the distant market. For example, sugar is generally milled and cotton is usually ginned on the plantation. This combination of raising and partially processing the crop is a major distinguishing trait of the plantation system.

Paddy rice farming

Peasant farmers in the humid tropical and subtropical parts of Asia developed a highly distinctive type of agriculture called paddy rice farming. From the monsoon coasts of India through the hills of southeastern China and on to the warmer parts of Japan stretches a broad zone of tiny, mud-diked, flooded rice fields, or **paddies**, many of which are perched on terraced hillsides. These fields form a strikingly uniform cultural landscape that is the hallmark of this type of agriculture.

Irrigated rice accounts for over half of the cultivated acreage in the paddies. Often farmers also cultivate a second crop for cash, such as tea, sugar cane, mulberry bushes for silkworm production, or the fiber crop jute. Asian farmers also raise pigs, cattle, and poultry and maintain fish in the irrigation reservoirs. Pork is a favorite food among the Chinese. As we will see in Chapter 6, religious dietary taboos prevent Indians from eating most livestock products, but Indians use draft animals such as the water buffalo to a greater extent than do other Asian farmers. Only the Japanese have mechanized paddy rice farming to any major degree.

Most paddy rice farms outside the Communist areas of Asia are tiny. A 3-acre (about 1 hectare) landholding is considered adequate to support a farm family. Asian farmers can survive on such a small scale of operation partly because irrigated rice provides a very large output of food per unit of land. Still, the paddy farmers must till their small patches most intensively in order to harvest enough food. This means they must carefully transplant by hand the small rice sprouts from seed beds to the paddy (see Figure 3-3). They must also plant and harvest the same parcel of land two or three times each year—a practice known as **double-cropping**—while applying large amounts of organic fertilizer to the land. Asian farmers are now producing even greater yields per acre because of the recent introduction of improved varieties of *hybrid* rice.

Peasant grain and livestock farming

In colder, drier Asiatic farming regions, climatically unsuited to paddy rice farming, as well as in the river valleys of the Middle East and parts of Europe, farmers practice a system of semisubsistence plow agriculture based on bread grains and herd livestock. The dominant grain crops in these regions are wheat and barley, supplemented in some areas by millet, oats, corn, and rye. Other subsistence crops include grain sorghums, soybeans, and potatoes. Most farmers in these areas also raise a cash crop, such as cotton, flax, hemp, or tobacco.

FIGURE 3–3
Laborers plant wet rice shoots by hand in an irrigated paddy in Japan. This planting process is repeated two or three times a year in order to achieve the maximum crop production from each piece of land. In some parts of Japan, machines have been introduced to take over some of the labor in rice farming; but in most Asian paddies, rice still requires hours of stoop labor.

Along with tilling crops, these farmers also raise herds of cattle, pigs, and sheep. The livestock provide manure, power to pull the plow, milk, and meat. They also consume a portion of the grain harvest. In some areas, such as the Middle Eastern river valleys, the use of irrigation helps support this peasant-grain-livestock system. Although these peasant farmers work their land intensively, they are generally not as productive as the paddy rice growers.

Mediterranean agriculture

In the lands bordering the Mediterranean Sea, a truly distinctive type of peasant subsistence agriculture took shape in ancient times, and much of this system survives intact today. Traditional Mediterranean agriculture is based on wheat and barley cultivation in the rainy winter season; raising drought-resistant vine and tree crops like the grape, olive, and fig; and small-scale livestock herding, particularly of sheep, goats, and pigs (Figure 3-4). In recent times, farmers have begun using irrigation in a major way, which has led to the expansion of crops such as the citrus fruits.

Mediterranean farmers do not combine stock-raising with crop cultivation. They rarely raise feed, collect animal manure, or keep draft animals. Instead, they pasture their livestock in communal herds on high, rocky, mountain slopes, while they cover the valleys and gentler slopes below with vineyards, orchards, and grain fields. Because the Mediterranean farmers do not fertilize their land with collected manure, the grain fields must lie fallow every other year to regain their fertility.

All three of these basic enterprises—wheat and barley cultivation, vine and tree cultivation, and livestock herding—are generally combined on each small farm. From this diverse, unspecialized trinity, the Mediterranean farmer can reap nearly all of life's necessities, including wool and

FIGURE 3–4
Mediterranean agriculture combines grain cultivation with vine and tree crops, in addition to herding. Often the grain is raised in the orchards, as in this scene of intertillage from the island of Crete, where newly harvested wheat lies in sheafs amid the olive trees. The mountains in the distance provide range for the farmers' sheep and goats. (Photo by Terry G. Jordan, 1971.)

FIGURE 3–5
Mechanized grain farming looks much the same throughout the world. This is a view of harvest time on a state farm in the Soviet Union. There the use of machinery can be centrally planned. In North America, teams of workers and equipment move south and contract with individual farmers to harvest the crop.

leather for clothing, and bread, beverages, fruit, milk, cheese, and meat. Since about 1850, however, many Mediterranean agricultural areas have changed as commercialization and specialization of farming have replaced the traditional diversified system. In such areas, the present-day agriculture is better described as market gardening.

Market gardening

The growth of urban markets in the last few centuries has given rise to many commercial forms of agriculture. We have already mentioned one of these, plantation agriculture. Another kind of commercial agriculture is **market gardening,** which we sometimes refer to as truck farming. Truck farmers specialize in intensively cultivated fruits, vegetables, and vines. They do not raise livestock. Typically, each farm and district concentrates on a single product such as wine grapes, table grapes, raisins, oranges, apples, lettuce, or potatoes, and the entire farm output is raised for sale rather than for consumption on the farm. Many truck farmers participate in cooperative marketing arrangements and depend on migratory seasonal farm laborers to harvest their crops.

Market garden districts are common in most industrialized countries and often lie near major urban centers. In the United States, a broken belt of market gardens extends from California eastward through the Gulf and Atlantic coast states, with scattered districts in other parts of the country. These farms produce everything from wine and raisins to citrus, apples, tomatoes, and spinach.

Commercial grain farming

Commercial grain farming is another market-oriented type of agriculture in which farmers specialize in growing wheat, or less frequently rice or corn. Great wheat belts stretch through Australia, the plains of interior North America, the steppes of Russia, and the pampas of Argentina. Together, the United States, Canada, and the Soviet Union produce 45 percent of the world's wheat. Farms in these areas are generally very large. They range from family-run wheat farms of 1000 acres (400 hectares) or more in the American Great Plains to giant state farms in the Soviet Union, some of which exceed 100,000 acres (40,000 hectares) (see Figure 3-5). Extensive rice farms, maintained under the same commercial system, cover large areas of the Texas-Louisiana coastal plain and lowland floodplains in Arkansas and California.

Widespread use of machinery enables commercial grain farmers to operate on this large scale. Indeed, planting and harvesting grain is more completely mechanized than any other form of agriculture. Commercial rice farmers employ such techniques as sowing grain from airplanes. Perhaps the ultimate development is the **suitcase farm,** a post-World War II innovation in the wheat belt of the northern Great Plains of the United States. The people who own and operate these farms do not live on the land. Most of them own several suitcase farms, lined up in a south-to-north row through the plains states. They keep fleets of farm machinery, which they send north with crews of laborers along the string of suitcase farms to plant, fertilize, and harvest the wheat. The progressively later ripening of the grain toward the north allows these farmers to maintain crops on all their farms with the same crew and the same machinery. Except for these visits by migratory crews, the suitcase farms are uninhabited.

Such a highly mechanized, large-scale, far-flung operation is often called an **agribusiness.** With agribusiness, farming has entered the industrial age. Land, organized in larger and larger units, is monopolized by fewer and fewer owners. Typically, these owners are no longer farm families or even farmers, but corporations located at some place distant from the land. In this way, the traditional man-land linkage has been severed, and a distant corporate relationship set up in its place.

Commercial livestock fattening

Commercial livestock fattening developed hand-in-hand with commercial grain growing as the urban market increased. In this system, farmers raise and fatten cattle and hogs for slaughter. One of the most highly developed fattening areas is the famous Corn Belt of the midwestern United States, where farmers raise immense amounts of corn and soybeans to feed cattle and hogs. A similar system prevails over much of western and central Europe, though the feed crops there are more commonly oats, potatoes, and sugar beets. Smaller zones of commercial livestock fattening are found in overseas European settlement zones such as southern Brazil and South Africa.

One of the main characteristics of commercial livestock fattening has traditionally been the combination of crop and animal raising on the same farm. This has led some geographers to refer to this type of agriculture as mixed crop and livestock farming. Farmers typically bred many of the animals they fattened, especially the hogs. In recent years, commercial livestock farmers have begun to specialize their activities, some concentrating on breeding animals, others on fattening them for market. The most recent development has been the factory-like **feedlot,** where farmers raise imported cattle and hogs on purchased feed (see Figure 3-6). Such feedlots are most common in the western and southern United States, in part because winters are less severe there.

Although commercial livestock fattening is often organized with assembly-line precision and has proved extremely profitable, the specter of worldwide famine in recent years has brought its nutritional efficiency into question. Actual world grain production has risen significantly faster than world population growth, grain cereals providing 85 percent of the protein intake of most of the world's people. Yet in the last fifty years,

FIGURE 3–6
Six thousand cattle can be fed at this feedlot in Omaha, Nebraska. The operation is run by a company that specializes in fattening cattle for market.

meat eating has soared in the Western world, particularly in the United States, wiping out most of these gains. At least one-half of America's harvested agricultural land is planted with feed crops for livestock. Over 70 percent of the grain raised in the United States is used for livestock fattening. However, livestock are not an efficient method of protein production. A cow, for instance, must eat 21 pounds of protein to produce 1 pound of edible protein. Plants are far more efficient protein converters. It has been estimated that the protein lost through conversion from plant to meat could make up almost all of the world's present protein deficiencies. The billion people in the developed nations today use as much cereal grain to feed their livestock as the 2 billion people in the low-income nations use directly as food. Put another way, the food that today feeds 220 million Americans would feed 1.5 billion at the consumption level of China.

Commercial dairying

In many ways, the specialized production of dairy goods closely resembles commercial livestock fattening. In the large dairy belts of the northeastern United States, western and northern Europe, southeastern Australia, and northern New Zealand, the keeping of dairy cows depends on the large-scale use of pastures (see box, "Thomas Hardy on Dairying"). In colder areas, some acreage must be devoted to winter feed crops, especially hay. Dairy products vary from region to region, depending in part on how close the farmers are to their markets. Dairy areas near large urban centers usually produce fluid milk, while those further away specialize in butter, cheese, or processed milk. New Zealanders, remote from world markets, produce mainly butter.

As with livestock fattening, in recent decades a rapidly increasing number of dairy farmers have adopted the feedlot system and now raise their cattle on feed purchased from other sources. Feedlots are especially common in the southern United States. Often situated on the suburban

Livestock ranching

In the Americas, Australia, the Republic of South Africa, and New Zealand, the nearest equivalent to nomadic herding is **ranching**. Nevertheless, there are more differences than similarities between these two systems. Although both the nomadic herders and the livestock ranchers specialize in animal husbandry to the exclusion of crop raising, and even though both live in arid or semiarid regions, livestock ranchers have fixed places of residence and operate as individuals rather than within a tribal organization. In addition, ranchers raise livestock for market, not for their own subsistence.

Livestock ranchers, faced with the advance of farmers, have usually fallen back into areas climatically too harsh for crop production. There they raise only two kinds of animals in large numbers: cattle and sheep. Ranchers in the United States, tropical and subtropical Latin America, and the warmer parts of Australia specialize in cattle raising. Midlatitude ranchers in the Southern Hemisphere specialize in sheep, to the extent that Australia, New Zealand, South Africa, and Argentina produce 55 percent of the world's wool. In Australia, sheep outnumber people fifteen to one.

Cultural Diffusion in Agriculture

The various agricultural regions that we have just discussed, the spatial variations in agriculture, are the result of cultural diffusion. Agriculture and its many components are inventions; they arose as innovations in certain source areas and diffused to other parts of the world.

The origin and diffusion of plant domestication

The beginnings of agriculture apparently occurred with plant rather than animal domestication. A **domesticated plant** is one willfully planted, protected, and cared for by humans. In addition, it is genetically distinct from its wild ancestors due to its deliberate improvement through selective breeding by the people who raise it. As a result, domesticated plants tend to be bigger than wild species, bearing larger, more abundant fruit or grain. For example, wild Indian corn grows on a cob only 2 centimeters long—that is, one-tenth to one-twentieth the size of the cobs of domesticated corn.

Plant domestication was a process, not an event. It came as the gradual culmination of hundreds, or even thousands, of years of close association between humans and the natural vegetation that surrounded them. The first step in domestication was the perception that a certain plant had usefulness for people. The perception led initially to protection of the wild plant and eventually to deliberate planting. Cultural geographer Carl L. Johannessen suggests that the domestication process can still be observed today. He believes that by studying current techniques used by native subsistence farmers in places such as Central America, we can gain insight into the methods of the first farmers of prehistoric antiquity. Professor Johannessen points out that two steps are normally required to develop and improve plant varieties: (1) selection of seeds or shoots only from superior plants; and (2) genetic isolation from other, inferior plants to prevent cross-pollination. He believes we can see these processes still under way among American subsistence farmers. Johannessen's study of the present-day cultivation of the pejibaye palm tree in Costa Rica revealed that native cultivators are actively engaged in seed selection. All choose the seed of fresh fruit from superior trees, those which bear particularly desirable fruit, as determined by size, flavor, texture, and color. Such trees are often given personal names, an indication of the value placed on them. Superior seed stocks are built up gradually over the years, with the result that elderly farmers generally have the best selections. Seeds are shared freely within family and clan groups, allowing speedy diffusion of desirable traits.

Dr. Johannessen also reported that some American Indian groups were clearly aware of the need for genetic isolation to reduce contamination from cross-pollination in corn plants. In Panama, for example, one Indian tribe of shifting cultivators raised fourteen varieties of corn, each in a field separated from all the others by intervening forest.

When, where, how, and by whom were these processes of plant domestication developed? The answers are not known with certainty, but cultural geographers have been among those who have done research on this problem. Early leaders were the German geographer Eduard Hahn and the famous American cultural geographer Carl O. Sauer (see biographical sketch). Their theories, as well as the contributions of numerous other scholars, are suggested in Figure 3-8.

Sauer suggested that domestication probably did not develop in response to hunger. He maintained that necessity was not the mother of agricultural invention, because starving people must spend every waking hour searching for food and have no time to devote to the centuries of leisurely experimentation required to domesticate plants. Instead, it was accomplished by a people who had enough food to remain settled in one place and devote considerable time to plant care. Thus, the first farmers were probably sedentary folk, rather than migratory hunters and gatherers.

Sauer reasoned that domestication probably did not initially occur in grasslands or large river floodplains. In such areas, primitive cultures would have had difficulty coping with the thick sod and periodic floodwaters. Sauer also felt that the hearth area of domestication must have been in a region where many different kinds of plants were growing, providing abundant vegetative raw material for experimentation and crossbreeding. Such areas typically appear in hilly districts, where climates change with differing sun exposure and altitude.

Sauer found it useful to distinguish between two different means of reproducing plants. One method, perhaps the more familiar to you, is to plant seeds derived from the fruit of the plant. The other, called vegetative reproduction, involves propagation by breaking off a piece of the fruit and planting it or by transplanting shoots. The white potato and banana are examples of vegetatively reproduced plants. Some domesticated plants can be reproduced either way. Professor Sauer believed that the first plants to be domesticated were those that could be vegetatively reproduced. Such reproduction, particularly the transplanting of shoots, was easier for primitive folk to understand. Moreover, vegetative reproduction is asexual, eliminating the need for genetic isolation and the danger of cross-pollination.

This initial domestication of plants, Sauer concluded, may have occurred from 14,000 to 35,000 years ago, most likely in the wet-dry monsoon climate of southeastern Asia, among sedentary fishing and

CARL O. SAUER   1889-1975

Sauer, a native of the Missouri Ozarks and a graduate of the University of Chicago, was widely regarded as the most prominent American cultural geographer. For over half a century, he was associated with the University of California at Berkeley. His works were so diverse as to defy simple classification, but important themes in much of his research were (1) humans as modifiers of the earth, (2) the cultural landscape, and (3) cultural origins and diffusion. As a geographer his work took him on many field trips. He studied by looking at the land, examining archaeological finds, and talking to the residents. In his classic book *Agricultural Origins and Dispersals* he presented some new and stimulating ideas concerning the domestication of plants and animals, some of which are presented in this chapter. His concern for the environment began when he was a student, and throughout his career he argued for "humane" use of the earth.

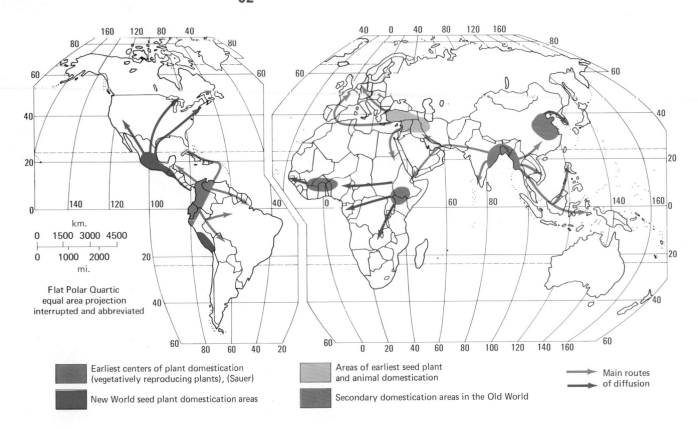

Earliest centers of plant domestication
(vegetatively reproducing plants), (Sauer)

New World seed plant domestication areas

Areas of earliest seed plant
and animal domestication

Secondary domestication areas in the Old World

Main routes
of diffusion

FIGURE 3–8
Centers of early agriculture and routes
of diffusion are shown on several
continents. Much of the information
shown on this map is speculative or
somewhat controversial because we
have no records of when or where
farming began. Using archaeological
finds, climatic patterns, and biological
information, scholars have pieced
together this tentative map of early
centers of domestication.

gathering people who lived in forests bordering freshwater streams.
Recent archaeological discoveries in Thailand and neighboring countries
lend some support to his proposal.

Some other scholars have suggested that the constantly wet tropical
rain forests were best suited to initial plant domestication because no
seasonal adjustments to temperature or rainfall are necessary in these
areas. Planting can be done at any time of year. In climates that have
pronounced seasonal differences, farmers must plant at a specific time of
year. This implies the use of some sort of calendar.

Domestication of plants reproduced by seed, Sauer believed, first
occurred in areas of Eurasia peripheral to the older vegetative domestication zone. Virtually all scholars, including Sauer, agree that southwestern
Asia was of monumental importance in this respect, in particular the hilly
fringe along the northern perimeter of the Tigris-Euphrates plain, part of
the so-called Fertile Crescent. They have devoted special attention to sites
in northern Iraq.

Perhaps most notable among the seed domesticates of this region were
the small grain crops, wheat and barley. In the moister climatic conditions
of 14,000 or more years ago, when scholars estimate that plant domestication began here, this hilly belt seemingly had many of the environmental
qualities favored by Sauer. In fact, the entire area from Asia Minor to the
borders of India is an agricultural hearth of great antiquity, and domestication of grains such as wheat and barley may have occurred repeatedly
throughout this southwestern Asian region.

To the east in China and Indochina, on the northeastern periphery of the
old vegetative crop zone, a secondary seed-plant domestication zone
developed, with rice as the principal grain domesticate. Indeed, China is

now viewed by some experts as a very important secondary center of early domestication.

In the Americas, said Sauer, parallel developments occurred. A vegetative domestication zone lay in northwestern South America, involving such crops as the white potato and manioc. Middle America was the great peripheral seed-plant domestication area, in which the Amerindian staple crop, corn (or maize), first entered agriculture. Some regard Peru as a second, less important American seed-plant hearth.

Controversy has long raged over the question of whether plant domestication was independently invented in Eurasia and America or whether the idea spread by cultural diffusion in ancient times from the Old World to the New. The fact that most American domesticates, such as corn, squash, tomatoes, pumpkins, and potatoes were seemingly unknown in the Eastern Hemisphere even as late as the time of Columbus strongly suggests independent invention, though stimulus diffusion could be responsible. Independent domestication may have occurred even *within* the Old World. In any case, the Amerindians domesticated a complex of crops superior in overall nutritional value to those developed by all Eastern Hemisphere peoples combined.

The widespread association of female deities with agriculture in the Old World suggests that women were the first people to work the land. We may assume this because of the traditional, almost universal division of labor in hunting-gathering-fishing societies. Under this system, men did the hunting and fishing, while women gathered harvests from wild plants. Since women were the ones in day-to-day contact with plants and stayed closer to home, it is reasonable that they initiated plant domestication. Only when farming began to supply the community with more food than hunting and fishing did men replace women as tillers of crops.

From the original hearths of plant domestication, agriculture spread gradually over much of the Old and New Worlds. Along the routeways of diffusion, secondary domestication centers developed and new crops were added to the agricultural inventory.

But the diffusion of domesticated plants did not end in antiquity. Only within the past century did crop farming reach its present territorial extent, completing the diffusion begun many millennia ago. The introduction of the lemon, orange, grape, and the date palm by Spanish mission fathers in eighteenth-century California is a recent example of relocation diffusion. This was part of a larger diffusion—the introduction of European crops that accompanied the mass emigrations of farmers from Europe to the Americas, Australia, New Zealand, and South Africa.

The origin and diffusion of animal domestication

A **domesticated animal** is one dependent on people for food and shelter, differing also from wild species in physical appearance and behavior, a result of controlled breeding and daily contact with humans. Animal domestication apparently occurred later in prehistory than did the first planting of crops, with the probable exception of the dog, whose companionship with people is seemingly much more ancient. Typically, people value domesticated animals and take care of them for some utilitarian purpose. Yet the original motive for domestication may not have been economic. People may have first domesticated cattle, as well as some kinds of birds, for religious reasons. Some domesticated animals, such as the pig and dog, perhaps attached themselves voluntarily to human settlements to feast on garbage, much in the manner of bears at Yellowstone National Park today. At first, perhaps humans merely tolerated these animals, later adopting them as pets. It may have been much later that economic functions were found for such pets.

Farmers of the vegetatively reproductive crop hearth in southern Asia apparently did not excel as domesticators of animals. The taming of certain kinds of poultry may be attributed to them, but probably little else. Seed cultivators of southwestern Asia seemingly deserve credit for the first great animal domestications, most notably the herd animals.

The wild ancestors of major herd animals, like cattle, pigs, sheep, and goats lived primarily in a belt running from Syria and southeastern Turkey eastward across Iraq and Iran to central Asia. Most animal domestication seems to have taken place in this general region or in adjacent areas. There in southwestern Asia, farmers first combined domesticated plants and animals into an integrated system, the antecedent of the peasant grain and livestock farming we described earlier. These people began using cattle to pull the plow, a revolutionary invention that greatly increased the acreage under cultivation. In turn, the farmers out of necessity began setting aside a portion of the harvest as livestock feed.

As the grain-herd livestock farming system continued to expand, particularly in the Fertile Crescent area, marginal lands were settled where crop cultivation was difficult or impossible. Population pressures forced people into these districts. The herd animals become more important to the occupants of the inferior margin lands, and they abandoned crop farming. They began wandering with their herds so as not to exhaust local forage. In this manner, nomadic herding was seemingly born long ago on the margins of the Fertile Crescent. Similarly, but in very recent times, livestock ranching may have arisen when herder-farmers retreated into inferior environments under pressure from crop-oriented agriculturists, in the process abandoning all crop raising because of the difficulty of raising plants in these inferior lands.

The Amerindian, who made superior contributions to plant domestication, was largely unsuccessful in taming animals, in part because suitable wild animals were less numerous. The llama, alpaca, and turkey were among the few American domesticates.

Modern innovations in agriculture

Innovation diffusion in agriculture did not end with the original spread of farming and herding. New ideas arose often during the succeeding millennia and spread through agricultural space as innovation waves. The nineteenth and twentieth centuries, in particular, have witnessed many such farming innovations and diffusions.

The spread of hybrid corn through the United States in the present century provides a good example of expansion diffusion (see Figure 3-9 and box, "Supercorn"). Such desirable agricultural innovations are often first accepted by wealthier, large-scale farmers, a clear case of hierarchical diffusion. In the pre-Civil War South, for example, the wealthier plantation owners maintained closest contact with the innovations of the "agricultural revolution" then under way in northwestern Europe.

One of the major innovation diffusions in twentieth-century American agriculture involved the spread of pump irrigation through many parts of the western Great Plains. A detailed study of this irrigation innovation was made in the Colorado Northern High Plains by the geographer Leonard Bowden. Farmers there were deciding more than whether or not to irrigate, because irrigation brought with it different crops, different

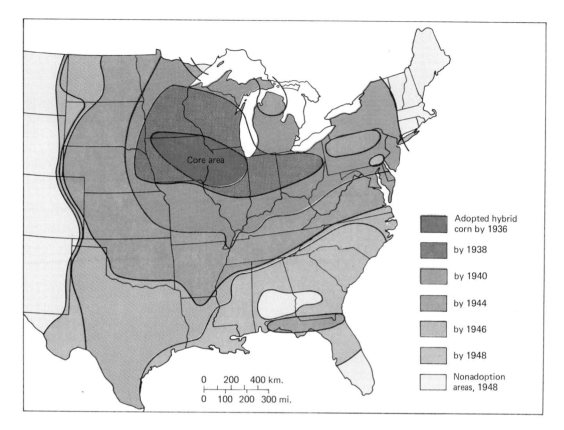

FIGURE 3-9

The spread of hybrid corn in the United States from 1936 to 1948 (see box) began from a core area of initial acceptance in Iowa and Illinois. The innovation spread by expansion (or contagious) diffusion throughout most of the eastern United States in little over a decade. Can you explain the barriers to this innovation encountered in New England, the South, and the Great Plains? (After Zvi Griliches, "Hybrid Corn and the Economies of Innovation," *Science,* 132 (July 26, 1960).)

SUPERCORN

Over 90 percent of all corn grown today in the United States is *hybrid,* a crossing of two or more pure strains of corn, accomplished by artificially controlled breeding. The resulting hybrids are "supercorn," producing up to one-third more corn per stalk than any other type. Experiments leading to the development of hybrids began just after World War I.

Acceptance of hybrid corn carries with it some major changes in farming operations. Traditionally, farmers simply saved some of their harvest to use as seed in the following year, selecting some of the better ears of corn for this purpose. Hybrid seed must be purchased each year because production declines rapidly from seed derived from hybrid plants. Moreover, hybrid plants require more care than do regular varieties. Thus the farmer adopting hybrid corn is committing himself to higher production costs, but he expects to be more than repaid through increased output.

The spread of hybrid corn in the United States (mapped in Figure 3-9) provides an excellent example of how innovation diffusion works in agricultural geog-

raphy. From a core area of early acceptance in Iowa and Illinois, hybrid corn spread rapidly by contagious expansion diffusion through most of the eastern United States. This spread was facilitated by the work of the United States Department of Agriculture and the local County Farm Agents. Hierarchical diffusion was also present on the local scale, as the more affluent, large-scale operators were generally quicker to adopt hybrid corn.

Barriers to the continued expansion of hybrid corn appeared in two main areas: The Great Plains and New England. The westward advance was blunted just west of the hundredth meridian, probably due mainly to increasing aridity to the west. Corn is a moisture-loving crop, and it is not widely raised in dry areas. Another barrier blocked the movement of hybrid corn into New England. In that case, the resistance was apparently due to the unimportance of corn in the dairy and market garden agriculture which dominates the New England region. Expansion into the less affluent rural districts of the South was retarded by lack of investment capital.

markets, and different farming techniques. The Colorado High Plains farmers were, in effect, deciding whether they wanted an entirely different system of agriculture from the one they had traditionally practiced.

The first irrigation well was in operation by 1935, but initial diffusion was retarded in part by the barrier imposed by shortage of investment capital in the Great Depression years. Beginning in 1948, irrigation spread quite rapidly. In studying this spread, Bowden observed contagion diffusion from the core area of initial acceptance and distance decay. The closer a potential irrigation site was to an existing irrigated farm, the more likely its owner was to accept the innovation. Hierarchical diffusion was evident also, for the earliest innovators were generally young farmers, while middle-aged farmers resisted irrigation for many years.

Some barriers to the diffusion of irrigation weakened through time. Banks and other moneylending institutions were initially reluctant to lend money to farmers for investment in irrigation. However, once the technique proved to be economically successful, loans were easier to obtain and interest rates were lowered.

Barriers such as this frequently operate to retard or block agricultural innovations of all types. Some barriers are cultural, others physical or environmental. Religious belief has served as a barrier—preventing old-order Amish farmers in Pennsylvania from accepting tractors, pickup trucks, and other agricultural machinery. Members of this sect will usually not adopt items of material culture unless they are mentioned in the Bible, although they sometimes depart from this restriction, as in their use of windmills. The Communist type of state-owned farm has not diffused to western Europe, the United States or other free-enterprise areas because its structure is based on a different political-economic philosophy from the capitalist system. Physical barriers, such as climate, blocked the continued northward expansion of hybrid corn and the westward movement of the boll weevil.

Agricultural Ecology

Because farmers and herders work and live on the land, there is a very close relationship between agriculture and the physical environment. In many ways, the map of agricultural regions reflects environmental influences. At the same time, thousands of years of agricultural use of the land have led to massive alterations in our natural environment. This interplay between humankind and the land is the substance of agricultural ecology.

Environmental influence

Weather and climate have had perhaps the greatest influence on the location and development of different forms of agriculture. For example, the cultivation of many crops sensitive to frost becomes prohibitively expensive outside tropical and subtropical areas. This is one reason why plantation agriculture has thrived. Plantation farmers in warm climates can produce cash crops desired by peoples in the middle latitudes, where such crops cannot be grown. Much market gardening in the southern and southwestern United States depends on a similar climatic advantage to produce citrus fruits, winter vegetables, sugar cane, and other crops that will not grow in areas closer to the large urban markets of the Northeast. In turn, the need for abundant irrigation water to flood the fields confines paddy rice farming to its present limits within Asia.

Soils can play an influential role in agriculture decisions. Shifting cultivation reflects in part an adaptation to poor tropical soils, which rapidly lose their fertility when farmed. Farmers practicing rudimentary sedentary agriculture often owe their superior farming status to the fertility of local volcanic soils, which are not so quickly exhausted.

Terrain can also affect agricultural development. As a general rule, farmers tend to practice crop farming in areas of level terrain, leaving the adjacent hills and mountains forested. In the United States, commercial wheat, rice, and corn farming is concentrated in the flattest areas, partly because such farmers are dependent on heavy machines, and, in the case of rice, on large-scale irrigation (Figure 3-10).

Agriculturists as modifiers of the environment

After the domestication of plants and animals, humankind began to alter the environment in a major way (see Figure 3-11). This is particularly evident in the treatment of natural vegetation. To the preagricultural hunter and gatherer, the forest was a friend that harbored valuable wild plants and animals. To the agriculturist, however, the woodland became an enemy to be destroyed. Over the millennia, as dependence on agriculture grew and as population increased, humans made ever larger demands on the forests. Farmers expanded small patches of cleared land until these areas merged with other clearings. They used ax and fire in their assault on the woodlands, with devastating effect. In many parts of China, India,

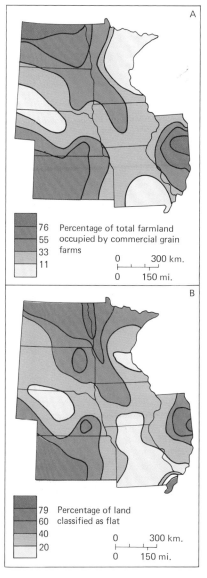

76 / 55 / 33 / 11   Percentage of total farmland occupied by commercial grain farms

0   300 km.
0   150 mi.

79 / 60 / 40 / 20   Percentage of land classified as flat

0   300 km.
0   150 mi.

FIGURE 3-10
The spatial relationship of commercial grain farming and flat terrain in the American Midwest. "Flat" land is defined as any with a 3° slope or less. Commercial grain farming is completely mechanized, and flat land permits more efficient machine operation. The result is this striking correlation between a type of agriculture and a type of terrain. What other factors might attract mechanized grain farming to level land? (After John J. Hidore, "Relationship Between Cash Grain Farming and Landforms," *Economic Geography*, 39 (1963), 86, 87.)

FIGURE 3-11
Millennia of grazing by sheep and goats have helped turn parts of the Greek Aegean island of Patmos into a rocky wasteland. Four thousand years ago this slope was probably forested with a scattering of live oaks and covered with a mantle of soil. Cacti and low shrubs now grow in the few remaining patches of thin soil. In this manner, traditional farmers practicing Mediterranean agriculture have largely destroyed the land. (Photo by Terry G. Jordan, 1971.)

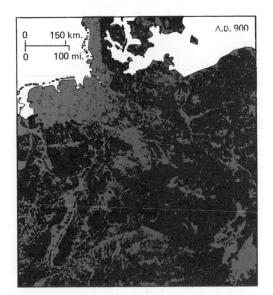

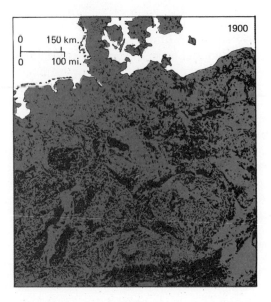

Forested

FIGURE 3–12

In these maps we see the agricultural impact on the forest cover of central Europe from A.D. 900 to 1900. Extensive clearing of the forests, mostly in the period before 1350, was tied largely to expansion of farmland. The forests survived best in hilly and mountainous areas, because these areas were less attractive to farmers. The map of forests for 1900 closely resembles maps of hills and mountain ranges in the same area. Where have forests survived best in North America? (Redrawn from H. C. Darby, "The Clearing of the Woodland in Europe," in William L. Thomas (ed.), *Man's Role in Changing the Face of the Earth*, Chicago: University of Chicago Press, 1956, pp. 202–203.)

and the Mediterranean lands, forests virtually vanished. In trans-Alpine Europe, the United States, and some other areas, they were greatly reduced. Figure 3-12 illustrates the clearing of the forests in central Europe over a 1000-year period.

Grasslands suffered similar modifications (see box, "The Dust Bowl"). Herders often allowed their livestock to overgraze prairie and steppe lands, causing deserts like the Sahara to expand. In some regions, farmers eventually displaced herders and plowed the grasses under to make way for crops. In the United States, one of the greatest transformations of a grassland area took place in California. Prior to the arrival of the first Spanish settlers, the California prairie lands were perhaps the most productive grasslands in North America. Covering 22 million acres, filled with native American grasses, they had a very high grazing capacity. However, Spanish settlers brought with them sheep, cattle, and uninten-

---

THE DUST BOWL

The "Dust Bowl" of the 1930s devastated the American Great Plains, in large part because farmers had plowed up the grasses that originally protected the soil from wind erosion. Woodie Guthrie, the great folk balladeer, captured the disaster in his song "The Great Dust Storm":

The storm took place at sundown
it lasted through the night.
When we looked out next morning
We saw a terrible sight.
We saw outside our window
Where wheatfields they had grown,
Was now a rippling ocean

Of dust the wind had blown.
It covered up our fences,
It covered up our barns,
It covered up our tractors
In this wild and dusty storm.
We loaded our jalopies
And piled our families in,
We rattled down the high-way
To never come back again.

"The Great Dust Storm" (Dust Storm Disaster), words and music by Woody Guthrie. TRO—Copyright © 1960 and 1963 by Ludlow Music, Inc., New York, N.Y. Used by permission.

tionally, their Mediterranean grasses. The grass seeds were inadvertently carried in hay on the ships, in sheep's wool, and in animal droppings. These hardy, lower-quality grasses established themselves initially around the Spanish missions and settlements and then slowly spread across the state as overgrazing and drought years threw the less hardy California grasses into retreat. After about 1850, American farmers and ranchers continued the destruction begun by the Spaniards and Mexicans. The grazing lands were flooded with sheep and cattle, far more than they could reasonably support. By the time the California livestock industry had peaked in the late nineteenth century, the grazing capacity of California's ranges had been cut in half due to soil erosion, overgrazing, and the invasion of mainly European low-quality weeds and grasses. The June grass, bluegrass, and oat grass were gone. In some areas, only tarweed, star thistle, or cheat grass was left. The transformation of the California grasslands by humans and their animals has been so total that today it is almost impossible to imagine what the original prairies were really like.

Irrigation is another very common environmental modification wrought by farmers. Artificial watering can have both intentional and unintentional impacts on the land. Obviously, the intended effect is to circumvent deficiencies in precipitation by importing water from another area, using dams and canals, or from another era, using deep wells and pumps to exploit groundwater accumulated over decades and centuries. Unfortunately, the beneficial effect of irrigation is often offset by unintentional environmental destruction. Ditch and canal irrigation can cause the local subsurface water table to rise, waterlogging the soil, and the mineral content of the water frequently salinizes the ground. In Pakistan, for example, the water table rose 10 to 30 feet (3 to 10 meters), and 800 to 2000 pounds of salt were added per acre of land (900 to 2200 kilograms per hectare), as a result of dam-and-ditch irrigation. Conversely, the water table has been drastically lowered by well and pump irrigation in parts of the American Great Plains, particularly Texas, causing ancient springs to go dry and promising an early end to intensive agriculture there.

The agricultural element in environmental perception

People perceive the physical environment through the lenses their culture fashions for them. Each person's agricultural heritage can be very influential in shaping these perceptions. This is not surprising, because human survival depends upon how successfully people can adjust their ways of making a living to environmental conditions.

As we saw in Chapter 1, the American Great Plains provide a good example of how an agricultural experience in one environment influenced farmers' environmental perception and subsequent behavior in another environment. A study made by geographer Thomas Saarinen in the 1960s revealed that, although the oldest and most experienced Great Plains farmers had the most accurate perception of drought, almost every farmer still underestimated the actual frequency of such dry periods. In addition, the study found that livestock ranchers on the Great Plains tend to be less aware of drought hazard than are commercial grain farmers. This suggests that the kind of farming practiced in an area can often mold the inhabitants' environmental perceptions according to the needs of their own livelihood.

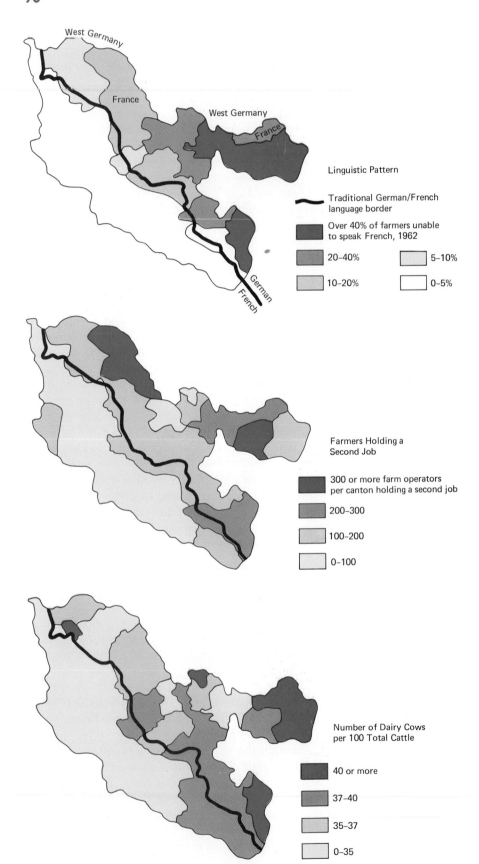

FIGURE 3–13

Agriculture and culture in France. In the northeastern border region of France, part of the old district known as the Lorraine, lies one segment of the German/French language border. Many agricultural features virtually duplicate the language pattern. On the German-speaking side of the line, farms are smaller and more fragmented, causing the farmers to seek second jobs to support their families. Dairy cattle and swine are more important among the German-speaking farmers. The causes of these differences lie in the respective cultures. Try to guess what they might be. (After Michel Cabouret, "Aperçus Nouveaux sur 1' Agriculture de la Lorraine du Nord-Est: Les Répercussions de la Division Linguistique dur Département de la Moselle," *Mosella*, 5 (Oct.–Dec. 1975), 51–58.)

Linguistic Pattern

Traditional German/French language border

Over 40% of farmers unable to speak French, 1962

20–40%   5–10%

10–20%   0–5%

Farmers Holding a Second Job

300 or more farm operators per canton holding a second job

200–300

100–200

0–100

Number of Dairy Cows per 100 Total Cattle

40 or more

37–40

35–37

0–35

Cultural Integration in Agriculture

In the preceding section, we concentrated on how human agricultural pursuits shape and are shaped by the physical environment. Now we turn to the ways cultural and economic forces can influence the distribution of agricultural activities. Religious taboos, politically based tariff restrictions, rural land-use zoning policies, and many other factors of human origin influence the distribution of agricultural activities (see Figure 3-13). Among some peoples, the system of crop and livestock raising is so firmly enmeshed in the culture that both society and religion are greatly influenced (see box, "Cultural Integration: The Example of Cattle Among the Dasanetch").

FIGURE 3–13 (Continued)

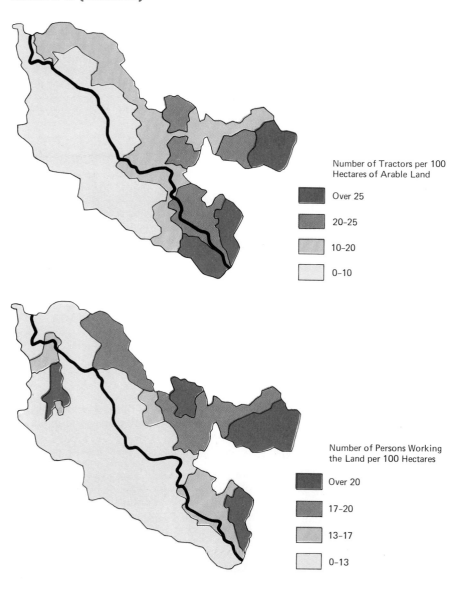

Number of Tractors per 100
Hectares of Arable Land

Over 25

20–25

10–20

0–10

Number of Persons Working
the Land per 100 Hectares

Over 20

17–20

13–17

0–13

CULTURAL INTEGRATION: THE EXAMPLE OF CATTLE AMONG THE DASANETCH

The Dasanetch are a herding people living close to Lake Rudolf in East Africa, where the borders of Ethiopia, Kenya, and Sudan meet. For them, cattle are more than mere domestic animals from which they derive milk, meat, blood, and skins. Instead, cattle occupy a central position in their society, serving religious and social roles in addition to the economic function. Dasanetch men identify closely with their cattle and sometimes even assume the personal name of a favorite ox. Cattle themes appear frequently in the song, dance, myth, and ritual of the Dasanetch. Cattle are also an essential aspect of the unmarried woman's dowry and serve as a medium of exchange. "Cattle are therefore central in the organization and functioning of Dasanetch society," bearing utilitarian, subjective, and monetary values. In this way, agriculture, religion, and society are thoroughly integrated.

Derived from data in Claudia J. Carr, Pastoralism in Crisis: The Dasanetch and Their Ethiopian Lands, (University of Chicago, Dept. of Geography, Research Paper No. 180, 1977, pp. 99–100.

JOHANN HEINRICH von THÜNEN
1783-1850

Von Thünen was not a professional scholar, but rather the landlord of an estate in the German province of Mecklenburg. He did attend several universities in Germany. A contemporary of von Humboldt and Ritter, he apparently never met them, and yet his contribution to geography has been very great. He was concerned with maximizing the agricultural profit from his extensive landholdings. This financial concern and his own curiosity led him to create the model of land use referred to as the "isolated state." Modern location theory in agricultural geography is based on von Thünen's model, and he is widely regarded as the originator of spatial models.

Dietary preferences

One potent cultural force at work in shaping the agricultural map is traditional dietary preference. The Germanic European fondness for bovine-derived dairy products, for example, helps explain the presence of commercial dairy belts in Europe, North America, and Australia, as well as their absence in Mediterranean and Latin American countries, where people are not as partial to milk products.

Coffee and tea consumption in the world displays some striking regional patterns from one country to another, as Figure 3-14 reveals. Notable in this pattern is the contrast between the preference for coffee in the United States and the British fondness for tea. In light of this contrast in beverage preference, it is hardly surprising that tropical highland plantations in the Western Hemisphere, nearer the United States, concentrate on coffee production, while in the Eastern Hemisphere similar hill plantations in the tropical areas in former British colonies such as India produce tea. The Dutch, like Americans, drink more coffee than tea, and during their rule of the East Indies, the name of their tropical island of Java became almost synonymous with coffee. In fact, most dictionaries still list *java* as a slang word for coffee, commemorating the traditional major highland plantation crop of the mountainous, formerly Dutch island.

The von Thünen model

An even more significant force influencing commercial agriculture is the transportation cost for farm produce. A century and a half ago, the German scholar-farmer Johann Heinrich von Thünen developed a European-oriented agricultural location theory based on the cost of transporting farm products to market (see biographical sketch). Von Thünen proposed that **intensive agriculture** would take place nearest to the market, since farmers could place almost all of their investment in the land in the form of labor and capital rather than in transportation. With increasing distance from market, farmers would spend progressively less per unit of land, because they would have to spend progressively more on transporting produce to market. Thus, they would be forced to use their land less intensively. In addition, according to von Thünen, higher land prices, taxes, and labor costs in areas near the market require farmers in those regions to maximize production and income per acre of land.

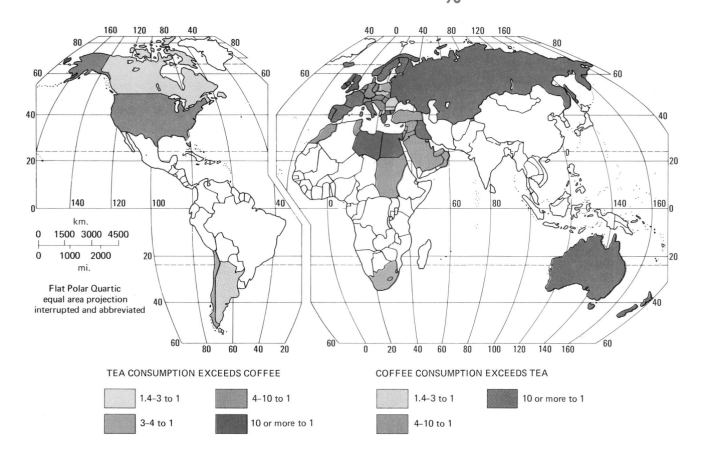

TEA CONSUMPTION EXCEEDS COFFEE

1.4–3 to 1	4–10 to 1
3–4 to 1	10 or more to 1

COFFEE CONSUMPTION EXCEEDS TEA

1.4–3 to 1	10 or more to 1
4–10 to 1	

The von Thünen model suggests that highly intensive commercial forms of land use, such as market gardening and feedlots, would be located nearest to large urban-industrial markets. Successive belts of progressively less intensive agriculture, represented by dairying, livestock fattening, commercial grain farming, and livestock ranching, would extend beyond this region. Livestock ranching, being the least intensive commercial type of agriculture, would therefore be relegated to the regions most remote from markets. Figure 3-15 diagrams an adaptation of von Thünen's model. The model can be applied on a variety of scales, from the local to the regional and international (Figure 3-16).

Of course, many factors other than transportation costs and cash yield per acre influence the map of agricultural regions. Models do not depict reality. Still, on a regional scale we can detect von Thünen's location pattern in the huge urban-industrial districts of the northeastern United States and in northwestern Europe. Zones of market gardening, dairying, livestock fattening, cash grain farming, and ranching do appear to be arranged at increasing distances from these major markets, as Figure 3-17 shows. We should regard plantations and market gardens that produce subtropical crops as intensive types of agriculture displaced to the south by the requirements of climate. We can find even more convincing evidence of the validity of von Thünen's theory if we note that the growth of urban markets and the importance of transportation facilities pushed the less intensive types of agriculture further and further to the hinterlands of nineteenth-century Europe and North America. Thus the American wheat belt moved westward from Pennsylvania and Ohio, through the

FIGURE 3–14

Tea and coffee consumption outside the major producing countries. Markets developed on the basis of these beverage preferences have helped shape the plantation producing areas in the tropical highlands. The huge market for coffee in the United States has encouraged planters in the tropical hill districts of South and Central America to grow coffee. What factors might explain the difference between the United States and Canada? Why are the British and Irish the only tea drinkers in western Europe? (After Norman Berdichevsky, "A Cultural Geography of Coffee and Tea Preferences," *Proceedings, Association of American Geographers,* 8 (1976), 25.)

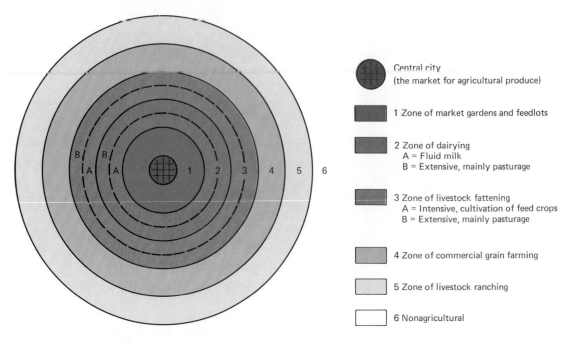

Central city
(the market for agricultural produce)

1 Zone of market gardens and feedlots

2 Zone of dairying
A = Fluid milk
B = Extensive, mainly pasturage

3 Zone of livestock fattening
A = Intensive, cultivation of feed crops
B = Extensive, mainly pasturage

4 Zone of commercial grain farming

5 Zone of livestock ranching

6 Nonagricultural

FIGURE 3–15
This simple model, slightly modified from von Thünen, shows the hypothetical distribution of types of commercial agriculture in an "isolated state." It is based on the following assumptions: (1) only one market (the central city) is available to farmers; (2) all farmers are market-oriented, producing goods for sale rather than for personal subsistence; (3) all aspects of the physical environment are uniform throughout the area; (4) all points the same distance from the central city have equal access to transportation to the city; (5) all farmers behave in an economically rational manner by maximizing their profits; and (6) the dietary preferences of the population are those of Germanic Europeans. These factors are held constant so that we may see the effect of transportation costs and differing distances from the market. The more intensive forms of agriculture, such as market gardening, are located nearest the market, while the least intensive form (livestock ranching) is most remote. Compare this model to the map of agricultural types in the United States (Figure 3–17).

FIGURE 3–16

Von Thünen's land-use principles can be applied on various scales. This pattern of agricultural clearings and surviving forest, near Munich in Bavaria, West Germany, reveals von Thünen's concentric zones at a local level. The village-dwelling settlers, beginning over 1100 years ago, cleared the forest in roughly circular areas closest to their villages, leaving the outlying areas wooded as range for their hogs. In this way, the most intensive land use—raising crops—was found nearest to the village, while the less intensive herding of livestock occupied peripheral lands. The suffix or prefix *brunn* refers to burning, suggesting that the settlers used fire to clear the land. (Adapted from Terry G. Jordan, *The European Culture Area: A Systematic Geography*, New York: Harper & Row, 1973, p. 48.)

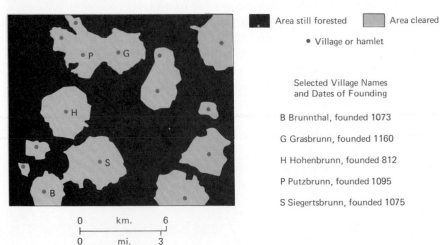

Area still forested   Area cleared

• Village or hamlet

Selected Village Names
and Dates of Founding

B Brunnthal, founded 1073

G Grasbrunn, founded 1160

H Hohenbrunn, founded 812

P Putzbrunn, founded 1095

S Siegertsbrunn, founded 1075

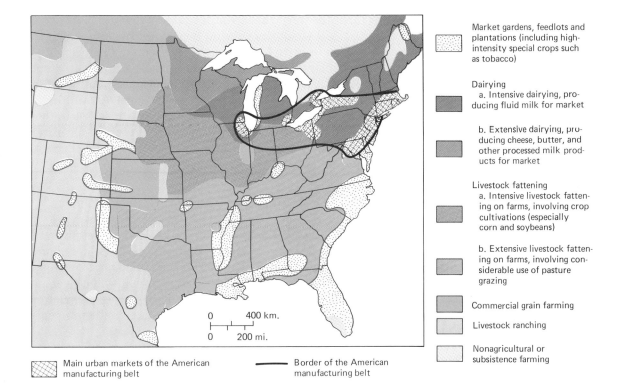

Market gardens, feedlots and plantations (including high-intensity special crops such as tobacco)

Dairying
a. Intensive dairying, producing fluid milk for market

b. Extensive dairying, producing cheese, butter, and other processed milk products for market

Livestock fattening
a. Intensive livestock fattening on farms, involving crop cultivations (especially corn and soybeans)

b. Extensive livestock fattening on farms, involving considerable use of pasture grazing

Commercial grain farming

Livestock ranching

Nonagricultural or subsistence farming

Main urban markets of the American manufacturing belt

Border of the American manufacturing belt

0   400 km.

0   200 mi.

Midwest, and finally to its present location in the Great Plains. It was replaced in the East by more intensive forms of agriculture such as dairying and livestock fattening.

Nor is evidence of the validity of von Thünen's model lacking in the underdeveloped countries of the world. Geographer Ronald J. Horvath made a detailed study of the African region centering on the Ethiopian capital city of Addis Ababa. While noting disruptions caused by ethnic and environmental contrasts, Professor Horvath found "remarkable parallels between Thünen's crop theory and the agriculture around Addis Ababa." Similarly, German geographer Ursula Ewald applied the model to the farming patterns of colonial Mexico during the period of Spanish rule, concluding that even this culturally and environmentally diverse land provided "an excellent illustration of von Thünen's principles on spatial zonation in agriculture."

Clearly, economic factors relating to location and distance from market help shape the spatial variations in agriculture. Culture and economy are firmly integrated, and their interaction helps produce the human mosaic.

FIGURE 3–17

Types of agriculture in the eastern and central portions of North America form a pattern based on major city markets. The main market for agricultural produce (comparable to the "central city" of Figure 3–16) lies in the urbanized zone from Boston and New York to Chicago. What similarities can you see between the distribution of types in the model and on this map? Why are the market garden and feedlot areas "displaced" to the south?

● ▬▬▬▬▬▬▬▬▬▬

The Agricultural Landscape

A great part of the world's land area is cultivated or pastured. In this huge area, the visible imprint of humankind might best be called the **agricultural landscape** (see box, "August Meitzen"). The agricultural imprint on the land often varies even over short distances, telling us much about local cultures and subcultures. Although this agricultural landscape changes constantly, it also remains in many respects a window on the past. Archaic features are everywhere. For this reason, the rural landscape can teach us a great deal about the cultural heritage of its occupants.

We have already discussed, in Chapter 2, some aspects of the agricultural landscape, in particular the rural settlement forms. We saw the different ways farming people situate their dwellings in various cultures. In Chapter 7, which deals with folk geography, we will consider traditional rural architecture, another element in the agricultural landscape. In this chapter, we will confine our attention to a third aspect of the rural landscape: the patterns of fields and properties created as people occupy land for the purpose of farming.

Traditional survey, cadastral, and field patterns

A **cadastral pattern** is one describing property ownership lines, while a field pattern reflects the way a farmer subdivides his land for agricultural use. Both can be much influenced by **survey patterns**, the lines laid out by surveyors prior to the settlement of an area. There are three major regional contrasts in survey, cadastral, and field patterns: (1) **unit-block** versus **fragmented landholding**; (2) regular, geometric survey versus irregular or unsurveyed property lines; and (3) private versus communal landownership.

Fragmented farms are the rule rather than the exception in non-Communist portions of the Old World. Under this system, farmers live in farm villages or hamlets. Their small landholdings are splintered into many separate fields that lie at varying distances and directions from the settlement. It is not uncommon for a farm to be divided into 100 pieces. Some farmers may even own 500 or more separate, tiny parcels of land. The individual plots may be roughly rectangular in shape, as in the Orient and southern Europe, or they may lie in long, narrow strips. The latter pattern is most common in western, northern, and eastern Europe, where farmers traditionally worked with a bulky, large plow that was difficult to turn (see Figure 3-18). The origins of the fragmented farm system go back to an early period of peasant communalism. One of its initial justifications was a desire for peasant equality. Each farmer in the village was to have land of varying soil composition and terrain. Distance of travel from the village was to be equalized. From the rice paddies of Japan and India to the pastures and fields of western Europe, the fragmented holding remains a prominent feature of the cultural landscape. Almost everywhere they are found, fragmented holdings display irregular property lines. If surveying was ever done in these areas, it occurred in dim antiquity and did not produce regular geometric shapes. The property lines seem a hopeless jumble to the outsider visiting such settlements.

Unit-block farms, by contrast, are those in which all of the farmer's property is contained in a single, contiguous piece of land. Such landholdings are typical mainly of the overseas area of European settlement, particularly the Americas, Australia, New Zealand, and South Africa. Most often, they display the imprint of regular geometric land survey. The checkerboard of farms and fields in the rectangular survey areas of the United States is a good example of this cadastral pattern (refer to Figure 2-25).

The American rectangular survey system was developed after the Revolutionary War as an orderly method for parceling out federally owned land for sale to pioneers. It imposed a rigid, square, graph-paper pattern on much of the American countryside, geometry triumphant over physical geography. All lines are oriented to the cardinal directions. The basic

FIGURE 3-18
Fragmented landholdings lie around a French farm village. The numerous fields and plots belonging to one individual farmer are shaded. Such fragmented farms are common in many parts of Europe and Asia. What advantages and disadvantages does this system have? (After Albert Demangeon, *La France,* Vol. 6 of *Géographie Universelle,* Paris: Armand Colin, 1946.)

Buildings

Holdings of one farmer

Garden, vineyards, and orchards

unit of the system is the section, a square of land one mile on each side and thus 640 acres in area (Figure 3-19). Sections were often bought and sold as half-sections (320 acres) or quarter-sections (160 acres). Larger squares, measuring six miles on each side and containing thrity-six square miles of land, are called townships, which also serve as political administrative subdistricts within counties. Roads follow section and township lines, adding to the square aspect of the American agricultural landscape. Canada adopted an almost identical rectangular survey system, which is particularly evident in the Prairie Provinces (Figure 3-20). Traces of more ancient rectangular survey systems can be seen in some European and Asian landscapes. The Roman **centuriation** pattern has left visual evidence in parts of the long-vanished empire; while in Japan, the **jori** rectangular survey system was begun in the seventh century A.D.

Equally striking in appearance are **long-lot** farms, where the landholding consists of a long, narrow unit-block stretching back from a road, river, or canal (Figure 3-21). Rather than occurring singly, long-lots are found lined up in rows, allowing this cadastral-survey pattern to dominate entire districts. Long-lots are found widely in the hills and marshes of central and western Europe, in parts of Brazil and Argentina, along the rivers of French-settled Québec and southern Louisiana, and in parts of Texas and northern New Mexico (Figure 3-22). The reason for elongating these unit-block farms was to provide each farmer with access to transportation facilities, either roads or rivers. In French America, long-lots were laid out in rows along streams, since water transport was the chief means of movement in colonial times. In the hill lands of central Europe, a road along the valley floor provides the focus, and long-lots reach back from the road to the adjacent ridgecrests.

Some unit-block farms have irregular shapes rather than the rectangular or long-lot patterns. Most of these result from **metes and bounds surveying**, a type that makes much use of natural features such as trees, boulders, and streams. Much of the eastern United States was surveyed under the metes and bounds system, with the result that farms there are much more irregular in outline than those where rectangular survey was imposed. The juncture of the two systems of survey is quite apparent from an airplane (Figure 3-23).

Field and cadastral patterns often vary greatly in accordance with the

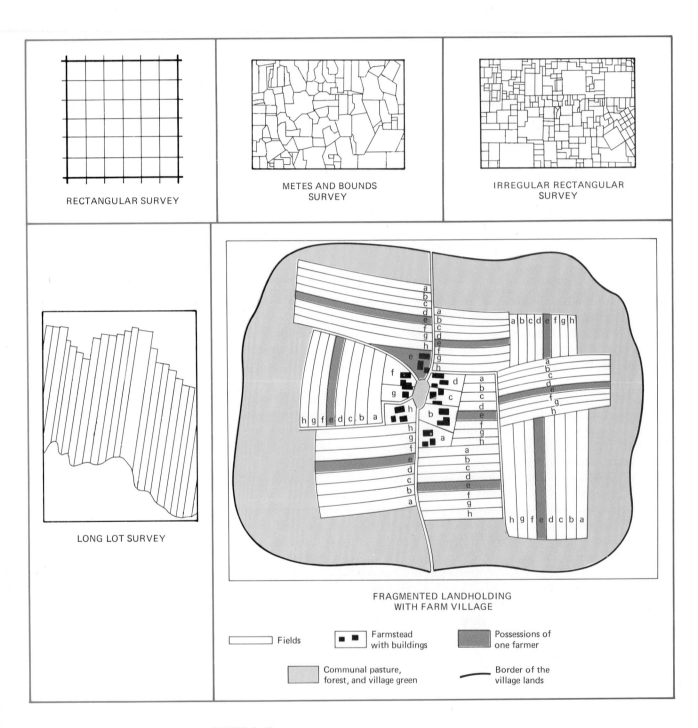

RECTANGULAR SURVEY

METES AND BOUNDS
SURVEY

IRREGULAR RECTANGULAR
SURVEY

LONG LOT SURVEY

FRAGMENTED LANDHOLDING
WITH FARM VILLAGE

Fields

Farmstead
with buildings

Possessions of
one farmer

Communal pasture,
forest, and village green

Border of the
village lands

FIGURE 3-19
Some types of original land division.

FIGURE 3–20
Original land survey patterns in the United States and southern Canada. The cadastral patterns still retain the imprint of the various original survey types. What impact on rural life might the different patterns have?

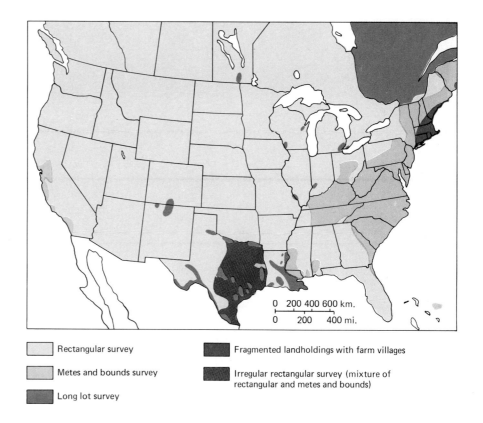

0 200 400 600 km.
0   200   400 mi.

☐ Rectangular survey

☐ Metes and bounds survey

■ Long lot survey

■ Fragmented landholdings with farm villages

■ Irregular rectangular survey (mixture of rectangular and metes and bounds)

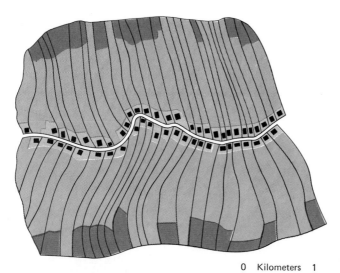

0   Kilometers   1

── Property lines

≈ The central road

■ Farmhouse and other buildings

☐ Farmyard and gardens

☐ Fields, meadow, and pasture

■ Forest

FIGURE 3–21
A long-lot settlement pattern in the hills of central Germany. Each property consists of an elongated unit-block of land stretching back from the road in the valley to an adjacent ridgecrest, part of which remains wooded.

FIGURE 3–22
Aerial view of riverine long-lot farms in French-settled southern Louisiana. Each farm consists of a narrow strip of land stretching back at right angles from the stream. The farmsteads are located at the front of the lot, near the banks and levees. (Photo courtesy of Professor Sam B. Hilliard, Louisiana State University.)

type of agriculture. In areas where shifting cultivation is practiced the pattern is one of scattered, irregularly shaped clearings that look like islands in a sea of forest. In commercial dairying and ranching regions, unit-block holdings cover the land. Other types of farming, such as paddy rice farming and grape-growing, lend themselves well to fragmented holdings.

Land reform and consolidation

In many parts of the world, particularly in Eurasia, major changes in cadastral and field patterns have occurred in the last century. In non-Communist areas, considerable progress has been made in consolidating fragmented holdings into farms that are either unit blocks or at least less fragmented than they were prior to consolidation (Figure 3-24).

Even more radical changes have occurred in most Communist countries. Large collective and state farms have replaced privately owned ones, and huge fields worked by large groups of laborers have taken the place of tiny individually worked parcels (Figure 3-25). Collective farms are owned either by the government or by a group of farmers, with proceeds or profits divided among the member farmers. State farms are government property and are worked by groups of hired laborers. In the Soviet Union, some state farms extend over 100,000 acres (40,000 hectares), providing employment for thousands of wage laborers.

Fencing and hedging

Property and field borders are often, but not always, marked by fences or hedges, heightening the visibility of these lines in the agricultural

ORIGINAL SURVEY LINES

PROPERTY LINES, ABOUT 1955
(Those which follow original survey
lines are shown by thicker lines)

FIELD AND WOODLOT BORDERS,
ABOUT 1955

U.S. RECTANGULAR SURVEY, HANCOCK AND HARDIN COUNTIES, OHIO

FIGURE 3–23
Two contrasting original survey patterns, rectangular and metes and bounds, were used in an area of west-central Ohio. Note the impact these survey patterns have had on cadastral and field patterns. What other features of the cultural landscape might be influenced by these patterns? (After Norman J. W. Thrower, *Original Survey and Land Subdivision*, Chicago: Rand McNally, 1966, pp. 40, 63, 84.)

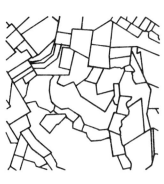
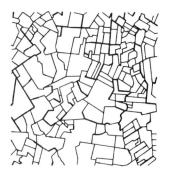

METES AND BOUNDS SURVEY, UNION AND MADISON COUNTIES, OHIO

FIGURE 3–24
Land consolidation in an Irish farm hamlet. The consolidation, carried out in 1909, greatly reduced fragmentation of holdings and produced unit-block farms for some inhabitants. Note that the consolidation caused the breakup of the hamlet and its replacement by isolated farmsteads. What advantages does the new cadastral pattern have over the old one? In what ways might the new be less advantageous than the old? (After James H. Johnson, "Studies of Irish Rural Settlement," *Geographical Review*, 48 (1958), 564.)

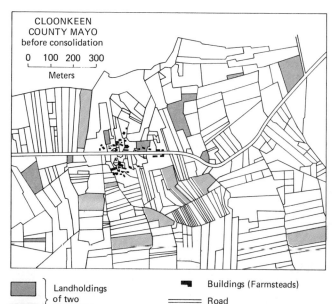
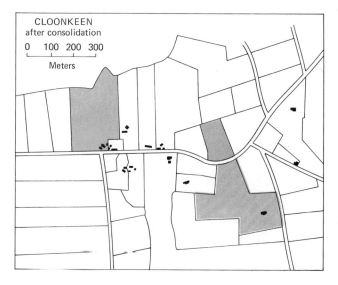

Landholdings of two sample farmers

Buildings (Farmsteads)

Road

Property lines

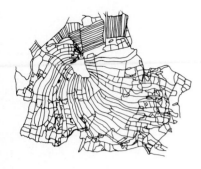

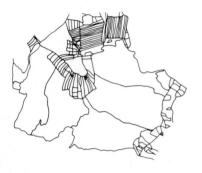

☐ Village

— Property and field borders

FIGURE 3–25
A village in Czechoslovakia before and after Communist collectivization. Six large blocks of land were set aside as the collective lands. Farmers were allowed to retain some small plots as private landholdings, and these cadastral lines were unchanged. But the greater part of the village farmlands were collectivized and the pattern greatly simplified (After R. Urban, "Die Strukturwandlung der tschechischen Landwirtschaft," *Zeitschrift für Ostforschung*, 1953, pp. 130–137, with modifications.)

landscape. Open-field areas, where the dominance of crop raising and the careful tending of livestock make fences unnecessary, are still the rule in India, Japan, much of western Europe, and some other Old World areas, but much of the remainder of the world's agricultural lands are enclosed.

Where present, fences and hedges add a distinctive touch to the cultural landscape (Figure 3-26). Different cultures have their own methods and ways of enclosing land, so that fences and hedges often can be linked to particular groups. Fences in different parts of the world are made of substances as diverse as steel wire, logs, poles, split rails, brush, rock, and earth. Those of you who have visited rural New England, western Ireland, or Yucatan perhaps retain as one of your visual memories the mile upon mile of stone fence that typify those landscapes. Barbed wire fences swept across the American countryside a century ago, but some remnants of older types can still be seen. In Appalachia, the traditional split rail zig-zag fence of pioneer times survives here and there, and pine jack leg fences are still in evidence in Rocky Mountain states such as Montana. Like most visible features of culture, fence types can serve as indicators of cultural diffusion.

The hedge is, in effect, a living fence. Few who have visited the mazelike hedgerow country of Brittany and Normandy in France or large areas of Great Britain and Ireland fail to perceive these living fences as a major aspect of the rural landscape. To walk or drive the roads of hedgerow country is to experience a unique feeling of confinement quite different from the openness of barbed wire or open-field landscapes.

Conclusion

We have seen that the ancient and honored form of livelihood called agriculture varies markedly from place to place, displaying the same tendency for spatial variation that we observed earlier for population. We expressed these regional patterns as twelve agricultural regions, ranging from traditional subsistence hand-labor farming systems of tropical rain forests to the highly mechanized cash grain operations of midlatitude wheat belts.

All of these diverse systems were rooted ultimately in the ancient innovations of plant and animal domestication, ideas that were diffused

FIGURE 3–26
This jack leg fence was built in Montana. It is made of lengths of lodgepole pine—a common fencing material for farmers in the area.

from multiple points of origin to occupy their present distributions. Subsequently, countless other agricultural innovations arose, diffused across agricultural space by expansion and relocation, collided with barriers, and settled finally into their present distributions.

Cultural ecology is implicit in the tilling of the soil and grazing of natural vegetation. Humankind cannot engage in agriculture, even on the most primitive level, without deliberately modifying the physical environment. The results, as we saw, include deforestation, soil erosion, and the expansion of deserts. By the same token, and because agriculturists work in such direct contact with the land, they are influenced in some measure by the physical environment in which they live and work. We observed the role of climatic advantage and disadvantage and the invitation of level terrain to large-scale mechanized farming as examples of this environmental influence.

Cultural integration taught us to look for cause-and-effect connections between agriculture and other cultural features. In particular, in the von Thünen model we saw the influence of transportation costs and nearness to market on types of farming.

We found the agricultural landscape to be particularly rich in spatial variations. The ways of dividing land for agricultural use proved to be diverse, ranging from large unit-block farms to tiny, fragmented ones. These spatial contrasts, added to the differences in rural settlement forms discussed in Chapter 2, help produce a highly varied agricultural landscape.

Glossary

Agribusiness highly mechanized, large-scale farming usually under corporate ownership.

Agricultural landscape the cultural landscape of agricultural areas.

Agricultural region a culture region based on characteristics of agriculture.

Agriculture the cultivation of domesticated crops and the raising of domesticated animals.

Cadastral pattern the shapes formed by property borders; the pattern of land ownership.

Centuriation an ancient Roman rectangular survey system, traces of which can still be seen in the cadastral pattern.

Domesticated animal an animal kept for some utilitarian purpose whose breeding is controlled by humans and whose survival is dependent on humans; differing genetically and behaviorally from wild animals.

Domesticated plant a plant willfully planted and tended by humans that is genetically distinct from its wild ancestors as a result of selective breeding.

Double-cropping harvesting twice a year from the same parcel of land.

Feedlot a factory-like farm, devoted to either livestock fattening or dairying; all feed is imported and no crops are grown on the farm.

Fragmented landholding one where the farmer's property is divided into two or more nonadjacent pieces of land.

Hybrid a special plant or animal that results from breeding two different varieties.

Intensive agriculture the expenditure of much labor and capital on a piece of land to increase its productivity. In contrast, extensive agriculture involves less labor and capital.

Intertillage the raising of different crops mixed together in the same field, particularly common in shifting cultivation.

Jori a traditional Japanese system of rectangular survey.

Long-lot a unit-block farm consisting of a long, narrow ribbon of land, stretching back from a road, river, or canal.

Market garden a farm devoted to specialized fruit, vegetable, or vine crops for sale rather than consumption.

Metes and bounds surveying a survey system producing irregularly shaped parcels and often oriented to physical environmental features.

Paddy a small flooded field enclosed by mud dikes, used for rice cultivation in the Orient.

Plantation a large landholding devoted to specialized production of a tropical cash crop.

Ranching commercial raising of herd livestock, on a large landholding.

Sedentary cultivation farming in fixed and permanent fields.

Shifting cultivation a type of agriculture characterized by land rotation, in which temporary clearings are used for several years and then abandoned to be replaced by new clearings; also known as slash-and-burn agriculture.

Subsistence agriculture farming to supply the minimum food and materials necessary to survive.

Suitcase farm in American commercial grain agriculture, a farm on which no one lives, that is planted and harvested by hired migratory crews.

Survey pattern pattern of original land survey in an area.

Unit-block landholding one where all of the farmer's property is contained in a single, contiguous piece of land.

Suggested Readings

Leonard W. Bowden. *Diffusion of the Decision to Irrigate.* Chicago: University of Chicago, Department of Geography, Research Paper No. 97, 1965.

Karl W. Butzer. *Early Hydraulic Civilization in Egypt: A Study in Cultural Ecology.* Chicago: University of Chicago Press, 1976.

Michael Chisholm. *Rural Settlement and Land Use: An Essay in Location.* London: Hutchinson University Library, 1962.

Ursula Ewald. "The von Thünen Principle and Agricultural Zonation in Colonial Mexico," *Journal of Historical Geography,* 3 (1977), 123–133.

Howard F. Gregor. *Geography of Agriculture: Themes in Research.* Englewood Cliffs, N.J.: Prentice-Hall, 1970.

David Grigg. "The Agricultural Regions of the World: Review and Reflections," *Economic Geography,* 45 (1969), 95–132.

Gerry A. Hale. "The Origin, Nature, and Distribution of Agricultural Terracing," *Pacific Viewpoint,* 3 (1961), 1–40.

Leslie Hewes. *The Suitcase Farming Frontier, A Study in the Historical Geography of the Central Great Plains.* Lincoln: University of Nebraska Press, 1973.

Ronald J. Horvath. "Von Thünen's Isolated State and the Area Around Addis Ababa, Ethiopia," *Annals, Association of American Geographers,* 59 (1969), 308–323.

Erich Isaac. *Geography of Domestication.* Englewood Cliffs, N.J.: Prentice-Hall, 1970.

Carl L. Johannessen. "The Domestication Processes in Trees Reproduced by Seed: The Pejibaye Palm in Costa Rica," *Geographical Review,* 56 (1966), 363–376.

Douglas L. Johnson. *The Nature of Nomadism: A Comparative Study of Pastoral Migrations in Southwestern Asia and Northern Africa.* Chicago: University of Chicago, Department of Geography, Research Paper No. 118, 1969.

Hildegard Binder Johnson. *Order Upon the Land: The U.S. Rectangular Land Survey and the Upper Mississippi Country.* New York: Oxford University Press, 1976.

Terry G. Jordan. "The Origin and Distribution of Open-Range Cattle Ranching," *Social Science Quarterly,* 53 (1972), 105–121.

K.H.W. Klages. *Ecological Crop Geography.* New York: Macmillan, 1942.

Fritz L. Kramer. "Eduard Hahn and the End of the 'Three Stages of Man'," *Geographical Review,* 57 (1967), 73–89.

Eugene Cotton Mather and John Fraser Hart. "Fences and Farms," *Geographical Review,* 44 (1954), 201–223.

Alan Mayhew. *Rural Settlement and Farming in Germany.* New York: Barnes & Noble, 1973.

Mushtaqur Rahman. "Ecology of Karez Irrigation: A Case of Pakistan," *GeoJournal,* 5 (1981), 7–15.

Brian K. Roberts. *Rural Settlement in Britain.* Hamden, Conn.: Archon Books, 1977.

Thomas F. Saarinen. *Perception of Drought Hazard on the Great Plains.* Chicago: University of Chicago, Department of Geography, Research Paper No. 106, 1966.

Carl O. Sauer. *Agricultural Origins and Dispersals.* New York: American Geographical Society, 1952.

Louis Seig. "The Spread of Tobacco: A Study in Cultural Diffusion," *Professional Geographer,* 15 (January 1963), 17–21.

Joseph E. Spencer and R. J. Horvath. "How Does an Agricultural Region Originate?" *Annals, Association of American Geographers,* 53 (1963), 74–92.

Dan Stanislawski. *Landscapes of Bacchus: The Vine in Portugal.* Austin: University of Texas Press, 1970.

Dorothy Sylvester. *The Rural Landscapes of the Welsh Borderland: A Study in Historical Geography,* New York: Macmillan, 1969.

Leslie Symons, *Agricultural Geography,* 2nd ed. Boulder, Col.: Westview Press, 1979.

Johann Heinrich von Thünen. *Von Thünen's Isolated State: An English Edition of Der Isolierte Staat.* Translated by Carla M. Wartenberg. Elmsford, N.Y.: Pergamon Press, 1966.

Harald Uhlig and Cay Lienau (eds.). *Types of Field Patterns,* Basic Material for the Terminology of the Agricultural Landscape, Vol. I Giessen, West Germany: W. Schmitz, 1967.

Derwent S. Whittlesey. "Major Agricultural Regions of the Earth," *Annals, Association of American Geographers,* 26 (1936), 199–240.

Political Patterns

4

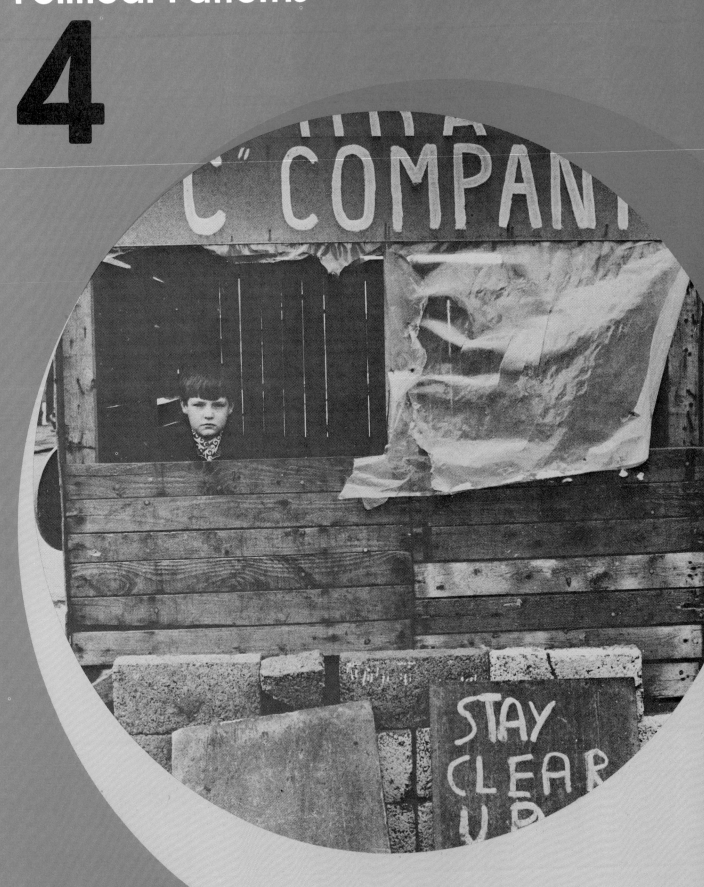

Perhaps you can remember as a child playing a "territorial" game in a field behind your house or out in the streets. You organized your "armies" and established strongholds in clumps of trees, on hilltops, or maybe on the metal fire escape that ran down the back of your apartment building. You demarcated your "turf," establishing your "borders" along creeks, ditches, alleyways, or other features of your special landscape—separating "them" from "us." In short, you organized people politically in a particular area.

Political geography involves the study of how, on an adult scale, territory is organized in different environments and under different cultural conditions. Traditionally, political geographers concentrated mainly on the development of the independent state, on theories of the international power balance, and on the possibilities of world conquest. Why does a nation develop in the first place? What factors in the environment and culture make it stronger or weaker, historically stable like England or unstable like Zaïre? What strategic advantages might one national territory have over another? This fascination is hardly surprising, because the independent nation-state has dominated the recent political development of the world. The rise of nationalism, the breaking down of older, multinational states, the destruction of colonial empires, and the shifting alliances among the world's industrial powers have involved humankind in two world wars. And the unstable, fluid mosaic of nation-states—each based in a specific locale, defending a "homeland," enveloped in a distinctive culture, and identifying an "us" and a "them"—shows no signs of disappearing from our lives. Geographers of the past century could hardly turn their backs on this important spatial reality.

But political geography involves much more than the independent state and the world power balance. Spatial differences of a political nature take many other forms and appear on a variety of scales, from small voting precincts to the mountain domain of a guerrilla force. The political organization of space *within* independent states has been found to be as interesting and significant as external relationships of the state. Spatial variations in political attitudes and behavior within the state, as reflected in voting patterns, for example, have proven to be fruitful topics for geographical research. In recent years, political geographers have devoted increasing attention to topics such as congressional redistricting and the spatial aspects of guerrilla warfare. For example, in 1972 the political geographer Richard Morrill was called by the state of Washington to direct reapportionment of legislative and congressional districts there.

Any aspect of political geography, any spatial political phenomenon, is the product of numerous causal forces, both cultural and environmental. The political geographer's main task is to identify and evaluate these forces in order to understand spatial variations. This chapter introduces many of the topics that interest political geographers, and it is structured by the themes of culture region, cultural diffusion, cultural ecology, cultural integration, and cultural landscape.

Political Culture Regions

Political geographers are interested in both formal and functional culture regions. The self-governing state and its political subdivisions constitute

◄ *Chapter-opening photo:* Ulster Defense Association (Protestant) street post in Belfast, Northern Ireland.

functional regions, and we can devise formal regions in studying such topics as voting patterns and legal systems. We will begin by considering formal culture regions in political geography and how they can be used to help understand the political structure of culture.

Formal culture regions in political geography

Since political attitudes and even government itself are cultural attributes, they can be categorized into formal culture regions (Figure 4-1). Perhaps most rewarding to the cultural geographer are regions based on voting behavior.

Voting patterns. A free vote of the people on some controversial topic can be one of the purest expressions of culture. Election returns can provide data on the distribution of cultural attitudes toward such topics as race relations, food taboos, and separatism. For example, the vote for Alabamian George Wallace in the United States presidential election of 1968 was the political expression of the Lower Southern culture region (compare Figures 4-2 and 1-5). This vote suggested that the political core of the old Confederacy was still intact over a century after the American Civil War. It also suggested that the culture and society that seceded from the Union in 1861 are still viable. To be sure, Wallace appealed to sizable numbers of voters in some areas outside the Lower South, but his success was greatest in that region.

We need not look to nationwide or sectional voting patterns to find important spatial variations in voting, to detect formal culture regions. There are many local examples within your own state, county, or city. California provides some excellent examples, both on the state and local level. As early as the 1850s, the people of northern and southern California differed noticeably in voting behavior, and these differences have persisted to the present. The north, settled largely by people of

FIGURE 4-1
Under Swiss democracy all adult citizens take part in regional parliamentary sessions. This open-air meeting is in Glarus.

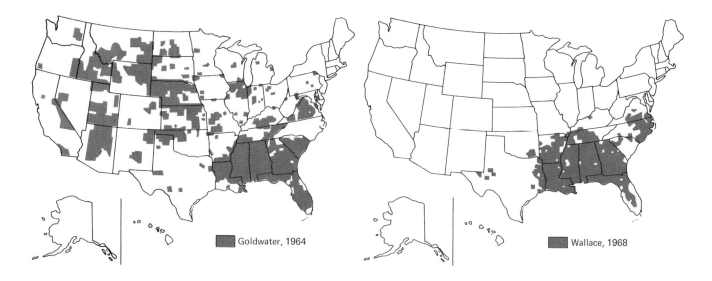

Goldwater, 1964

Wallace, 1968

Midwestern and New England background, acquired a liberal political image, while southern California, peopled from the Upper and Lower South, as well as Mexico, became a conservative stronghold. Geographers Stanley D. Brunn and Robert M. Pierce, using multivariate statistical analysis, identified these political culture regions, and their findings are shown in Figure 4-3.

On a still more local level, we can seek formal culture regions based on voting within individual cities. For example, the vote for mayor in Los Angeles in 1969 revealed some striking spatial variations. Tom Bradley, later elected mayor of the city, was defeated in the 1969 election by incumbent Sam Yorty. The election provided a rather clear-cut choice, even though both candidates were registered Democrats. Bradley, a black, had a liberal philosophy and felt that the city police needed to be more tightly controlled. He championed the right to assemble and demonstrate. Yorty, a white, campaigned on a "law-and-order" platform and made an issue of student demonstrations and street riots. Bradley got more votes in the primary election, but Yorty won the final vote with a majority of 53.2 percent. An analysis of the voting pattern revealed that Bradley's support had been strongest in black neighborhoods, high-income white districts, and university neighborhoods. Indeed, Bradley claimed over 90 percent of the black vote. Yorty's strength was greatest in white neighborhoods next to black areas. The Mexican-American vote was also strongly for Yorty. In sum, the vote varied greatly from one precinct to another, which provided an excellent glimpse of the human mosaic on the local level.

Legal systems. Legal systems provide another revealing political facet of culture and are reflected in formal culture regions. Figure 4-4 shows the distribution of such bodies of law. Some legal systems are of ancient origin, and often we can trace migrations that occurred long ago by studying legal traditions. The Moors, for example, left behind them in Spain many Islamic laws pertaining to irrigation and water rights. Overlapping of legal systems is common, and confusion often results when different cultures each impose their own body of laws on an area.

For example, Spanish settlers implanted their largely Roman legal

FIGURE 4-2

Two recent political expressions of the Lower Southern culture region (see Figure 1-4). Goldwater, the Republican presidential candidate in 1964, found his major support in the Lower South, as did independent candidate George Wallace in 1968. What might explain the differences between the two maps, as for example in South Carolina? The similarities? (Adapted from Stanley D. Brunn, *Geography and Politics in America,* New York: Harper & Row, 1974, pp. 279, 281.)

FIGURE 4-3

Liberal and conservative strongholds in California, as revealed by recent voting patterns. Most of the south, anchored in Los Angeles and San Diego, is a conservative region, while San Francisco is the center of a northern liberal region. What factors might explain this contrast? (Adapted from Robert M. Pierce and Stanley D. Brunn, "The Classification and Regionalization of California Politics," *California Geographer,* 15 (1975), 22.)

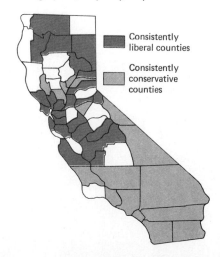

Consistently liberal counties

Consistently conservative counties

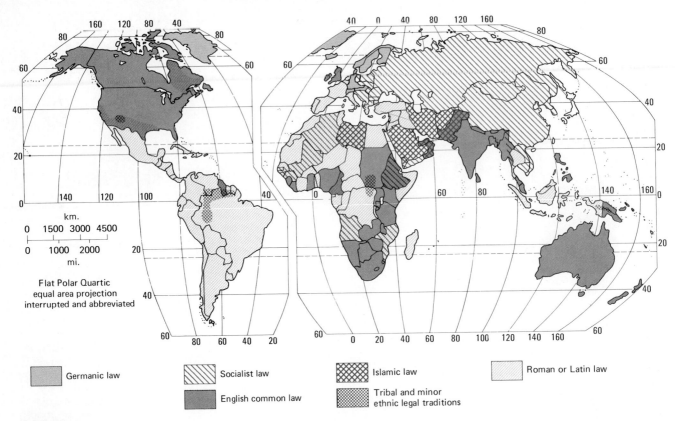

Germanic law

English common law

Socialist law

Islamic law

Tribal and minor
ethnic legal traditions

Roman or Latin law

FIGURE 4–4

In the major legal systems of the world there has been considerable blending and overlapping of legal tradition. This blending is partly because European powers established overseas empires. (In part, after John H. Wigmore, "A Map of the World's Law," *Geographical Review*, 19 (1929), pp. 114–120, and Ernst S. Easterly III, "Global Patterns of Legal Systems," *Geographical Review*, 67 (1977), 209–220.)

system in Texas in the eighteenth century. Then, in the 1800s, Anglo-American settlers seized political control of the province and superimposed their system of English common law, retaining some Hispanic laws. The mixture was confusing enough to assure employment for generations of lawyers. But confusing or not, the laws of Texas provide an index of the diffusion of Spanish and British cultures. A similar blending of English common law and Roman law is found in Québec, Louisiana, South Africa, and the Philippines.

In contrast to these traditional legal systems are others of recent origin. Most notable is Socialist law, which has supplanted or been superimposed upon more ancient systems in much of the Eastern Hemisphere in this century.

Functional culture regions in political geography

The functional culture region is rather different from the formal type. It deals with a region that is organized to function in some way, a region that may well be heterogeneous in its cultural makeup.

Independent states. The independent state is such a culture region. It is organized to function politically; when political power is organized to control a particular piece of territory, an independent state can be the result. This organization, this functioning, makes the independent state a functional rather than a formal region.

One of the most basic human needs, whether inherited genetically or learned culturally, is to belong to a group. That group needs to control its own piece of earth, its own territory. This need is sometimes called the **territorial imperative** (see box, "The Territorial Imperative"). Social scientists cannot agree whether this territorial drive, this seeming compulsion to possess and defend a homeland, is instinctive or learned, but it does appear to be common in humankind. Throughout history, the territorial imperative has taken many forms. It can be discovered in loyalty to homestead, neighborhood, hometown, province, or nation.

Think of your own territorial attachments and allegiances. Even in the mobile American culture, attachments to neighborhood, town, baseball or football team, university and high school can be detected. These loyalties are territorial, rooted deeply in people's psychological makeup. And if such allegiances are found in such a migratory people as the Americans, imagine the territorial attachments of less mobile peoples in other countries. Try to comprehend the feelings of a peasant in India whose great-great-grandfather may have tilled the same land he now tills, whose ancestral memories layer the countryside, filling each landmark with a mythic depth. If you can do that, you can also understand the powerful emotions that are unleashed when such a person's attachment to the land is threatened.

One of the most advanced expressions of human territoriality is the independent state. Thousands of years of human organization lie behind it, beginning in prehistoric times with the small, loosely organized territories of hunting bands. Today, political geographers study independent states in order to learn how and why each comes to occupy a particular area. They are also interested in each state's stability and chances for long-term survival. They explore the character of a national territory as well as the bonds that cause a nation's people to feel like and function as a group.

Distribution of national territory. Many factors help determine the fate of independent states. Not the least of such influences is the state's shape. The more compact a nation's territory, the more cohesive it is likely to be. Theoretically, the most desirable shape for a nation is circular or hexagonal. These two geometric forms maximize compactness and allow particularly short communication lines within a country. Of course, no states

THE TERRITORIAL IMPERATIVE

Zoologists have for some time recognized that animal behavior in many species is in part motivated by a territorial instinct, a need to possess and defend a home area as individuals or as members of a group. Territory provides a sense of identity to these animals and satisfies a basic need for belonging. Such an instinct is found in animals as diverse as the mockingbird, lemur, crab, and prairie dog. For these animals and others, the attachment to territory is genetic, a need perhaps even stronger than the sex drive.

Robert Ardrey, in his book *The Territorial Imperative,* says that humans are territorial animals, motivated by the same instinct that affects mockingbirds and prairie dogs. In other words, the political organization of territory into states, provinces, countries, and the like is the product of animal instinct—as are nationalism,

patriotism, and the desire to defend territory against invaders. On the smallest scale, the territorial imperative finds human expression in the homestead and family. Then it ranges upward through clan and tribe, through neighborhood, district, and province, to reach humankind's ultimate territorial creation—the independent state. The territory involved may be a family's suburban yard, the domain of a street gang in the ghettos of New York City, the hilly refuge of a Stone Age tribe in New Guinea, or the expanses of an empire. In Ardrey's words, "the dog barking at you from behind his master's fence acts for a motive indistinguishable from that of his master when the fence was built."

Is human territorialism learned or instinctual? Ardrey argues for instinct, but some social scientists do not agree. The question is still being debated.

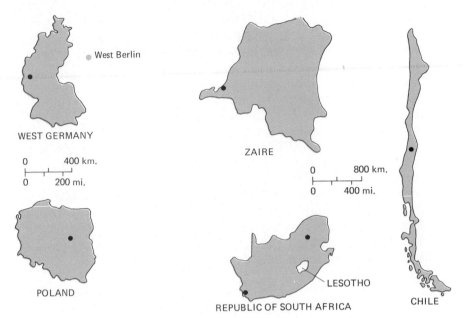

FIGURE 4–5
These differences in the distribution of national territory, drawn from Europe, Africa, and South America, show wide contrasts in territorial form. Poland and, to a lesser extent, Zaïre approach the ideal hexagonal shape. But West Germany is elongated and has an exclave in West Berlin. The Republic of South Africa has a foreign enclave, Lesotho. Chile must overcome extreme elongation. What problems can arise from elongation, enclaves, and exclaves? How might these problems be overcome?

WEST GERMANY

ZAIRE

POLAND

LESOTHO

REPUBLIC OF SOUTH AFRICA

CHILE

West Berlin

● Capital city (in South Africa, function divided between several cities)

actually enjoy this ideal degree of compactness, although some—such as France, Poland, Zaïre, and Brazil—come close to it (see Figure 4-5).

Any one of several unfavorable territorial distributions can inhibit national cohesiveness. Particularly damaging to a state's future are **enclaves** or **exclaves**. An enclave is a district surrounded by a state but not ruled by it. It can be either self-governing or a part of another state. In either case, its presence can be an actual or potential menace to the surrounding state. For instance, the independent black African state of Lesotho is completely surrounded by the Republic of South Africa. Yet mountainous Lesotho may someday become a perfect base of operations for black nationalist guerrillas who wish to destroy the surrounding republic's white supremacist government.

Exclaves are pieces of national territory separated from the main body of a country by the territory of another. Alaska is an exclave of the United States. Of course, exclaves are particularly undesirable if a hostile power holds the intervening territory. Defense of such an isolated area is always difficult and may stretch national resources to the breaking point. Moreover, an exclave's population, isolated from their fellow countrymen, may themselves develop separatist feelings, causing additional problems. Pakistan provides a good recent example of the national instability created by exclaves. Pakistan was created in 1947 as two main bodies of territory separated from each other by almost 1000 miles (1600 kilometers) of northern India. West Pakistan had the capital and most of the territory, but East Pakistan was home to most of the people. West Pakistan hoarded most of the nation's wealth, exploiting East Pakistan's resources and giving little in return. Ethnic differences between the peoples of the two sectors further complicated matters. In 1973, a quarter of a century after its founding, Pakistan disintegrated. The Indian army intervened, and West Pakistan found itself unable to defend its distant exclave, which seceded to become the independent nation of Bangladesh. Enclaves and exclaves can also exist within states, provinces, and even municipalities (see box, "Municipal Exclaves").

Even when a national territory is one piece, instability can develop if the shape of the state is awkward. Narrow "shoestring" nation-states, such as Chile and Norway, can be difficult to administer, as can island nations such as Indonesia, which consists of many separate islands. In such situations, transportation and communications are often difficult, causing administrative problems. The West Indies Federation, a short-lived union of islands in the Caribbean, disintegrated in part because the sea encouraged islanders to develop local rather than national allegiances.

Boundaries. The boundaries that define political territories are of different types. Until fairly recent times, many boundaries were not sharp, clearly defined lines, but instead zones or *frontiers*. Another term for such frontier zones is *march* or *marchland*. Today, about the nearest equivalent to the marchland is the *buffer state*, an independent but small and weak country lying between two powerful, potentially belligerent states. The Peoples' Republic of Mongolia, for example, is a buffer state between the Soviet Union and China; Nepal occupies a similar position between India and China.

Most modern boundaries are lines rather than zones. We can distinguish several types. **Natural boundaries** are those that follow some

MUNICIPAL EXCLAVES

Enclaves and exclaves do not relate only to independent states. Yonkers, New York, is a good example of a city's exclave.

Before railroads, the boundary of Yonkers followed the Hudson River in the west and the Bronx River in the east. The Hudson was a large, navigable river, but the Bronx River was no more than a winding brook about ten feet (three meters) wide that flowed through a swampy valley. As railroads and highways were built, the brook was twice "relocated"—straightened to fit human needs—and the swamp was filled.

Today, despite these changes, the boundary of Yonkers still follows the old Bronx riverbed, crisscrossing the highway, the present river, and the railroad. As a result, isolated municipal exclaves have been created to the east of highway, river, and railroad. Someone who lives in Yonkers can reach these exclaves only by long detours through the adjoining city of Mount Vernon, the New York City borough of the Bronx, or the villages of Eastchester Township. A fuel depot, warehouses, and a manufacturing plant in these exclaves, which logically should be part of Mount Vernon or the Bronx, are officially part of Yonkers.

As in larger nation-states, these tiny exclaves create a variety of problems. Such seemingly simple matters as providing police protection, sewers, and postal service for the exclaves become enmeshed in a web of difficulties and confusion. For instance, a manufacturing plant has its mailing address in Yonkers. Yet the Yonkers post office does not deliver its mail because the plant is far from normal postal routes. The firm must pick up its own mail in Yonkers. A supermarket that straddles the

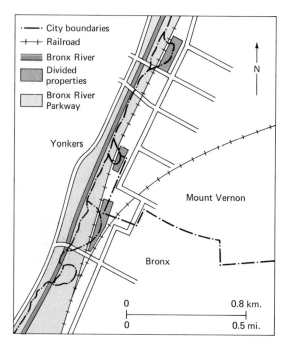

Yonkers-Mount Vernon line has had similar problems. A thief seen in the Yonkers part of the store was arrested by Mount Vernon police because of the obvious problems of getting quick protection from "far away" Yonkers.

Adapted from Alexander Melamid, "Municipal Quasi-Exclaves: Examples from Yonkers, N.Y." Reproduced by permission from The Professional Geography, *Volume 18, 1966.*

feature of the natural landscape, such as a river or mountain ridge. **Ethnographic boundaries** are based on some culture trait, such as language or religion. And **geometric boundaries** are regular, often perfectly straight lines drawn without regard for physical or cultural features. The United States—Canada boundary west of the Lake of the Woods is a geometric border. So are most county and state borders in the western United States and Canada. Some boundaries are of mixed type, composites of two or more of the types listed. Some others are arrived at by historic accident and correspond to none of these types.

Another way of classifying boundaries is genetic. **Antecedent boundaries** are those determined prior to settlement—the western part of the United States—Canada boundary is, once again, a good example. **Superimposed boundaries**, by contrast, follow settlement and are often decided by the fortunes of war. The United States-Mexico boundary is superimposed. When established, it severed numerous established Spanish-speaking settlements from their traditional ties with Mexico. **Relic boundaries** are those that no longer exist but may still be evidenced by local cultural contrasts.

Regardless of their type, political boundaries can greatly influence other cultural features. They can even help shape our perception and retard our knowledge of nearby areas (see box, "What's in a Boundary?").

Core areas. National territories have taken shape in a variety of ways. Some states have sprung full-grown into the world, often as the result of international compromises in times of stress. Others, including many of the stablest and oldest, grew outward from a small nucleus called a **core area**, incorporating adjacent lands, often over many centuries. Generally, such core areas have, like the Nile River valley of Egypt, some particularly attractive set of resources for human life and culture, (Figure 4-6). Larger numbers of people are more likely to cluster there than in surrounding districts, particularly if the area has some measure of natural defense against aggressive neighboring political entities. This denser population, in turn, may produce enough wealth to support a large army, which then provides the base for further expansion of the core area. Finally, the core

---

WHAT'S IN A BOUNDARY

Political boundaries can strongly affect how we look at the world. For instance, geographers have shown that a political boundary can be a strong barrier against the flow of information from one area to another. A study of schoolchildren in Dals Ed, in Sweden, and Halden, just across the border in Norway, shows that the children can easily recall place-names in their own country but not those of the neighboring country. Although language differences between Sweden and Norway are slight, the border puts a powerful barrier between school children only miles apart.

When the children of Dals Ed and Halden drew mental maps of both countries, each group showed a marked preference for its own national locations. On the Swedish maps, areas of desirability sloped gently away from Swedish places that the children were familiar with. The nearby Norwegian border looked like a geological fault line. Preference suddenly dropped away.

A partial explanation for this is that the children on each side of the border are open to quite different sources of information. The Swedish geographer T. Lundén has analyzed textbooks on both sides of the border and has demonstrated clearly how the geographic content in them differs, always offering the readers more information about *us* than about *them*.

Can you think of any boundaries that might have changed how you think about the world? Are they national boundaries? Or have state or even local boundaries sometimes acted as barriers to the free flow of information to you or to others outside?

Adapted from Peter Gould and Rodney White, Mental Maps (Baltimore: Penguin, 1974), pp. 143–146.

FIGURE 4–6
The Nile River Valley, clearly visible on this satellite photograph, has long served as the political core area for Egypt. Its densely-populated, irrigated farmland stands in marked contrast to the barren deserts on either side.

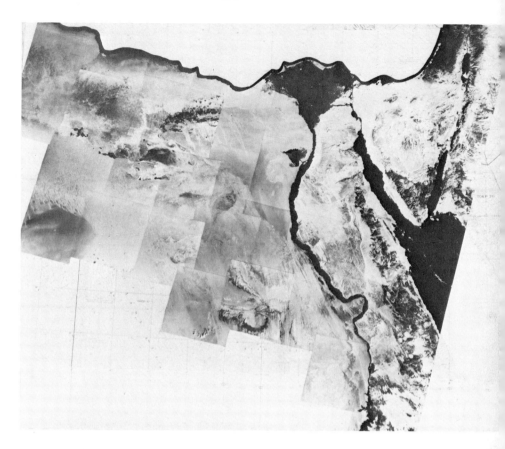

area requires an organized government headed by ambitious and able leaders bent on enlarging their territory.

During this state-building process, the core area often remains the state's single most important district, housing the capital city and the cultural and economic heart of the nation. France expanded to its present size from a small core area around the capital city of Paris. China evolved from a nucleus in the northeast. And the Soviet Union originated in the small principality of Moscow, as Figure 4-7 shows. At the end of this process, the core area may remain roughly at the center of the national territory. Or if growth occurred mainly in one direction, it may find itself at the edge of the nation. For example, the United States grew westward from a core between Massachusetts and Virginia on the Atlantic coastal plain, an area that still has the national capital, the densest population, and the greatest concentration of industry.

Nations that expanded around core areas are generally more stable than those created all at once to fill a political void. The absence of a core area, to which citizens can look as the national heartland, can leave a state's national identity blurred. This makes it easier for various provinces to develop strong local or even foreign allegiances. Try to imagine the destructive impact on political unity if Americans were deprived of their core area—if they did not think of Washington, D.C., as their national capital or of the Battle of Yorktown as a national victory. Belgium, West Germany, and Zaire are examples of states without core areas.

Potentially, states with multiple, competing core areas are the least stable of all. This situation often develops when two or more independent states are united. The main threat is that one of the competing cores will form the center of a separatist movement and thus dissolve the state. In

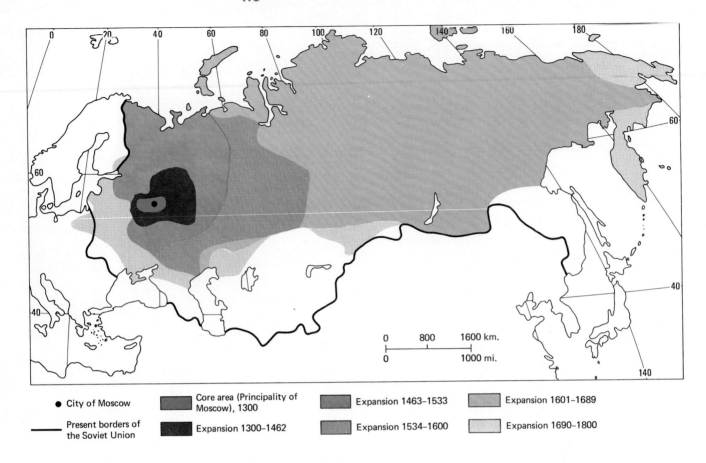

- ● City of Moscow
- ── Present borders of the Soviet Union
- Core area (Principality of Moscow), 1300
- Expansion 1300–1462
- Expansion 1463–1533
- Expansion 1534–1600
- Expansion 1601–1689
- Expansion 1690–1800

FIGURE 4–7

Note the territorial development of the Russian state from a core area. Can you think of reasons why expansion to the east was greater than to the west? What environmental goals might have motivated Russian expansion?

the Republic of South Africa, the province of Transvaal competes with the Cape Province, centered in Cape Town. This rivalry reflects the forced union of these areas after the Boer War in the early twentieth century. In Spain, Castile and Aragon united in 1479, but the union is still shaky—in part because the old core areas of the two states, represented by the cities of Madrid and Barcelona, continue to compete for political control and to symbolize two cultures, the Castilian and Catalonian.

Capital cities. A typical core area contains the capital of the nation, a city that is often also the largest in population and has the greatest concentration of economic and cultural functions. We call such dominant capitals **primate cities**. Moscow, Paris, and Mexico City are all core-area primate capitals.

Often, however, the capital city has been moved from the original core area. Several factors might prompt such a relocation. Territorial loss has been one cause. For example, Turkey's capital was moved in 1923 from coastal Istanbul to Ankara in the interior, partly in response to Turkey's continued loss of its Balkan territories.

Economic and cultural factors can also influence the movement of a capital. For instance, a capital might be moved closer to a border in order to be near the main routes of commerce and cultural exchange. The result is a **head-link capital**. St. Petersburg, now Leningrad, lies on the northwestern edge of Russia. For two centuries (1703-1918), it replaced Moscow as the Russian capital because the czars wanted more contacts with Europe. In the same way, independent states that are conquered and become colonies sometimes move their capitals to the port cities nearest the ruling country, only to return them to the traditional location after they regain independence.

In certain cases, a country's political headquarters are moved nearer to its expanding frontier. A new capital such as this is a **forward-thrust capital**. A modern example is Brasilia, present capital of Brazil. Traditionally, Brazil's main population has clung to the nation's elongated seacoast. Rio de Janeiro, a world-famous port city, was the capital. However, Brazil's leaders, realizing the resource wealth of their country's vast interior, were determined to break the ocean's hold on the Brazilian people. At a spot in the interior wilderness, they built from scratch a capital city. Brasilia was meant to symbolize their nation's new interior-directed, continental attitude. Throwing cost aside and employing the most modern architecture, they attempted to create a new national ego for a whole country. However, the experiment was not totally successful. Even government employees were reluctant to move away from their nation's core area, from their "homelands."

Spatial organization of territory. Independent states differ greatly in the way their territory is organized for purposes of administration. Political geographers recognize two basic types: the **unitary state** and the **federal state**. Unitary states are characterized by power being concentrated in the central government, with little or no provincial authority. All major decisions are made in the central government, and policies are applied uniformly through the national territory. France and China are both unitary states, even though one is democratic and the other totalitarian. A federal state, by contrast, is a more geographically expressive political system. It acknowledges the existence of regional cultural differences and provides the mechanism by which the different regions can perpetuate their individual characters. Power is diffused and the central government surrenders much authority to the individual provinces. The United States, Canada, Australia, and Switzerland are all federal states, though with varying degrees of federalism. The trend in the United States, particularly since the defeat of the Confederacy in the Civil War, has been toward a more unitary, less federal government, with fewer states' rights. In Canada, on the other hand, increasing federalism has resulted from French-Canadian demands for Québec's autonomy.

Whether federal or unitary, a state functions through some system of political subdivisions, normally on several different levels. In federal systems, these subdivisions sometimes overlap in authority, with confusing results. For example, the Indian reservation in the United States occupies a unique and ambiguous place in the federal system of political subdivisions. These semiautonomous enclaves are legally sanctioned political territories that only indigenous Americans can possess. While not sovereign, they do have certain self-government rights that conflict with other local authority. Reservations do not fit neatly into the American political system of states, counties, townships, precincts, and incorporated municipalities. They add to the confusion that so often typifies federal systems.

The boundaries and size of political subdivisions are sometimes redrawn to decrease overlap of authority or to produce units of optimum size. Some planners in the United States, for example, suggest that counties are too small and should be consolidated. Most American counties were drawn small enough that a farmer in the most distant reaches could journey on horseback to the county seat, transact business, and return home in one day. In the modern era of rapid transportation, it is argued, the county has become an obsolete, overly small administrative subdivision. Along these lines, England recently redrew many of its county borders, some of which were many centuries old, to increase administrative efficiency.

Centrifugal and centripetal forces. The spatial organization of territory, degree of compactness, presence or absence of a core area, type of boundaries, and the type of capital all can influence an independent state's stability. However, stronger forces are also at work. Whatever its size and shape, the human factor often makes or breaks a state. Political geographers have long recognized that the most viable independent states, the states least troubled by internal discord, are those that developed and retained a strong feeling of group solidarity among their populations. Group identity is the key; the size and shape of a state can operate to its advantage only when its population possesses such cohesiveness.

Political geographers refer to factors that promote national unity and solidarity as **centripetal forces**. Whatever disrupts internal order and encourages destruction of the state is called a **centrifugal force**. Many nations have one principal centripetal force that, more than any other single factor, provides fuel for nationalistic sentiment. Such a unifying force, which stands out above all others in any given state, is referred to as the **raison d'être**—the "reason for being." This applies not only to the independent state, but also to another type of political functional culture region—the insurgent state.

Insurgent states

The **insurgent state**, a product of guerrilla warfare, in recent years has commanded more attention from political geographers. If successful, guerrilla war passes through roughly three stages, each of which has particular territorial traits and can be treated as a functional political region. Indeed, when geographers discuss the development of insurgent states, they are really dealing with the emergence of independent states from within the body of old ones. In fact, guerrillas themselves must become good geographers. They must be keenly aware of both the physical and the cultural environment. They are usually less well-armed than their adversaries. Therefore, if they do not know the land they are moving across, they will be trapped and destroyed. Just as important, if they cannot tap the basic stresses and strains in the cultural groups they wish to win over, they are bound to lose.

The raison d'être of insurgencies lies in deep dissatisfaction with the existing order and the belief that needed changes can be accomplished only by force. The dissidents need not be numerous, but they need the sympathy of a sizable segment of the population. The first stage of insurgency is mobile warfare, in which small guerrilla bands are unable to seize permanent control over territory and are constantly on the move to avoid capture. These bands confine their operations to specific, carefully chosen regions, usually in mountains or other inaccessible lands where the guerrillas can easily conceal themselves. At the same time, this chosen area should be largely self-sufficient economically, discontent politically, and located near key military objectives, such as cities and transport lines. The Cuban insurgency, led by Fidel Castro, provides a good example of the guerrilla's geographical consciousness (Figure 4-8). The Sierra Maestra provided Castro's forces with concealment in the rugged mountain terrain and dense vegetation, access to such key population centers as

FIGURE 4–8
Fidel Castro began his rise to power as a guerrilla based in the rugged Sierra Maestra of Cuba. The terrain sheltered his forces until they were able to take control of the cities.

nearby Santiago, and contact with a mountain people who had had experience in guerrilla warfare during the period of Spanish rule (see Figure 4-9).

In the second stage, the guerrillas become strong enough to establish permanent bases that they continuously control. These bases form the core area of the evolving insurgent state. The insurgent movement adds political administration to its functions and forms a government. The command base becomes a "capital." The ideas the insurgency is based on are disseminated to the local people. In this way the guerrillas publicize the raison d'être of the state. The base area expands outward into surrounding areas, and guerrillas are dispatched to establish new bases in other suitable regions. As a result, the insurgent state has bases scattered throughout the country. Such fragmentation, although necessary, often produces the same weakness that plagues territorially fragmented independent states. Communication between the bases is difficult, and there is real danger that each base will become a separate insurgent state, more and more out of touch with the leadership and goals of the original revolution.

In the final stage of a successful insurgency, the revolutionary forces

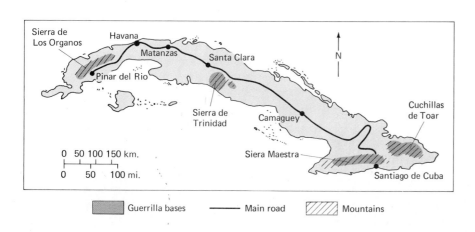

FIGURE 4–9
Cuba was peppered with guerrilla bases in 1958, shortly before the overthrow of the government. Why did the Castro guerrillas choose these areas for bases? What geographic advantages and disadvantages do they have? (Adapted from an article by R. W. McColl in the *Annals, Association of American Geographers,* 59 (1969), 617.)

abandon guerrilla tactics and engage in conventional warfare. In effect, the rival governments are now military equals competing for territory. At this stage, the guerrillas make major efforts to enlist the support of all dissident elements in the country and to portray the revolution as inevitably successful. The insurgents may carry out promised reforms in lands they already control in order to set up attractive models.

The sequence of insurgency described here has most typically been carried out in the rural areas of agrarian states or colonies. In industrial societies, the scene of activity is more likely to be urban areas. However, much of the same basic sequence applies to urban guerrilla warfare. Examples of urban-based insurgencies include the revolt of Jews in the Warsaw ghetto during the German occupation of Poland and, more recently, the Irish Republican Army's ongoing activities in the cities of Northern Ireland.

For us, the central point of insurgencies is that the leaders are geographically conscious at every stage of their campaign. Conditions of the physical environment and patterns of local cultures and economies have the same vital role in success of failure of insurgent states that they have in the stability of independent states.

Multinational political bodies

A third major type of political functional culture region, in addition to independent and insurgent states and their subdivisions, is composed of multinational bodies. Independent states for many centuries have formed international associations of one kind or another for purposes of trade, military assistance, or mutual security (Figure 4-10). Many of the city states of ancient Greece, for example, formed leagues and associations.

In the twentieth century, multinational organizations have increased in number and importance. Increasingly, independent states seem willing to give up some of their sovereignty in return for economic advantage, protection, or similar benefit. Some of these, such as the British Commonwealth or the French Community, are the relics of former colonial empires. Some others, including the North Atlantic Treaty Organization (NATO), are largely military in function. The Common Market, established to create a tariff-free zone in western Europe, may eventually achieve some measure of political union among its member nations. The Council for Mutual Economic Assistance (COMECON) constitutes what amounts to a Russian-dominated economic empire in Eurasia. Still other multinational organizations are ethnic in concept, as for example the Arab League, which links most Arabic-speaking nations.

The extent to which individual states have given up sovereignty to belong to these multinational bodies varies from one organization to another. Most have sacrificed very little independence. NATO membership, for example, has not prevented fellow members Greece and Turkey from engaging in military confrontation with one another, just as Arab League members Morocco and Algeria have fought border skirmishes.

The most ambitious international undertaking is the United Nations, a multinational body that claims all but a very few of the world's independent states as members. In this sense, it has achieved greater success than its ill-fated predecessor, the League of Nations.

Are these multinational organizations forerunners of political union on a large scale? It is too early to tell, but most likely the answer is No. If the "territorial imperative" is instinctual in humans rather than learned, there can be little hope for world political unity.

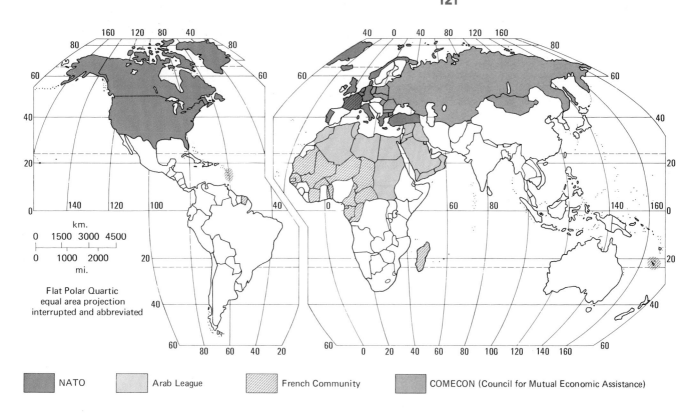

NATO   Arab League   French Community   COMECON (Council for Mutual Economic Assistance)

FIGURE 4–10
Some multinational political
organizations.

Diffusion of Political Innovations

Political ideas and institutions spread from place to place by means of
cultural diffusion. Therefore, we can apply the concepts outlined in
Chapter 1 to the spatial movement of political innovations. Relocation
diffusion and both types of expansion diffusion occur in politics, and
barriers to spread are also encountered.

Instances of political ideas, systems, and states carried by relocation
diffusion are very numerous. Empires are typically built in this way. The
presence of "British-type" governments and English common law in
Australia and New Zealand, on the opposite side of the world from
Britain, is explained by relocation diffusion accomplished in the nineteenth century by settlers from Great Britain. Similarly, the establishment
of the Republic of Texas (1836-1845) with an "American-type" government can be attributed to immigrants from the South, as can the subsequent union of Texas and the United States. The Boers of coastal South
Africa, people of Dutch descent whose government had been taken over
by the British Empire, migrated to the interior in the nineteenth century
and established new self-ruling Boer states.

Relocation diffusion is not always the result of mass migrations,
however. Small groups or even individual migrants with political ideas
can accomplish the same political diffusion, although it is harder for
small groups and they do not always succeed. For example, "Ché"
Guevara was sent by the Communist government of Cuba to the South
American nation of Bolivia, where he unsuccessfully tried to organize a
Communist guerrilla movement. Lenin, under somewhat similar condi-

tions a half-century earlier, was able to gain control of the Russian government.

Contagious expansion diffusion frequently operates in the political sphere. It can be seen in the spread of political independence in Africa, in voting patterns and approval of women's suffrage in the United States, and in many other cases. In 1914, only two African states—Liberia and Ethiopia—were fully independent of European colonial or white minority rule. Ethiopia later fell temporarily under Italian control. Influenced by developments in India and Pakistan, the Arabs of North Africa began a movement for independence. Their movement began to gain momentum in the 1950s and swept southward across most of the continent between 1960 and 1965, as Figure 4-11 shows. Since 1970, African independence has spread into all remaining colonies. Only the white minority rule of South Africa now bars the path of continued diffusion of this political idea southward to the Cape of Good Hope. No colonies ruled from Europe exist in present-day Africa. A less-welcomed political idea—military coup—has seemingly followed the same route of contagious diffusion in Africa. The majority of the newly independent African states are now ruled by armed forces.

FIGURE 4–11

Independence from European colonial rule (or white minority rule) has diffused through most of Africa. Independence for Africans was an idea first implanted in the northeastern and western reaches of the continent. Since 1959, independence has spread rapidly to the south.

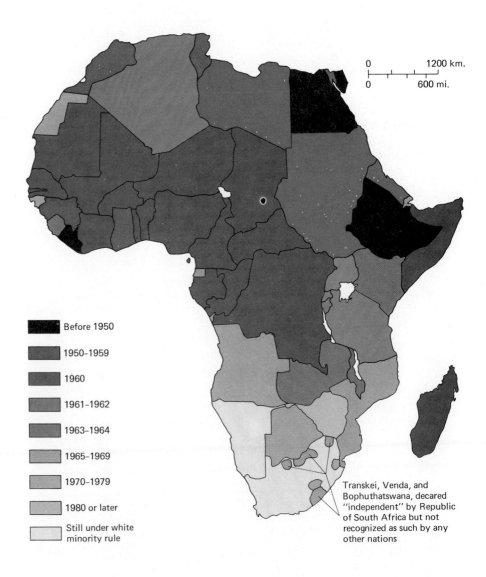

0   1200 km.

0   600 mi.

Before 1950

1950–1959

1960

1961–1962

1963–1964

1965–1969

1970–1979

1980 or later

Still under white minority rule

Transkei, Venda, and Bophuthatswana, decared "independent" by Republic of South Africa but not recognized as such by any other nations

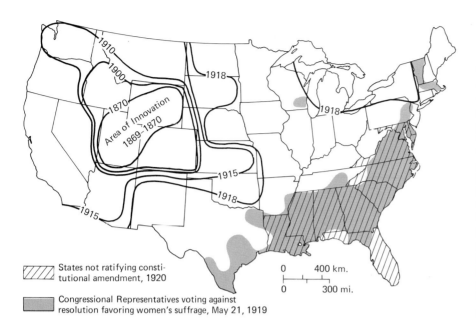

FIGURE 4-12
The diffusion of suffrage for women of the United States, 1870–1920, began in the western United States. It spread steadily for five decades and finally gained nationwide acceptance through a constitutional amendment in 1920. The area of most prolonged resistance to women's suffrage was the Lower South. Compare this map to Figure 1–5. Can you think of any reasons why this movement arose in the West? What were the barriers in diffusion in the Lower South? Compare this pattern to a map showing states where opposition to the ERA is strongest. (Adapted from C. Paulin, *Atlas of the Historical Geography of the United States,* New York: American Geographical Society and the Carnegie Institute, 1932.)

American politics abound with examples of cultural diffusion. A classic case is the spread of full suffrage for women, a movement that began in the interior West just after the Civil War and culminated in 1920 with the ratification of a constitutional amendment (see Figure 4-12). Opposition to women's suffrage was strongest in the Deep South, a region where today the greatest resistence to ratification of the ERA is found. On the local and state level, political scientists have long recognized the "friends and neighbors" voting effect. This principle is based on the fact that support for particular candidates is generally strongest in their home district and weakens with distance. The "friends and neighbors" effect is contagious diffusion that results from interpersonal communication with a small area. However, the growing importance of mass media has allowed candidates to reach a larger audience, which makes "friends and neighbors" diffusion outdated in many elections.

Barriers of various types can halt or slow the diffusion of political ideas. The spread of independence in Africa in the 1950s and 1960s was very rapid because most European powers had grown disenchanted with colonialism and viewed their African colonies more as burdens than assets. In effect, then, few barriers were thrown in the path of African independence. Portugal, by contrast, clung tenaciously to its African colonies until a change in government in Lisbon reversed a 500-year-old policy and the colonies were quickly freed. However, white minority rule in southern Africa, controlled by African-born people of European ancestry, is proving to be much more of a barrier to black self-government than was European colonial rule. But the Republic of South Africa, the last white minority-ruled bastion, is having to cope with the contagious diffusion of the self-rule idea, an idea already implanted in the minds of its restive black majority. Time will tell whether white minority rule was a permeable or absorbing barrier to this diffusion, or whether white rule is swept away altogether by military force. In fact, permeability is already evident. The Republic of South Africa recently granted a quasi-independence to several Bantu native reservations within the country.

Political Ecology

Political culture regions do not exist, nor do political ideas diffuse, in an environmental vacuum. Spatial variations and the spread of political phenomena often can be linked to terrain, soils, climate, vegetation, and other facets of the physical environment. Conversely, established political authority can be a powerful instrument of environmental modification, providing the framework for organized alteration of the landscape. This established authority enacts and enforces laws that allow large populations to have a great impact on the environment, for better or worse. Thus political entities influence and are influenced by the physical surroundings.

The political geographer's view of humankind's relationship to the land has changed over the years. In the early part of the twentieth century, the concept of environmental determinism prevailed among English and American political geographers. The writings of the English geographer Vaughan Cornish are representative of the period. In his classic work *The Great Capitals*, first published in 1923, Cornish argued that the existence of western Europe's oceanic colonial empires was "easily explained" on physical environmental grounds. The indented coastline of Europe, he pointed out, offered many natural harbors. Moreover, European countries on the Atlantic coast enjoyed the shortest sailing distances to the main trade areas of the world and stood at the gateway to the easiest routes to the interior of Eurasia via the plains of northern Europe and the Mediterranean Sea. As Cornish saw it, the insularity of the British provided an extra spur to seamanship. Maritime empires, then, were seen as the inevitable result of good natural harbors, short sea routes, and access to the Eurasian interior. But we must be cautious in accepting such environmentalist pronouncements. We might ask why England remained a backward, underdeveloped country even as late as the 1600s and why the "inevitable" maritime empire was so long in coming. What is there in the environmentalist argument that would explain the subsequent collapse of the British Empire? Did sailing distances change and harbors disappear?

In the decades following 1940, political geographers have adopted a less rigid viewpoint when considering how the physical environment affects political features. Possibilists acknowledge that environmental forces influence political life, but they deny that these forces are the only influence. We should approach the study of such physical influences as the folk fortress with this view in mind.

Folk fortresses

Before modern air and missile warfare was developed, a state's survival was enhanced by some sort of natural protection, such as surrounding mountain ranges, deserts, or seas; bordering marshes or dense forests; or outward-facing escarpments. Political geographers called natural strongholds **folk fortresses**. The folk fortress might shield an entire state or only its core area. In either case, a folk fortress was a valuable asset. Surrounding seas sheltered the entire British Isles from invasion for the last 900 years. In Egypt, desert wastelands on east and west insulated the fertile, well-watered Nile Valley core. The Netherlands was traditionally protected by low-lying wetlands, which also threatened the country itself with floods. In the same way, Russia's core area was shielded for centuries by dense forests, expansive marshes, bitter winters, and vast distances.

States without any sort of natural defense have often been hard-pressed to maintain their independence. Korea, a land bridge leading from China to Japan, has repeatedly attracted invaders from both directions. Only rarely has Korea achieved unity and full independence. Poland, which lies on the open plains of northern Europe, has been overrun and partitioned many times by hostile neighbors.

Landform patterns

Closely related to the concept of the folk fortress is the distribution of landforms. Ideally, a state should have rugged mountains and hills around its edges and plains in the interior (see box, "Terrain and Political Geography"). Such a pattern not only facilitates defense but also provides a natural unit of enclosed plains as the basis for a cohesive state. Few countries enjoy entirely satisfactory landform patterns, although France—centered on the plains of the Paris basin and flanked by border mountains and hills such as the Alps, Pyrenees, Ardennes, and Jura Mountains—comes very close to the ideal. Figure 4-13 shows how France is sheltered. Mountain-ridge borders are also desirable, because they stand out on the landscape and cross thinly populated country. Rivers, by contrast, are much less suitable as borders. They often change course and generally flow through densely settled valleys, creating all sorts of potentially provocative situations for the nations on either bank.

An undesirable arrangement of physical features may disrupt a state's internal unity. A mountain range, a desert, or some other barrier cutting through the middle of the state's territory forms perhaps the worst pattern imaginable. Such barriers can disrupt communications within the state and often isolate one part of a population from another. Separatist

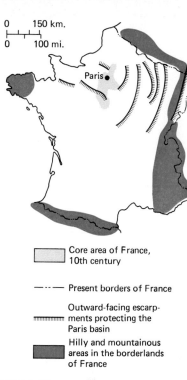

☐ Core area of France, 10th century

—·—· Present borders of France

▨ Outward-facing escarpments protecting the Paris basin

■ Hilly and mountainous areas in the borderlands of France

FIGURE 4–13
The French distribution of landforms is linked to the protection of such terrain features as ridges, hills, and mountains. Sheltering, outward-facing escarpments formed a folk fortress protecting the core area and capital of the French state until as recently as World War I. Hill districts and mountain ranges have lent stability to French boundaries in the south and southeast.

TERRAIN AND POLITICAL GEOGRAPHY

The Bavarian town of Berchtesgaden is known today mainly because Adolf Hitler and some other high Nazi officials had resort homes nearby. To the political geographer, Berchtesgaden has another significance: It is an example of the political importance of terrain.

Berchtesgaden is situated in the Bavarian Alps, in the midst of a wreath of high mountains. In the era before modern transportation and communication, these mountains isolated and sheltered the valley. It was shielded from both cold winter winds and invading armies.

In this setting, Berchtesgaden developed as an independent principality ruled by a religious order. For seven centuries, from 1156 to 1803, Berchtesgaden maintained its independence. The borders of the principality, which followed the surrounding mountain ridges, scarcely changed at all during this long period. And even after Berchtesgaden lost its independence and was annexed by Bavaria and Germany, most of its mountain-marked border survived as part of the international boundary between Germany and Austria. In this way, terrain and the political pattern often are linked.

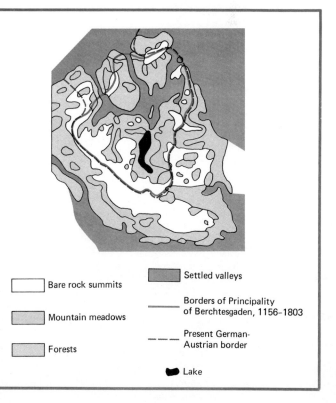

☐ Bare rock summits

▨ Mountain meadows

☐ Forests

■ Settled valleys

—— Borders of Principality of Berchtesgaden, 1156–1803

--- Present German-Austrian border

● Lake

HALFORD J. MACKINDER   1861-1947

Mackinder developed a fascination for spatial patterns and maps at a young age. At school in England, he was caned by a teacher for drawing maps instead of writing Latin exercises. His interest in geography persisted, and in 1887 he became one of Oxford University's first lecturers in geography. He thus led the way for the growth of geography in British universities and became a founding father of British geography.

Much influenced by the scientific geography found in nineteenth-century German universities, Mackinder introduced many of the German concepts into England. Previously, the Royal Geographical Society of London had been interested mainly in exploration rather than in analytical studies and theories. Mackinder's famous heartland theory was first proposed in a scholarly address to the society in 1904 and was later enlarged to book form. He served as a member of Parliament for twelve years, and after World War I he helped redraw the boundaries of Europe. In 1945, he was awarded the Royal Geographical Society's highest honor, the Patron's Medal. His influence on analytical political geography has been very great indeed.

sentiments grow more easily when shielded by environmental barriers. In addition, internal mountain ranges provide excellent potential guerrilla bases where insurgents can live in relative safety. Peru, which straddles the Andes with fringes of territory in the Amazon basin and the Pacific coastal lowlands, faces such a problem. So does Spain, which consists of a number of plains areas separated by hills and mountains. Both Peru and Spain have problems of internal unity, partly because of their unfavorable physical settings. It is interesting to note that Portugal is the only area in the Iberian Peninsula to escape Castilian Spanish rule. It may owe its freedom in part to the thinly populated hills and mountains separating it from Spain.

For nation-states, perhaps the best borders of all have proved to be those marked by seacoasts. Islands, and the small continent that hosts Australia, have been excellent natural barriers to expansive or acquisitive neighbors. Among others, Iceland, Sri Lanka and the Malagasy Republic have benefited from their island location. However, island nations are not totally free from attacks by neighbors, as the histories of Hawaii, Cuba, and the Philippines show. In addition, disputes still arise among nations about the placement of borders in adjacent ocean areas. Icelanders are presently arguing bitterly with the United Kingdom and other nations about fishing rights in the ocean near Iceland. Peninsular location provides some of the same advantages for such countries as Italy, India, and Turkey, although peninsulas are usually harder to defend than are islands. The advantage of peninsulas lies in their "natural" seacoast borders.

Expanding states often regard coastlines as the logical limits to their territorial growth, even if they belong to other states. This was true of the United States' drive to the Pacific Ocean in the first half of the nineteenth century, an expansion justified by the doctrine of **manifest destiny**. This doctrine was based on the belief that the Pacific shoreline was the logical and predestined western border for the United States. A somewhat similar doctrine has long led Russia to seek expansion in the direction of the Mediterranean Sea and Indian Ocean.

Environment and the balance of power

Discussions of environmental influence, manifest destiny, and the outward probings of the Russian state lead naturally to one of the earliest theories proposed by a political geographer, the so-called **heartland theory** of Halford J. Mackinder, a British geographer (see biographical sketch). As early as 1904, Mackinder was concerned with the balance of power in the world and in particular with the possibility of world conquest. His writings reflected imperial Britain's fear that czarist Russia might challenge its empire in Asia, specifically India. His theory of **geopolitics** was heavily tinged with environmental determinism.

Mackinder thought that the continent of Eurasia would be the most likely base from which a successful campaign for world conquest could be launched. Eurasia dwarfs all other continents in size and natural resources and is home to almost four-fifths of the human race. In examining this huge landmass—this "world island," as he called it—Mackinder discerned two environmental regions. The **heartland** or interior of Eurasia was isolated from the sea. The coastland fringes along the Atlantic Ocean, Mediterranean Sea, Indian Ocean, and Pacific Ocean—that is, the maritime lands, oriented to the sea—were walled off from much of the heartland by mountain ranges (see Figure 4-14). Of these two areas, Mackinder judged the heartland to be potentially better as a base for world

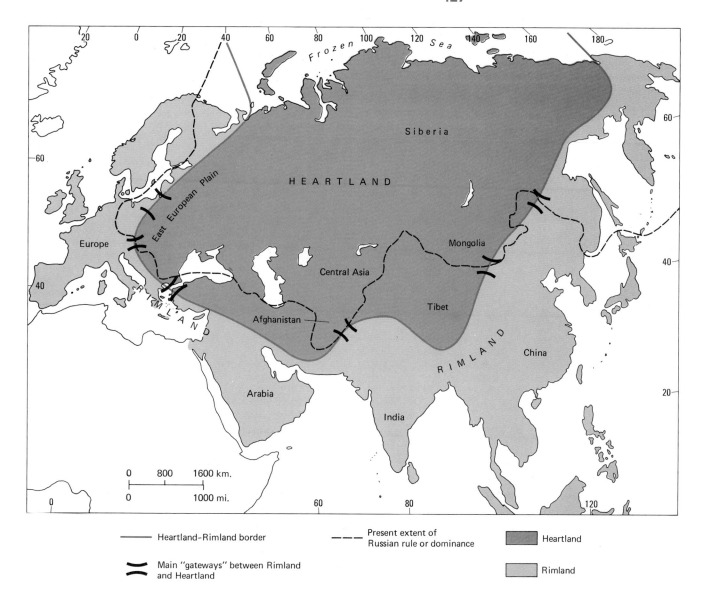

Heartland-Rimland border

Main "gateways" between Rimland and Heartland

Present extent of Russian rule or dominance

Heartland

Rimland

FIGURE 4–14

The huge interior of the Eurasian continent, isolated from maritime influences and partially walled off by mountain ranges and frozen Arctic seas, stands in marked contrast to the ocean-fringed rimland. The theories of Mackinder and Spykman are based on this environmental contrast. (After Mackinder and Spykman, with modifications.)

conquest, mainly because it was immune to sea power. A navy is the main strength of the coastland countries, especially, of course, England. The coastlands, however, were not invulnerable to infantry and cavalry thrusts from the heartland. For this reason, in Mackinder's view, a unified heartland power could with impunity probe into the coastlands, eventually conquering the maritime countries and annexing their navies. This sea power could then be turned against the outlying continents and islands until the entire world was subject to the heartland.

Mackinder felt that the initial unification of the heartland could best be achieved from the East European plain, which is the most densely populated and economically productive part of the heartland. Mackinder proposed, in effect, that

Who rules the East European plain rules the heartland.
Who rules the heartland rules Eurasia.
Who rules Eurasia rules the world.

By 1904, the Russian state had largely accomplished the first step, having spread over six centuries from a small core area in the East European plain to most of the heartland (look again at Figure 4-7). The rise of a Communist regime and consequent fears of Russian-inspired "world revolution" brought considerable attention to the heartland theory after 1917. The recent Russian invasion of Afghanistan could be viewed as an attempt to extend control over one of the few remaining parts of the heartland. Mackinder implied that Russian rule of the world was an eventual probability.

The heartland theory has several fallacies. In particular, it neglects the consequences of air power and overestimates the potential of the thinly settled Eurasian interior, which consists largely of frozen tundra and parched desert. In past decades, Mackinder's ideas were probably more important for the people they influenced, including Adolf Hitler, than for their overall validity. In the final analysis, the greatest value of the heartland theory was its stimulation of controversy and thought among scholars.

One result of this ferment was Nicholas Spykman's **rimland theory**, proposed in 1944 in his book *The Geography of the Peace*. Although Spykman shared Mackinder's belief that Eurasia was the key to world conquest, he placed greater value on the coastlands, which he called the **rimland**. Spykman felt that the huge population of the rimland, amounting to about two-thirds of the human race, coupled with the area's sizable mineral and agricultural resources, made these coastal lands far more important than the thinly populated and environmentally harsh heartland. He stressed that land power was no monopoly of the heartland, that the masses of the rimland could invade the interior of Eurasia through any number of natural gateways. Spykman concluded that

Who rules the rimland rules Eurasia.
Who rules Eurasia rules the world.

Fortunately, in Spykman's view, the rimland is one of the most thoroughly fragmented political zones in the world. Its great potential for power is diffused among numerous independent states. Spykman felt that both the United States and Russia could maintain their independence by keeping the rimland divided politically. He saw the German and Japanese thrust prior to and during World War II as a serious attempt to unify the rimland.

Much of American foreign policy since 1946 has been based on the Mackinder and Spykman theories, aimed at keeping the rimland divided and the rimland states either pro-West or neutral. In the "domino theory," "containment" policy, and other common phrases of America's postwar foreign policy, we can hear the echoes of both Mackinder's and Spykman's pronouncements. American military involvement in Korea, Vietnam, and western Europe were all intended to prevent rimland areas from falling under Communist rule. Events have suggested, however, that Americans have neither the need nor the will to police the rimland.

Theories of Russian world conquest have splintered on the rocks of Chinese, Vietnamese, and even European nationalism. Spykman's fear of rimland unification has proven illusory among nations that have historically shown little inclination to work together. In fact, warfare, not cooperation, seems to be the normal order within the rimland area. Finally, traditional strategies have been overtaken by technology, particularly by missile warfare, which has in some ways rendered environmental location militarily insignificant.

Cultural Integration in Political Geography

Although we can learn a great deal from studying how the physical environment and political phenomena interact, we can gain an even broader perspective by examining the ties between politics and other facets of culture in an area. State building, voting patterns, and other topics that interest political geographers, although often influenced by physical environmental factors, are largely explained in cultural terms. In addition, political decisions often have far-reaching effects on the distribution of such cultural elements as religion, type of economy, land use, and migration. Indeed, the political organization of territory, both past and present, is revealed to some degree in almost every facet of culture.

Religion and language

Political stability is closely bound up with the spatial distribution of religions and languages. In fact, religion and language are perhaps the most potent forces in the modern and independent state. If the whole population in a country speaks the same tongue and adheres to the same faith, national unity is fostered. Indeed, language or religion provides the raison d'être for many states. In contrast, instability frequently develops when two or more sizable religious or linguistic groups share citizenship in a single state. Such differences have prompted historic and recent conflicts in areas as diverse as India, Lebanon, Ireland, Canada, Israel-Palestine, and Guyana (Figure 4-15). Some states and empires have collapsed under these divisive pressures. Examples from this political obituary list the Austro-Hungarian Empire and the Turkish Ottoman Empire.

FIGURE 4–15

When bitterly opposed religious groups occupy the same political unit, and particularly when the groups are highly segregated residentially, political instability can result. This map shows residential segregation of Catholics and Protestants in a section of Belfast, Northern Ireland, about 1958. What administrative problems might a pattern such as this present to the authorities? Would the pattern likely be more, or less, segregated today? (After F. W. Boal, "Territoriality on the Shankill-Falls Divide, Belfast," *Irish Geography*, 6 (1969), 37.)

0   500

Feet

+ Roman Catholic residence   • Protestant residence   Nonresidential land

When religious and linguistic diversity are combined in the same state, the situation becomes even more critical, especially if languages and religions display similar spatial variations, thus reinforcing one another. Precisely such a problem plagues the island nation of Cyprus in the eastern Mediterranean. The struggle there pits Greek-speaking Christians against Turkish-speaking Muslims, with the Christians constituting about four-fifths of the total population. War has broken out between these factions on several occasions during Cyprus's brief existence as an independent state, and the nations of Greece and Turkey have become involved. Turkish invasion and population relocations have added to the bitter hatred between Greek and Turkish Cypriots. It no longer seems likely that the two groups will be able to coexist in the same state. Linguistic and religious diversity will possibly destroy Cyprus and lead to permanent partition of the island between Greece and Turkey. In nearby Lebanon, an Arab nation, Christians and Moslems have very nearly succeeded in partitioning the territory of the state.

In nations where free elections are held, voting patterns repeatedly record the symptoms of such internal discord. Even in the nations where linguistic and religious differences have not produced separatist senti-ments, the voting map often duplicates the pattern of language and religion (see Figure 6-15).

Population distribution

How a population is distributed over a national territory can also influence political stability. Traditionally, a clustering of people in the interior of the state, with a sparser population in border regions, was considered particularly desirable. Such a pattern tends to create a feeling of community within the state and keeps contacts with residents of foreign areas at a minimum. The least advantageous population distribu-tion is a concentration of people around the country's borders, leaving a thinly settled core. This pattern tends to retard contacts with the interior and to encourage closer ties with people across the borders in other states. People living near borders may in fact establish international contacts stronger than those binding them to their own state. However, with modern advances in communications, population distribution is much less important today, although it may still be influential.

Favorable population distribution characterizes such states as Egypt, where 95 percent of the people occupy about 3½ percent of the land constituting the Nile Valley core area (see Figure 4-16). In Chile, a clustering of population in the central region partly compensates for the country's unwieldy shape. Unfavorable distributions appear in the con-centrations of people around the edges of Canada, Brazil, Australia, and Spain. As already noted, Brazil has tried to change this situation by actively encouraging its people to move to the interior.

Ideology

Ideally, there should be no great differences in political and economic philosophy within a state, especially if a diverging view is strong in one specific region. To maintain a strong state, people should be fairly united in their approval of democracy, republic, monarchy, theocracy, or dicta-torship; of free enterprise, socialism, or communism. In free societies, voting patterns can reflect regional differences in political and economic

SPAIN

EGYPT
(UNITED ARAB REPUBLIC)

● Capital city

Population 50 or more per square kilometer
(125 or more per square mile)

Population less than 50 per square kilometer
(less than 125 per square mile)

FIGURE 4–16
Population distributions within independent states vary widely. Spain has an unfavorable distribution of people. Most Spaniards are clustered around the edges of the state, even though the capital is centrally located. The fact that Portugal is independent of Spain is partly a consequence of the coastal concentration of Iberian population. Egypt, by contrast, has the overwhelming majority of its people concentrated in one central corridor, the Nile Valley and delta. What difficulties might this population distribution cause if Egypt were successful in uniting with countries to the east and west—as, for example, union with Libya to the west?

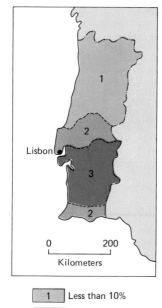

Lisbon

0   200
Kilometers

1 Less than 10%
2 10–30%
3 More than 30%

FIGURE 4–17
Portugal: Communist votes as a percentage of the total, 1976. When democracy was restored to Portugal in the mid-1970s, free elections showed Communist strength to be greatest in the southern half of the nation, duplicating the pattern of some other cultural features. For example, the Moorish imprint is much more apparent in the south. Why might the Communists have the greatest appeal there?

philosophy. For example, France, Italy, Portugal, and some other democratic countries contain certain districts that regularly vote Communist. Figure 4-17 shows a recent Portuguese voting pattern suggesting Communist sectionalism. If major rival political-economic factions divide a state, and if each draws support from one or more regions, the resulting struggle for control can lead to secession, civil war, and destruction of the state.

The United States was very nearly destroyed by such a civil war in the 1860s, when advocates of slavery and weak central government seceded and established the southern Confederacy. Although the South collapsed and was forced to rejoin the union—a victory for those in favor of abolition and a strong central government—the rift has never completely healed.

Common historical experiences

National unity gets much of its strength from past experiences "shared" by the population. Ideally, a people should feel that their state exists because they or their ancestors willfully established it and defended it against alien enemies. The common memory of a war of independence, struggles against invaders, and the deeds of national heroes all serve the cause of group cohesiveness and, consequently, national unity. These memories, even if historically inaccurate, tend to emphasize a people's heroic struggle for independence (see Figure 4-18). Even defeats and long periods of subjugation may well be the glue that binds a people together. The French, for instance are well aware of recent and ancient struggles against German and English invasions and oppression. They learn in early childhood about the legendary anti-English exploits of their great national heroine, Jeanne d'Arc.

FIGURE 4–18
Americans share many folk heroes, such as Paul Revere. This heritage binds people together and contributes to national unity. Think about how national symbols are used to promote unity in a time of political crisis.

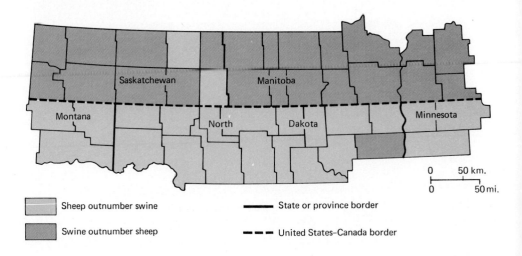

FIGURE 4-19
The political impact on economy can be revealed in the choice of livestock—in this case, the border area between the United States and Canada. Sheep are more numerous than swine on the United States side of the boundary, in part because of government-backed price incentives for wool. What other factors might account for this contrast? (Based on data in Hendrik J. Reitsma, "Crop and Livestock Production in the Vicinity of the United States–Canada Border," *Professional Geographer*, 23 (1971), 220–221.)

Sheep outnumber swine

Swine outnumber sheep

State or province border

United States–Canada border

Economy

The cultural factors discussed in the preceding sections all influence the stability of political states. But equally important influences flow in the opposite direction, leaving a political imprint on other facets of culture. Laws and government policies can have far-reaching effects on a nation's cultural patterns (see box, "Politics and Prostitution"). This political influence is evident in the distribution of economic features. For example, the United States-Canada border in the Great Plains crosses an area of environmental and cultural sameness. The land and people on both sides of the boundary are very similar. Yet the presence of the border, representing two different bodies of law and regulations, has fostered differences in agricultural practices. In the United States, an act passed in the 1950s encourages sheep raising by guaranteeing an incentive price for wool. No such law was passed in Canada. As a result, sheep are far more numerous on the American side of the border, while Canadian farmers rely more on hogs. Figure 4-19 illustrates the difference.

The Political Landscape

The cultural landscape clearly shows the relationships between politics and culture. This physical manifestation is so pronounced that, in some areas, geographers can speak of a political landscape. There are at least

POLITICS AND PROSTITUTION

Certain forms of economic activity are legal in some areas and illegal in others. Gambling and prostitution fall into this category. Both are widely practiced in many areas where they are illegal, but there is a concentration of such activities in counties, states, and countries where they are permitted by law.

The people of Nevada have maintained a more permissive attitude toward gambling and prostitution than is true in most of the rest of the United States. Nevada laws permit both of these activities, with important

economic results for the state. All but five of Nevada's counties permit prostitution, and some thirty-three brothels containing as many as 250 prostitutes presently exist in small towns and rural areas of the state. In this way, the distribution of laws has a direct effect on the spatial distribution of a form of economy. The map of political subdivisions reflects the distribution of houses of prostitution.

Based on Richard Symanski, "Prostitution in Nevada," Annals, Association of American Geographers, 64 (1974), 357–377.

three major categories of visible political phenomena: the imprint made on the land by the legal code, the physical traits of borders, and the visible expressions of government authority.

Imprint of the legal code

Many laws find their way into the cultural landscape. Among the most noticeable are those that regulate the land-surveying system, because the law often requires that land be divided into specific geometric patterns. In most of the United States, as was discussed in Chapter 3, a rigid rectangular system was imposed on the land, producing a distinctive checkerboard appearance that is striking from the air. In Canada, the laws of the French-speaking province of Québec encourage land survey in long, narrow parcels, but English-speaking provinces, such as Ontario, adopted a rectangular system. As a result, the political border between Québec and Ontario can be spotted easily from the air.

Even legal decisions made long ago by vanished governments can remain imprinted on the landscape. For example, Denmark ruled the provinces of Schleswig and Holstein, now held by West Germany, until the 1860s. During that period, Danish laws broke up farm villages and dispersed the rural population in isolated farmsteads. At the same time, many fragmented landholdings were combined into large block farms. In nearby German-ruled provinces, different laws prevailed, and the population and property lines remained unchanged. Today, even though Germany has ruled Schleswig-Holstein for over a century, the old border is still clearly visible in the settlement landscape.

Legal imprint can also be seen in the cultural landscape of urban areas. In Rio de Janeiro, height restrictions on buildings have been enforced for a long time. The result is a waterfront lined with buildings of uniform height. By contrast, most American cities have no height restrictions, allowing skyscrapers to dominate the central city. The consequence is a jagged skyline, like that of San Francisco or New York City (see Figure 4-20).

Physical properties of boundaries

Political borders vary greatly in the degree to which they stand out in the landscape. On one extreme are highly visible boundaries marked by walls, cleared strips, and barbed-wire barriers. The famous Berlin Wall, first erected in 1961, is an excellent example (see Figure 4-21). As a general rule, political borders are most visible where tight restrictions limit the movement of people and goods between neighboring states. Sometimes such boundaries are even lined with pillboxes, tank traps, and other obvious defensive installations. At the opposite end of the spectrum are international borders, such as that between the United States and Canada, that are unfortified, thinly policed, and very nearly invisible. But even undefended borders of this type are usually marked by regularly spaced boundary pillars or cairns and by customs houses and colorfully striped guardhouses at crossing points.

Relics of boundary defenses, some dating from ancient times, are common in certain areas. Hadrian's Wall in England marks the northern border during one stage of Roman occupation and parallels the modern border between England and Scotland. The Great Wall of China and the elaborate concrete and steel installations of France's Maginot Line are two other reminders of boundaries of the past.

FIGURE 4–20
Legal height restrictions, or their absence, can greatly influence urban landscapes. New York City lacks such controls and its skyline is punctuated by spectacular sky scrapers. In Rio de Janeiro, by contrast, height restrictions allow the natural environment to provide the "highrises."

▼FIGURE 4–21
The Berlin Wall divides a city that was once whole. The brick and barbed wire visually mark the limits of political control. Are political boundaries visible in your area?

A quite different type of boundary, marking the territorial limits of urban street gangs, is also evident in the central areas of many American cities. The principal device used by these teenaged gangs to mark their "turf" is graffiti. Geographers David Ley and Roman Cybriwsky studied this phenomenon in Philadelphia. They found that borders were marked by externally directed, aggressive epithets, taunts, and obscenities, placed there for the benefit of neighboring gangs. A street gang of white youths, for example, plastered their border with a black gang with slogans like "White Power," "Do Not Enter [District]21-W,—," and similar graffiti painted on walls. The gang's "core area," their "home corner," contains internally supportive graffiti, such as "Fairmount Rules" or a roster of gang members. Thus a perceptive observer can map the gang territories on the basis of these political landscape features.

The impress of central authority

The attempt to impose centralized government appears in many facets of the landscape (Figure 4-22). Railroad and highway patterns focused on the national core area, and radiating like the spokes of a wheel to reach the hinterlands of the state, are good indicators of central authority. In Germany, the rail network was developed largely before unification of the country in 1871. As a result, no focal point stands out. On the other hand, the superhighway system of autobahns, encouraged by Hitler as a symbol of national unity and power, tied the various parts of the Reich to such focal points as Berlin and the Ruhr industrial district.

Central authority backed by military power tends to produce a landscape in which the rural population is dispersed and the cities are without defense installations. Clustered farm villages and walled towns can be physical signs of an absence of central authority, of a need to provide defense on the local level. In England, where effective central government has prevailed for a thousand years, few cities retain their former walls, and the villages have shrunk as farmers have dispersed into the countryside. However, in Central Europe, which remained politically fragmented until very recent times, numerous town walls can still be seen, and the farmers remain concentrated in farm villages. To be sure, other factors also helped shape these contrasts between Britain and mainland Europe, but the different concentration of authority definitely played an important role. In the same way, the inability of the now-deposed government in South Vietnam to effectively protect the rural areas from the insurgent Viet Cong caused many farm folk to move to "fortified hamlets," enclosed with barbed wire, creating an altered rural settlement landscape.

The visibility of provincial borders within a nation can also reflect the central government's strength and stability. Stable, secure nations, such as the United States, often permit considerable display of provincial borders. Most state boundaries within the United States are marked with signboards or other features announcing the crossing. In contrast, insecure countries, where sectionalism threatens national unity, often suppress such signs of provincial borders.

FIGURE 4–22
One of the United States government's most massive modifications of the landscape was undertaken by the Tennessee Valley Authority. The Fontana Dam in North Carolina is the tallest dam in the project. Thousands of acres of land were flooded when the dam was completed.

Some of the most visible central governments are those that have recently taken power. They try to assure their survival by saturating the landscape with evidence of their existence. The Greek military leaders who took power in 1967 soon placed placards with the risen-phoenix symbol of their government in every town, village, and hamlet. They supplemented the placards with countless slogans painted on signs, spelled out in white rocks on hillsides, and commemorated in changed street names. These visible symbols of the government were just as quickly removed when the military junta fell from power in 1974.

Conclusion

Political spatial variations—from local voting patterns to the spatial arrangement of international power blocs—add yet another dimension to the complex human mosaic. In particular, independent and insurgent political states function as vital culture regions. They help shape many other facets of culture. Political culture regions constantly change as political innovations ebb and flow across their surface. Political phenomena as varied as guerrilla movements, women's suffrage, and territorial expansion of nations move along the paths of diffusion.

Cultural ecology helps us understand the links between systems of power and the physical environment. States do not exist in an environmental vacuum. The spatial pattern of landforms, hydrogeography, and vegetation are frequently reflected in boundaries, core areas, folk fortresses, and global strategies. Although the environment molds the political state, the state also molds the environment. Governments can act as agents of destruction or conservation.

The cultural-integration approach underscores the relationships between politics and other facets of culture. Harmony and stability within nations often depend on relative cultural homogeneity of the population. This is so critical that leaders sometimes seek to impose homogeneity by force. The integration of politics and culture is also revealed in the economy. A map of agricultural contrasts in the border zone between the United States and Canada illustrates this point.

Finally, politics leaves an imprint on the cultural landscape. The imprint is often overlooked, as in the patterns of survey systems or highways. Occasionally the imprint is brutal, as in the Berlin Wall. Frequently it is overt, as in the billboards and banners of totalitarian regimes.

Glossary

Antecedent boundary a political border drawn prior to the settlement of an area.

Centrifugal force any factor that disrupts the internal order of a state.

Centripetal force any factor that supports the internal unity of a state.

Core area the territorial nucleus from which a state grows in area and through time, often containing the national capital and the main center of commerce, culture, and industry.

Enclave a piece of territory surrounded by, but not part of, a state.

Ethnographic boundary a political boundary that follows some cultural border, such as a linguistic or religious border.

Exclave a piece of a state separated from the main body of it by the intervening territory of another state.

Federal state an independent state in which considerable autonomy and power are given to individual provinces and the central government is relatively weak.

Folk fortress a stronghold area with natural defensive qualities, useful in the defense of the state against invaders.

Forward-thrust capital a capital city situated near the frontier of the most rapid territorial expansion or new settlement in a state.

Geometric boundary a political border drawn in a regular, geometric manner, often a straight line, without regard for environmental or cultural patterns.

Geopolitics the study of the relationship between the physical environment and political patterns.

Head-link capital a capital city situated near the border along the main route of foreign trade and cultural contact.

Heartland the interior of a state or land mass, removed from maritime connections; in particular, the interior of the Eurasian continent.

Heartland theory a 1904 proposal by Mackinder that the key to world conquest lay in control of the interior of Eurasia.

Insurgent state a state within a state, the result of a guerrilla insurgency directed toward secession or overthrow of the existing government.

Manifest destiny the belief that a nation should follow its natural course by expanding to some clear geographic limits.

Natural boundary a political border that follows some feature of the natural environment, such as a river or mountain ridge.

Primate city a capital city of a nation, which also contains the greatest concentration of population, cultural activities, and economic functions.

Raison d'être in French, literally "reason for being"; the main unifying force within a state, the principal basis of nationalism.

Relic boundary a former political border, no longer functioning as a boundary.

Rimland the maritime fringe of a country or continent; in particular, the western, southern, and eastern edges of the Eurasian continent.

Rimland theory a 1944 proposal by Spykman that the key to world conquest lay in domination of the Eurasian rimland.

Superimposed boundary a political border drawn after the settlement of an area.

Territorial imperative the need to possess and defend territory; observed in many animal species and perhaps also inherent in humans.

Unitary state an independent state in which power is highly concentrated in the central government.

Suggested Readings

Anouar Abdel-Malek. "Geopolitics and National Movements: An Essay on the Dialectics of Imperialism," in Richard Peet (ed.), *Radical Geography: Alternative Viewpoints on Contemporary Social Issues*. Chicago: Maaroufa Press, 1977.

Robert Ardrey. *The Territorial Imperative: A Personal Inquiry into the Animal Origins of Property and Nations*. New York: Atheneum, 1966.

Edward F. Bergman. *Modern Political Geography*. Dubuque, Iowa: Wm. C. Brown, 1975.

Mark Blacksell. *Post-War Europe: A Political Geography*, Boulder, Col.: Westview Press, 1977.

Stanley D. Brunn. *Geography and Politics in America*. New York: Harper & Row, 1974.

Stanley D. Brunn. "Geography and Politics of the United States in the Year 2000," *Journal of Geography*, 72 (1973), 42–49.

Saul B. Cohen. *Geography and Politics in a World Divided*, 2nd ed. New York: Oxford University Press, 1973.

Vaughan Cornish. *The Great Capitals: An Historical Geography*. London: Methuen, 1923.

Kevin R. Cox, David R. Reynolds, and Stein Rokkan (eds.). *Locational Approaches to Power and Conflict*. New York: Halsted Press, 1974.

Harm J. de Blij and Martin Ira Glassner. *Systematic Political Geography*, 3rd ed. Toronto: John Wiley, 1980.

Ernst S. Easterly, III. "Global Patterns of Legal Systems: Notes Toward a New Geojurisprudence," *Geographical Review*, 67 (1977), 209–220.

Jean Gottmann. *The Significance of Territory*. Charlottesville: University of Virginia Press, 1973.

Rex Honey. "Political Geography: A Behavioral Framework," *Geographical Perspectives*, 37 (Spring 1976), 3–11.

James H. Johnson. "The Political Distinctiveness of Northern Ireland," *Geographical Review*, 52 (1962), 78–91.

Roger E. Kasperson and Julian V. Minghi (eds.). *The Structure of Political Geography*. Chicago: Aldine, 1969.

David Ley and Roman Cybriwsky. "Urban Graffiti as Territorial Markers," *Annals, Association of American Geographers*, 64 (1974), 491–505.

William S. Logan. "The Changing Landscape Significance of the Victoria-South Australia Boundary," *Annals, Association of American Geographers*, 58 (1968), 128–154.

Robert W. McColl. "The Insurgent State: Territorial Base of Revolution," *Annals, Association of American Geographers*, 59 (1969), 613–631.

Halford J. Mackinder. "The Geographical Pivot of History," *Geographical Journal*, 23 (1904), 421–437.

Richard L. Morrill. "Ideal and Reality in Reapportionment," *Annals, Association of American Geographers*, 63 (1973), 463–477.

Richard Muir. *Modern Political Geography*. New York: Wiley, 1975.

G. H. Pirie, C. M. Rogerson, and K.S.O. Beavon. "Covert Power in South Africa: Geography of the Afrikaner Broederbond," *Area*, 12 (1980), 97–104.

J. Douglas Porteous. "Home: The Territorial Core," *Geographical Review*, 66 (1976), 383–390.

J.R.V. Prescott. *The Geography of Frontiers and Boundaries*. London: Hutchinson University Library, 1965.

J.R.V. Prescott. *The Geography of State Policies*. Chicago: Aldine, 1968.

Nicholas J. Spykman. *The Geography of the Peace*. New York: Harcourt Brace, 1944.

Glen V. Stephenson. "Cultural Regionalism and the Unitary State Idea in Belgium," *Geographical Review*, 62 (1972), 501–523.

Imre Sutton. "Sovereign States and the Changing Definition of the Indian Reservation," *Geographical Review*, 66 (1976), 281–295.

Peter J. Taylor. "Political Geography," *Progress in Human Geography*, 1 (1977), 130–135; 2 (1978), 153–162.

Peter J. Taylor and R. J. Johnston. *Geography of Elections*. New York: Holmes & Meier, 1979.

Derwent Whittlesey. "The Impress of Effective Central Authority Upon the Landscape," *Annals, Association of American Geographers*, 25 (1935), 85–97.

Chapter-opening photo: Bilingual road sign in an Irish *Gaeltacht*, 1974, with the English names obliterated.

The Babel of Languages

5

You are in a seafood restaurant in Miami. Behind you, a man asks the waiter for an order of oysters. Someone else walks over to his table and says with a smile: "Flatbush Avenue!" The man laughs. "Close," he replies, "but I actually grew up on Ocean Avenue!" Of course, they are talking about streets in Brooklyn, New York, not Miami, Florida. That may sound like ESP or just sound absurd, unless you know that the man pronounced "oysters" as "ersters." His accent identified him to his fellow Brooklynite, who acted as a cultural geographer. The eavesdropper isolated a single culture trait, a Brooklyn **dialect;** identified a formal culture region, the area where Brooklynese is spoken; and drew the appropriate conclusions.

Every time you go to a dance, ride a bus, or listen to a radio talk show, you probably automatically make some pretty good guesses about where the people you hear came from. You base a lot of these guesses on how they talk. To do so, you unconsciously take a number of subtle factors into account: accent, pronunciation, stress, inflection, word choice, and others. We can often distinguish out-of-towners from local residents, rich from poor, black from white, suburbanite from city dweller, immigrant from native-born, and one neighborhood from another.

For geographers, language is particularly important, because speech is so basic an aspect of culture. It is a major means by which cultural elements pass from one generation to the next. Thus language is one of the principal means of preserving a way of life. Nearly every cultural group and subgroup has its own distinctive speech. For this reason, geographers often use language to identify different cultures. Because language is essential to communication, it influences the sort of political, social, and economic institutions we create. As a result, economic and religious systems frequently follow patterns of language distribution, and political borders quite often parallel language boundaries. Environmental features such as mountains, plains, and bodies of water can also affect the distribution of languages. In short, human linguistic patterns form a highly varied mosaic whose design both affects and is affected by many elements of culture and the physical environment.

Linguistic Culture Regions

Many different kinds of culture regions can be devised on the basis of speech. They can range from those that reflect the distribution of individual words to those that reflect the broad range of differences in vocabulary, grammar, and pronunciation among separate dialects and languages.

The borders of word usage or pronunciation are called **isoglosses.** No two words, phrases, or pronunciations have exactly the same spatial distribution; that is, no two isoglosses are duplicates. Figure 5-1 provides an example of how isoglosses crisscross one another. Geographers commonly devise multitrait linguistic culture regions, seeking borders where numerous features of speech change. Isoglosses often cluster together, and these "bundles" serve as the most satisfactory dividing lines among dialects and among languages. Using this approach, the cultural geographer can prepare maps of the German-language culture area, the culture area of the Southern dialect of American English, and so on.

Few, if any, borders between languages are sharp, in keeping with the

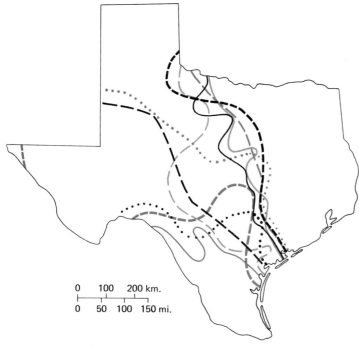

EASTERN AND NORTHERN BORDERS OF:

———————— Remuda (group of saddle horses)

— — — — Mesa (flat-topped hill)

———————— Morral (feed bag)

———————— Resaca (channel)

• • • • • • • • Vaquero (cowboy)

■ ■ ■ ■ ■ ■ Arroyo (dry creek)

— — — — Frijoles (pinto beans)

• • • • • • • • Pilón (something extra)

— — — Toro (bull)

■ ■ ■ ■ ■ Acequia (irrigation ditch)

FIGURE 5–1
Many words have been adopted from Spanish into English in the western and southern parts of Texas. Note that the isogloss for each word is slightly different from every other one but that the result is a typical "bundle" of isoglosses, dividing Texas into two dialect regions. (Based on data in Elmer B. Atwood, *The Regional Vocabulary of Texas,* Austin: University of Texas Press, 1962.)

general character of cultural borders. Rather than a dividing line, the geographer usually encounters a zone of bilingualism or perhaps a thorough spatial mixing of speakers of two different languages. Linguistic "islands," separated from the main body of a language, often further complicate the drawing of borders. Similarly, dialect terms often overlap considerably, making it difficult to draw isoglosses. Indeed, linguistic geographers often disagree about how many dialects are present in an area and where isoglosses and dialect borders should be drawn. One scholar surveys the speech of the American South and detects two major dialects; another equally qualified linguist surveys the same vocabulary evidence in the same area and concludes that only one dialect, containing four subdialects, exists. Still another expert asks, in all seriousness, "Do dialect borders exist?" You should be aware, then, that linguistic borders shown on maps, like most cultural boundaries, are often arbitrarily drawn, oversimplified, and potentially misleading.

In spite of these shortcomings, the linguistic culture region is a convenient and necessary device to facilitate the spatial study of language. One of the most useful types of culture region depicts **language families.**

Language families

Certainly, the mixture of languages across the globe reflects the long, turbulent history of humankind. Look at the map in Figure 5-2 showing world language distribution. As you can see, the linguistic pattern looks like a crazy quilt. In reality, of course, the distribution is far more complex than this, encompassing literally thousands of dialects and languages, each spoken in its own distinct area. Some order can be brought to this seeming chaos only if we recognize that most individual languages belong to families, related tongues derived from a common ancestral speech. As you read the following section, you may want to refer to Figure 5-2.

The Indo-European language family. The largest and most widespread language family is the **Indo-European,** which is dominant in Europe, the Soviet Union, North and South America, Australia, and parts of southwestern Asia and India. Subgroups such as Romance, Slavic, Germanic, Indic, Celtic, and Iranic are part of the Indo-European family, and they in turn are subdivided into individual languages. For example, English is a

FIGURE 5-2
This map shows the major linguistic culture areas of the world. Although there are hundreds of languages and thousands of dialects in the world, they can be grouped into a few linguistic families. Note particularly the broad extent of the Indo-European language family. English-speaking Americans share Indo-European language roots with a wide variety of other cultural groups.

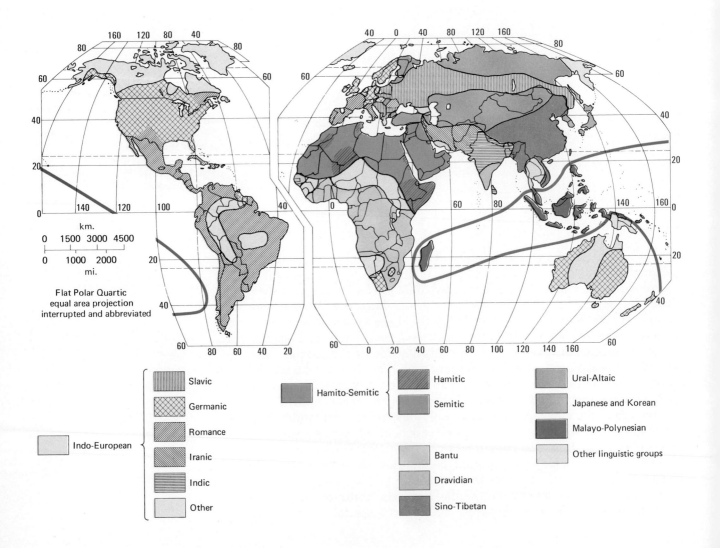

TABLE 5-1 Major Indo-European Languages, Ranked by Number of Speakers

Language	Subdivision	Number of Speakers (in millions)	Main Areas Where Spoken
English	Germanic	310	British Isles, Anglo-America, Australia, New Zealand, South Africa, Philippines, former British colonies in tropical Asia and Africa
Russian	Slavic	190	Soviet Union
Hindi	Indic	180	India
Spanish	Romance	175	Spain, Latin America, southwestern United States
Bengali	Indic	100	Bangladesh, eastern India
German	Germanic	95	Germany, Austria, Switzerland, Luxembourg, eastern France, northern Italy
Portuguese	Romance	95	Portugal, Brazil, southern Africa

Germanic Indo-European language. Indo-European tongues claiming the largest number of speakers are shown in Table 5-1.

If we compare the vocabularies of various Indo-European tongues, we can readily see the kinship of these languages. For example, the English word *mother* is similar to the Polish *matka*, the Greek *meter*, the Spanish *madre*, the Armenian *mair*, the Avestan (spoken in Iran) *matar*, and the Sinhalese (spoken in Sri Lanka) *mava*. Such similarities in vocabulary suggest that these languages had a common ancestral tongue.

Using words as clues, geographers and linguists have concluded that the earliest speakers of the original Indo-European language probably lived in interior Eurasia or eastern Europe about 5000 or more years ago. Figure 5-6 shows how these speakers then spread west and south. As they lost contact with one another, different Indo-European groups gradually developed variant forms of the language. Today's widespread distribution of Indo-European languages is partly the result of political empire building and the resulting migrations. The Romance languages, which are derived from Latin, owe their broad distribution to the empires of the Romans, Spaniards, and Portuguese; English spread with the creation of the British Empire. However, some Indo-European linguistic groups retreated to refuge areas and declined, as did the speakers of the Celtic tongues, who today occupy only the hilly western fringes of the British Isles and France.

The Hamito-Semitic family. A second language family, completely unrelated to the Indo-European, is the **Hamito-Semitic.** The Semitic languages originated before recorded time. Ancient Babylonians, Assyrians, and the Phoenicians were Semites. Historically, the Semitic languages have been closely linked with monotheism, or the worship of a single god. In fact, in Chapter 6 you will find that Semitic tribes developed Judaism, Christianity, and Islam, the three major monotheistic religions of the world. The Semitic languages cover the area from the Arabian peninsula and the Tigris-Euphrates river valley in the Fertile Crescent of Iraq westward through Syria and North Africa to the Atlantic Ocean. Despite the considerable size of this domain, there are fewer speakers of the Semitic languages than of the other major language families, mainly because most of the areas they inhabit are sparsely populated deserts.

Arabic is by far the most widespread Semitic language and has the greatest number of speakers, about 115 million. Although many different dialects of Arabic are spoken, the written form is standard.

Hebrew also is a Semitic tongue, closely related to Arabic (Figure 5-3). For many centuries, Hebrew was a "dead" language, used only in religious ceremonies by millions of Jews scattered around the world. With the creation of the state of Israel in 1947, a common language was needed to unite the immigrant Jews, who spoke the languages of many different countries. Hebrew was revived and made the official national language of what otherwise would have been a **polyglot,** or multilanguage, state. However, Hebrew had lain dormant for 2000 years. It had to be modernized. To make the transition to the twentieth century, words had to be coined for *telephone, airplane, rifle,* and the like.

Migrants from southwestern Arabia brought Semitic speech to Ethiopia about 3000 years ago. There, in the isolation of the East African mountain highlands, it gradually evolved into Amharic, a third major Semitic tongue.

Smaller numbers of linguistically related people who speak Hamitic languages share North and East Africa with the Semites. These people originated in Asia and today include the Berbers of Morocco and Algeria, the Tuaregs of the Sahara, and the Cushites of East Africa. The Hamitic speech area was formerly much larger than it is now. It once covered the lands of the ancient Egyptians, but it was greatly reduced and fragmented by the expansion of Arabic over a thousand years ago.

Languages of sub-Saharan Africa. Immediately south of the Hamito-Semitic zone in Africa is a linguistic **shatter belt** of diverse languages. A shatter belt is a zone of cultural diversity, populated by a great variety of small cultural groups, each in its separate homeland. Beyond this area lies the domain of Bantu speech. There are at least eighty-three individual Bantu tongues, each spoken by one tribe or clan. Among the most important are Swahili, widely used in East Africa; Zulu, found in southern Africa; and Congolese, spoken in western equatorial Africa. The

FIGURE 5-3
Hebrew has become the common language for all immigrants to Israel as well as for Jews all over the world. Posters in Hebrew provide news of events and entertainment in the city of Tel Aviv. Hebrew is read from right to left.

Bantu group, part of a larger Niger-Congo-Bantu language family, apparently began in tropical Africa and spread eastward and southward from there (refer to Figure 5-6).

Among the linguistic groups retreating before the Bantu were the Hottentots and Bushman, who speak related languages distinguished by peculiar clicking sounds. The few surviving speakers of Bushman and Hottentot live in the Kalahari Desert of southwestern Africa.

Oriental language families. The **Sino-Tibetan language family** is the major linguistic group in the Orient. This language family, dominated by Chinese, has one of the largest groups of speakers in the world. Over 500 million more people speak a Sino-Tibetan language than speak English. The Sino-Tibetan speech area extends throughout most of China and Southeast Asia. Chinese itself is spoken in a variety of dialects by perhaps 700 million people in China and in scattered locales from Singapore to San Francisco. Mandarin Chinese, originally spoken only in northeastern China, has now been adopted as the official form of speech for the People's Republic of China. Other Sino-Tibetan languages include Thai, Burmese, and Tibetan. These languages collectively border the Chinese speech area on the south and west.

Japanese and Korean constitute another Oriental language family that occupies the midlatitude peninsular and insular strongholds of Korea and Japan in eastern Asia. Japanese alone has over 100 million speakers. The adoption of Chinese written characters in both areas has led many casual Western observers to assume that Japanese and Korean are related to Chinese speech. Actually, they belong to entirely different language families.

Malayo-Polynesian languages. One of the most remarkable language families in terms of distribution is the **Malayo-Polynesian,** also referred to as Austronesian. Representatives of this group live mainly on tropical islands stretching from Madagascar, off the east coast of Africa, through Indonesia and the Pacific Islands, to Hawaii and Easter Island. This east-west, or longitudinal, span is more than half the distance around the world. The language area also covers a north-south, or latitudinal, range from Hawaii and Taiwan in the north to New Zealand in the south. Such a far-flung distribution, divided as it is by vast stretches of open ocean, is a testimonial to the navigational skills of the Malayo-Polynesian people, who spread their language as they traveled from island to island in small boats.

Other language families. Other linguistic groups include the **Ural-Altaic** and the **Dravidian**. The Ural-Altaic group flanks the Indo-Europeans on the north and south. They inhabit the inhospitable desert, tundra, and taiga lands of Eurasia, with major settlements as far west as Turkey, Hungary, and Finland. The tundras, found mainly near the Arctic Circle, are bitterly cold and treeless. The taiga is a vast expanse of thinly settled coniferous forest just south of the tundra in the Soviet Union. The Dravidian languages are spoken by the numerous darker-skinned peoples of southern India. Remnant native languages such as Amerindian dialects, Eskimoan, Papuan, and Caucasian fill out the rest of the linguistic map.

English dialects in the United States

Most of the people in the United States speak English. Yet American English is hardly uniform from region to region. At least three major dialects, corresponding to the three major culture regions, had developed in the eastern United States by the time of the American Revolution: the Northern, Midland, and Southern dialects (compare Figures 5-4 and 1-5). As the three subcultures expanded westward, their dialects spread and fragmented. Nevertheless, the dialects retained much of their basic character even beyond the Mississippi River, although mixing occurred. The three dialects have distinctive vocabularies and pronunciations, as Table 5-2 suggests. Even so, it is often difficult to draw the dialect boundaries, even east of the Mississippi (see Figure 5-5).

Today, many of the regional words are becoming old-fashioned, and American English is tending to be standardized into a form of the Midland dialect. Even so, new words that display regional variations are still being coined. For instance, the following terms are all used to describe a controlled-access divided highway: *freeway, turnpike, parkway, thruway, expressway,* and *interstate.* Of these, *parkway* and *turnpike* seem to be mainly northeastern and midwestern words, whereas *freeway* is the preferred California word. In England, *motorway* is the preferred term.

America's black minority speaks its own distinctive form of English. Black English, once dismissed by linguists as no more than inferior substandard English, is in reality a blend of the Southern dialect of English and a variety of African languages. This subdialect, which seems to have developed from the early pidgin and plantation Creole English of the slaves, is spoken by perhaps 80 percent of America's black population. The structures of Black English, with their African heritage, can be heard in the speech of black ghetto dwellers who have yet to make their compromises with the mainstream culture in America. The use of

FIGURE 5–4

Dialects of American English in the eastern United States. These correspond to the three culture regions described in Chapter 1: New England, Middle-Atlantic, and Lower South. Compare this map to Figure 1–5. (After Kurath, Allen, Wood, and E. B. Atwood, *The Regional Vocabulary of Texas,* Austin: University of Texas Press, 1962.)

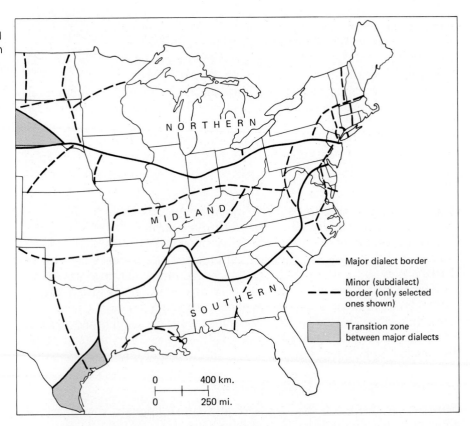

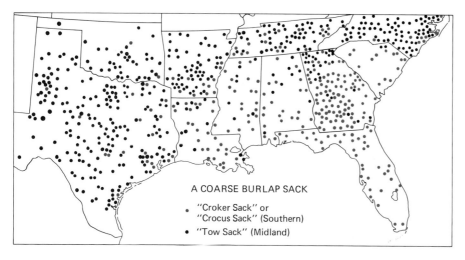

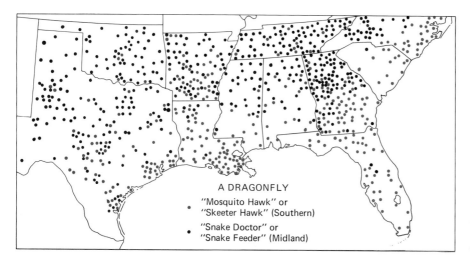

FIGURE 5-5
Some Midland and Southern words in the South. Each dot represents one person interviewed who gave the response indicated. If you were drawing the isoglosses for these words, where exactly would you place them? If these two maps were your only evidence, where would you draw the Midland-Southern dialect border? These are common problems for the linguistic geographer, and they illustrate how "artificial" dialects and dialect maps are. (After Gordon R. Wood, *Vocabulary Change: A Study of Variation in Regional Words in Eight of the Southern States.* Carbondale and Edwardsville, Ill.; Southern Illinois University Press, 1971, pp. 325, 337–339; and E. Bagby Atwood, *The Regional Vocabulary of Texas,* Austin: University of Texas Press, 1962, pp. 196, 199.)

TABLE 5-2   Three Major Dialects of American English, as Indicated by Vocabulary Samples

Meaning	Northern Dialect	Midland Dialect	Southern Dialect
Food eaten between meals	bite	piece	snack
Dragonfly	darning needle	snake feeder, snake doctor	mosquito hawk, skeeter hawk
Fence built of stone	stone wall	stone fence	rock fence
Cottage cheese	Dutch cheese, pot cheese	smear cheese	curds, clabber cheese
Green beans	string beans	green beans	snap beans
Worm in ground	angleworm	fish worm, redworm	earthworm

undifferentiated pronouns ("Me help you?"); the lack of pronoun differentiation between genders ("He a nice little girl"); the "he"/"she" pronoun possessive ("Ray sister she got a new doll baby"); "been" in special sentence structures ("I been wash the car"); and many other features of Black English separate it very distinctly from standard English. There are numerous local variants of Black English.

In the American school system, such dialect forms are usually considered mistakes—evidence of the verbal inability or impoverishment of blacks—rather than as part of the proper grammar of a separate linguistic group. In the same way, linguists have often been unwilling to admit the contributions that blacks and other minorities have made to American English. Black English seems to have been a repressed but innovative linguistic force that probably produced some of the evident differences between Southern white dialect and Northern white dialect—a possibility that many whites are reluctant to admit.

FIGURE 5-6

Linguistic hearths and diffusions are shown here. Indo-European, Bantu, Semitic, and Malayo-Polynesian languages spread from relatively small hearth areas to occupy expansive linguistic domains. Until about A.D. 1500, the Malayo-Polynesian family was the most widespread linguistic group, but Indo-European tongues have explosively expanded across the world since that time. What do the different patterns and routes of diffusion tell you about the transportation technologies of the four language groups?

Linguistic Diffusion

The most common form of linguistic cultural diffusion has been through relocation. Indo-European, Semitic, Malayo-Polynesian, and most other widespread language families owe their far-flung distribution to the migrations of peoples who spoke these tongues. Figure 5-6 shows the relocation diffusion of four major language families.

However, relocation and expansion diffusion are not mutually exclusive. Relocation diffusion often involved a relatively small number of

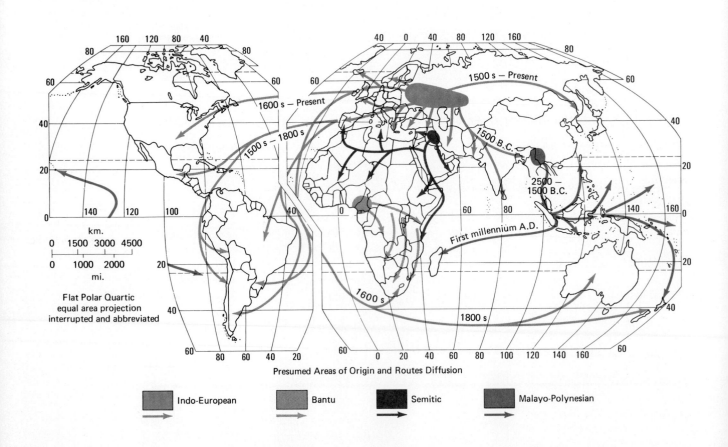

km.
0 1500 3000 4500
0 1000 2000
mi.

Flat Polar Quartic
equal area projection
interrupted and abbreviated

Presumed Areas of Origin and Routes Diffusion

Indo-European   Bantu   Semitic   Malayo-Polynesian

speakers, a conquering elite who came to rule an alien people. In this way, Arabic spread across much of North Africa. The language of the conqueror, implanted by relocation diffusion, often gained wider acceptance through expansion diffusion. Typically, the conqueror's language spread hierarchically—adopted first by the more important and influential persons and by city folk. The diffusion of Latin with Roman conquests frequently occurred in this manner.

Occasionally such circumstances resulted in a linguistic blend. French was introduced into England by the Norman conquerors in 1066 and became the speech of the ruling class. But in time, Norman French merged with the Anglo-Saxon speech of the conquered people to form the English language. Perhaps a third of all English words are of French origin.

Not infrequently, the process of linguistic diffusion was reversed, particularly when a conqueror or immigrant group lost its dominance over the native speakers. Swedish was implanted in coastal Finland by Swedish soldiers and settlers during a brief period of political greatness centuries ago. Now Swedish retreats steadily before Finnish there through the device of contagious expansion diffusion.

Hierarchical expansion diffusion can be seen at work in the spread of slang words and phrases. Terms such as *rap*, *grass* (for marijuana), *far out*, *heavy*, *stoned*, and countless others come and go in American English. Who are the first users of such vocabulary in your peer group? As a rule, are they the more popular persons, those who function as natural leaders and entertainers? Use of slang terms typically begins with such persons and then spreads down to those in lower social hierarchies. In a similar way, such fad words may be abandoned.

Barriers to linguistic diffusion also exist. Church groups and persons in positions of authority generally oppose obscenities and curse words. People who use such terms in their speech may be punished or ostracized, and books containing them may be excluded from libraries. Movies containing certain obscenities are often legally restricted from being shown to certain age groups. Similarly, Mexican-American schoolchildren were traditionally punished by teachers in some southwestern states for speaking Spanish on the playground.

Linguistic Ecology

The theme of cultural ecology, especially the environment's influence on culture, is quite relevant to the study of languages. The following section, from the viewpoint of the possibilist, suggests some ways that the environment influences vocabulary and the distribution of language.

The environment and vocabulary

Humankind's relationship to the land has played a strong role in the development of linguistic differences (see box, "Naming the Wind"). The environment even affects vocabulary. For example, the Eskimoan tongue has many different words for "seal," depending on whether the seal is old or young, on land or in the water. This reflects the seal's importance to the Eskimos' livelihood. Eskimoan also has many words for "snow," each describing a different type. Similarly, in the rural South, from Virginia to Texas, there are many terms to describe and distinguish streams: *river*, *creek*, *branch*, *fork*, *prong*, *run*, *bayou*, and *slough*. This indicates that the

NAMING THE WIND

When you relate to the world you live in, what do you do? Do you see it? Hear it? Smell it? Feel it? Think about your answer, because it will probably help explain why you use many of the words you do. Your perception of the environment influences your vocabulary.

When you go out in the morning to walk your dog, buy the paper, or catch your first class, do you smell the street you walk along? Then, as you move along it, always in contact with it, do you feel it? Or might you say that you hear the direction you are going by listening to your own footsteps, the sounds of traffic, the words of other pedestrians? Although to some extent we do all those things, people in modern industrial societies have come to rely more and more on their eyes, on "seeing" the world. For us, space is bounded or static, a rectangle, an ever-present framework or matrix for viewing objects. It you walked out tomorrow morning and all the objects you were used to had disappeared, you would feel helpless, disabled. For most of us, without things to see, space is merely an empty frame. We have no words to describe it except perhaps empty, even though it might be filled with wind.

The geographer Yi-fu Tuan has compared this view of the world with that of the Aivilik Eskimos on South-ampton Island. Note the linguistic consequences of relating in a different way to the environment: "To the Eskimo, space is not pictorial or boxed in, but something always in flux, creating its own dimensions moment by moment. He learns to orient himself with all senses alert. He has to during certain times in winter when sky and earth merge and appear to be made of the same substance. There is then 'no middle distance, no perspective, no outline, nothing that the eye can cling to except thousands of smokey plumes of snow running along the ground before the wind—a land without bottom or edge.' Under such conditions the Eskimo cannot rely on the points of reference given by permanent landmarks: he must depend on the shifting relationships of snow contours, on the types of snow, wind, salt air, and ice crack. The direction and smell of the wind is a guide, together with the feel of ice and snow under his feet. The invisible wind plays a large role in the life of the Aivilik Eskimo. His language includes at least twelve unrelated terms for various winds. He learns to orient himself by them. On horizonless days he lives in an acoustic-olfactory space."

Quote from Yi-Fu Tuan, Topophilia *(Englewood Cliffs, N.J.: Prentice-Hall, 1974), p. 11.*

area is a well-watered land with a dense network of streams. The Spanish language, derived from Castile, a land rimmed by hills and high mountains, is especially rich in words describing rough terrain, allowing speakers of this tongue to distinguish even subtle differences in the shape and configuration of mountains, as Table 5-3 reveals. English, by contrast, developed in coastal plains and marshes, and our language is as a consequence very poor in words describing mountainous terrain.

The environment: provider of refuge

One of the most obvious environmental influences on language is the protection and isolation offered by "inhospitable" environments. Such areas often provide hard-pressed, outnumbered linguistic groups refuge from aggressive neighbors. Rugged hill and mountain areas, excessively cold or dry climates, impenetrable forests, islands, and extensive marshes and swamps all offer refuge to minority language groups. For one thing, unpleasant environments rarely attract conquerors. Also, mountains tend to isolate the inhabitants of one valley from those in adjacent ones, retarding the contacts that might lead to linguistic diffusion.

Examples of these **linguistic refuge areas** are numerous. The rugged Caucasus Mountains and nearby ranges in the borderlands between the Soviet Union, Iran, and Turkey are populated by a large variety of peoples (see Figure 5-7). They form a living museum of declining and dying linguistic stocks (see Figure 5-8). Similarly, the Alps, Himalayas, and highlands of Mexico are linguistic shatter belts, and the American Indian

TABLE 5-3 Some Spanish Words Describing Mountains and Hills

Spanish Word	English meaning
Candelas	literally "candles"; a collection of peñas
Ceja	steep-sided breaks or escarpment separating two plains of different elevation
Cejita	a low escarpment
Cerrillo or Cerrito	a small cerro; a hill
Cerro	a single eminence, intermediate in size between English hill and mountain
Chiquito	literally "small," describing minor secondary fringing elevations at the base of and parallel to a sierra or cordillera
Cordillera	a mass of mountains, as distinguished from single mountain summits
Cuchilla	literally "knife"; the comblike secondary crests that project at right angles from the sides of a sierra
Cumbre	the highest elevation or peak within a sierra or cordillera
Eminencia	a mountainous or hilly protuberance
Loma	a hill in the midst of a plain
Lomita	a small hill in the midst of a plain
Mesa	literally "table"; a flat-topped eminence
Montaña	equivalent to English mountain
Pelado	a barren, treeless mountain
Pelon	a bare conical eminence
Peloncilla	a small pelon
Peña	a needle-like eminence
Picacho	a peaked or pointed eminence
Pico	a summit point, English peak
Sandia	literally "watermelon"; an oblong, rounded eminence
Sierra	an elongated mountain mass with a serrated crest
Teta.	a solitary, circular mountain in the shape of a woman's breast
Tinaja	a solitary, hemispherical mountain shaped like an inverted bowl

*Source: Robert T. Hill, "Descriptive Topographic Terms of Spanish America," *National Geographic Magazine,* 7 (1896), 292–297.

tongue Quechua clings to a refuge in the Andes Mountains of South America. Bitterly cold tundra climates of the far north have sheltered certain Uralian, Altaic, and Eskimoan peoples, and the dry desert has shielded speakers of Hottentot and Bushman from Bantu invaders. In short, hostile environments protect linguistic groups who are willing to endure the hardships they offer.

In a similar manner, lush tropical rain forests allowed a few small tribal groups to remain hidden from the outside world until the 1970s (see Figure 5-9). Outsiders only recently discovered the Philippine refuge of the Tasaday, a Malayo-Polynesian remnant tribe. But once found, the Tasaday quickly were introduced to helicopters, television crews, and a variety of new objects that they, naturally enough, had no words for. The long-term effects on the Tasaday language are bound to be significant.

Even in the United States, there are linguistic refuge areas. For instance,

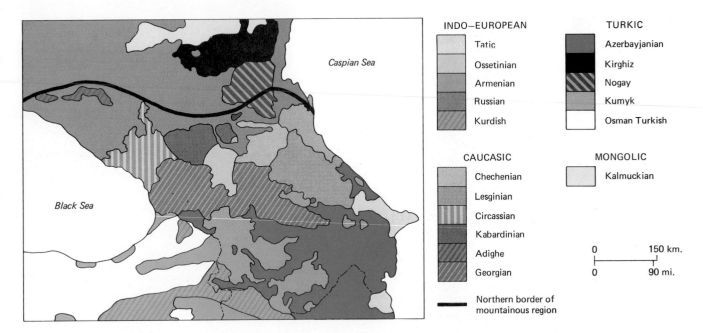

INDO-EUROPEAN
- Tatic
- Ossetinian
- Armenian
- Russian
- Kurdish

TURKIC
- Azerbayjanian
- Kirghiz
- Nogay
- Kumyk
- Osman Turkish

CAUCASIC
- Chechenian
- Lesginian
- Circassian
- Kabardinian
- Adighe
- Georgian

MONGOLIC
- Kalmuckian

0   150 km.

0   90 mi.

— Northern border of mountainous region

FIGURE 5-7

The environment is a linguistic refuge in the Caucasus Mountains. The rugged mountainous region between the Black and Caspian seas, on the border between the Soviet Union, Turkey, and Iran, is peopled by a great variety of linguistic groups, representing three major language families. Mountain areas are often linguistic shatter zones, because the rough terrain provides refuge and isolation. (After C. S. Coon, *The Races of Europe,* New York: Macmillan, 1954, with modifications.)

the Cajuns, living in the marshy bayou areas of Louisiana, have clung to a form of French despite a heavy dose of Americanization in recent decades. Unquestionably, their isolation has helped them hang onto their old linguistic identity, a holdover from the time when Louisiana was French territory. Environmental isolation can no longer be the determining linguistic force it once was. It becomes harder and harder to discover spots on the earth so isolated that they remain untouched by outside influences. Today, inhospitable lands may offer linguistic refuge but it is no longer certain that they will in the future. Even an island situated in the middle of the vast Pacific Ocean can offer no reliable refuge in an age

FIGURE 5-8

The Georgians are one of the ethnic groups whose language and culture are sheltered by the Caucasus Mountains. Even the sweeping political changes within the Soviet Union have not caused the disappearance of this language. The Georgians occupy one of the fifteen separate linguistic republics within the Soviet Union, the Georgian Soviet Socialist Republic.

FIGURE 5-9
Contemporary Western
civilization enters many
remote regions. The traditional
language and culture of this
Peruvian group may not be
able to survive the invasion.

FIGURE 5-9
Contemporary Western
civilization enters many
remote regions. The traditional
language and culture of this
Peruvian group may not be
able to survive the invasion.

of airplanes. Similarly, marshes and forests will provide refuge only if they are not drained and cleared by farmers who want new farmlands. The reality of the world is no longer isolation but interaction.

The environment: guide for migration

Migrating people often are attracted to new lands that seem environmentally similar to their homelands. Germanic Indo-Europeans sought familiar temperate zones in America, New Zealand, and Australia. Semitic peoples rarely spread outside arid and semiarid climates. Ancestors of the modern Hungarians, a Uralian-Altaic linguistic stock, left the grasslands of inner Eurasia in the tenth century and found a new home in the grassy Alföld, one of the few prairie areas of Europe.

Environmental barriers and natural routeways have often guided linguistic groups in certain paths. The wide distribution of the Malayo-Polynesian language group, and particularly their presence in Hawaii and Madagascar, cannot be fully understood without studying prevailing winds and water currents in the Pacific and Indian oceans. And migrating Indo-Europeans entering the Indian subcontinent through low mountain passes in the northwest were deflected by the Himalayas and the barren Deccan Plateau into the rich Ganges-Indus river plain. Even today in parts of India, according to Charles Bennett, the Indo-European/Dravidian "language boundary seems to approximate an ecological boundary" between the water-retentive black soils of the plains and the thinner, reddish Deccan soils.

Because such physical barriers as mountain ridges can retard groups from migrating from one area to another, they frequently serve as linguistic borders. In parts of the Alps, speakers of German and Italian live on opposite sides of a major ridge. The mountain rim along the northern edge of the Fertile Crescent in the Middle East forms the border between Semitic and Indo-European tongues. Linguistic borders that follow such physical features generally tend to be stable, and they often endure for thousands of years. Language borders that cross plains and major routes of communication are frequently unstable.

Linguistic Cultural Integration

Language is intertwined with all aspects of culture. The theme of cultural integration permits us to probe some of these complex links between speech and other cultural phenomena. In particular, this section focuses on the links between language and politics, economics, and religion (see box, "The French Canadians").

Empire building and the spread of language

"Dust to Dust/Ashes to Ashes/Into the grave/The great queen dashes," wrote an Asian Indian poet on the death of Britain's Queen Victoria. This poet's attempt to grapple with a foreign language, English, is but one

---

THE FRENCH CANADIANS: AN ILLUSTRATION OF LINGUISTIC CULTURAL INTEGRATION

The theme of cultural integration in relation to language is well illustrated by the French-speaking Canadians. Concentrated in the province of Québec and numbering over 6 million, these *Canadiens* are descended from French colonists who arrived in the 1600s and 1700s. From 1760 to 1867, they lived under English rule; and since 1867, Québec has been part of Anglo-dominated Canada. Throughout the period of English rule, the French Canadians maintained their language and culture, successfully resisting assimilation.

The French language survived in large part because of religious factors. Its survival is an excellent example of the integration of speech and faith within a culture. Most other Canadians are Protestant. The French Canadians are Roman Catholics, and the Church provided social cohesion, a cultural rallying point. French language and culture were preserved in the numerous rural Catholic churches and church schools of Québec.

In time, the linguistic and religious solidarity of the French Canadians found a political expression centered in their attachment to the province of Québec. For many decades, government of the province was dominated by English-speaking administrators, but a political awakening allowed the *Canadiens* to gain political control of Québec. As a result, the province is politically different from the rest of Canada, and in some ways it now resembles a state within a state. The laws of Québec retain a dominantly French influence, but the remainder of Canada adheres to English common law. The provincial flag, adopted in 1948, preserves the old fleur-de-lis symbol of the French kings. French is a legal language in Québec (and throughout Canada), and most

Canadiens cannot speak any other language. French is used in newspapers, schools, churches, radio, television, court proceedings, and legislative gatherings. An attempt is presently under way to abolish all use of English in Québec. The province even has its own distinctive land-survey pattern, derived from French colonial times and preserved in provincial law. The political expression of the Québec French has in recent years led to increasing demands for independence.

The economic expression of French Canada has historically been class division between English and French. People who spoke English came to occupy an economic upper class, dominating managerial and other high positions. To a remarkable degree, the wealth of the province was in the hands of the English. Even the old French fur-trapping interests, which dated back to the early 1600s, came under English and Scottish ownership. Moreover, the French Canadians were slower to be absorbed into the industrial life of the cities, and many remained in the rural areas until recent times. The traditional economic role of the *Canadiens* as second-class citizens now lies largely in the past, because the longtime English dominance of Québec's economy is rapidly fading. Perhaps economic equality will weaken *Canadiens'* desire for political independence.

Thus language, religion, politics, and economics are closely interwoven in Canada. Such interdependence is found in many culture regions. In 1980 about half of the French-speaking population of Québec voted in favor of seeking sovereignty for their province.

result of the British conquest of India. The aggressive expansion of European and American power across the globe in the last four centuries has affected the linguistic patterns of millions of people. The United Kingdom, France, the Netherlands, Belgium, Portugal, Spain, the United States, and Japan all controlled overseas empires. This empire building superimposed Indo-European tongues on the map of the tropics and subtropics. The areas most affected were Asia, Africa, and the Malayo-Polynesian island world. In South America as well, two alien tongues—Spanish and Portuguese—were imposed on most of an entire continent.

Even though the imperial nations have given up part or all of their colonial empires, the languages they transplanted overseas have survived. As a result, English still has a foothold in much of Africa, the Indian subcontinent, the Philippines, and certain areas of the Pacific islands. French persists in the former French and Belgian colonies, especially in north, west, and central Africa, Madagascar, Indochina, and Polynesia. In some of these areas, English and French are still the languages of the educated political elite and enjoy a role as languages of government, commerce, and higher education. In fact, they often enjoy official legal status.

In South America, two expanding empires—Spain and Portugal—clashed in the fifteenth century. Their compromise had far-reaching linguistic consequences. In 1494, Spain and Portugal signed the Treaty of Tordesillas. Under this treaty, Spain received control over all colonial lands west of a certain meridian (mapped in Figure 5-10), and Portugal gained control over the lands east of this line. This line through South America gave Portugal only a small eastern portion of the continent. In this way, Brazil eventually became a Portuguese-speaking land. Most of the rest of South America remains a Spanish language area.

Language and conquest

Conquering armies have often carried their own languages with them. After Christian forces conquered the Moors in Iberia, Arabic disappeared from southern Spain and Portugal. In the American West, a long series of military campaigns caused the retreat or extinction of many American Indian populations and their languages. Conquests have often uprooted entire ethnic groups from ancestral homelands and forced them to settle elsewhere, carrying their languages with them. For example, 10 million German-speaking residents were evacuated and expelled from the eastern provinces of Germany during and after World War II. This area was then recolonized by Polish- and Russian-speaking settlers. As a result, some 50,000 square miles (130,000 square kilometers) of territory quickly changed from Germanic to Slavic speech.

Language can even more directly be a weapon of conquest. The imposition of a foreign language is a powerful way to break a people's self-esteem and national or cultural pride and identity. One typical strategy of control is to forbid the use of native languages in the conquered country's educational system. Japan took this course in Korea after it annexed the peninsula in 1910; the United States did the same thing after its conquest of the Philippines in the late 1890s.

The linguistic history of the United States is a running tale of the suppression and destruction of non-English languages. One of the early tricks slavers learned was to mix captured blacks from different African language areas in the same ship. This practice cut down the ability of the slaves to communicate with one another and thereby lessened the

SPAIN | PORTUGAL

N

Approximate Line
of Demarcation,
Treaty of
Tordesillas, 1494

0   800   1600 km.

0   600   1000 mi.

_____ Present Border of Brazil
(Portuguese as official language)

▨ Area of Portuguese Speech

FIGURE 5–10

This map depicts the mesh of language and politics in South America. The Treaty of Tordesillas, cosigned by Spain and Portugal in 1494, established the political basis for the present linguistic pattern in South America. Portugal was awarded the eastern part of the continent, and Spain the west. The Portuguese language was implanted in Portuguese territory, and today it has diffused westward from its source.

possibility of coordinated slave revolts. The result seems to have been the early acceptance of Africanized English as the speech of American blacks. Almost up to the present day, American Indians have been subjected to linguistic assaults from the dominant culture (see box, "Conquering the Indian with Words"). Large numbers of Indian children have traditionally been taken from their families and placed in special boarding schools often hundreds of miles from their homes. In these schools, run by the white-controlled Bureau of Indian Affairs, the Indian children have often been forbidden on pain of punishment to speak their own language.

Language and nationalism

In Europe, speech and nationality became increasingly synonymous after the early 1800s. As a result, European political boundaries often coincide with linguistic borders, as Figure 5-11 shows. This concept has spread to other parts of the world. In this context, it is not surprising that many colonial peoples, on freeing themselves from imperial control, have tried to free themselves from the **colonial languages** as well. For newly independent third-world nations, throwing off a colonial language has presented certain problems. Although most of these countries want to adopt a single native tongue as their national language, such an approach is often unrealistic for several reasons. When the European powers claimed their empires in Asia and Africa, they drew borders with little or no regard for linguistic boundaries. As a result, the ex-colonial nations must cope with these arbitrarily drawn borders. Their boundaries typical-

---

CONQUERING THE INDIANS WITH WORDS

Wilfred Pelletier, an Odawa Indian, was born on Manitoulin Island, Ontario, Canada. He remembers what problems language caused him when, as a child, he first had to leave the Indian reservation and enter the English-speaking world that surrounded and dominated it:

"Many of us as children . . . were not even permitted to speak our own language. Of course, we still tried to speak our own language, but we were punished for it. Four or five years ago they were still stripping the kids of their clothes up around Kenora and beating them for speaking their own language. It is probably still happening in many other institutions today. I was punished several times for speaking Indian not only on the school grounds but off the school grounds and on the street, and I lived across from the school. Almost in front of my own door my first language was forbidden me, and yet when I went into the house my parents spoke Indian.

"Our language is so important to us as a people. Our language and our language structure related to our whole way of life. How beautiful that picture language is where they only tell you the beginning and the end, and you fill in everything, and they allow you to feel

how you want to feel. Here we manipulate and twist things around and get you to hate a guy. The Indian doesn't do that. He'll just say that some guy got into an accident, and he won't give you any details. From there on you just explore as far as you want to. You'll say: 'What happened?' and he'll tell you a little more. 'Did he go through the windshield?' 'Yep' He only answers questions. All of the in-between you fill in for yourself as you see it. We are losing that feeling when we lose our language at school. We are taught English, not Indian, as our first language. And that changes our relationship with our parents. All of a sudden we begin saying to our parents 'you're stupid.' We have begun to equate literacy [in English] with learning, and this is the first step down. It is we who are going down and not our parents, and because of that separation we are going down lower and lower on the rung because it is we who are rejecting our parents; they are not rejecting us. The parents know that, but they are unable to do anything about it. And we take on the values, and the history of somebody else."

From Wilfred Pelletier, "Childhood in an Indian Village," in Satu Repo (ed.), This Book Is About Schools, pp. 23–24. Copyright © 1969 by Pantheon Books, a Division of Random House, Inc. With permission.

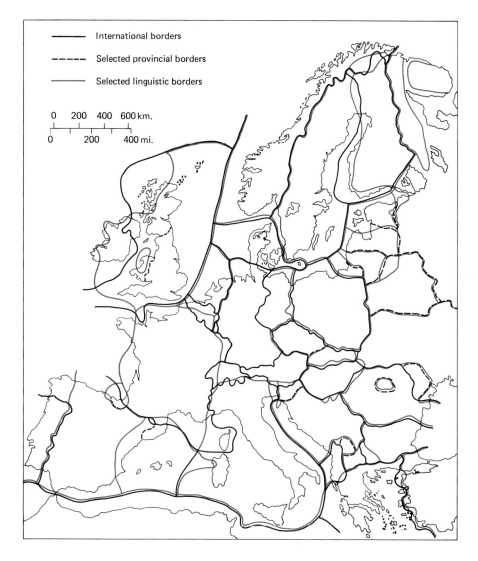

FIGURE 5-11
This map presents political borders and language borders in Europe. Note the close correspondence between the two types of borders today. Why are linguistic and political borders more similar in eastern Europe than in the western part?

ly encompass peoples speaking many different native languages.

Such polyglot nations are difficult to administer. National or tribal jealousies can easily explode if governments single out one native language as the official national speech. Moreover, the adoption of a native language can isolate an underdeveloped country from the huge body of scientific writings in Indo-European languages, which were easily accessible through the rejected colonial tongue.

However, retention of the colonial language causes even more serious difficulties. The vast mass of the population does not know the colonial language and would have to learn it as a foreign language. Still more serious, the colonial language itself represents a bitter and humiliating national experience. Retaining it simply emphasizes that a nation has broken with its own cultural roots. Political decisions like this are of great significance for both the fate of a language and the destiny of a culture.

A language's legal status in the area where it is spoken can greatly influence its rise or fall. A language is most likely to survive when it is the official language of a nation. Languages such as French (in France), English (in the United Kingdom, the United States, and several other countries), and Portuguese (in Brazil and Portugal) enjoy this position. At the opposite extreme are minority languages within nations that grant them no legal standing or where government forces work actively to exterminate them. The fate of such minority tongues is often a gradual death.

An unofficial suppression of minority languages has occurred in the United States. As late as 1910, one out of every four Americans could speak some language other than English with the skill of a native. This was a result of the mass immigrations from Germany, Polish-speaking lands, Italy, Russia, China, and many other foreign areas. By the 1980s, much of this linguistic diversity has given way to English, partly because these imported languages lacked legal status. Only Spanish-speaking immigrants experienced any long-term success in preserving their speech in the United States. They achieved this, however, at the price of discrimination and lower socioeconomic status. Linguistically, America has been not a melting pot, but rather a destroyer of languages.

The Soviet Union has, superficially at least, taken a different approach to its large number of diverse linguistic minorities. The boundaries of many political subdivisions within the country are based on language. The fifteen largest linguistic groups occupy separate republics, equivalent to states within the United States. Ukrainian speakers live in the Ukrainian Soviet Socialist Republic, the speakers of Latvian in the Latvian Soviet Socialist Republic, and so on. Smaller linguistic groups, although not granted full republican status, are recognized politically in subdivisions that include Autonomous Soviet Socialist Republics, autonomous *oblasts*, and national *okrugs*. Although the Soviet system is designed to preserve linguistic distinctiveness, it seems to have masked a campaign of Russianization. All schools in the Soviet Union require years of instruction in Russian, and the best jobs generally require fluency in the Russian language.

Even in polyglot states that tolerate or give full legal standing to minority languages, the trend is often toward assimilation into the majority linguistic group. This is true in Finland, where Swedish retreats before Finnish, and in the United Kingdom, where Celtic languages have declined (see Figure 5-12). Geographer Keith Buchanan refers to the Celtic decline as cultural "liquidation" and feels it is in part a side-effect of industrialization. He believes the English used their educational system, which forbade the use of Welsh and other Celtic tongues, to acculturate the Celts and convert them into a loyal labor force for the mines and factories.

Language and religion

Language and religion are often closely associated, expanding and contracting together. Perhaps Arabic provides the best example of this cultural link. Arabic spread from its original core area on the Arabian peninsula with the Muhammadan faith. Had it not been for the evangelical fervor of the Muslims, Arabic would not have spread so widely. The other Semitic languages also correspond to particular religious groups. Hebrew-speaking people are of the Jewish faith, and the Amharic speakers in Ethiopia are Coptic Christians. Indeed, we can attribute the preservation and revival of Hebrew to the tenacity of the Jewish faith.

Certain languages have even acquired a religious status. Latin survived mainly as the ceremonial language of the Roman Catholic Church and Vatican City. In non-Arabic Muslim lands, such as Iran, Arabic is still

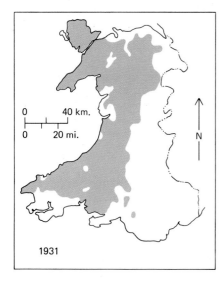
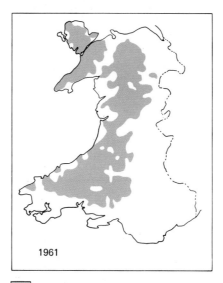
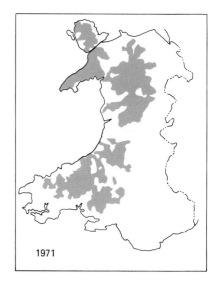

80% or more of the population
(over three years of age)
able to speak Welsh

used in religious ceremony. Even in English, the seventeeth-century language of the King James Bible, replete with *thee, thou,* and various second-person singular verb forms, survives in spoken prayers:

Great religious books can also shape languages by providing them with a standard form. Luther's translation of the Bible led to the standardization of the German language, and the Koran is the model for written Arabic. The appearance of a hymnal and the Bible in the Welsh language greatly aided the survival of that Celtic tongue.

Economics and language

Economic forces also help transform linguistic maps. Languages often migrate along transportation routes. Railroads and highways usually spread the languages of the cultural groups who build them, sometimes spelling doom for the speech of technologically less-advanced peoples whose lands are suddenly opened to outside contacts. The Trans-Siberian Railroad, built around the turn of the century, spread the Russian language eastward to the Pacific Ocean. The Alaska Highway through Canada has carried English into Amerindian refuges. At present, the construction of highways into Brazil's remote Amazonian interior threatens the Indian languages of that region.

In other cases, languages may develop or expand largely because of commercial needs. When groups from different linguistic backgrounds transact business, **pidgin** languages often result. These consist of relatively few words, some borrowed from each language group involved. The word *pidgin* derives from a Chinese pronunciation of the English word *business.* Because England was so widely involved in trade during its colonial era, many pidgin languages are simplified forms of English. In other commercial situations, one existing language is elevated to the status of **lingua franca**, or language of communication and commerce, over a wide area where it is not a mother tongue. The Bantu tongue Swahili enjoys this status in much of East Africa.

FIGURE 5–12

Retreat of the Welsh Language in the mid-twentieth century. Welsh is a Celtic Indo-European language spoken in the region of Wales. For centuries the Welsh have been dominated by English-speaking people in the United Kingdom. As a result, the language is dying. Between 1931 and 1961 the number of Welsh speakers declined from 900,000 to 660,000, and by 1971 only 542,000 Welsh speakers remained. The 1981 estimate is 489,000. Meanwhile, the district known as the *Bro Gymraeg*, where Welsh is spoken, shrank and began to fragment. English is penetrating along the coast and valleys, causing Welsh to retreat into the hilliest terrain. (Based on data in D. Trevor Williams, "A Linguistic Map of Wales According to the 1931 Census, with Some Observations on Its Historical and Geographical Setting," *Geographical Journal*, 89 (1937), 146–151; Emrys Jones and Ieuan L. Griffiths, "A Linguistic Map of Wales, 1961," *Geographical Journal*, 129 (1963), 192–196; and E. G. Bowen and H. Carter. "The Distribution of the Welsh Language in 1971: An Analysis," *Geography*, 60 (1975), 1–15.)

The Linguistic Landscape: Names on the Land

The cultural landscape, the visible man-made landscape, bears the imprint of language in various ways. Figure 5-13 shows one example of a linguistic landscape. Most striking perhaps are the names people have placed on the land, the names they have given to settlements, terrain features, streams, and various other aspects of their surroundings. These place-names, or **toponyms,** often directly reflect the spatial patterns of language, dialect, and national origin. Toponyms become part of the cultural landscape when they are placed on one of the signs and placards that dot the countryside. As you drive through English-speaking portions of North America, you read highway signs such as "Huntsville City Limits," "Harrisburg 25," "Ohio River," "Newfound Gap, Elevation 5048," or "Entering Cape Hatteras National Seashore." For the linguistic geographer, toponyms often provide an excellent visible index to the distribution of cultural traits.

Many place-names consist of two parts—the **generic** and the specific. For example, in the American place-names we listed above—Huntsville, Harrisburg, Ohio River, Newfound Gap, and Cape Hatteras—the specific names are *Hunts, Harris, Ohio, Newfound,* and *Hatteras.* The generic parts, which tell what kind of place is being described, are *ville, burg, river, gap,* and *cape.*

Generic names are of greater potential value to the cultural geographer than are specific names. Generic names appear again and again throughout a culture region. There are literally thousands of generic place-names,

FIGURE 5–13
Language dominates a street scene in Japan. The characters used to write Japanese have been borrowed from Chinese script. The result is a distinctive linguistic landscape.

and every culture or subculture has its own distinctive set of them. They can be particularly valuable in tracing the spread of a culture, and they often aid in the reconstruction of culture regions of the past. Sometimes they provide information about changes that people once wrought in their physical surroundings. We will look at each of these ways cultural geographers use generic place-names.

Generic toponyms of the United States

The three previously mentioned dialects of the eastern United States (Figure 5-4)—Northern, Midland, and Southern—illustrate the value of generic toponyms in cultural geographical detective work. For example, New Englanders, speakers of the Northern dialect, frequently used the term *center* in the name of the town or hamlet near the center of a township. Outlying settlements then bore the prefix *east, west, north,* and *south* with the specific name of the township as the suffix. Thus in Randolph Township, Orange County, Vermont, we find settlements named Randolph Center, South Randolph, East Randolph, and North Randolph. These generic usages and duplications are peculiar to New England, and we can locate colonies founded by New Englanders as they migrated from their homeland by looking for such place-names in other parts of the country. Westward from New England—through upstate New York, Ontario, and into the upper Midwest—we can observe a trail of "Centers" and name duplications that clearly indicate their path of migration and settlement (Figure 5-14). Thus we can see the toponymic evidence of New England in areas as far afield as Walworth County, Wisconsin—where Troy, Troy Center, and East Troy are clustered. Other

FIGURE 5-14
The migration of New Englanders and the spread of the Northern dialect is revealed by generic place-names. Two of the most typical place-name characteristics in New England are the use of *Center* in the names of the principal town in a township and the tendency to duplicate the names of settlements within townships by adding the prefixes *East, West, North,* and *South* to the town name. As the concentration of such place-names suggests, Massachusetts, the first New England colony, is where these two New England traits originated. Note how these traits moved westward with New England settlers, but thinned out rapidly to the south, in areas not colonized by New Englanders. Some of the names on this map come from nineteenth-century atlases and are no longer in use.

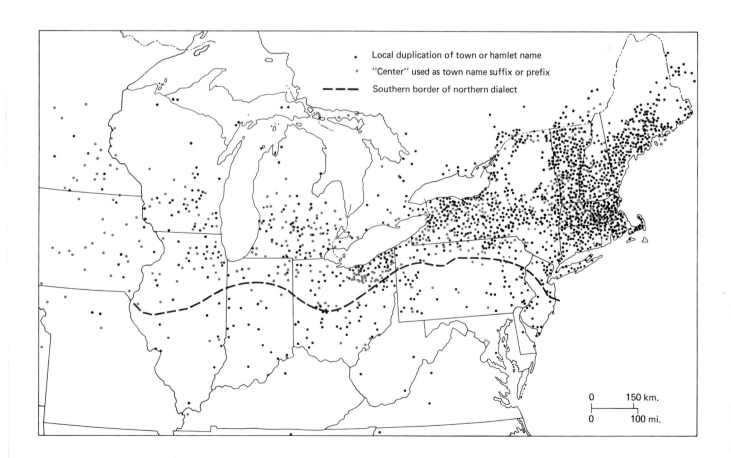

- Local duplication of town or hamlet name
- "Center" used as town name suffix or prefix
- Southern border of northern dialect

0   150 km.

0   100 mi.

W.T.R. Pryce. "Migration and the Evolution of Culture Areas: Cultural and Linguistic Frontiers in North-East Wales, 1750 and 1851," *Transactions, Institute of British Geographers*, 65 (1975), 79–108.

George R. Stewart. *Names on the Land: A Historical Account of Place-Naming in the United States*, Boston: Houghton Mifflin, 1958.

Peter Trudgill. "Linguistic Geography and Geographical Linguistics," *Progress in Geography: International Reviews of Current Research*, 7 (1975), 227–252.

Philip L. Wagner. "Remarks on the Geography of Language," *Geographical Review*, 48 (1958), 86–97.

Robert C. West. "The Term 'Bayou' in the United States: A Study in the Geography of Place Names," *Annals, Association of American Geographers*, 44 (1954), 63–74.

Ronald Wixman. *Language Aspects of Ethnic Patterns and Processes in the North Caucasus*, University of Chicago, Dept. of Geography Research Paper No. 191, 1980.

Gordon R. Wood. *Vocabulary Change: A Study of Variation in Regional Words in Eight of the Southern States.* Carbondale and Edwardsville, Ill.: Southern Illinois University Press, 1971.

Wilbur Zelinsky. "Generic Terms in the Place Names of the Northeastern United States," *Annals, Association of American Geographers*, 45 (1955), 319–349.

Chapter-opening photo: A praying member of the Tenri sect uses symbolic hand gestures in Osaka, Japan.

Religious Realms

6

Your first reaction to a chapter on the geography of religions may well be: "What does geography have to do with religious faith?" You might be inclined to award the study of religion in its entirety to philosophers and theologians—after all, the word *theology* means literally "the study of God," while the exact original Greek meaning of *geography* is "description of the earth." It probably never crossed your mind that geographers might also have a legitimate interest in this topic. And, admittedly, cultural geographers do not deal with personal religious experience, the very heart of religion.

Still, religion is part of culture. Indeed, in some cultures, religion is the essential trait, the one about which the other aspects of life are arranged. **Religion**, a set of beliefs and practices designed to allow humans to achieve mental and physical harmony with the powers of the universe, has been an essential aspect in the development of culture. In some cultural groups, religion has amounted to little more than a protective buffer between humans and the mysterious, potentially destructive forces of nature. Others have, over centuries, developed highly articulated systems of belief with elaborate moral codes.

The appropriateness of the study of religion in cultural geography will be revealed through our five themes. Religion differs from one place to another, producing variations that can be mapped as culture regions. These spatial variations were produced by cultural diffusion and reflect a complex interplay between religion, the environment, and other aspects of culture. In turn, the spatial pattern of religion is visibly imprinted on the cultural landscape. You will agree after reading this chapter, we believe, that religion is not only relevant to cultural geography, but that to ignore it would produce a greatly distorted spatial view of culture. Religion is an essential hue in the human mosaic.

Religious Culture Regions

Since students of culture have often ranked religion as one of the more important shapers of people's values and customs, cultural geographers have frequently used religion to define culture regions. Both formal and functional regions can be devised for religion.

Some religions are highly organized spatially, having created an elaborate political hierarchy of subdivisions, each occupying a specific piece of territory—that is, functional culture regions. Perhaps no other faith has developed such regions as fully as has the Roman Catholic Church. This religious group has extended a network of administration and service over most of the inhabited earth. The basic Catholic functional region is the *parish*, under the care of a priest. Anywhere from several tens to several hundreds of parishes comprise a *diocese*, administered by a bishop who has headquarters in a principal city, or *see*, located within the region. Several dioceses, usually about four, form an *archdiocese*, under the direction of an archbishop. Through these functional regions, the Catholic Church operates a variety of religious services, including hospitals, convents, schools, seminaries, and parish churches. Clearly, such religious organization of space is of interest to the cultural, and particularly the political, geographer.

We can devise all kinds of formal culture regions based on religion. We may, for instance, define culture regions on the basis of a single religious trait. An example would be a map of all areas where **monotheism**, the worship of a single god, is prevalent. We would find that much of the world is in such a culture region, since monotheism is typical of a number of major religions. We may choose instead to set up religious culture regions based on a combination of traits. The most basic kind of multitrait formal religious culture region depicts the spatial distribution of generally acknowledged religious groups, such as Christians, Jews, Muslims, and Hindus. Figure 6-1 reveals the worldwide patterns of such groups. On a different scale, a similar map, Figure 6-2, shows the distribution of the leading Christian **denominations** in the United States. The boundaries of formal religious culture regions such as these, like most cultural borders, are rarely sharp. Persons of different faiths live in the same province or town, and individuals can belong to a number of different religious sects in a lifetime. Religions, competing with one another, adopt the traits of other religious groups. Geographer Wilbur Zelinsky suggests, for instance, that America's "imported" religions, including Catholicism, Judaism, and various sects of Protestantism, are becoming increasingly Americanized. That is, they now resemble one another much more than they resemble the same religions in Europe.

There are two major categories of religion, both of which are further divided into various groups, sects, and denominations. The first category includes **universalizing religions**, those that actively seek new members and have as a goal the conversion of all humankind. Universalizing religions instruct their faithful to spread the Word to all the earth, using

FIGURE 6–1

The world distribution of major religions is shown on this map. Which religions cover the largest geographic area? Do these religions also have the largest number of followers?

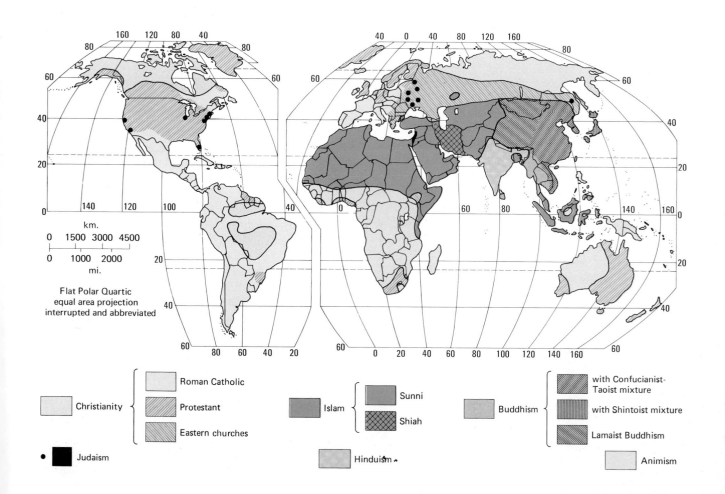

km.
0 1500 3000 4500

0 1000 2000
mi.

Flat Polar Quartic
equal area projection
interrupted and abbreviated

Christianity
Roman Catholic
Protestant
Eastern churches

• Judaism

Islam
Sunni
Shiah

Hinduism

Buddhism
with Confucianist-Taoist mixture
with Shintoist mixture
Lamaist Buddhism

Animism

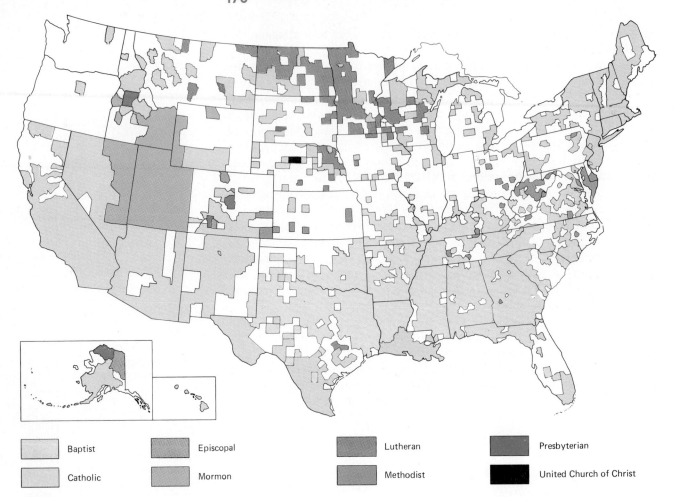

Baptist		Episcopal		Lutheran		Presbyterian	
Catholic		Mormon		Methodist		United Church of Christ	

FIGURE 6–2

Leading Christian denominations in the United States are shown by countries. In the shaded areas, the church indicated claimed 50% or more of the total church membership. The most striking features of the map are the "Baptist belt" through the South, a Lutheran zone in the upper Midwest, Mormon (Latter-Day Saints) dominance in Utah, and the zone of mixing in the Midland area from Pennsylvania through Nebraska and Kansas. The Roman Catholic presence is probably exaggerated in some areas, especially the West, because of the church's more inclusive membership criteria. Can you explain the religious pattern in Louisiana, Florida, and Illinois? (Redrawn with permission from Douglas W. Johnson, Paul R. Picard, and Bernard Quinn, *Churches and Church Membership in the United States: 1971,* Washington, D.C.: Glenmary Research Center. Copyright © 1974 by the National Council of the Churches of Christ in the USA, Inc.; with modifications; and Dean R. Louder and Lowell Bennion, "Mapping Mormons Across the Modern West," in Richard H. Jackson (ed.), *The Mormon Role in the Settlement of the West,* Provo, Utah: Brigham Young University Press, 1978, 164.)

one method or another to convert the heathen. The Gospel of Matthew, for instance, urges: "Go ye therefore, and teach all nations, baptizing them in the name of the Father, and of the Son, and of the Holy Ghost: teaching them to observe all things whatsoever I have commanded you." The Koran tells Muslims to "do battle against them until there be no more seduction from the truth and the only worship be that of Allah."

Contrasted to universalizing religions are **ethnic religions**, each of which is identified with some particular ethnic or tribal group and does not seek converts. Universalizing religions grow out of ethnic religions—the evolution of Christianity from its parent Judaism is the primary example. This change usually occurs within an ethnic religion when a charismatic leader or reformer emerges whose revelations are so profound and whose personality is so dynamic that persons beyond the immediate cultural group are attracted. Once the evangelical spirit of such a universalizing religion is spent, a fragmentation and reversion to ethnic status sometimes occurs.

Christianity

Christianity is by far the largest universalizing religion, both in area and in number of believers. From its humble Palestinian beginnings as a reform movement within the ethnic religion Judaism, the Christian faith spread across a large part of the earth, winning countless millions of converts and overrunning whole cultures. Early converts carried it to Greek lands, and from there to many other parts of the world. At a very early date, however, Christianity began to fragment into separate churches. A major schism between Eastern and Western Christianity became final in A.D. 1054, when the Eastern leaders were excommunicated by the Roman Pope. The Eastern Church, in turn, split repeatedly into a number of local Christian groups. One of these, the Eastern Orthodox Church, found mainly in the Greek- and Slavic-speaking areas of eastern and southeastern Europe, fragmented into a variety of national sects, including Greek Orthodoxy and Russian Orthodoxy. Since the late 1940s, Eastern Orthodoxy, under considerable governmental pressure from Communist regimes in the Slavic countries, has retreated toward the Grecian refuge from which it spread a thousand years ago. Other branches of Eastern Christianity include the Coptic Church, originally a nationalistic church of Christian Egyptians, which survives today mainly among the highland peoples of Ethiopia; and the Maronites, Semitic descendants of seventh-century heretics who retreated to a mountain refuge in Lebanon. Remnants of the Nestorian Church, derived from an even earlier "heresy" concerning the dual personality of Christ, can presently be found in the mountains of Kurdistan north of the Fertile Crescent and in India's Kerala State. The Nestorian Church was largely destroyed by the Asiatic conqueror Tamerlane in the Middle Ages. Though Maronites and many Nestorians acknowledge the supremacy of the Roman Pope, they continue to remain separate churches.

The Western or Roman Catholic Church rose to prominence in western and central Europe by sending missionaries to convert the Germanic and Celtic peoples (Figure 6-3). Western Christianity splintered also, most notably in the Protestant breakaway of the 1500s. Since then, the Roman Catholic Church has remained strongly unified, but Protestantism has tended from its beginnings to divide into a bewildering array of sects. Both Catholic and Protestant missionaries have worked tirelessly to spread Christianity to other parts of the world.

The map of religious groups in the United States vividly reflects the fragmented nature of Western Christianity (see Figure 6-2). Early policies

FIGURE 6-3

Each religion has its own set of rituals, pageants, and symbols. The celebrations of the Roman Catholic Church are especially rich in pomp and display. In this procession, the pope is surrounded by attendants and church officials in costumes designed centuries ago. What religious symbols, costumes, and art can be seen in your community?

of official religious toleration in Rhode Island and Pennsylvania encouraged oppressed religious groups to emigrate to America. The numerous faiths imported from Europe were later joined by Christian sects developed in America. The American frontier was a breeding ground for new religious groups, as individualistic pioneer sentiment found expression in new Christian denominations. The number of denominations in the United States today is considerable. Moreover, many of these groups, though united at the national level, are split at the regional or congregational level. In numerous parts of the country, a relatively small community may contain the churches of half a dozen religious groupings, with individual families sometimes split along religious lines. In addition, a single family member may belong to a number of these churches in his or her lifetime.

As a result of this local fragmentation and mixing, the religious map of the United States displays less regionalization of faiths than is found in much of the rest of Christendom. Still, we can find some patterns in Figure 6-2. In a broad "Bible belt" across the South, Baptist and other conservative fundamentalist denominations are dominant, and Utah is at the core of a Mormon realm. A Lutheran belt stretches from Wisconsin westward through Minnesota and the Dakotas, and Roman Catholicism dominates southern Louisiana, the southwestern borderland, and the heavily industrialized areas of the Northeast. The Midwest is a thoroughly mixed zone, though Methodism is generally the largest single faith.

Another way of mapping formal religious regions in the United States is to cut across denominational lines and group churches and sects by philosophy, intensity, and local diversity. Geographer James R. Shortridge used such an approach, and Figure 6-4 shows some of the results he obtained. Dr. Shortridge divided the individual churches into "liberal"

FIGURE 6–4
Some regional religious types in the United States. These regions were devised by measuring (1) the relative degree of liberalism and conservatism, (2) the strength of religious belief or commitment, and (3) the degree of religious diversity within an area. The classification crosses denominational lines to some extent. For example, Southern Baptists are considered "conservative," while Northern Baptists are "liberal." Compare the Southern "Bible Belt" of intense, conservative Protestantism with the Lower Southern culture region shown in Figure 1–5. Geographer James R. Shortridge prepared this map using the same data as in Figure 6–2, correcting some of the omissions and exaggerations and reorganizing denominational groupings. (Derived in part from James R. Shortridge, "A New Reorganization of American Religion," *Journal for the Scientific Study of Religion,* 16 (1977), 146–147. Canadian areas were added by Jordan, without statistical basis.)

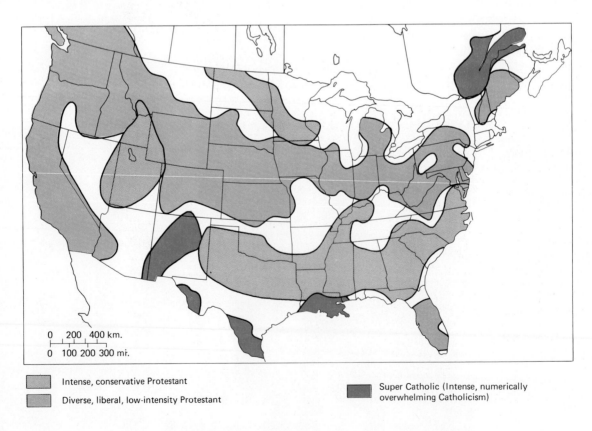

Intense, conservative Protestant

Diverse, liberal, low-intensity Protestant

Super Catholic (Intense, numerically overwhelming Catholicism)

and "conservative" categories. Some Baptist, Methodist, and Lutheran sects, for example, were judged to be liberal, while others, such as the Lutheran Church-Missouri Synod, the Southern Baptist, and the Free Methodist, were placed in the conservative category. Measurements were made to determine how many churches were present in each county and how strong religious belief or commitment was. The results revealed a Lower Southern "Bible Belt" of intense, conservative Protestantism; a northern belt of diverse, liberal, low-intensity Protestantism; and several "Super Catholic" areas, where the Roman Catholic Church was overwhelmingly dominant.

Islam

Islam, another great monotheistic, universalizing faith, claims perhaps as many as 500 million followers. Like Christianity, Islam originated among Semites of the Middle East. It arose in western Arabia in the seventh century. With militant fervor, Arabs spread it westward across North Africa and eastward through the Fertile Crescent (Figure 6-5). Arab warriors also carried Islam into the Indo-European-populated highlands of the Middle East, mainly Iran and Afghanistan, and beyond into the Indus Plain of the Indian subcontinent. Figure 6-6 maps the Old World religious hearths and diffusions. In later centuries, Muslim missionaries following the trade routes spread the faith as far as the southern Philippines, Indonesia, the interior of China, and tropical Africa. The Turks accepted Islam from the Arabs and carried it through Asia Minor into parts of southeastern Europe.

Although it is not as severely fragmented as Christianity, Islam too has split into separate groups. Two major sects prevail: the Shiite Muslims,

FIGURE 6–5
Muslims in Senegal, Africa, stop in the street to mark a time of prayer. Each man has unrolled his prayer rug and faces Mecca. This ritual is repeated several times a day throughout the Islamic world. In your area, what kinds of religious practices occur in public places?

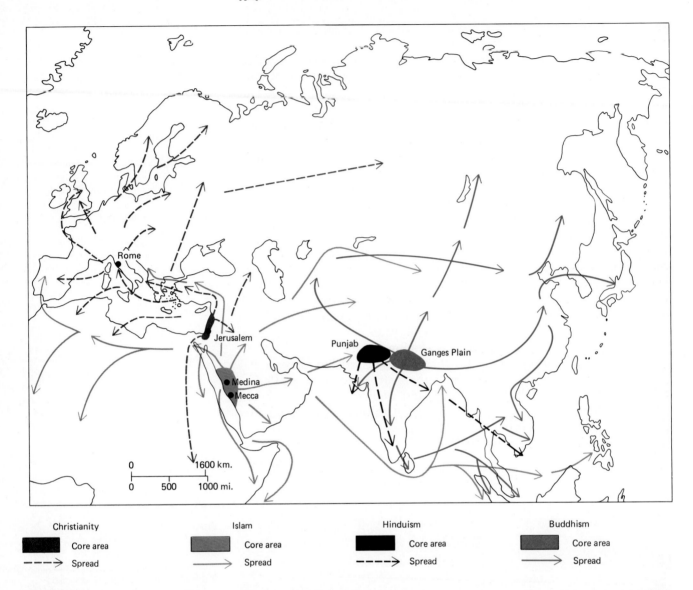

FIGURE 6–6

The origin and dispersal of four major religions are plotted on a map of Eurasia. Christianity and Islam, the two great universalizing monotheistic faiths, arose in southwestern Asia and spread throughout the Old World. Hinduism and Buddhism both originated in the northern reaches of the Indian subcontinent and were widely diffused.

living mainly in Iran and parts of Iraq and numbering about 50 million; and the Sunni Muslims, forming most of the remaining majority within the Islamic world. Originally, these two groups disagreed on the proper method of appointing a successor to Muhammad after his death.

Judaism

Judaism, the oldest monotheistic faith, is the parent of Christianity and is closely related to Islam. The origins of Judaism lie 4000 years in the past, probably on the fringes of the Fertile Crescent. In contrast to the other monotheistic faiths, Judaism does not actively seek new converts and has remained an ethnic religion throughout most of its existence. It has split into a variety of subgroups, partly as a result of the dispersal of the Jews in Roman times and the subsequent loss of contact between the various colonies. Jews, dispersed to many parts of the Roman Empire, became a minority group wherever they were found. In later times, they spread through much of Europe, North Africa, and even southern Arabia. Those Jews who resided in Spain and Portugal were called the Sephardim, while those in central and eastern Europe were known as the Ashkenazim. The late nineteenth and early twentieth centuries witnessed large-scale Jewish migration from Europe to America. The disaster that befell European Judaism during the Nazi years involved the systematic murder of perhaps a third of the entire Jewish population of the world, mainly Ashkenazim. Europe ceased to be the primary homeland of Judaism as many of the survivors fled overseas, mainly to Israel and America (Figure 6-7).

Judaism has close to 14 million adherents throughout the world. At present, almost half of the World's Jewish population lives in the United States; another 30 percent in Europe and the western Soviet Union; and 20 percent in Asia, mainly Israel. The large majority of American Jews settled in cities and towns rather than rural areas. Most Jews in the larger urban centers, such as New York City, are descendants of Ashkenazim from eastern Europe, especially Poland and Russia, who immigrated between 1880 and 1915. Those found in towns and small cities of the Midwest and the South immigrated largely from Germany in the period before 1880. Low fertility rates among American Jews and increasing intermarriage with gentiles have raised concern about the long-term future of Judaism in America.

Hinduism

Rivaling the Middle Eastern desert as a spawning ground for the world's great religions is northern India, in the plains and foothills adjacent to the Ganges and Indus rivers (see Figure 6-6). The earliest religion to derive from this hearth on the Indian subcontinent was Hinduism, which is at least 4000 years old. Hinduism spread from the Punjab region to dominate the entire Indian subcontinent. Missionaries later carried this faith to Indonesia and other parts of Southeast Asia. Subsequently, most of the overseas areas, with the exception of the Indonesian island of Bali, adopted other religions, while large parts of the Indian subcontinent were converted to Islam. In spite of these losses, Hinduism still claims about

FIGURE 6–7
Three Jewish men are seen in Jerusalem—the historic center of world Judaism. The clothing and beards are typical for orthodox Jewish men, the most traditional group in the Jewish religion. Most Jews in other lands belong to the Conservative or Reform groups.

500 million followers, who compose a large majority of the Indian population. Although Hinduism once displayed universalizing traits, it has long since reverted to the status of an ethnic religion.

Hinduism is decidedly **polytheistic**, involving the worship of hundreds of deities. It also includes features such as the **caste system**, a rigid segregation of people according to ancestry and occupation; the belief in reincarnation; and the veneration of all forms of life, called **ahimsa**, with severe restrictions on killing and eating animals of any kind. However, no standard set of beliefs prevails, and Hinduism has many local forms. Some Hindus are actually monotheistic, others permit the eating of fish, still others venerate military powers and are highly skilled as soldiers.

Buddhism

Buddhism began in the Himalayan foothills of northern India about 500 B.C. as a reform movement within Hinduism. Its founder was Prince Siddhartha, later known as the Buddha (Figure 6-8). The faith is based on the four "noble truths": life is full of suffering; desire is the cause of this suffering; cessation of suffering comes with the quelling of desire; and an "Eight-Fold Path" of proper personal conduct and meditation permits the individual to overcome desire. The resultant state of escape and peace is known as Nirvana.

For centuries, Buddhism remained confined to the Indian subcontinent, but missionaries later carried Buddhism to China (100 B.C.-A.D. 200), Korea and Japan (A.D. 300-500), Southeast Asia (A.D. 400-600), Tibet (A.D. 700), and Mongolia (A.D. 1500). Like Christianity, Buddhism almost completely disappeared from its place of origin, its followers being slowly reabsorbed into Hinduism. In China and Japan, Buddhism fused with native ethnic religions such as Confucianism, Taoism, and Shintoism to form composite faiths (see box, "Buddhism in China"). Southern Bud-

FIGURE 6-8
Kamakura's praying Buddha in Japan attracts many pilgrims and tourists. Compare the style, setting, and size with statutes used in Christian religions.

BUDDHISM IN CHINA

Only centuries after Buddhism first entered China along the central Asian trade routes, it became the common faith of most Chinese. In Ch'ang-an, the great capital of the T'ang dynasty (A.D. 618-907), Buddhism was omnipresent.

Yet as Buddhism profoundly changed Chinese society, so China too changed Buddhism. Unlike Christianity entering "barbarian" Europe, Buddhism invaded a giant, self-contained civilization. China may have affected Buddhism more deeply than Europe affected Christianity.

A few examples will illustrate what happened. Early Chinese translations quickly changed the relatively high position Buddhism had granted women. The "husband supports his wife" became, in Chinese, "The husband controls his wife." "The wife comforts her husband" became "The wife reveres her husband." In addition, the Chinese cult of the family was soon interwoven with Buddhist observances. A typical inscription from a Buddhist temple of the fourth century might read: "We respectfully make and present this holy image in honor of the Buddhas, Bodhisattvas, and pray that all living creatures may attain salvation, and particularly that the souls of our ancestors and relatives may find repose and release."

Among the Chinese masses, Buddhism fused with other popular cults. The Buddhist heavens and hells of India, for instance, were retained, but given a Chinese bureaucratic structure. Over time, Chinese artists transformed the Indian sculptural ideal, the half-naked ascetic, into the potbellied, earthy "happy Buddha" that can be bought in gift shops today.

Such merging of religions is a common occurrence when adherents of one faith attempt to supplant a traditional religion. In this way, spatial variation develops even within the same religious faith, and each culture or subculture places its own distinctive mark on the belief system.

Source: Arthur F. Wright, Buddhism in Chinese History *(Palo Alto, Calif.: Stanford University Press, 1959).*

dhism, dominant in Sri Lanka and mainland Southeast Asia, retains the greatest similarity to the religion's original form, while a special variation known as Lamaism prevails in Tibet and Mongolia. Buddhism's tendency to merge with native religions, particularly in China, makes it difficult to determine the number of its adherents. Estimates range from 170 million to 600 million people. While Buddhism in China has become enmeshed with local faiths to become part of an ethnic religion, elsewhere it retains a decidedly universalizing character. Along with Christianity and Islam, Buddhism remains one of the three great universalizing religions in the world.

Buddhism has won some converts in the United States, making inroads mainly among well-educated young intellectuals. Perhaps the most popular form of Buddhism in America is Zen, derived from Japan and ultimately from China. The essence of Zen Buddhism is acquiring a new way of looking at life and things generally. Zen Buddhists seek to realize the nature of things, the nature of being, and their oneness with the universe. In their search they try to break from the everyday, logical thought processes that, as they see it, shackle and confine the human mind.

Animism

Tribal peoples who do not adhere to any of the world's major ethnic or universalizing religions are usually referred to collectively as **animists**. Animists believe that certain inanimate objects possess spirits or souls. These animistic spirits live in rocks and rivers, mountain peaks and heavenly bodies, forests and swamps. Each tribe has its own characteristic form of animism and has vested a particular set of objects with spirits. Usually a tribal religious figure serves as an intermediary between the people and the spirits. To some other animists, the objects in question do

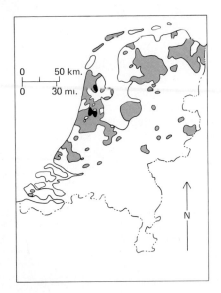

20–50% of population reporting no religious affiliation, 1960

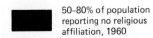
50–80% of population reporting no religious affiliation, 1960

FIGURE 6–9
Secularization in the Netherlands is mapped for 1960. The deepest inroads against traditional religion have been made in the northern part of the Netherlands, formerly a Calvinist Protestant stronghold. In the Catholic south, which is less urbanized and industrialized, few have defected from the Christian faith.

not actually possess spirits, but rather are valued because they have a particular potency to serve as a link between a person and the omnipresent god. It is easy but deceptive to classify such systems of belief as "primitive" or "simple," but they can be extraordinarily complex—far more intricate, in fact, than any set of religious practices we may take part in.

Animism is in retreat almost everywhere. It survives in remote areas where tribal peoples have found refuge, such as interior Africa, the Amazon Basin, and the mountains of New Guinea. Not surprisingly, many of these are the same places we identified as linguistic refuge areas in Chapter 5. As we will see later, many animistic beliefs survive in universalizing religions.

Secularized areas

In some parts of the world, especially in urban and industrial areas, traditional religions are declining. Secularization is taking place in lands as different as India, the Netherlands, and the Soviet Union. Figure 6-9 shows the decline of traditional religion in the Netherlands. In some instances, the retreat from organized religion has resulted from a government's active hostility toward a particular faith or toward religion in general. In other cases, we can attribute the decline to the failure of religions oriented to the needs of rural folk to adapt to the urban scene. Whatever the reason, people are leaving their traditional religions in growing numbers.

For many Americans, religion today plays a minimal role in their daily lives. To some extent, this change is reflected in the way churches are built. Unlike the great cathedrals of Europe's past and the churches in Québec or Mexico today, churches in the United States are almost never built at the functional center of a city. Instead, they are usually constructed on peripheral sites where land values are lower or in the suburbs where fragmenting urban congregations have moved in large numbers. This suggests that our lives, like our cities, revolve around business and commerce, not religious activities. Along with this new pattern of secularization is a growing emphasis on the commercialization of religion itself, as is seen in the Last-Supper tablecloths advertised on a West Virginia radio station, the soaring cost of a funeral, and the creation of drive-in churches.

Quasi-religions, or systems of belief similar to religions but lacking worship services, often fill the emotional vacuum produced by secularization. Perhaps the most widespread quasi-religion is Communism, which owes much to the Judeo-Christian world from which it sprang. The Communist image of a victorious proletariat parallels the Christian belief that "the meek shall inherit the earth," and both Communists and Christians value sexual morality and hard work. A quasi-religion can also take a nationalistic form, as in Nazi Germany. In Israel, Judaism may be evolving toward quasi-religious nationalism.

Religious Diffusion

The distribution of religions (Figure 6-1) is the product of countless innovations and the result of innumerable compromises. To understand how such diffusion occurs, we will look at expansion and relocation diffusion, for religions are spread in both ways. Relocation diffusion is one method of the universalizing religions, which send missionaries to new lands. The European settlers who brought Christianity with them to America are another example of relocation diffusion.

Expansion diffusion

As you recall, expansion diffusion can be subdivided into hierarchical and contagious types. In hierarchical diffusion, ideas are implanted at the top of a social structure and spread down later. They leapfrog across an area, seizing the largest cities, the most important people, while temporarily bypassing "lesser" people, smaller towns, or intervening rural territory. The spread of early Christianity through southern Europe splendidly illustrates hierarchical diffusion, since the early congregations were in towns and cities, temporarily producing a pattern of Christianized urban centers and pagan rural areas. Indeed, traces of this process were left in our language. The Latin word *pagus* ("countryside") is the root of both "pagan" and "peasant," suggesting the "heathen" connotation of rural areas. Contagious diffusion means the spread of ideas in the manner of contagious disease by personal contact through areas and populations without regard to hierarchies. Such diffusion, when applied to religious belief, is called **contact conversion** and is the result of everyday contact between people.

Religious ideas move in the manner of all innovation waves. They weaken with increasing distance from their place of origin and with the passage of time. Barriers often retard or halt their spread. Similarly, religion itself can act as a barrier to the spread of nonreligious innovations. Religious taboos occasionally function as absorbing barriers, preventing diffusion of foods and practices that violate the taboo. In this way, cigarette smoking, an innovation introduced into the United States mainly during World War I, has been unable to penetrate Mormon communities in Utah. Similarly, the relocation diffusion of a religious doctrine encounters an absorbing barrier if laws are passed to forbid immigration by the doctrine's believers. More commonly, barriers are of the permeable type, allowing part of the innovation wave to diffuse through it, but weakening it and retarding its spread. The partial acceptance of Christianity by various Indian groups in Latin America and the western United States, serving in some instances as a camouflage beneath which many aspects of the tribal religions survive, is an example. A permeable barrier can also be seen in the commercial cultivation of tobacco by certain Pennsylvania farmers who belong to sects that forbid smoking.

Relocation diffusion blocked: China and Christianity

When Catholic and Protestant missionaries reached China from Europe and the United States in the nineteenth century, they expected to find fertile ground for conversion—millions of people ready to receive the word of God. However, they had crossed the boundaries of a culture region whose civilization extended back thousands of years and whose basic social ideas left little opening for Christianity. For instance, the missionaries were left in a quandary about how to translate *sin* into Chinese. They could find no equivalent concept in the Chinese language. They tried out a number of possibilities: a word meaning "not good"; a Chinese negative particle, the equivalent of the word *not*; a word carrying the idea of something abhorrent or corrupt. Finally, they settled on the word *tsui*, borrowed from popular Buddhist sects. It meant to do something wrong and was tied to a newly developing Buddhist idea of keeping personal internal ledgers of merit and demerit.

However, even *tsui* could not solve the problem. Centuries before, the Chinese had settled to their own satisfaction the question of what is basic human nature. As they saw the matter, humans were basically good. Evil desires represented merely a deviation from that natural state. People only had to shrug them off and they would return to the basic nature that they share with heaven. Consequently, the idea of "original sin" left the Chinese completely baffled. The Christian image of humankind as flawed, of a gap between creator and created, of the Fall and the impossibility of returning to godhood, was culturally almost incomprehensible to the Chinese. Other aspects of Christianity simply added to the cultural gap. How could the fall from grace come from too much knowledge, a commodity highly prized in China? What was wrong with a giant snake in the garden of Eden to a people whose art was filled with reptilian dragons, the imperial symbol? Even an adequate word for Jehovah, the personalized, single god of the West, was lacking.

In short, many concepts of Christianity fell on rocky soil in China. Moreover, Westerners first appeared neither as conquerors nor as superior beings, but as crude "barbarians." The thought that they would have anything to offer in the realm of ideas did not occur to the Chinese, secure in their own civilization. Only in the early twentieth century, as China's social structure crumbled under Western assault, did a significant, though still small, number of Chinese convert to Christianity. Many of these were "rice Christians," poor Chinese who were willing to become Christians for the rice the missionaries could give them. In 1949, with the triumph of the Communists, Christianity left mainland China, hardly more successful than when it had first arrived. For the geographer, this is a good example of an attempted relocation diffusion of a major religion that simply did not work because of cultural barriers.

Religious Ecology

One of the main functions of many religions is the maintenance of a harmonious relationship between a people and their physical environment. Naturally, then, the physical environment has had a particularly powerful influence on the development of various religions. Environmental influence is most readily apparent in the tribal animistic faiths. In fact, an animistic religion's principal goal is to mediate between the people and the "spirit-infested" forces of nature. Animistic ceremonies often are intended to bring rain, quiet earthquakes, end plagues, or in some other way manipulate environmental forces by placating the spirits believed responsible for these events (see box, "How to Intercede with the Cloud People").

While the physical environment's influence on the major religions is less pronounced than in animistic faiths, it is still evident. Animistic nature-spirits lie behind certain practices found in the great religions, such as the veneration of rivers, mountains, rocks, and forests. For

HOW TO INTERCEDE WITH THE CLOUD PEOPLE

The following songs or prayers derived from animistic groups are typical pleas aimed at influencing environmental conditions. From the Pueblo Indians of the Sia Pueblo, near Bernalillo, New Mexico, a plea for rain:

White floating clouds
Clouds like the plains
Come and water the earth.
Sun embrace the earth
That she may be fruitful.
Moon, lion of the north,
Bear of the west,
Badger of the south,
Wolf of the east,
Eagle of the heavens,
Shrew of the earth,
Elder war hero,
Warriors of the six mountains of the world,
Intercede with the cloud people for us.

From the Haida Indians of coastal British Columbia, Canada, a plea for fair weather:

O good Sun,
Look thou down upon us;
Shine, shine on us, O Sun,
Gather up the clouds, wet, black, under thy arms—
That the rains may cease to fall.
Because thy friends are all here on the beach
Ready to go fishing—
Ready for the hunt.
Therefore look kindly on us, O Good Sun.

Reprinted from American Indian Poetry: An Anthology of Songs and Chants, *edited by George W. Cronyn, with the permission of Liveright Publishing Corporation. Copyright 1934 Liveright Publishing Corporation.*

PROMISES TO KEEP

A somewhat more assertive prayer for rain, by an elderly Anglo-American woman in the rural area of central Texas:

Mr. Creator, up there! Yew hear me! I'm lookin' in yore Book rah't now, an' in it Yew say Yew'll take care of us in time of need. Well, cain't Yew see we're in need rah't now? Cain't Yew hear thuh cows jest a' yellin' and a' bellerin' from bein' so dry? Well, we need Yew. An' we're goin' to hold Yew to yore promiss, so Yew'd better not forget it!

Note: There came a big rain at her place three days later. (From Jean M. Hayes, "Recollections of the Past: A Study of the Early Pioneer Life in Northeastern Erath County," July 1974. Unpublished seminar paper in cultural geography, available in the Special Collections Department of the North Texas State University Library.)

instance, the River Ganges is holy to the Hindus (see Figure 6-10), and the Jordan River has a special meaning to Christians. In the same category is the veneration of high places—for example, Mount Fujiyama, sacred in Japanese Shintoism, and holy volcanos in Mexico. Rocks and stones sometimes retain holy status. The famous Black Stone at Mecca has a special significance for Muslims (see Figure 6-11), who believe that this stone was sent down from heaven by Allah. In fact, it is probably a meteorite. Trees and forests have an honored position in certain major religions. In some areas, Christians use evergreen trees in Christmas celebrations and plant evergreens in cemeteries as symbols of everlasting life—both are relics of the pre-Christian tree worship that covered much of heavily forested northern Europe. We can also see the survival of animistic worship of the heavenly bodies in the placement of the Christian day of worship on Sun-day and the celebration of Christmas near the winter solstice. Perhaps the widespread sacred or semisacred status of cattle is related to the former worship of the moon. This phenomenon, most notable in Hinduism, also appears elsewhere in the Old World. Scholars have suggested that the crescent shape of cattle horns led early humans to associate these animals with the crescent moon.

FIGURE 6–10
Hindus bathe in the River Ganges in Varanasi (Benares), India. Hindus regard this as a holy river. Many travel to Varanasi to cremate relatives along the banks of the river, and millions come for religious festivals.

FIGURE 6–11
This small building, the *kaaba,* houses the sacred Black Stone in Mecca, Saudi Arabia. Pilgrims come from afar to this site, for they believe the stone was sent down from Heaven by Allah, the Islamic god.

Indeed, humans may have originally domesticated cattle because of this animal's sacred quality.

The calendar of major religious celebrations often reflects the importance of seasonal changes. For instance, the Jewish New Year takes place in the fall, at the time when the annual summer drought of the Mediterranean region ends and a new agricultural year begins with the coming of autumnal rains. In the Northern Hemisphere, the celebration of Easter corresponds with the coming of spring. Indeed, the very word *easter* is derived from *Ostar,* a pre-Christian Germanic goddess of spring.

Even today, environmental stress can evoke a religious response not so different from that of animistic cults. Local ministers and priests often attempt to alter unfavorable weather conditions with special services, and there are few churchgoing people in the Great Plains of the United States who have not prayed for rain in dry years. In northeastern China, repeated plagues of crop-destroying locusts gave rise over the centuries to a number of "locust cults," complete with temples. Almost 900 such temples were built, providing a place of worship for the locust and locust-gods (see Figure 6-12). Suitable sacrifices and rituals were developed in an effort to avert the periodic infestations.

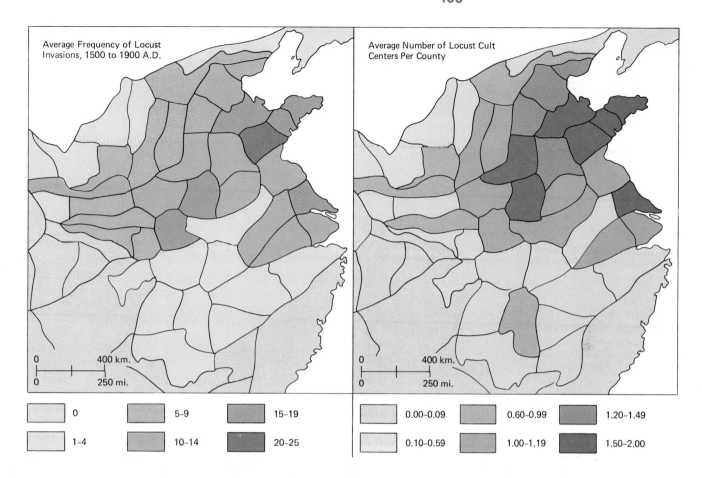

Average Frequency of Locust Invasions, 1500 to 1900 A.D.

0
400 km.
0
250 mi.

Average Number of Locust Cult Centers Per County

0
400 km.
0
250 mi.

0	5–9	15–19
1–4	10–14	20–25

0.00–0.09	0.60–0.99	1.20–1.49
0.10–0.59	1.00–1.19	1.50–2.00

FIGURE 6–12
The frequency of locust infestations and the number of "locust cults" in China are shown here. These cults arose in response to an environmental hazard. The worship of locusts was grafted onto the Buddhist-Confucianist-Taoist composit religion of China. (Redrawn with permission from Shin-Yi Hsu, *Annals, Association of American Geographers,* 59 (1969), 734, 745.)

The environment and monotheism

On a much broader scale, some geographers have sought to explain the origins of monotheism by environmental factors. The three major monotheistic faiths—Christianity, Islam, and Judaism—all have their roots among the desert dwellers of the Middle East. Lamaism, the most nearly monotheistic form of Buddhism, flourishes in the deserts of Tibet and Mongolia. In all of these cases, the people involved (Hebrews, Arabs, Tibetans, Mongolians) were once nomadic herders (see Chapter 3), wandering from place to place in the desert with flocks and herds of livestock. The geographer Ellen Churchill Semple argued in the early twentieth century that such desert-dwelling peoples "receive from the immense monotony of their environment the impression of unity" (see biographical sketch). Semple believed that the unobstructed view of the stars and planets provided by the clear desert skies allowed the herders to see that the heavenly bodies moved across the sky in an orderly, repeated progression. This revelation supposedly suggested to the desert stargazers that a single guiding hand was responsible for the orderly system. Semple, in the classic style of environmental determinism, concluded that desert dwellers "gravitate inevitably into monotheism."

Other possibilistic rather than deterministic explanations have been proposed for the origins of monotheism. Some cultural geographers feel that we should look at the social structure of nomadic herding people for answers. Desert nomads are organized into tribes and clans ruled by a male chieftain who has dictatorial powers over the members of the group.

ELLEN CHURCHILL SEMPLE 1863-1932

Born in Louisville, Kentucky, of a well-to-do family, Semple received a master's degree in history from Vassar and then went to Germany to study. At that time, few women attended universities in Germany, and some claim she had to listen to geography lectures from outside the classroom door. When she returned to America, she brought some of the ideas of German geography. She wrote eloquently and voluminously on environmental determinism. Best known, perhaps, is her book *Influences of Geographic Environment*, published in 1911. Among the ideas presented in her works is the theory that religions are largely the product of the physical environment. Her books gained a very wide readership, both among professional geographers and educated laypersons. She was on the geography faculties at the University of Chicago and Clark University for many years and was a well-known personality in geography.

It is possible that the all-powerful male deity of Middle Eastern monotheism is simply a theological reflection of the all-powerful, secular, male chieftain. Significantly, female deities are usually associated with farming societies, probably because woman represents fertility, while male deities are linked with herding or hunting peoples.

Other geographers have noted that these nomadic peoples lived on the edges of larger, more established culture regions. New ideas, these scholars feel, have a tendency to develop at the borders, not at the core or the regions where older structures and ideas are firmly entrenched. The fact is, however, that we do not know enough about early monotheism to say with certainty why or even where it arose. We are not even certain that the first monotheists were desert nomads. And we do know that some desert dwellers were polytheistic.

Religion and environmental modification

Just as the physical environment can influence religious belief and practice, so the religious outlook of a people can help determine the extent to which they will modify their environment. In the words of Professor Lynn White, "human ecology is deeply conditioned by beliefs about our nature and destiny—that is, by religion." White goes on to suggest that the **teleology** of Judeo-Christian religious tradition teaches that people have dominion over Nature. Teleologists believe the earth was created especially for humans. This view is implicit in God's message to Noah after the Flood promising that "every moving thing that lives shall be food for you, and as I gave you the green plants, I give you everything." The same theme is repeated in the Psalms, where Jews and Christians are told that "the heavens are the Lord's heavens, but the earth he has given to the sons of men." Within the teleological view is the belief that humans are not part of nature, but are separate, forming one member of a God-Nature-Human trinity.

Believing that the earth was given to humans for their use, Christian thinkers in medieval Europe adopted the view that humans were God's helpers in finishing the task of creation. These theologians believed that human modifications of the environment were God's work. Small wonder that the medieval period in Europe witnessed an unprecedented expansion of agricultural acreage, involving the large-scale destruction of woodlands and drainage of marshes. Nor is it surprising that Christian monastic orders, such as the Cistercian Fathers, supervised many of these projects, directing the clearing of forests and the establishment of new agricultural colonies.

Christianity, according to White's view, destroyed classical antiquity's feeling for the holiness of natural things. Subsequently, he argues, scientific advances permitted the Judeo-Christian West to modify the environment at an unprecedented rate and on a massive scale. This marriage of technology and teleology is, White proposes, the root of our modern ecological crisis. By contrast, the great religions of the Orient and many animistic tribal faiths contain teachings and beliefs that are protective of Nature (see box, "The Yanoama World View"). People are part of and at harmony with Nature. Such religions do not threaten the ecological balance, says Professor White.

Geographer Yi-Fu Tuan disagrees. He points to a discrepancy between the stated ideals of religions and reality. Even though China enjoys an "old tradition of forest care" based in its composite religion, the Chinese woodlands have been systematically destroyed through the millennia.

THE YANOAMA WORLD VIEW

We of Judeo-Christian religious heritage need to be reminded that most other cultures do not perceive Humans, God, and Nature as a trinity of distinct entities. The world-view of the Yanoama, an animistic Indian tribe of the Brazilian-Venezuelan borderland, is instructive.

"Religion impinges on all aspects of life, without the conceptual distinction between *man, nature,* and the *divine* that characterizes Judeo-Christianity. No omnipotent God exists. There is no material world surrounding the Yanoama and existing independently of them, no world that they view as capable of being dominated and turned to satisfy their own needs. . . . Mysteriously, man can share a common life with an animal, or even with some natural phenomenon, such as the wind or thunder. People not only live now in intimate association with the monkeys, tapirs, deer, and birds of the forest, but also have been—or might be—these very creatures

"There is an easy transmutability among the Yanoama between what [we] commonly define as different realms: the human, natural, and divine. . . . Thus, adult males share spirits, or souls, with other creatures. Among these, the harpy eagle and the jaguar are particularly prevalent. The alter egos of females are associated spiritually with totally different creatures, such as butterflies."

From William J. Smole, The Yanoama Indians: A Cultural Geography *(Austin and London: University of Texas Press, 1976), p. 23.*

Nor are the Oriental and tribal religions consistently protective of the environment. Buddhism, for example, protects temple trees but demands huge quantities of wood for cremations. Animistic shifting cultivators sometimes make offerings to appease the woodland spirits before destroying huge acreages of forest with machete and fire. Civilization itself, argues Tuan, is the exercise of human power over Nature. Religion can resist but not overcome that exercise.

Other ecologists point out, too, that the Judeo-Christian tradition is not lacking in concern for environmental protection. In the Book of Leviticus, for example, farmers are instructed by God to let the land lie fallow one year in seven and not to gather food from wild plants in that "sabbath of the land."

Religion and environmental perception

Religion can also influence the way people perceive their physical environment. Nowhere is this more evident than in the perception of environmental hazards such as floods, storms, and droughts. Hinduism and Buddhism teach followers to accept such hazards without struggle, to regard them as natural and unavoidable. Christians are more likely to view storm, flood, or drought as unusual and preventable. As a result, they will generally take steps to overcome the hazard. Sometimes, however, Christians see natural disasters as divine punishment for their sins, in which case worshipers feel they can prevent future disasters by repenting.

Within a single major religion, people's relationship with the land can vary from one sect to another. We have already discussed the overall Judeo-Christian view of the God-Nature-Human trinity. A study conducted in several small southwestern settlements in the United States by Florence Kluckhohn suggests that individual religious groups see this trinity differently. The large majority (72 percent) of Spanish-American Catholics interviewed felt that humans are subject to nature. Most Mormons (55 percent) saw humans in harmony with nature, a relationship preserved by proper living and hard work. The most common response from Protestant Anglo-Texans (48 percent) held that humans control nature and can overcome environmental hazards. Two-thirds of the Zuni and Navaho Indians, most of whom cling to animism, favored the view of humans in harmony with natural forces. Similarly, a study by John Sims and Duane Baumann revealed that residents of Alabama, where intense, conservative Protestantism prevails, were more likely to react to a tornado threat fatalistically, relying on God to see them through, while Illinoisans, as adherents of a liberal, low-intensity Protestantism, felt in control of their own destiny and took more measures to protect themselves. Perhaps partly as a result, the mortality rate in tornadoes is markedly lower in the Midwest than in the South.

Cultural Integration in Religion

While the interaction between religious belief and the environment can shape both religions and the land, religious faith is similarly intertwined with other aspects of culture. Spatial variations in religious belief influence and are influenced by social, economic, and political patterns in countless ways. Religions and languages often travel together, and religious belief is sometimes at the root of nationalism. In the economic sphere, religion can determine what crops and livestock are raised by farmers, what foods and beverages people consume, and even what type of employment a person has.

Religion and economy

People make their living in many different ways, and these forms of livelihood vary greatly from one area to another. Religion is partially responsible for these variations. Try to place yourself in the position of the Hindu street sweeper of Calcutta, whose religion discourages him from aspiring to any higher position in life. Try to imagine what job you might get if your town suddenly attracted religious pilgrims from all over the country. Consider the possible economic effect of religious-based food taboos on the agriculture of your area. In these ways and many more, religion and economics are bound together (see box, "A Marriage of Religion and Economy"). This relationship is evident in agriculture.

A MARRIAGE OF RELIGION AND ECONOMY: THE CARGO CULTS OF MELANESIA

Cultural integration is perhaps nowhere more startlingly revealed than in the so-called cargo cults of the western Pacific tropical islands, the area known as Melanesia. There, a religion has arisen based on the hoped-for arrival of Western material goods delivered in American cargo-laden ships. Savior-like Americans will bring the cargo to the islands. Dr. Kal Muller tells of one such cult on the New Hebridean island of Tanna: "On the volcano's rim looms a blood-red cross. Nearby, men with 'U.S.A.' daubed on their bodies shoulder make-believe rifles of bamboo. Soldiers of Christ? Hardly. On the New Hebridean island of Tanna, both cross and marchers herald a hoped-for messiah of material riches—a savior cryptically called John Frum.

"Some followers of the mythical Frum consider him a beneficent spirit; others see him as a god come to earth, or as the "king of America." All believe he will some-

day usher in a prosperous, work-free millennium of unlimited 'cargo'—pidgin English for Western material goods. . . .

"In 1942, World War II reached Tanna's shores. U.S. troops landed on nearby islands, bringing food, arms, prefabricated houses, jobs, and legions of jeeps. . . . But with the war's end, the cargo disappeared, and islanders . . . turned to mock military drills in the hope of luring GIs—and cargo-laden Liberty ships—back to Tanna. . . .

"Although Frum fails to materialize—as has been the case for 35 years—his followers remain devout, often attributing his absence to their own shortcomings or to governmental intervention."

From Kal Muller, "Tanna Awaits the Coming of John Frum," National Geographic Magazine, *145 (1974), 707, 714.*

WINE AND RELIGION IN GERMANY

Even back into prehistoric times in Europe, wine has been linked to religion. In early Christian times, vineyards were introduced into southwestern Germany by Roman monks, who desired ceremonial wine for the holy sacrament. This close attachment of church to wine in Germany left vestiges discernible even today. Among these vestiges are the religious names given to many individual vineyards, names that in turn appear on the wine bottle labels. Some are listed below. Some generic wine names also reveal the link to religion. One of the most famous of these is *Liebfraumilch*: mild, semisweet blends from German Rheinhessen. The name means "milk of the Holy Virgin."

Derived from Hugh Johnson, The World Atlas of Wine (New York: Simon & Schuster, 1971), pp. 124–144.

German Wine District	Town or Village	Name of Vineyard	(Translation)
Rheingau	Rüdesheim	Mönchspfad	("Monks' Path")
Rheingau	Rüdesheim	Magdalenenkreuz	("Cross of Mary Magdalen")
Rheingau	Oestrich	Gottesthal	("God's Valley")
Rheinpfalz	Forst	Jesuitengarten	("Jesuits' Garden")
Rheinpfalz	Forst	Mariengarten	("Virgin Mary's Garden")
Rheinpfalz	Deidesheim	Paradiesgarten	("Garden of Paradise")
Rheinpfalz	Deidesheim	Herrgottsacker	("Lord God's Field")
Mosel	Graach	Himmelreich	("Heaven")
Mosel	Klüsserath	Bruderschaft	("Monastic Brotherhood")
Nahe	Bad Kreuznach	Mönchberg	("Monks' Hill")
Nahe	Niederhausen	Pfaffenstein	("Pope's Rock")
Nahe	Bad Kreuznach	Kapellenpfad	("Chapel Path")
Saar	Wiltingen	Klosterberg	("Convent Hill")

Religion and agriculture. Within some religions, certain plants and livestock, as well as the products derived from them, are in great demand because of their role in religious ceremonies and traditions. When this is the case, the plants or animals tend to spread with the faith. For example, in some Christian sects in Europe and the United States, celebrants drink from a cup of wine that symbolizes the blood of Christ during the sacrament of Holy Communion. The demand for wine created by this ritual aided the diffusion of grape growing from the sunny lands of the Mediterranean to newly Christianized districts beyond the Alps in late Roman and early medieval times. When you drink German Rhine wine, you are benefiting from this diffusion because the vineyards of the Rhine were the creation of monks who arrived from the south between the sixth and ninth centuries (Figure 6-13; see also box, "Wine and Religion in Germany"). For the same reason, Catholic missionaries introduced the cultivated grape to California. In fact, wine was associated with religious worship even before Christianity arose. Vineyard-keeping and wine-making spread westward across the Mediterranean lands in prehistoric times in association with worship of the god Dionysus.

Religion also can often explain the absence of individual crops or domestic animals in an area. The environmentally similar lands of Spain and Morocco, separated only by the Strait of Gilbraltar, show the agricultural impact of food taboos. On the Spanish, Roman Catholic, side of the strait, pigs are common, but they are not found in Muslim Morocco

FIGURE 6–13
A label from a bottle of German Rhine wine depicting a religious connection with the vineyards.

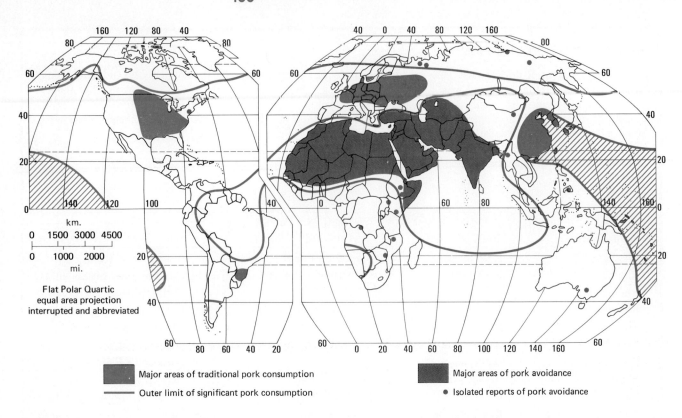

Major areas of traditional pork consumption

—— Outer limit of significant pork consumption

Major areas of pork avoidance

• Isolated reports of pork avoidance

FIGURE 6–14

Consumption and avoidance of pork is influenced by religion. Some religions and churches—such as Islam, Judaism, and Seventh-Day Adventism—prohibit the eating of pork. Cultural groups with a traditional fondness for pork include central Europeans, Chinese, and Polynesians. How can you explain the pattern in North America? (Based in part on Simoons.)

on the African side. The Islamic avoidance of pork underlies this contrast. Figure 6-14 maps the pork taboo. Judaism also has restrictions against pork and other meats, as is stated in the following passage from the Book of Leviticus:

> These shall ye not eat, of them that chew the cud, or of them that divide the hoof: as the camel, because he cheweth the cud, but divideth not the hoof; he is unclean unto you. And the coney, because he cheweth the cud, but divideth not the hoof; he is unclean unto you. And the hare, because he cheweth the cud, but divideth not the hoof; he is unclean unto you. And the swine, though he divide the hoof, and be cloven-footed, yet he cheweth not the cud, he is unclean unto you.

Scholars have attempted to explain the Islamic and Judaic pork taboos in various ways. Some have suggested that these two cultures were primarily concerned with the danger of intestinal parasites (trichinosis), or that they considered pigs unclean. However, it is unlikely that the cause-and-effect relationship between poorly cooked pork and intestinal parasites could have been detected prior to the days of modern medical technology. Other scholars have suggested a theory based on economy and ecology, after observing that pork avoidance is characteristic of the monotheistic faiths that arose among desert nomads. The proponents of this view believe that nomadic herding originated on the borders of the great farming areas of the ancient Middle East, near the Tigris, Euphrates, Nile, and other rivers. Population pressures forced people to settle farther and farther from the river banks, so that eventually some groups lost access to irrigation waters. As we saw in Chapter 3, these people were forced to abandon most crop farming and turn to animal husbandry. The poor quality of the range required them to wander from place to place in the desert, in nomadic fashion, seeking forage for their livestock. Pigs, which were valuable animals to the sedentary farmers of the river valleys, could not travel long distances, and there was little for them to eat in the desert. As a result, the nomad relied instead on sheep, goats, horses, camels, and, in some areas, cattle. Since environmental conditions prevented the nomads from owning pigs, they may have declared pork undesirable in a "sour grapes" reaction. In time, this declaration may have found religious expression as a taboo. Ages later, as a final "revenge" in the seventh century A.D., the Muslim nomads imposed their religion, complete with the pork taboo, on the farming people of the river valleys.

Muslims are also not permitted any alcoholic beverages. The Koran states: "O ye who have believed, wine, games of chance, idols, and divining arrows are nothing but an infamy of Satan's handiwork. Avoid them so that ye may succeed." Christians, however, have failed to reach a consensus on this taboo. Some Christian denominations prohibit all consumption of alcohol, in the belief that it is detrimental to health, welfare, and behavior, while others even use wine in religious ceremonies. In the United States, such groups as the Baptists, Methodists, Mormons, and Seventh-Day Adventists support prohibition, while Roman Catholics, Lutherans, and several other churches tolerate alcohol. The economic imprint of these different attitudes can be seen in a map of "wet" and "dry" areas in the United States. Texas provides an excellent example, since it is religiously diverse and by law allows each community to decide in local-option elections whether alcohol may be sold or served (Figure 6-15). Almost without exception, Catholic and Lutheran areas in Texas are "wet", while Baptist and Methodist counties are "dry."

Religion and fishing. Food taboos also strongly affect the fishing industry. Practices such as the traditional Roman Catholic avoidance of meat on Friday greatly stimulated fishing, since fish became the standard Friday fare in Catholic areas. Indeed, the Christian tradition has always honored fishermen. We can perhaps trace this back to the apostle Peter, a fisherman by profession. The fish was an early symbol of Christianity, initially

FIGURE 6–15
The distributions of religion and alcohol sales in Texas show a spatial correlation. Catholic and Lutheran areas generally choose to be "wet," and Baptist-Methodist areas retain prohibition. Both the Baptist and Methodist churches have traditionally taken a stand against alcoholic beverages. (From *38th Annual Report of the Texas Alcoholic Beverage Commission,* Austin, 1972, p. 49; and *Churches and Church Membership in the United States: 1971,* National Council of Churches, 1974.

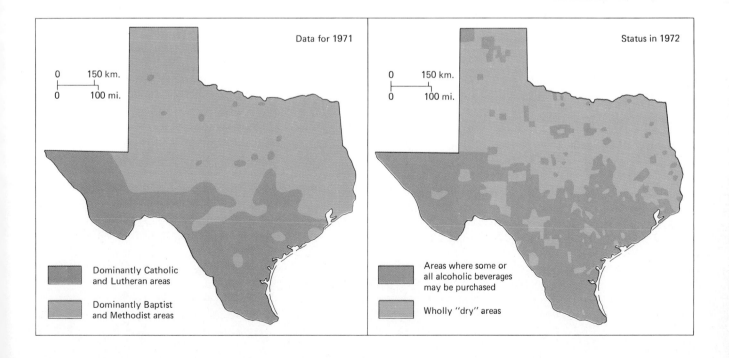

Data for 1971

0 — 150 km.
0 — 100 mi.

■ Dominantly Catholic and Lutheran areas
■ Dominantly Baptist and Methodist areas

Status in 1972

0 — 150 km.
0 — 100 mi.

■ Areas where some or all alcoholic beverages may be purchased
■ Wholly "dry" areas

exceeding the cross in importance. Use of this symbol stimulated the fishing industry, particularly in Catholic countries, and a lively trade in shipping preserved fish from coast to interior developed.

Other cultures place religious taboos on fish consumption and produce an opposite economic result. Most Hindus will not eat fish. India regularly suffers food shortages and dietary deficiencies while the nearby ocean teems with protein-rich fish. Among Christians, the Seventh-Day Adventists have a finless fish taboo. When missionaries of this church converted the population of Pitcairn Island in the South Pacific to their faith, the island's economic self-sufficiency collapsed, because the people had previously depended heavily on pork and finless fish for their diet.

Religious tourism: the pilgrim trade. For many religious groups, sites of particular importance to the faith have become the goal of **pilgrimages**. Journeys to these places often involve the movement of large numbers of people. Pilgrimages are typical of both ethnic and universalizing religions. They are particularly significant to followers of Islam, Hinduism, Shintoism, and Roman Catholicism.

The sites vary in character: some have been the setting for miracles; some are the source regions of religions or areas where the founders of the faith lived and worked; others contain sacred physical features such as rivers and mountain peaks; and still others are believed to house gods or are religious administrative centers where leaders of the church reside. Examples include the Arabian cities of Mecca and Medina in Islam; Rome and the French town of Lourdes in Roman Catholicism; the Indian city of Varanasi on the holy Ganges River, a goal of Hindu pilgrims; and Ise, the hearth of Shintoism in Japan. The distribution of pilgrimage shrines in Mexico is shown in Figure 6-16.

Religion provides the stimulus for pilgrimage by offering those who participate the reward of soul-purification or the attainment of some desired objective in their lives. Pilgrims often come from great distances

FIGURE 6–16
This map displays the distribution of religious pilgrimage shrines in Mexico and south Texas. These shrines vary greatly in importance and age. Some date from pre-Christian times, and others have arisen in recent years. Pilgrimages are a facet of religious life in most Roman Catholic countries, including Mexico. The concentration of sites in central Mexico corresponds to an area of greatest population density. What kinds of major religious sites are located in the rest of North America and in your own region? (Redrawn with modifications from Mary Lee Nolan, "The Mexican Pilgrimage Tradition," *Pioneer America*, 5, 2 (July 1973), 16, with permission.)

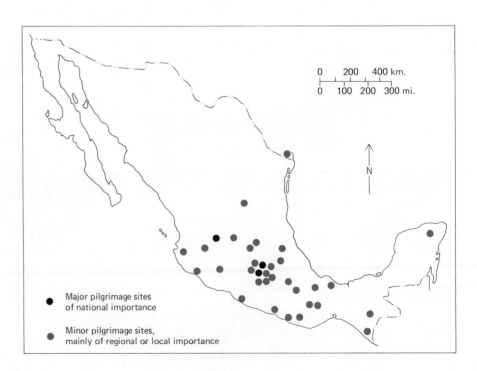

- ● Major pilgrimage sites of national importance
- ● Minor pilgrimage sites, mainly of regional or local importance

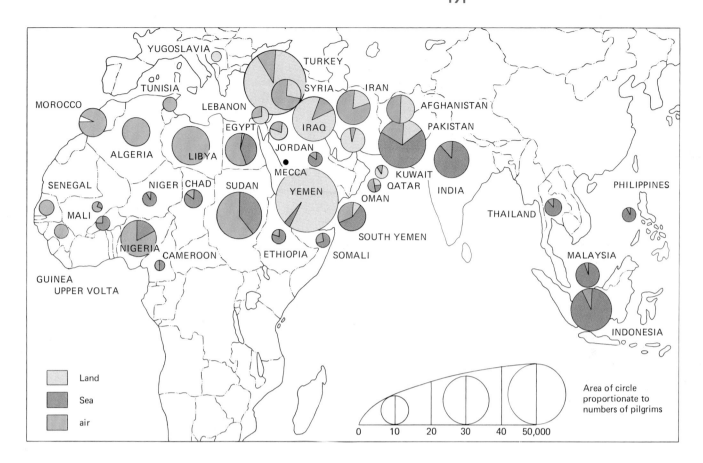

Land

Sea

air

Area of circle
proportionate to
numbers of pilgrims

0   10   20   30   40   50,000

FIGURE 6–17

The pilgrimage of foreign Muslims to Mecca, 1968. 375,000 Muslim pilgrims converged on the holy city of Mecca in 1968, in spite of the blockage of the Suez Canal that resulted from the Arab-Israeli war of the previous year. Saudi Arabians, in whose nation Mecca is situated, are not shown. (After Russell King, "The Pilgrimage to Mecca: Some Historical and Geographical Aspects," *Erdkunde,* 26 (1972), 70.)

to see major shrines. Other sites, of lesser significance, draw pilgrims only from local districts or provinces. Pilgrimages can have tremendous economic impact, since the movement of pilgrims amounts to a form of tourism. In some favored localities, the pilgrim trade provides the only significant source of revenue for the community. Lourdes, a town of 16,000 in the south of France, attracts about 2 million pilgrims each year, many seeking miraculous cures at the famous grotto where the Virgin Mary supposedly appeared. Not surprisingly, among French cities, Lourdes ranks second only to Paris in number of hotels, although most of these are small. Mecca, a small city of 185,000 residents, attracted 375,000 Muslim pilgrims in 1968 from every corner of Islamic culture region, as is shown in Figure 6-17. By land, sea, and air, the faithful come to this hearth of Islam, a city closed to all non-Muslims. As you might expect, such massive pilgrimages have a major impact on the development of transportation routes and carriers. To facilitate the pilgrimage to Mecca and Medina, steamships connect the Arabian port of Jidda with overseas Muslim areas in East Africa, Indonesia, Malaysia, and other lands. Chartered and scheduled airline service is also available to Mecca pilgrims. In medieval Europe, many roads and bridges were built to accommodate pilgrims. Monks often helped maintain these routes and established shelters at regular intervals as way stations. Some of these hospices still survive, as at the summit of St. Gotthard Pass in the Swiss Alps.

Religion and profession. Often religion and employment are closely connected. In Hinduism, persons in each caste traditionally had a

Less than 35% of Catholics regularly attend mass

More than 60% of Catholics regularly attend mass

—— International border

FIGURE 6–18

Attendance at Mass along the Franco-Belgian border, about 1950. The people on both sides of the boundary speak French and share many other cultural traits; yet Catholicism remains a vital force only on the Belgian side. The political border has become a religious border. What developments in the respective countries might help explain this striking pattern? (Adapted from Fernand Boulard, *An Introduction to Religious Sociology*, trans. M. J. Jackson, London: Darton, Longman and Todd, 1960.)

prescribed economic role to play. To follow any occupation other than that dictated by caste was a violation of moral obligations. In southern India alone, over 2000 castes and subcastes developed, most with rigidly determined occupational requirements. The caste system apparently originated about 1500 B.C., when Indo-Europeans invaded and conquered northern India. These conquerors formed a light-skinned, elite upper class, while the vanquished native population was kept by law in a subservient position. From this segregation of conqueror and native grew the caste system. More recently, however, this system has been made illegal. A total correspondence between caste and occupation no longer exists. However, the caste system has by no means disappeared in rural India, where the greater part of the population lives, although it has waned in urban areas.

In medieval Europe, Christians were generally restricted from loaning money for interest. Jews, outcasts in Christian Europe, found most professions closed to them by law. As a result, while most of the Jewish population remained in poverty, individual Jews found an economic niche as moneylenders. They then used this occupation as a capitalist foothold from which they developed skills as retailers, and in time some even became important businessmen.

Religion and political geography

Americans, accustomed by their heritage to the doctrine of separation of church and state, are usually unaware how closely religion and politics are intertwined in much of the world. Religious practices and traits often change abruptly at political boundaries, as along parts of the Franco-Belgian border in western Europe (Figure 6-18), and political parties are often identified with religious denominations.

In some nations, religion has been the rallying point for nationalistic sentiment and has even provided a justification for national existence. In 1947, when Britain granted independence to her colonial holdings in India, the area split to form a Hindu state (India) and a Muslim state (Pakistan). Those who created this division felt that the two religious groups could not coexist peacefully within the same state. Time has since shown that Hindus and Muslims have difficulty living together on the same subcontinent, even in separate states. However, the sizable Muslim population left in India has lived rather peacefully in the dominantly Hindu state in the last three decades. Israel and the Republic of Ireland are two other nations based on religion. In Israel, automatic citizenship is available only to Jews. In cases where religion is an important basis of nationalism, a **state church** is often created. Such a church is recognized by law as the only one in the state, and the government controls both church and state. In Norway, for example, the constitution establishes the Lutheran faith as the state church, and pastors and officials are appointed government employees.

In still other cases, the church is actively involved in governing countries. Such a government is known as a **theocracy**, (see box, "The Mormon Region"). The head of the church is often also the head of state. Vatican City, ruled by the Pope, is a fully independent state occupying parts of Rome. Similar to theocracies, but less rigid, are countries where the secular ruler is the nominal head of the state church, as was true of prerevolutionary Russia. Until 1974, Greek Orthodox bishops were actively involved in the government of Cyprus. The danger for the church in such a situation is that the religion may fall with the government.

THE MORMON REGION: A CASE STUDY IN CULTURAL INTEGRATION

An excellent example of the interworkings of religion, politics, economy, and population is provided by the Mormon culture region in the Great Basin of the American West. Established by members of the Church of Jesus Christ of Latter-Day Saints in 1847, the Mormon culture region spread from the Salt Lake City area to encompass Utah and parts of all bordering states. The population was originally derived from New York and New England, but later immigrants came from Europe and other areas.

Initially, and through most of the nineteenth century, a theocratic government ruled in the Mormon culture region, giving a political expression to the faith. The church leader, Brigham Young, was also the territorial governor of Utah. Repeated efforts were made to create the state of Deseret, to be part of the United States but still under church administration. While the power of the United States government was finally employed to destroy the Mormon theocracy, the tie between church and government remained strong for many years.

In the economic sphere, the church leadership exerted an immense influence on development of the Great Basin area. A goal of economic self-sufficiency was proclaimed. Everything needed in Deseret was to be produced there. Artisans possessing necessary craft skills were actively recruited in Europe and elsewhere. Agricultural colonies were established in southern Utah, the "Mormon Dixie," to produce cotton and other warm-climate crops that did not grow in the colder Salt Lake area. Most facets of the economy were directly or indirectly controlled by the church, even to the point of ownership in some cases. To a remarkable degree, the plan of economic self-sufficiency succeeded, and through organized hard labor the desert of the Great Basin was made to produce abundantly.

The church also profoundly influenced the population geography of the Great Basin. Indeed, the very settlement of the area was undertaken as a result of a decision by church leaders to migrate from Illinois. After colonization of the Salt Lake area, new colonies were founded, also under church direction. Sites for the new colonies were chosen by the church, and even the selection of colonists was made by the religious leaders. From a very early time, the Mormon church has encouraged large families, thereby further influencing the population distribution of the Great Basin.

In this way, an integration of religion, politics, economy, and demography developed in the Great Basin. To this day, the Mormon culture region retains the distinctive imprints of this interplay.

The presence of two hostile religious groups within the same country can lead to disruption, and perhaps even civil war. States currently threatened by religious divisions include Cyprus, where Greek Orthodox Christians and Turkish Muslims are at odds; Lebanon, where Christians and Muslims are fighting a civil war; the United Kingdom, which has sought unsuccessfully to reconcile warring Catholics and Protestants in Northern Ireland; and the Philippines, where Catholics are at war with a Muslim minority on the island of Mindanao (Figure 6-19; see also box, "The Politics of Religion").

In some nations, political parties are linked to particular church groups. As a result, voting returns often duplicate the religious map. Such ties are particularly common in Europe, where political parties have names like Catholic People's Party or Christian Democrats. It is common in these countries for churchgoers to be advised from the pulpit on how they should vote. Even in countries like the United States, where legal separation of church and state is maintained, voting patterns often correspond to religion.

The Religious Landscape

Because religion is so vital an aspect of culture, its impress on the cultural landscape is often quite striking. In some regions, the religious element is the dominant visible evidence of culture, producing what we might call

FIGURE 6–19
Slogans on a wall depicting the political and religious strife in Northern Ireland.

THE POLITICS OF RELIGION: LIVING IN BELFAST

You don't have to be a professional geographer to map the religious politics of Belfast, Northern Ireland. All you have to do is live there. Northern Ireland is torn between a politically powerful Protestant majority and a Catholic minority, between the Catholic Republic of Ireland to the south and England across the Irish Sea, between the guerrilla Irish Republican Army (IRA) of the Catholic community and the paramilitary organizations of the Protestant community, between these two groups and an occupying British army. Belfast, the capital, is an embattled city. Bomb blasts, sniper attacks, and assassinations leave the scent of civil war always in the air.

The separation between Belfast's Catholics and Protestants is almost total. It extends to housing, schools, jobs, and even entertainment. Imagine that you are a resident of the Catholic Falls area. Your bus to work stops only two blocks away, but the bus stop is in the Protestant Shankill district, so you don't take it. You prefer a far longer walk to a bus stop in your "own" area. Right around the corner from your house, the Protestant district begins. You can tell without looking at a map. Why? Because as you pass from Catholic to Protestant areas, the graffiti, the dates and slogans

painted on the walls, change. In some places the change is even more clearly marked by barricades or by carefully painted curbstones and lamp posts, as well as by murals depicting historic flags, emblems, and personalities from one of the religious communities.

In religiously segregated Belfast, intermarriage between Protestants and Catholics is rare and strongly disapproved of by both communities. Children are educated in segregated schools, and visits to friends and relatives, as surveys have shown, are almost entirely confined to people of one's "own" outlook. So if you were an inhabitant of Belfast, where you walked and talked, or even whether you lived or died when a bomb went off or a bullet ricocheted off a wall, would be determined by your religion. As a result, your politics would be the politics of religious nationalism.

Can you think of any way in which religious segregation in America might have played a part in your life? Do you think a comparison could be made between the effects of religious segregation in Northern Ireland and racial segregation in the United States?

Source: M.A. Busteed, "Northern Ireland: Geographical Aspects of Crisis," Research Papers, School of Geography, University of Oxford, 1972, pp. 17–27.

sacred landscapes or holy places. At the opposite extreme are landscapes almost purely secular in appearance. Religions, then, differ greatly in visibility, but even those least apparent to the eye normally leave some mark on the countryside. The content of religious landscapes is varied, ranging from houses of worship to cemeteries, wayside shrines, and place-names. Moreover, religion can help shape other landscape features such as settlement patterns.

Religious structures

The most obvious religious contributions to the landscape are the buildings erected to house divinities or to shelter worshipers. These structures vary greatly in size, function, style of architecture, construction material, and degree of ornateness (see Figure 6-20). To Roman Catholics, for example, the church building is literally the house of God, and the altar is the focus of vitally important ritual. Partly for these reasons, Catholic churches are typically large, elaborately decorated, and visually imposing. In many towns and villages, the Catholic house of worship is the focal point of the settlement, exceeding all other structures in size and grandeur.

To most Protestants, on the other hand, the church is simply a place to assemble for worship. God visits the church but does not live there. The result is a smaller, less ornate structure. The simpler church buildings of Protestantism appeal less to the senses and more to the personal faith. Many fundamentalist Protestant sects hold that salvation is best attained through sacrifice and an austere life-style. For this reason, fundamentalist Protestant structures are typically not designed for comfort, beauty, or high visibility.

Paralleling this contrast in church styles are attitudes toward wayside shrines and similar manifestations of faith. Catholic culture regions typically abound with shrines, crucifixes, crosses, and assorted visual

FIGURE 6–20
Religious architecture takes many forms. *Left:* St. Basil's church on Red Square in Moscow reflects the distinctive Russian religious architecture. *Right:* The mosques of Islam are characterized by domes and tall minarets. This mosque stands in Cairo. (Moscow photo by Terry G. Jordan, 1981.)

FIGURE 6-21
A wayside shrine in rural Germany. Such shrines are a highly visible part of the religious landscape in some Christian areas. (Photo by Terry G. Jordan, 1978.)

reminders of religion, as do some Eastern Orthodox Christian areas. One of the writers of this textbook vividly recalls driving along a mountain road in southern Bavaria on a summer night some years ago, when suddenly the headlights illuminated a realistic, life-sized crucifix in a shrine bordering the pavement. Instinctively his foot went to the brake, and it was several seconds before he could adjust to the reality of this German Catholic religious landscape (Figure 6-21). Protestant areas, by contrast, are bare of such symbols and do not startle the night driver. Their landscapes do, however, occasionally display such features as signboards advising the traveler to "Get Right With God," a common sight in the southern United States. A billboard on the interstate highway near Montgomery, Alabama, advises the traveler: "Go to Church or the Devil will get you."

Muslims and Jews rely much less on houses of worship than do Christians. An assembly of the faithful is all that is required for worship. Thus, the synagogue and the mosque are typically unimposing structures. In fact, they are often indistinguishable from other buildings and houses in a community. In Muslim areas, the minaret, the needlelike tower from which the faithful are called to worship, takes precedence over the mosque as the major feature of the religious landscape. Jews who have lived as a minority group among Christians for many years are often influenced to build impressive, churchlike synagogues, but these buildings represent a break with Jewish tradition.

Hinduism has produced large numbers of visually striking temples for its multiplicity of gods, but much worship is practiced in private households. Another Hindu landscape feature is the wayside shrine with the image of a god or goddess adorned with flowers. In some religions, temples are exclusively the residences of gods and entry is restricted to the priestly class.

Most tribal ethnic religions do not stand out in the cultural landscape. Animistic groups regard many objects as sacred, but these items are commonplace and would not reveal their religious significance to the eyes of an outsider. Tribal religions often do not have separate houses of worship.

The building materials chosen for a religious structure often demonstrate the value a religion places on its visibility in the landscape. Sects that wish to call attention to their sacred structures typically build them of different materials than those used in the construction of houses and other nonreligious buildings. In some parts of Europe, for example, churches are built of stone, while secular structures in the same communities are made of brick or wood.

Landscapes of the dead

Religions differ greatly in the type of tribute they award to the dead. This variation appears in the cultural landscape. Hindus, Buddhists, and Japanese Shintoists cremate their dead. Having no cemeteries, their dead leave no obvious mark on the land (Figure 6-22). In the same way, the few remaining Zoroastrians, called Parsees, who preserve a once-widespread Middle Eastern faith now confined to parts of India, have traditionally left their dead exposed to be devoured by vultures. In Egypt, on the other hand, spectacular pyramids and other tombs were built to house dead leaders. These monuments were generally placed on land not suitable for

FIGURE 6–22
Hindus burn the bodies of their dead in funeral pyres on the bank of the holy River Ganges in the pilgrimage city of Varanasi, India. What environmental impact might the use of firewood to cremate the dead have in a nation with over 500 million Hindus?

crop farming. Christians and Muslims, as well as Chinese who practice the composite Confucianist-Buddhist religion, typically bury their dead, setting aside land for that purpose and erecting monuments to the deceased kin (see Figure 6-23). In parts of pre-Communist China, as much as 10 percent of the land in some districts was covered by cemeteries and ancestral shrines, greatly reducing the acreage available for agriculture.

Traditionally, Chinese grave sites were chosen for their *Feng Shui*, literally "wind and water," the perfect combination of tangible and intangible elements that would leave the dead in harmony with their surroundings (Figure 6-24). It is believed that if the Feng Shui of a grave site is wrong, the dead will be restless and their descendants will suffer. Ideally, for a grave site in China, the configuration of the earth should be perfect—neither featureless and flat, nor steep and rugged. The active and passive forces of Chinese cosmology, *Yin* and *Yang*, should correctly surround the site. As Chuen-yan David Lai, a Canadian geographer, has written: "The *Yang* energy is expressed as a lofty mountain range, symbolically called the 'Azure Dragon,' and the *Yin* energy as a lower ridge called the 'White Tiger.' The most auspicious model of *Feng Shui* topography is a secluded spot where these two energies converge, interact vigorously, and are kept together in abundance and in harmony by surrounding mountains and streams."

Cemeteries often preserve truly ancient cultural traits, for people as a rule are reluctant to change practices relating to the dead. The traditional rural cemetery of the southern United States provides a case in point. All

FIGURE 6–23

A striking landscape of the dead has been created in the Sahara Desert by the Nubian peoples of the Sudan. The burials are mounded and covered with hundreds of small rounded rocks. A very different landscape is seen in the French cemeteries of southern Louisiana, including New Orleans, where the dead rest in above-ground crypts.

FIGURE 6–24

The model shows an ideal tomb site according to the Chinese principles of *Feng Shui.* The tall mountain range represents the spirit of the "Azure Dragon," a figure of active Yang energy. The lower hills symbolize the "White Tiger," a figure of the complementary passive Yin energy. The winding stream represents wealth. (After Lai.)

grass is chopped from the southern cemetery, exposing the bare earth, and freshwater mussel shells are placed atop elongated grave mounds. Rose bushes and cedars are planted through the cemetery. Recent research suggests that the use of shells and roses may be derived from the worship of the ancient, pre-Christian mother goddess of the Mediterranean lands. The seashell and rose were two major symbols of this great goddess, who could restore life to the dead. Similarly, the cedar evergreen is an age-old Mediterranean and Germanic symbol of death and eternal life. While the present Christian population of the South is unaware of the pagan origins of this cemetery symbolism, it seems likely that their landscape of the dead contains visible elements thousands of years old.

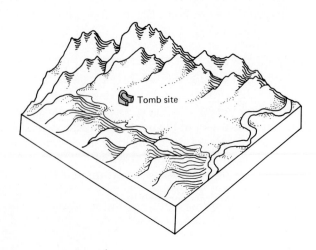

Tomb site

Religion and rural settlement pattern

As we saw in Chapter 2, most farming peoples live either in clustered villages or in dispersed farmsteads separated from one another. Religion often helps determine which of these patterns will prevail. In the United States and Canada, many highly cohesive religious groups have traditionally formed village settlements, in contrast to the more typical American pattern of dispersed farmsteads. The farm village tradition in Anglo-America was introduced by the Puritans of New England and later perpetuated by Mennonites in Canada, Mormons in the Great Basin of the American West, and the Amana colonists in Iowa (Figure 6-25). The large majority of utopian communities, so common on the American frontier, also utilized the farm village pattern. These sects, religious and utopian alike, typically placed a high value on group interaction and mutual support, and they felt that the clustered village was necessary to provide the daily contacts essential to the practice and perpetuation of their faith.

If the sect weakened and declined, or if factionalism developed, the clustered farm settlements often broke up. In Colonial New England, where some Puritan settlements had developed as villages, the power of church leaders in Boston waned after about 1700, and the Puritan movement began to fragment. Thereafter the farm villages gave way to scattered farmsteads, for religious individualism and scattered farmsteads had replaced the cohesive, village-based theocracy.

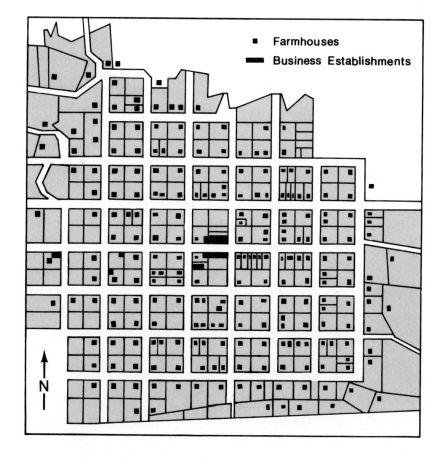

■ **Farmhouses**
▬ **Business Establishments**

N

FIGURE 6–25
A Mormon farm village in Utah. Cohesive religious faiths often encourage clustering of the rural population, as occurred often in the United States. What advantages for the faith are offered by clustered villages? (After Lowry Nelson, *The Mormon Village: A Pattern and Technique of Land Settlement*, Salt Lake City: University of Utah Press, 1952, p. 121.)

Religious names on the land

"St.-Jean," "St.-Aubert," "St.-Damase-des-Aulnaies," "Ste. Perpétue de L'Islet," "St.-Pamphile," "St.-Adalbert," "Ste.-Lucie," "St.-Fabien-de-Panet," "St.-Juste-de-Bretenières," "Ste.-Camille-de-Bellechasse"—so read the town-name placards as one drives from the St. Lawrence River south on Highway 24 in Québec, paralleling the Maine border. All this saintliness is merely a part of the French Canadian religious landscape, as Figure 6-26 shows. The point is that religion often inspires the names people place on the land. Within Christianity, the use of saints' names for settlements is very common in Roman Catholic and Greek Orthodox areas, especially in overseas colonial lands settled by Catholics, such as Latin America and French Canada. In areas of the Old World that were settled long before the advent of Christianity, saints' names were often grafted onto pre-Christian names, as in Alcazar de San Juan, in Spain, which combines Arabic and Christian elements.

Toponyms in Protestant regions display less religious influence, but some imprint can usually be found. In the southern United States, for example, the word *chapel* as a prefix or suffix, as in Chapel Hill, and Ward's Chapel, is very common in the names of rural hamlets. Names like this accurately convey the image of the humble, rural Protestant churches that are so common in the South.

FIGURE 6-26
Religious place-names dot the map of French Canada. In the French Canadian province of Québec, the dominant Roman Catholic religion finds an expression in the names given to towns and villages. Saintly names are dominant in the areas of purest French settlement. Nearer the United States-Canada border, in townships settled by English-speaking people, religious place-names are rare.

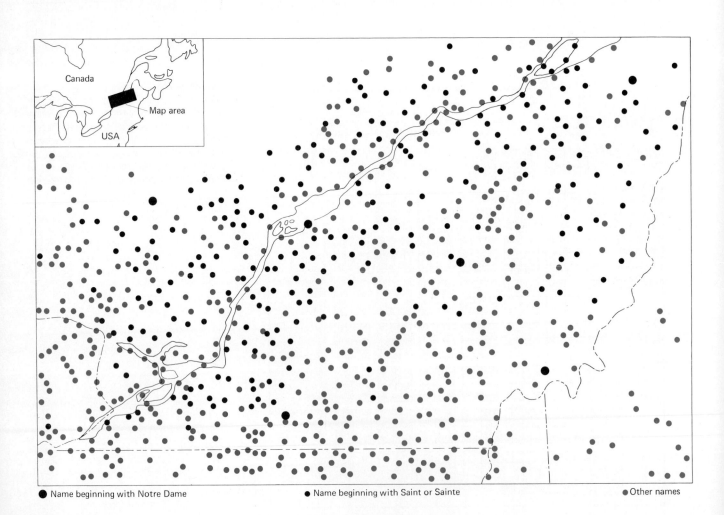

● Name beginning with Notre Dame   ● Name beginning with Saint or Sainte   ● Other names

Conclusion

Religion is firmly interwoven in the fabric of culture, a bright hue in the human mosaic, for religions and individual religious elements vary greatly from one area to another. Several major religions and many minor ones form a variety of culture regions. We illustrated some of these spatial variations with maps.

Such religious spatial variation led us to ask how these distributions came to be, a question best answered through the methods of cultural diffusion. Some religions, universalizing denominations, actively encourage their own diffusion. Most Christian churches, for example, send out missionaries to "spread the word." Other religions erect barriers to expansion diffusion by restricting membership to one particular ethnic group. Jews, for instance do not seek converts. The spatial diffusion of religious ideas often parallels and accompanies other, nonreligious elements of culture, such as language, crops, and political systems.

The theme of cultural ecology reveals some fundamental ties between religion and the physical environment. One major function of many religious systems, particularly the animistic faiths, is to appease and placate the forces of nature and to achieve harmony between the people and the physical environment. Religions differ in their outlook on environmental modification by humans. Christianity incorporates the doctrine that environmental alteration is good and is the will of God. Thus Christians, assuming divine approval, cleared forests, drained marshes, and plowed native grasslands. Some other religious groups view such alterations as an affront to the gods. We need to face the question of whether the Christian ecological outlook is leading us to environmental disaster.

Religion is culturally integrated—that is, causally related to economy and politics, among other things. Everything from tourism to nationalism can have a religious component. This further strengthens the view of culture as a functioning whole.

The cultural landscape abounds with expressions of religious belief. Places of worship—temples, churches, and shrines—differ in appearance, distinctiveness, prominence, and frequency of occurrence from one religious culture area to another. These buildings provide a visual index to the various faiths. Cemeteries and religious place-names also add a special effect to the landscape that tells us about the religious character of the population.

Glossary

Ahimsa The Hindu doctrine that places restrictions on killing and eating animals; a veneration of all forms of life.

Animism the belief that inanimate objects, such as trees, rocks, and rivers, possess souls.

Caste system in traditional Hinduism, the rigid segregation of people according to ancestry and occupation.

Contact conversion the spread of religious beliefs by personal contact.

Denomination a subdivision of a major religion, such as Lutheran or Baptist.

Ethnic religion a religion identified with a particular ethnic or tribal group; does not seek converts.

Monotheism the worship of only one god.

Pilgrimage a journey to a place of religious importance.

Polytheism the worship of many gods.

Quasi-religion a system of belief similar to a religion but lacking worship services.

Religion a set of beliefs and practices designed to allow humans to achieve mental and physical harmony with the powers of the universe.

State church one designated by the government as the official, legal faith in a political state, usually receiving financial support from the government.

Teleology a philosophy proposing that the earth was created specifically as the abode for humans, that the earth belongs to humans by divine intention.

Theocracy a government guided by a religion.

Universalizing religion a religion that actively seeks converts and has the goal of converting all humankind.

Suggested Readings

Surinder M. Bhardwaj. *Hindu Places of Pilgrimage in India.* Berkeley and Los Angeles: University of California Press, 1973.

Daniel Doeppers. "The Evolution of the Geography of Religious Adherence in the Philippines Before 1898," *Journal of Historical Geography,* 2 (1976), 95–110.

R. A. Donkin. "The Cistercian Order and the Settlement of Northern England," *Geographical Review,* 59 (1969), 403–416.

Isma'il R. al-Fārūqi and David E. Sopher. *Historical Atlas of the Religions of the World,* New York: Macmillan, 1974.

Robert H. Fuson. "The Orientation of Mayan Ceremonial Centers," *Annals, Association of American Geographers,* 59 (1969), 494–511.

John D. Gay. *The Geography of Religion in England.* London: Gerald Duckworth, 1971.

Clarence J. Glacken. *Traces on the Rhodian Shore.* Berkeley: University of California Press, 1967.

Peter L. Halvorson and William M. Newman. *Atlas of Religious Change in America, 1952-1971.* Washington, D.C.: Glenmary Research Center, 1978; and their accompanying volume, *Patterns in Pluralism: A Portrait of American Religion.* Washington, D.C.: Glenmary Research Center, 1980.

Manfred Hannemann. *The Diffusion of the Reformation in Southwestern Germany, 1518-1534,* Chicago: University of Chicago, Department of Geography, Research Paper No. 167, 1975.

Charles A. Heatwole. "Exploring the Geography of America's Religious Denominations: A Presbyterian Example," *Journal of Geography,* 76 (1977), 99–104.

Shin-Yi Hsu. "The Cultural Ecology of the Locust Cult in Traditional China," *Annals, Association of American Geographers,* 59 (1969), 731–752.

Terry G. Jordan. "Forest Folk, Prairie Folk: Rural Religious Cultures in North Texas," *Southwestern Historical Quarterly,* 80 (1976), 135–162.

Florence R. Kluckhohn et al. *Variations in Value Orientations.* Evanston, Ill.: Row, Peterson, 1961.

Chuen-yan David Lai. "A Feng Shui Model as a Location Index," *Annals, Association of American Geographers,* 64 (1974), 506–513.

Emanuel Maier. "Torah as Movable Territory," *Annals, Association of American Geographers,* 65 (1975), 18–23.

Donald W. Meinig. "The Mormon Culture Region: Strategies and Patterns in the Geography of the American West, 1847-1964," *Annals, Association of American Geographers,* 55 (1965), 191–220.

Ellen Churchill Semple. *Influences of Geographical Environment.* New York: Henry Holt, 1911.

James R. Shortridge. "Patterns of Religion in the United States," *Geographical Review,* 66 (1976), 420–434.

Frederick J. Simoons. *Eat Not This Flesh: Food Avoidances in the Old World.* Madison: University of Wisconsin Press, 1961.

Paul Simpson-Housley. "Hutterian Religious Ideology, Environmental Perception, and Attitudes Toward Agriculture," *Journal of Geography*, 77 (1978), 145–148.

John H. Sims and Duane D. Baumann. "The Tornado Threat: Coping Styles of the North and South," *Science*, 176 (1972), 1386–1392.

David E. Sopher. *The Geography of Religions*. Englewood Cliffs, N.J.: Prentice-Hall, 1967.

Dan Stanislawski. "Dionysus Westward: Early Religion and the Economic Geography of Wine," *Geographical Review*, 65 (1975) 427–444.

Yi-Fu Tuan. "Discrepancies Between Environmental Attitude and Behavior: Examples from Europe and China," *Canadian Geographer*, 12 (1968), 176–191.

Yi-Fu Tuan. "Sacred Space: Explorations of an Idea," in Karl W. Butzer (ed.), *Dimensions of Human Geography: Essays on Some Familiar and Neglected Themes*, Chicago: University of Chicago, Dept. of Geography, Research Paper No. 186, 1978, pp. 84–99.

Stephen W. Tweedie, "Viewing the Bible Belt," *Journal of Popular Culture*, 11 (1978), 865–876.

Ingolf Vogeler. "The Roman Catholic Culture Region of Central Minnesota," *Pioneer America*, 8 (1976), 71–83.

Lynn White Jr. "The Historical Roots of Our Ecologic Crisis," *Science*, 155: 3767 (March 10, 1967), 1203–1207.

Wilbur Zelinsky. "An Approach to the Religious Geography of the United States: Patterns of Church Membership in 1952," *Annals, Association of American Geographers*, 51 (1961), 139–167.

The Geography of Folk Culture

7

Students of culture, geographers included, recognize two major classes of
cultural groups: (1) the popular, consisting of large masses of people who
conform to and prescribe ever-changing norms; and (2) the **folk,** made up
of people who retain the traditional. The word *folk* conjures up many
images for citizens of the urban, industrialized world. It describes a rural
people who live in an old-fashioned way—a people holding to a simpler
lifestyle little influenced by the industrial revolution, modern technology,
and the flight to the cities. Many disillusioned American urban young
people were seeking this simpler way of life when they "dropped out"
and moved to rural communes in the late 1960s and early 1970s. But in
reality one cannot choose to be part of a folk tradition—one must be born
into it.

Closely related to the concept of "folk" are the concepts of folk culture,
folk society, folklore, folklife, and folk geography. A **folk society** is a
small, isolated, cohesive, conservative, nearly self-sufficient group that is
homogeneous in custom and race, with a strong family or clan structure
and highly developed rituals. Order is maintained through sanctions
based in the religion or family, and interpersonal relationships are strong.
Tradition is paramount, and change comes infrequently and slowly. There
is little division of labor into specialized duties. Rather, each person is
expected to perform a great variety of jobs, though duties may differ
between the sexes. Most goods are handmade, and a subsistence economy
prevails. Individualism is generally weakly developed in folk societies, as
are social classes. Unaltered folk societies no longer exist in industrialized countries such as the United States and Canada. Perhaps the nearest
modern equivalent in Anglo-America is the Amish, a German-American
farming sect that largely renounces the products and labor-saving devices
of the industrial age (Figure 7-1). In Amish areas, horse-drawn buggies
still serve as the main transportation facilities. The Amish's central
religious concept of *demut,* "humility," clearly reflects the weakness of
individualism and social class so typical of folk societies, and there is a

◄ *Chapter-opening photo:* An Amish
barn-raising.

FIGURE 7–1
The Amish in the United States retain
many aspects of folk culture in their
everyday lives.

corresponding strength of Amish group identity. Rarely do the Amish marry outside their sect. Their religion, a variety of the Mennonite faith, provides the principal mechanism for maintaining order.

By contrast, a **popular society** is a large, heterogeneous group, often highly individualistic and constantly changing. Interpersonal relationships tend to be impersonal, and a pronounced division of labor exists, leading to the establishment of many specialized professions. Secular institutions of control such as the police and army take the place of religion and family in maintaining order, and a money-based economy prevails. Because of these contrasts, "popular" may be viewed as clearly different from "folk." The popular is replacing the folk in industrialized countries and in many developing nations. Folk-made objects give way to their popular equivalent, usually because the popular item is more quickly or cheaply produced, is easier or time-saving to use, or lends more prestige to the owner.

While folk society refers to a cohesive group of people, **folk culture** involves individual persons who do not necessarily belong to a cohesive social group. Bearers of folk culture can live in cities, surrounded by the popular society, but still retaining many folk practices and material objects. In the United States, few folk societies survive, but folk culture on the individual level is far more persistent and is likely to be perpetuated. Typically, such bearers of folk culture combine folk and nonfolk elements in their lives. The proportion of folk to nonfolk characteristics in an individual's cultural makeup varies from one person to another, but most of us bear at least some folk traits. Are children's games such as "London Bridge" part of your heritage? Have you ever chanted the ancient count-out phrase "eenie, meenie, miney, moe"? Have you placed a horseshoe over a door for good luck? If so, then you retain some folk elements in your cultural makeup.

Folklife refers to the totality of the folk culture and society, including both material and nonmaterial elements. **Material culture** includes all objects or "things" made and used by members of a cultural group: tools, utensils, buildings, furniture, clothing, artwork, musical instruments, vehicles, and other physical objects. Material elements are visible. By contrast, **nonmaterial culture,** including **folklore,** can be defined as oral, including the wide range of tales, songs, beliefs, superstitions, and customs that is passed from generation to generation as part of an oral or written tradition. Folk dialects, religions, and world-views can also be regarded as aspects of nonmaterial culture.

Cultural geographers adopt the folklife approach in their study of folk groups, although emphasis traditionally has been placed on the material aspects of culture, particularly folk architecture. **Folk geography,** a term coined by the cultural geographer Eugene Wilhelm, may be defined as the study of the spatial patterns of folklife. Folk geography is an integral, growing branch of cultural geography, and our five themes are well suited to it.

Folk Culture Regions

As a rule, elements of folklife exhibit major variations from place to place and minor variations through time, while popular society displays less difference from region to region but changes rapidly through time. The natural divisions of folklife, then, are spatial—that is, geographic. For this reason, the theme of culture region is well suited to the study of folklife.

Formal regions of folklife can be delimited on the basis of material or nonmaterial elements. Cultural geographers have tended to emphasize material culture in most of their studies, but recently some have turned to nonmaterial topics.

Material folk culture regions in eastern North America

Figure 7-2 shows the material folk culture regions of the eastern United States as delimited by Henry Glassie, to which have been added those of eastern Canada. Not surprisingly, these regions bear a close resemblance to the traditional rural culture regions shown in Chapter 1 (Figure 1-5), since material folk culture is obviously a major component of rural cultural geography. Glassie considered many artifacts before devising the map—everything from dolls and outdoor ovens to tombstones, bean pots, homemade boats, folk architecture, and blackbird pies. Using this evidence, he identified five folk regions in the eastern United States: the North, Mid-Atlantic, Midwest, Upland South, and Lowland South. To these we can add French Canada and Upper Canada. As popular culture spread during the last century or so, folk culture retreated and very nearly vanished in much of the area included in the study. Nevertheless, we can find many interesting remnants of folk culture in all of the regions.

The Mid-Atlantic folk culture region, though the smallest of the five, is possibly the most important, since through relocation diffusion it exerted influence on the Midwest, Upper Canada, and the Upland South. Encompassing the greater part of Pennsylvania, the southern half of New Jersey, northern Maryland, and most of Delaware, the Mid-Atlantic region

FIGURE 7–2
Material folk culture regions of the eastern United States. Compare this map with Figure 1–5. (After Henry Glassie, *Pattern in the Material Folk Culture of the Eastern United States,* Philadelphia: University of Pennsylvania Press, 1968, p. 39.)

reveals a material folk culture that combines continental European and British contributions. From the German-language areas of central Europe came such diverse material items as log construction, large barn types, elaborate and brightly colored birth and baptismal certificates, the "long rifle" made famous by the likes of Daniel Boone, and a type of pottery decoration called *sgraffito*, made by pouring a thin layer of liquid clay over unfired red pottery and then scratching designs through the clay layer to expose the red color underneath (Figure 7-3).

The material folk culture of the North is more purely English in origin, reflecting the background of the early Puritan settlers of New England. Typically English are such folk items as tombstones adorned with a winged death's head and the village greens, or "commons," that lie at the core of many villages and towns (Figure 7-4). Beans baked with molasses, salt pork, and onions in a large pot set in a stone-lined pit are a typical northern folk food, particularly in New England. The folk region is an extensive one, reaching from the Canadian Maritime Provinces to Wisconsin.

In the Lowland South, centered in the coastal plains of the Atlantic and the Gulf of Mexico, the material folk culture reflects a mixture of British and African influences. Among the distinctive material items of this culture region are: the African-style head kerchiefs worn by black women;

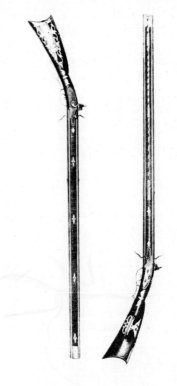

FIGURE 7–3
The photograph on the left shows three examples of sgraffito pottery. On the right is a double-barrel superposed long rifle from the period following the Revolutionary War. The building is a typical Pennsylvania barn, complete with German hex signs. All three of these items are derived from the German-language areas of Europe.

the mule-powered syrup mill in which cane or sorghum is crushed; the "dogtrot" folk house, distinguished by an open-air breezeway through the middle; the banjo, an important instrument in the folk music of the region; the scraped-earth cemetery, from which all grass is laboriously chopped to expose the bare ground; and the typically British fireplace and exterior chimney.

The material folk culture of the Upland South is derived from both the Mid-Atlantic and the Lowland South, although the former region seems to have been its most important source. Both British and continental European influences are strong here. The Appalachian and Ozark highlands, which form the eastern and western centers of the Upland South, provided the shelter and isolation that permitted a greater survival of material folk culture here than in the other regions. Abundant log structures, split-rail fences, whiskey stills, and tobacco barns are among the material folk items surviving in the Upland South. Perhaps for this reason, students of folklife have long been attracted to the Upland South, and many of the examples presented in this chapter will be drawn from this culture region.

The Midwest, a narrow, wedge-shaped material folk culture region, is a complex patchwork of Mid-Atlantic, Northern, and Upland Southern influences, to which were added a host of items derived directly from Europe. As such, it might be regarded as the most thoroughly "American" region of the eastern United States, more closely akin to the West than the East. The Midwest has long been a progressive farming area, where the products and methods of the industrial age were quickly adopted, with the result that popular culture has almost entirely replaced the earlier folk forms in many areas. But here and there in the Midwest you may still glimpse a large Pennsylvania barn type, an Upland Southern log house, a continental German half-timbered structure, or a typical New England town meeting hall.

Completing the map of eastern North America are two Canadian folk regions. French Canada was implanted in the seventeenth century by settlers from northern France. The highly distinctive French Canadian material folk culture is revealed in features as diverse as traditional house architecture (see Figure 7-27); fence types (Figure 7-5); grist windmills

FIGURE 7–4
A variation of the winged death's head tombstone found in upstate New York.

FIGURE 7–5
French folk fences in Europe (left) and Québec (right), illustrate both the French Canadian folk culture and the process of cultural diffusion. (Source: Jean Brunhes, *Human Geography*, London: George G. Harrap & Co., Ltd., 1955, Figures 71 and 72.)

with sturdy stone towers; *pétanque*, a bowling game played with small metal balls; and maple sugar pies. Some items were adopted by the French from Indian tribes of the St. Lawrence Valley, as for example the snowshoe, which has for three centuries been manufactured by folk artisans of ash wood and strips of cowhide. Upper Canada, occupying the southern part of the province of Ontario, is similar to the Midwest in that it is a folk region where different cultural traditions mixed. Perhaps the major shaping influences came from the Mid-Atlantic and the North, particularly Pennsylvania, the Maritime Provinces, and upstate New York. Adding additional diversity were numerous settlers coming directly from Europe. In this way, Pennsylvania German log construction, Northern folk foods, and a host of other items of material folk culture were implanted in Ontario. Curiously, very few features of French Canadian material folk culture penetrated Upper Canada, in spite of the proximity of the two regions.

Folklore regions

Nonmaterial folk culture displays regional contrasts in much the same manner as material folk culture does. Increasingly, folk geographers have become concerned with nonmaterial phenomena, such as folktales and folk music, organizing them into culture regions. In general, nonmaterial culture closely corresponds spatially to material culture regions. The North, Lowland South, Mid-Atlantic, and other American folk regions can be recognized through a study of nonmaterial folk culture. But other regional classifications are also possible, as we shall see.

Joan Wilson Miller was one of the first cultural geographers to display an interest in folklore. Her area of interest was the Ozark highlands, one of the Upland Southern folk domains, where she sought to delimit the Ozark culture region on the basis of folktales. Using existing collections of Ozark folktales, collections that contained data on the place of residence of the informants from whom the tales were obtained, Miller mapped the spatial distribution by counties (Figure 7-6). Her map identifies a cluster of twelve counties straddling the western part of the Arkansas-Missouri border as the main source of recorded Ozark folktales. Each of these counties was home to at least ten informants. Collectively, the twelve counties constitute the Ozark folk culture region as defined by folktales. One might conclude from Dr. Miller's map that Ozark folk culture remains most nearly intact in the western part of the highland area.

Folk music, another aspect of nonmaterial culture, can also be used as the basis for delimiting culture regions. Alan Lomax, a leading expert on the English-language folk songs of North America, recognizes four folk-song culture regions in the United States: the Northern, Southern, Western, and Black song families (Figure 7-7). The Northern tradition, characterized by unaccompanied solo singing in hard, open-voiced, clear tones with unison on the refrains, is based largely in British ballads and has not deviated greatly from the English prototype. In the Southern folk-song tradition, by contrast, unison singing is rare and the solo is high-pitched and nasal. Combining English and Scotch-Irish elements, the Southern style features ballads that are more guilt-ridden and violent than those of the North. The Western style, according to Lomax, is simply a blend of the Southern and Northern traditions. The Black folk-song family contains both African and British elements, featuring polyrhythmic songs of labor and worship with instrumental accompaniment,

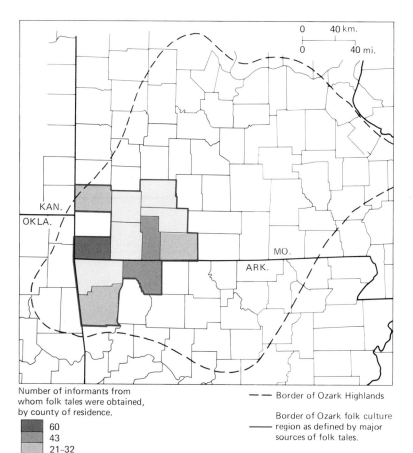

FIGURE 7–6
The Ozark folk culture region, as defined by the major source area of recorded folk tales. This use of nonmaterial folk culture suggests that surviving Ozark folkways may be best preserved in the southwestern part of the mountain zone. What possible explanations are there for this concentration? (After E. Joan Wilson Miller, "The Ozark Culture Region as Revealed by Traditional Materials," *Annals, Association of American Geographers,* 58 (1968), 63.)

Number of informants from whom folk tales were obtained, by county of residence.

60
43
21–32
10–18
0–6

– – – Border of Ozark Highlands

——— Border of Ozark folk culture region as defined by major sources of folk tales.

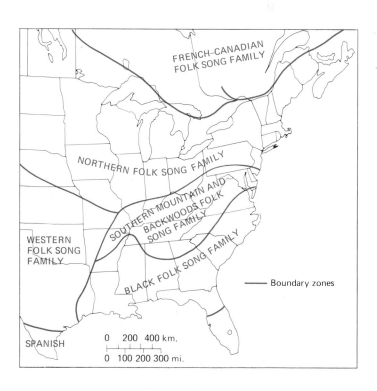

Boundary zones

FIGURE 7–7
Folk-song culture regions of the eastern United States and Canada. Compare this map to Figures 1–5 and 7–2. Folk music is rarely used as a criterion for devising culture regions, but is well-suited to this purpose. (Modified from Alan Lomax, *The Folk Songs of North America in the English Language,* Garden City, New York: Doubleday, 1960, frontispiece.)

FIGURE 7-8

Switzerland: Where do newborn children come from? When you were little and asked your parents where babies come from, did you get the old run-around about storks or some other equally absurd answer? If so, don't judge them too harshly, for they were only perpetuating an old folk custom of deception. This map of Switzerland reveals that different provinces and districts are characterized by distinctive evasive answers to this age-old question. The map provides us another example of how nonmaterial folk culture can provide an index to culture regions. Where exactly would you draw the boundaries of the culture regions on this map? How many culture regions would you designate? Cultural geographers always face the same difficult decisions in delimiting culture regions. Most French-speaking Swiss parents prefer the cabbage-pumpkin explanation, German-Swiss children are more likely to hear the stork story, and Italian-Swiss youngsters are usually told that their siblings come by purchase from the store. (After Elsbeth Liebl, "Herkunft der Kinder," in Paul Geiger et al., *Atlas der Schweizerischen Volkskunde*, Basel: Schweizerische Gesellschaft für Volkskunde, Vol. 2, part 4, plates 202–205.)

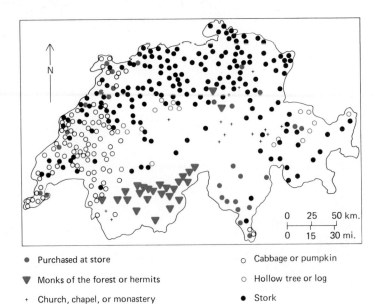

● Purchased at store	○ Cabbage or pumpkin
▼ Monks of the forest or hermits	○ Hollow tree or log
+ Church, chapel, or monastery	● Stork

chorus group singing, clapping, swaying of the body, and a strong, surging beat. Black and Southern styles coexist across much of the coastal plain South, each still closely linked to its respective racial group. In addition to the folk-music regions delimited by Lomax, we can recognize a Mexican-American and a French-Canadian region, each displaying distinctive instrumentation, melodies, and motifs. Some of the French-Canadian fur trader songs, such as "Alouette, gentile Alouette," have spread to the North American population at large. The music of traditional Mexican mariachi street bands is commonly heard on radio stations in the southwestern states.

Many other facets of folklore can be categorized into culture regions. Figure 7-8 depicts an example from the rich folklore of Switzerland, a meeting ground of German, French, Italian, and Rhaeto-Romanic peoples. The great *Atlas der schweizerischen Volkskunde* (Atlas of Swiss Folklore), perhaps the best of its kind in the world, contains hundreds of maps of value to the folk geographer in formulating culture regions.

Cultural Diffusion in Folk Geography

Folk culture, both material and nonmaterial, spreads by the same processes of diffusion as do other types and elements of culture. The material folk culture regions described earlier in this chapter (Figure 7-2) were produced mainly by relocation diffusion, as different groups of settlers moved west from major source areas and implanted their folk cultures in new lands (Figure 7-9; see also box, "A Transatlantic Fish Story").

Diffusion of religious folk songs

Expansion diffusion can also be at work in the spread of folk culture. An interesting example is the diffusion of Anglo-American religious folk

A TRANSATLANTIC FISH STORY

Cultural diffusion is often revealed by comparing folktales in different regions. The following tale, presented in a much-abridged form, occurs both in Celtic Wales on the island of Great Britain and among people of British extraction in the Ozark Mountains of Missouri and Arkansas. It apparently spread by relocation diffusion to America and halfway across the continent, changing somewhat in the process.

Ozark Mountain Version
A man living up the Meramec River
caught a yellow catfish using only
his hands
he took it home and put it in a rain
barrel
the fish turned into a woman
she became a fish again
he put it back in barrel
and took it back to the river

Welsh Version
A man living
on the River Towey
caught a salmon
from a small boat with a rod
the fish spoke Welsh and English,
                                and
turned into a naked girl with a
                        fish-hook in her lip
she became the man's wife

Adapted from E. Joan Wilson Miller, "The Ozark Culture Region as Revealed by Traditional Materials," Annals, Association of American Geographers, 58 (1968), 59.

FIGURE 7–9

Diffusion of folk cultures through eastern North America. The material folk culture regions shown in Figure 7–2 were produced by ideas carried along the routes of diffusion shown here. In large part, folk culture was spread by relocation diffusion, as settlers moved west. What factors might have caused the currents of diffusion to flow as they did? (In part after Henry Glassie, *Pattern in the Material Folk Culture of the Eastern United States*, Philadelphia: University of Pennsylvania Press, 1968, pp. 37, 38, with modifications.)

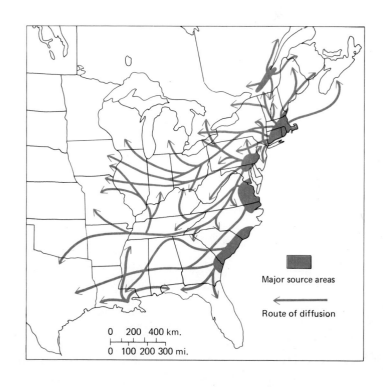

Major source areas

Route of diffusion

0   200 400 km.
0 100 200 300 mi.

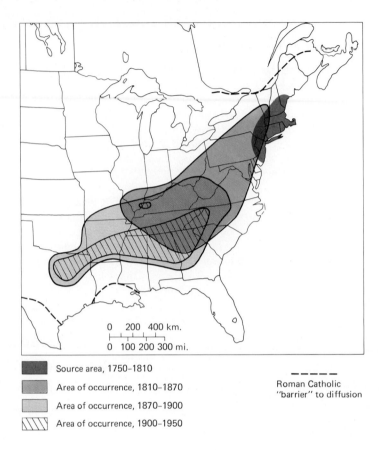

FIGURE 7-10

Spatial diffusion of Anglo-American religious folksongs, 1750–1950. These songs, white spirituals, spread by expansion diffusion from New England to the South, eventually disappearing from the source region. (After George P. Jackson, "Some Factors in the Diffusion of American Religious Folksongs," *Journal of American Folklore,* 65 (1952), 367.)

songs in the United States (Figure 7-10). From an eighteenth-century core area based mainly in the New England, or Northern, culture, these white spiritual songs spread southwest into the Upland South and finally into the Lowland South, where such songs retain their greatest acceptance today. In the meantime, religious folk songs largely disappeared from the Northern source regions, possibly because of the rapid urbanization and popularization of culture in that area. The white spiritual movement began as an expression of protest against the entrenched Protestant establishment. Simple folk melodies were the main musical device of the spirituals, and they spread rapidly by means of outdoor "revivals" or "camp meetings." Non-English-speaking peoples and non-Protestants were little influenced by the spiritual movement, for language and religion proved effective barriers to diffusion. The French Canadians and Louisiana French were not affected by the movement.

Diffusion of the agricultural fair

Another element of folk culture that originated in the Northern region and spread west and southwest was the American agricultural fair, a custom rooted in medieval European folk tradition. According to folk geographer Fred Kniffen (see biographical sketch), who researched the subject, the first American agricultural fair was held in Pittsfield, Massachusetts, in 1810, and the idea quickly gained favor throughout western New England and the adjacent Hudson Valley (Figure 7-11). From that source region it diffused westward into the American heartland, the Midwest, where it gained its widest acceptance. Normally promoted by agricultural societies, the fairs were originally educational in purpose, and farmers could learn about improved methods and breeds. Soon an entertainment function was added, represented by a racetrack and midway, and competition for prizes for superior agricultural products became common. By the early twentieth century, the agricultural fair had diffused through most of the United States, though farmers in culture regions such as the Upland South and Lowland South did not accept it as readily or fully as did the Midwesterners. The spread of the agricultural fair followed a more northerly route than that of white spiritual songs, although the source areas of the two were almost identical.

The blowgun: diffusion or independent invention?

Often the past diffusion of an item of folk culture is not clearly known or understood, presenting folk geographers with a problem of interpretation. An example is provided by the blowgun, a long, hollow tube through which a projectile is blown by the force of the breath. The cultural geographer Stephen C. Jett mapped the distribution of this hunting weapon and found it among folk societies in both the Old and New Worlds, all the way from the island of Madagascar off the African coast to The Amazonian jungles of South America, over halfway around the world (Figure 7-12). Apparently the blowgun was first invented by Malaysian peoples, probably on the island of Borneo in the East Indies. It became the principal hunting weapon of this folk society and was diffused with the Malayo-Polynesian linguistic group through much of the equatorial island belt of the Eastern Hemisphere. But how do we account for its presence

FIGURE 7–11
Diffusion of the American agricultural fair, 1810–1910. Both the agricultural fair and the white spiritual arose in the same general area. Compare the diffusion of the fair and the spiritual. What differences can you detect in the routes of diffusion? Why might these differences have developed? (After Fred B. Kniffen, "The American Agricultural Fair," *Annals, Association of American Geographers*, 41 (1951), 45, 47, 51.)

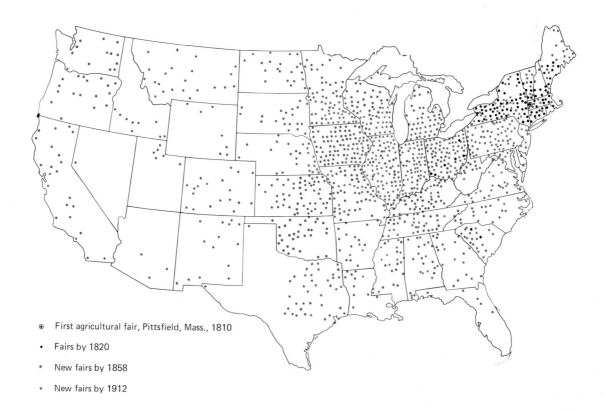

⊙ First agricultural fair, Pittsfield, Mass., 1810

· Fairs by 1820

· New fairs by 1858

· New fairs by 1912

among Amerindian groups in the Western Hemisphere? Was it independently invented by the Amerindians? Was it brought by relocation diffusion in pre-Columbian times to the Americas? Or did it spread to the New World only after the European discovery of America? The answers to these questions are not known, but the problem presented is one common to cultural geography, and particularly to folk geography, since the nonliterate condition of most folk societies precludes written records that might reveal diffusion.

If you choose to believe that the blowgun had a single origin and spread to America, then you must explain the wide gaps where it is not found in the South Pacific island world and Africa, which lie between the two zones of occurrence. If you choose instead to support the independent invention theory, then you have to accept the proposition that an identical device was invented two times, in very different folk societies. The study of cultural diffusion often presents such problems. In the case of the blowgun, additional research will be required to solve the mystery.

Cultural Ecology in Folk Geography

Cultural ecology is an especially appropriate theme in folk geography, because folk societies enjoy a very close relationship with their physical environment (Figure 7-13). The ties to the soil are not just economic, but social and religious as well. It is easy, in studying such groups, to be tempted by the easy answers offered by environmental determinism and to interpret the close ties between man and land as simply a human response to the environment. But while folk societies may be more sensitive to the qualities of the soil, climate, and terrain, it does not follow that they are enslaved and wholly shaped by their physical surroundings. Nor is it necessarily true that folk groups are in close harmony with their environment, for often soil erosion, deforestation, and overkill of wild animals can be attributed to traditional rural folk.

Folk foods: the example of geophagy

Most folk societies consume natural foods derived directly from the land either through husbandry of domesticated plants and animals or through hunting and gathering of wild species. The large majority of people in such societies are directly involved in food production and are therefore intimately in contact with the land. Each folk group has its own distinctive selection of foods and means of food preparation.

Perhaps no food habit intertwines environment and culture more closely than **geophagy,** the deliberate eating of earth. While found among many different cultures, dirt-eating is most common in black Africa and among Americans of African ancestry. Certain kinds of clay are the preferred earth material for geophagy. In the African source regions of this folk custom, clays are consumed for a variety of reasons (Figure 7-14). Some African earth-eaters feel that the clay is an effective treatment for certain diseases and parasites, while others believe it provides needed nutrients for pregnant women and growing children. Some consume clay as part of religious ceremonies. In Holmes County, Mississippi, an

FRED B. KNIFFEN   1900-

A native of Michigan, Fred Kniffen is of New England ancestry and spent much of his boyhood in the transplanted New England folk culture of the upper Midwest. At the University of California, Berkeley, Kniffen studied under the famous cultural geographer Carl O. Sauer and the renowned anthropologist Alfred Kroeber. This combination of geography and anthropology in his doctoral degree work provided the basis of Kniffen's interest and expertise in folk geography. He is acknowledged as the founder and kindly "father figure" of American folk geography. His circle of influence is wide.

From 1929 to the present, Dr. Kniffen has been associated with the Department of Geography and Anthropology at Louisiana State University, Baton Rouge, where he is presently professor emeritus. He has authored some 125 titles, and his range of interest has been great. In his list of publications are works on folk houses, agricultural fairs, covered bridges, outdoor folk ovens, log construction, and other fascinating items of material culture. Dr. Kniffen's regional interests have been centered in Anglo-America, with special focus on Louisiana. His 1936 article on the folk houses of Louisiana is regarded as a classic, seminal work, and his 1968 book *Louisiana: Its Land and People* has been widely praised. Dr. Kniffen has received many honors and tributes, most notably the honorary presidency of the Association of American Geographers in 1966–1967 and membership in Phi Beta Kappa.

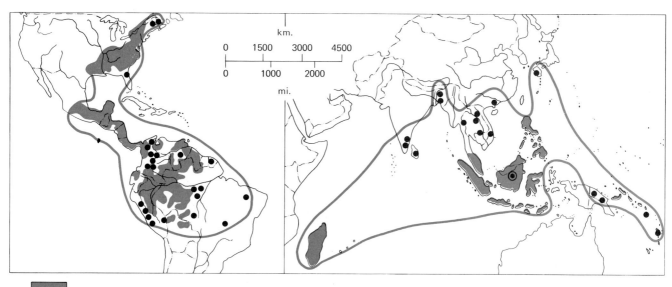

Major occurrence   ● Isolated occurrence   ◉ Probable Old World place of origin

FIGURE 7–12

Present distribution of the blowgun in the Americas, Pacific, and Indian Ocean lands. The blowgun was found among folk societies in two widely separated areas of the world. Was this the result of cultural diffusion or independent invention? (After: Stephen C. Jett, "The Development and Distribution of the Blowgun," *Annals, Association of American Geographers,* 60 (1970), 668, 674.)

FIGURE 7–13

The ecology of folk architecture in northern New Mexico. Buildings erected by people belonging to folk societies consist of materials locally available. So it is among the Hispanic and Indian folk of northern New Mexico, where the type of wall construction changes with elevation above sea level, reflecting in part the progression of microenvironments encountered at different heights. (Adapted from Charles O. Gritzner, "Construction Materials in a Folk Housing Tradition: Considerations Governing Their Selection in New Mexico," *Pioneer America,* 6 (January 1974), 26.)

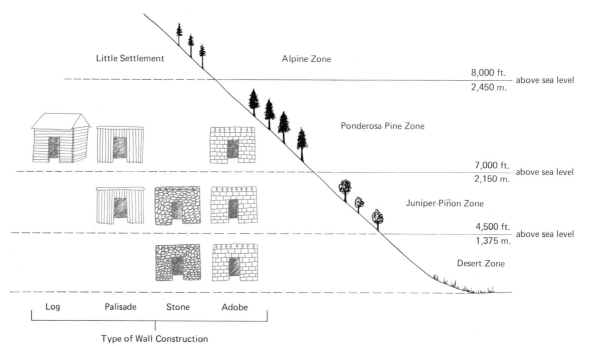

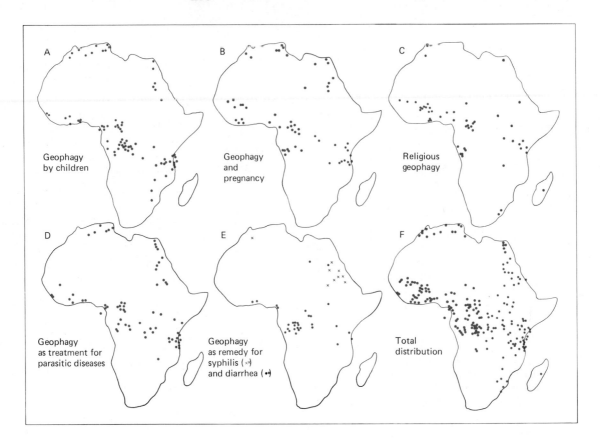

FIGURE 7–14

Geography in Africa. Clay eating is a widespread folk custom in Africa, especially in the West African region where many of the slaves brought to America originated. African geophagy is associated by its practicioners with both health and religion. (After John M. Hunter, "Geophagy in Africa and in the United States: A Culture-Nutrition Hypothesis," *Geographical Review*, 63 (1973), 172, and Sture Lagercrantz and B. Anell, "Geographical Customs," *Studia Ethnographica Upsalensia*, 17(1958), 24–84.)

intensive study made by cultural geographer Donald E. Vermeer and health expert Dennis A. Frate found that geophagy is confined mainly to pregnant black women and to black children under the age of five. By way of comparison, 28 percent of pregnant black women and 7 percent of pregnant whites in the county consume clay. The average intake is about fifty grams per day. The preferred clays, obtained from digs or highway cuts in the upland section of the county, are fine-textured and grit-free, light gray or whitish in color, and sour in taste. The clay is heated in a pan on a stove for several hours; some add salt and vinegar before baking. Geophagy in Holmes County is apparently unrelated to dietary deficiencies or intestinal parasites. Rather, it is best regarded as a folk custom that persists for cultural reasons.

Geophagy is deeply rooted in Afro-American folk culture and has survived in spite of persistent attempts to abolish it. In slavery times, some white masters put mouthlocks on the blacks to prevent geophagy, and local health officials today generally oppose it. In Alabama, the consumption level is so great that the Highway Department has posted signs forbidding digging at road cuts because of the damage it causes. Often southern rural blacks send packages of geophagical clays to kinfolk in northern or western cities.

The barrier preventing a wider diffusion of geophagy in America seems to be the social stigma attached to the practice. Yet it is a permeable barrier: many persons who do not eat clay will consume commercial, store-bought starch, which is perceived as a more respectable substitute. In addition to the 28 percent of pregnant black women in Holmes County who consume clay, another 19 percent eat box starch, as do an additional 10 percent of the pregnant whites.

Folk medicine and the environment

In geophagy we find an intimate tie between folk culture and the environment, but close links are also typical of folk medicine. It is common in folk societies to treat diseases and disorders with drugs and medicines derived from the root, bark, blossom, or fruit of plants. In the United States, folk medicine is best preserved in the Upland South, particularly southern Appalachia; on some Indian reservations; and in the Mexican borderland. Many of the folk cures have proven effectiveness.

The outlook of the Upland Southerner toward cures is well expressed in the comments of an eastern Tennessee mountaineer root digger who, in an interview with cultural geographer Edward T. Price, said that "the good Lord has put these yerbs here for man to make hisself well with. They is a yerb, could we but find it, to cure every illness." Root digging has been popularized to the extent that much of the produce of the Appalachians is now funneled to dealers, who serve a larger market outside the folk culture (Figure 7-15). But root digging remains at heart a folk enterprise, carried on in the old ways and requiring the traditionally thorough knowledge of the plant environment.

Along the Texas-Mexico border, on both sides of the Rio Grande, folk medicine is still widely practiced by **curanderos** or "curers." Over 400 medicines are derived from both wild and domestic plants growing in the border region, perpetuating a tradition rooted in sixteenth-century Indian and Spanish sources. The local folk medicine is based on the belief that health and welfare depend on harmony between the natural and supernatural; disease and misfortune are thought to involve some disharmony. The *curandero*, through the use of counseling and botanical medicines, strives to restore harmony. In recent years, fewer border folk have sought herbal remedies for infections, sprains, or broken bones, choosing instead to go to doctors and hospitals, but *curanderos* are treating more cancer, diabetes, and hypertension than previously. The thriving *curandero* business along the Rio Grande is best viewed as a persistent folk element in a culture undergoing considerable change and popularization. Some *curanderos* have responded to change by becoming virtual paramedics and employing antibiotics in some cures.

Folk culture and environmental perception

An intimate knowledge of the environment, then, provides food and medicines for people in a folk society or folk culture. It is not surprising, in view of this close association with the land, that members of such groups, when migrating, seek lands similar to those they leave behind (Figure 7-16). They function best in environments like those their ancestors have occupied for centuries, because the lore of the land passed down to them relates to one particular locale.

When overpopulation or some other "push" factor causes folk groups to seek a new homeland, they are often "pulled" to places that are similar in terrain, soils, vegetation, and wildlife. A good example can be seen in the migrations of southern highland folk from the mountains of Appalachia in the century between 1830 and 1930. As the Appalachians filled up, many highlanders began looking elsewhere for similar areas to pioneer. In their migrations, they normally moved in clan or extended-family groups.

FIGURE 7-15
An Appalachian root digger holding ginsing.

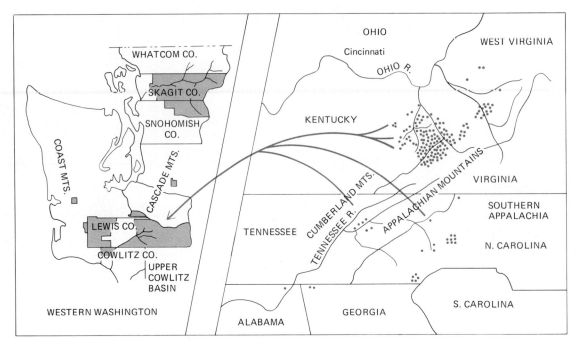

•   Appalachian place of origin of families or individuals migrating to the Upper Cowlitz Basin

     Settlement areas of Appalachian hill folk in Washington state

FIGURE 7–16

The migration of Appalachian hill folk to western Washington. Each dot represents the former home of an individual or family that migrated to the upper Cowlitz River basin in the Cascade Mountains of Washington State between 1884 and 1937. Some 3,000 descendants of these migrants lived in the Cowlitz area by 1940. What does the high degree of clustering of the sources of the migrants and the subsequent clustering in Washington suggest about the processes of folk migrations? How should we interpret their choice of familiar terrain and vegetation for a new home? If you migrated, would you look for a place similar to the one where you now live? Why might members of a folk society choose a similar land? (After Woodrow R. Clevinger, "The Appalachian Mountaineers in the Upper Cowlitz Basin," *Pacific Northwest Quarterly*, 29 (1938), 120; and Woodrow R. Clevinger, "Southern Appalachian Highlanders in Western Washington," *Pacific Northwest Quarterly*, 33 (1942), 4, with modifications.)

Initially they found an environmental twin of the Appalachians in the Ozark-Ouachita Mountains of Missouri and Arkansas. Somewhat later, others sought out the hollows, coves, and gaps of the central Texas hill country. The final migration of Appalachian hill folk brought some 15,000 members of this culture to the Cascade and coastal mountain ranges of Washington state between 1880 and 1930 (Figure 7-16). The role of environmental perception and clan ties in directing these migrations can be seen in the following remarks by a Kentucky mountaineer, recorded by W. R. Clevinger in 1937: "I've been figurin' fer a right smart time about leavin' fer Washington. I hear there's a good mountin country out thar where a man can still hunt, git work in mills and loggin', and git a piece of land right cheap. Some of my kin out thar have writ back, wantin' me to jine 'em."

People so close to nature are also sensitive to what they perceive as very subtle environmental qualities. Nowhere is this sensitivity more evident than in the practice of "planting by the signs," found among folk farmers in the United States and elsewhere (see box, "Planting by the Signs of the Zodiac"). Reliance on the movement and appearance of planets, stars, and the moon might seem absurd to the managers of huge, corporation-owned farms, but these beliefs and practices are still widespread among the members of folk cultures.

All in all, folk groups are much more observant of their local physical environment than are most people in the popular and academic cultures. They strive for harmony with nature, though they do not always achieve it, and often ascribe animistic religious sanctity to the forces of the environment and to particular parts of their habitat. Some members of the popular culture, from Henry David Thoreau to disenchanted American

PLANTING BY THE SIGNS OF THE ZODIAC

Each day of a month is said to be dominated by one of the signs of the zodiac. Every sign appears at least once a month, holding sway for two or three days at a time. The signs were long ago assigned traits, such as masculine or feminine; fiery, airy, earthy, or watery; barren or fruitful.

Many rural folk in America, and elsewhere as well, use the signs as indicators of the proper planting time. The following are some "rules" for farming "by the signs," collected from interviews in rural north Georgia and from various other sources. They illustrate the intimate ties between people and the physical environment so typical in folk cultures:

"Planting is best done in the fruitful signs of Scorpio, Pisces, Taurus, or Cancer."

"Plow, till, and cultivate in Aries."

"Always set plants out in a water or earth sign [Taurus, Cancer, Virgo, Scorpio, Capricorn, or Pisces]."

"Graft just before the sap starts to flow, while the moon is in its first or second quarter, and while it is passing through fruitful, watery sign, or Capricorn. Never graft or plant on Sunday as this is a barren, hot day."

"Plant flowers in Libra, which is an airy sign that also represents beauty."

"Corn planted in Leo will have a hard, round stalk and small ears."

"Crops planted in Taurus and Cancer will stand drought."

"Don't plant potatoes in the feet [Pisces]. If you do, they will develop little nubs like toes all over the main potato."

"Plant all things which yield above ground during the increase or growing of the moon, and all things which yield below the ground (root crops) when the moon is decreasing or darkening."

"Never plant on the first day of the new moon, or on a day when the moon changes quarters."

From Eliot Wigginton (ed.), The Foxfire Book *(Garden City, N.Y.: Doubleday, 1972), pp. 215–218.*

youth of the 1970s, have lamented the loss of closeness to nature that accompanied the rise of nonfolk culture, and they have sought to recapture that intimacy by withdrawing to rural retreats. But to reestablish the close ties, they, like folk groups, will have to depend on nature for their day-to-day livelihood, a risk and sacrifice that relatively few are able or willing to take or make. Such intimacy is the product of centuries of trial and error and, once lost, is not easily regained.

Cultural Integration in Folk Geography

In reading the discussion of culture regions, diffusion, and ecology, you perhaps got the impression that folk groups are completely self-sufficient and totally segregated from the popular culture. Rarely is that true. Few folk societies are so isolated and remote as to escape altogether from interaction with the larger world. The theme of cultural integration will allow us to see how groups can retain their folk character and yet be in almost daily contact with popular cultures—that is, how folk groups are integrated into the nonfolk world. There is a lively exchange constantly under way between the folk and the popular cultures. Perhaps most commonly, the folk absorb ideas filtering down from the popular culture, but occasionally elements of the folk culture penetrate the popular society. Even peasants can innovate, despite the relatively unchanging character of folk society, and these innovations and ideas can spread upward to other classes of society. Two examples from the culture of the Appalachian hill folk of the southern United States will illustrate the integration of folk and popular, showing the impact that these two cultures can have on each other. These examples are mountain "moonshining" and "country" music.

The mountain moonshine whiskey industry

Corn whiskey has been manufactured since the earliest days of Anglo-American pioneering in the southern Appalachians in the eighteenth century. Very likely its origins lie still further back, in the Scottish folk tradition of making whiskey from barley. The word *whiskey* is itself of Celtic origin, probably from the Scottish Gaelic *uisge beatha* ("water of life"), and the techniques of making the beverage were likely diffused to America and to the Appalachians with the Scotch-Irish, a people of Scottish origin who came from Northern Ireland. Home manufacture of whiskey has prevailed in many Appalachian hill settlements for two hundred years and is a deep-rooted folk custom (Figure 7-17). Whiskey-making withstood the prohibitionist attitudes of the great nineteenth-century religious revival, and even though many mountaineers are devout Baptists or Methodists, they continue to defy the anti-liquor teachings of these and other Protestant churches. The mountain folk were more than willing to vote their areas legally "dry," but they were not prepared to give up distilling and drinking hard liquor. Much like the geophagy of southern blacks, corn whiskey among the mountain whites is very persistent in the folk diet.

Traditionally, corn liquor was intended mainly for consumption within the family, not for market. In other words, the manufacture of "white lightning" was still purely in the folk tradition. Gradually over the years, however, some Appalachian moonshine began finding its way to market. Whiskey provided the best opportunity for the hill folk to participate in the money economy of the country, since its manufacture converted a bulky grain crop of low cash value into a beverage that was compact and of high value per unit of weight. As early as 1791, the United States federal government had begun taxing manufacturers of whiskey, but from the beginning the mountaineers found ways to avoid the tax. Stills were concealed in remote coves and hollows to escape detection by the federal revenue collectors; if the stills were discovered and destroyed, new ones in different locations soon replaced them. The revenuers proved no more successful in abolishing the making of whiskey than the churches had been. In effect, the mountain folk accepted the markets offered by the popular culture but rejected its legal and political institutions.

The mountain people proved more than capable of evading the law. By the 1950s, some 25,000 gallons of white lightning were reaching the market each week from the counties of eastern Tennessee alone (Figure 7-18). In spite of numerous raids by the federal authorities, production continued unabated. Today, a substantial amount of illicit whiskey still reaches market from southern Appalachia. This production, coupled with that of the legal taxpaying whiskey manufacturers of Kentucky and Tennessee, represents an impressive survival of a folk industry in a popular society.

Interaction with the popular culture in the production of illegal whiskey led to other kinds of contact, providing still more examples of cultural integration. To market the produce, after about 1930 at least, fast vehicles were required in order to outrun the law. The result was a "folk automobile," a souped-up jalopy quite humble in appearance but capable

FIGURE 7-17
An Appalachian whiskey still.

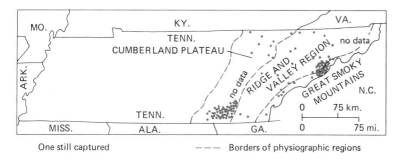

One still captured   — — — Borders of physiographic regions

FIGURE 7-18
Approximate number and location of illegal stills captured monthly in eastern Tennessee in the mid-1950s. The rugged Smoky Mountains and Cumberland Plateau offer more abundant hiding places for stills than does the ridge and valley region. What might account for the clustering in two main areas? (After: Loyal Durand, Jr., "Mountain Moonshining in East Tennessee," *Geographical Review*, 46 (1956), 171.)

of very high speeds. Some claim that the mountaineer's whiskey-running automobile was the forerunner of the basic American stock car and that stock car racing is simply a legal form of the traditional flight from revenuers (Figure 7-19). The Ford flathead V-8 of the 1930s and 1940s owed much of its commercial success in the South to the fact that it was the easiest and best engine to modify for these purposes. Thus, stock car racing is another result of the interplay between folk and popular cultures.

FIGURE 7-19
Stock car racing in the American South may be a product of interaction between folk and popular culture.

The bluegrass country music industry

Country music is derived, to a great degree, from the folk ballads of the English and Scotch-Irish who settled the southern Appalachians in colonial times. Some experts have even hypothesized that the use of the fiddle (violin) to produce the shrill sounds so typical of mountain music is an effort to recapture the sound of the Celtic Scottish bagpipe. Gradually, Appalachian folk music absorbed influences of the American social experience, becoming a composite of Old World and New World folk traditions. Like whiskey-making, Appalachian music long remained confined to the traditional society that had developed it. As folk music, it gave expression to a unique lifestyle and a particular land, while dealing with such universal themes as love and hate, happiness and sorrow, comedy and tragedy.

Entry of country music into the popular culture began about the time of World War I and was facilitated by the invention and diffusion of the radio. Popularization brought changes to country music. The number of tunes and songs, which had been relatively small and slow to increase in the folk society, exploded in a few decades into tens of thousands. Performers in crowded, noisy night spots soon resorted to electrical amplification to achieve the needed volume, producing such curious folk-popular mixtures as the electric guitar. The themes of lyrics were addressed to life in the popular rather than the folk culture. But at its core, country music remained folk.

Bluegrass, one of many styles of country music, emerged in the 1930s during the process of popularization of Appalachian folk music. It was developed by Bill Monroe, a Kentuckian. The unique bluegrass sound is achieved by the joining of a lead banjo with a fiddle, guitar, mandolin, and string bass. In many ways, bluegrass remains faithful to its folk origins. Only nonelectric instruments are used, and the high-pitched, emotional vocal sound clearly reveals derivation from Scottish church singing. The acceptance of bluegrass music remains greatest in its Appalachian core area in Kentucky, Tennessee, Virginia, and North Carolina (Figure 7-20). Most bluegrass performers are drawn from this core area, and the music retains a strong identification with Appalachian places, both in the titles and lyrics of songs and in the names of performing groups. Thus we find songs like "Hills of Roane County" (Tennessee) performed by groups like the Clinch Mountain Boys.

The nineteenth-century migration of Appalachian hill folk to Missouri, Arkansas, Texas, and Oklahoma, coupled with the Depression-era movement of "Okies" and "Arkies" to the Central Valley of California, provided natural areas for bluegrass expansion in the mid-twentieth century. The distribution of bluegrass music festivals, mapped by cultural geographer George O. Carney, accurately reflects these migrations (Figure 7-20).

Thus, music of the folk tradition has been modified, popularized, and spread by means of technology that is part of the popular culture. Such music provides yet another example of the interaction of cultural forces that underlies the cultural integration theme.

Folk Architecture in the Cultural Landscape

Every folk society produces its own distinctive cultural landscape, and one of the most obvious and visible aspects of the folk landscape is the architecture. The products of **folk architecture** are derived not from the drafting tables of professional architects, but from the collective memory of a traditional people. These buildings, whether dwellings, barns, churches, mills, or inns, are not based on blueprints, but on mental images that change little from one generation to the next. In this sense, we can

• Home of professional bluegrass music performer, 1972

• Bluegrass music festivals held, 1972

FIGURE 7-20

The geography of "bluegrass" country music. The Southern Appalachian core area of bluegrass music is clearly revealed by the location of major performers; the distribution of festivals indicates both the popularization of this style of country music and the migration of Appalachian people to other states. How many of the festival sites are in hill or mountain areas? What barriers, if any, might prevent the continued diffusion of bluegrass? (After George O. Carney, "Bluegrass Grows all Around: The Spatial Dimensions of a Country Music Style," *Journal of Geography*, 73 (April 1974), 37, 46.)

BUILDING A FOLK HOUSE: A GEORGIA LOG CABIN

Folk houses are built without architects, often by communal labor. Here is a description of a log cabin "raising":

"Most of 'em we built was log houses, and we'd pitch in and in a couple a' days we'd have a man a house built. Ever'body 'd just go in and help a man. Wasn't countin' on gettin' a dime out of it. 'Course they'd have a big supper, and when we got done we always had somethin' at th' end—some kinda big party 'r dance in th' house 'fore they ever moved in. . . .

"You take fifty men and it didn't take but a little bit t'

build a dadblame house. It went up fast. Some done th' notchin'. Some done th' layin' up. Some carryin' th' logs. Some peelin' th' logs. They 'uz always a job fer every bunch, and ever'body 'uz on their job and they kep' ever'thing goin', y' know. God, it didn't take long t' build a *big* house. Puttin' down th' floorin' was th' biggest job in it."

From Lawton Brooks, as quoted in Eliot Wigginton (ed.), Foxfire 2 (Garden City, N.Y.: Doubleday, 1973), pp. 367–368.

---

speak of an "architecture without architects" (see box, "Building a Folk House"). Folk buildings are extensions of a people and their region. They help provide the unique character or essence of each district or province and are a highly visible aspect of the human mosaic. Do not look to folk architecture for refined artistic genius or spectacular, revolutionary design. Seek in it instead the traditional, the conservative, and the functional. Expect from it a simple beauty, a harmony with the physical environment, a visible expression of folk culture (see box, "The Cultural Ecology of a Folk House").

THE CULTURAL ECOLOGY OF A FOLK HOUSE

Folk houses, as a rule, are beautifully suited to their physical environment. Centuries of trial and error taught their builders how to construct dwellings that provide comfort and protection from the extremes and hazards of the local weather. Nowhere are these attributes of folk architecture better displayed than on Lan Yü (Orchid Island), located in the Pacific Ocean forty miles off the coast of Taiwan.

The Malay-Polynesian inhabitants of Lan Yü, the Yami, build their folk houses mostly below ground level, in stone-lined pits, for protection from hurricanes. The sketch shows a cross section of a Yami

house. A strongly reinforced, streamlined roof projects partly above ground level, exposing a section of an elongated slope to the brunt of the hurricane winds. The force of the storm wind presses down on the roof and slides by, keeping it in place. To escape the midday heat when no storms are blowing, each Yami builds a "cool tower" above ground level. These are easily replaced when hurricanes blow them away.

Adapted with permission from Chang Shuhua, "The Gentle Yamis of Orchid Island," National Geographic Magazine, 151 (January 1977), 107.

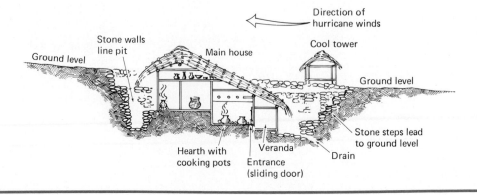

Direction of hurricane winds
Stone walls line pit
Ground level
Main house
Cool tower
Ground level
Stone steps lead to ground level
Hearth with cooking pots
Veranda
Entrance (sliding door)
Drain

The house, or dwelling, is the most basic structure erected by people, regardless of their culture. For most persons in nearly all folk cultures, a house is the single most important thing they will ever build. Folk cultures as a rule are rural and agricultural. For these reasons, it seems appropriate to focus on traditional farmstead architecture, and particularly on the folk house, in this treatment of the cultural landscape.

Traditional building materials

One way we can classify folk houses and farmsteads is by the type of building material used in construction (see Figure 7-13). Farm dwellings range from massive houses of stone, endowed with as much permanency as humans can give to a structure, to temporary brush and thatch huts. Figure 7-21 maps the traditional building materials used in rural folk architecture in different parts of the world. Environmental conditions, particularly climate, vegetation, and the types of building material locally available, strongly influence the choice of construction materials (Figure 7-22).

Shifting cultivators of the tropical rain forests typically build houses of poles and leaves. Sedentary subsistence farming peoples of the adjacent highlands and the oases and river valleys of the Old World desert zone rely principally on earthen construction, in the form of sun-dried (adobe) bricks or pounded earth. In some more prosperous regions, kiln-baked bricks are available. Herders and farmers of the semiarid, tropical savanna grasslands, particularly in Africa, construct thatched houses from coarse

FIGURE 7–21

Traditional building materials in rural areas vary from the relative permanence of stone to cloth tents. What factors might explain this pattern?

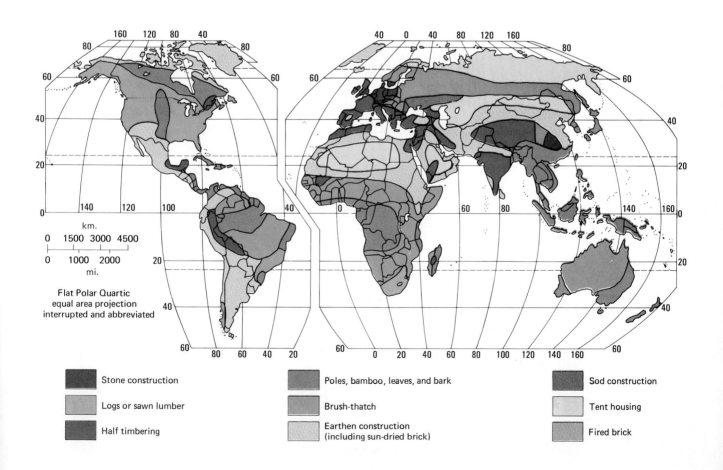

Stone construction	Poles, bamboo, leaves, and bark	Sod construction
Logs or sawn lumber	Brush-thatch	Tent housing
Half timbering	Earthen construction (including sun-dried brick)	Fired brick

FIGURE 7-22
Rural architecture can be as simple as the tent of the nomads in Afghanistan shown in upper left. In Niger, West Africa, rural folk cooperate to secure the framework for a hut. Each rib is a bundle of tree limbs lashed together (upper right). The small stone house with rock fence is in a New Mexico Hispano settlement and reflects the local dominance of one building material. (Photo courtesy of Professor Charles F. Gritzner of South Dakota State University.)

grasses and thorn bushes. Mediterranean farmers, most of whom live in rocky, deforested lands, use stones as their principal building material, as do some rural residents of interior India and the Andean highlands of South America. Entire landscapes of stone, including walls, roofs, terraces, streets, and fences, lend an air of permanence to the cultural landscapes of these regions.

In middle and higher latitudes, in areas where timber remains abundant, farm folk traditionally built their houses of sawn lumber or unmilled logs. The log cabin of the United States and its frame successors fit in this category, as do the folk houses of northern Europe and most of the Soviet Union. In some partially deforested temperate regions, including lands as diverse as central Europe and parts of China, farmers once built half-timbered houses, raising a framework of hardwood beams and filling the interstices with some other material. Sod or turf houses are typical of some prairie and tundra areas, such as the Russian steppes and, in pioneer times, the American Great Plains. Nomadic herders generally live in portable tents made of skins or wool.

Floorplan and layout

Another way to classify traditional farmsteads is on the basis of the floorplan and layout. One style is the **unit farmstead,** in which people, farm animals, and storage facilities are all under one roof in a single structure (Figure 7-23). Such houses, in their simplest form, are rectangular and single-storied. People and livestock occupy different ends of the structure. Often not even a dividing wall separates human and animal quarters. More complex unit farmsteads are multistoried and arranged so that people and livestock live on different levels. Unit farmsteads of both types are widely distributed in Europe.

More common are farmsteads in which the house, barn, and stalls occupy separate buildings. The **courtyard farmstead** is a common type within this category (See Figure 7-24). The various structures of the

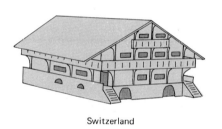
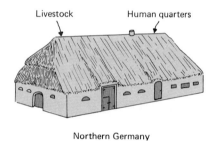

Livestock   Human quarters

Switzerland

Northern Germany

FIGURE 7–23

Two examples of unit farmsteads from Europe. The northern German folk structure is single story, with people and livestock occupying different ends separated by an open hearth. The Swiss chalet is multistory; the ground floor houses livestock and the upper stories are for people.

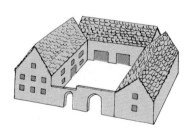

Adobe wall, thatched at top for protection from weather

German Frankish farmstead, Central Europe
(half-timbering, multistory house)

Inca Marca farmstead, Peru and Bolivia
(stone construction, single story)

Chinese farmstead, Szechwan province
(adobe brick, thatched roof, single story)

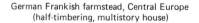

FIGURE 7–24

These three multistructure courtyard farmsteads come from widely divergent cultures. What could account for the similarity? Is it a case of cultural diffusion? Or did the obvious advantages of the courtyard farmstead for defense and privacy lead to its independent invention by folk societies in Germany, South America, and China?

courtyard farmstead cluster around an enclosed yard. This type appears in several seemingly unrelated culture regions, such as the Inca-settled portions of the Andes Mountains, the hills of central Germany, and eastern China. Courtyard farmsteads have a wide distribution in part because they offer both privacy and protection.

In most countries where Germanic Europeans immigrated and settled, including Anglo-America, Australia, and New Zealand, the **strewn farmstead** prevails. The various farm buildings, instead of being linked together around a central courtyard, are spaced apart from one another in no consistent pattern. Strewn farmsteads are especially common in zones of wooden construction, where the danger of fire is greatest. Spacing the buildings reduces the danger that fire will spread from one building to another. Since they are poorly suited to defense, they are often associated with rural regions of greater than average tranquility.

Other characteristics

Material composition, floorplan, and layout are all important ingredients of folk architecture, but there are numerous other characteristics that can be used to classify farmsteads and dwellings. The form or shape of the roof, the placement of the chimney, and even such details as the number and location of doors and windows can be important classifying criteria. Professor Estyn Evans (see biographical sketch), the noted expert on Irish folk geography, considered roof form and chimney placement, among other traits, in devising an informal classification of Irish folk houses (Figure 7-25). He discerned three major folk-housing culture regions, as

FIGURE 7–25

Some folk houses of Ireland. The Irish houses, while basically similar, differ in roof form, chimney placement, location of windows, material composition, and floorplan. Some are unit farmsteads, such as the barrel-roofed type, in which people lived in one end and the livestock in the other. What architectural features do all these houses have in common? The western coastal fringe of Ireland is the windiest part of the country. What effect might wind have had on roof form? (After various publications of E. Estyn Evans.)

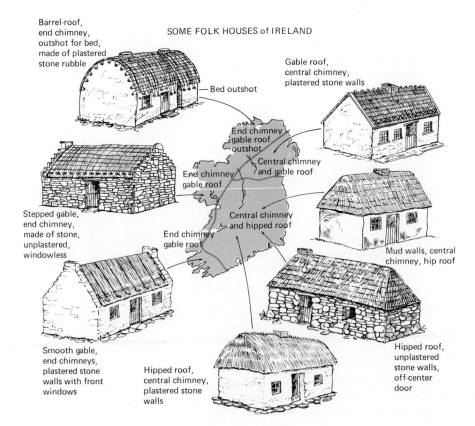

SOME FOLK HOUSES of IRELAND

Barrel-roof, end chimney, outshot for bed, made of plastered stone rubble

Bed outshot

Gable roof, central chimney, plastered stone walls

End chimney gable roof outshot

Central chimney and gable roof

End chimney gable roof

Central chimney and hipped roof

Stepped gable, end chimney, made of stone, unplastered, windowless

End chimney gable roof

Mud walls, central chimney, hip roof

Smooth gable, end chimneys, plastered stone walls with front windows

Hipped roof, central chimney, plastered stone walls

Hipped roof, unplastered stone walls, off-center door

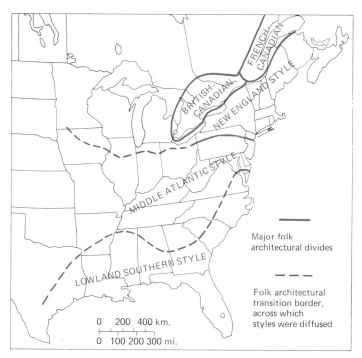

FIGURE 7-26

Eastern American folk architecture culture regions. Compare this map to Figure 1–4. For examples of folk houses typical of some of these regions, see Figure 7–27. (After Kniffen and Lewis, with modifications.)

determined by chimney and roof, on the small island of Ireland. If floorplan and material composition had been included, additional culture regions would have been identified, based on local architectural features such as the bed outshot of far north Ireland, the mud wall constructions of the interior counties, and the off-center door found in several districts (Figure 7-25).

Folk housing in the United States

In the United States and Canada, folk architecture is largely a relict form in the cultural landscape. Popular culture, with its mass-produced, commercially built houses, has so overwhelmed the folk tradition that few if any folk houses are being built today. But many survive in the landscape, reminders of the rich American legacy in folk architecture.

Geographers recognize five major folk architecture culture regions in eastern North America, three of which are in the United States (Figure 7-26). The names given to the culture regions in the eastern United States should by now be familiar to you: New England, Middle Atlantic, and Lowland South. You have encountered similar terms and regions in Chapters 1 and 5 as well as earlier in this chapter.

The New England folk houses are all of wooden frame construction. Among the oldest of New England types, dating to colonial times, is the "large" house, a huge dwelling of two-and-a-half stories built around a central chimney. The floorplan consists of four full-sized rooms on each story. The addition of a one-and-a-half story shed on the rear of a New

E. ESTYN EVANS   1905-

Though born in Shropshire, England, Evans is of Welsh heritage and received his education in Wales, where he studied under H. J. Fleure in geography and anthropology at Aberystwyth. At the young age of twenty-three, he was invited to establish a Department of Geography at Queen's University in Belfast, Northern Ireland, and he remained with that institution of higher learning throughout his forty-four-year career.

The marriage of geography and anthropology in his training led him to specialize in the field of folk geography, and he was one of the first geographers in the English-speaking world to pursue the study of material folk culture. Evans's Celtic background was a factor in the deep attachment he developed for Ireland, his adopted home. He is best known to cultural geographers for numerous books and articles about the folk material culture of Ireland, in particular *Irish Heritage* (1943), *Mourne County* (1951), *Irish Folk Ways* (1957), *and The Personality of Ireland* (1973). Evans long served as Chairman of Geography at Queen's and for a time as Dean of the Faculty of Arts. He became the first director of the Institute of Irish Studies, which he helped to establish in 1965. He is president of the Ulster Folk Life Society and trustee of the Ulster Folk and Transport Museum, of which he was the founder-father. In 1970 he was honored by being appointed Commander of the Order of the British Empire, and in 1973 he received the Victoria Medal of the Royal Geographical Society. He holds honorary doctorates from five universities.

England "large" produced the **saltbox house,** so named because the roof profile has a longer slope at the rear, duplicating the shape of an old-fashioned salt container (Figure 7-27). The New England "large" and "saltbox" are massive houses, well suited to the extremely cold New England winters, when most work must be done indoors (Figure 7-28). Somewhat later, New England folk developed the smaller **Cape Cod house,** similar to the earlier central-chimney saltbox and large houses but only one-and-a-half stories tall. Still later came the **upright and wing**

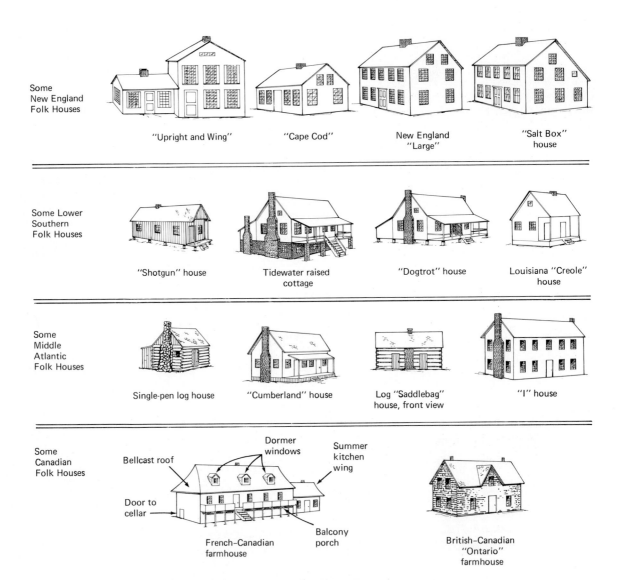

Some
New England
Folk Houses

"Upright and Wing"   "Cape Cod"   New England "Large"   "Salt Box" house

Some Lower
Southern
Folk Houses

"Shotgun" house   Tidewater raised cottage   "Dogtrot" house   Louisiana "Creole" house

Some
Middle
Atlantic
Folk Houses

Single-pen log house   "Cumberland" house   Log "Saddlebag" house, front view   "I" house

Some
Canadian
Folk Houses

Bellcast roof   Dormer windows   Summer kitchen wing   Door to cellar   French-Canadian farmhouse   Balcony porch   British-Canadian "Ontario" farmhouse

EXAMPLES of EASTERN AMERICAN FOLK HOUSES

FIGURE 7-27
Examples of American folk houses. Each of the five folk architecture regions in eastern North America (Figure 7–26) has characteristic house types. In floorplan, many of these are derived from the British Isles. What similarities can you detect between these American types and the Irish types shown in Figure 7–25? What differences? (After Kniffen, Glassie, Lewis, and Georges Gauthier-Larouche, *Évolution de la maison rurale traditionnelle dans la région de Québec,* Québec: Presses de l'Université Laval, 1975.)

FIGURE 7–28
A New England folk house and New England generic place name, in the Western Reserve area of northeastern Ohio. The cultural landscape of this section of Ohio bears the unmistakable imprint of the Northern, or New England, folk culture. The folk house is a "New England Large" (see Figure 7–27), and the "Center" suffix is also a good indicator of New England's influence, as is the "Classical Revival" Mediterranean prefix, Mantua, derived from Mantova, Italy. See Figures 5–14 and 8–10. (Photo 1977 by Terry G. Jordan.)

house, essentially one-story and two-story houses facing different directions and joined together as one dwelling.

Lowland Southern folk houses, like those of New England, are generally of wooden frame construction. They differ, however, in their much smaller size, the addition of front porches, and their high foundations, all of which reflect a warmer climate. Many have exterior rather than interior chimneys, to minimize the heat retention in this hot, subtropical zone. The **tidewater raised cottage** consists of two full-sized rooms, side by side, with rear shed rooms and a front porch, all raised high above ground level on a brick superstructure to escape periodic floodwaters. The **dogtrot house** is even better suited to the hot climate by virtue of the open roofed passageway, or dogtrot, placed between the two main rooms to pick up cooling breezes (Figure 7-29). Louisiana **Creole houses** are often of half-timbered rather than frame construction, and they have a central chimney and a distinctive roof style consisting of two unbroken slopes covering the two main rooms, shed rooms, and porch. The **shotgun house** has gables facing the front and rear rather than the sides, and it is two or more rooms and a porch long but only one room wide. Its name derives from the folk saying that you can fire a shotgun through the entire length of the house without hitting anything, since the doors are all lined up in a row. According to John M. Vlach, a scholar of American folklife, the shotgun house is an African folk house, brought initially by slaves to Haiti in the West Indies and later, about 1800, from Haiti to Louisiana.

The most distinguishing trait of Middle Atlantic folk architecture is log construction, formed by laying logs horizontally and notching them together to form the walls. Introduced by Germans, Swedes, and Finns in the Delaware Valley and southeastern Pennsylvania in the 1600s and 1700s, log construction remained confined largely to the Middle Atlantic architectural zone. The simplest folk house of the Middle Atlantic is the

FIGURE 7–29

A dogtrot house, typical of the Lowland South. The distinguishing feature is the open passageway, or dogtrot, between the two main rooms. This house, still occupied by descendants of the builder, was built in the mid-nineteenth century and is located in Newton County, East Texas. (Photo 1978 by Terry G. Jordan.)

log **single-pen house,** or one-room dwelling (Figure 7-27). The addition of a second log room to the chimney end of a single-pen house forms the **saddlebag house,** a type common in the Ohio Valley. Adding a room to the gable end opposite from the chimney produces the **Cumberland house,** a common folk house of middle Tennessee and some other Upland Southern regions. The Middle Atlantic folk revealed affluence by adding a full second story to the Cumberland, saddlebag, or other one-story types. The resulting folk dwelling, one room deep, two rooms wide, and two full stories tall, is called an **"I" house** (Figure 7-30). Its name derives from the fact that it is very common in Indiana, Illinois, and Iowa, states that begin with the letter I.

Canada also offers a variety of traditional folk houses (Figure 7-26). In French-speaking Québec, one of the common types consists of a main story atop a cellar, with attic rooms beneath curved, bell-shaped, or "bellcast" roof (Figure 7-27). A balcony-porch with railing extends across the front, sheltered by the overhanging eaves. Attached to one side of this French-Canadian folk house is a summer kitchen that is sealed off during the long, cold winter. Often the folk houses of Québec are built of stone. To the west, in the British-Canadian region, one type of folk house occurs so frequently that it is known as the "Ontario farmhouse." One-and-a-half stories in height, the Ontario farmhouse is usually built of brick and has a distinctive gabled front dormer window (Figure 7-27).

Many other folk-built structures are part of the landscape and have been

FIGURE 7–30
An "I" house on the American prairies. This typical Middle Atlantic house was built on the Blackland Prairie of Texas by a settler from Ohio. Typical features of the "I" house include two full stories, single-room depth (excluding the real addition), double-room with side-facing gables, and matched exterior chimneys. (Photo 1833, from the J. E. Taulman collection, University of Texas Archives, Austin, with permission.)

studied by cultural geographers. A rich literature exists, for example, on folk barns, covered bridges, grist windmills, traditional fences, and folk churches. The preceding material on folk houses should be regarded as only an introduction to and small sample of the kinds of landscape features studied by folk geographers.

Conclusion

Folk geographers study traditional cultures and are interested both in material and nonmaterial aspects of folklife. Because folk culture displays major variations from one place to another, the device of culture region is a useful starting point for the study of traditional lifestyles. We saw how, by employing the theme of culture region, we could bring spatial order to the myriad of folk traits that survive, in vestige at least, in the United States.

The study of cultural diffusion allowed us to see how, even in conservative, change-resistant folk societies, innovations and traits spread across geographical space, how a Welsh folktale reaches Missouri or a New England agricultural fair reaches the Pacific Coast. Our study of the blowgun presented us with the kind of spatial problem that leads to speculation concerning diffusion versus independent invention. We also suggested that many problems remain to be solved, that the study of folklife is still wide open to imaginative scholars of the future.

By using the theme of cultural ecology, we explored the fundamental, almost religious tie that binds folk groups to the land. We glimpsed and began to appreciate the intimate knowledge, far surpassing that of the popular culture, that folk groups have of their physical surroundings.

The study of cultural integration revealed the many connections and causal relationships that exist between folk and popular cultures. We saw how elements of folk culture can penetrate and influence the popular realm and the kinds of changes they undergo in the process.

Through our study of folk architecture, we saw an example of the visible imprint of folk groups on the cultural landscape. The folk house, perhaps the most basic type of structure ever built, served as our guide to the incredibly varied landscapes created by folk groups. We learned that even in industrialized, urbanized societies like that of the United States, the folk architecture, in relic form, remains clearly imprinted on the land.

In America, the study of folk culture, particularly material folk culture, is still in its infancy. It needs the diligent research of a new generation of cultural geographers, folklorists, anthropologists, and archaeologists; of psychologists, sociologists, linguists, and historians. For those who are intrigued by the study of folklife, the future offers an abundance of needed research and fieldwork. It promises the rich satisfaction that comes from discovery, personal contacts with folk groups, and the recording and preservation of endangered traditional customs and objects.

Glossary

Bluegrass a type of popular country music, derived from Appalachian folk music in Kentucky, with a distinctive sound achieved by combining a banjo, fiddle, guitar, mandolin, and string bass.

Cape Cod house a New England folk house of frame construction, one-and-a-half stories, with a central chimney.

Courtyard farmstead a clustering of farmhouse, barn, and other farm buildings around a central courtyard or open place.

Creole house a Lowland Southern folk house of half-timbered construction, with a central chimney and two unbroken roof slopes.

Cumberland house a Middle Atlantic folk house consisting of two rooms side by side, with chimneys on the ends.

Curandero in Mexican folk medicine, a curer, or healer.

Dogtrot house a Lowland Southern folk house distinguished by an open, roofed passage or breezeway between the two main rooms.

Folk traditional, rural, nonpopular.

Folk architecture structures built by members of a folk society or culture in a traditional manner and style, without the assistance of professional architects or blueprints, using locally available raw materials.

Folk culture the body of folk traditions and practices found in individual persons who no longer belong to a cohesive social group.

Folk geography the study of the spatial patterns of elements of folklife; a branch of cultural geography.

Folklife the totality of the material and nonmaterial folk culture.

Folklore the teaching and wisdom of a folk group; the traditional tales, sayings, beliefs, and superstitions that are transmitted orally.

Folk society a small, cohesive, stable, isolated, nearly self-sufficient group that is homogeneous in custom and race; characterized by a strong family or clan structure; order maintained through sanctions based in the religion or family; little division of labor other than between the sexes; frequent and strong interpersonal relationships; and a material culture consisting mainly of hand-made goods.

Geophagy   the deliberate eating of earth.

"I" house   a Middle Atlantic folk house characterized by single-room depth, two-room width, and two full stories of height.

Material culture   includes all physical, material objects made and used by members of a cultural group, such as clothing, buildings, tools and utensils, instruments, furniture, and artwork; the visible aspect of culture.

Nonmaterial culture   includes the oral aspect of a culture, such as songs, dialect, tales, beliefs, and customs.

Popular society   a large, heterogeneous, weakly united group permitting considerable individualism, innovation, and change; having a money-based economy, division of labor into professions, and secular institutions of control; producing and consuming machine-made goods.

Saddlebag house   a two-room Middle Atlantic folk house with a chimney positioned between the two rooms.

Saltbox house   a large New England folk house, so named because the roof profile has a longer slope at the rear of the house, duplicating the shape of an old-fashioned salt container.

Shotgun house   a Lowland Southern folk house of African origin, distinguished by single-room width and a depth or length of two or more rooms, producing a long, narrow house.

Single-pen house   a house consisting of one room, such as the single-pen log folk house of the Middle Atlantic architectural region.

Strewn farmstead   a farmstead in which the house, barn, and other buildings are spaced apart from one another.

Tidewater raised cottage   a Lowland Southern folk house consisting of two frame rooms and a porch elevated on a tall brick foundation structure.

Unit farmstead   a farmstead in which the living quarters, stables, and barn are combined under one roof in a single structure.

Upright and wing house   a New England folk house consisting of a one-story section joined to a two-story section, with roof lines at right angles to one another.

Suggested Readings

Jan H. Brunvand (ed.). *The Study of American Folklore: An Introduction*, 2nd ed. New York: Norton, 1978.

Ronald H. Buchanan. "Geography and Folk Life," *Folk Life*, 1 (1963), 5–15.

George O. Carney. "T for Texas, T for Tennessee: The Origins of American Country Music Notables," *Journal of Geography*, 78 (1979), 218–225.

George O. Carney. *The Sounds of People and Places: Readings in the Geography of Music*, Washington, D.C.: University Press of America, 1978.

E. Estyn Evans. "The Cultural Geographer and Folklife Research," in Richard M. Dorson (ed.), *Folklore and Folklife: An Introduction*. Chicago: University of Chicago Press, 1972, pp. 517–532.

E. Estyn Evans. "The Ecology of Peasant Life in Western Europe," in William L. Thomas (ed.), *Man's Role in Changing the Face of the Earth*. Chicago: University of Chicago Press, 1956, pp. 217–239.

E. Estyn Evans, *Irish Folk Ways*, London: Routledge and Kegan Paul, 1957.

Larry R. Ford and Floyd M. Henderson. "The Image of Place in American Popular Music: 1890–1970," *Places*, 1 (1974), 31–37.

George M. Foster. "What Is Folk Culture?" *American Anthropologist*, 55 (1953), 159–173.

Henry Glassie. *Pattern in the Material Folk Culture of the Eastern United States*. Philadelphia: University of Pennsylvania Press, 1968.

John M. Hunter. "Geophagy in Africa and in the United States: A Culture-Nutrition Hypothesis," *Geographical Review*, 63 (1973), 170–195.

Stephen C. Jett. "The Development and Distribution of the Blowgun," *Annals, Association of American Geographers*, 60 (1970), 662–688.

Terry G. Jordan, "Alpine, Alemannic, and American Log Architecture," *Annals, Association of American Geographers*, 70 (1980), 154–180.

Terry G. Jordan. " The Texan Appalachia," *Annals, Association of American Geographers*, 60 (1970), 409–427.

Terry G. Jordan. *Texas Log Buildings: A Folk Architecture*. Austin: University of Texas Press, 1978.

Clarissa T. Kimber. "Plants in the Folk Medicine of the Texas-Mexico Borderlands," *Proceedings, Association of American Geographers*, 5 (1973), 130–133.

Fred B. Kniffen. "American Cultural Geography and Folklife," in Don Yoder (ed.), *American Folklife*. Austin: University of Texas Press, 1976, pp. 51–70.

Fred B. Kniffen. "Folk-Housing: Key to Diffusion," *Annals, Association of American Geographers*, 55 (1965), 549–577.

Peirce F. Lewis. "Common Houses, Cultural Spoor," *Landscape*, 19:2 (January 1975), 1–22.

Alan Lomax. *The Folk Songs of North America*, Garden City, N.Y.: Doubleday, 1960.

E. Joan Wilson Miller. "The Ozark Culture Region as Revealed by Traditional Materials," *Annals, Association of American Geographers*, 58 (1968), 51–77.

Campbell W. Pennington, *The Tarahumar of Mexico: Their Environment and Material Culture*. Salt Lake City: University of Utah Press, 1963.

Pioneer America: The Journal of American Historic Material Culture. Published by the Pioneer America Society and the Department of Geography and Anthropology at Louisiana State University, Baton Rouge, this is the leading American periodical on the subject of material folk culture and folk geography. Volume 1 was published in 1969.

Edward T. Price. "Root Digging in the Appalachians: The Geography of Botanical Drugs," *Geographical Review*, 50 (1960), 1–20.

Amos Rapoport. *House Form and Culture*. Englewood Cliffs, N.J.: Prentice-Hall, 1969.

Ellen Churchill Semple. "The Anglo-Saxons of the Kentucky Mountains: A Study in Anthropogeography," *Geographical Journal*, 17 (1901), 588–623.

Karl A. Sinnhuber. "On the Relations of Folklore and Geography," *Folk-lore*, 68 (1957), 385–404.

Roger T. Trindell. "American Folklore Studies and Geography," *Southern Folklore Quarterly*, 34 (1970), 1–11.

Donald E. Vermeer and Dennis A. Frate. "Geophagy in a Mississippi County," *Annals, Association of American Geographers*, 65 (1975), 414–424.

Peter O. Wacker. "Folk Architecture as an Indicator of Culture Areas and Culture Diffusion: Dutch Barns and Barracks in New Jersey," *Pioneer America*, 5 (July 1973), 37–47.

Eugene J. Wilhelm, Jr. "Field Work in Folklife: Meeting Ground of Geography and Folklore," *Keystone Folklore Quarterly*, 13 (1968), 241–247.

Don Yoder (ed.). *American Folklife*. Austin: University of Texas Press, 1976.

Chapter-opening photo: A camper ➤
club in the Red Rock Canyon,
California.

The Geography of Popular Culture

8

What do quiche Lorraine, a neatly manicured suburban grass lawn, a collegiate basketball game, and levis have in common? How are they, in turn, linked to fraternity house frisbee tossing, a can of beer from a Milwaukee brewery, CB radios, punk rock, or a rodeo? The answer is that all are aspects of the **popular culture**.

The preceding chapter dealt with folk culture. We suggested there that folk and popular could be regarded as contrasting cultural alternatives. As you may recall, we described popular culture as constantly changing, based in large, heterogeneous groups of people concentrated mainly in urban areas. Popular material goods are mass-produced by machines in factories, and a money economy prevails. Relationships between individuals are more numerous but less personal than in folk societies, and the family structure is weaker. People are more mobile, less attached to place and environment. A distinct division of labor, reflected in myriad, highly specialized "professions" and "jobs," characterizes the earning of a livelihood, and considerable leisure time is available to most people. Secular institutions of control, such as the police, army, and courts, take the place of family and church in maintaining order.

If there is a single hallmark of popular culture, it is *change*. Words such as *growth*, *progress*, *fad*, and *trend* crop up frequently in newspapers and conversations. So pervasive is change that some persons are unable to cope with it, leading them to an insecurity expressed in the term *future shock*. In a humorous debunking of popular culture and his own inability to change quickly enough, *Dallas Morning News* columnist John Anders recalled that he "danced the Twist when others had moved on to the Swim, wore Old Spice after the rest of the guys had graduated to English Leather, donned corduroy during the burlap frenzy, and ate Big Boy Hamburgers while my peers moved into Quiche Lorraine. . . ."

If all these characteristics seem rather commonplace and "normal," it should not be surprising. You are, after all, firmly enmeshed in the popular culture, or else you would not be attending college or reading a book. The large majority of people in Europe, the United States, Canada, and other "developed" countries now belong to the popular rather than the folk culture. Industrialization, urbanization, the rise of formal education, and the resultant increase in leisure time have all contributed to the spread of popular culture and the consequent retreat of folklife. We and our recent ancestors abandoned the hidebound, secure, stable, traditional folk culture to embrace with enthusiasm the free, open, dynamic lifestyle offered by popular culture. Tradition and superstition gave way to change and knowledge; science challenged religion for dominance in our daily lives. We profited greatly in material terms through this transition, but we also forfeited much, as Chapter 7 suggested. Indeed, it would not be proper to regard popular culture as somehow superior to folk culture. We might best regard the two as cultural extremes, and we should be aware that adoption of popular culture brings certain disadvantages. Certainly, the weakened family structure and personal relationships would be among these. One prominent cultural geographer, Fred B. Kniffen (see box in Chapter 7), who has lived in both folk and popular settings, feels that of all the elements of popular culture and the age of technology, "only two would I dislike to give up: inside plumbing and medical advances."

Cultural geographers could hardly ignore the impressive triumph of popular culture in the Western world. While geographers, as we have seen, do not neglect folk studies, they devote an ever-increasing proportion of their energies to the study and understanding of the spatial characteristics of popular culture. They do so not only because of the ascendant position of popular culture in our own society, but also because elements of popular culture vary from one place to another. While it is generally true that popular culture varies less across space than does folk culture, regional patterns can be detected, even on the local scale (Figure 8-1). The popular culture of New England is different in many ways from that of California, western Canada, or the South (Figure 8-1a). The geographer wants to know what these spatial variations are and how they came to be. Equally interesting to geographers are spatial uniformities produced by popularization of culture. Our five themes facilitate such a study.

Popular Culture Regions

The spatial variations of popular culture can be portrayed by culture regions, and we will find that formal and vernacular regions are particularly relevant to the study of popular culture. The geographic study of sports in the United States provides an excellent first example of the usefulness of culture regions in the analysis of popular culture.

Formal culture regions in American sport

Few aspects of popular culture are as widely publicized as our games, both amateur and professional. From Little League through high school,

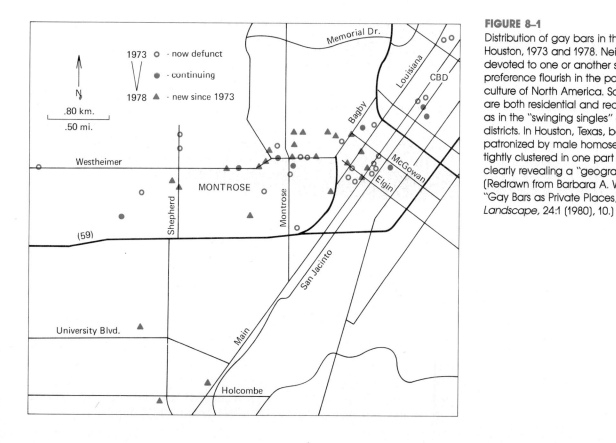

FIGURE 8–1

Distribution of gay bars in the city of Houston, 1973 and 1978. Neighborhoods devoted to one or another sexual preference flourish in the popular culture of North America. Some of these are both residential and recreational, as in the "swinging singles" apartment districts. In Houston, Texas, bars patronized by male homosexuals are tightly clustered in one part of the city, clearly revealing a "geography." (Redrawn from Barbara A. Weightman, "Gay Bars as Private Places," *Landscape*, 24:1 (1980), 10.)

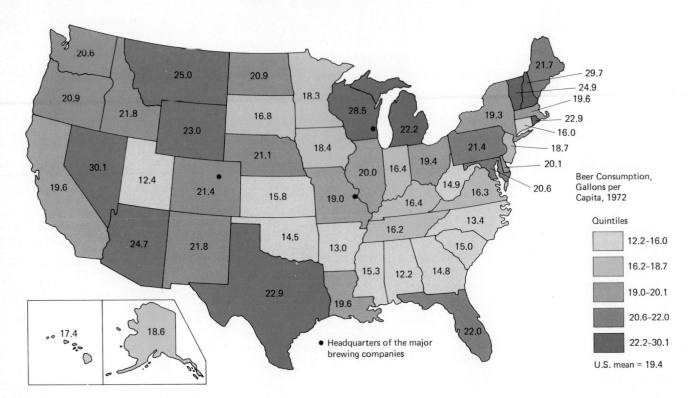

FIGURE 8-1a

The cultural geography of commercial beer consumption. Looking at Figures 6-2 and 9-2 may help explain the regional pattern displayed on this map. What other causal factors might be at work? (Adapted from John F. Rooney, Jr., and Paul L. Butt, "Beer, Bourbon and Boone's Farm: A Geographical Examination of Alcoholic Drink in the United States," *Journal of Popular Culture*, 11 (1978), 832–856.)

college, Olympic, and professional contests and leagues, athletics receive almost daily attention from many members of the popular culture. In fact, the rise of competitive spectator sports parallels closely the development of popular culture in North America and Europe. The further we withdrew from our folk tradition, the more important organized games became for us. It is no accident that the nineteenth century, which witnessed the industrialization and resultant popularization of our culture, also gave us football, ice hockey, baseball, soccer, and basketball—our major spectator sports. While our folk ancestors played a variety of games, these were limited mainly to children or helped hone skills needed in everyday life; relatively little time or attention was devoted to them. Certainly, the concept of professional athletes and admission-paying spectators is unique to the popular culture and is not to be found in folk societies. Hard as it may be for us to realize, our folk ancestors knew nothing even remotely like our Super Bowl, World Series, Stanley Cup, or N.C.A.A. tournaments.

As commercial spectator sports spread through North America, distinct regional contrasts developed. "Hotbeds" of football developed in some regions, basketball became a winter mania in certain areas, baseball came to rule supreme in some states, and ice hockey ascended to reign in still other provinces. Participant sports reveal similar regionalization. Skiing, tennis, bowling, and golf vary greatly in popularity from one region to another.

The geographer John F. Rooney, an expert on the spatial aspects of American sport, has found pronounced regional differences, some of which are summarized in Figure 8-2. He discovered, for example, that most leading states in the production of football players for the major professional and college teams, both in terms of total numbers and on a

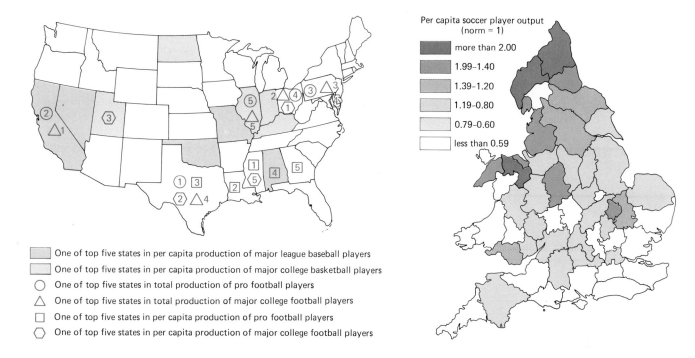

Per capita soccer player output
(norm = 1)

- more than 2.00
- 1.99–1.40
- 1.39–1.20
- 1.19–0.80
- 0.79–0.60
- less than 0.59

One of top five states in per capita production of major league baseball players

One of top five states in per capita production of major college basketball players

◯ One of top five states in total production of pro football players

△ One of top five states in total production of major college football players

☐ One of top five states in per capita production of pro football players

⬡ One of top five states in per capita production of major college football players

FIGURE 8–2
Major source regions of American athletes playing football, baseball, and basketball by state, and of English and Welsh professional soccer players by county. What cultural or environmental factors might explain these patterns? (After data in John F. Rooney, Jr., "Up From the Mines and Out From the Prairies: Some Geographical Implications of Football in the United States," *Geographical Review,* 59 (1969), 483; and John F. Rooney, Jr., *A Geography of American Sport,* Reading, Mass.: Addison-Wesley, 1974, pp. 118, 152, 179, and John Bale, "The Football (County) League," *Geographical Magazine,* 50 (1977–1978), 488.)

FIGURE 8–3
Football arose with the thread of popular culture in North America and has become an important leisure-time activity for many. The intensity of interest varies from one region to another.

per capita basis, were grouped together in clusters, in rather confined areas of the country (Figure 8-3). The top five states in per capita production of National Football League players are Texas, Louisiana, Mississippi, Alabama, and Georgia, all in a contiguous belt across the Deep South (Figure 8-2). Texas also ranks among the top five states in per capita production of major college football players and in total production of both college and pro "gridders." Ohio, Pennsylvania, Illinois, and California also rank high as contributing states. Significantly, some populous states, such as New York, do not rank high as producers of football players. New York, second ranking in population, does not rank among the top ten states in production of professional football players. Neighboring Pennsylvania, by contrast, is the fourth most populous state and ranks third as a producer of pro players. Oklahoma, not among the leading states in per capita production of college and pro players, draws heavily upon high schools in neighboring Texas to man traditionally excellent football teams at the University of Oklahoma.

The highest per capita production of major college basketball players is concentrated in an Ohio Valley cluster of three states: Indiana, Kentucky, and Illinois (Figure 8-2). As we might expect, colleges and universities in these three states are more often known as basketball rather than as football powers. Major league baseball players, on a per capita basis, are drawn mainly from California, Nevada, Oklahoma, Missouri, and Alabama (Figure 8-2).

The regionalization evident in men's athletics is also evident in the leading women's intercollegiate sports (Figure 8-4). The Midwest is a basketball area, the Northeast is ruled by field hockey, tennis is the major sport in the South, and softball and volleyball share distinction as popular women's games in the West (Figure 8-5).

American sport, then, displays marked areal variations, and we can best reveal these contrasts in formal culture regions. A quite different applica-

FIGURE 8–4
Leading women's intercollegiate sports, by census region and major centers. (After data in John F. Rooney, Jr., *A Geography of American Sport*, Reading, Mass.: Addison-Wesley, 1974, pp. 249–252.)

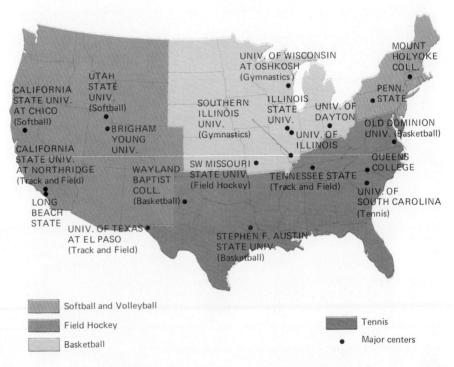

Softball and Volleyball

Field Hockey

Basketball

Tennis

Major centers

tion of the culture region theme to the study of popular culture is seen in vernacular regions.

Vernacular culture regions

"Exciting Green Country," proclaims a brochure published by Green Country, Inc., and the Oklahoma Tourism and Recreation Commission, "where a blend of natural beauty, ideal climate and frontier heritage offers visitors a memorable vacation experience." News media based in Tulsa repeatedly drum "Green Country" into the minds of local Oklahomans; billboard advertisements and businesses with "Green Country" as part of their name spread the same message: northeastern Oklahoma is Green Country (Figure 8-6).

Green Country is but one example of hundreds of **vernacular regions** in America. A vernacular region may be defined as one perceived to exist by its inhabitants, one existing as part of the popular or folk culture. Rather than being the intellectual creation of the professional geographer, a vernacular region is the product of the spatial perception of the population at large. Rather than being a formal region based on carefully chosen criteria, a vernacular region is a composite of the mental maps of the

FIGURE 8-5
Basketball reigns supreme in some parts of North America, particularly the Ohio Valley.

FIGURE 8-6
"Green Country," a popular culture vernacular region, includes all of northeastern Oklahoma and manifests itself in promotional billboards and business names in the town of Tahlequah. Once the proud capital of the Cherokee Indian Nation, Talequah is today merely a small town in Green Country. Promotional regions such as this are becoming increasingly common in America. (Photos by Terry G. Jordan, 1977.)

WILBUR ZELINSKY   1921–

Wilbur Zelinsky, professor at Pennsylvania State University, is one of America's most prominent cultural geographers. An Illinoisan by birth, but a "Northeasterner by choice and conviction," Dr. Zelinsky received his education at the University of California at Berkeley, where he was a student of the famous geographer Carl O. Sauer. His doctorate was awarded in 1953.

As the frequent references in this chapter to his work will attest, Dr. Zelinsky has made numerous important geographical studies of American popular culture, ranging the gamut from the diffusion of classical place-names to the spatial patterns of personal given names. One of his most ambitious and imaginative projects was a provocative assessment of the impact of increasingly powerful personal preference on the spatial character of American society (see the box entitled "Personal Preference and the Changing Map of American Society" in this chapter). In 1973, Professor Zelinsky published his widely acclaimed book *The Cultural Geography of the United States*. In addition to his research in popular culture, Dr. Zelinsky has made substantial contributions in the fields of population and folk geography.

In 1966, Professor Zelinsky received the Award for Meritorious Contributions to the Field of Geography, presented by the Association of American Geographers. He served as President of the Association in 1972-1973.

people. Such regions vary greatly in size, from small districts that cover only part of a city or town to huge, multistate areas. Like most other geographical regions, they often overlap and usually have poorly defined borders.

Almost every part of the industrialized Western world offers examples of vernacular regions based in the popular culture. Figure 8-7 shows some province-sized popular regions in North America. Geographer Wilbur Zelinsky (see biographical box) compiled these regions by determining the most common provincial name appearing in the white pages of urban telephone directories. One curious feature of the map is the sizable, populous district in New York, Ontario, eastern Ohio, and western Pennsylvania where no affiliation to province is perceived. Using a quite different source of information, geographer Joseph Brownell in 1960 sought to delimit the popular "Midwest" (Figure 8-8). Professor Brownell, in this pioneering study, sent out questionnaires to postal employees in the midsection of the United States, from the Appalachians to the Rockies. He asked each employee whether, in his or her opinion, the community lay in the "Midwest." The results revealed a core area in which the residents looked upon themselves as Midwesterners. It is interesting to compare the "Midwest" detected by Zelinsky with that detected by Brownell and to speculate concerning differences between them.

Vernacular regions exist on many different scales. A resident of Alabama's "Black Belt," for example, might also claim to reside in "Dixie" and "the South" (see Figure 1-8). Regardless of size or origin, vernacular regions of America are perceptual in character. They exist because members of the popular or folk culture perceive them. As befits an element of popular culture, the vernacular region is often perpetuated by the mass media, especially radio and television. In fact, many are initially diffused through the media.

Cultural Diffusion and Popular Culture

Culture regions, as you know by now, imply cultural diffusion. The same processes of cultural diffusion described in previous chapters permit the spread of items of popular culture. But the rate of diffusion is more rapid. In ancient times, thousands of years were normally required for innovations to complete their areal spread, and even as recently as the early nineteenth century, the normal time span was still measured in decades. In the popular culture, modern transportation and communications networks now permit cultural diffusion to occur within weeks or even days. The propensity for change makes diffusion extremely important to the popular culture. It may also be true that the availability of devices permitting rapid diffusion is one of the major causes of change in the popular culture.

Geographer Wilbur Zelinsky, in his book *The Cultural Geography of the United States*, described a personal experience with the lightninglike diffusion of a classic item of popular material culture, the hula hoop. "In August, 1958," he wrote, "I drove from Santa Monica, California to Detroit at an average rate of about 400 miles per day; and display windows in almost every drugstore and variety store along the way were being

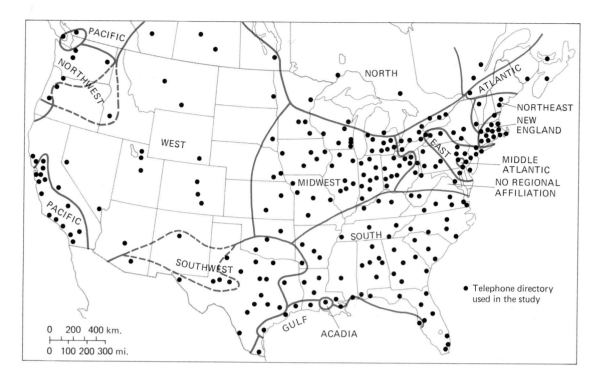

FIGURE 8–7
Some vernacular regions in North America. Cultural geographer Wilbur Zelinsky mapped
these regions on the basis of business names in the white pages of metropolitan
telephone directories. Why are "West" names more widespread than those containing
"East"? What might account for the areas where no region name is perceived?
(Adapted with permission from Wilbur Zelinsky, "North America's Vernacular Regions,"
Annals, Association of American Geographers, 70 (1980), 14.)

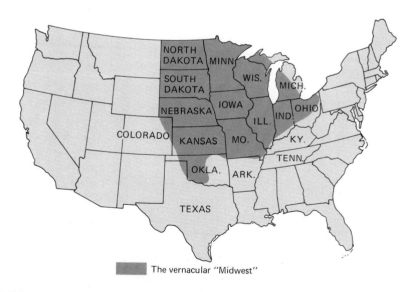

The vernacular "Midwest"

FIGURE 8–8
The vernacular "Midwest." Borders were determined by asking postmasters and
postmistresses whether their locales were in the Midwest. Is a regional name such as
"Midwest," "Southwest," "Northwest," or "Southeast" used to describe the area where you
live? Are such terms used in Canada, Australia, and similar countries? (After Joseph W.
Brownell, "The Cultural Midwest," *Journal of Geography,* 59 (1960), 83.)

hastily stocked with hula hoops just off the delivery trucks from Southern California. A national television program the week before had roused instant cravings. It was an eerie sensation, surfing along a pseudo-innovation wave."

Diffusion of classical place-names

A much earlier cultural diffusion, also researched by Professor Zelinsky, provides us an even more detailed look at the spread of popular culture and the different types of diffusion. This example involves the origin and spread of classical town-names in the United States. If you have traveled much in the United States, particularly in the North and Midwest, you have no doubt encountered town, county, and township names such as Rome, Athens, Syracuse, Troy, Corinth, Arcadia, Euclid, or Homer (Figures 8-9 and 7-28). If you live in the United States, these may not have seemed unusual to you, because they are so common. But is it not strange that, in a country with no direct ties to ancient Greece and Rome, so many names of this type appear? They are a product of the so-called Classic Revival, based in the view that America is the latter-day successor to the glories of the Greco-Roman world. This view, which arose with the independence of the United States, persisted through the nineteenth century. Because of it, Americans adopted a neoclassical architecture for public buildings, Latin mottoes and inscriptions (for example, *E Pluribus Unum*), and even Latin and Greek personal names such as Horace, Virgil, and Ulysses. American popular culture took on a decidedly Greco-Roman flavor. The use of place-names derived from Greece and Rome was merely one aspect of this Classic Revival.

Central New York state was the hearth area where the innovation of classical town-names first appeared in the 1780s. The cities of that region bear witness to the innovation—Syracuse, Ithaca, Utica, Troy, Rome, and others. In the decades that followed, on through the nineteenth century, classical names diffused over much of the United States, most commonly in a "classical belt" stretching westward from New York state to central Nebraska and Kansas. Some 1500 such names are still in use (Figure 8-10).

More important, the spread of classical place-names illustrates many of the types and principles of cultural diffusion. Contagious expansion diffusion is suggested by the compact clusters of classical names that occur here and there, as in southern Iowa. The implantation of one or several classical names apparently influenced founders of nearby communities to adopt similar names for their settlements. Relocation diffusion is also apparent, for it is no accident that the density of classical names is greatest along the pathway leading from central New York, the route of thousands of westward-moving settlers. Utica, New York, for example, has namesakes in Ohio, Indiana, Michigan, Illinois, Kansas, and Nebraska —all perpetuating the name of an ancient Phoenician-Roman city in North Africa.

The spread of classical names also suggests hierarchical expansion diffusion. For example, some such names appeared in southern Maine after 1800, east of the core area in central New York. Relocation diffusion is not likely in this instance, since the flow of migrants was westward, and Maine is too remote from central New York to have been affected by contagious diffusion. In all probability, the idea reached Maine through written communications between elite, educated individuals—a perfect example of hierarchical diffusion.

FIGURE 8-9
The influence of the Classic Revival and the New England tradition of adding directional prefixes on toponyms (see Figure 5-14) can both be seen in the upper highway sign. The lower sign suggests the important English influence in the culture of New England.

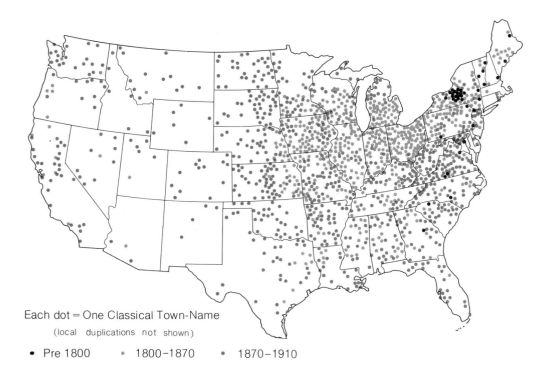

Each dot = One Classical Town-Name

(local duplications not shown)

● Pre 1800   • 1800–1870   • 1870–1910

The Canadian-United States boundary between New York and Ontario acted as an absorbing barrier to the diffusion of classical town-names. Canadians, still under British rule as late as 1867, did not envision their country as a latter-day Greece or Rome and were thus not attracted to classical place-names. To cross into Canada at Niagara or Detroit is to leave "Greece" and "Rome" behind.

Diffusion of the rodeo

From the Classic Revival to the rodeo may seem a quantum jump, yet popular culture is so diverse as to include both. The American commercial rodeo provides another good example of cultural diffusion (Figure 8-11). Like so many elements of popular culture, the modern rodeo had its origins in folk tradition. Rodeos began simply as roundups of cattle in the Spanish livestock ranching system in northern Mexico and the American Southwest. In fact, the word *rodeo* is derived from the Spanish *rodear*, "to surround" or "to round up."

When Anglo-Americans adopted certain Mexican cowboy skills in the nineteenth century, the foundation for riding and roping contests was laid. Cowboys from adjacent ranches began holding contests at roundup time. No prizes were awarded, and these competitive tests of skills remained folk in character initially. After the Civil War, some cowboy contests on the Great Plains were formalized, with prizes awarded (Figure 8-12). Still, no admission was charged, preserving much of the folk aspect of the event.

The transition to commercial rodeo, with admission tickets and grandstands, came quickly as an outgrowth of the formal cowboy contests. One such contest, at North Platte, Nebraska, in 1882, led to the inclusion of some rodeo events in a "Wild West Show" at Omaha in 1883. These shows, which moved by railroad from town to town in the manner of circuses, were probably the most potent agent of early rodeo diffusion.

FIGURE 8–10
Diffusion of classical town names in the United States, 1780–1910. From a hearth area in upstate New York in the 1780s, classical names diffused across much of America. What might explain the uneven distribution of such names? Do classical town names occur in your home area? If so, who implanted them there? (After Wilbur Zelinsky, "Classical Town Names in the United States: The Historical Geography of an American Idea," *Geographical Review*, 57, (1967), 480, 490, 491.)

FIGURE 8-11
Commercial rodeos, an aspect of popular culture, developed from informal cowboy contests, a folk tradition in the American West.

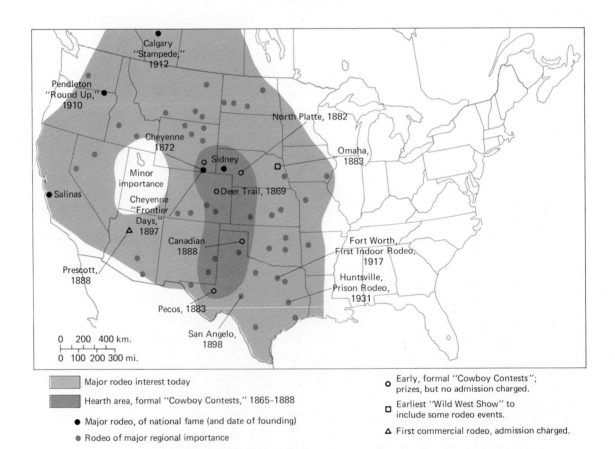

FIGURE 8-12
Origin and diffusion of the American commercial rodeo. Derived originally from folk culture, rodeos evolved through formal "cowboy contests" and "Wild West shows" to emerge, in the late 1880s and 1890s, in their present popular culture form. The border between the United States and Canada proved no barrier to the diffusion, though Canadian rodeo, like Canadian football, differs in some respects from the American type.

Within a decade of the Omaha affair, commercial rodeos were being held independently of Wild West shows at several towns, apparently first at Prescott, Arizona, in 1888. The spread was extremely rapid, as is typical of cultural diffusion in the popular culture. By the turn of the century, commercial rodeos were being performed in much of the West. At Cheyenne, Wyoming, the famous "Frontier Days" rodeo was first held in 1897. By the time of World War I, the rodeo had also become an institution in provinces of western Canada, where the Calgary "Stampede" began in 1912.

Today, rodeos are held in almost every community of any size in the western United States. For example, the state of Oklahoma's calendar of events for the period April through September, 1977, listed no fewer than ninety-eight rodeos scheduled. Racial and sexual lines have been crossed by the rodeo in culturally diverse Oklahoma, producing such events as the Creek Nation All Indian Rodeo at Okmulgee, the All Girls Rodeo at Duncan, and the All Black Rodeo at Wewoka. In Texas and some other states, rodeo competition has become an official high-school sport.

The diffusion of the commercial rodeo has carried it even into New York's Madison Square Garden. Professional rodeos are now held in thirty-six states and three Canadian provinces. Its major acceptance in the popular culture is found west of the Mississippi and Missouri rivers (Figure 8-12).

Barriers to the diffusion of commercial rodeo were encountered at the border of Mexico, south of which bullfighting occupies a dominant position, and in the Mormon culture region centered in Utah. Nor, except in California, did rodeo popularity penetrate the Cascade and coastal mountain ranges to reach the Pacific shore. However, a uniquely Mexican form of rodeo, the *charreada*, is growing rapidly in popularity in central Mexico today. As we might expect, the greatest strength of commercial rodeo in the United States lies in the beef cattle areas.

International diffusion

Cultural diffusion, even among folk societies, has never respected international borders. But in popular culture, innovations are diffused between countries and continents as rapidly as jet airplanes and satellite-beamed television programs. As a result, the popular cultures of North America and western Europe have become rather similar and are constantly in contact with one another. Country-western music is now heard in Northern Ireland's pubs, levi-clad Yugoslavs in small towns flock to American-made movies, Americans wait in line to hear touring British rock musicians, Rocky Mountain ski resorts are built in Alpine-Swiss architecture, and the latest Paris clothes fashions appear in American department stores. Even in many underdeveloped countries, acceptance of Western popular culture occurs among a socioeconomic elite, so that the visitor to a provincial town in India may find a thriving local Lions Club. The international diffusion of popular culture has been so successful that many people now share aspects of a global culture.

A communications barrier

While the communications media have the potential to allow almost instant diffusion over very large areas, spread can be greatly retarded if access to the media is denied (see box, The Geography of 'Rock and Roll'"). A recent issue of *Billboard*, a magazine devoted largely to popular

THE GEOGRAPHY OF "ROCK AND ROLL"

Diffusion occurs rapidly in popular culture. A style of music, "rock and roll," arose in the early 1950s, achieved its maximum diffusion within a decade, then gave way to other music forms. Its chief personality, Elvis Presley, was only 42 years old at the time of his death in 1977, yet the heyday of rock and roll had ended a decade and a half before he died.

The hearth of rock and roll, about 1952 or 1953, was the "Upper Delta" country along the Mississippi River, centered on Memphis, Tennessee. Elvis, Little Richard, Fats Domino, Chuck Berry, and Jerry Lee Lewis, the chief practitioners of rock and roll, all hailed from the Upper Delta. The style developed as a blending of black "rhythm and blues" and hill southern white "rockabilly," a fast-tempo country and western style. Diffusion was achieved both through the radio and sales of inexpensive 45 r.p.m. records, coupled with live concerts. The spread occurred most rapidly between 1955 and 1958; after 1963, rock and roll was in decline.

Barriers were encountered in the diffusion. Parental opposition to the music and lyrics as "degraded" led to the banning of rock and roll on radio stations in some cities. The barriers proved to be permeable—explicit sexual references, so common in rhythm and blues and vintage rock and roll, were softened. "Roll with me, Henry" became the less suggestive "Dance with me, Henry."

Hierarchical diffusion was clearly evident. Early adopters were inquisitive, gregarious young people, trend-setters in their generation. From them acceptance spread down through lower hierarchies until the hard core of nonaccepters remained. Similar trend-setters abandoned rock and roll for other rock styles after about 1963, and the major musical phenomenon of the 1950s went into decline. The influence of rock and roll is seen in later styles, but in its pure form it is rarely performed today.

Adapted from Richard V. Francaviglia, "Diffusion and Popular Culture: Comments on the Spatial Aspects of Rock Music," in David A. Lanegran and Risa Palm (eds.), An Invitation to Geography (New York: McGraw-Hill, 1973), pp. 87–96; and from research by Larry Ford.

music, described such a barrier to diffusion. In the May 14, 1977, issue, record company executive Seymour Stein complained that radio stations and disk jockeys were refusing to play "punk rock" records, denying the style an equal opportunity for exposure. Stein claimed that punk devotees were concentrated in New York City, Los Angeles, Boston, and London, where many young people had found the style reflective of their feelings and frustrations. Without access to radio stations, punk rock could diffuse from these centers only through live concerts and the record sales they generated. The publishers of *Billboard* noted that "punk rock is but one of a number of musical forms which have had problems breaking through nationally out of regional footholds," since *pachanga*, *ska*, pop/gospel, and more recently *reggae*, experienced similar difficulties. To control the programming of radio and television is to control much of the diffusionary apparatus in the popular culture.

The Ecology of Popular Culture

Popular culture, no less than folk, has a cultural ecology. People, functioning within popular cultures, both influence and are influenced by their physical surroundings.

Environmental influence

Because popular culture is largely the product of industrialization and the rise of technology, it is less closely tied to the physical environment than is folk culture. Gone is the intimate association between people and land known by our folk ancestors. Gone, too, is our direct vulnerability to many environmental forces. But even though technology, with its machines and communications media, has removed us from close contact with nature and reduced many environmental hazards, the physical surroundings can still exert influence on popular culture.

Our previous example of American sports provides some suggestion, at least, of environmental influence. Is the greater popularity of basketball and the higher per capita production of players in the North partly a result of colder winters there? Presumably the cold weather might make basketball, a traditional indoor sport, more desirable for spectators. Does cold weather likewise favor bowling and ice hockey, perhaps explaining their greater popularity in northern states and Canada? Surely it is not mere chance that the four major college football bowl games—Cotton, Rose, Orange, and Sugar—are all played in Sun Belt states on the southern border of the United States, or that until 1982 the professional Super Bowl had never been played outside the Sun Belt.

Even in these instances, though, climatic influence is waning. Huge covered stadiums now make it possible to play football and baseball indoors, and artificial wave-making machines permit surfboarding in the Arizona desert (Figure 8-13). Migrating northerners bring their interest in ice hockey to the South, where the game is played in refrigerated arenas while outside temperatures soar into the nineties. But as these examples suggest, the popular way of life has become a high-energy culture. Even the devices of diffusion in the popular culture require large amounts of electricity and gasoline, and countless labor-saving machines add to the seemingly insatiable need for fossil fuels and other energy supplies. Recently, we have witnessed a sharp rise in energy costs. Should these costs continue to rise, we might conceivably reach a point where many aspects of the popular culture could no longer be maintained.

Impact on the environment

Popular culture makes some heavy demands on the physical environment. This is true even in the realm of recreation. Since World War II, leisure time and related recreational activities have increased greatly in the United States, Canada, Europe, and other developed countries. Much leisure time is now spent by members of the popular culture in some space-consuming activity in areas outside the cities. The demand for

FIGURE 8-13

Surfing, once tied to beach locations, can now be practiced in places like the desert, where artificial wave-making machines have been installed. This scene is in Tempe, Arizona, hundreds of miles from the nearest coast.

"wilderness" recreation zones has risen sharply in the last quarter-century, and no end to the increase seems at hand (Figure 8-14).

Hikers, campers, hunters, fishers, bikers, dune buggy and snowmobile enthusiasts, weekend cottagers, surfers, spelunkers, mountain climbers, boaters, sightseers, and others are making unprecedented demands on the open country. Such a massive presence of people in our open areas cannot help damaging the physical environment. National parks such as Yosemite in California now suffer from traffic jams, residential congestion, litter, and noise pollution—very much like the urban areas (Figure 8-15). In less congested wilderness districts, as few as several hundred hikers a month can beat down trails to the extent that vegetation is altered, erosion encouraged, and wildlife diminished. Even the best-intentioned, most conservation-minded visitors do some damage. One of the paradoxes of the modern age and popular culture seems to be that the more we cluster in cities and suburbs, the greater our impact on open areas. We carry our popular culture with us when we vacation in such regions.

Some countries have reacted to the recreational tourist boom merely by making natural areas ever more accessible, ever more crowded and

damaged. Others, including the United States, have now drawn a distinction between national park tourism and wilderness areas. Access to many wild districts is now greatly restricted, in hopes that they can be saved from the damage that necessarily accompanies recreational activity. In some national parks, access by private automobile and camper pickup is now restricted. But for the greater part of the countryside, the recreational assault on the environment continues.

Cultural Integration in Popular Culture

The interaction of popular culture and physical environment, while significant, is overshadowed in importance by the internal workings of the culture. The most potent forces shaping any element of popular culture are other elements of the same popular culture. Thus we turn to the theme of cultural integration to increase our understanding of cause-and-effect relationships.

The impact of communications media

The impact of the communications media provides an excellent example of cultural integration. Geographer Ronald F. Abler concluded that our modern communications system, a product of the industrialized popular culture, is the most potent force for spatial change that people presently command. It was long assumed that the overall effect of efficient, rapid communications, particularly radio and television, was to homogenize popular culture and reduce the differences between places. Indeed, impressive evidence can be marshaled to support this **convergence hypothesis**. Geographer Wilbur Zelinsky, for example, found by comparing the given names of persons in various regions of the eastern United States for 1790 and 1968 that a more pronounced regionalization existed in the eighteenth century than today (see box, "The Geography of Personal Given Names"). The personal names bestowed on children by our generation of parents vary less from place to place than did those of our

---

THE GEOGRAPHY OF PERSONAL GIVEN NAMES

Does your given name give you a geographical label? Within the popular culture of America, can we identify regions on the basis of the names parents choose for their children? Maybe, according to cultural geographer Wilbur Zelinsky, who published the first geographical study of personal names in America. His findings, however, also give some support to the **convergence hypothesis** (see Glossary).

Regionalization is suggested by the following selection of given names, belonging to students who completed graduate degrees at universities in one region of America during the period 1960-1975: Ruzelle, Dailis, Norence, Lenola, LaVerta, Pearlean, Jessyetene, Homoizelle, Jamesetta, Fedies, Jearl, Zerline, Christella, Vernice, and Bevelyn. Imaginative and out of the ordinary?

Indeed they are! Did you correctly identify them as names of students at black universities in the American South? Do compound names like Billy Joe, Eddie Mae, Mary Alice, Donna Jean, and John Henry similarly remind you of the South? How about the use of initials instead of names, such as J. B., J. D., and C. L.?

While the trend in American popular culture may be toward less regional diversity in personal names, some contrasts apparently remain. The American South, both black and white, provides evidence to support this conclusion.

Inspired by Wilbur Zelinsky, "Cultural Variation in Personal Name Patterns in the Eastern United States," Annals, Association of American Geographers, 60 (1970), 743–769. Black personal names are from thesis directories at Prairie View A & M and Texas Southern universities in Texas.

ancestors two centuries ago. Similarly, daily exposure to the Midland dialect favored by national television and radio announcers is causing the decline of other dialects, presenting the rather dreary prospect that our grandchildren may all speak the English of Walter Cronkite. The possible end product of the convergence would be a national or even planetary culture.

Professors Abler and Zelinsky, however, both suggest that the media have a potential for reinforcing or even promoting regional cultural differences. Popular culture, to a degree previously unknown, through leisure, wealth, and rapid communications, allows the individual personality to come to the forefront (see box, "Personal Preference and the Changing Map of American Society"). Increasingly, free exercise of individual preferences, with each person "doing his own thing," is creating a new spatial order in countries such as the United States and Canada. The number of special-interest groups and publications has exploded in recent decades. Many radio stations now cater to very special clienteles, as do almost countless magazines and clubs. For example, the number of black-oriented radio stations in the United States increased from only 32 in 1956 to 130 in 1970 and 239 by 1980.

The media, in effect, are helping to create new subcultures and to sustain some traditional ones. They are assisting the rise of consciousness and even militance along ethnic, racial, age, and sexual lines by putting persons of similar backgrounds, interests, preferences, or beliefs into

PERSONAL PREFERENCE AND THE CHANGING MAP OF AMERICAN SOCIETY

"Take a large human population. After it has been stirred and seasoned well for two centuries, relax traditional social and economic constraints. Give many of its individual members enough leisure time and money so that they can do pretty much what they wish to please themselves. Add several dashes of new social and technological forces; let the mixture simmer for a couple of decades; then ask: what sorts of choices will be made by the millions of participants in such a macro-experiment? What things will how many persons do, and *where* will they do them?

"The ingredients for this recipe are, of course, to be found in the United States. . . . Our nation has witnessed the attainment of a degree of affluence and freedom of attitude and action, of a range of individual and social options, on the part of a quite massive fraction of its total adult population that is unprecedented in human history, yet may be predictive of things to come in other highly advanced countries. . . . The increasingly free exercise of individual preferences as to values, pleasures, self-improvement, social and physical habitat, and general life-style in an individualistic, affluent national community may have begun to alter the spatial attributes of society and culture in the United States to a significant extent.

"This notion happens to be imbedded in an even more fundamental proposition, namely, that we are now engaged in a process of deep, perhaps revolutionary, structural change in human society, the causes and consequences of which are still unclear. The geographer has been accustomed to seeking the sources for a real diversity in human activities in three sets of factors . . . : the laws of economic behavior; the still dimly apprehended laws of socio-cultural behavior; and the opportunities and constraints of an exceedingly complicated physical environment. Perhaps we can no longer afford to ignore a fourth major set of less familiar factors: the differences in personality structure . . . among a growing number of human beings in quest of self-fulfillment. . . .

"Are the newly emergent, often vicarious communities of self-selected individuals superior, or even acceptable, replacements for the confining, womblike certitudes of traditional local societies? Are we trudging down the road to utopia or dystopia? May not individual alienation or the burden of constant choice be too stiff a price to pay for the intoxication of almost limitless mobility and personal experimentation? Putting it boldly: Is what we are winning worth what we are losing?"

Excerpted, with minor changes, from Wilbur Zelinsky, "Selfward Bound? Personal Preference Patterns and the Changing Map of American Society," Economic Geography, *50 (1974), 144, 176, with permission.*

frequent contact with one another. Will such subcultures segregate spatially? Will regionalization within the popular culture be the end product? It is really too early to tell for certain, since the massive impact of special-interest media "narrowcasting," to use Professor Abler's term, is too recent to have produced a final result. But there are suggestions that the media are, indeed, helping to create a spatially diverse popular culture. Hints of this trend are seen in the segregated communities where only elderly people live, as in Sun City, Arizona; or in the concentration of people favoring a "swinging singles" lifestyle in certain apartment districts within cities such as Dallas.

Planetary culture, then, may well be illusory. Popular culture, under the shaping influence of special-interest communications media, may be drifting toward a regionalization as pronounced as any found in folk society. In any case, the media are unquestionably fostering and strengthening subcultural identities.

Why football fever?

The cultural integration theme may also permit us to better understand some of the spatial patterns presented earlier in the discussion of culture regions. For example, some of the differences between places in American sport may be explained in part by other elements of culture. "Football fever" is a case in point.

Why do certain districts exceed others in football interest and per capita player production? Part of the answer, as suggested earlier, may lie in the realm of cultural ecology. But even more important causal forces are likely to be found in other elements of the popular culture. The four major football "hotbeds," according to Professor Rooney, are: (1) western Pennsylvania, eastern Ohio, and northern West Virginia; (2) parts of Texas and western Oklahoma; (3) northern Utah and portions of adjacent states; and (4) southern Mississippi. Interestingly, the Pennsylvania-Ohio-West Virginia region, which seems to be the original American football "hotbed," corresponds well to a zone of heavy industry, particularly steelmaking. Are such blue-collar workers the hard-core supporters of football? If so, it is more than appropriate that the professional team located in the core of this region is nicknamed the "Steelers". Other "blue-collar" type nicknames for sports teams around the country, such as "Packers," "Brewers," "Boilermakers," and "Mariners," imply a working-class clientele.

Texas football fever apparently originated among oil field roughnecks, another blue-collar group, and the support of high-school football seems even today to be most fanatical in oil towns. Texas professional teams are owned by oil-rich families, and the Houston franchise is nicknamed "Oilers." It is possible, as Dr. Rooney suggests, that roughnecks coming from the Pennsylvania oil fields implanted football fever in Texas. These examples would suggest that there is a tie between one's interest in football and one's type of employment, at least in some areas.

Northern Utah, on the other hand, presents a quite different situation. There football fever rages in a largely nonindustrial region, among affluent, well-educated people. The key seems to be the local dominance of the Mormon faith, which places great emphasis on physical fitness and group-team cooperation. Southern Mississippi is a rural, thinly populated region with many poor people and blacks. The reasons for its prominence as a producer of football players is not clear, but they are likely cultural. Clearly, factors other than type of employment can cause football fever.

The Landscape of Popular Culture

Landscape mirrors culture. We are what we see and what we build for others to see. Popular culture permeates the landscape of countries such as the United States and Canada, including everything from mass-produced suburban houses to golf courses and neon-lighted "strips." So overwhelming is the presence of the popular culture in most American settlement landscapes that an observer must often search diligently to find visual fragments of the older folk cultures. The popular landscape is in continual flux, for change is a hallmark of popular culture.

American front yards

As an example of the popular cultural landscape and the changes that occur in it, let us consider a truly American institution: the front yard, (Figure 8-16). A dwelling set back from the street, with the nonfunctional intervening space covered by an expanse of grassy lawn, has since the early 1800s been one of the most pervasive symbols of the urban and suburban Anglo-American popular landscape. Homeowners who neglect to tend these lawns properly, or who put the space into some functional use such as vegetable gardening, invite the animosity and contempt of their neighbors, not to mention the lowering of property value. For most of us, the grass-covered front yard is so universally accepted that we assume it to be a part of the natural order of things in suburbia.

Anglos migrating west in the nineteenth century brought the front lawn with them, even into the desert areas of the American Southwest, where irrigation was necessary to maintain the grass. The desert became dotted with green suburban oases. In cities such as Tucson, the Anglo dwellings flanked by lawns stood in marked contrast to the older Hispano houses, which either lacked yards altogether or had bare-earth areas. Geographer Melvin E. Hecht has studied the popular culture yard landscape that resulted from the Anglo-Hispano contact, and he has documented the decline of the grass lawn tradition. Increasingly, Anglo-Tucsonians are turning to "desert front" yards, where grass is replaced by gravel, crushed rock, desert plants, paving, or undisturbed desert (Figure 8-16). A few innovators among the Anglos adopted such yards even in the early part of

FIGURE 8-16
The grass-covered front yard and the more recently developed "desert front" are both elements of the landscape of popular culture.

this century, but the rapid rise of the desert front yard began in the 1950s, spurred by a new wave of urban immigrants who found the desert beautiful rather than repulsive. In the manner of typical hierarchical diffusion, acceptance occurred earliest in the higher-priced subdivisions and spread gradually to the middle-class districts. Professor Hecht found that fully one-half of all houses built in Tucson between 1965 and 1975 had desert front yards. Some of these are covered with gravel dyed green, a simulation of the lawn, but most represent complete departures from the older custom. Hecht concluded that the decline of the lawn tradition heralded the emergence of a new, distinct popular culture region, one which reflected an appreciation of Arizona's natural setting and Hispanic heritage. Desert fronts have since diffused to become part of the popular cultural landscape in neighboring states and even beyond. It is perhaps symptomatic of the visual excesses of popular culture that desert fronts are now appearing in high-rainfall states such as Florida, where plastic sheets have to be installed under the gravel layer to prevent grass and weeds from emerging. But, then, desert fronts in Florida are no more absurd than grass lawns were in desert Arizona.

Gentleman farms

Another element of the American popular cultural landscape is the "gentleman farm," an agricultural unit operated for pleasure rather than profit (Figure 8-17). Typically, gentleman farms are owned by affluent city people as an avocation, and such farms help to create or maintain a high social standing for those who own them. Some rural landscapes in American now contain many such gentleman farms; perhaps most notable among these areas are the inner Bluegrass Basin of north-central Kentucky, the Virginia Piedmont west of Washington, D.C., Long Island in New York, and parts of southeastern Pennsylvania. Gentleman farmers engage in such activities as breeding fine cattle, racing horses, or hunting foxes.

Geographer Karl Raitz made a study of gentleman farms in the Kentucky Bluegrass Basin, where the concentration is so great that they constitute a dominant feature of the cultural landscape (Figure 8-18). The result is an idyllic scene, a rural landscape created more for appearance than for function. Professor Raitz provided a list of visual indicators of Kentucky gentleman farms: wooden fences, either painted white or creosoted black, a type costing upwards of $7000 per mile to build; an elaborate entrance gate; a fine hand-painted sign giving the name of the farm and owner; a network of surfaced, well-maintained driveways and pasture roads; and a large elegant house, visible in the distance from the public highway through a lawnlike parkland dotted with clumps of trees and perhaps a pond or two. So attractive are these estates to the eye that tourists cruise the rural lanes to view them, convinced they are seeing the "real" rural America, or at least rural America as it ought to be.

The American scene

Front yards and gentleman farms are but two features of the American popular landscape. One very perceptive and sensitive cultural geographer, David Lowenthal, attempted a broader analysis, an overall evaluation of the visible impact of popular culture in the American countryside. In an article entitled "The American Scene," Professor Lowenthal lists the

FIGURE 8–17
Gentleman farms in the Kentucky Bluegrass region near Lexington. The photos reveal some typical landscape features, such as board fences and imposing mansions. (Photos courtesy of Professor Karl B. Raitz).

main characteristics of popular landscape in the United States. Among these are the "cult of bigness"; the tolerance of present ugliness to achieve a supposedly glorious future; zoo-like enclaves of historical artifacts, either genuine or fake; emphasis of individual features at the expense of aggregates, producing a "casual chaos"; and the preeminence of function over form.

The fondness for massive structures is reflected in structures such as

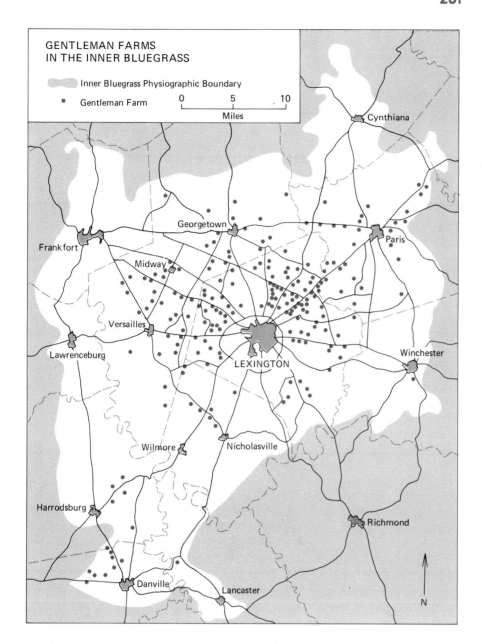

FIGURE 8–18
The gentleman farm is a major landscape feature in central Kentucky. Why might a concentration have developed there? How does such a landscape differ from one that might be produced by a folk culture? (Copied, with permission, from Karl B. Raitz, "Gentleman Farms in Kentucky's Inner Bluegrass," *Southeastern Geographer*, 15 (1975), 44.)

the Empire State Building, Salt Lake City's Mormon Temple, the Pentagon, or the San Francisco-Oakland Bay Bridge (Figure 8-19). Americans have dotted their cultural landscape with the world's largest of this or that, perhaps in an effort to match the grand scale of the physical environment, which offers such superlatives as the Grand Canyon, the redwoods, and the Yellowstone geysers. Americans apparently admire these structures more for their size than their beauty.

FIGURE 8–19
The landscape of American popular culture is characterized by massive structures, such as the Mormon Temple in Salt Lake City, and by functionality, well exemplified by the unsightly oil derrick on the Oklahoma State Capitol grounds.

Americans, says Professor Lowenthal, tend to regard their cultural landscape as unfinished. Because of this, they are "predisposed to accept present structures that are makeshift, flimsy, and transient," resembling, in Lowenthal's view, "throwaway stage sets." Similarly, the hardships of pioneer life perhaps preconditioned Americans to value function more highly than beauty. A shopping center, junk car lot, or mobile home park may seem ugly to the passerby, but so long as it is functional it seems to give no serious cause for complaint (Figure 8-20). For many years, the state capitol grounds in Oklahoma City were adorned with little more than oil derricks, standing above busy pumps drawing wealth from the

Sooner soil—an extreme but revealing view of the American landscape (Figure 8-19).

Individual landscape features, says Dr. Lowenthal, take precedence over groupings. Five buildings or houses in a row may display five different architectural styles, and rarely is an attempt made to erect assemblages of structures that "belong" together. "Places are only collections of heterogeneous buildings." To be worthy, each structure must be unique and eye-catching, and architects in the popular culture vie with one another in producing attention-grabbing edifices. Each fast-food chain seems to require its own outlandish style of structure to facilitate instant visual recognition by potential customers.

The past, reflected in archaic landscape relics, has traditionally been confined by Americans to zoo-like "historylands," often enclosed by imposing wire-link fences and open only during certain seasons or hours (see box, "The Bicentennial Landscape"). If the desired bit of visual history has by accident perished, Americans do not hesitate to rebuild it from scratch, undisturbed by the lack of authenticity, as for example at Jamestown, Virginia. Normally the history zoos are segregated and sanitized to the extent that people no longer live in them. Europeans have incorporated historic buildings into their functioning landscape; Americans have chosen to keep them at arm's length.

Lowenthal, a resident both of the United Kingdom and the United States, sees the American landscape partially with the eyes of a visitor. People who create the landscape and live in it full-time are likely to perceive it differently than do visitors. For example, geographer Yi-Fu Tuan suggests that a commercial "strip" of stores, hamburger joints, filling stations, and used-car lots may appear as visual blight to an outsider, but the owners or operators of the businesses may be very proud of them and of their role in the community. Hard work and hopes color their

FIGURE 8–20
Trailer park inhabitants live in a makeshift part of our functional environment.

THE BICENTENNIAL LANDSCAPE

"Needing an admirable past, Americans have extended it, reinterpreted it, and reinvented it. The process of historical revision is not peculiar to America; most new nations seek to manufacture images of their countries as new creations, uncontaminated and untrammeled by Old World memories and mistakes. In the late nineteenth century, many Americans first realized that the United States was no longer rural, egalitarian, thrifty, Anglo-Saxon. National progress had outdated that ideal. Americans therefore began to look for an enviable American past to set against the defects of the present. Even in so brief a nationhood, selective memory makes it easy to remodel the past in the image of present ideals. Thus the Bicentennial landscape largely reflects today's ideas of what the Republic's origins should have been. . . .

"The Bicentenary mood combines a renewed desire to draw sustenance from the past with a growing suspicion that the effort is farcical. However extravagant our rededication, however eloquent our appeals to return to the past, there is no going back. Not only are most of the landscapes touted by Bicentennial hawkers historically false, they are unconvincing either as imitations or as evocations of the past. No one really believes in them, but their popularity as entertainment lends support to the suggestion that the true Father of the modern United States is no longer George Washington but Walt Disney.

"Williamsburg and Disneyland are two of America's greatest make-believe landscapes. A recent visitor found it hard to remember the difference between them. So much of Williamsburg is fantasy; so much of Disneyland is historical. . . .

"Until recently, Americans tended to segregate history safely out of the mainstream of modern lives and landscapes. The museumized past was a rare feature, to be viewed on special occasions at special places where its content and meaning were carefully controlled. The Bicentennial epoch, coupled with current disillusionment, has changed this perspective. Increasingly enamored of the past, Americans no longer wish to fence it off; they long to see it everywhere. Historical flavor now permeates even the most modern aspects of life. Every landscape and townscape advertises its unique heritage. . . .

"The new embrace of all this historical freight does not, however, mean that Americans are now historically minded. On the contrary, events and landscapes from the past become ever more like what we prefer the present to be. The authority of the past justifies every innovation in architecture and planning, in exterior design and interior decor. Pedestrianized shopping enclaves, high-rise condominiums, "heritage" villages, suburban communal fortresses all supposedly derive inspiration from Puritan settlements, Southern plantations, Western missions, or pioneer wagon encampments. Developers attempt to make you believe that you can escape from the shoddiness of modern building and the stresses of modern milieus by being transported to some dreamland in the past. . . .

"The artifacts as well as the archives of the recent past dominate our landscapes. Manufacturers may have aimed at instant obsolescence, and twentieth-century buildings and clothing, cars and highways do crumble and corrode quite rapidly. But this does not mean that they sink out of sight. On the contrary, they remain impressive features in the landscape, lasting monuments to recent follies. They loom so large partly because they were built to loom large and partly because their components, unlike their utility, are virtually imperishable—plastic, metal, reinforced concrete. Much of our urban fabric is a mass of decaying buildings less than half a century old. Indeed, structures of the 1950s and 1960s, many of them already ruined or obsolete, comprise our most formidable visible past, an impediment alike to historical vision and of future planning. . . .

"Psychoanalytic patients reexplore their memories to free themselves from being determined by their past; collectively, Americans must become more conscious of their past history to gain a larger measure of future choice. To experience and create present-day landscapes that reflect a concern with continuity, rather than nostalgic yearning, we need to reconstruct a coherent and believable past. Coming truly to terms with the past means neither deliberately rejecting and forgetting it, as Americans did during much of their first century of nationhood; nor falling in love with it, as we have more recently been prone to do; but accepting it, good and bad alike, and realizing that while we cannot recapture that past, its influence endures to magnify all our landscapes, actions, and ideals."

Excerpted from David Lowenthal, "The Bicentennial Landscape: A Mirror Held Up to the Past," Geographical Review, 67 (1977), 255–258, 267, with permission.

perception of the landscape. Similarly, what is an unsightly sprawl of suburban houses to the passerby may be a beautiful realization of a desire for home ownership to the inhabitant.

America, then, has a distinctive popular cultural landscape. Some perceive it to be ugly and dismaying. Others see it as dynamic and reflective of a self-confident, future-oriented people. And still others, perhaps even the majority, simply take it for granted and pay little heed.

Conclusion

Geographers clearly have a role to play in the study of popular culture. The examples we have presented, drawn mainly from North America, reveal that our five themes permit a distinctly geographical approach to the subject. Culture regions reveal some spatial contrasts; diffusion allows us to glimpse the movement of elements of popular culture through geographic space; ecology and integration explain some of the processes and factors involved in the development of spatial diversity; and landscape makes us more aware of the visible impact of popular culture. Hopefully, too, this chapter and the one preceding have broadened your perspective concerning the popular culture lifestyle you now pursue. If you are a typical member of the popular culture, your way of life is an extreme one—as extreme as that of the self-sufficient farmers who belong to folk society.

Glossary

Convergence hypothesis holds that cultural differences between places are being reduced by improved transportation and communication systems, leading to a homogenization of popular culture.

Popular culture a dynamic culture based in large, heterogeneous societies permitting considerable individualism, innovation, and change; having a money-based economy, division of labor into professions, secular institutions of control, and weak interpersonal ties; producing and consuming machine-made goods.

Vernacular region a region perceived to exist by its inhabitants; based in the collective spatial perception of the population at large; bearing a generally accepted name or nickname.

Suggested Readings

Ronald F. Abler. "Monoculture or Miniculture? The Impact of Communication Media on Culture in Space," in David A. Lanegran and Risa Palm (eds.), *An Invitation to Geography.* New York: McGraw-Hill, 1973, pp. 186–195.

Peter Blake. *God's Own Junkyard: The Planned Deterioration of America's Landscape.* New York: Holt, Rinehart & Winston, 1979.

Alvar W. Carlson, "The Contributions of Cultural Geographies to the Study of Popular Culture," *Journal of Popular Culture.* 11 (1978), 830–831.

George O. Carney. "Country Music and the Radio: A Historical Geographic Assessment," *Rocky Mountain Social Science Journal,* 11 (April 1974), 19–32.

George O. Carney. "From Down Home to Uptown: The Diffusion of Country-Music Radio Stations in the United States," *Journal of Geography,* 76 (1977), 104–110.

Larry R. Ford and Floyd M. Henderson. "The Image of Place in American Popular Music: 1890-1970," *Places,* 1 (1974), 31–37.

Richard V. Francaviglia. "Diffusion and Popular Culture: Comments on the Spatial Aspects of Rock Music," in David A. Lanegran and Risa Palm (eds.), *An Invitation to Geography.* New York: McGraw-Hill, 1973, pp. 87 96.

James K. Good. "A Perceptual Delimitation of Southern Indiana," *Professional Paper No. 8,* Department of Geography and Geology, Indiana State University, Terre Haute, 1976, pp. 3–10.

Ernst C. Griffin and Larry R. Ford. "Tijuana: Landscape of a Culture Hybrid," *Geographical Review,* 66 (1976), 435–447.

Charles F. Gritzner, "Country Music: A Reflection of Popular Culture," *Journal of Popular Culture,* 11 (1978), 857–864.

Melvin E. Hecht. "The Decline of the Grass Lawn Tradition in Tucson," *Landscape,* 19 (June 1975), 3–10.

John A. Jakle and Richard L. Mattson. "The Evolution of a Commercial Strip," *Journal of Cultural Geography,* 1 (Spring-Summer 1981), 12–25.

Terry G. Jordan. "Evolution of the American Windmill: A Study in Diffusion and Modification," *Pioneer America,* 5 (July 1973), 3–12.

Journal of Popular Culture. An interdisciplinary journal published by the Popular Culture Association and Bowling Green State University. Volume 1 appeared in 1967. See in particular Volume 11, No. 4 (Spring 1978), a special issue on cultural geography and popular culture.

Fred B. Kniffen. "Milestones and Stumbling Blocks," *Pioneer America,* 7 (January 1975), 1–8.

David Lowenthal. "The American Scene," *Geographical Review,* 58 (1968), 61–88.

David Lowenthal. "The Bicentennial Landscape: A Mirror Held Up to the Past," *Geographical Review,* 67 (1977), 253–267.

Richard Pillsbury. "Carolina Thunder: A Geography of Southern Stock Car Racing," *Journal of Geography,* 73 (January 1974), 39–47.

Karl B. Raitz. "Gentleman Farms in Kentucky's Inner Bluegrass," *Southeastern Geographer,* 15 (1975), 33–46.

John F. Rooney, Jr. *A Geography of American Sport.* Reading, Mass.: Addison-Wesley, 1974.

John F. Rooney, Jr. "Up From the Mines and Out From the Prairies: Some Geographical Implications of Football in the United States," *Geographical Review,* 59 (1969), 471–492.

Neil L. Shumsky and Larry M. Springer. "San Francisco's Zone of Prostitution, 1880-1934," *Journal of Historical Geography,* 7 (1981), 71–89.

Norman R. Yetman and D. Stanley Eitzen. "Some Social and Demographic Correlates of Football Productivity," *Geographical Review,* 63 (1973), 553–557.

Wilbur Zelinsky. "Classical Town Names in the United States: The Historical Geography of An American Idea," *Geographical Review,* 57 (1967), 463–495.

Wilbur Zelinsky. *The Cultural Geography of the United States.* Englewood Cliffs, N.J.: Prentice-Hall, 1973.

Wilbur Zelinsky. "Cultural Variation in Personal Name Patterns in the Eastern United States," *Annals, Association of American Geographers,* 60 (1970), 743–769.

Wilbur Zelinsky. "Selfward Bound? Personal Preference Patterns and the Changing Map of American Society," *Economic Geography,* 50 (1974), 144–179.

Chapter-opening photo:
A Mexican graveyard in southern Texas. ➤

Ethnic Geography

9

A fine statue of the American national hero Paul Revere, mounted on his trusty horse, towers over a pedestrian mall near the Old North Church in Boston. Close by is the Revere home, carefully and lovingly preserved. As American as apple pie, you may say, a shrine to national independence. But what language are the elderly women speaking as they sit on benches near the statue and go about their knitting? Certainly it is not good Yankee English, by the sound of it. And the same tongue dominates conversation in a nearby barbershop. Can it be Italian? Indeed it is. Closer inspection reveals Italian family names on almost every business establishment in Revere's neighborhood, like Giuffre's Fish Market, Italian pizza parlors, an Italian-dominated outdoor vegetable market, a Sons of Italy lodge hall, and Italian-American women leaning out of upper-story windows on opposite sides of the street to converse, Naples-style. Revere, himself of French ethnic extraction, would be astounded. Boston's North End is Italian! A pilgrimage to the site where the American Revolution began has become a trip to Little Italy.

"America's Little Switzerland," proclaims a brochure from the New Glarus, Wisconsin, Chamber of Commerce. This small town, founded by Swiss immigrants in 1845, invites prospective visitors to attend a Heidi Festival in June and an outdoor performance of the Wilhelm Tell drama in September. They are urged to eat Swiss food at restaurants such as the Schweizerhof, Alpine Cafe, Hofmann's Wilhelm Tell, and Glarner Stube; to spend the night at the Swiss-Aire Motel; to purchase Swiss cheese, Swiss music records, Swiss hayshirts, Swiss chocolate bars, and even Swiss army knives at gift shops like The Swiss Maid; and to bowl at the Swiss Lanes. "Traces of Switzerland are everywhere," claims the brochure; "Swiss homes bear Swiss family crests, the melodies of Switzerland are perpetuated in the yodels and folk songs of twentieth-century New Glarus. The language of Old Glarus is still spoken in homes and on the street." Summing it up, New Glarus is "Heidiland, U.S.A.," "America's best-known Swiss settlement," "a brilliant cameo of ancient Switzerland and modern America set in the gentle hills and valleys of Southern Wisconsin."

The small midwestern town of Wilber, settled by Bohemian immigrants beginning about 1865, is somewhat more modest, claiming only to be "The Czech Capital of Nebraska" and inviting visitors to attend in 1977 the sixteenth "Annual Czech Festival of Nebraska Czechs, Incorporated, of Wilber, Nebraska." Celebrants are attracted by promises of eating Czech foods like *koláče*, *jaternice*, poppyseed cake, and *jelita*; seeing Czech folk dancing; purchasing glassware, "colored Czech postcards and souvenirs" imported from Czechoslovakia, or handicraft items made by Nebraska Czechs (and bearing an official seal and trademark to prove authenticity). "Czech Foods, Czech Refreshments, Czech Bands," proclaim the festival leaflets, and "breathtaking pageants of old world history" as well. "Many shops are decorated in the Czech motif and music can be heard on the streets during most hours of the day. Many items of Czech heritage . . . are sold. Czech baking and meat items are offered daily by local merchants who use authentic recipes." Thousands of visitors from the United States, Canada, and overseas attend the festival each year. Indeed, the visitor to the state of Nebraska can see much of "Europe" without ever leaving this American heartland, for besides the Wilber festival, Nebraska offers "Swedish Days" at the town of Holdrege in May, "Danish Days" at Minden in June, "German Heritage Days" at McCook in April, "Czech Festival" at Clarkson in June, "Swedish Festival" at Stromsburg in June, and "St. Patrick's Day Celebration" at O'Neill in March, in addition to five Indian Tribal "pow wows" and assorted additional European ethnic festivals.

As long ago as 1893, the famous American historian Frederick Jackson Turner claimed that "the frontier promoted the formation of a composite nationality for the American people; . . . immigrants were Americanized, liberated, and fused into a mixed race. . . ." For generations we have been taught that America is a "melting pot" in which various ethnic groups were blended to produce something homogeneously American.

How then do we explain the Italians at Paul Revere's feet, "America's Little Switzerland," the incorporated Czechs of Wilber, and thousands of similar ethnic enclaves? The fact is that Turner was wrong about the formation of a composite nationality. The United States, Canada, and many other countries retain, in both urban and rural areas, an ethnic crazy-quilt pattern, and ethnic groups remain an important aspect of the human mosaic.

What exactly is an **ethnic group**? Much controversy has surrounded attempts to formulate an accepted definition. *Ethnic* is derived from the Greek word *ethnos*, meaning a "people" or "nation," but that definition is too broad for our use. To narrow it down, we can define an ethnic group as one possessing a common ancestry and cultural tradition, with a strong feeling of belonging and cohesiveness, living as a minority in a larger society. The main problem encountered in defining *ethnic* is that different groups base their identity on different traits. For some, such as the Amish, it is religion; for the Swiss-American it is ancestral nationality; for the blacks it is principally race; for the German-American it is ancestral language; for the French-Canadian it is mother tongue; for the Cuban-American it is political philosophy; for the Appalachian southerner it is folk culture. Indeed, no two ethnic groups establish their identity in exactly the same way. In this sense, we can see that ethnic identity is very similar to nationalism, discussed in Chapter 4. Just as a nation has a *raison d'être*, a reason for being, a basic unifying force, so do ethnic groups. Just as the main unifying force differs from one nation to another, so it differs from one ethnic group to another.

Ethnic groups are the keepers of distinctive cultural traditions and the focal point of various kinds of social interaction. They can provide not only group identity, but also friendships, marriage partners, recreational facilities, business success, and a political power base. They offer the cultural security and reinforcement so essential for minorities, but they can also give rise to suspicion, friction, distrust, clannishness, and even violence. Ethnicity, in America at least, produces one of the brighter hues in the human mosaic.

This is not to say that North American ethnic minorities have remained unchanged by their host culture. **Acculturation** occurs, meaning that the ethnic group changes sufficiently to be able to function within the host society. On the other hand, full **assimilation**, the loss of all ethnic traits and complete blending into the host society, is very rare. Although it was long assumed by students of American culture that immigrant ethnic groups would be fully assimilated, it is increasingly clear that few if any have been. In fact, the past quarter century has witnessed a resurgence of ethnic identity, both in the United States and Canada. In Europe, too, ethnic minorities in countries as diverse as France, the United Kingdom, and Spain have raised demands for cultural autonomy.

The study of ethnic groups has given rise to numerous terms that you

HALLOCK F. RAUP   1901-

Credit for some of the earliest studies in ethnic geography by an
American scholar belongs to Dr.
Hallock F. Raup, Professor Emeritus
of Geography at Kent State University in Ohio. During the quarter-
century span from 1930 to the mid-
fifties, Dr. Raup published
geographical studies of the Pennsylvania Germans (1938) and of
such California groups as the Ana-
heim Germans (1932) and the
Italian-Swiss of the Coastal Ranges
(1935). A later study measured the
Spanish cultural imprint left in California from colonial times.

Professor Raup was attracted to
the study of ethnic geography
through his Pennsylvania German
heritage and the encouragement
offered him by the great cultural
geographer Carl O. Sauer at Berkeley (see Chapter 3). Raup's doctoral dissertation in geography, written
under Sauer's direction, was entitled "The Pennsylvania-Dutch at the
Forks of the Delaware." Though Dr.
Raup later turned to other interests
in cultural geography, the influence of his pioneering research
can be detected among the generation of ethnic geographers presently at work.

may encounter, such as ethnology, ethnography, ethnicity, and ethnic
geography. **Ethnology**, which developed mainly within anthropology, is a
science dealing with the origin, distribution, and characteristics of cultures, with traditional emphasis on more primitive folk societies. **Ethnography** is a branch of ethnology and is the purely descriptive treatment of
cultures. Until recently, ethnologists have rarely studied the ethnic
groups found in industrialized Western cultures. Instead, they have done
research more closely akin to folk geography. **Ethnicity** is the state of
being ethnic; that is, of possessing ethnic quality or affiliation.

Ethnic geography is the study of the spatial aspects of ethnicity. It is
based in the fact that ethnic groups are highly territorial in organization.
They occupy clearly defined areas, whether rural or urban, and place is an
essential aspect of ethnicity. An ethnic group, no less than a political
state, cannot exist without its own territory. In other words, the study of
ethnicity has a built-in geographical dimension, and ethnic geography is
the result. Cultural differences from one place to another can often be
explained in terms of ethnicity.

The beginnings of the academic subdiscipline of ethnic geography lie in
the period during and just after World War I, when numerous ethnic
groups in Europe were clamoring for political self-determination. American and European geographical journals during that period contained
numerous articles on ethnic patterns. German cultural geographers in the
1930s continued this interest in ethnic groups, but unfortunately much of
their work served the purposes of Nazi propaganda. A few American
geographers devoted attention to ethnic studies through the thirties,
forties, and fifties, but it was not until the mid-1960s that ethnic
geography began to grow and thrive as a subdiscipline, a rise that
coincided with and resulted from increasing ethnic awareness in the
United States and Canada (see biographical sketch of Hallock F. Raup).

Ethnic Culture Regions

Our five themes of cultural geography are well adapted to the study of
ethnic groups. Since such groups typically occupy compact, clearly
definable territories, culture region is a particularly appropriate theme.
The United States and Canada furnish examples of ethnic culture regions,
both rural and urban.

Mapping ethnic groups

In America, the task of mapping ethnic groups is often a difficult one for
geographers. The reason is that the United States census does not
enumerate religious groups or the later descendants of foreign-born
immigrants. Only the Spanish-surnamed, Amerindian, and black ethnic
groups can be mapped with any precision on the basis of the census.
Canada, by contrast, takes a much more complete ethnic census that
reveals most minorities.

The American ethnic geographer must often resort to means other than
the census to obtain ethnic data. Some have used the interview method.
Harold F. Creveling used this technique with success in mapping ethnic
groups within a Massachusetts city in the 1950s. The cultural geographer

Peveril Meigs was even more ingenious in his attempt to map the Louisiana French in the 1930s. He counted surnames in telephone directories and supplemented those data by reading family names from rural mailboxes. In this way, Meigs was able to produce an accurate map of the Louisiana French (Figure 9-1). It should be noted, however, that the use of surnames as an index of ethnicity can be misleading in the case of mixed marriages, where the cultural influence of the mother is concealed.

Ethnic culture regions in rural North America

In the eighteenth and nineteenth centuries, massive numbers of non-English European peoples migrated to North America, constituting the greatest migration of all time. A great many of these immigrants settled in rural areas, forming thousands of ethnic farming communities. The bulk of the rural settlers were German and Scandinavian, with lesser numbers of Dutch, Catholic Irish, Swiss, Poles, Ukrainians, Czechs, and other groups. Most chose the agricultural lands of Pennsylvania, the Midwest, and the Canadian Prairie Provinces. The South, with the exception of southern Louisiana, central Texas, and parts of Missouri, was not greatly influenced by this migration. By the end of the nineteenth century, successive waves of immigrants had established colonies, representing almost every linguistic area of Europe, throughout much of the American countryside.

The rural ethnic settlement areas of the United States and Canada can be divided into two categories: **ethnic provinces** and **ethnic islands**. The difference is in size, both in terms of area and population. Ethnic provinces cover large areas, usually including all or part of several states and containing hundreds of thousands or even millions of people, while ethnic islands, sometimes also referred to as **folk islands**, are small dots in

FIGURE 9-1
The Louisiana French ethnic province, as mapped by two different methods. The 1939 map was compiled by sampling the surnames in telephone directories. The ten most common names in each directory were determined and the percentage of these ten that was of French origin was recorded. When no telephone directories were available, surnames on mailboxes were used. Look through the telephone directory for your home town. What are the ten most common family names? What ethnic background do the names reveal? What distortions or inaccuracies might result from using only telephone directories to enumerate ethnic groups? The 1970 map is based on the U.S. census data for the white population's "mother tongue," defined by the Bureau of the Census as the language spoken in the home during the respondent's childhood. (After Peveril Meigs, 3rd, "An Ethno-Telephonic Survey of French Louisiana," *Annals, Association of American Geographers,* 31 (1941), 245; and a map produced by James P. Allen of the Department of Geography, California State University, Northridge, for distribution at the 1978 meeting of the Association of American Geographers at New Orleans.)

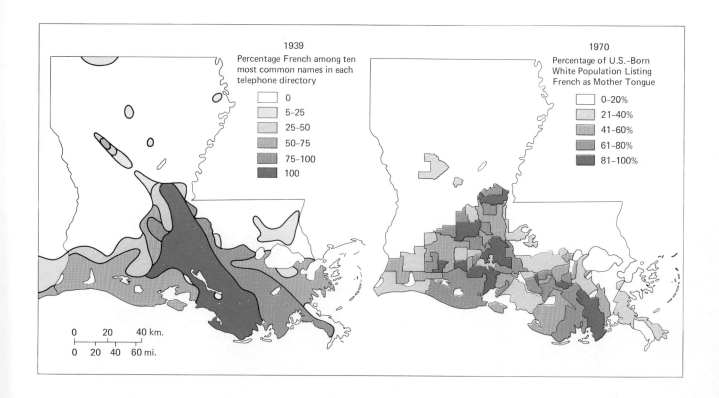

the countryside, typically occupying an area smaller than a county and housing anywhere from several hundred to several thousand people.

Only a few ethnic provinces can be found in North America (Figure 9-2). They include the expansive Mexican-populated borderland of the American Southwest, French Canada, French Louisiana, and the Afro-American or black area of the American South. These districts, in most cases, are large enough in area and population to retard acculturation. Indeed, many French-speaking people in Québec are presently agitating for political independence. Ethnic provinces can be weakened by emigration, as has occurred in the black South, or strengthened by continued immigration, as in the Mexican borderland. In fact, the influx of over one million Mexicans each year represents the greatest ethnic immigration presently under way in North America and is permitting the Mexican ethnic province in the United States to expand northward.

Ethnic islands, by contrast, are much more numerous. Large areas of rural North America have many ethnic islands, as Figure 9-2 suggests. Figure 9-3 provides some Midwestern examples of ethnic islands, revealing the crazy-quilt pattern typical of much of the American heartland. Germans, the largest single group in American ethnic islands, are clustered principally in southeastern Pennsylvania and in Wisconsin, with lesser concentrations in Minnesota, Illinois, Missouri, Texas, Kansas, and

FIGURE 9–2
Ethnic provinces and ethnic islands in the United States and southern Canada. An ethnic province is a large area dominated by a single ethnic group. The Hispanic-American borderland has no sharp boundary, but is spreading north as immigration from Mexico continues. At present, French Canada is probably the purest and most powerful ethnic province; by contrast, French Louisiana is probably the weakest and most subject to acculturation. The Black Belt has been greatly weakened in the last half-century by out-migration.

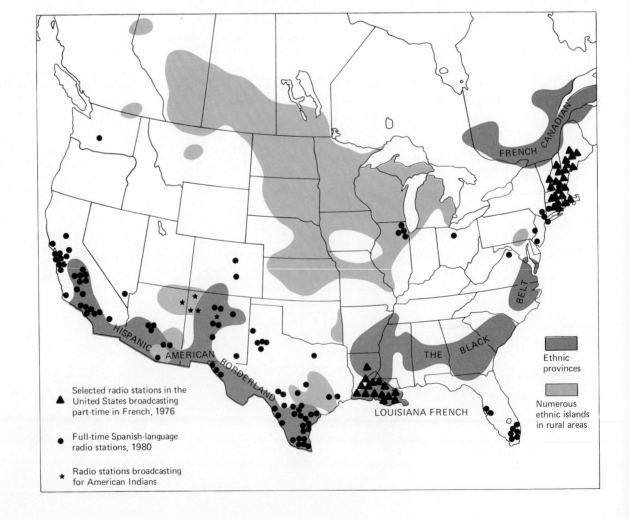

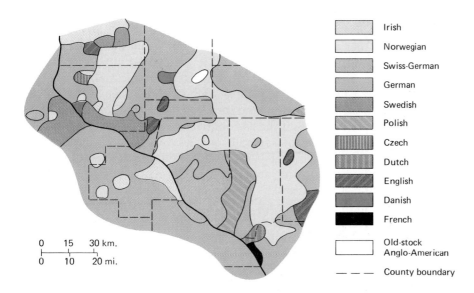

Irish
Norwegian
Swiss-German
German
Swedish
Polish
Czech
Dutch
English
Danish
French

Old-stock Anglo-American

– – – County boundary

0 15 30 km.
0 10 20 mi.

FIGURE 9–3
Ethnic islands in the rural American heartland are illustrated in the distribution of ethnic groups in a small portion of western Wisconsin and southeastern Minnesota during the 1940s. Although not all parts of the United States display this many ethnic islands, it is typical of much of the Midwest. Are ethnic islands found in your home area? How are they distinctive? (After G. W. Hill, "The People of Wisconsin According to Ethnic Stocks, 1940," *Wisconsin's Changing Population,* Madison: Bulletin of the University of Wisconsin, Serial no. 2642, October 1942; and Douglas Marshall, "Minnesota's People," *Minneapolis Tribune* (August 28, 1949), Part 4, p. 1; with modifications.)

several other states, as Figure 9-4 shows. Scandinavians, primarily Swedes and Norwegians, came mainly to Minnesota, the eastern Dakotas, and western Wisconsin. Ukrainians were drawn mainly to the Canadian Prairie Provinces, particularly Manitoba. The other Slavic groups, consisting mostly of Poles and Czechs, did not establish as many large rural clusters as did the Germans and Scandinavians, but they are found scattered about the Midwest and Texas.

Ethnic islands survive from one generation to the next because most land is inherited. In addition, the sale of land is typically confined within the ethnic group, helping preserve the identity of the island. A social stigma is often attached to the sale of land to outsiders. Even so, the smaller size of ethnic islands makes their population more susceptible to acculturation.

FIGURE 9–4
The distribution of the German element in the United States, including Germans, German-Swiss, Russian-Germans, Austrians, and Alsatians. Descendants of German-speaking immigrants are concentrated in the north-central parts of the country, both as farmers and city folk. Although on a map of this scale, the German-settled area seems to constitute a sizeable ethnic district, in reality it consists of thousands of ethnic islands. Why are so few German-Americans found in the rural South and West? [After Jordan; Marshall (see caption for Fig. 9–3); Gerlach; Hill (see caption for Fig. 9–3); Max Hannemann, "Das Deutschtum in den Vereinigten Staaten," *Petermanns Mitteilungen Ergänzungsheft,* No. 224, Gotha: Justus Perthes, 1936; Wilbur Zelinsky, *The Cultural Geography of the United States,* Englewood Cliffs, N.J.: Prentice-Hall, 1973, p. 30; J. F. Thaden, "The Farm People of Michigan According to Ethnic Stocks," Michigan State College, Agricultural Experiment Station, Section of Sociology and Anthropology, 1946 (map); and Justice N. Carman, *Foreign-Language Units of Kansas:* I. Historical Atlas and Statistics, Lawrence: University of Kansas Press, 1962.]

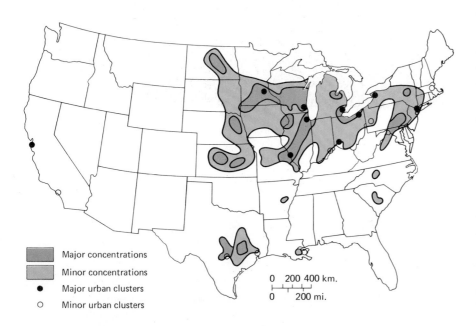

Major concentrations
Minor concentrations
● Major urban clusters
○ Minor urban clusters

0 200 400 km.
0 200 mi.

Urban ethnic neighborhoods and ghettos

Ethnic culture regions are typical both of the cities and the rural areas of North America. An ethnic neighborhood is an area within a city where members of an ethnic group are concentrated. Ethnic neighborhoods became typical in the United States and Canada after about 1840, coinciding with the urbanization and industrialization of North America. Instead of dispersing through the residential areas of the city, the ethnic groups clustered together in separate quarters of the city. The ethnic groups involved were, to a degree, derived from different parts of Europe than the immigrants to rural areas. While Germany and Scandinavia supplied most of the rural settlers, the cities drew much more heavily on Ireland and eastern and southern Europe. Catholic Irish, Italians, Poles, and East European Jews became the main urban ethnic groups, though lesser numbers of virtually every nationality in Europe came to the cities of North America. In the United States, these groups were later joined by French Canadians, southern blacks, Puerto Ricans, Filipinos, Chinese, Appalachian whites, Amerindians, Cubans, and other groups not of European birth.

America was not the first society to have urban ethnic neighborhoods. Rather, distinct ethnic quarters have long been a part of urban history. In cities built by conquerors during periods of empire expansion, the native people often were forced to live in specific districts. Sometimes walls

FIGURE 9–5
Ethnic neighborhoods in the Cleveland area, 1960s. What similarities and differences are revealed by comparing this map with the one of Chicago (Figure 9–6)? Compare both to the model shown in Figure 9–8 and see if you can detect the outlying clusters. Note the movement to suburbs that is underway. (After Allen G. Noble and Albert J. Korsok, *Ohio—An American Heartland,* Bulletin 65, State of Ohio, Division of Geological Survey, Columbus, 1975, p. 176, with modifications.)

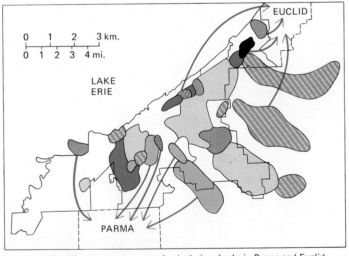

Arrows indicate movements to mixed-ethnic suburbs in Parma and Euclid

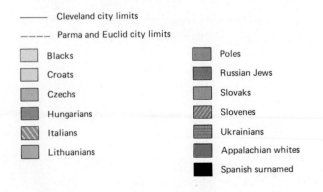

———— Cleveland city limits

– – – – Parma and Euclid city limits

Blacks		Poles	
Croats		Russian Jews	
Czechs		Slovaks	
Hungarians		Slovenes	
Italians		Ukrainians	
Lithuanians		Appalachian whites	
		Spanish surnamed	

were built around such quarters to set them off from the rest of the city. Roman cities had distinct Christian neighborhoods; Islamic cities had Christian quarters; and Christian cities have long had Jewish quarters. But cities in the United States and Canada are perhaps more ethnically diverse than any others in the world. The census in 1870 showed that the populations of New York, Chicago, and San Francisco were about 45 percent foreign-born. Even after legislation was passed in the 1920s to effectively close the door to European and Asian immigrants, large numbers of southern blacks, Appalachian whites, Puerto Ricans, and Mexicans migrated to North American cities. Figures 9-5 and 9-6 show concentrations of ethnic groups in Cleveland and Chicago.

The heritage of these ethnic neighborhoods continues to play an important role in urban affairs. In the 1970s, the offspring of Irish immigrants zealously guarded their ethnic turf in South Boston against blacks. Japanese in San Francisco fought against a redevelopment plan that would replace neighborhood housing with hotels and convention centers. In East Los Angeles, the residents of a Mexican-American community attempted (but failed) to incorporate their neighborhood so that they could achieve self-rule, and a similar movement in South Tucson, Arizona, succeeded.

A neighborhood is a voluntary community where people reside by choice. Members of an ethnic group may choose to live near one another, thereby forming an **ethnic neighborhood**. The benefits of an ethnic neighborhood are many: common use of language, nearby kin, stores and services specially tailored to a certain group's taste, and institutions important to the group—such as churches and lodges—which remain viable only when a number of people live close enough to participate frequently in their activities (see box, "The Whites Out There").

There is a difference between a **ghetto** and an ethnic neighborhood. The term *ghetto* has traditionally been used to describe an area within the city where a certain ethnic group has been forced to live. The term perhaps originated in medieval Venice, where Jews were required to live in an undesirable part of the city near the ironworks. This section was known as "ghetto," perhaps taking its name from the foundry's owner. Later, it was common to refer to the Jewish section of any European city as the ghetto. Often these quarters were walled and set off from the rest of the city by a gate that was locked at sundown, thereby physically reinforcing the segregation of the Jewish population. Use of the term today should be reserved for areas of residential segregation where an ethnic group lives because it has very little choice in the matter—options are limited or nonexistent. In other words, a ghetto is an involuntary community.

Whether an ethnic group lives in a ghetto or voluntarily forms its own neighborhood usually depends on how discriminatory the majority society acts toward it. For example, because American society discriminates more against blacks than Italians, a black ghetto is more likely to exist than an Italian ghetto. This was revealed in a study of Cleveland, Ohio, by John F. Kain. The Cleveland blacks are confined to a ghetto by discriminatory housing practices and are much more highly segregated residentially than are white ethnic groups (Figure 9-6). Italians, Poles, Jews, Appalachian folk, and other white ethnic groups in Cleveland occupy neighborhoods rather than ghettos and are more likely to disperse to the suburbs than are blacks. Even so, the American urban blacks are in a far superior position to the city-dwelling blacks of the Republic of South Africa. There, the mandatory racial segregation act of 1923, with subsequent

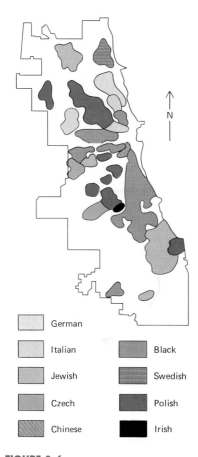

German
Italian   Black
Jewish   Swedish
Czech   Polish
Chinese   Irish

FIGURE 9–6
Ethnic neighborhoods remain intact in Chicago. This map shows their distribution in 1957. Black areas are defined as neighborhoods with 25% or more black residents. Do ethnic groups cluster in neighborhoods in your city? (St. C. Drake and H. Cayton, *Black Metropolis*, New York: Harper & Row, 1962.)

"THE WHITES OUT THERE": MOVING INTO A NON-CHINESE NEIGHBORHOOD

What does it feel like to be the "different" family moving into a new neighborhood? Here is one account of what it felt like to a young Chinese girl, moving from San Francisco's Chinatown to a white neighborhood in the late 1930s.

"When I was three and a half my family moved out of Chinatown to the Mission District. . . . I was very conscious that Chinatown was a long way from the Mission District and I was coming from another world. . . . When my parents would talk about the outside being a bad place, they would refer sort of generally to 'the whites out there,' they always called them *sai yen*. To me, of course, that meant the whites right around us. It meant the bar downstairs where there was an Irish tavern, Cavanaugh's, that we could hear coming up through the floor every night. We'd hear this crashing, singing, people being thrown around down there, they would have brawls and they would pee on our doorstep. Every other day we would go down there with a bucket to wash it off. But at the same time my parents kept reminding us that 'the whites out there,' the same people who would vomit and pee on our doorstep, were the people who had the power to take our home away from us. We had to do a little placating of them. Every Easter, every Christmas, every American holiday, I would be sent on a little tour of all the local businesses.

I would go to the bakery across the street, the barbershop down the street, the realty company, and the bar. I would deliver a little cake to each one. We wanted to be known as that nice Chinese family upstairs or down the street, you know, whom you wouldn't ever want to hurt in any way. My family was very aware that they were embattled Chinese in a white district, that they had spent many years finding that place to live, and that at any moment they would be asked to leave. And somehow a quality I sensed out of all this, about being Chinese, was a vulnerability. At any moment you could be thrown out. So you had to watch your step and you had to be very clever, you had to placate, you had to maneuver. And no matter what happened you did not get openly angry, because if you did, you would have lost your dignity. No matter what they did you had to be stronger than they, you had to outlast them."

This is what it was like for one nonwhite family to move "up" into the white residential world. What do you think were the benefits from their point of view? What were the costs?

From Victor G. Nee and Brett de Bary Nee, Longtime Californ': A Documentary Study of an American Chinatown *(New York: Pantheon, 1973), pp. 162–166. Copyright © 1973 by Pantheon, a Division of Random House, Inc. With permission.*

amendments, has created quite distinct ethnic quarters. The only blacks allowed by law to reside in white neighborhoods of Johannesburg, for example, are domestic live-in servants, and even their numbers have declined in recent decades, in part because they are not allowed to have their families with them.

Although an ethnic neighborhood or ghetto may seem homogeneous to outsiders, it is a diverse area. A typical ethnic urban area has four different sectors. Figure 9-7 shows all four in diagram form: the core, middle, fringe, and outlying cluster. The core is the original area dominated by the ethnic group, normally on the edge of the central business district. Here, housing is oldest and, as a result, deteriorating. Rents are generally low. Often residences have been broken up into small apartments, rooming

FIGURE 9-7
Zones within an ethnic area are depicted in this diagram. A typical immigrant might first settle in the ghetto core. Gradually in a series of short moves the immigrant progresses to the middle area, the fringe, and at last to an outlying cluster. Many members of the ethnic community remain behind.

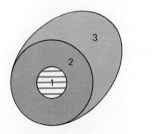
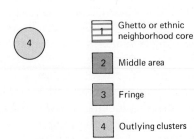

1   Ghetto or ethnic neighborhood core

2   Middle area

3   Fringe

4   Outlying clusters

houses, or transient hotels. The core is usually the "**port of entry**" for migrants new to the city. It is populated by a large number of single men who have come to the city without their families. Generally the new migrants lack skills and information about jobs, making this an area of high unemployment (Figure 9–8).

If core-area residents land a steady job, they may seek more permanent dwellings—a flat or a larger apartment in the middle zone, with higher rents and more available space. Here you would likely find families instead of only single men.

The fringe area is the transition between ghetto and neighborhood. Here, homes come at premium prices. The non-ethnic residents who surround the ghetto fear the group's expansion and try to contain it by economic barriers. Those group members who can afford the higher rents are more skilled and better-educated than the rest of their ethnic group. Because some of them live on the fringe out of choice rather than necessity, it probably can be called a neighborhood instead of a ghetto.

Some ethnic areas lack the fringe. Often it cannot develop because nearby tightly knit ethnic groups strongly resist expansion into their territory. In this case, outlying clusters take over the fringe's role. But a new emotional element also enters the picture. Some group members, having achieved a degree of economic success, want to remove themselves, literally and symbolically, from their ghetto past. Consequently, as the outlying cluster develops, it often becomes a desirable goal for those who are still trapped in the ghetto core. For example, San Francisco has two distinct areas of Chinese settlement outside of Chinatown, the original ethnic ghetto. These began to develop in the late 1940s, when federal law made it illegal to restrict ethnic groups from living in FHA-financed housing. Gradually, the Chinese bought homes in areas outside Chinatown. As more and more Chinese moved to these fringe areas, true ethnic neighborhoods emerged, complete with shops, services, and restaurants. The white neighborhood now shows signs of fear that the Chinese will dominate the area, and some whites have suggested real estate moratoriums and other means of inhibiting Chinese home ownership.

The organization of the ethnic area into a spatial pattern of four zones—core, middle, fringe, and outlying cluster—relates to the **immigrant's ladder**, a metaphor for the way new migrants supposedly enter society at the bottom and climb progressively higher and higher in status. The bottom rungs of the ladder are in the ghetto core; the middle rungs, in the ethnic fringe or outlying cluster. Typically, earlier-arrived ethnic groups eventually abandon poorer residential areas altogether and are replaced by newcomers of different ethnic background. We can see this historic process in action in the succession of groups that dominated certain neighborhoods and then passed on to more desirable areas. Boston's West End was mainly an Irish area in the nineteenth century. As the twentieth century began, the Irish were replaced in this deteriorating neighborhood by the Jews, who in turn were replaced in the late 1930s by Poles and Italians. The list of groups that passed through Chicago's Adams area from the nineteenth century to the present provides an almost complete history of American migratory patterns: First came the Germans and Irish, who were succeeded by the Greeks, Poles, French Canadians, Czechs, and Russian Jews, who were soon hard-pressed by the Italians. They in turn were challenged by Chicanos and even a small group of Puerto Ricans. Blacks, who have played such a great role in urban

FIGURE 9–8
A scene in the Chicano ethnic core of Los Angeles. Such districts serve as "ports of entry" for immigrants newly-arrived from Mexico.

migration, were the only major group absent from this list. As a rule, the tendency to leave an ethnic neighborhood and settle in a mixed residential area increases as acculturation progresses. The more acculturated the person, the less likely he or she is to live in an ethnic neighborhood.

Cultural Diffusion and Ethnic Groups

Glancing at the maps of North American ethnic provinces, islands, and neighborhoods, you might conclude that the seemingly haphazard spatial pattern is the result of pure chance. In reality, though, orderly processes created the ethnic mosaic, processes we may refer to as "dominant personality," "emigrant letters," and "cluster migration." These processes all fit quite well the concept of relocation diffusion.

Migration processes

Most voluntary migrations are begun by a **dominant personality**, sometimes also referred to as a "true pioneer." This individual is a forceful, ambitious type, a natural leader, who perceives emigration as a solution to economic, social, political, or religious problems in the homeland, and, by the force of his or her personality, convinces others to migrate. It is usually possible in retrospect to point to the activities of one such dominant personality and conclude that, had it not been for that person, the migration in question would not have occurred or would have been inconsequential.

The main device used by dominant personalities to promote migrations is the **emigrant letter**. After choosing a settlement site, the dominant personality exerts influence by writing letters back to the homeland, extolling the virtues of the new country and urging friends and relatives to follow. In such letters, positive aspects of the adopted country are stressed and the negative are downgraded or omitted altogether, with the result that the new homeland is made to sound like a second Garden of Eden (see box, "An Emigrant Letter from an American Land of Milk and Honey"). Others are induced to follow in a sort of **chain migration**. Once begun, such migrations tend to snowball. Those who follow the dominant personality in turn influence others to do the same. Friends and relatives are most susceptible to this kind of influence. The number of emigrant letters rapidly increases, and among the secondary migrants are other forceful personalities who also wield persuasive powers.

Cluster migration describes the tendency of people to move in clusters, leaving certain small districts in the homeland to settle similarly confined colonial areas overseas. It is a natural and expected result of dominant personalities and their use of emigrant letters (Figure 9-9). In this manner, people from several parishes in rural Germany can be responsible for occupying a township or small district in the United States or Canada. Typically neighbors in the new homeland had been neighbors in the Old World. The influence of dominant personalities spreads most easily among people they know, and the decision to emigrate spreads by contagious diffusion through a population. In the last half of the nineteenth century, and particularly after the American Civil War, large-scale advertising campaigns added another dimension to ethnic migration, but the basic processes remained unchanged.

AN EMIGRANT LETTER FROM AN AMERICAN LAND OF MILK AND HONEY

The following excerpts are from a letter written in 1832 by the first German settler in Texas to a friend back in Germany. The letter was eventually published in a German newspaper and prompted a large migration from northwestern Germany to Texas. How would you have reacted to the letter?

"In February of last year I embarked on a brig to New Orleans, where . . . I received favorable news of Austin's Colony in Texas. I embarked again . . . and landed after an eight-day voyage . . . in this colony.

"Each married immigrant who wishes to engage in farming receives a *league* of land, and a single person gets one-quarter of a *league*. . . . A *league* of land contains 4,440 acres of land, including hills and valleys, woods and meadows with creeks flowing through. . . . He must pay in installments a fee of $160 for surveying . . . and must take an oath of citizenship. After one year he becomes a citizen of Mexico. . . . A father of a family . . . receives on his arrival a land grant that is virtually a count's estate, and within a short time the land will be worth $700 to $800. . . . The expenses for the land need not be paid immediately. Many obtain the money by raising cattle. . . . Farmers who own 700 head of cattle are common hereabouts. . . . Europeans are especially welcome in the colony, and I was given an excellent *league* of land, upon which I built my home. . . .

"The land here is hilly, covered partly with forest and partly with natural prairies. There are various types of trees. The climate is similar to that of Sicily. . . . There is no real winter, and the coldest months are almost like March in Germany. Bees, birds, and butterflies stay all through the winter season. . . . The soil requires no fertilizer. . . . The main crops are tobacco, rice, indigo, sweet potatoes, melons of special good-ness, watermelons, wheat, rye, and vegetables of all kinds. Peaches are found in abundance growing wild in the forest, as are mulberries, . . . walnuts, plums, persimmons as sweet as honey, and wine grapes in great quantity. . . . There is much . . . wild game, and hunting and fishing are free. The prairies are filled with the most lovely flowers. There are many snakes here, . . . but each farmer knows how to protect himself against them. . . . The more children you have, the better, for you will need them as field laborers. . . . Mosquitos and gnats are common only near the coast. Formerly there were no taxes at all, and now we have only community taxes. Each year you need work barely three months to make a living. . . .

"There is freedom of religion here, . . . and English is the prevailing language. . . . Up the river there is much silver to be found, but Indians still live there.

"Col. Austin promised me recently to see that all Germans who come to the colony will be given land at once. When you arrive at San Felipe, ask for Friedrich Ernst of Mill Creek. It is thirty miles from there to my place, and you will find me without any difficulty. . . . For my friends and former countrymen, I have built a shelter on my estate where they can stay while selecting their *league* of land."

Your friend,
Fritz Ernst

Translated, adapted, and rearranged from Hermann Achenbach, Tagebuch meiner Reise nach den Nordamerikanischen Freistaaten, oder: Das neue Kanaan [*Diary of My Trip to the North American Free States, or The New Canaan*] (Düsseldorf: G. H. Beyer and J. Wolf, 1835), pp. 132–135; and Detlef Dunt, Reise nach Texas, nebst Nachrichten von diesem Lande; für Deutsche, welche nach Amerika zu gehen beabsichtigen [*A Trip to Texas, Together with News of That Country, for Germans Who Plan to Come to America*] (Bremen: Carl W. Wiehe, 1834), pp. 4–16.

The American Indian reservations represent another kind of ethnic island, created by quite different forces and 'processes. They are the remnant refuges of displaced peoples, driven by military conquest from former ethnic provinces into remnant ethnic islands. As a rule, Amerindians occupy marginal environments not wanted by the whites. Like the European ethnic islands, those of the Indians add human diversity to the North American countryside, but their development has been largely different.

Diffusion of ethnic traits

As ethnic groups migrated from Europe and elsewhere to North America, they had the potential to introduce, by relocation diffusion, all of the traits of their Old World culture. Conceivably they could have perpetuated all

FIGURE 9-9

Ethnic cluster migration from French Canada to the United States. Ethnic islands and urban neighborhoods typically result from cluster migration. One of the more significant ethnic migrations of the last century has been the movement of French-Canadians to the factory towns of New England, a migration accomplished by numerous small clusters of people. This map shows the clustered sources of French Canadians who migrated to the towns of Brunswick and Waterville in Maine in the 1880-1925 period. The parish of Beauce supplied most of the Waterville French, while L'Islet Parish was the leading source of Brunswick French. Try to reconstruct in your own mind the sequence of events which might have led to this clustering of migration source and destination. If you were migrating to a foreign country, would you seek out people of your own nationality who had preceded you there? (After James P. Allen, "Migration Fields of French Canadian Immigrants to Southern Maine," *Geographical Review,* 62 (1972), 377.)

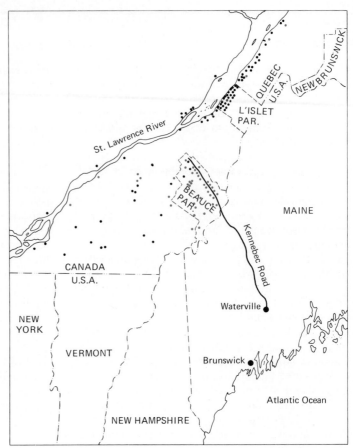

• Birthplace of ten immigrants to Brunswick, Maine, 1880–1900

• Birthplace of one immigrant to Waterville, Maine, 1890–1925

facets of their ancestral way of life, both material and nonmaterial. Had they done so, then a visit to a North American ethnic province, island, or neighborhood would indeed be a visit to Europe, Africa, or Asia.

However, the ethnic immigrants did not reproduce their Old World cultures overseas. Only selected traits were successfully introduced, and others underwent considerable modification before becoming established in the new homeland. In other words, absorbing barriers existed that prevented the diffusion of many Old World traits to America, and permeable barriers caused changes in many other traits (Figure 9-10).

When an ethnic group migrates into a new environmental and cultural setting, the members have four choices. They may retain traditional ways, borrow alien ways from the groups they encounter in the New World, invent new techniques better suited to the adopted homeland, or modify traditional or alien ways as they see fit. Most immigrant ethnic groups resort to all four devices, in varying degrees. The displacement of a group and relocation in a new homeland can have widely differing results. Perhaps most commonly, the relocation weakens tradition and upsets an age-old balance, causing a rapid discarding of Old World traits and accelerated borrowing, invention, and modification—in short, acculturation.

The economic barrier

Several factors are very important in determining whether tradition is maintained by a relocated ethnic group or whether borrowing, invention, and modification occur. Perhaps the overriding factor in the successful or unsuccessful cultural diffusion of homeland traditions to a new homeland is economic. The large majority of ethnic immigrants to the United States, Canada, Australia, and other overseas European settlement zones migrated in order to improve their economic condition. Some few, such as the Florida Cubans or the Hungarians of the late 1950s, came for political freedom. Other small groups, including the Mennonites and French Huguenots, sought religious freedom. But most came for economic reasons. They readily discarded Old World traits that interfered with economic success in America. Whether traits were transferred, borrowed, invented, or modified was very often determined by economic considerations.

For example, a non-English language stood in the way of economic success in America, while religious affiliation, as a rule, presented no such hindrance. Therefore, we should not be surprised to learn that most American ethnic groups largely abandoned their traditional languages but generally retained affiliation with ancestral religious sects (Figure 9-11). Few younger-generation urban Italian-Americans today speak Italian, but most remain at least nominally Roman Catholic. Few rural German-American farmers speak German, but most perpetuate the Lutheran, Reformed, or Catholic traditions of their forefathers. For the same reason, many immigrant farmers in the ethnic islands of North America aban-

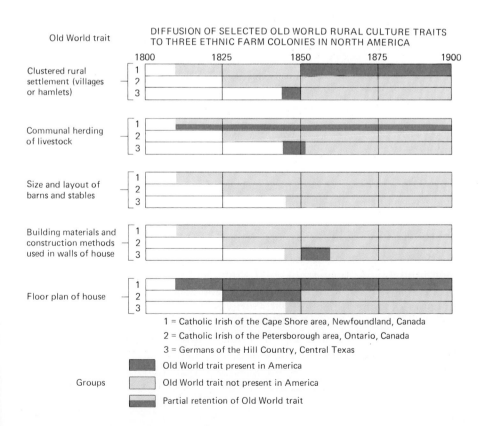

DIFFUSION OF SELECTED OLD WORLD RURAL CULTURE TRAITS TO THREE ETHNIC FARM COLONIES IN NORTH AMERICA

Old World trait

Clustered rural settlement (villages or hamlets)

Communal herding of livestock

Size and layout of barns and stables

Building materials and construction methods used in walls of house

Floor plan of house

1 = Catholic Irish of the Cape Shore area, Newfoundland, Canada
2 = Catholic Irish of the Petersborough area, Ontario, Canada
3 = Germans of the Hill Country, Central Texas

Groups

Old World trait present in America
Old World trait not present in America
Partial retention of Old World trait

FIGURE 9–10

Diffusion of selected Old World rural culture traits to three ethnic farm colonies in North America. Note the interesting similarities and differences between the three settlement areas. The Cape Shore Irish were very isolated and the Hill Country Germans moderately so, but the Petersborough Irish had frequent contacts with non-Irish Catholics. The two Irish colonies were in climates colder than that of Ireland, while the Texas Germans found their new homeland warmer and drier than Germany. The Irish, from a deforested country, moved to densely wooded colonies, while the Germans found timber only slightly more abundant in the new homeland. What effects might these contrasts have had on the diffusion and retention of Old World traits? (After Mannion, pp. 166–167 and Jordan, *German Seed*, pp. 118–191.)

FIGURE 9–11
National origin and religious affiliation in Nova Scotia, Canada. By 1871, the Canadian province of Nova Scotia had been settled by a variety of ethnic groups speaking English, French, German, and Scottish Gaelic. By the mid-twentieth century, English had become the prevailing speech. German and Gaelic had largely died out, but the various ethnic groups had remained true, for the most part, to their ancestral religions. Anglican and Baptist membership was indicative of English ancestry, Lutheranism of German origin, and Presbyterianism of Scotch-Irish and most Scottish people. About a third of the original Scottish settlers, mainly those in the east and north of Nova Scotia, were Catholic, as were six-sevenths of the French. Blurring of ethnic lines had occurred to some extent, however. The United Church combined Methodists and many Presbyterians, joining many people of English, Scottish, and Scotch-Irish heritage. Numerous Lutheran Germans converted to the Anglican faith. But the majority of people in 1941 still adhered to the churches of their immigrant ancestors. Which would you more willingly give up if you migrated to a foreign land, your language or your religion? (After Andrew H. Clark, "Old World Origins and Religious Adherence in Nova Scotia," *Geographical Review*, 50 (1960), 320, 327, with modifications.)

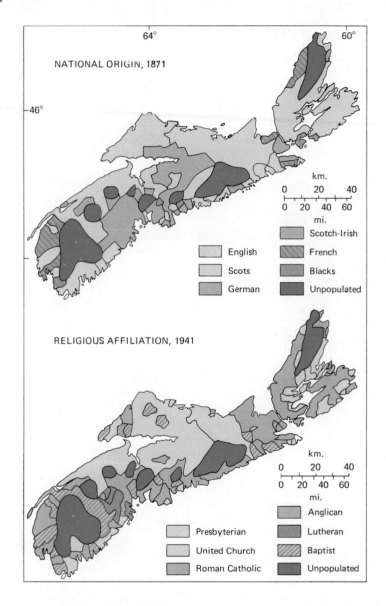

doned the traditional crops they had raised in Europe and shifted to corn, cotton, or some other previously unknown crop. They did so in order to produce what the market demanded.

The factor of isolation

The degree of isolation of an ethnic group in the new homeland also helps determine if traditional traits will be retained, modified, or abandoned. If the new settlement area is remote and contacts with outsiders are few, diffusion of traits from the Old World is more likely. Because contacts with alien groups are rare, little borrowing of traits can occur. Isolated ethnic groups often preserve in archaic form cultural elements that disappear from their former homeland; that is, they may, in some respects, change less than their kinfolk back in the homeland. Language and dialects offer some good examples of this preservation of the archaic. The

Polish Dialect spoken by descendants of immigrants who came from the province of Silesia to south-central Texas in the 1850s, although infiltrated with English words, is closer to mid-nineteenth-century Silesian Polish than is the speech found today in Silesia itself, prompting Polish linguists to come halfway around the world to Texas to learn more about the spoken Polish of the previous century. Similarly, Germans living in ethnic islands in the Balkan region of southeastern Europe preserve archaic South German dialects better than in Germany itself, and some Elizabethan-age English usages are more common in southern Appalachia than in England.

Isolation can be either physical, the result of spatial remoteness, or cultural, the product of clannishness. The Old Order Amish Germans of Pennsylvania provide an example of deliberate, self-imposed isolation. Because of it, they perpetuate a lifestyle devoid of electricity, automobiles, and tractors.

The effect of isolation on cultural diffusion can be seen in Figure 9-10. The Newfoundland Irish are the most isolated of the three groups included. Note that they have introduced and preserved more Old World ways than either of the other two groups. As a rule, the earlier an ethnic community was established, the more likely its members were to introduce Old World ways. As the decades passed, particularly in the nineteenth century, transportation and communication systems were rapidly improved, breaking down isolation.

Cultural rebound

Cultural diffusion in ethnic settlements is often delayed by a third factor, a temporary barrier imposed by the struggle for survival and related difficulties during the early years of pioneering in the new homeland. Years later, after the immigrants establish a more comfortable existence, they often revert to homeland ways, a process we can call **cultural rebound**. Figure 9-10 illustrates two examples of cultural rebound, or belated cultural diffusion. The Newfoundland Irish, who had lived in clustered clan hamlets in Ireland, initially established scattered farmsteads in America, probably because they were generally not blood kin of the other Irish in their neighborhood. After several generations, however, natural population increase and intermarriage produced extended families and clans, and the Irish clan hamlet reappeared. In Texas, German settlers built crude log cabins in the Anglo-American style to serve as temporary houses until they could get their farms established. After a few years, when the most difficult pioneering was behind, they reverted to the typically German half-timbered construction in building their homes (see Figure 9-19).

The environmental factor

A fourth factor influencing cultural diffusion from the Old World was the physical environment. Many immigrant ethnic groups coming to North America settled lands different in some important environmental respect from the old country, even though they often sought similar areas. For city dwellers the environmental differences were of relatively little consequence, but for farmers the contrasts usually meant cultural borrowing, invention, and modification. If the climate was warmer, for example, smaller barns and less winter feed for livestock were needed; if the new land was unsuited to a traditional crop, farmers stopped raising it and abandoned the traditional tools, implements, and customs associated with its cultivation, adopting new crops and the means for their raising.

Cultural Ecology and Ethnicity

Our discussion of the physical environmental barriers to cultural diffusion leads naturally into a consideration of cultural ecology as it relates to ethnicity. Two topics will concern us in this section of the chapter: the ethnic factor in the selection of sites for non-urban colonies and the perception of the new environment by ethnic groups.

Selecting a site

In the eighteenth and nineteenth centuries, many factors influenced ethnic immigrants as they chose settlement sites for colonies in the North American countryside. Some immigrants were prompted by a desire to find lands similar to those of the old country. Others sought lands better than those they had left behind, since they were intent upon economic advancement.

Some ethnic immigrant groups developed a reputation as very good judges of soil fertility in America. Germans and Czechs, in particular, are reputed to have chosen consistently the best farmland, a choice that helped them become prosperous and superior farmers. The ethnic geographer Russel L. Gerlach, researching the German communities of the Ozarks, found that while Appalachian southern settlers in that region chose easy-to-work sandy and bottomland soil, Germans often chose superior soils that were harder to work. In Lawrence County, Missouri, for example, the Germans were relative latecomers but still got some of the best land when they selected dark-soiled prairie lands that had been avoided by earlier Anglo-American settlers. In Gerlach's words, "a map showing the distribution of Germans in the Ozarks can also be a map of the better soils in the region."

A similar ability to select choice soils can be detected among the Czechs in Texas, the state containing the largest rural Czech population in the United States. Figure 9-12 reveals, to a quite remarkable degree, that the Czech farming communities in Texas are concentrated in prairie regions underlain by dark, fertile soils. Nothing comparable to the Texas prairie soils is found in Czechoslovakia, but the Czechs quickly recognized the great potential of such land.

Many ethnic groups sought environments resembling the homeland. The state of Wisconsin, dotted with hundreds of ethnic islands, provides some fine examples. In particular, the choice of settlement sites by the Finns, Icelanders, English, and Cornish who came to Wisconsin is revealing (Figure 9-13). The Finns, coming from a cold, thin-soiled, glaciated, lake-studded, coniferous forest zone in Europe, chose to settle the North Woods of Wisconsin, a land very similar in almost every respect to the one from which they had departed. Icelanders, from a bleak, remote island in the North Atlantic, located their only Wisconsin colony on Washington Island, as isolated outpost surrounded by the waters of Lake Michigan. The English, accustomed to good farmland, generally founded

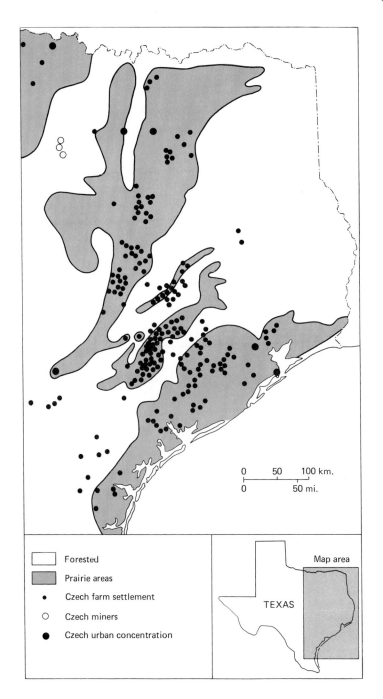

Forested

Prairie areas

• Czech farm settlement

○ Czech miners

● Czech urban concentration

TEXAS

Map area

0   50   100 km.

0   50 mi.

FIGURE 9–12

The ecology of Czech settlements in Texas.
Note the tendency of Czechs to settle in
prairie regions. The prairie grasses were
underlain by rich soils that have supported a
prosperous Czech farming class for a
century. (After Henry R. Maresh, "The Czechs
in Texas," *Southwestern Historical Quarterly,*
50 (1946–47), 236–240 and map.)

ethnic islands in the better agricultural districts of southern and southwestern Wisconsin. Many of the English were Cornish, miners from the
Celtic highlands of western Great Britain, and they sought out the
lead-mining communities of southwestern Wisconsin, where they continued their traditional occupations. On a broader scale, thousands of ethnic
Germans from wheat-growing communities on the open steppe grasslands
of south Russia, the so-called Russian-Germans, chose to settle the
prairies of the American and Canadian Great Plains, where they established fine wheat farms not unlike those of their east European homeland.

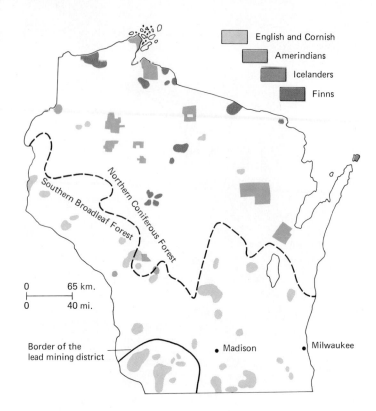

FIGURE 9-13
The ecology of selected ethnic islands in Wisconsin. Notice that Finnish settlements are concentrated in the infertile North Woods section, as are the Amerindian reservations. The Finns went there by choice, the Indians survived there because few whites were interested in such land. The English, by contrast, are found more often in the better farmland south of the border of the North Woods. Some of the English were miners from Cornwall, and they were drawn to the lead mining country of southwestern Wisconsin, where they could practice the profession already known to them. Icelanders, an island people, chose an island as their settlement site in Wisconsin. (After G. W. Hill, "The People of Wisconsin According to Ethnic Stocks, 1940," *Wisconsin's Changing Population*, Madison: Bulletin of the University of Wisconsin, Serial No. 2642, October 1942.)

Environmental perception

Often, as in the cases just described, there was some striking similarity between the physical environments of the old and new homelands. But sometimes the dissimilarities were even more striking. In such cases, members of immigrant ethnic groups in the rural areas of North America generally tended to perceive their new environments as being more like the European lands they had abandoned than was actually the case. Their perception of the new country emphasized the similarities and downgraded the differences.

Perhaps for this reason, L. Unstad, a Norwegian in subtropical, unglaciated central Texas, on the fringe of the semiarid lands, reported that he "found the lay of the land, the woods on the hills, the farms on the hillsides and in the valleys very similar to rural scenes in the eastern part of Norway." He could overlook the major differences in climate and vegetation, the pronounced visible differences between unglaciated and glaciated terrain, and be impressed instead by the similarities. Perhaps the seeking for similarity was a symptom of homesickness or an unwillingness to admit that migration had brought them to a largely alien land. Perhaps growing to adulthood in a particular kind of physical environment retards one's ability to accurately perceive a different setting.

Whatever the reason, the distorted perception occasionally caused problems for ethnic farming groups. Sometimes crops that had thrived in the old homeland were not well suited to the particular American setting. A period of trial and error was often necessary to come to terms with the

New World environment. In a few instances, the misperception was of such magnitude that economic disaster resulted and the ethnic island had to be abandoned.

Cultural Integration and Ethnicity

The complicated spatial pattern of ethnic islands, provinces, ghettos, and neighborhoods is related to a variety of other cultural geographical phenomena. Ethnicity can play a role in deciding what people buy, how they vote, how they make a living, where they do their shopping, how they spend their free time, or whom they choose as their marriage partners. In other words, ethnicity is causally related to many other facets of culture, and therefore we can profitably apply the theme of cultural integration to the geographic study of ethnic groups. To illustrate how ethnicity is integrated into the cultural fabric of North America, we will use three examples from economic geography: choice of employment, types of business activity, and farming practices. Examples are drawn from both urban and rural settings.

Ethnicity and urban business activity

Differential ethnic preferences give rise to distinct patterns of purchasing goods and services. This in turn is reflected in the types of businesses and services available in different ethnic settlement areas in a city. The geographer Keith D. Harries made a detailed study of businesses in the Los Angeles urban area, comparing Anglo-American, black, and Mexican-American neighborhoods (Figure 9-14).

He found that an East Los Angeles Mexican-American neighborhood has unusually large numbers of food stores, eating and drinking places, personal services, and repair shops. This Mexican area has, in fact, three times as many food stores as the Anglo neighborhoods. In large part, this is due to the dominance of small corner grocery stores and the fragmentation of food sales among several different kinds of stores, such as *tortillerias*. The large number of eating and drinking places is related to the Mexican custom of gathering in *cantinas* (bars), where much of the social life is centered. Numerous small barbershops are one reason why personal service establishments rank so high.

Black south Los Angeles ranks highest in personal service businesses, and vacant stores there rank second. Eating and drinking places there are the third most numerous. In contrast to the Mexican eastern part of town, the south has relatively few bars but a large number of liquor stores and liquor departments in food and drug stores. Secondhand shops are very common, but there are no antique or jewelry stores and only one book-stationery shop. A distinctive black personal service enterprise, the shoeshine parlor, is found only in south Los Angeles.

The Anglo neighborhoods, more affluent on the average than either the Mexican or black areas, rank very high in professional and financial service establishments, such as doctors, lawyers, and banks. These services are much less common in the non-Anglo neighborhoods. Furniture, jewelry, antique, and apparel stores are more numerous among the Anglos, as are full-scale restaurants. In short, Dr. Harries found major

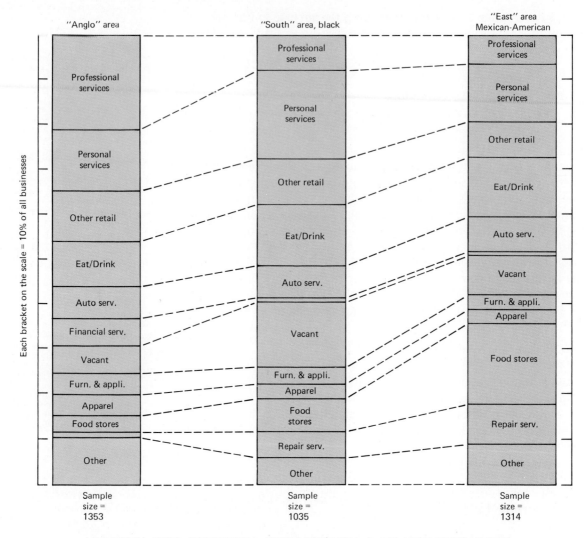

VARIATION in TYPES of BUSINESSES by ETHNIC DISTRICTS in the LOS ANGELES URBAN AREA

FIGURE 9–14

Variation in types of businesses by ethnic districts in the Los Angeles urban area. "Professional services" include such persons as doctors and lawyers, while "personal services" are represented by businesses like barbershops and shoeshine parlors. Do such differences exist between ethnic neighborhoods in your city? (After Keith D. Harries, "Ethnic Variations in Los Angeles Business Patterns," *Annals, Association of American Geographers,* 61 (1971), 739.)

differences between the three ethnic areas. Though due in part to economic rather than ethnic contrasts, these differences are also related to dietary and social customs.

Ethnicity and rural-small town businesses

The contrasts observed by Dr. Harries in the urban scene can also be found in rural and small town areas. An example can be taken from a study by the geographer Elaine M. Bjorklund of an ethnic island in southwestern Michigan. The island was settled in the mid-nineteenth century by Dutch Calvinists (Figure 9-15). Their descendants adhered to a strict moral code, and they tended to regard the non-Dutch Reformed world outside their ethnic island as sinful and inferior. The Calvinist Reformed Church was clearly the key to their ethnicity, since the Dutch language died out in the area. The impact of the Calvinist code of behavior on business activity in this Dutch ethnic island could be seen in various ways. There were, as recently as 1960, no taverns, dance halls, or movie theaters except in the city of Holland, and no business activity was permitted on Sunday. In most towns and villages, businesses are still restricted to grocery stores and filling stations. Since Calvinists believe that leisure and idleness are evil, most present-day farmers work at second jobs during slack seasons in the agricultural year.

Ethnicity and type of employment

Closely related to type of business is type of employment. In many urban ethnic neighborhoods, individual groups early gravitated to particular kinds of jobs. These job identities were never rigid, and they were stronger in the decades immediately following immigration than they are today, due to advancing acculturation, but some notable examples can be found. In some cases, the identification of ethnic groups and job types was sufficiently strong to produce stereotyped images in the American popular mind, such as Irish policemen, Italian grocers and restaurant owners, and Jewish retailers.

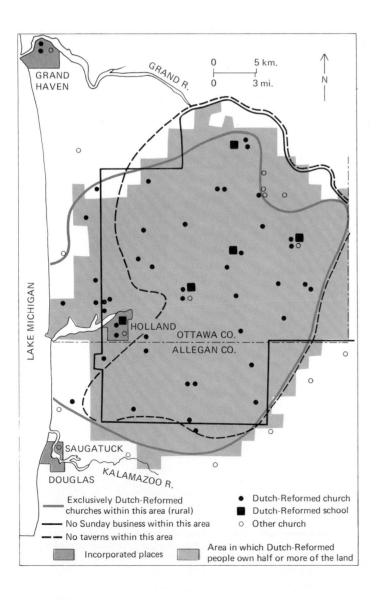

FIGURE 9-15
The impact of ethnicity in southwestern Michigan, about 1960. A colony of Dutch Reformed (Calvinist) immigrants was established here in the 1840s, and the ethnic island has survived to the present. The Calvinists kept taverns, movie theaters, non-Calvinist churches, and Sunday business activity out of their area. What other economic activities might be influenced by strict religious groups such as the Calvinists? (After Elaine M. Bjorklund, "Ideology and Culture Exemplified in Southwestern Michigan," *Annals, Association of American Geographers*, 54 (1964), 235.)

In Boston, the Irish once provided most of the laborers in the warehouse and terminal facilities near the central business district, the Italians dominated the distribution and marketing of fresh foods, the Germans gravitated to the sewing machine and port supply trades, and the Jews found employment in merchandising and the manufacture of ready-made clothing. Italians in the northeastern United States still control the terrazo and ceramic tile unions, and Czechs dominate the pearl button industry. In many cases, these ethnic job identities were related to occupational skills developed in the European homeland. A recent example is the immigration of Basques from Spain to serve as professional *jai alai* players in the cities of southern Florida, where this ancient Basque ball game has become a major medium of legal gambling.

Ethnicity and farming practices

Even within the same occupation, different ethnic groups can retain distinctiveness. For example, there has long been a popular belief in the United States that farmers of German ethnic origin are superior to Anglo-Americans as tillers of the soil. As early as 1789, Benjamin Rush, describing the Pennsylvania Germans, enumerated sixteen ways "in which they differ from most of the other farmers" of that state. Similar remarks can be found in accounts dealing with German ethnic islands in other parts of America.

A number of cultural geographers have tested the claim of German agricultural distinctiveness in the United States (Table 9-1). One such study focused on the Hill Country of central Texas in the nineteenth century. Germans settled there, it was found, farmed the land more intensively, derived more income from their land, and were more likely to be landowners than were the Anglos. German-owned sheep yielded 24 percent more wool per capita, and German poultry laid 15 percent more

TABLE 9-1   German-American and Anglo-American Farmers Compared

	Texas Hill Country 1860–1880		Cullman County Alabama, 1930		Missouri Ozarks, 1972	
	Germans	Anglos	Germans	Anglos	Germans	Non-Germans
% owning land	96%	75%	91%	46%	88%	80%
% owning slaves	0%	11%	—	—	—	—
% of cropland in small grains	25%	10%	—	—	15%	3½%
% of cropland in cotton and corn	52%	60%	73%	89%	—	—
average farm size, acres	557	323	60	45	180	162
average cropland, acres	33	33	23	23	103	79
average value of farm produce	$233	$176	$1341	$1032	—	—
average number of cattle owned	55	52	3.4	2.2	—	—

Sources: Terry G. Jordan, German Seed in Texas Soil; *Russel Gerlach,* Immigrants in the Ozarks; *Walter M. Kollmorgen,* The German Settlement in Cullman County, Alabama: An Agricultural Island in the Cotton Belt *(Washington, D.C.: U.S. Department of Agriculture, Bureau of Agricultural Economics, 1941).*

eggs than their Anglo livestock counterparts, due to better feeding and care.

Perhaps the major reason for these differences was that Anglo farmers, for several centuries, had been faced with a superabundance of land on the frontier, which blunted the traditional European "land hunger" and permitted large landholdings, thus making intensive land use and soil conservation unnecessary. The Germans, newly arrived from Europe, retained the more intensive European system. This explanation received added support from a study of colonial Pennsylvania by geographer James T. Lemon. He found that the farming practices of the Germans, English, and Scotch-Irish—all recently arrived from Europe—did not differ in any significant way.

Germans in the South still retained their agricultural superiority in the 1930s, according to a study by Professor Walter M. Kollmorgen, a pioneer in the field of ethnic geography (see biographical sketch). His research on a German ethnic island in Alabama revealed that the German-Americans there practiced a more diversified agriculture, had higher incomes, and were more often landowners than Anglos in the same county (Table 9-1). "Agricultural practices in the county," he concluded, "represent to a considerable extent a projection of patterns introduced by the Germans and the non-Germans."

An even more recent study, by ethnic geographer Russel L. Gerlach, revealed that in the 1970s farmers of German descent living in the Missouri Ozarks were distinct in many respects from non-Germans (Table 9-1). They had larger farms, had more acreage under cultivation, and were more likely to be landowners. It seems, then, that German-Americans continue even to the present day to farm differently from their non-German neighbors. They are, indeed, superior agriculturists, at least when compared to old-stock Anglo-Americans.

Similar differences along ethnic lines can be detected in present-day Canada. In a recent study of southern Manitoba, geographers D. Todd and J. S. Brierley compared the rural economies in German Mennonite, Slavic, British, French, and Dutch communities there. After detecting contrasts between these groups in type of agriculture, level of education, and kinds of nonfarm employment, Todd and Brierley concluded that fundamental functional linkages between ethnicity and the regional economic structure exist.

America's Ethnic Landscapes

Ethnicity is often, or even generally, visible, and we can properly speak of ethnic landscapes. Ethnic groups frequently differ in styles of traditional architecture, in the patterns of surveying the land, in the distribution of houses and other buildings, and in the degree to which they "humanize" the land. In particular, many rural areas of the United States and Canada bear an ethnic imprint on the cultural landscape. Frequently this is a relict landscape: visible features produced by previous generations and surviving to the present. Other ethnic landscape elements are apparently still being produced today. Often the ethnic imprint is subtle, discernible only to those who pause and look closely; sometimes it is quite striking, immediately visible even to the untrained eye (see box, "The Face of the Fox").

WALTER M. KOLLMORGEN 1907-

Dr. Kollmorgen, Professor Emeritus of Geography at the University of Kansas and noted agricultural geographer, made some early contributions to the study of American ethnic groups. Beginning in the late 1930s, he undertook research on the farming practices of ethnic minorities in the United States, resulting in some thirteen scholarly publications in the period 1940 to 1947. The subjects of his research included the Germans in Alabama and Pennsylvania, the German-Swiss in Tennessee, the French in Louisiana, and other ethnic minorities located mainly in the American South. Professor Kollmorgen's detailed statistical comparisons of ethnic and nonethnic farmers provided geographers with the first conclusive evidence of ethnic distinctiveness in agriculture and established a model of rigorous scholarship for later ethnic geographical studies.

Like so many geographers, Professor Kollmorgen received the inspiration for his research while traveling through the countryside and carefully observing what he saw. In the 1930s, he made numerous tours through the southern Appalachians. He "soon found the conspicuous cultural landscape area developed by the German Swiss in Franklin County, Tennessee, and the German settlement in Cullman County, Alabama." Intrigued by the visual contrasts he saw between the settlement areas of Germans and non-Germans, Kollmorgen decided to make a comparative study as his doctoral dissertation in geography at Columbia University.

THE FACE OF THE FOX: INDIAN AND NON-INDIAN LANDSCAPES IN IOWA

America's Indian reservations have distinctive land-scapes. Below is one visitor's reaction to the Fox Indian countryside, surrounded by Anglo-American farm land in central Iowa:

"One fall day I chanced to drive through the Iowa countryside, the landscape wrought by white Iowa farmers: rolling hills stretched out, and impressed upon the hills were rectangular shapes, sharp and precise, each shape its own color. An Iowa farmer looking out upon his handiwork must have sensed, it seemed to me, his enormous power and must have felt great pride. Here and there, along a river or on some steep slope, nature was allowed to hold forth—trees and grass and brush—but not to encroach. Then I drove onto the roads of the Fox community. Immediately nature leapt up: the terrain was formed of hills and bluffs and streams; trees were seen in any direction in small and large clusters and covering whole hills, and some reached high. In the spaces that remained, grass and weeds and brush threatened to reach as high. Growth was beneath me, around me on all sides, and overhead.

"There, I recognized, was the difference. Passing through the countryside of white Iowa, one senses, as the Iowa farmer must sense, that he stands on top of what he sees, and a relationship is compellingly conveyed: man and his works. Entering the Fox community, one senses, as a Fox must sense, that he is enveloped."

Quoted from Frederick O. Gearing, The Face of the Fox (Chicago: Aldine, 1970), p. 47.

The Finnish sauna in rural America

A good example of ethnicity in the cultural landscape of America is provided by the *sauna*. In Finland, these small steam bathhouses normally built of logs are seen at almost every farmstead. The Finns find it refreshing in cold weather to take a steam bath in the superheated sauna, often followed by an undressed romp in the snow. The European sauna is an important element in the cultural landscape of Finland.

When Finns came to America, they brought the preference for the sauna with them. The cultural geographers Matti Kaups and Cotton Mather made a study of this Finnish landscape feature in Minnesota and Michigan (Figure 9-16). They found the sauna to be an excellent visual indicator of Finnish-American ethnic islands. In one sample area, an almost purely Finnish rural district in the Upper Peninsula of Michigan, Kaups and Mather found that 88 percent of all Finnish-American residences had a sauna out behind. In an area of greater ethnic mixture in northern Minnesota, 77 percent of Finnish houses had saunas adjacent, as contrasted to only 6 percent of non-Finnish residences in the same district (Figure 9-16).

Land survey systems

Most immigrant ethnic groups in the areas of overseas European colonization had to accept predetermined survey systems, usually some form of rectangular land survey. These groups obviously had no chance to introduce their own distinctive system. However, a few ethnic groups arrived in colonial times, before standard survey systems had been adopted. These early arrivals were able to impose distinctive patterns on the land.

The best example is provided by the French. Wherever they settled in colonial America, whether in Québec, Detroit, Green Bay, Louisiana, or one of the scattered fur-trading colonies in the valleys of the Mississippi-Ohio River basin, the French almost always surveyed the land in *long-lots* (see Chapter 3). The Franco-American long-lots were long, narrow farms

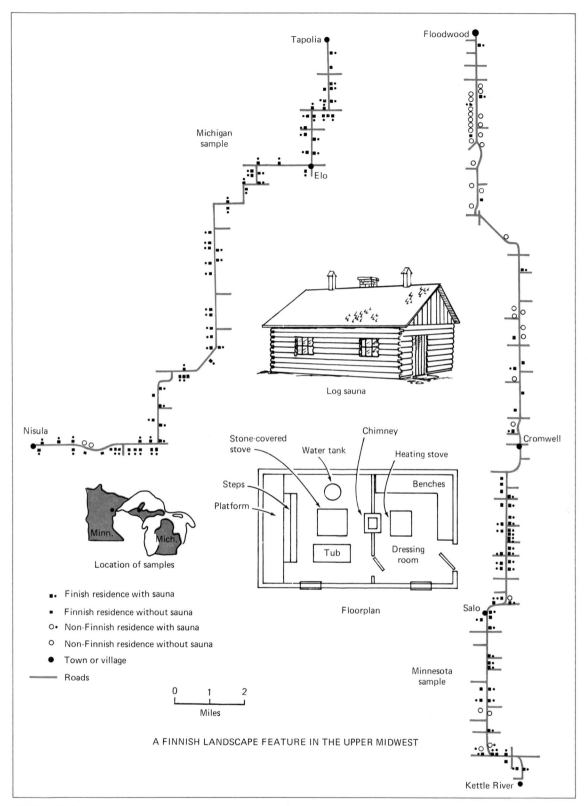

Tapolia

Floodwood

Michigan
sample

Elo

Nisula

Log sauna

Location of samples

Minn.

Mich.

Stone-covered
stove

Water tank

Chimney

Heating stove

Steps

Benches

Platform

Tub

Dressing
room

Cromwell

■• Finish residence with sauna

■ Finnish residence without sauna

○• Non-Finnish residence with sauna

○ Non-Finnish residence without sauna

● Town or village

—— Roads

Floorplan

Salo

Minnesota
sample

0   1   2

Miles

A FINNISH LANDSCAPE FEATURE IN THE UPPER MIDWEST

Kettle River

FIGURE 9–16

A Finnish landscape feature in the upper Midwest. In two traverses through Finnish ethnic islands in northern Minnesota and Michigan, two geographers found that the *sauna,* a small steam bathhouse, was an almost unfailing visual sign of Finnish settlement. In this way, ethnicity is imprinted on the cultural landscape. (After Cotton Mather and Matti Kaups, "The Finnish Sauna: A Cultural Index to Settlement," *Annals, Association of American Geographers,* 53 (1963), 495, 499.)

with a narrow frontage on a river. The farmer's landholding stretched back away from the stream in a ribbon-shaped parcel, and the dwelling was built at the front of the lot, near the waterway. The French apparently brought the long-lot survey system from northern France to the St. Lawrence Valley in the 1600s, and they carried it with them into the American heartland and down the Mississippi. Today the visual evidence of their distinctive system remains imprinted on the land, even in some areas where the French culture has otherwise disappeared. In Québec, this French survey system was long ago made the legal type for new land settlement.

Settlement patterns

Even within the constraints of a governmentally imposed survey system, some ethnic groups were able to produce their own distinctive settlement patterns. Often this was accomplished even where a rigid checkerboard survey was present.

In the Missouri Ozarks, for example, Germans and non-Germans alike settled a region of rectangular survey. In a close look at present-day

FIGURE 9–17

Distribution of farmsteads in German and non-German rural parts of Gasconade County, Missouri, 1970. Both areas have identical survey systems and similar road patterns, yet the German farmers generally situate their houses further from the public roads than do non-Germans. Can you think of any reasons why the German-Americans are distinctive in this way? (After Gerlach, p. 71.)

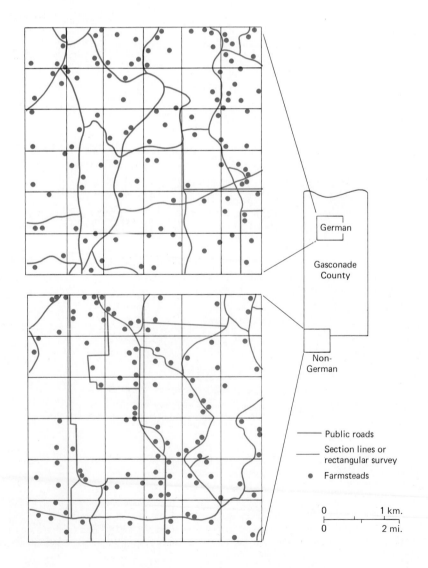

German

Gasconade County

Non-German

Public roads

Section lines or rectangular survey

Farmsteads

0   1 km.

0   2 mi.

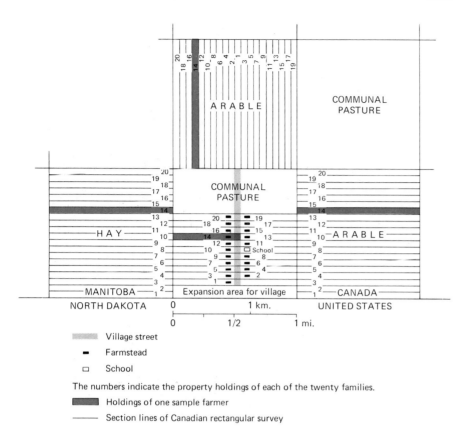

FIGURE 9–18
A Mennonite farm village in Manitoba, Canada. The Mennonites, a German-speaking religious sect from Russia, settled this area in 1875. Accustomed to living in street villages (see Chapter Two) in Russia, the Mennonites created similar farm villages, lined up along a central street, in Canada. The fragmentation of landholdings and communal pasture are also Old World customs. The Mennonites created this village, named Neuhorst, in spite of the Canadian rectangular survey system, which encouraged scattered farmsteads and unit-block holdings. While many such villages later disappeared, some survive as part of the Mennonite ethnic landscape. From a distance, these surviving villages are revealed by long rows of cottonwood trees which line the central street. What advantages would clustered village settlement offer to an ethnic group? What disadvantages? (After John Warkentin, "Mennonite Agricultural Settlements of Southern Manitoba," *Geographical Review,* 49 (1959), 359.)

settlement maps, geographer Russel L. Gerlach found that rather different patterns have developed. German-American farmsteads are much less frequently situated on public roads than are non-German houses (Figure 9-17). Farmhouses lie in many cases a half-mile from the nearest public road. To be precise, over three-quarters of all non-German farmhouses are within a hundred yards of public roads, as contrasted to just over half of the German-owned houses.

Similarly, some Russian-German Mennonite colonists in the prairie provinces of Canada were able to create clustered farm villages in a rectangular survey area, in marked contrast to their non-Mennonite neighbors (Figure 9-18). Mennonites duplicated the street villages they had known in Russia, while other farmers in the area lived out on their land in dispersed farmsteads. Numerous other rural ethnic groups, both in Canada and the United States, settled in clustered farm villages. Apparently the cohesive bond of ethnicity encouraged these immigrants to live in clustered communities, where they could be in close daily contact with people of their own kind. In most cases, however, the villages later broke up as acculturation progressed, and the farmers moved out to build homes on their farmland.

Traditional architecture

The architecture of houses and outbuildings in rural areas in many instances provides a visual index of ethnicity. Most often, the distinctive structures are old and survive as relics in the landscape. Typically, they represent folk architecture (see Chapter 7). In ethnic islands, at least, it is uncommon for folk architectural styles and building methods to be employed after the foreign-born generation dies off, but the early structures are so well built that some persist in the landscape.

As you travel about North America, you can see this ethnic architecture in diverse landscapes: southeastern Pennsylvania offers the massive "Dutch" barns, built of stone and equipped with a *forebay*, an overhang on one side of the second story of the barn; the Mexican borderland is dotted with adobe structures; the French St. Lawrence Valley is lined with neat stone farmhouses of a distinctive style (see Chapter 7); Pueblo Indian communities of northern New Mexico display spectacular "apartment" dwellings built of mud bricks; and scattered German ethnic islands reveal aged half-timbered houses (Figure 9-19). In some cases, the similarity between structures in the Old and New Worlds is quite striking, extending even to minor details of construction (Figure 9-20).

Even if Old World architectural styles are not present, it is still often possible to discern architectural differences between ethnic and non-ethnic areas. For example, while purely American in style, German-owned farmhouses in the Missouri Ozarks are on the average larger, older, in better condition, and more often equipped with lightning rods than are non-German homes, according to Gerlach's survey.

The visible ethnic imprint also extends to landscape elements other than buildings. For example, traditional fence types sometimes suggest the ethnic background of the local population, as in French Canada, where fences like those of French Europe are occasionally seen (Figure 7-5). Ethnicity is, indeed, visible.

FIGURE 9–19

An example of relict ethnic architecture in America: a half-timbered (Fachwerk) house in a German settlement in Texas. Built about 1848 by immigrants to the town of Fredericksburg, this house reveals German influence not only in its half-timbered construction, but also in the casement type windows and decorative trim. Such ethnic architecture is most typical of the early settlement period in pre-Civil War American ethnic islands. (Photo by Terry G. Jordan.)

FIGURE 9-20
A striking example of architectural transferral from Europe to America. The top illustration shows a folk house in the Opole district of Poland, the bottom a dwelling built in south-central Texas by a Polish immigrant from the Opole area. The architectural style is that of Upper Silesia. (Photos by T. Lindsay Baker, Associate Curator, Panhandle-Plains Historical Museum, Canyon, Texas. Used with permission.)

Conclusion

Through the theme of culture region, we saw how ethnic groups, whether rural or urban, tend to cluster spatially. In fact, we could say that spatial identity is a prerequisite of ethnicity, so that the study of ethnic groups is inherently geographic. Cultural diffusion allowed us to see the selective process by which immigrating ethnic groups introduce only some of their Old World traits while abandoning or modifying others and adopting some new traits. Cultural ecology taught us that migrating ethnic groups often look for familiar physical environments in choosing new homes and tend, as a rule, to perceive greater similarity between their old and new homelands than is actually the case. The imprint of ethnicity on economic activity was revealed through the theme of cultural integration. Examples of the visual aspects of ethnicity, some obvious and some quite subtle, became evident in our discussion of the cultural landscape.

The "melting pot," in North America and elsewhere, has apparently not reached a high enough "temperature" to dissolve ethnic minorities into a homogeneous mixture. Maybe it never will. There are "lumps" in the stew. By adopting the viewpoint of the cultural geographer, we have been able to look at many spatial facets of ethnicity, decipher some of the reasons why the ethnic mosaic has come to be, and interpret the cultural imprint of ethnic groups.

Glossary

Acculturation the process by which an ethnic group changes in order to function in the host society.

Assimilation loss of all ethnic traits and complete blending into the host society.

Chain migration the snowballing process whereby immigrants, by writing letters back to the homeland, induce other members of their ethnic group to migrate; such chains, if active over a period of time, typically produce cluster migration.

Cluster migration the tendency of people, including ethnic groups, to migrate in clusters from specific source areas to specific destinations.

Cultural rebound the belated appearance, after the early difficult years of pioneering are past, of Old World cultural traits among ethnic groups that have migrated.

Dominant personality a forceful, ambitious, influential person, a natural leader, who emigrates and is able to convince others to follow.

Emigrant letters or "America letters" are those written back to friends and relatives in their former homes by early immigrants, describing their new homeland in glowing terms, serving to induce others to follow them.

Ethnic geography the study of the spatial aspects of ethnicity.

Ethnic group a cultural group possessing a common tradition and strong feeling of belonging, living as a minority in a larger host society of a different culture.

Ethnic island a small ethnic area in the rural countryside; sometimes called a "folk island."

Ethnic neighborhood an area within a city containing members of the same ethnic background; a voluntary segregation of urban people along ethnic lines.

Ethnic province large districts dominated by a single ethnic group, usually including both rural areas and cities.

Ethnicity possessing ethnic quality or affiliation; the state of being ethnic.

Ethnography a branch of ethnology; the purely descriptive treatment of cultures.

Ethnology a science dealing with the origin, distribution, and characteristics of cultures, with emphasis on analysis and comparative study.

Folk island the same as ethnic island.

Ghetto a segregated ethnic area within a city, caused by residential discrimination against the will of the people involved.

Immigrant's ladder the movement of people from a core ethnic neighborhood to progressively higher-status neighborhoods.

"Port of entry" the area at the core of an ethnic neighborhood in a city where recent migrants to the city are likely to seek housing.

Suggested Readings

James P. Allen. "Franco-Americans in Maine: A Geographical Perspective," *Acadiensis*, 4 (1974), 32–66.

Daniel D. Arreola. "The Chinese Role in Creating the Early Cultural Landscape of the Sacramento-San Joaquin Delta," *California Geographer*, 15 (1975), 1–15.

Bruce Bigelow. "Marital Assimilation of Polish-Catholic Americans: A Case Study in Syracuse, N.Y., 1940-1970," *Professional Geographer*, 32 (1980), 431–438.

William A. Bowen. "American Ethnic Regions, 1880," *Proceedings of the Association of American Geographers*, 8 (1976), 44–46.

John W. Cole and Eric R. Wolf. *The Hidden Frontier: Ecology and Ethnicity in an Alpine Valley*. New York and London: Academic Press, 1974.

Harold F. Creveling. "Mapping Cultural Groups in an American Industrial City," *Economic Geography*, 31 (1955), 364–371.

G. A. Davis and O. F. Donaldson. *Blacks in the United States: A Geographic Perspective*. Boston: Houghton Mifflin, 1975.

C. A. Dawson. *Group Settlement: Ethnic Communities in Western Canada*. Toronto: Macmillan, 1936.

Russel L. Gerlach. *Immigrants in the Ozarks: A Study in Ethnic Geography*. Columbia: University of Missouri Press, 1976.

T. Hart. "Patterns of Black Residence in the White Residential Areas of Johannesburg," *South African Geographical Journal*, 58 (1976), 141–150.

Leslie Hewes. "Cultural Fault Line in the Cherokee Country," *Economic Geography*, 19 (1943), 136–142.

Wsevolod W. Isajiw. "Definitions of Ethnicity," *Ethnicity*, 1 (1974), 111–124.

John A. Jakle and James O. Wheeler. "The Changing Residential Structure of the Dutch Population in Kalamazoo, Michigan," *Annals, Association of American Geographers*, 59 (1969), 441–460.

Hildegard Binder Johnson. "The Location of German Immigrants in the Middle West," *Annals, Association of American Geographers*, 41 (1951), 1–41.

Terry G. Jordan. *German Seed in Texas Soil: Immigrant Farmers in Nineteenth-Century Texas*. Austin: University of Texas Press, 1966.

Terry G. Jordan. "Population Origin Groups in Rural Texas," *Annals, Association of American Geographers*, 60 (1970) 404–405 and colored fold map.

Walter M. Kollmorgen. "A Reconnaissance of Some Cultural-Agricultural Islands in the South," *Economic Geography*, 17 (1941), 409–430; 19 (1943), 109–117.

Leszek A. Kosínski. "Changes in the Ethnic Structure in East-Central Europe, 1930-1960," *Geographical Review*, 59 (1969), 388–402.

Trevor R. Lee. *Race and Residence: The Concentration and Dispersal of Immigrants in London*. Oxford: Clarendon Press, 1977.

James T. Lemon. "The Agricultural Practices of National Groups in Eighteenth-Century Southeastern Pennsylvania," *Geographical Review*, 56 (1966), 467–496.

David Ley. *The Black Inner City as Frontier Outpost*. Washington, D.C.: Association of American Geographers, Monograph Series, No. 7, 1974.

John J. Mannion. *Irish Settlements in Eastern Canada: A Study of Cultural Transfer and Adaption*. University of Toronto, Department of Geography, Research Publication No. 12, 1974.

Richard L. Morrill. "The Negro Ghetto: Problems and Alternatives," *Geographical Review*, 55 (1965), 339–361.

Richard L. Nostrand. "The Hispanic-American Borderland: Delimitation of an American Culture Region," *Annals, Association of American Geographers*, 60 (1970), 638–661.

"The Peoples of China," Map Supplement, *National Geographic Magazine*, Vol. 158 (July 1980). A splendid color map showing China's ethnic mosaic.

Edward T. Price. "The Melungeons: A Mixed-Blood Strain of the Southern Appalachians," *Geographical Review*, 41 (1951), 256–271.

Karl B. Raitz, "Ethnic Maps of North America," *Geographical Review*, 68 (1978), 335–350. A valuable listing of maps that reveal ethnic distributions.

Karl B. Raitz. "Themes in the Cultural Geography of European Ethnic Groups in the United States," *Geographical Review*, 69 (1979), 77–94.

H. F. Raup. "The Italian-Swiss Dairymen of San Luis Obispo County, California," *Yearbook, Association of Pacific Coast Geographers*, 1 (1935), 3–8.

Tommy W. Rogers. "Race and Geographic Differentials in Mississippi Housing Characteristics," *Mississippi Geographer*, 6 (1978), 19–31.

Stephan Thernstrom (ed.). *Harvard Encyclopedia of American Ethnic Groups*. Cambridge, Mass.: Harvard University Press, 1980.

D. Todd and J. S. Brierley. "Ethnicity and the Rural Economy: Illustrations from Southern Manitoba," *Canadian Geographer*, 21 (1977), 237–249.

Ingolf Vogeler. "Ethnicity, Religion, and Farm Land Transfers in Western Wisconsin," *Ecumene*, 7 (1975), 6–13.

David Ward. "The Emergence of Central Immigrant Ghettoes in American Cities: 1840-1920," *Annals, Association of American Geographers*, 58 (1968), 343–359.

Chapter-opening photo: ➤
Manchester, England.

The City in Time and Space

10

If the time humankind has spent on earth were compared to a twenty-four-hour day, then only in the last half hour have there been settlements of more than a hundred people. Only a few minutes have elapsed since towns and cities first emerged, and large-scale urbanization has been going on for less than sixty seconds. Yet such has been the impact of those "minutes" on humans that the very word we use for society's total cultural complex—*civilization*—is inextricably connected with the city. *Civitas*, the Latin root word for "civilization," was first applied to settled areas of the Roman empire. Later it came to mean a specific town or city within an area. "To civilize" in Western terms means literally "to citify," although this was not true of all cultures.

The urbanization of the last 200 years has deepened the links among culture, society, and the city. An "urban explosion" has gone hand in hand with the industrial revolution. Cities have grown at unprecedented rates, and the ways of the countryside are increasingly replaced by urban lifestyles. Recent United Nations estimates show that the world's urban population has doubled since 1950 and will double again before the year 2000 (see Figure 10-1). By then about 75 percent of the developed world's population will live in cities. Today, only 33 percent of the less developed world's population lives in cities, but because of the high rate of urbanization—coupled with rapid population increases—this figure will increase to 50 percent by the turn of the century.

This is the first of two chapters on urban geography. In this chapter, we will consider the overall pattern of urbanization. We will attempt to learn why cities are distributed as they are and how the idea of urbanization arose and spread. We will see the extent of urbanization in different cultures. Chapter 11 will deal with *internal* geographic aspects of the city.

Culture Region

As we look at a world map (see Figure 10-2), we see that the urban revolution has produced a diverse pattern that shows some countries to be highly urbanized while others are still predominantly rural. We shall apply the concept of culture region to this pattern and group countries into five broad categories based on their **urbanized population,** which is the percentage of the total population living in towns and cities.

However, we must be sensitive to limitations in the data. First, not all of the world's countries have accurate census data for their urbanized populations. While some have accurate figures, others used estimates based upon decade old censuses. Consequently, while Figure 10-2 draws upon the most recent data available, the level of accuracy varies among countries. Second, and equally important, definitions of urbanized populations differ from country to country. For example, in the United States, the Census Bureau defines a city as a densely populated area of at least 2500 people. India, on the other hand, uses 5000 people as the minimum figure for their urban definition, whereas South Africa counts as a city any settlement of more than 500. This variation in definitions suggests that we treat world urbanization data only as a general outline, data from which we can generate broad comparisons, not as up-to-the-minute, accurate data.

In spite of these shortcomings in the data, it is possible to group the

FIGURE 10-1
Urbanization, one of the most
Important forces affecting the world,
is now responsible for pressing
problems in all countries. Shown here
are scenes from the business district in
Calcutta (upper left), squatter
settlements in Rio de Janeiro (upper
right), and the residential district of
Bombay (bottom). For further
discussion of non-Western cities, see
the section beginning on p. 329.

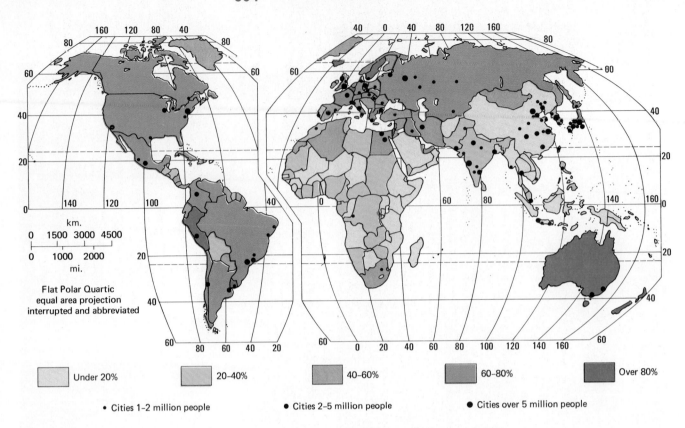

| Under 20% | 20–40% | 40–60% | 60–80% | Over 80% |

• Cities 1–2 million people   ● Cities 2–5 million people   ● Cities over 5 million people

FIGURE 10-2

This map depicts different levels of urbanization throughout the world. What factors are responsible for countries having 90 percent of their populations in cities? Why are some countries less than 30 percent urbanized? (United Nations, *Demographic Yearbook*, 1977)

world's countries into several broad categories that generate ideas about patterns and principles of urbanization. Six countries make up the highest category (see Figure 10-1). Belgium is the most urbanized country in the world with 95 percent of its population in cities; Iceland is a second with 87 percent, followed by Australia (86 percent), Sweden (83 percent), Israel (82 percent), and New Zealand (81 percent). What do these countries have in common? Although each is industrialized with a fairly high standard of living, similarities—and differences—in the settlement pattern are of prime interest. Except for Belgium, which has a dense network of towns and villages, all the other countries have one or two major cities with immense populations, surrounded by large expanses of sparsely settled land of marginal value, such as deserts, mountains, or tundra. The high rate of urbanization comes from clustering in the major cities, not from large numbers of smaller settlements.

In the next category—countries with 60 to 80 percent of the population urbanized—fall the bulk of the industrialized countries, such as the United Kingdom (77 percent), Japan (76 percent), Canada (76 percent), the United States (74 percent), and the USSR (62 percent). All of these countries have their urban populations spread out across thousands of cities of all sizes and are supported by more densely settled rural areas than those countries in the highest category.

Nations with the smallest urbanized populations (under 20 percent) are those generally called "third world," "emerging," or "lesser developed" countries (LDCs). Often they are former European colonies that have a history of rural exploitation. Only recently have these countries entered the industrialization process. Examples are Kenya (10 percent), Mali (17 percent), and Uganda (7 percent). It is in this category that urbanization is taking place most rapidly.

Often those countries in the lower categories are dominated by one city of extraordinary size. Political and economic power is concentrated in these cities, which, because of their primary importance to the functioning of the countries, are called **primate cities.** Such cities are most likely to dominate countries that were former political and economic dependencies, or countries that were formerly larger but have recently lost territory. Vienna, Austria, is an excellent example of the latter case; Kampala, Uganda, the former. Many former European colonies are dominated by primate cities.

Let us now look at the rise and spread of the earliest urban settlements.

Origin and Diffusion of the City

As we seek explanations for the origin of cities, we see a relationship between areas of early agriculture, permanent village settlement, the development of new social forms, and urban life. The first cities resulted from a long and complicated transition that took thousands of years.

Early people were nomads, constantly moving in their search for sustenance. But at some point, campsites became more permanent, first being occupied for months at a time, later for years. In most areas, this change to permanent settlement was closely tied to the domestication of plants and animals (see Chapter 3). In the Near East, which is where the first cities appeared, a network of permanent agricultural villages developed about 10,000 years ago.

These farming villages were modest in size, rarely having more than 200 people, and were probably organized on a kinship basis. Jarmo, one of the earliest villages, located in present-day Iraq, had 25 permanent dwellings clustered together in a compound centered around grain storage facilities. Even though the people did not have plows, agriculture was based on wheat and barley cultivation. It is thought that domestic dogs, goats, and sheep were used for meat, and food supplies were augmented by hunting and gathering.

Although small farming villages like Jarmo are found predating cities in different parts of the world, it is wrong to assume that a simple quantitative change took place whereby villages slowly grew into towns, then into cities. Instead, we are dealing with major qualitative changes that nurtured true urban life.

The two crucial elements behind this change were the generation of an agricultural surplus and the development of a stratified social system. Surplus food is a necessary prerequisite for supporting nonfarmers—that is, people who work at administrative, military, or handicraft tasks. Social stratification, where there are distinct differences between an elite class and a lower class, facilitates the collection, storage, and distribution of resources through well-defined channels of authority that can exercise control over goods and people. At some point, early settlements grew by gaining advantage over their neighbors, and they were able to dominate their region by controlling access to vital resources. This might have been done through pure military force. Or, possibly, power could have been expanded by forcing tribute to a religious figurehead, such as a god-king. Or perhaps a settlement's sphere of power expanded simply because it controlled a needed resource, such as water, and others had to assume secondary roles to gain access to the resource.

In the search for understanding the transition from village to city life, some scholars prefer to construct models for the development of urban life based on one single factor as the "trigger" behind the change. Four of these models are discussed below.

The **hydraulic civilization** model sees the development of large-scale irrigation systems as the prime mover. Higher crop yields resulted from irrigated agriculture, and, in turn, this food surplus could support the development of a large nonfarming population. A strong, centralized government, backed by an urban-based military, expanded power into the surrounding areas. Those farmers who were tempted to resist the new authority were denied water. Continued reinforcement of the power elite came from the need for organizational coordination to assure continued operation of the irrigation system.

So, because of irrigation, a surplus was created that was able to support nonfarmers. Class distinctions were reinforced by power differences as well, and labor specialization developed. Some people were farmers, some worked on the irrigation system, others became artisans creating the implements needed to maintain the system, and still others became adminstrative workers in the direct employ of the power elite's court.

Some writers have also used this model to explain the decline of urban-based civilizations. If there is disruption in the political system, a breakdown of power, then the irrigation facilities might not be maintained. Canals silt up, water supplies are lost through dam breakages, and, as the irrigation system loses effectiveness, the urban-rural support system breaks down, leading to reduced agricultural output and subsequent population stress.

Although the hydraulic model fits several areas where cities first arose—namely, China, Egypt, and Mesopotamia—it cannot be applied to all urban hearths. In Mesoamerica, for example, an urban civilization blossomed without widespread irrigated agriculture. This model also begs the question of how or why a culture might first develop an irrigation system.

Other writers have suggested what we might call the *innovation model*, which sees one group gaining advantage over others by exploiting new technology or a new resource base. A new trait, such as irrigated agriculture, or a plow, might be invented by one group, and this could lead to increased agricultural yields. An expanded food supply might also come from **domestication** of a new animal or crop, or by moving into a productive, yet previously unoccupied ecological niche. In Mesopotamia, the first farming villages were on the hillsides above the river floodplain. Some writers argue that the first groups to move into the floodplain quickly developed a more productive agricultural system than their neighbors who remained on the river valley flanks. A surplus food supply was generated in the floodplain that could support nonfarmers—people who could specialize in the kinds of occupations necessary to support city life. Perhaps some specialized in the making of agricultural tools that in turn could be traded to surrounding villages.

This model assumes a certain degree of inventiveness. Some critics feel that humans invent new technologies or new tools, or move into new areas, only when they must. In other words, "necessity is the mother of invention." Consequently, these critics seek explanations as to *why* new areas were occupied or new systems innovated.

One explanation is the *environmental stress model*. Although this model has numerous variations, all concern changes in the physical environment leading either to further innovations or to one group controlling resources at the expense of others. Some scholars believe that a change in climate has been a major factor behind invention and movement. They argue that original crop domestication took place in Mesopotamia under conditions that were wetter and cooler than those that currently exist in the area. Then, beginning about 10,000 years ago, the climate became warmer and drier. Early hillside farmers were forced down from the valley flanks to draw upon river water for irrigation. Of course, this was a gradual process, taking hundreds of years, but the result was that the groups first able to adapt to the new climatic conditions monopolized the floodplain resource base.

But supporting evidence is not convincing. There is no question that our climate has become increasingly warmer in the last 10,000 years; however, it does not automatically follow that precipitation has lessened. In some parts of the world, rainfall has actually increased as the climate warmed. We must await more precise supporting data from Mesopotamia before giving serious consideration to this particular variation of the stress model.

However, there are other kinds of environmental stress that can be considered, such as the effect that human activities might have on a fragile ecosystem. Activities such as cultivation or grazing might lead to soil depletion or erosion, thereby depriving a group of its agricultural resource base. Some writers suggest that increased population from an initial innovation might stress the existing resource base. Once again, those groups that can successfully adapt to changing conditions ascend to positions of power, able to dominate their less innovative neighbors, and able to build upon surplus and trade in a way leading to population growth, dense settlement, and stratified society.

Implicit in the previously mentioned models is the extension of political power by one group over others, so it is not surprising that some writers place major emphasis on *coercion and warfare* as the trigger behind the rise of cities. They argue that competition among groups for scarce resources such as land or water leads to conflict, and that the group most able to dominate others will control the resources. By controlling resources, the dominant group can demand allegiance and tribute.

Proponents of this model suggest that a town is the most easily defended settlement. It can be surrounded by walls and fortifications. Wealth, be it grain or gold, can be stored in a central place and guarded against intruders. Urban dwellers can easily be pressed into service in defense of their city, since surrender or defeat will have dire consequences for all. A clustered settlement, then, might be an effective adaptation to pervasive conflict; once people are clustered together, the extension of power over these city people is relatively easy.

Critics of this model note that cities have developed in areas where warfare was not common or widespread. In fact, some scholars maintain that warfare became widespread only *after* the rise of cities. Others argue that cooperation—not conflict—is a necessary prerequisite for interaction of towns and villages.

Obviously, then, all single-factor models have their limitations when it comes to explaining the qualitative change from agricultural villages to true cities. A wiser course is to accept the idea that multiple factors are responsible for changes leading to urban life. For example, in an area such as Mesopotamia, it appears that an initial advantage may have gone to those groups first exploiting the unoccupied river bottoms. They may have experimented with primitive watering systems on the hillsides; with vast amounts of river water available, invention of a sophisticated irrigation system may have resulted. This would have consolidated power in the hands of one or two groups, and they may have extended control over the hinterland through coercion and warfare. Yet, at a later stage, sedimentation may have reduced the effectiveness of irrigation. Food shortages may have resulted, thus weakening the political system, and a change of power or demise of the settlement could result. Then, those settlements best able to adapt to the new conditions might rise to dominance. So the cycle would repeat itself.

In summation, it is probably unwise to think that one single-factor model can explain the rise of cities in all areas of the prehistoric world. Instead, we must appreciate the complexities of the transition period from agricultural village to true city; what explains this change in one area may not apply in another.

Urban hearth areas

We have already mentioned that the first cities appeared in distinct areas such as Mesopotamia, the Nile valley, Pakistan's Indus river valley, the Yellow River valley (or Huang Ho) of China, and Mesoamerica. These are called the **urban hearth areas** (see box, "Cahokia"). Figure 10-3 gives the general dates for the emergence of urban life in each region.

CAHOKIA: AN EARLY URBAN CENTER ON THE MISSISSIPPI

Cahokia, a pre-Columbian urban center on the Mississippi, shows that not all early cities were found in the five urban hearth areas mentioned in the text. Instead, Cahokia illustrates the process of independent city origin and can be taken as an example of events duplicated in hundreds of areas around the world.

The Cahokia settlement is an aggregation of mounds and living structures dating from about A.D. 100, located in the American Bottoms region of the Mississippi valley, close to St. Louis. It is the largest of ten large population centers and some fifty smaller farming villages that flourished between A.D. 900 and 1500.

How did this city arise? Archaeologists maintain that the city resulted from a complicated feedback process that involved population growth and an increase in agricultural productivity. In the late eighth century, the hoe replaced a less effective digging stick and a new variety of maize diffused into the American Bottoms region better suited to environmental conditions of the warm river valley.

Peak population came centuries later, probably between 1150 and 1250, when Cahokia may have approached a population of 40,000. Archaeological evidence suggests that houses were mainly of pole-and-thatch construction and varied in size according to the status of the occupants. The settlement also contained many ceremonial structures, most notably large earthen mounds similar to the pyramids of Mesoamerican cities. Close to the largest mound was an enclosed area of large public structures that reminds one of the citadel areas of Mesopotamian cities.

Cahokia flourished because it was an ideally located central place, situated on fertile agricultural lands, with access to local and long-distance trade moving through the network of sloughs and rivers. Scholars who have investigated the site believe that Cahokia declined in importance around A.D. 1250. Perhaps this was due to exhaustion of local resources, perhaps because its trade hinterland was eclipsed by the growing strength of other Mississippi river cultures. Whatever the reason, further investigation is bound to shed light on the complicated processes that lead to the rise and fall of cities.

Adapted from Melvin Fowler, "A Pre-Columbian Urban Center on the Mississippi," Scientific American, (August 1975) 93–102.

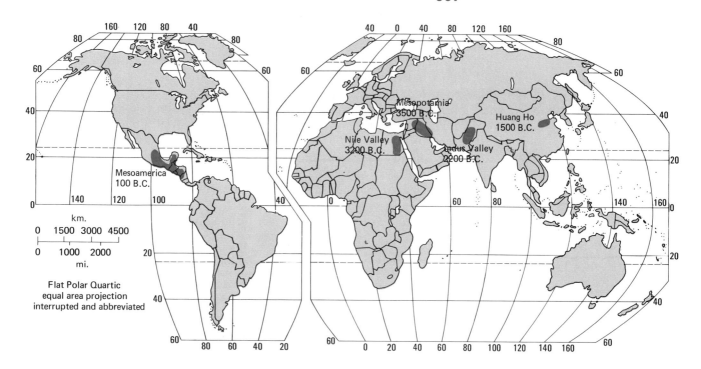

FIGURE 10-3

The world's first cities arose in five urban hearth areas. The dates are conservative figures for the rise of urban life in each area; some scholars would, for example, suggest urban life in Mesopotamia existed by 5000 B.C. New discoveries are constantly being made which suggest that urban life appeared earlier in each of the hearth areas. Note, however, that the latest date is in Mesoamerica.

It is generally agreed that the first cities arose in Mesopotamia, the river valley of the Tigris and Euphrates in what is now Iraq. These cities, small by current standards, covered one-half to two square miles (1.28 to 5.12 square kilometers) and embraced populations that rarely exceeded 30,000. Nevertheless, with such a population concentrated in such a small area, the densities within these cities could easily reach 10,000 people per square mile (4000 per square kilometer). This is comparable to many contemporary cities. Detroit, for example, has a population density of roughly 12,000 per square mile (4500 per square kilometer). Congestion and crowdedness have apparently been urban problems since the first cities were formed.

If we were to look at the landscape of the Mesopotamian cities, we would first see that most of the urban population was contained within a wall, which provided both physical protection and a symbolic boundary for the inhabitants. Beyond the wall, directly outside the main gates, we might find a few clusters of houses—the first suburbs. These would probably house visitors to the city. Within the wall, the central part of the city would be dominated by the citadel, the seat of the power elite. Here we would find three important buildings, which symbolize the functions of the early cities: the **ziggurat** or temple, the palace, and the granary.

The temple made up the religious core of the ancient Mesopotamian city. This precedent was repeated in different forms—the pyramid, the dome, the cathedral—right up to our own age. Over time, the Mesopotamian ziggurat developed from a temple complex open to believers into an imposing structure mounted on a raised platform, overseen by priestly guardians. In other words, it was slowly withdrawn from the people. The well-known Tower of Babel was a gigantic ziggurat rising 200 feet (61.5 meters). The immense scale of these later temples evidently was meant to reflect the power that lay menacingly behind them. Because the urban power structure almost surely based its rule on religion, the palace, the actual seat of power, was usually close to the temple. The granary, too, was enclosed in the citadel, which suggests that this storehouse for the agricultural surplus of the population was often guarded from that population itself.

Inside the walled and guarded citadel, in a city within a city, lived the king and his court, as well as his military forces. Even today, the Pentagon, the Kremlin, and similar sites prove that the citadel persists in the city. Before 2000 B.C., within the citadels, the streets were paved, drains and running water were provided, private sleeping quarters were built, bathtubs and water closets were installed, and spacious villas were constructed. But the privileges of the ruling class and their retainers did not extend to the city as a whole.

Outside the citadel, and covering most of the city, lay the cramped residential quarters of the masses. Houses were one or two stories tall, were composed of clay brick, and contained three or four rooms. They fronted on narrow streets that were unsurfaced and without drainage and that served as the community dump. Excavations at Ur, one of the earliest Mesopotamian cities, show that the level of garbage rose so high that new entrances had to be cut into the second stories of the houses. The only open spaces were the small market squares dotting the city. Here artisans clustered to trade their goods; here food was distributed; and here the military herded the urban population to hear the latest edict from their rulers. Just inside the walls of the city were the first ghettos. Here, the lowest classes lived in huts of mud and reed rather than houses of fired clay.

Cities found in the other hearth areas demonstrate essentially the same spatial characteristics. Usually they were walled, with a citadel monopolizing the central place. Streets were crooked and narrow, with tightly clustered dwellings of one or two stories lining them. The poor lived on the outskirts, nearest the wall, where they were most vulnerable during times of attack. But there have been some differences between hearth areas. For example, the early cities of the Nile were not walled, which suggests that a regional power structure kept individual cities from warring with one another.

The most important differences are found in the Mesoamerican hearth area (see box, "City Planning in the New World: Teotihuacán"). Here, cities were less dense and covered larger areas. Furthermore, these cities arose without benefit of the technological advances found in the other hearth areas, most notably the wheel, the plow, metallurgy, and draft animals. However, the domestication of maize compensated for these shortcomings. Maize is a grain that yields several crops a year without irrigation in the tropical climate, and it can be cultivated without heavy plows or pack animals. Probably most striking is the relatively recent (200 B.C.) date of urban life in Central America. All other urban hearth areas arose by at least 2000 B.C. Did the Mesoamerican cities arise later because they lacked technological innovations? Or did they evolve only after Old World urbanites had crossed the oceans and planted the seeds of city life? This question opens the door to a discussion of how cities have spread across the face of the earth.

The diffusion of the city from hearth areas

Urban life originated at specific places in the world. Yet cities are now found everywhere—North America, Africa, Southeast Asia, Latin Ameri-

CITY PLANNING IN THE NEW WORLD: TEOTIHUACÁN

Teotihuacán was a Mesoamerican city created by a society that had no metal tools, had not invented the wheel, and had no pack animals. At its height, Teotihuacán covered eight square miles (twenty square kilometers), which made it larger than imperial Rome. Its central religious monument, the Temple of the Sun, was as broad at its base as the great pyramid of Cheops in Egypt. Its population may have reached 100,000.

Strategically located astride a valley that was the gateway to the lowlands of Mexico, Teotihuacán flourished for 500 years as a great urban commercial center. Yet it was more than that. It was the Mecca of the New World, a religious and cultural capital that probably housed pilgrims from as far away as Guatemala. Not a trace of fortification has ever been unearthed. Perhaps most startling, Teotihuacán was a totally planned city. Its two great pyramids, its citadel, its hundred lesser religious structures, and its 4000 other dwellings were laid out according to an exact design. Its streets (and many of its buildings) were organized on an exact grid aligned with the city center. Even the shape of the river that divided the city was changed to fit the grid pattern.

Planning for the construction of Teotihuacán's major temples must have been an incredible undertaking. The Temple of the Sun, for instance, rises to a height of 215 feet and has a base of 725 square feet. These dimensions mean that it took about one million tons of sun-baked mud bricks to build the temple. When the Spaniards conquered Mexico in the sixteenth century, they were amazed to find Teotihuacán's ruined temples. Local inhabitants claimed that the temples had been built by giants. They showed the Spaniards the bones of giant elephants (which had lived there in prehistoric times) to prove their point.

But the small as well as the large was cleverly conceived in Teotihuacán. Houses were apparently planned for maximum space and privacy. Apartments were constructed around central patios, with each patio designed to give dwellers light and air, as well as an efficient drainage system. In a Teotihuacán housing complex, a person could indeed have lived in relative comfort.

ca, Australia. How did city life come to these regions? There are two possibilities. The first is that cities evolved spontaneously as native peoples created new technologies and social institutions. A second possibility is that the preconditions for urban life are too specific for most cultures to invent without contact with other urban areas. They must have learned these traits through contact with city dwellers. This school of thought emphasizes the diffusion of ideas and techniques necessary for city life.

Diffusionists strongly suggest that the complicated array of ideas and techniques that gave rise to the first cities in Mesopotamia were shared with other people, in both the Nile and the Indus river valleys, who were on the verge of the **urban transformation.** There is no question that these three civilizations had contact with one another. Archaeological evidence documents trade ties. Soapstone objects manufactured in Tepe Yahyā, 500 miles (800 kilometers) to the east of Mesopotamia, have been uncovered in the ruins of both Mesopotamian and Indus Valley cities, which are separated by thousands of miles. Indus Valley writing and seals have also been found in Mesopotamian urban sites. However, it is possible that trading took place only after cities were rather well advanced in each of the regions.

But what about the cities of Mesoamerica? Did they evolve in isolation, or did they have cultural contact across the oceans with the urban dwellers of Asia and Africa? This topic is controversial, yet some evidence strongly suggests that Japanese fishers visited the coasts of North and South America before the rise of urban cultures in Mesoamerica. Contact with Mediterranean cultures is another possibility. In voyages on replicas of ancient seagoing rafts across both the Atlantic and Pacific oceans, the anthropologist Thor Heyerdahl has shown that there may have been a wide variety of contacts between continents. He maintains that the symbol of his transatlantic expedition—the sun god Ra—was common to both Mesoamerican and North American civilizations. Further discoveries may well show the extent of sharing among the urban civilizations of Asia and Africa and strengthen the diffusionist argument. Until then, the controversy continues.

Nonetheless, there is little doubt that the diffusion process has been responsible for the dispersal of the city in historical times. This is because the city has commonly been used as the vehicle for imperial expansion. The sociologist Gideon Sjoberg, in his book *The Preindustrial City*, states: "The extension of the power group's domain, notably through empire-building, is the primary mechanism for introducing city life into generally non-urbanized territories." Typically, urban life is carried outward in waves of conquest as the borders of an empire expand. Initially, the military controls newly won lands and sets up collection points for local resources, which are then shipped back into the heart of the empire and used for its economy. As the surrounding countryside is increasingly pacified, the new settlements lose some of their military atmosphere and begin to show the social diversity of a city. Artisans, merchants, and bureaucrats increase in number. Families appear. The native people are slowly assimilated into the settlement as workers and may eventually dominate the city. Finally, the process repeats itself as the empire pushes farther outward: first a military camp, then a collection point for resources, then a full-fledged city expressing true **division of labor** and social diversity.

Examples of imperial city-building dot history. Alexander the Great, in the course of his conquests, ordered his architects to establish at least seventy cities. The Roman Empire, a power expanding from a single urban center, built literally thousands of cities, changing the rural face of Europe, North Africa, and Asia Minor in the process. In other times, the Persians, the Maurya Empire of India, the Han civilization of China, the Greeks, and others performed the same city-spreading task. In more recent times, European empires have used the resources of cities to expand and consolidate their power in colonies in the Americas, Africa, and Asia. England, France, and Spain contained the key hearth areas; North America's first cities were simply military outposts of a sort.

Think of the westward expansion of North American cultures launched from the eastern coast. First, military posts were built to control and administer frontier lands. These became central points for trade with and exploitation of the surrounding areas. Other kinds of activities clustered around the original forts. The new settlements had all the diversity necessary to call them cities. Such was the case with Detroit, Pittsburgh, Chicago, San Francisco, and many other American cities. As the American nation spread, so did cities.

This sort of expansion diffusion is, then, a major process in dispersing urban life over the surface of the earth. Figure 10-4 shows some of the routes the city took in this diffusion process.

Evolution of Urban Landscapes

Understanding urban landscapes necessitates an appreciation of urban processes both past and present. The patterns we see today in the city, like

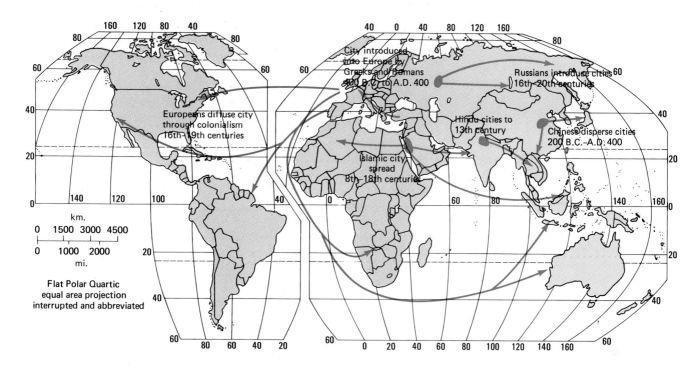

FIGURE 10-4

This map illustrates how cities have spread with the expansion of certain empires.

building form, architecture, street plans, and land use, are a composite of past and present cultures; they reflect the needs, ideas, technology, and institutions of human occupance. This section, then will examine major stages in the evolution of urban landscapes in both Western and non-Western cities.

Two concepts underlie our examination of urban landscapes. The first is **urban morphology,** or the physical form of the city, which consists of street patterns, building size and shape, architecture, and density. The second concept is **functional zonation.** This refers to the pattern of land uses within a city, or the existence of areas with differing functions, such as residential, commercial, or governmental. Functional zonation is also concerned with social patterns—whether an area is occupied by the power elite or by low-status persons, by Jews or by Christians, by high-income persons or by low. Both concepts are central to the cultural landscape of cities, because both make statements about how cultures occupy space.

We will begin our study of urban landscapes with Western cities, examining the evolution of urban patterns from Greek times to the postindustrial. Following that will be a discussion of non-Western cities.

The Greek city

Western civilization and the Western city both trace their roots back to ancient Greece. City life diffused to Greece from the Near East. By 600 B.C., there were over 500 towns and cities on the Greek mainland and surrounding islands. As Greek civilization expanded, cities spread with it throughout the Mediterranean—to the north shore of Africa, to Spain, to southern France, and to Italy. These cities were of modest size, rarely containing more than 5000 inhabitants. Athens, however, may have reached 300,000 in the fifth century B.C.. This figure includes perhaps 100,000 slaves, the labor power behind Greek society.

FIGURE 10-5
The historic core of Athens—the agora—is still visible in the urban landscape. This area was the focus for schools, libraries, theaters, social interaction, and commerce. How does the Greek agora compare with the civic center of a contemporary town?

Greek cities had two distinctive functional zones—the **acropolis** and the **agora.** In many ways, the acropolis was similar to the citadel of Mesopotamian cities. Here were the temples of worship, the storehouse of valuables, and the seat of power. The acropolis also served as a place of retreat in time of seige. If the acropolis was the domain of the power structure, the agora was the province of the citizens. As originally conceived, the agora was a place for public meetings, education, and social interaction, and judicial matters. In other words, it was the civic center, the hub of democratic life for Greek men (women were excluded from political life). During the classical period, commercial activities were not considered fitting for the agora, but later it became the major marketplace of the city—without losing its atmosphere of a social club (see Figure 10-5). In Latin countries, the social function of the agora has carried over to the plaza, with its open space surrounded by cafés and restaurants.

Early Greek cities were messy, despite their outstanding public buildings and temples. Narrow muddy streets littered with garbage became obstacle courses for pedestrians. Private housing was often crude at best, miserable at worst. The earlier Greek cities probably were not planned but rather grew spontaneously, without benefit of formal guidelines. Yet the Greeks, concerned as they were with aesthetics and humankind's total environment, may have been the first to formulate the principles of city planning. Many of the later Greek colonial cities around the Mediterranean clearly were planned. For instance, Greek cities in Italy were built on a checkerboard pattern, with streets of uniform width and city blocks of relatively uniform dimensions. However, it seems unlikely that the Greeks were the only ancient people to approach city building this way. It does not seem possible that all the earlier cities in Mesopotamia, the Nile, China, and the Indus evolved without some degree of planning. For example, the street pattern of Indus cities was a gridiron, with straight streets meeting at right angles. Such a pattern required some degree of planning. Nevertheless, Greek cities were held up as models of urban planning during the later Renaissance period (A.D. 1500–1700) and stimulated artists and engineers of the sixteenth century to think about a totally planned environment.

Roman cities

By 200 B.C., the focus for the Western city had shifted from Greece to Rome. The Romans adopted many urban traits from the Greeks, as well as from the Etruscans, a civilization of northern Italy that the Romans had conquered. As the Roman Empire expanded, city life was diffused into France, Germany, England, interior Spain, the Alpine countries, and parts of eastern Europe. The military camp, or *castra*, was the basis for many of these new settlements. In England, the Roman trail of city building can be found by looking for the suffixes *-caster* and *-chester*—as in Lancaster or Winchester, cities originally founded as Roman camps. Figure 10-6 shows the diffusion of urban life into Europe as the Greek and Roman frontiers advanced.

The landscape of these Roman cities shared several traits with their Greek predecessors. The gridiron street pattern, used in later Greek cities, was fundamental to Roman cities. This can still be seen in the heart of

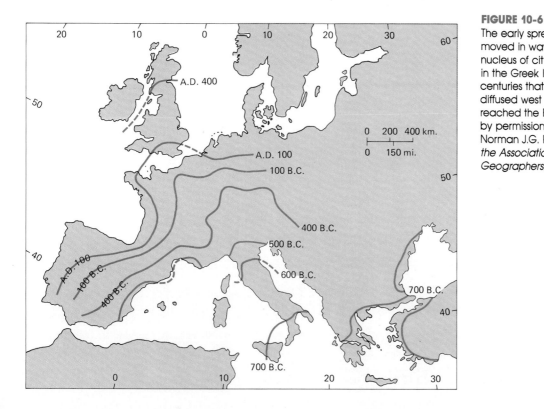

FIGURE 10-6

The early spread of urban development moved in waves across Europe. The nucleus of city life was well established in the Greek lands by 700 B.C. In the centuries that followed, urbanization diffused west and north until it finally reached the British Isles. (Reproduced by permission from an article by Norman J.G. Pounds in the *Annals of the Association of American Geographers*, 59, 1969.)

such Italian cities as Verona and Pavia (see Figure 10-7). These straight streets and right-angle intersections make a striking contrast to the curved, wandering lanes of the later medieval quarters or the streets of Rome itself. At the intersection of a city's two major thoroughfares was the **forum,** a zone combining elements of the Greek acropolis and agora. Here were not only the temples of worship, administrative buildings, and warehouses, but also the libraries, schools, and marketplaces that served the common people.

Clustered around the forum were the palaces of the power elite. For comfort, the West had nothing like these palaces and suburban villas of the wealthy until the twentieth century. They were sanitary, well heated in winter, and spacious—marvels of domestic architecture. These Roman rulers in their comfortable houses sat at the center of a gigantic empire.

Despite the architectural accomplishments of the Roman engineers, the Roman masses lived in squalid conditions. The homes of the rich spread horizontally across the landscape, but the homes of the poor rose vertically. They lived in shoddy apartment houses, often four or five stories high, called *insula*. These tenements seem to be the first Western example of high-density dwellings. With this Roman "invention," two human urban types arrived on the scene—the land speculator and the slum landlord. The elaborate system of aqueducts and underground sewers did not extend to the poor. The result, probably a low in urban sanitation, was that the garbage of perhaps a million Romans was thrown into open pits around the city. Thus, even in its best days, Rome's population was continually at the mercy of plagues.

Rome's most important legacy probably was not its engineering feats, although they remain landmarks in European cities to this day (see Figure 10-8). Rather, the Romans developed a lasting method for choosing the site of a city. They consistently chose sites with transportation in mind. That is, the Roman Empire was held together by a complicated system of

FIGURE 10-7

The Roman grid street pattern still survives in Pavia, Italy, and the original city site is still used. Many of the straight streets from Roman times remain in use twenty centuries after they were first built. The dotted lines indicate the Roman streets that do not exist today. Beyond the Roman core the streets developed in irregular patterns.

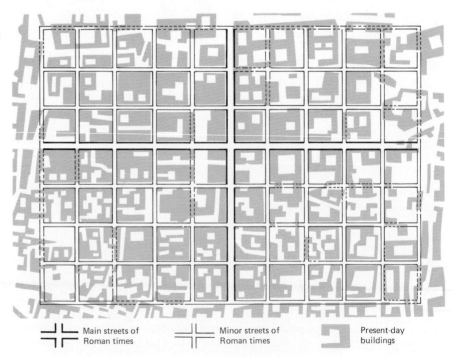

⌐⌐ Main streets of   ⌐⌐ Minor streets of   Present-day
⌐⌐ Roman times   ⌐⌐ Roman times   buildings

FIGURE 10-8
The coliseum in Rome was an important center of activity, where crowds of 60,000 were entertained by mock battles, circuses, gladiators fighting, and sports events. Most large Roman cities had similar structures. Today, most cities have stadiums and coliseums that continue the tradition of public spectacles started by the Romans.

roads and highways, which linked the towns and cities. In choosing a site for a new settlement, access was a major consideration. Some cultures have situated their settlements with defense in mind. Hence, their towns might be located in the most inaccessible places, such as marshes, hilltops, or islands. Even though urban life declined in Europe with the collapse of the Roman Empire, numerous cities, including Paris, London, and Vienna, were later refounded on old Roman sites because they offered the advantages of access.

Urban decline in the Dark Ages

With the decline of the Roman Empire (by A.D. 400), urban life also declined. Historians attribute the fall of Rome to internal decay, the invasions of the Germanic "barbarians," and other factors. Cities were sapped of their vitality. The highway system that linked them fell into disrepair, so that cities could no longer exchange goods and ideas. Cities were increasingly invaded by wandering tribes, yet they could no longer count on outside military support as the administrative structure of the empire collapsed. Isolated from one another, they lost vital functions. Within 200 years, many of the cities founded by the Romans withered totally away. There were exceptions. Cities of the Mediterranean survived because they established trade with the Byzantine civilization centered in Constantinople. After the eighth century, some cities—particularly those in Spain—were infused with new vigor by the Moorish Empire, which spread across the Mediterranean from northern Africa. But the cities of northern regions were unable to survive. Cities became small villages. Where thousands had formerly thrived, a few hundred eked out a subsistence living from agriculture.

The medieval city

The medieval period, lasting roughly from A.D. 1000 to 1500, was a time of renewed urban expansion in Europe and a period that deeply influenced the future structure of urban life. Urban life spread beyond the borders of the former Roman Empire, into the north and east of Europe, as the Germanic and Slavic peoples expanded their empires. In only four centuries, 2500 new German "cities" were founded, although they were tiny compared to those of the Roman Empire. Most cities of present-day Europe were founded during this period. Many were on old Roman sites; others were new.

Five symbols—the fortress, the charter, the wall, the market, and the cathedral—signify the major functions of the medieval city. The fortress expresses the importance of defense. Usually the cities were clustered around a fortified place. The importance of this role is expressed today in many place-names. This is demonstrated by cities in Germanic lands ending in -burg, such as Salzburg or Würzburg; in France with -bourg, as in Strasbourg; and in English with -burgh, as in Edinburgh. Each suffix has the same meaning—a fortified castle. The terms burgher and bourgeoisie, which now refer to the middle class, originally referred to a citizen of the medieval city.

The charter was a governmental decree from a regional power, usually a feudal lord, granting political autonomy to the town. This act had several important implications. It freed the population from feudal restrictions, made the city responsible for its own defense and government, and allowed it to coin money. Thus city life become even freer than life on rural feudal estates. These rights and responsibilities contributed to the development of urban social, economic, and intellectual life and, in turn, to the development of civilization.

The wall was important for defense, but it was more important as a symbol of the sharp distinction between country and city. Within the wall, most inhabitants were, by charter, free; outside, most were serfs, "City air sets a man free" went the medieval proverb. Indeed, even though the medieval city had feudal characteristics, it generally was a community of citizens able to move about with little restriction, free to buy and sell property and goods. A city of "free" citizens, not based on a vast pool of slave labor, was a first in the history of the Western city.

It was at the wall's gates that the division between city residents and nonresidents was sharpest. Here, goods entering the city were inspected and taxed. Here, nonresidents were issued permits for entry and undesirables were excluded. And here, at sunset, the gates were closed, shutting out the rural world until sunrise. Often nonresidents were required to leave the city at dusk and seek accommodations outside the wall. As a result, suburbs—called faubourgs, meaning "beyond the fortress"— sprang up. In time, these communities demanded to be included in the true city. If their petition was accepted, the walls would be expanded to encompass the former suburb. By this process, the medieval cities grew, much as modern cities annex their sprawling suburbs. Then, in the sixteenth century, the increasing use of gunpowder and the invention of accurate artillery made the building of elaborate permanent fortifications a necessity. The wall lost its "mobility." Even so, within the walls the medieval city was never a giant. At its widest point, it was probably no more than half a mile from the city center to the wall, easy walking distance even for citizens of a modern industrial city.

Another key zone was the marketplace. It symbolized the important role of the medieval city in economic activities (see box, "The Greatest City in the World: Hangchow"). The city depended on the countryside for its food and produce, which were traded in the market. The market also was a center for long-distance trade, which linked city to city. Textiles, salt, ore, and other raw materials were bought and sold in the marketplace. Usually the market "square" (seldom square-shaped) became the focus for guild houses and the residences of wealthy merchants, so that it was the heart of the commercial zone. One important aspect of the medieval market is still found in Europe. Even today, open-air markets are held at least one day a week, and many European housewives do their shopping there. In some cities, the strength of the market tradition has inhibited development of suburban supermarkets. Residents seem to prefer the activity and human

---

THE GREATEST CITY IN THE WORLD: HANGCHOW

The Chinese city Hangchow, wrote the Italian Marco Polo, "is the greatest city . . . in the world, where so many pleasures may be found that one fancies himself to be in Paradise." According to a contemporary Chinese account, in the markets of thirteenth-century Hangchow one could buy "beauty products (ointments and perfumes, eyebrow-black, false hair), pet cats and fish for feeding them with, . . . bath wraps, fishing tackle, . . . chessmen, oiled paper for windows, fumigating powder against mosquitos," and other merchandise unobtainable elsewhere in China (or probably anywhere else on earth). In addition, one could visit any of fifteen big specialized markets—including the principal pig market, which was right in the center of town—or the scores of smaller markets for products ranging from flowers and oranges to pearls and precious stones.

Indeed, to the European visitor, Hangchow was a wonder that his medieval city had not prepared him for. As French historian Jacques Gernet comments, "The largest cities of Europe, with a population of several tens of thousands, were nothing but petty market towns in comparison with the 'provisional capital' of China." Its vast ramparts were pierced by five gateways for canals that carried boats loaded with products from all over the country. Its great thoroughfares (the largest sixty yards or fifty-six meters wide and three miles or five kilometers long) terminated at the ramparts in thirteen monumental gates. It had a population of about 1 million people, which made it "the biggest urban concentration in the world at the time."

Visually, the city had a modern urban look. An unbroken line of dwellings stretched as far as the eye could see. As one of its inhabitants wrote, "The city of Hangchow is large . . . and overpopulated. The houses are high and built close to each other. Their beams touch and their porches are continuous. There is not an inch of unoccupied ground anywhere." Yet almost all the streets of Hangchow were paved, and the level of public cleanliness was probably higher than anywhere in the Western urban world before our own time. The authorities in Hangchow jealously guarded the purity of the water in its giant artificial lake. They realized something that nineteenth-century Europeans had not yet grasped: Polluted water leads to epidemics. "The townspeople who drink no other water but this," wrote a city official, "run the risk of epidemics [if it becomes impure]."

The population was so large (and space so tight) that it spilled beyond the ramparts into giant suburbs. It seems fitting to end this description of thirteenth-century Hangchow with the awe-struck words of Oderic de Pordenone, another visitor from medieval Europe, on seeing these suburbs: "At each of [Hangchow's] gates . . . are cities larger than Venice or Padua might be, so that one will go about one of those suburbs for six or eight days and yet will seem to have travelled but a little way."

Adapted from Jacques Gernet, Daily Life in China on the Eve of the Mongol Invasion, 1250–1276 (Stanford, Cal.: Stanford University Press, 1962), pp. 13–58.

contact of a market in the city's heart to modern decentralized shopping facilities.

The town's crowning glory, its great church, ordinarily was close to the market. Religion had a far more central place in medieval European life than it has today. The church was a community center for medieval citizens.

The urban morphology of the medieval city is of interest because the centers of many modern-day European towns are remnants of this period. The streets were typically narrow wandering lanes, rarely more than fifteen feet (four and one-half meters) wide, in contrast to the straight streets of the Roman gridiron patterns. The narrowness of the streets in these medieval cores constrains twentieth-century automobile use. For example, in 141 West German cities, 77 percent of the streets are too narrow for safe and efficient two-way traffic. As a result, some cities, such as Vienna, Salzburg, and Munich, have excluded auto traffic from the old areas, turning them into pedestrian zones where cars may enter only during certain hours (see Figures 10-9 and 10-10).

Many central-city buildings are also remnants of this period. These structures were originally built three stories high, with the bottom floor reserved for work space and the upper floors for dwelling and storage. This is still a common pattern. Many European shop owners and artisans live above their workplaces. However, many of the medieval buildings are hardly adequate for twentieth-century use. They are cramped by modern standards—as anyone who has seen a medieval suit of armor knows, people were physically smaller then—and they lack adequate heating and plumbing. Of course physical deterioration is also a problem. These factors have turned some inner-city medieval quarters into modern low-rent districts. As a result, most are occupied by lower-income people who are often retired and on a fixed pension. A move to a modern apartment would be too expensive for these people, so they put up with the hardships of life in a fourteenth-century dwelling.

There are three important points about the role of the medieval period in the evolution of the Western city: (1) This was the period when most European cities were founded; (2) many of the traditions of Western urban life were begun then; and (3) the medieval landscape is still with us, giving a visible history of the city and physically constraining twentieth-century activities.

The Renaissance and baroque periods

During the Renaissance (1500–1600) and baroque (1600-1800) periods, the form and function of the European city changed. Absolute monarchs arose to preside over a unified nation-state. The burghers, or rising middle class, of the cities slowly gave up their freedoms to join with the king in pursuit of economic gain. City size increased rapidly because the bureaucracies of regional power structures came to dominate cities and because trade patterns expanded with the beginnings of European imperial conquest. A new concern with city planning and military technology also acted to remold and constrain the physical form of the city.

Cities and the surrounding countryside began to combine into nation-states, ruled by all-powerful monarchs. One city, the national capital, rose to prominence in most countries. Provincial cities were subjected to its tastes, and power was centralized in its precincts. The first office buildings, those structures that came to stretch from Washington, D.C., to

FIGURE 10-9

The typical narrow and winding street pattern of the medieval period still persists in Salzburg, Austria, along with the pattern of street-level shops with residences above. Recently the total inner city of Salzburg was closed to auto traffic, allowing pedestrians free rein within the historic core.

FIGURE 10-10

The townscape of Salzburg, Austria, illustrates two important periods of urban development. The tightly compact housing closest to the river is medieval, while the larger buildings set off by squares and courtyards were constructed later during the baroque period.

Moscow, were built to house a growing new government bureaucracy. Most important, the capital city was restructured to reflect the power of the central government and to ensure its control over the urban masses.

Hand in hand with these developments went a new interest in city planning. This concern grew from a revival of all things classical, including Greek and Roman urban planning; from a new philosophical emphasis on humankind's earthly home; and from new aesthetic concepts that gave urban planners a foundation to work from. Most of these planning measures were meant to benefit the privileged classes. They considered the city a stage on which to act out their destinies, and if the city was a stage, it could be rearranged at will. Typical of the time was the infatuation with wide, grandiose boulevards. The rich could ride along them in carriages, and the army could march along them in an impressive display of power. Other features of the baroque city were large open squares, palaces, and public buildings. Statues were everywhere. This environment was strikingly different from the dark, closed world of the medieval quarters, where the middle classes still resided. The spacious new aristocratic sections often were created at the expense of the middle class, whose homes were demolished to make way for a new palace or boulevard.

This rebuilding process reached a peak in nineteenth-century Paris. There, Napolean III had Baron Haussmann build a system of boulevards designed to control the populace. Cobblestone streets were carefully paved so that there would be no loose ammunition available for rioting Parisians. Streets were straightened and widened and cul-de-sacs were broken down to give the army, should the people arise, space to maneuver and ordered sight lines for its artillery. Whole neighborhoods were torn down to build wide avenues. Thousands were displaced as their apartment buildings were demolished. They had to seek new shelter on their own, and many ended up in the congested working-class sections of east and north Paris. These areas are still overcrowded, and much of the blame can be assigned to the baroque planners.

In these developments, we can see the coming of the modern city. The masses of city dwellers are sacrificed to the traffic pattern. Neighborhoods are overwhelmed by the straight line. The rise of the urban planner coincides with the loss of a sense of the needs of most urban dwellers. In our own times, the highway has replaced the avenue as the yardstick of the urban planner, but the results have been the same—the wholesale destruction of inner-city neighborhoods. As a result, the needs of most urban dwellers are not met.

The new military technology aggravated the problems of congestion and high density within the city. Extensive urban fortifications were needed as a defense against artillery bombardment. These fortifications could not easily be extended outward to encompass new urban growth. Instead, new stories were added to medieval buildings. As a result, population densities increased within the walls, and urban overcrowding became a reality. The walls also threatened the independent financial status of the city. They were so expensive to erect that, without outside aid, urban bankruptcy always remained a possibility. Moreover, the wall was no longer the simple dividing line between city and countryside that it had been in medieval times. The area outside the walls became a military no-man's-land, a dangerous space subject to artillery fire in time of war. People who settled there did so at their own risk, because the military reserved the right to torch all structures in time of war to deprive the enemy of shelter and cover. Figure 10-11 contrasts the morphology or physical form of typical medieval and baroque cities. In particular, note the differences in the street patterns and fortifications.

Today, the Renaissance and baroque urban landscapes offer mixed blessings to the city dweller. The boulevards help traffic circulation in some cases and hinder it in others, depending on whether the boulevard system is linked together. Most boulevards were built as disjointed entities. The palaces and mansions of the period still dominate the central part of many cities. Most of these structures are now museums, government buildings, or banks and other financial institutions. The spacious gardens, meant for the private pleasure of aristocrats, are now usually open to the public and offer the inner-city resident much-appreciated open space. Figures 10-12 and 10-13 show typical modern-day use of the baroque landscape.

Renaissance and baroque planning had a profound effect on many American cities, as well as European cities. For example, Washington, D.C., was originally designed by a French planner during the height of the baroque period. Although the original plan has been compromised somewhat, its intent is still visible in the wide boulevards, open spaces, public buildings, and monuments of the city. Other examples of the baroque spirit can be found in such cities as Philadelphia, Williamsburg, Virginia, and Columbia, South Carolina.

The industrial city and urbanization

The function, structure, and landscape of the Western city has changed dramatically since the industrial revolution. Furthermore, the industrial

FIGURE 10-11
Contrasts in medieval and baroque city planning can be seen in two West German cities. Heilbronn developed in medieval times around a castle-fortress. The church, town hall, marketplace, and fortress were clustered at the center of the town, surrounded by an irregular street pattern. Saarlouis was founded in 1681 by Louis XIV of France, and exhibits the typical baroque concern with symmetry, boulevards, squares, and elaborate water fortifications.

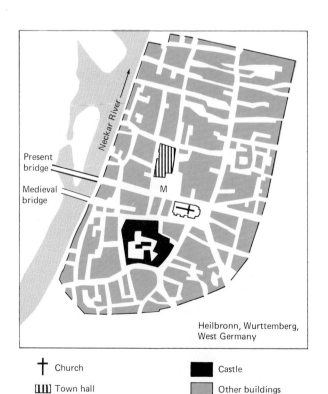

Heilbronn, Wurttemberg, West Germany

Saarlouis in the Saarland, West Germany

† Church

[III] Town hall

■ Castle

■ Other buildings

▨ River and water fortifications

M – Marketplace

FIGURE 10-12

The boulevard was a favorite of the baroque planners. The avenues often led to public buildings or monuments and were lined by upper-income housing. Unfortunately, the boulevards were usually created at the expense of thousands who were displaced as older housing was destroyed by the street builders. Has a similar situation occurred in your city as freeways have been built?

FIGURE 10-13

An important part of the baroque consciousness was expressed in the planned garden, such as this one in London. Although the gardens were originally the province of the aristocracy, today most of them are open to the public and serve as much needed recreation space for the central city population.

city has profoundly altered the fabric of society itself. It has given the world its first societies with urban majorities, where more people live in cities than in the countryside. All indications are that this trend will continue.

Up to the industrial period, the rate of urbanization in Western countries was relatively low. For example, in 1600, urban dwellers made up only 2 percent of the German, French, and English populations; the Netherlands and Italy were 13 percent urban dwellers. However, as millions of people migrated to the cities during the past 200 years, the rate of urbanization skyrocketed. By 1800, England was 20 percent urbanized, and it became the world's first urban society around 1870. By the 1890 census, 60 percent of its people lived in cities. The United States was 3 percent urbanized in 1800, 40 percent in 1900, 51 percent in 1920 (when it became an urban country), and now has about 75 percent of its population in towns and cities. The link between urbanization and industrialization is clear, because the United States industrialized later than England.

Western cities often grew too fast, without planning or guidelines, and at the expense of the working class. (see box, "Living Conditions in the Industrial Age: London 1849"). The industrial revolution and the triumph of capitalism turned the city from a public institution into private property—spoils to be divided with an eye to maximum profits. New urban symbols—the factory, the railroad, and the slum—appeared with the emergence of the commercial city. The old marketplace was replaced by the merchants' exchange, the bank, and finally the stock market. Bisected by the railroad and captured by the land speculator, the city fragmented. Overall planning for the efficient use of land disappeared. Instead, a new philosophy emerged, **laissez-faire utilitarianism.** Lewis Mumford, in his book *The City in History*, defines this as a belief that divine providence ruled over economic activity and ensured the maximum public good through the unregulated efforts of every private, self-seeking individual.

One expression of this new philosophy was a changed attitude toward land and the buildings on that land. Once raw materials such as coal and iron ore could be brought to the city by rail, factories began to cluster together to share the benefits of **agglomeration**—that is, to share labor, transportation costs, and utility costs and to take advantage of financial institutions found in the city. Industry concentrated in the city itself, around labor, the commercial marketplace, and capital. Land use intensified drastically. In medieval Europe, land was leased for long periods (99

LIVING CONDITIONS IN THE INDUSTRIAL AGE: LONDON 1849

Henry Mayhew was a journalist who spent part of his life investigating poverty, labor, and living conditions in nineteenth-century England. In *London Labour and the London Poor*, he has left us a classic account of life in industrial England. The summer of 1849, when Mayhew started his work, was a period of particular tension in England, because a cholera plague was sweeping the country. Within three months, 13,000 people were estimated to have died of the disease in London alone. Mayhew visited the cholera areas, which were mainly the districts where the laborers and unemployed poor lived. At the time, the way cholera spread was still being debated, but Mayhew's conclusions seem clear. "So well-known are the locations of fever and disease," he wrote, "that London would almost admit of being mapped out pathologically, and divided into its morbid districts and deadly cantons." Here is part of his account of his trip to one of the "deadly cantons":

"We then journeyed on to London-street, down which the tidal ditch continues its course. In No. 1 of this street the cholera first appeared seventeen years ago, and spread up it with fearful virulence; but this year it appeared at the opposite end, and ran down it with like severity. As we passed along the reeking banks of the sewer the sun shone upon a narrow slip of the water. In the bright light it appeared the colour of strong green tea, and positively looked as solid as black marble in the shadow—indeed it was more like watery mud than muddy water; and yet we were assured this was the only water the wretched inhabitants had to drink. As we gazed in horror at it, we saw drains and sewers emptying their filthy contents into it; we saw a whole tier of doorless privies in the open road, common to men and women, built over it; we heard bucket after bucket of filth splash into it, and the limbs of the vagrant boys bathing in it seemed by pure force of contrast, white as Parian marble. . . .

"In this wretched place we were taken to a house where an infant lay dead of the cholera. We asked if they *really did* drink the water? The answer was, 'They were obliged to drink the ditch, without they could beg a pailful or thieve a pailful of water.' [It was not uncommon for the poor to go from house to house in wealthier sections begging for water.] But have you spoken to your landlord about having it laid on for you? 'Yes sir; and he says he will do it, and do it, but we know him better than to believe him.'"

From Eileen Yeo and E. P. Thompson, The Unknown Mayhew *(New York: Schocken, 1971), p. 21. Copyright© 1971 by Pantheon Books, a Division of Random House, Inc.*

to 999 years) and was rarely sold. After the seventeenth century, land came to be treated as a commodity. With the increased competition for land in the industrial period, land transactions and speculation became an everyday part of the city. Land parcels became the property of the owner, who had no obligations toward society in deciding how to use them. The historic urban core was often destroyed, the older city replaced. The result was a chaotic mosaic of mixed land uses: factories directly next to housing; slum tenements next to public buildings; open spaces and parks violated by railroad tracks. A planned attempt to bring order to the city came only in the twentieth century with the concept of zoning. Yet even this idea was rooted in some of the same forces—profit, bigotry, and individualism—that had already made the industrial city unresponsive to the needs of most of its inhabitants (see box, "The Origins of Zoning in America: Race and Wealth").

Laissez-faire industrialism in the "age of invention" did surprisingly little for the human fodder that fueled its shops and plants. If the wholesale distribution of such utilities as gas and water is excluded, the industrial city made no improvements in human living standards beyond what had already been available in the seventeenth-century city. The industrial city did take sunlight and air from the new working class. In their slum dwellings, direct sunlight was seldom available, and open spaces were nonexistent (see Figure 10-14). In Liverpool, for instance, one-sixth of the population reportedly lived in "underground cellars." Vast tenement areas quickly grew to accommodate new migrants from the countryside. It was common for a large family to share a single room. A

THE ORIGINS OF ZONING IN AMERICA: RACE AND WEALTH

"The standard zoning ordinance of American cities was originally conceived from a union of two fears—fear of the Chinese and fear of skyscrapers. In California a wave of racial prejudice had swept over the state after Chinese settlers were imported to build the railroads and work in the mines [in the mid-nineteenth century]. Ingenious lawyers in San Francisco found that the old common law of nuisance could be applied for indirect discrimination against the Chinese in situations where the constitution of the state forbade direct discrimination. Chinese laundries of the 1880s had become social centers for Chinese servants who lived outside the Chinatown ghetto. To whites they represented only clusters of 'undesirables' in the residential areas where Chinese were living singly among them as house servants. By declaring the laundries nuisances and fire hazards, San Francisco hoped to exclude Chinese from most sections of the city. . . . Such nuisance-zone statutes spread down the Pacific coast. They were directed against laundries, livery stables, saloons, dance halls, pool halls, and slaughterhouses. . . .

"[Meanwhile,] in New York [City] the Fifth Avenue Association, a group composed of men who owned or leased the city's most expensive retail land, demanded that the city protect their luxury blocks from encroach-ment by the new tall buildings of the garment district. . . . The Fifth Avenue Association feared that the ensuing decades would see the [skyscraper] lofts invading their best properties, bringing with them [lower-class] lunch-hour crowds and a blockade of wagons, trucks, and carts. In short, they feared that skyscraper lofts, low-paid help, and traffic congestion would drive their middle-class and wealthy customers from the Avenue."

The combination of West Coast racism plus the fears of wealthy New York merchants resulted in the New York Zoning Law of 1916, a prototype zoning statute for the nation. These were the roots of the first American attempts to deal coherently with urban growth. Not surprisingly, the zoning law was no sooner passed than it was seized on in the South and elsewhere "as a way to extend [the] laws and practices of racial segregation. . . . A land or structure limitation . . . became a financial, racial, and ethnic limitation by pricing certain groups out of particular suburbs. Italians were held at bay in Boston, Poles in Detroit, blacks in Chicago and St. Louis, Jews in New York."

Abridged and adapted from Sam Bass Warner, Jr., Urban Wilderness. (New York: Harper & Row, 1972), pp. 28–32, 117–118. Copyright © 1972 by Sam Bass Warner, Jr.

study from the middle of the nineteenth century in Manchester, England, showed that there was but one toilet for every 212 people. Running water was usually available only on the ground floors of apartment buildings. Sometimes a whole neighborhood depended on a corner well and pump that already was polluted by the runoff from outhouses. Disease was pervasive, and mortality rates ran high. In 1893, the life expectancy of a male worker in Manchester was twenty-eight years; his country cousin might live until fifty-two. The death rate in New York City in 1880 was 25 per thousand, whereas it was half that in the rural counties of the state. The infant mortality rate per thousand live births rose from 180 in 1850 to 240 in 1870. Legislation correcting such ills came only in the latter part of the century, and only after the 1890 census did the mortality rates in the United States once again head downward.

But not all city dwellers had to live in the industrial landscape. New transportation modes—particularly the electric trolley, perfected in the 1880s—triggered a suburban explosion. The middle class left the central city in large numbers, now that they had a cheap and efficient means of travel, and they created a haven of large homes, spacious lots, and tree-lined streets on the outskirts of the city. The social differences between central city and suburbs became significant, because only the wealthy could afford suburban dwellings. The central city was left for the working class. The influx of European immigrants to American cities in the last decades of the nineteenth century coincided with the middle-class flight to the suburbs (and in part triggered it). Areas that had seen middle-class families move to the suburbs often saw large numbers of blue-collar migrants move into the city's old residential core. The middle-class houses were broken up into small apartments, so that where one family had lived previously, now five or six immigrant families resided (see box, "Reviving Old Neighborhoods: German Village, Columbus, Ohio").

FIGURE 10-14
This London scene shows a typical working-class slum of the nineteenth century. Sunlight, fresh air, clean water, and sewers were often lacking, opening the area up to epidemics of typhoid and cholera. Many American cities had similar sections.

Megalopolis

In the nineteenth century, cities grew at unprecedented rates because of the concentration of people and commerce. Movement away from the central city quickened in the last decades of the century. The inner city became increasiingly dominated by commerce and the working class. By the turn of the century, the change in the industrial city was so apparent that H. G. Wells wrote:

> Many of the railroad begotten "giant cities" will reach their maximum in the coming century and in all probability are destined to such a process of dissection and diffusion as to amount almost to obliteration. . . . These coming cities will not be, in the old sense, cities at all; they will present a new and entirely different phase of human distribution.

Wells was right, because a new form of city has emerged in the twentieth century. It is the dispersed and decentralized city, brought about by new forms of transportation—the auto, truck, bus, airplane, and pipeline—and new methods of communication—radio, television, tele-type, and airmail. With decentralization, instead of being concentrated in dense, compact areas, the new cities sprawl until they merge with their neighbors. One metropolitan area blends into another, until supercities are created that stretch for hundreds of miles.

The prototype of this new form is found on the eastern seaboard of the United States, stretching from Boston in the north to Washington, D.C., in

REVIVING OLD NEIGHBORHOODS: GERMAN VILLAGE, COLUMBUS OHIO

During the past decade, historic preservation has become a significant force in halting inner-city decay. Yet, as with all urban issues, preservation is deeply intertwined with complicated community issues, as is illustrated by this case study of a historic district in the center of Columbus, Ohio.

Settled by German immigrants between 1820 and 1860, the German Village population reached 10,000 in 1872 and manifested all the aspects of a typical nineteenth-century ethnic community. But by 1920, hastened in part by the anti-German feelings of World War I, both the quality of life and the ethnic nature of the Village had declined drastically. Physical deterioration of the small, red-brick cottages were widespread; much of the land was zoned for commercial or industrial land use. By the mid-1950s, German Village exhibited the classic symptons of urban blight; overcrowding, poor sanitary conditions, an excess of renter-occupied housing, and a low-income population. In 1956 the city of Columbus made plans for widespread redevelopment and clearance.

Talk of restoration as an alternative to renewal began and a few property owners renovated their buildings as an example. As a result of intensive promotional efforts, a German Village society was formed in 1960 and soon afterward the mayor established a commission to review building permits and recommend legislation needed to protect and restore the Village. Boundaries for a historic district were established the following year, and the area was rezoned from industrial to residential. Private investment increased as the threat of redevelopment ended. A "certificate of appropriateness" became a prerequisite to apply for a building permit, and restoration manual was issued describing "appropriate" construction. Over 600 certificates had been issued by 1967.

The housing market changed drastically as well-off, well-educated young professionals moved in. Living in "the Village" gave identity in a sprawling city and today the area is the of the most prestigious districts in Columbus.

But many see German Village as a classic case of **gentrification**—the displacement of poor people by higher-income groups as older buildings are renovated. However, a survey by Ford and Fusch of low-income residents in surrounding neighborhoods found these people felt far more positively toward the German Village development than previously imagined. One of the major factors was that they felt German Village had been instrumental in changing the city's view of inner-city neighborhoods, which, not insignificantly, had led to more financial support for central city areas. While it is true that low-income people may be forced from the core of a historic district, perhaps this dislocation is a small price to pay for increased stability in surrounding neighborhoods.

Adapted from Larry R. Ford, "Saving the Cities: Urban Preservation in America," Focus, 30:1 (September–October 1979).

the south. Some call it the supercity of Boswash. The geographer Jean Gottmann coined the term **megalopolis** to describe it. This term is now used worldwide in reference to giant metropolitan regions. Aside from Boswash, there are Chipitts, stretching from Chicago to Pittsburgh, Ciloubustonis, consisting of Cincinnati, Louisville, Columbus, Dayton, and Indianapolis; and San San, the California supercity that someday may reach from San Diego to San Francisco. In Europe, the Ruhr area in Germany, most of the Netherlands, the Midlands of England, and the Po Valley of northern Italy could qualify as megalopolises. Other highly industrialized, highly urbanized countries, such as Japan, have new supercities.

The characteristics that these urban regions share are high population densities, extending over hundreds of square miles or kilometers; concentrations of numerous older cities; transportation links formed by freeway, railroad, air routes, and rapid transit; and an extremely high proportion of the nation's wealth, commerce, and political power. As noted, the prototype is in the northeastern section of the United States, from New Hampshire to Virginia. Here, 20 percent of the American population lives on 2 percent of the land area, at a density of almost 600 persons per square mile (240 per square kilometer). No other state outside this area's core has a density higher than 300 per square mile (120 per square kilometer). The high level of urbanization in this area reflects the advantages of an early start. The area itself is not particularly well endowed with natural resources and from early times has specialized in trading, manufacturing, and services. As the resources of the interior were opened up to them, these cities grew until they formed what Jean Gottmann calls "the financial and managerial Main Street of the modern world."

The megalopolitan form has major drawbacks, because problems come on a giant scale with such an immense concentration of people and activities. Common problems in the supercities are congestion, high land prices, overcrowding, financial insolvency, deteriorating inner cores, a poor and disenfranchised population in contrast to the affluent in the suburbs, and air and water pollution. Unfortunately, solutions to these problems will not soon be found, because another characteristic of megalopolitan areas is political fragmentation. Because most of the problems are regionwide, they go beyond the legal jurisdiction of the smaller towns and counties. Often they cross state borders. Solutions will come only with increased cooperation between all political units and the formation of regional agencies. Until then, the megalopolis will continue to grow, and its problems will increase.

Now that we have examined the evolution of the Western city, let us look at the development of non-Western cities.

The landscape of non-Western cities

Most of the world's population lives in non-Western countries, and it is in these areas that we see the greatest potential for dramatic change in urban patterns. This change is mainly a function of high natural population growth coupled with enormous rates of migration from countryside to cities. Recent growth in these non-Western cities has been staggering. In 1950, only four of the fifteen largest cities of the world were in non-Western countries; it is estimated that by the year 2000 twelve of the fifteen largest cities will be in emerging countries. In 1980 there were twenty-six cities with over 5 million people, sixteen of them in non-Western countries. Accompanying this rapid growth are serious economic, political, and social problems (see Figure 10-15). In this section, we will examine these non-Western cities in order to gain better understanding of the urban landscape, processes, and problems.

But first, we must think about terminology. Up to now, we have simply differentiated between Western and non-Western cities. However, such a simplistic dichotomy has limitations. Western culture has profoundly influenced urban life throughout the world, first through colonialism and presently through capitalistic industrialism (see Figure 10-16). Many African cities, for example, were founded as colonial outposts of the French or British empires (see Figure 10-17). Their form and function articulate ties to Europe, and even through the period of independence, the Western influence remains strong; references to these cities as "non-Western" therefore involves some hesitation and qualification.

However, it would be equally mistaken to overlook local influences. Because many of these cities have been strongly stamped by Western culture does not mean they will follow the path taken by Western cities. Local political, economic, and social patterns affect these cities in unique ways. Though they face similar problems found in Western cities, their solutions may differ. In fact, local influences are so strong that it is

FIGURE 10-15
Migration to cities has been so rapid that
often illegal squatter settlements have
been the only solution to housing
problems. The top photograph is from the
Persian Gulf, the bottom from Manila.

FIGURE 10-16
Monuments, parks, and palaces—often
designed by European planners—can be
found in former colonial cities. This is
the Plaza de Mayo, Buenos Aires.

difficult to generalize about non-Western cities as a single category; more
detailed study must examine them at a much finer scale in order to
appreciate how African cities, for example, differ from Asian cities.

So the following is admittedly a broad-brush treatment of a complex
topic. References listed at the end of the chapter will guide the student
interested in learning more about this complicated theme.

Three urban models: indigenous, colonial, and emerging cities

The preceding section on the evolving landscape of Western cities was
able to delimit specific evolutionary periods, such as medieval and
industrial. This is more difficult to do with non-Western cities because
local influences have been so important and city histories are so varied.
Instead, we will generalize about non-Western cities by using three
models representing idealized or hypothetical stages that a typical non-
Western city might experience.

The first model is that of the **indigenous city,** referring to one created by
purely local forces, removed, say, from the influences of the West.
Examples would be early Islamic cities in Africa developed in the
eleventh century, or the precolonial cities of Mexico and Central America.

The second model is that of the **colonial city.** This refers both to those
cities founded by colonialism and to those precolonial or indigenous

FIGURE 10-17
State-owned high-rise buildings are common solutions to the chronic housing shortage in Third World cities. This scene from Nigeria is typical of urban landscapes in many emerging countries.

cities whose existing structure was deeply influenced by Western colonialism. Cities in this category are far more common and widespread than indigenous cities.

The third model is that of the **emerging city.** This is the city of the present—the settlements of those nations that we call "emerging," "third world," or "less developed countries."

Although each model will be discussed in turn, suggesting that cities have experienced each of the three stages, this might convey a faulty impression. Some cities in the world were untouched by colonialism. Kabul, Afghanistan, is an example. On the other hand, there are also a few cities today that might still qualify as colonial cities, such as Hong Kong. And still other cities are products of only the last decades; that is, they have been developed to meet contemporary needs, so they have not been either indigenous or colonial cities. They are true "emerging" centers.

The indigenous city

Indigenous cities developed without contact with Western influences. Most of them predate European colonialism; a very few, as mentioned earlier, may have been untouched by the landscape and structure of the later colonial period.

If we were to examine the worldwide distribution of precolonial indigenous cities, we would see urban centers in the New World restricted to Mexico, Central America, and the Andean highlands. In Africa, there would be small cities in the west, a band of Islamic empires in the north, and some more small cities in the eastern highlands, again associated with Islamic empires. Most of the continent would be without citylike settlements until the European colonial period. Asia would have the largest number of indigenous cities, reaching from the Near East, across present-day Pakistan and India, to China and Japan. The least number of cities within the continent would be found in southwest Asia.

The landscape and structure of the indigenous city are very similar to those already described in the section on the Western medieval city. In fact, some would argue that cities could be generalized into a "preindustrial" urban model, suggesting that cities in both Western and non-Western countries were essentially the same in form and function before the industrial period. The major proponent of this argument is the sociologist Gideon Sjoberg, who first formulated and presented generalizations on the preindustrial city. The fact that his terminology is not used in this text does not imply rejection of his concepts. Indeed, much information on both medieval and indigenous cities has been drawn from his works.

Let us examine some of the landscape characteristics of the indigenous city. Street patterns are narrow and winding, being built for cart and foot traffic, and also expressing the slow, unplanned development of the city through time. Land use is mixed, particularly when compared to the colonial and emerging city. Residences and workplaces generally occupy the same one- or two-story structures, often with the shop closest to the street and residences either in back rooms or on the upper floor.

Like the medieval city, there is some occupational and ethnic clustering. All silver merchants might be found on one street, gold workers on another. But many activities do not have permanent locations. We call these **floating activities;** goods are sold from pushcarts plying the streets, or from a regular spot on the marketplace. (Another less fortunate floating activity is common in contemporary emerging cities: the thousands of homeless urban dwellers living on the streets. The street people in modern Calcutta are legendary.)

Ethnic groups may dominate certain areas. Sometimes this is formalized into "quarters" that form semiautonomous villages within the city. For example, it was common in an Islamic city to have one quarter for Jews, another for Christians. Foreign traders and merchants were also usually restricted to certain areas of the city.

The central part of the city is dominated by the marketplace or bazaar, religious buildings, monuments, government buildings, and the homes of the elite. As a consequence, the city demonstrates a much higher density in the center than on the outer edges. As one moves away from the core, one generally finds decreasing wealth and social status. The disadvantaged are found close to the city's edges. Groups of recent urban migrants might be found there, or neighborhoods of unassimilated ethnic groups.

This model of the city's social structure, with the elite at the center and the disadvantaged on the outskirts, is usually referred to as the **preindustrial model,** because it was first generalized and presented in Sjoberg's works. This scheme describes not only non-Western indigenous cities, but also North American urban social patterns up until the time that the railroad and electric streetcar facilitated suburbanization in the second half of the nineteenth century.

Few cities today would fit the indigenous model. Most were profoundly altered by European colonialism, so let us now turn to a model of colonial cities.

The colonial city

A colonial city, by definition, is an administrative and commercial outpost for an external power. As we look at the landscape of the colonial city, we will see expressions of these two functions. Another important characteristic is the separation of colonial and indigenous activities.

When colonial cities were built near indigenous cities, the Europeans would either weld their city onto the existing settlement or, in a few extreme cases, build a totally new city nearby. The British built New Delhi across from original Delhi, and today the two still illustrate the contrast between colonial and indigenous cities. In old Delhi, gross density is 213 persons per acre; in New Delhi, 13 persons per acre. This results from the very difficult urban morphology. New Delhi has wide streets, gardens surround the spacious houses of administrative staff, and parks and squares ring government buildings. All of this reminds one of the baroque period in Western urban development. And well it should. Remember that much European colonialism was coincidental with the baroque era, therefore, it is not surprising that colonial cities express these planning ideas.

As the baroque was used in Europe to express the power of the elite, so it was used in colonial cities. Grandiose boulevards were often cut through native residential quarters, large monumental buildings demonstrated the presence of the new power structure, and the Europeans were housed in elaborate residences that constantly reminded locals of their new masters. Architecture and urban planning have long been used by power structures to reinforce their status and control.

When new colonial cities were founded, they were often based on a standardized plan. For example, all Spanish cities in the New World were constructed according to the Laws of the Indies, drafted in 1573. The document explicitly outlined how colonial cities were to be constructed. Law 114, quoted in Vance, *This Scene of Man,* stated:

> From the plaza the four principal streets are to diverge, one from the middle of each of its sides and two streets are to meet at each of its corners. The four corners of the plaza are to face the four (cardinal) points of the compass, because thus the streets diverging from the plaza will not be directly exposed to the four principal winds, which would cause much inconvenience.

The Laws go on to say that this gridiron street plan should be centered on a church and central plaza and that all individual lots should be walled. Smaller plazas were to dot the neighborhoods, occupied by parish churches or monasteries, so that religious teaching would be evenly spread across the new city. In many ways, the formal guidelines for Spanish colonial cities duplicate the planning rules used by the Romans.

France and England also used the gridiron street plan as the basis for many of their colonial cities. It is found in former colonial towns across both Africa and Asia. Remember also that the United States spread colonial towns across the country during the westward movement. As in other colonial cities, the rectangular gridiron plan was often used, demonstrating that a simple, orderly street plan, fitting for the military, which so often initiated early colonial settlement, could be easily extended and was extremely effective for colonial town planning.

Another important characteristic of the colonial city is that the landscape expresses a greater degree of functional zonation than precolonial indigenous cities. Unlike the earlier city, colonial settlements would have distinct districts dominated by one particular land use. A commercial district would have warehouses, docks, and small factories; the administrative section would have government buildings, the governor's mansion, banks, insurance firms, and monuments. Very often a retail district would grow close to the colonial residential area, complete with shops and stores. This would be quite different from the mosaic of land uses found in the indigenous city, where the marketplace, the carts, and the dispersed houses of the merchants served local retail needs.

In summation, several themes make up the colonial city model. First, if a colonial city was built close to an existing city, the two would be very different in form and function. This difference is not just physical; the cities would be socially separate as well. Colonialism, after all, is by definition a power structure controlling another culture, so this class distinction would pervade all aspects of the city. An extreme contemporary example might be Capetown, South Africa, which, through the policy of apartheid, continues a colonial tradition. Secondly, colonial cities were often built to a standardized plan and frequently used the gridiron street pattern. Lastly, the colonial city demonstrated much more functional zonation than did indigenous cities. This resulted both from the administrative and commercial goals of the city and from the social distance between native and colonial cultures.

The emerging city

With the end of colonialism and the movement toward political and economic independence, non-Western countries entered a period of rapid, sometimes tumultuous, change. Cities have often been the focal point of change. Millions of people have migrated to cities in search of a better life. Economic activities clustered in and around cities have often changed their orientation from external to local markets. As well, political and social unrest has been centered in the cities. So the emerging city model is a fluid one; it is still in the process of forming, and the end results cannot be known.

Some scholars think that non-Western cities will duplicate the changes experienced by Western cities as the latter underwent industrialization. Though there are similarities, the differences are much greater. William Hance has written on the differences between contemporary African urbanization and that experienced earlier in Europe, and most of his conclusions can be extended beyond Africa to include emerging cities in Asia and Latin America.

First, Hance notes that population growth is more rapid in African cities than it was in Europe. This results not only from a high natural increase, but mainly from an extremely high rate of migration to the cities. And although the people flock to the cities in search of jobs, Hance points out that there is less of a correlation between economic growth and urbanization than there was in Europe. Cities increase in size not because there are jobs to lure workers, but rather because conditions in the countryside are so bad. People leave in hopes that urban life will offer a slight improvement. This results in high urban unemployment. Often 25 percent of the labor force is without work. In Europe during the nineteenth century, workers could migrate to the New World to find work or land. No such safety valve exists today in the emerging countries. The city is the last hope.

Hance goes on to point out that emerging cities have weaker ties with their domestic hinterlands than did European cities. They are dependent on the outside world for raw materials. This means that the local countryside is excluded from the kind of development that could offer employment to rural populations. A vicious circle must be broken: people will leave the countryside for cities until jobs are available; yet it will be difficult to develop rural employment as long as economic activities continue to cluster around cities.

The combination of high numbers of immigrants coupled with widespread unemployment leads to overwhelming pressure for low-rent housing. Governments have rarely been able to meet these needs through housing projects, so one of the most common folk solutions has been construction of illegal housing or squatter settlements. In Lima, Peru, the *barriadas* house fully a quarter of the urban population; in Caracas, Venezuela, about 35 percent. Similar figures are found in emerging cities in Africa and Asia (see Figure 10-15).

These squatter settlements usually begin as collections of crude shacks constructed from scrap materials, and gradually they become increasingly elaborate and permanent. Paths and walkways link houses, vegetable gardens spring up, and often water and electricity are bootlegged into the area so that a common tap or outlet serves a number of houses. At later stages, economic activities such as handicrafts or small-scale artisan activities take place in the squatter settlement.

Governments treat squatter settlements in various ways. Some bulldoze them down periodically, not simply because they are illegal, but also to discourage migration to the city. Their reasoning is that if squatter settlements are destroyed, fewer migrants will come to the city, knowing that any housing solution they find will only be temporary. On the other hand, some city governments turn their backs on the squatter settlements, viewing them as satisfactory solutions to the problem of low-cost urban housing. Zambia has what is called a "site and service" scheme where a settlement is laid out and prospective residents are given about $50 in order to buy basic materials needed for a crude house. Usually this includes concrete for the floor and a corrugated iron roof. After that, the occupants are on their own. The government knows that housing will be improved as the dweller finds work and has a regular paycheck.

Regardless of official policy, be it to destroy or condone, squatter settlements are an important part of the emerging city landscape. They occupy vacant land both on the outskirts and in the city center. Parks are often taken over. More frequently they spread over formerly unwanted land, such as steep slopes and river banks.

The outskirts of the growing cities manifest activities other than squatter settlement. This is often where new economic activities are located, so a landscape of factories and warehouses is common. When government money is available, large high-rise apartment houses are built nearby for workers. There are also signs of middle-class suburbs growing up, which is a function both of jobs in the outlying area for white-collar workers and of "push" forces driving the affluent out of the city center. Traffic noise, air pollution, and congestion make the central city less desirable than before, so those who can afford new housing often relocate. This is obviously similar to the suburbanization of North American cities in the last decades.

Another parallel with the American experience is that the large central-city dwellings vacated by the middle class are often subdivided into smaller apartments for lower-income families. Where previously one middle-class family lived, the dwelling may now house six or seven families. Whether this structural change will eventually lead to the social disparity and ghetto pattern characteristic of North American cities remains to be seen.

It must be emphasized once again that it is dangerous to assume that non-Western emerging cities will replicate the Western urban experience. Although we have noted some similarities with North American cities, the differences must also be kept in mind. As an example, many emerging cities will not undergo the same evolution of transportation systems found in Europe or America. They may evolve directly from foot and cart traffic systems to autos and trucks, skipping the electric streetcar and railroad period so important in molding the Western urban pattern.

Let us also appreciate how different national policies may affect emerging cities. China, for example, has been one of the few countries to contain urban growth. In 1963, China's leaders decided to stabilize the urban population. By requiring young people to locate in the countryside, they created massive changes in the population distribution. It is estimated that by 1973, some 25 million people were permanently resettled in rural villages. This kind of planning can be effected only with a strong autocratic government; yet we must remember that many of the emerging countries are experimenting with socialistic or communistic institutions, and therefore they may have the power to force strong policies upon their population. Decisions regarding the nature and location of economic activities can also dramatically affect a country's urban pattern.

So, in conclusion, the future of the emerging city is unclear (see box, "Calcutta: Portrait of an Emerging City"). Certainly the urban problems faced in non-Western countries are some of the most important facing the world. Some solutions may come from the Western experience; most will not. They will be local solutions, designed to meet specific needs; and

CALCUTTA: PORTRAIT OF AN EMERGING CITY

Although all cities are unique in their own ways, Calcutta illustrates many of the problems faced by hundreds of emerging cities around the globe. Thousands of migrants pour into Calcutta each day, leading to overburdened services, scarce housing, and high unemployment—in short, an overcrowded city.

Calcutta is India's largest urban center, with some 8 million people crowded into an area that sees population densities climbing to 177,000 people per square mile in the city center. This is three times the density of central Manhattan. United Nation estimates forecast that population will top 12 million by 1983.

Three-quarters of the city's population live in crowded tenements or *bustees*. These are mostly built of unbaked brick and lack adequate sanitary services. It is reported that generally 30 persons must share one water tap and that 20 share a single latrine. More than half of the city's families share one-room accommodations. But they are the lucky ones: estimates on the homeless run well over half a million. These are the people who sleep on the city streets.

A recent study shows that 30 percent of the working force is unemployed. However we can assume the figure to be much higher among the young, new migrants, and certain ethnic groups. As in many third-world cities, scarce economic resources aggravate tensions between ethnic groups, with the result that certain groups monopolize specific sectors of the economy, while others do without. For example, lower-class Moslems have been traditionally employed in soap and leather industries, work regarded by Hindus as polluting therefore reserved for low-status people. Ethnic and kinship networks are tightly drawn so that group members share resources and exclude nonmembers. This is a typical pattern found in other emerging cities where the social fabric is made up of different ethnic and social groups.

What about Calcutta's future? It is difficult to be optimistic. City planners, working hand in hand with technical agencies of the United Nations, have constructed a two-tier plan. The first phase focuses on the immediate needs of the city, such as sewage, water, housing, and transportation. The second phase looks at the future of the city in the broad context of its hinterland and assumes responsibility for planning over a resource region encompassing some 500,000 square miles of the country. Ideally, such broad planning can control the flow of migrants by offering economic alternatives to city life. If Calcutta's growth can be slowed, then perhaps the city's services can be expanded to serve the existing population.

therefore it is faulty to assume that non-Western cities will follow Western urban patterns. A totally new and unique urban landscape may emerge.

The Ecology of Urban Location

The theme of cultural ecology is useful in understanding locational aspects of cities by examining how cultures have used and modified the physical environment during urban development. We should appreciate that interaction with the environment is a two-way street: humans may respond to different physical characteristics; yet, equally, humans may modify those characteristics to suit their needs.

Site and situation

There are two components of urban location, **site** and **situation.** Site refers to the local setting of a city, whereas the situation is the regional setting. Both are dynamic and change through time. This can result from changes in the physical environment, or, more commonly, from changes in cultural capabilities. To illustrate, think of San Francisco. The original site of the Mexican settlement was on a shallow cove on the eastern or inland shore of a peninsula. The importance of its situation, or regional location, was that it drew upon water-borne traffic coming across the bay from other, smaller settlements. Hence the town could act as a transshipment point. Hides and tallows were loaded onto deep-water clippers plying world trade routes.

But, through time, both the site and the situation of the city have changed. During the frantic Gold Rush activity, the small cove was filled to create flatland for warehouses and to facilitate stretching wharves into deeper bay waters. The filled-in cove is now occupied by the heart of the central business district (see Figure 10-18). The situation has also changed as patterns of trade and transportation technology have evolved. The original transbay situation was quickly replaced during the Gold Rush by the city's role in supplying the mines and settlements of the gold country. Access to the two major rivers leading to the mines, plus continued access to ocean trade routes, were the important components of the city's situation.

However, the situation has changed dramatically in the last decade. San Francisco is no longer the major port on the bay. The change in technology to containerized cargo was adopted more quickly by Oakland, the rival city on the opposite side of the bay, resulting in San Francisco's decline as a port city. One of the reasons that Oakland was able to adjust to containerized cargo was that it filled in huge tracts of shallow baylands, creating a massive area for the loading, unloading, and storage of cargo containers. This once again illustrates how urban sites and situations are continually changing.

Certain attributes of the physical environment have been important in the location of cities. Those cities with distinct functions, like defense, have sought out specific physical characteristics in their original siting. The location of many contemporary cities can be partially explained by decisions made in the past that capitalized on advantages of certain sites. Trade and defense needs have been particularly important. The following classification examines some of the different location possibilities.

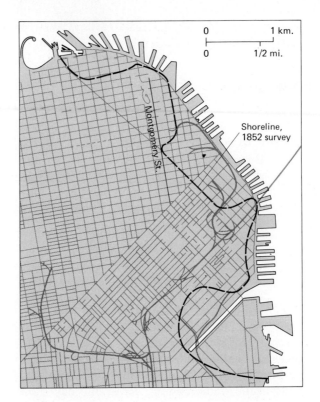

FIGURE 10-18
San Francisco's financial district was once located on the waterfront. Although the shoreline of the city has changed, the financial institutions remain on Montgomery Street.

Defensive sites

There are many types of **defensive sites** (some are diagramed in Figure 10-19). The river-meander site, with the city located inside a loop where the stream turns back on itself, leaves only a narrow neck of land unprotected by the waters. Cities as widely separated as Bern, Switzerland, and New Orleans are situated inside river meanders. Indeed, the nickname for New Orleans, Crescent City, refers to the curve of the Mississippi River.

Even more advantageous was the river-island site, which often combined a natural moat with an easier river crossing, because the stream was split into two parts. Paris began as a small settlement on the Ile de la Cité, or "island of the city," in the middle of the Seine River (see Figure 10-20). Similarly, Montreal is situated on a large island surrounded by the St. Lawrence River and other water channels. Islands lying off the seashore or in lakes offered similar defensive advantages. Mexico City began as an Indian settlement on a lake island. Venice is the classic example of a city built on an offshore island in the sea. New York City began as a small Dutch town on Manhattan Island.

Peninsular sites were almost as advantageous as island sites, because they offered natural water defenses on all but one side. Boston was founded on a peninsula for this reason, and a wooden palisade wall was built across the neck of the peninsula. Bombay is also built on a peninsula.

Danger of attack from the sea often prompted sheltered-harbor urban sites, where a narrow entrance to the harbor could easily be defended. Examples of sheltered-harbor cities include Rio de Janeiro, Tokyo, and San Francisco.

High points also were sought out. These are often referred to as

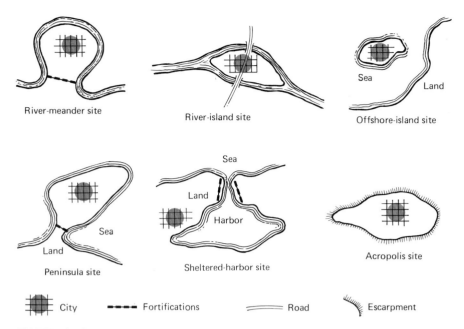

River-meander site

River-island site

Sea
Land

Offshore-island site

Peninsula site

Sea
Land

Sea
Land
Harbor

Sheltered-harbor site

Acropolis site

City   - - - - Fortifications   ══════ Road   Escarpment

FIGURE 10-19
Defensive city sites make use of the natural protection offered by physical features such as water or hills. Can you find a place in your area that might have made a good defensive site for a small town?

FIGURE 10-20
The city of Paris originated on an island in the Seine River. A Celtic tribe occupied the island before the Romans. The Romans placed their temple on the island and later, in the Dark Ages, it became the site of a Christian church. The island is still the heart of present-day Paris, being the site of Notre Dame Cathedral and numerous government buildings, as well as high-rent residences.

LE PLAN DE LA VILLE, CITE, VNIVERSITE FAVXBOVRGS DE PARIS AVEC LA DESCRIPTION DE SON ANTIQVITE

acropolis sites, meaning "high city." Originally the city developed around a fortification on the high ground and then spilled out over the surrounding lowland. Athens is the prototype of acropolis sites, but many other cities are similarly situated. Québec and Salzburg, Austria, occupy acropolis sites.

Trade-route sites

In many other instances, defense was not a prime consideration. Urban sites were frequently chosen because they lay at important points on trade routes. Here, too, the influence of the physical environment can be detected (Figure 10-21).

Especially common types of **trade-route sites** (see Figure 10-22) are bridge-point and river-ford sites, places where major land routes could easily cross over rivers. Typically, these were sites where streams were narrow with firm banks or shallow with firm beds. Occasionally, such cities even bear in their names the evidence of their sites, as in Frankfurt ("ford of the Franks"), West Germany, and Oxford, England. The site for London was chosen because it is the lowest point on the Thames River where a bridge, the famous London Bridge, could easily be built to serve a trade route running inland from Dover on the sea.

Confluence sites are also common. They allow cities to be situated at the point where two navigable streams flow together. Pittsburgh, at the confluence of the Allegheny and Monongahela rivers, is a fine example. So is St. Louis, near the confluence of the Mississippi and Missouri rivers. Head-of-navigation sites, where navigable water routes begin, are even more common, because goods must be transshipped at such points.

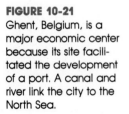

FIGURE 10-21
Ghent, Belgium, is a major economic center because its site facilitated the development of a port. A canal and river link the city to the North Sea.

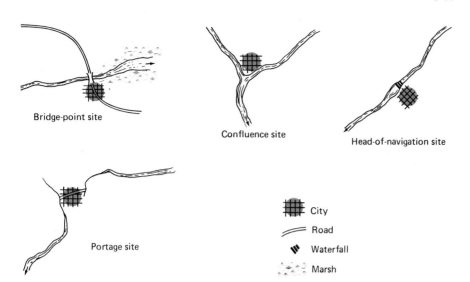

Bridge-point site

Confluence site

Head-of-navigation site

Portage site

City
Road
Waterfall
Marsh

FIGURE 10-22
Trade-route city sites are at strategic positions along transportation arteries. Is your city located on a trade-route site?

Minneapolis-St. Paul, at the falls of the Mississippi River, occupies a head-of-navigation site. Basel, Switzerland, is on the Rhine River, and Louisville, Kentucky, is at the rapids of the Ohio River. Portage sites are very similar. Here, goods were portaged from one river to another. Moscow is on a portage site where the headwaters of streams flowing north and south are close. Similarly, Chicago is near a short portage between the Great Lakes and the Mississippi River drainage basin.

In these ways and others, an urban site can be influenced by the physical environment. There are, of course, many nonenvironmental factors that can influence the choice of site.

At this point, it is useful to distinguish between the specific urban site and the general location or **spatial distribution** of cities. Spacing or location implies a broader, overall view of the pattern of urban centers. Site is frequently influenced by the environment, but general location or spacing of cities is less likely to be. The theme of cultural integration will allow us to gain a better idea of why cities are spaced as they are.

Cultural Integration in Urban Geography

In recent decades, urban geographers have paid considerable attention to the distribution or spacing of towns and cities in order to determine some of the economic and political factors that influence the pattern of cities. In doing so, they have created a number of models that collectively make up "central-place" theory. These models represent a fine example of cultural integration.

Most urban centers are engaged mainly in the third, or **tertiary,** stage of production. Primary economic activities are agriculture, forestry, and mining. Construction and manufacturing are secondary activities. The tertiary activities of urban centers are to facilitate the distribution of manufactured goods to the people living in their vicinity and to provide political, medical, educational, transportational, communicational, and other services for consumers. Towns and cities that support such tertiary activities are called **central places.**

WALTER CHRISTALLER   1893-1969

Christaller said that as a child in Germany his favorite plaything was an atlas, yet it was not until he was nearly forty years of age that he resumed his study of geography at a university. Christaller became a "maverick" among the geographers in Germany. His ideas on models were too radical for most of his fellow geographers in Nazi Germany to accept. As a result, he was never offered a professorship. Christaller's classic work, *The Central Places of Southern Germany*, was written in the early 1930s as his doctoral dissertation in geography. In it, he proposed the central-place theory described in this chapter. Acceptance of central-place theory came belatedly, among American and Swedish geographers. Only in his later years did Christaller receive the honors due him.

In the early 1930s, the German geographer Walter Christaller (see biographical sketch) first formulated **central-place theory,** a series of models designed to explain the spatial distribution of tertiary urban centers. Crucial to his theory is the fact that different goods and services vary both in **range,** the average maximum distance people will travel to purchase a good or service, and in **threshold,** the size of the population required to make provision of the service economically feasible. For example, it requires a larger number of people to support a hospital, university, or department store than to support a gasoline station, post office, or grocery store. Similarly, consumers are willing to travel a greater distance to consult a heart specialist, record a land title, or purchase an automobile than to buy a loaf of bread, mail a letter, or visit a movie theater. People will normally spend as little time and effort as possible in making use of services and purchasing goods in a central place, but they will be obliged to travel farther to use those services that require a large market.

Because the range of central goods and services varies, tertiary centers are arranged in an orderly hierarchy. Some central places are small and offer a limited variety of services and goods; others are large and offer an abundance. At the top of this hierarchy are regional metropolises, huge urban centers that offer all services associated with central places and that have very large tributary areas, or **hinterlands.** At the opposite extreme are small market villages and roadside hamlets, which may contain nothing more than a post office, service station, or café. Between these two extremes are central places of various degrees of importance. Each higher rank of central place provides all the goods and services available at lower-ranked centers plus one or more additional goods and services. Central places of lower rank greatly outnumber the few at the higher levels of the hierarchy. One regional metropolis may contain thousands of smaller central places in its tributary market area (see Figure 10-23). The size of the market area is determined by the distance range of the goods and services it offers.

With this hierarchy as a background, Christaller then tried to measure the influence of three forces in determining the spacing and distribution of tertiary centers. He accomplished this by creating models. His first model measured the influence of market and range of goods on the spacing of cities. To simplify the model, he assumed that the terrain, soils, and other environmental factors were uniform; that transportation was universally available; and that all regions would be supplied with goods and services from the minimum number of central places. In such a model, the shape of a market area was circular, encompassing the range of goods and services, with the city at the center of the circle. However, when central places of the same rank in the hierarchy were nearby, the circle became a hexagon (see Figure 10-24a). If market and range of goods were the only causal forces, the distribution of tertiary towns and cities would produce a pattern of interlocking hexagons, each with a central place at its center.

Then Christaller created a second model. In this model, he tried to measure the influence of transportation on the spacing of central places. He no longer assumed that transportation was universally and equally available in the hinterland. Instead, Christaller assumed that as many demands for transport as possible would be met with the minimum expenditure for construction and maintenance of transportation facilities. As many high-ranking central places as possible would thus be on

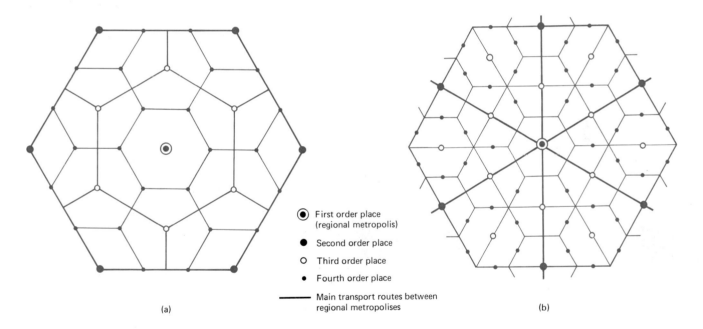

○ First order place
  (regional metropolis)
● Second order place
○ Third order place
· Fourth order place

FIGURE 10-23

Christaller's hierarchy of central places shows the orderly arrangement of towns of different size. This model is an idealized presentation of places performing central functions. For each large central place many smaller central places are located within the larger place's hinterland.

straight-line routes between important central places (see Figure 10-24b). The transportation factor causes a rather different pattern of central places from the pattern caused by the market factor. This is because direct routes between adjacent regional metropolises do not pass through central places of the next lowest rank. As a result, these second-rank central places are "pulled" from the points of the hexagonal market area to the

○ First order place
  (regional metropolis)
● Second order place
○ Third order place
· Fourth order place
— Main transport routes between
  regional metropolises

(a)

(b)

FIGURE 10-24a

The influence of market area on Christaller's arrangement of central places is shown in this diagram. If marketing were the only factor controlling the distribution of central places, this diagram would represent the arrangement of towns and cities. Why, in this model, would hexagons be the shape to appear as opposed to a square, circle, or some other shape? (After Christaller, p. 66, by permission of the publisher.)

FIGURE 10-24b

This diagram shows the distribution of central places according to Christaller's model. If the availability of transportation is the determining factor in the location of central places, their distribution will be different than if marketing were the determining factor. Note that the second-order central places are pulled away from the apexes of the hexagon and become located on the main transport routes between regional metropolises. (After Christaller.)

midpoints in order to be on the straight-line routes between adjacent regional metropolises.

Christaller felt that the market factor would be the greater force in rural countries, where goods were seldom shipped throughout a region, and that the transportation factor would be stronger in densely settled industrialized countries, where there were greater numbers of central places and more demand for long-distance transportation.

A third model devised by Christaller measured a type of political influence, the effect of political borders on the distribution of central places. Christaller recognized that political boundaries, especially within independent countries, would tend to follow the hexagonal market-area limits of each central place that was a political center. He also recognized that such borders tend to separate people and retard the movement of goods and services. Such borders necessarily cut through the market areas of many central places below the rank of regional metropolis. Central places in such border regions lose rank and size because their market areas are politically cut in two. Border towns are thus "stunted," and important central places are pushed away from the border, which distorts the hexagonal pattern.

Obviously, many other forces influence the spatial distribution of central places. Market area, transportation, and political borders are but three of them. For example, in all three of these models, the physical environment is assumed to be uniform. Of course, it is not. But the actual distribution of central places shows how important these factors are.

Conclusion

The first cities arose as new technologies—particularly the domestication of plants and animals—facilitated the concentration of people, wealth, and power in a few specific places. This transformation from village to city life was accompanied by new social organizations, a greater division of labor, and increased social stratification. These characteristics still distinguish rural and urban lifestyles. Although the first cities developed in specific places, urban life has now been diffused worldwide and all suggestions are that our planet will become increasingly urban in the decades to come. Therefore an understanding of the city and its problems is crucial to understanding the human mosaic.

Many of the problems now plaguing the Western city are expressions of uncorrected ills from the past. Circulation and housing problems in Europe, for example, must often be understood in the context of the medieval urban landscape, for even though the landscape evolved 500 years ago, the narrow streets and cramped housing conditions of that period still pervade the typical European central city. Understanding the past is definitely necessary for correcting current problems.

This is also true of the North American city. Much of our urban environment evolved only during the last 200 years, when industrialism was the dominant force; yet this has in no way given us immunity from urban ills. Problems of land use, housing, transportation, and social services often trace their origins from the past century, and it is wise to attempt to understand the forces resonsible for their rise before we attempt solutions that may be unrelated to the true cause.

On the other hand, the problems of non-Western cities are mainly products of this century. Cities are bursting at the seams as thousands of new migrants crowd into urban places each day, seeking houses, jobs, and schooling. But jobs are scarce, so unemployment rates are often over 25 percent. Housing is also a problem. In some cities, over a third of the population lives in hastily constructed squatter settlements.

The future of the world's cities is unsure. Strong governmental planning measures might alleviate many of the present-day ills, but the long-range hope lies with decreased population growth and increased economic opportunities. Whether this is possible or not under contemporary conditions remains to be seen.

This chapter has examined the city at a broad-brush, worldwide level; the next chapter will look at cultural patterns within the city.

Glossary

Acropolis the fortified zone of an ancient Greek city, containing the temples, storehouse, and seat of the power structure.

Agglomeration the clustering of economic activities in urban areas, to share market, labor, transportation costs, and utility costs.

Agora the social gathering place in the ancient Greek city, used for public meetings, education, social activity, judicial matters, and marketing.

Central place a town or city engaged primarily in the tertiary stage of production; a regional center.

Central-place theory a set of models designed to explain the spatial distribution of tertiary urban centers.

Colonial city a city founded by colonialism, or an indigenous city whose structure was deeply influenced by Western colonialism.

Decentralization the movement of households, business, and industry away from the central city.

Defensive site an easily defended place to locate a city.

Division of labor a social system that divides work into specialized occupations for people within the society.

Domestication the taming and selective breeding of animals and the cultivation and selective breeding of plants by humans.

Emerging city a city of a current developing or emerging country.

Floating activities those not tied to a specific location.

Forum the public place at the intersection of two major roads in an ancient Roman city, combining the functions of the Greek agora and acropolis.

Functional zonation the division of the city into different areas for different functions, such as industry and housing.

Gentrification replacement of lower-income groups by higher-income people as buildings are restored.

Hinterland the area surrounding a city and influenced by it.

Hydraulic civilization one based on large-scale irrigation.

Indigenous city a city formed by local forces.

Laissez-faire utilitarianism the belief that economic competition without government interference produces the most public good.

Megalopolis a large urban region formed as several urban areas spread and merge, such as Boswash, the region including Boston, New York, and Washington, D.C.

Preindustrial model a city scheme that places the highest status groups in the city center: group status lessens towards the periphery.

Primate city a city of large size and dominant power.

Range in central-place theory, the average maximum distance people will travel to purchase a good or service.

Site the local setting of a city.

Situation the regional setting of a city.

Spatial distribution the general pattern of location, as opposed to specific sites.

Tertiary production economic activities concerned with the provision of services, such as product distribution, medicine, education, government, transportation, and communication.

Threshold the population required to make provision of services economically feasible.

Trade-route site a place for a city that is at a significant point on transportation routes.

Urban hearth areas the five regions—Mesopotamia, the Nile Valley, Pakistan's Indus Valley, China's Yellow

River area, and Mesoamerica—where the world's first cities evolved.

Urbanized population   the proportion of a country's population living in cities.

Urban morphology   the form and structure of cities, including street patterns and the size and shape of buildings.

Urban transformation   the change from rural to urban life.

Ziggurat   in ancient Mesopotamia, a temple shaped as a tall pyramidal tower.

Suggested Readings

Brian J. Berry. *The Human Consequences of Urbanization.* New York: St. Martin's Press, 1973.

Terry Christensen. *Neighborhood Survival: The Struggle for Covent Garden.* London: Prism, 1979.

Gerald Breese (ed.). *The City in Newly Developing Countries.* Englewood Cliffs, N.J.: Prentice-Hall, 1969.

Walter Christaller. *The Central Places of Southern Germany,* trans. C. W. Baskin, Englewood Cliffs, N.J.: Prentice-Hall, 1966.

Kingsley Davis. *Cities: Their Origin, Growth and Human Impact.* San Francisco: Freeman, 1973.

Thomas Detwyler and Melvin Marcus (eds.). *Urbanization and Environment: The Physical Geography of the City.* Belmont, Ca.: Duxbury Press, 1972.

Robert Dickinson. *The West European City.* London: Routledge and Kegan Paul, 1961.

Arthur Field (ed.). *City and Country in the Third World.* Cambridge, Mass.: Schenkman, 1970.

Larry Ford. "Saving the Cities: Urban Preservation in America," *Focus,* 30 (1979).

Jean Gottmann. *Megalopolis.* Cambridge, Mass.: M.I.T. Press, 1961.

Erwin A. Gutkind. *International History of City Development.* 4 vols. New York: Free Press, 1964-1969.

William Hance. *Population, Migration, and Urbanization in Africa.* New York: Columbia University Press, 1970.

Jorge Hardoy (ed.). *Urbanization in Latin America: Approaches and Issues.* Garden City, N.Y.: Doubleday (Anchor Books), 1975.

Arnold S. Linsky. "Some Generalizations Concerning Primate Cities," *Annals, Association of American Geographers,* 55 (1965), 506–513.

William Mangin. "Squatter Settlements," *Scientific American,* (1967), 21–29.

Lewis Mumford. *The City in History.* New York: Harcourt Brace Jovanovich, 1961.

John Palen. *The Urban World.* New York: McGraw-Hill, 1975.

John Pfeiffer. *The Emergence of Society.* New York: McGraw-Hill, 1977.

Henri Pirenne. *Medieval Cities.* Garden City, N.Y.: Doubleday (Anchor Books), 1956.

Charles Redman. *The Rise of Civilization.* San Francisco: Freeman, 1978.

Lester Rowntree and Margaret Conkey. "Symbolism and the Cultural Landscape," *Annals, Association of American Geographers,* 70 (1980), 459–474.

Howard Saalman. *Medieval Cities.* New York: Braziller, 1968.

Gideon Sjoberg. *The Preindustrial City.* New York: Free Press, 1960.

James E. Vance, Jr. *This Scene of Man: The Role and Structure of the City in the Geography of Western Civilization.* New York: Harper & Row, 1977.

Sam Bass Warner, Jr. *The Urban Wilderness: A History of the American City.* New York: Harper & Row, 1972.

Chapter-opening photo: The urban mosaic of old and new, of rich and poor, and of residential and commercial shows clearly in this photo of Boston.

The Urban Mosaic

11

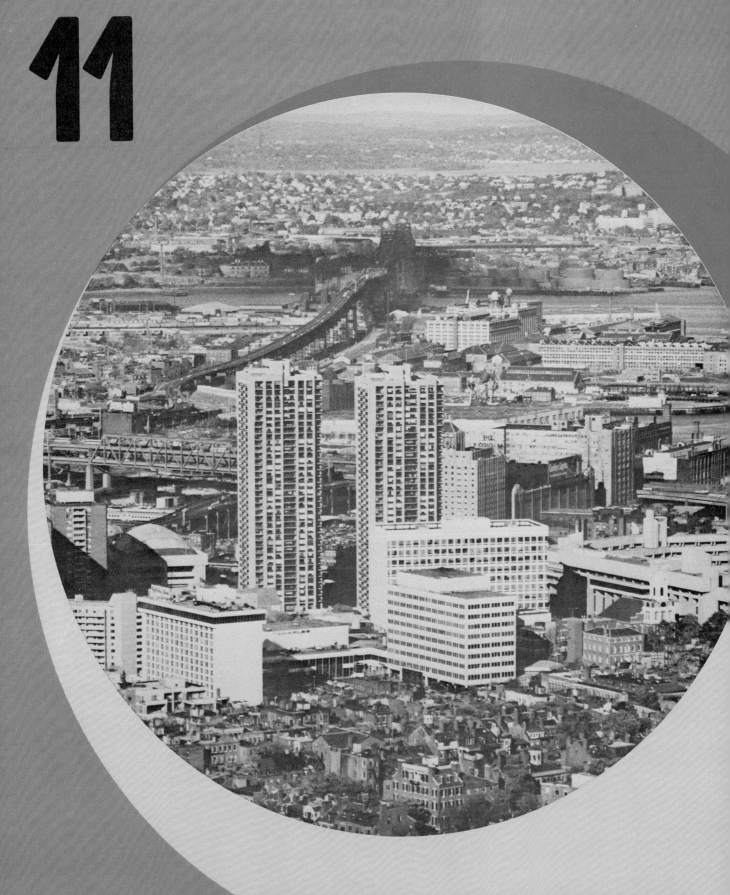

Picking out patterns in your own city is, in some ways, a difficult matter. As you walk or drive through your city, its intricacy may dazzle, and its form may sometimes seem puzzlingly chaotic. It is often hard to imagine why city functions are where they are, why people cluster where they do. Why does one block have high-income housing and another, slum tenements? Why is a new factory so near the airport? Why is the black ghetto next to the central business district? Why does the highway run through one neighborhood and around another? Why does the subway system connect the suburbs to the downtown area but provide no transportation to and from inner-city neighborhoods? And just when you think you are beginning to see some patterns in your city, you may also note that those patterns are swiftly changing. The house you grew up in is now part of the business district. The row of houses across the street from your old grade school has been replaced by a bowling alley, laundromat, high-rise office building, or perhaps a giant parking lot. The central city that you roamed as a child looks dead. A suburban shopping center thrives on what was once rubble-strewn vacant lots. If you go back to visit the Little Italy of your childhood, you may find a thriving soul-food restaurant where the Italian grocery store once stood.

Chapter 10 focused on cities as points in geographic space. The goal of this chapter is geographically quite different. We will try to orient ourselves within cities to gain some perspective on the patterns in them. In other terms, the two chapters differ in scale. The earlier chapter let us see cities from afar, as small dots diffusing across space and interacting with one another and with their environment. In this chapter, we will study the city as if we were walking its streets.

Our tour guides in this close-up view of the city will be five familiar themes of cultural geography. Through culture region, we will examine spatial differences within cities. Cultural diffusion will show how these internal and regional differences develop. Cultural ecology will permit us to see the role of the physical environment within the structure of the city. And through cultural integration, we will see what a finely woven fabric the city really is. Of course, the visual impact of these elements is revealed in the urban landscape, a "townscape" perceived in different ways by different people.

Urban Culture Regions

Like society, the city is composed of many different groups. And just as people of similar interests seek one another out for conversation, people of like mind and like circumstances tend to cluster together in neighborhoods. Consequently, the theme of culture regions can be applied to those parts of the city where people live who share similar traits—such as values, income, language, religion, or race. Most city dwellers are intuitively aware of these urban culture regions. Visual clues—such as size and condition of housing, dress styles, or kinds of cars on a street—help categorize some areas as high-income, others as slums, some as Polish neighborhoods, others as Chinese.

Looking at these urban regions, the cultural geographer seeks answers to such questions as: Why do people of similar values cluster together? How can urban culture regions be defined? What patterns are apparent within culture regions?

Social areas

To begin answering these questions, we should distinguish between **social culture regions** and **ethnic culture regions.** In a social area, people share such social traits as income, education, and stage of life. An ethnic area is shared by people of similar ethnic background, who share race or language. An example of a social area would be an upper-income neighborhood. An example of an ethnic area is a Chicano neighborhood. Material on ethnic regions is found in Chapter 9.

One way to define social areas is to isolate one social trait and plot its distribution. The United States census is a common source of such information because the districts used to count population, called **census tracts,** are small enough to allow the subtle texture of social areas to show. For example, Figure 11-1 shows the rough distribution of income in Berkeley, California. Census tracts with similar average incomes have been lumped together, showing areas of high, middle, and low income. These areas, in a crude way, correspond to the social stratification of the city. High-income areas are mostly in the hilly area to the east, where whites dominate. Lower-income areas are on the flatlands, closer to the bayfront industrial areas, and are made up of students and minorities. Similar mapping could be done with other social traits taken from the census, such as age, education, or percentage of families below poverty level. A visual field check is often a simple first step in mapping social areas (see Figures 11-2 and 11-3).

Another approach is to correlate various social indicators. For example, politicans have long known that districts with certain demographic characteristics (such as age, income, and occupation) tend to vote certain ways. There might be a correlation between, say, Democratic voting and Catholic working-class neighborhoods. What politicians know from experience, urban analysts try to formalize through statistical studies. They look at the degree of correlation between factors such as income, occupation, age, and ethnicity, and then their results can be translated into a pattern of multiple-factor urban social areas.

But it is easy to misinterpret these results. A statistical correlation between groups exhibiting certain characteristics says nothing about an individual. This misinterpretation is called the **ecological fallacy,** because it surfaced from statistical studies done in the field of human ecology. An illustration of this fallacy follows.

Data from the 1930 census on the percentage of blacks in each state and the percentage of illiterates show a high statistical correlation. One might conclude that a large number of blacks are illiterate. But that is not true. When the data are examined closely, one sees that southern states with the highest number of blacks are also those with the highest number of illiterate whites. Similar misinterpretations can come from correlation studies done comparing urban groups.

Neighborhoods

Social areas are not merely statistical definitions. They are also areas of shared values and attitudes, of interaction and communication. The concept of a **neighborhood** is often used to describe small social and ethnic areas where people with shared values and concerns interact on a daily basis. For example, if we consider only census figures, we might find that parents between thirty and forty-five years of age, with two or three children, and earning between $30,000 and $50,000 a year cover a fairly

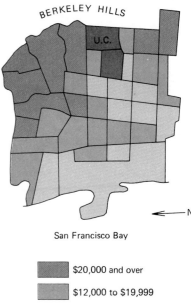

San Francisco Bay

$20,000 and over

$12,000 to $19,999

Under $11,999

FIGURE 11-1
The map shows the high- and low-income areas of Berkeley based on the median family income for each census tract. The areas of highest income are located in the Berkeley-Oakland hills, whereas the areas of lowest income are either directly adjacent to the UC campus on the south or in the flatlands on the west, where low-income housing is mixed with industrial and commercial uses. Students and ethnic minorities dominate the low-income areas and compete for the limited stock of low-rent housing in the city. The upper-income areas are predominantly white families living in newer housing.

FIGURE 11-2
One of the most pressing problems facing the United States is reversing the continued decay of inner cities. This is the South Bronx.

FIGURE 11-3
Social areas within the city can be delimited by certain traits taken from the census, such as income, education, or family size. How would the social characteristics of this neighborhood differ from those in Figure 11-2?

wide area in any given city. Yet, from our own observations, we know that this broad social area is probably composed of smaller units of interaction —areas where people gather for social events, where they know they can find friends or advice. These units would be neighborhoods.

People of similar values cluster together in neighborhoods to reduce social conflict. Where neighbors share values about home maintenance, child rearing, and public order, there is little need to worry about these topics from day to day. People can rest secure that their neighbors feel the same way. Any "deviants" will face such social coercion that they will probably choose to live elsewhere. Consequently, some of the minor conflicts of daily life lose their importance in a neighborhood. People can turn their attention to work, home, or broader social issues. Public order is protected by the neighborhood.

People usually choose a place to live with this in mind. Most people seek areas where people like themselves live. If there is a big difference in the backgrounds of neighbors, they must then constantly worry about potential conflict. Perhaps you have seen firsthand the unsettling effect on a neighborhood when a distinctly different family—in income, background, or race—moves in.

In short, a neighborhood is a place where a resident can feel at ease. The importance of living in a congenial neighborhood often overwhelms the disadvantages an area may offer. For instance, a study of Durham and Greensboro, North Carolina, found that when people had to choose between "a very good but inconveniently located neighborhood" and "a less desirable but conveniently located neighborhood," the residents chose the good neighborhood by a three-to-one margin. Even bad housing conditions may not erase from people's minds the benefits of living in a certain neighborhood. One study discovered that, although half of New York City's Puerto Rican immigrants were dissatisfied with their living quarters, only 26 percent were also dissatisfied with their neighborhoods. This also reflects the fact that in urban, rather than suburban, neighborhoods, much living and human interchange take place in the streets and not at home.

In viewing neighborhoods geographically, one warning should be issued. People living in neighborhoods defined by outsiders often do not hold the same definition. The sociologist Herbert J. Gans studied a largely Italian working-class area in Boston known as the West End. By all external criteria—economic, social, and cultural—the West End was a neighborhood. But Gans found that the concept of the West End as a single neighborhood was foreign to the West Enders themselves. Although the area had long been known to outsiders as the West End, the residents themselves divided it up into many subareas. Ironically, only the threat of "redevelopment"—that is, the destruction of the neighborhood—led residents to think of the West End as a single entity (see box, "Boston's West End and Urban Renewal").

Cultural Diffusion in the City

The patterns of activities we see in the city result from thousands of individual decisions made regarding location. Where should we locate our store, in the central city or in the suburbs? Where should we live,

BOSTON'S WEST END AND URBAN RENEWAL

The West End, an aging Boston neighborhood dominated by Italians, was seen by outsiders as a slum. Planners and government officials viewed it as an eyesore contaminating elegant, upper-class Beacon Hill and the downtown shopping area. "Real estate men," according to sociologist Herbert Gans, "had long felt that the area was 'ripe' for higher—and more profitable uses." In the late 1950s, the West End was slated for "urban redevelopment." This meant that the neighborhood's old, low-rent structures would be torn down and a new neighborhood of luxury apartment houses would be built—not, of course, for the West Enders, who would be "relocated" elsewhere.

Planners felt that, in addition to rebuilding the central city, they would be doing a favor to the West Enders by moving them out of a human cesspool. Unfortunately, the West Enders failed to agree. The vast majority of them had no desire to leave their "slum," which they saw as an attractive low-rent community. The day after the government gave the go-ahead signal for redevelopment, one young Italian told Gans: "I wish the world would end tonight . . . I wish they'd tear the whole damn town down, damn scab town . . . I'm going to be lost without the West End. Where the hell can I go?" A typical West Ender comment was: "It isn't right to scatter the community to all four winds. It pulls the heart out of a guy to lose all his friends."

To the West Enders, according to Gans, "the idea that the city could clear the West End, and then turn the land over to a private builder for luxury apartments seemed unbelievable." The average West Ender thought: "The whole thing is a steal, taking the area away from the people, and giving it to some guys who had paid off everyone else. . . . It is just someone making money at our expense."

In fact, the West Enders were not far wrong in defining the social injustice done to them. The financial effort expended on their needs (including relocation) amounted to about 1 percent of the clearance and rebuilding cost for the whole neighborhood. Yet, as Gans points out, "The real cost of relocation . . . was very much higher, and was paid in various ways by the people who had to move. In short, the redevelopment of the West End was economically feasible only because of the hidden subsidies which the residents provided—involuntarily, of course. . . ."

"I was told," Gans adds, "that before the West End was totally cleared—and even afterwards—West Enders would come back on weekends to walk through the old neighborhood and the rubble-strewn streets."

Adapted from Herbert J. Gans. The Urban Villages. Copyright© 1962 by The Free Press of Glencoe, Illinois, a Division of The Macmillan Company.

downtown or outside the city? The end result of such decisions might be expansion at the city's edge or the relocation of activities from one part of the city to another. The cultural geographer looks at such decisions in terms of expansion and relocation diffusion.

To understand the role of diffusion, let us divide the city into two major areas—the inner city and the outer city. Those diffusion forces that result in residences, stores, and factories locating in the inner or central city are **centralizing forces.** Those that result in activities locating outside the central city are called **decentralizing forces.** The pattern of homes, neighborhoods, offices, shops, and factories in the city results from the constant interplay of these two kinds of forces.

Centralization

Examining the advantages of centralization can best be accomplished by breaking them into two categories: economic and social advantages.

Economic advantages. An important economic advantage to central-city location has always been accessibility. For example, imagine that a department store seeks a new location. Its success depends on whether customers can reach the store easily. If its potential market area is viewed as a full circle, then naturally the best location is in the center. There, customers from all parts of the city can gain access with equal ease. Before the automobile, a central-city location was particularly necessary because public transportation—such as the streetcar—was usually focused there. A central location is also important to those who must deliver their goods to customers, because it provides equal transportation time and costs to all the customers. Bakeries and dairies usually located as close as possible to the center of the city so that their daily deliveries would be most efficient.

Location near regional transportation facilities is another aspect of accessibility. Many a North American city grew up with the railroad at its center. Hence, any activity that needed access to the railroad had to locate in the central city. In St. Louis, Chicago, Minneapolis–St. Paul, Buffalo, and other urban areas, giant wholesale and retail manufacturing districts grew up around railroad districts. Thus they became "freight-yard and terminal cities" for the produce of the nation. Today, although these areas have often been abandoned by their original occupants, a walk by the railroad tracks will give the most casual pedestrian a view of the modern "ruins" of the railroad city.

Another major economic advantage of the inner city is agglomeration, or clustering, which results in mutual benefits for businesses. For example, retail stores locate near one another to take advantage of the pedestrian traffic each generates. A large department store generates a good deal of foot traffic, so that any nearby store will also benefit. A number of cities around the world, including Atlanta, Pittsburgh, Montreal, and Munich, have actually closed specific downtown areas to motorized traffic, thereby creating pedestrian malls for downtown strollers and shoppers, hoping to create a pleasant environment that will attract more foot traffic.

Historically, offices have clustered together in the central city because of their need for communication. Remember, the telephone was invented only in 1875. Before that, messengers hand-carried the work of banks, insurance firms, lawyers, and many other services. Clustering was essential for rapid communication. Even today, there is a distinct tendency for office buildings to cluster, because face-to-face communication is still important for the business community. In addition, central offices take advantage of the complicated support system that grows up in a central city and aids everyday efficiency. Printers, bars, restaurants, travel agents, office suppliers, and others must be in easy reach.

Social advantages. Three social factors have traditionally reinforced central-city location: historical momentum, prestige, and the need to locate near work. The strength of historical momentum should not be underestimated. Many activities remain in the central city simply because they began there long ago. For example, the financial district in San Francisco is located mainly on Montgomery Street. This street originally lay along the waterfront. San Francisco's first financial institutions were established there in the Gold Rush of 1849 because it was the center of commercial action. Goods were being shipped from there to the Mother Lode region by river barge, and gold was being brought down by packet. In later years, however, land filling extended the shoreline. Today, the financial district is several blocks from the bay. The financial district that began at wharfhead remained at its original location, even though other activity moved with the changing shoreline.

The prestige associated with the downtown area is also a strong centralizing force. For some activities, it is still necessary to have a central-city address. Think how important it is for some advertising firms to be on New York's Madison Avenue or for a stockbroker to be on Wall Street. This extends to many activities in cities of all sizes. The "downtown lawyer" and the "uptown banker" are examples. Residences have often been located in the central city because of the prestige associated with it. Most cities have remnants of high-income neighborhoods close to the downtown area. Although this trend has weakened in North America —downtown areas have become more congested and noisy, and transportation has encouraged suburban residences—it still is important elsewhere. London and Paris have very prestigious neighborhoods directly in the downtown area. The same is true for Latin American cities, where the power elite have traditionally lived in the city center.

Probably the strongest social force for centralization has been the desire to live near one's employment. Until the development of the electric trolley in the 1880s, there was little alternative for most urban dwellers but to walk to work. This meant that most people had to live near the central city, because most employment was there. Upper-income people had their carriages and cabs, but others had nothing. In his book, *Topophilia,* Yi-fu Tuan notes that in early Victorian London, "pedestrians rather than carriages dominated the street scene. Clerks, tradesmen, and workers thronged the sidewalks on their way to and from work in central London. Some 100,000 people a day, for example, walked over the toll-free London Bridge across the Thames, and about 75,000 over the toll-free Blackfriars Bridge."

The "horsecar," which came along in the 1850s, somewhat reduced central-city residential congestion. It was essentially, a bus drawn along tracks by horses, and it traveled about four miles (six and a half kilometers) in three-quarters of an hour. However, only with the trolley— which covered six to eight miles (nine and a half to thirteen kilometers), with stops, in one-half hour—did the middle class begin its exodus from the inner city. This electric-powered streetcar, first introduced in Richmond, Virginia, in the late 1880s, may have been an early factor in the declining prestige of the downtown area (see Figure 11-4). According to Sam Bass Warner, Jr., the electric streetcar's major failing "was its grinding gears and pounding steel wheels. . . . By raising the sound levels of urban streets to intolerable heights the streetcars drove the rich from their customary conspicuous locations on the city's main thorough-

FIGURE 11-4
This photograph of Oakland in 1916 shows the important role played by the electric streetcar in urban development. The straight avenues radiate out from the downtown and were planned to facilitate subdivision along streetcar lines. Residents could then use the streetcar for access to work and shopping opportunities in the central city while living in a less congested suburban environment.

fares. Quiet isolation became a fundamental amenity in wealthy neighborhoods and the goal of middle-class homeowners."

The working poor had no possibility of escaping the noise. They simply had to accept the unacceptable. They accepted as well the elevated train whose tracks passed over (and through) their neighborhoods, creating a sunless world below. These poor, who still walked to work, were left in inner-city residences. Their residences were often the oldest in the city and consequently the most deteriorated and the cheapest to be found. Thus, as the middle class moved out to the "streetcar suburbs" on the edges of the city, the low-income workers increasingly dominated the inner city. Here began the clear-cut separation of rich and poor that we still see in urban areas today. In North American cities, this exodus of the middle class coincided with a period of great flow of European and Asian workers. Many inner-city areas became the ethnic neighborhoods that were discussed earlier.

Decentralization

Decentralizing forces encourage relocation diffusion, such as the movement of a shop or residence from the downtown to the suburbs. Decentralizing forces also promote expansion diffusion, such as the location of a new shop in the suburbs. The forces behind decentralization fall into the same two general categories (economic and social) that were used to explain centralization. Now, however, everything is reversed. People and businesses are moving from the city instead of into it.

Economic advantages. Changes in accessibility have been a major reason for decentralization. The department store that originally located in the central city may now find that its customers have moved to the suburbs. They no longer shop downtown. As a result, the department store may move to a suburban shopping center. The same process also occurs among industries such as food-processing plants. They must move away to minimize transportation costs. The activities that were located downtown because of the railroad may now find trucking more effective. They relocate closer to a freeway system that only skirts the downtown area. And many offices now locate near airports so that their executives and salespeople can fly in and out more easily.

Although agglomeration once served as a centralizing force, its former benefits have now become liabilities in many downtown areas. These disadvantages involve such things as increased rents as a result of the high demand for space; congestion in the support system, which means delays in getting supplies or standing in endless lines for lunches; and traffic congestion, which makes delivery to market time-consuming and costly. Some downtown areas are so congested that traffic moves more slowly today than it did at the turn of the century. Traffic studies of midtown New York City show that the average automobile moves at a snail's pace of six miles (nine and a half kilometers) per hour. According to a 1907 study, horse-drawn vehicles moved through the same area at an average speed of eleven and a half miles (eighteen and a half kilometers) per hour, almost twice as fast.

Employees, experiencing high rents, traffic jams, and other inconveniences of central-city living, demand higher wages as compensation. This adds to the cost of doing business in the central city, and many firms choose to leave rather than bear such additional costs. As a result, many firms have left New York City. Most have chosen to locate in smaller suburbs removed from Manhattan. They claim that it costs less to locate there and that their employees are happier and more productive because they do not have to put up with the turmoil of city life.

There can also be benefits of clustering in new suburban locations, such as in industrial parks, where the costs of utilities and transportation links are shared by all the occupants. Similar benefits can come from residential agglomeration. Suburban real estate developments take advantage of clustering by sharing costs of schools, parks, road improvements, and utilities. New residents much prefer moving into a new development when they know that a full range of services is available nearby. Then they will not have to drive miles to find, say, the nearest hardware store. It is to the developer's advantage to encourage construction of nearby shopping centers.

Social advantages. A number of social factors reinforce decentralization, such as loss of downtown prestige, sentiment attached to the suburbs, and new employment patterns and transportation systems (see Figure 11-5).

The downtown area might once have lured people and businesses into the central city because it was a prestigious location. But once it begins to decay, once shops close and office space goes begging, there may be a certain stigma attached to it. This may drive residents and commercial activities away. Investors will not sink money in a downtown area that they think has no chance of recovery, and shoppers will not venture downtown when streets are filled with vacant stores, transients, pawnshops, and secondhand stores. One of the persistent problems faced by cities is how to reverse this image of the downtown area so that people will once again consider it the focus of the city. Chambers of commerce spend millions of dollars each year putting out literature that tries to create a new image of the central city.

Sentiment and prestige attached to the suburbs is a significant decentralizing force. There has been a long-standing preference in the United States and Canada for the single-family dwelling and large lot. These have been most readily obtained where land values are lower, away from the city center. And because the suburbs were originally dominated by upper-income people, socially mobile families have considered a move in that direction a step upward.

The need to be near one's workplace has historically been a great centralizing force, but it can also be a very strong decentralizing force. At first the suburbs were "bedroom communities," from which people commuted to their jobs in the downtown area. This is no longer the case. In most metropolitan areas, most jobs are not in the central city but in outlying districts. Now people work in suburban industrial parks, manufacturing plants, office buildings, and shopping centers. Thus a typical journey to work involves **lateral commuting**—that is, travel from one suburb to another. As a result, most people who live away from the city center actually live closer to their workplace. A testimony to this is a freeway system at rush hour; traffic is usually heavy in all directions, not just to and from the city center.

The costs of decentralization

Unfortunately, decentralization has taken its toll. Many of the urban problems now burdening North American cities are direct products of rapid decentralization that has taken place in the last thirty years (see

FIGURE 11-5
Transportation systems are an important force in the urban structure, not simply for the delivery of goods to the central city, but also to convey those who work and shop downtown, as illustrated in this picture of New York City commuters.

NORTH AMERICAN URBAN FUTURES: TRENDS OF THE EIGHTIES

There are several important trends that bear watching during the 1980s for their effect on population patterns, resource use, urban morphology, and city livability.

Slow Growth and Population Loss in the Industrial Belt

A list of shrinking cities (among the largest 100 urban centers) is dominated by cities of the northeastern industrial belt—cities such as Cleveland, Detroit, Buffalo, Pittsburgh. Although some of the population decline can be explained as continued movement into the suburbs from the central city, there is little question that these areas are experiencing severe problems due to industrial relocation, the contraction of traditional manufacturing activities, obsolete physical facilities, high taxes, and sky-rocketing fuel and energy costs. As jobs become scarce, people either suffer from unemployment or leave for better opportunities in other regions.

Rapid Growth in the Sun Belt

The other side of the population- industrial movement in North America is the rapid growth of Sun Belt cities—those urban areas found in the belt stretching across the South to Arizona and southern California. Industry is lured into these areas by attractive land prices, tax breaks, lower labor costs, less unionization (in the case of the South), and abundant, lower-cost fuel and energy. And following industry and jobs have come people. Until the late 1960s, southern states were exporters of people, but this trend was reversed by the late 1970s, and the 1980s saw these states become the fastest growing in North America. But along with this population explosion go problems of providing services (such as schools), urban sprawl, transportation congestion, and pervasive real estate speculation. Whether these areas can do a better job of planning than the rapid-growth cities of the 1960s remains to be seen.

Energy Boom Towns

With the new emphasis on developing domestic energy supplies a boom town landscape has come to much of the continent. Small crossroad towns have exploded overnight with the opening of new mine sites, power production facilities, and transportation nodes. Hundreds of mobile homes might be trucked in within a week to provide housing, yet goods and services take months—and years—to catch up, leaving the population without shopping facilities, libraries, schools, entertainment. Chain stores and supermarkets seem reluctant to move into these new boom towns until some indication of population stability is evident; the boom-and-bust cycle of the past nurtures a definite reluctance to expand facilities. Furthermore, the population of the boom towns might fluctuate widely as thousands of construction workers leave town after plants and facilities are built, leaving a small cadre of caretaker workers.

Other trends worth watching are the much publicized "return-to-the-city" movement of white-collar workers, the effect of increasing gasoline prices, and the impact of record-high housing prices on social structure, employment patterns, and growth rates of our major urban areas.

---

box, "North American Urban Futures"). These problems plague both inner cities and suburbs.

Vacant storefronts, empty offices, and deserted factories testify to the movement of commercial functions from central cities to suburbs. Retail sales in North American central cities have steadily declined, losing business to suburban shopping centers. Industries have relocated in spacious suburban industrial parks where taxes are lower, land costs cheaper, and transportation connections better. Even offices are finding advantages to suburban location. Like industry, offices capitalize on lower costs and easier access to new transportation networks.

What are cities doing to reverse this trend? Many cities have mounted special campaigns to combat central-city desertion. They offer tax incentives to those who stay or wish to locate in the downtown, and permits for new central buildings are often rushed through special channels that cut planning red tape. But most common is the downtown redevelopment project.

Urban renewal can have several goals, ranging from revival of retail trade, to construction of new central-city office space, to redevelopment of inner-city housing. The most common redevelopment strategy focuses on three interconnected components of city life: jobs, housing, and retail sales. The first task is to revive downtown employment patterns, often by constructing new office facilities competitive with outlying centers, or by concentrating on a specialized function. Many cities design redevelopment projects that cluster new financial institutions together. Banks, insurance firms, and stock brokerage houses can be found in the new high-rises.

Once people work in the city, they might be tempted to move back from the suburbs if appealing housing is available. So a second goal of redevelopment is construction of middle-income inner-city housing. Usually these projects will be located close the new office complex. Finally, with people both working and living in the downtown once again, retail sales can be expected to pick up. This is the third phase of many renewal plans. Pedestrian malls, shops clustered around fountains and open spaces, restaurants, and numerous specialty shops can be found in the newly planned redevelopment shopping areas. These new retail centers are usually located near both offices and new housing so as to draw workers during lunch hours and the new residents on their way home from work. In fact, many redevelopment projects combine all three elements into one superblock: residences, shops, and workplaces connected by elevated pathways removed from street-level congestion.

Urban redevelopment can also be designed to renew the deteriorated housing stock of low-rent residences. However, because some see the continued presence of lower-income people in the central city as conflicting with revival of a viable retail sector, politicians are often reluctant to approve such plans. A constant criticism of renewal projects has been that they destroy low-rent housing and replace it with middle- or high-rent dwelling units. Poor people—who are usually the elderly and minorities—are displaced and forced to move into other low-rent areas of the city, simply aggravating the problem of urban poverty.

This is not to judge all urban renewal as bad. There are many humane renewal projects that have combined economic revitalization of the inner city with housing and jobs for society's less fortunate. It can be done. Yet all agree that it is politically and economically more difficult than the project that simply constructs housing for high- and middle-income city dwellers.

Decentralization has also cost society millions of dollars in problems brought to the suburbs. Where rapid suburbanization has been the case, sprawl has usually resulted. A common pattern is leapfrog or checkerboard development, where housing tracts jump over parcels of farmland resulting in a mixture of open lands with built-up areas. This pattern results because developers buy cheaper land farther away from built-up areas, thereby cutting their costs. Furthermore, home buyers often pay premium prices for homes in subdivisions surrounded by farmlands (see Figure 11-6).

This form of development is costly because it is more expensive to provide city services, such as police, fire protection, sewers, and electrical lines, to those areas lying beyond open, unbuilt parcels. Obviously, the most cost-efficient form of development is adding new housing directly adjacent to built-up areas. That way the costs of providing new services are minimal. Costs are considerably higher when parcels of open land must be bridged.

Furthermore, sprawl extracts high costs because of increased usage of cars. Public transportation is extremely costly and inefficient when it must serve a low-density checkerboard development pattern; so costly that many cities and transit firms cannot extend lines into these areas. This means that the auto is the only form of transportation there. More energy is consumed for fuel, more air pollution is created by exhaust, and more time is spent in commuting and everyday activities. Hence, society pays again for the costs of decentralization.

We shouldn't overlook the costs of losing valuable agricultural land to urban development. Farmers cultivating the remaining checkerboard parcels have a hard time making ends meet. They are usually taxed at extremely high rates, since their land has high potential for development, and few can make a profit when taxes eat up all their resources. Often the only recourse is to sell out to subdividers. So the cycle of leapfrog development goes on.

But many cities are now taking strong measures to curb this kind of sprawling growth. Some cities, like San Jose, California, one of the fastest-growing cities of the 1960s, now try to focus new development on the empty parcels of the checkerboard pattern. This is called "in-filling."

Instead of new growth extending the sprawling outer edge of the city, it will take place within the existing urban area, where services are already available and can be provided at lower costs.

Other cities are tying the number of building permits granted each year to the availability of urban services. If schools are already crowded, water supplies inadequate, and sewer plants overburdened, the number of new dwelling units approved for an area will reflect this lower carrying capacity (see box, "Controlling Urban Growth").

So, in summary, the costs of decentralization are many. Decayed central cities and overburdened suburbs are part of the toll. Higher energy consumption and increased air pollution are also products of our sprawling cities. Social costs, such as inner-city poverty and ghettoization, can also be attributed to urban decentralization.

CONTROLLING URBAN GROWTH

Although the first urban growth control measures were written more than a decade ago, the controversy goes on with the issue enmeshed in drawn-out legal battles and bureaucratic red tape.

One of the earliest and best-known growth control plans was developed in Petaluma, California, a small town of 40,000 lying 40 miles north of San Francisco. Once a sleepy center of chicken ranches, the town began sprawling beyond its Victorian downtown in the late 1960s. A few years later the city council took strong measures to limit growth by adopting a plan whereby only 500 home-building permits would be issued each year. This was roughly half the number granted in earlier years, so growth was effectively slowed by 50 percent. Each permit would be awarded only after careful evaluation of the proposed structure. Was it of moderate cost? Did it have an adverse effect on the environment? Was it close to existing city services?

Reaction and opposition to the plan was immediate. Not only did the building industry object, but they were joined by civil rights groups who saw growth control as a possible vehicle of discrimination. Since some types of suburban zoning—such as large-lot minimums and bans against apartment houses—generally push up housing prices and discriminate against lower-income people, civil rights groups saw the Petaluma plan as a threat to minority groups.

So the Petaluma plan was challenged in court as violating the constitutional "right to travel," a legal right traced to the Magna Carta. While a collection of building industries, labor unions, and civil liberties groups pushed a legal challenge against the Petaluma plan, the city, with financial support from other cities interested in a legal precedent for growth control, stood by its plan. Lower-court decisions were reversed by higher courts until the final decision was made in 1978 by the U.S. Supreme Court.

However, even if the legal foundation for the Petaluma plan is sound, there remain an array of other problems faced by cities with growth management plans. Probably most important is the question of whether growth control forces up the price of houses. Evidence is mixed. A recent California study shows housing prices rise about 5 to 8 percent with growth control, both because of the market demand for a scarce supply and because delays in approval from a more complicated permit-granting process cost developers dearly during times of fluctuating interest rates and rising wage and materials costs. Another question is whether growth control discourages developers from building lower-priced and moderately priced housing. With only a limited number of permits available, many developers choose to maximize their profits by building higher-priced homes. Even though some plans, such as Petaluma's, give bonus points for moderately priced homes, some evidence suggests this incentive is still not enough to assure a broad range of prices.

Another question is how are permits to be limited? Some cities have adopted lotteries; others a complicated point system designed to permit only those with the most-desired attributes. Still other cities designate areas that are off-limits to building, and permit development only where city services exist or can be cheaply provided.

Working out an effective, yet equitable, growth control plan will be one of the challenges faced by cities in the 1980s.

The Cultural Ecology of the City

Cities are affected by the physical environment and, equally, urbanization profoundly alters the effects of natural processes. The theme of cultural ecology is helpful in organizing information about these city-nature relationships.

The urban ecosystem

In the first chapter of this book, ecology is defined as the study of the relationship between an organism and its physical environment. To study this relationship, we examine both organism and environment as one unit through which the flow of energy or matter can be traced. This is called the **ecosystem**. We can apply this concept to the city in order to better understand the relationships between urban populations and the physical environment.

There are four important concepts related to the ecosystem approach: input, storage, output, and feedback. To illustrate, let us examine just one component of the urban ecosystem: water. Obviously, a city needs water to survive, so it imports a given amount each day, either from local sources, such as lakes and reservoirs, or from long distances via canals and aqueducts. This is the **input** of the system. What happens to it as it moves through the city?

Water is used in households, industry, stores, and offices; using the terminology of the ecosystem, we say that it is transformed and leaves the system in other forms. These are the **outputs.** Some water is consumed by people; hence it temporarily becomes part of the body systems. Other water becomes part of different products, such as cheese or drinks, and, after transformation, may leave the city's system as goods are exported to other markets. Still other water is used for industrial cooling and, as it evaporates, returns to the atmospheric system as vapor. And a small amount of water is not used, but rather is stored within the system for future use, just the way organisms store energy. But most of the water—about 95 percent—is simply used to convey wastes from one point to another; from home to sewer plant, from factory to river, from sidewalk to gutter. This output is a most troublesome aspect of the urban system.

Feedback is a crucial part of any system. It is the repercussions on a system when an element is returned in modified or changed form by other components of the system. A simple example would be if a city used water from a lake both for its water supply and also as a dumping area for sewage. As more effluent is discharged into the lake, water quality decreases, and the city must expend more energy (measured both in money and activity) to protect its fresh-water supply.

A more complicated example—and in no way has this relationship been conclusively proven—is the way that city-produced air pollution may alter weather patterns so that a water supply system is strained, either by drought or by flooding. Further examples of the interconnectivity within the urban ecosystem will be apparent in the following discussion of the geologic, meteorologic, and hydrologic components of the urban environment.

The urban geologic environment

In the previous chapter, under the discussion of site and situation, we saw that cities are both affected by—and affect—the physical environment. Let us explore further the relationships between urbanization and the geologic environment.

To begin with, topography can influence urban development in three ways: the direction of city growth, the routing of transportation, and the patterning of social areas. However, we must emphasize that these potential effects are dependent on a number of cultural variables. The most important variables concern a society's technological level, the amount of energy and capital available for modification of the geologic environment, and, lastly, the stage in a city's development. In other words, the geologic environment may have a great effect on those cities in early stages of growth, where there are alternatives to expending energy and money on modifying terrain, or where the technology is lacking for bulldozing, landfill, or high-stress building construction. Whereas at later stages of growth, in a rich, highly industrialized culture, there will be far more examples of humans modifying the geologic environment (see Figure 11-7).

Let us look at the way terrain might influence early stages of city growth. Cities usually expand first on those areas where building costs are lowest. This means that flat, well-drained lands that are close to transportation and adjacent to existing urban activities will be built upon first. These site characteristics are also attractive to other uses, such as agriculture, and the competition between farming and urban growth remains an important issue today (see the discussion in this chapter on costs of decentralization). But as topography varies, building costs increase. Areas of hills, marshes, and floodplains may be built upon only at later stages of a city's growth when there are fewer alternatives.

The increased costs of site preparation, such as grading hills or draining swamps, can have two very different consequences. On the one hand, the increased cost of building may be passed on to the consumer—meaning

FIGURE 11-7
When land values are high and pressure for housing intense, terrain rarely stands in the way of the developer, as illustrated by this cut-and-fill in California.

that those who buy the houses pay more, and the area will be occupied by higher-income groups. On the other hand, other aspects of construction may be cut in order to compensate for increased site preparation costs. Lots may be smaller, houses undersized, and shortcuts taken in construction methods so that the finished product is of lower quality. This means that lower-income groups will probably occupy the area.

Environmental feedback may also blemish an area. Former swamps or marches may have flooding problems; hillsides may slide; or unstable foundations and flooded basements may lower market prices so that an area of former middle-price homes becomes accessible to lower-income people. Unfortunately, they are the ones least able to bear the costs of pumping out basements or reinforcing foundations. It seems unjust that they must bear the costs of poor environmental planning.

Lastly, transportation systems can be affected by terrain; and since there is a close link between transportation and urban development, the resulting urban pattern may express these relationships. The first urban transportation system was the horse-drawn streetcar, which was obviously restricted to level parts of the city, since horses could not pull car and passengers up or down hills. Slight gradients could be negotiated by smaller horse-drawn carriages; those who could afford such conveyances had access to hilltop building sites. But it was only with the cable car that hills became accessible to the middle class. Starting in San Francisco in 1873, cable cars came into widespread use in American cities. However, cable cars had problems in cold, wet climates because of freezing in the cable conduits, so a better solution to public transportation needs was sought.

Electric trolley systems profoundly altered the pattern of urban development beginning in the 1890s. But, like the horse-drawn carriage, they had limited hill-climbing abilities. Only slight gradients could be negotiated, so trolley lines ascended slopes only when it was possible to follow hillside contours. Often a network of steep stairways and paths connected neighborhoods with streetcar lines. In the end, it was only the automobile that led to widespread building on steep urban slopes. And even this form of development has been influenced by factors such as frequency of heavy snowfalls and ice storms.

The possibility of serious environmental feedback can influence urban patterns. In some parts of the world, the potential of damage from earthquakes is severe. The threat of destruction from earthquakes has always been great in California; however, if one examines the pattern of development, it is appalling to see how much construction has taken place in vulnerable areas. Filled lands, such as on bay margins, are areas where ground shaking will be worst, yet millions of people reside on these areas in California. Other construction has taken place directly on major faults where continual movement—known as creep—slowly rips buildings apart. Widespread development is found in floodplains immediately downstream from huge dams that could collapse from a major quake.

Only in the last decade has California taken steps to prevent construction on the hundreds of active faults crisscrossing urban areas. When the inevitable major earthquake comes, the toll will be high.

Although California is notorious for its earthquake hazard, the possibility of major damage from a quake is not limited just to that area. Some of the strongest recorded earthquakes have been in the central and eastern portions of the United States. But few measures are being taken in those areas to protect urban dwellers from potential disaster, either by requiring adjustments to existing buildings or planning growth for areas less vulnerable to earthquake damage.

Urban weather and climate

Cities alter just about all aspects of local weather and climate. Temperatures are higher in cities, rainfall increases, as does fog and cloudiness, and atmospheric pollution is much higher near cities.

The cause behind these alterations is no mystery. Because cities pave over large areas of streets, buildings, parking lots, and rooftops, about 50 percent of the urban area is a hard surface. Rainfall is quickly carried into gutters and sewers, so that little standing water is available for evaporation. This means that temperatures will be higher, since heat is removed from the air during the normal evaporation process.

Furthermore, cities generate enormous amounts of heat. This comes not just from heating systems of buildings, but also from automobiles, industry, and even from human bodies. One study shows that on a winter day in Manhattan, the amount of heat produced in the city is 2 1/2 times that reaching the ground from the sun. (During the summer, solar heating is greater than human-produced heat.) The end result of this heat generation is to produce a large mass of warmer air sitting over the city. This is called the urban **heat island** (see Figure 11-8).

As a result of the heat island, yearly temperatures will average 3.5 degrees F. warmer than in the countryside; they can easily be twice as much warmer during the winter, when city-produced heat is greatest.

There will also be significant temperature differences within the city. In winter, heavily traveled streets will be 2 or 3 degrees F. warmer than untraveled side streets; places where autos stand for a while, like stoplights, can be another 3 degrees F. warmer. Furthermore, low spots in the city, where cold air collects, will be much colder than higher places. And wooded areas are warmer than bare blocks.

During the summer, the city center is warmer than the suburbs. Often there can be a 10 degree F. difference between downtown and outlying

FIGURE 11-8
The London heat island forms a dome over the city. Notice the marked contrast in temperature between the built-up central part of the city and the surrounding "Green Belt." (After Chandler.)

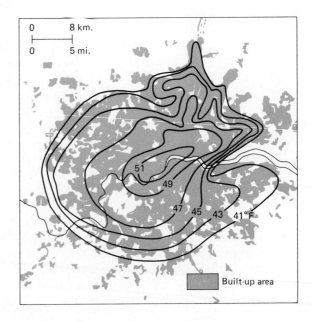

residential areas, which is a result of suburban lawns and parks stabilizing temperatures by using up heat through evaporation and releasing heat at night faster than paved areas. Concrete areas tend to store heat longer at night, which leads to a build-up of temperatures over a series of warm days.

Precipitation (rain and snowfall) is also affected by urbanization. Because of higher temperatures within the urban area, snowfall will be about 5 percent less than in the surrounding countryside. However, rainfall can be 5 to 10 percent higher. This is a function of two factors: first, the large number of dust particles in urban air, and, second, the higher city temperatures. Dust particles are a necessary precondition for condensation, for they offer a focus around which moisture can adhere. So where there is a greater number of dust particles, condensation will take place more easily. That is why fog and clouds are usually more frequent around cities (see Figure 11-9).

And once condensation takes place, rainfall is not far behind. Rainfall increases on the order of 10 percent have been documented immediately downwind from cities. For example, thunderstorms in the London area produce 30 percent more rainfall than in the countryside. Some urban climatologists argue that they can see a weekday rainfall increase pattern:

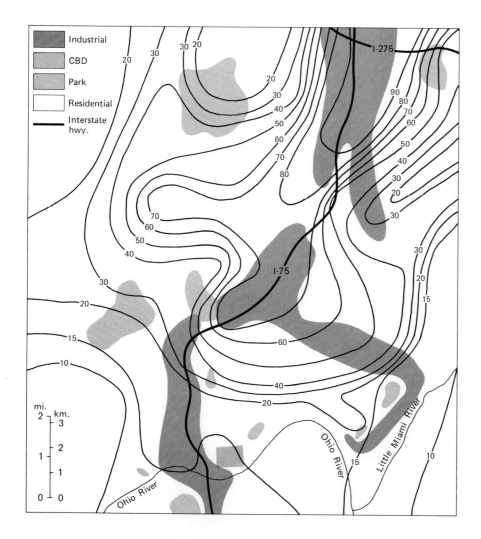

FIGURE 11-9
The dust dome over Cincinnati, Ohio. Values show the concentration of particulate matter in the air at 3000 feet elevation on May 27, 1970. The higher the value, the greater the amount of particulate matter. (After Bach and Hagedorn.)

rainfall is less on weekends because dust particle generation—from autos and industry—is reduced.

City-generated air pollution is one of the most serious problems of our times. No longer is air pollution simply a nuisance. It can cause serious illness, at times death; it damages agriculture near cities; and it extracts a high cost from every urban dweller. Unless pollution can be halted, it may actually be the limiting factor on growth. Some suggest that fresh air—not water—will determine the ultimate carrying capacity of the Los Angeles basin (see box, "Cities, Autos, and Air Pollution"). Federal and local air quality agencies are experimenting with regulations limiting further growth and development in those areas suffering from persistent air pollution.

Much has been written about air pollution, and we refer readers to references listed at the end of this chapter for additional material.

Urban hydrology

The city is not only a great consumer of water, but it also alters runoff patterns in a way that increases the frequency and magnitude of flooding. We will first discuss urban water demands, then the problems of urban flooding.

Within the city, residential areas are usually the greatest consumers of water. This could vary depending on the kind of industry found in a city, but as a general statement, we see each person using about 60 gallons per

---

CITIES, AUTOS, AND AIR POLLUTION: THE LESSONS OF LOS ANGELES

Air pollution affects virtually all of the world's cities. For simplicity, pollution-suffering urban centers can be broken down into two categories: "brown air" cities, which suffer from photochemical smog produced mostly by autos; and "grey air" cities, where industrial smog generated by coal and oil burning is the major pollution problem. Most of what we know about brown air cities comes from lessons learned in Los Angeles over the last 30 years.

Air pollution first became troublesome in the 1940s, when particulate matter increased to some 400 tons per day. This came mostly from outdoor burning and industrial smokestacks, so strict emission ordinances were passed in 1947. Although particulate fallout decreased, the city was still bothered by increasing amounts of yellow-brown haze. Its source remained a mystery until the early 1950s, when a professor at Cal Tech accidentally identified the Los Angeles smog as a mixture of complex hydrocarbons. Southern California sunlight baked the original pollution until secondary pollutants, such as ozone, were produced; hence the name "photochemical smog."

But the source of the hydrocarbons was not known. At first the city pointed the finger at the numerous oil refineries in the area and ordered them to control their emissions. But the smog still worsened. Only in 1953 was the auto identified as the major producer of hydrocarbons in the United States.

Los Angeles turned to the auto industry, which agreed to study the problem, but its research was given a low priority in Detroit. Only after constant prodding by Los Angeles did the industry respond. Eight years later, the first simple crankcase emission control devices appeared on California cars. These eliminated about 20 percent of the hydrocarbons discharged by an auto, and only after more elaborate devices were required in 1966 did total hydrocarbon emissions in the Los Angeles airshed begin decreasing.

Unfortunately, another problem arose. Although hydrocarbons decreased, nitrogen oxides increased. This resulted from higher temperatures inside high-compression engines triggering a reaction that ended in the discharge of harmful nitrogen. One pollution problem had been replaced by another. The solution to the nitrogen oxide problem may come with lead-free gasoline and catalytic converters. However, since only newer cars will carry these devices, the millions of older cars will continue to discharge nitrogen dioxide. Furthermore, experts predict that emissions can be cut 50 to 75 percent in the next 10 to 15 years, but that the auto population will increase 100 percent, thereby putting us back at square one. The only successful solution lies with decreased usage of autos and an alternative to the internal-combustion engine.

day in a residence. This contrasts with commercial areas, where there is only a 26 gallon per day use rate per person.

Of course, residential demand varies. It is higher in drier climates than where rainfall is adequate for garden water; it is greater where lots are larger: and it is also higher in middle- and high-income neighborhoods than in lower-income areas. Higher-income groups usually have a larger number of water-using appliances, such as washing machines, dishwashers, and swimming pools.

However, price influences water demand. People use less water when price increases. Recent periods of drought in the West demonstrate that residents can both use considerably less water and find alternatives to fresh-water consumption. Many of the rationing plans adopted during the California drought of the mid-1970s restricted per capita daily use to around 40 gallons. Toilets (which use about seven gallons per flush) were flushed less, showers were shortened, and household "grey water" was used for gardens.

This is not to suggest that only Western cities are vulnerable to drought. The eastern United States experienced severe water shortages in the mid-1960s, and England suffered from a two-year drought in the mid-1970s. In both cases, city dwellers were forced to ration water.

As meteorologists forecast increased climatic variability, meaning that more frequent droughts are a distinct possibility, cities must prepare for more efficient water usage. Some politicians and planners argue that storage capacity must be increased through building more dams and reservoirs. Others see this as a faulty strategy, for these increased water supplies might trigger rapid growth that will put the city in an even more vulnerable position during inevitable periods of drought. More water leads to more people; more people consume more water; and reduced rainfall means that more people will suffer from less water. The best strategy will combine development of ample storage and delivery systems with reduced residential and commercial consumption.

Let us turn now to the problem of urban floods. It was noted earlier that urbanization seems to increase both the frequency and the magnitude of flooding. Why might this be? Cities create large impervious areas where water cannot soak into the earth. Instead, precipitation is converted into immediate runoff. It is forced into gutters, sewers, and stream channels that have been straightened and bared of vegetation, resulting in more frequent high-water levels than are found in a comparable area of rural land. Furthermore, the time period between rainfall and peak runoff is reduced in cities; there is less lag than in the countryside, where water runs across soil and vegetation into stream channels and then into rivers. So, because of hard surfaces and artificial collection channels, runoff is concentrated and immediate.

Several studies show that flooding becomes five or six times more frequent in an urbanized watershed, and because pressures on land from city growth often lead to the development of floodplains, the scenario is set for disaster. Floodplains are, by definition, areas subject to natural flooding, so it should come as no surprise that rivers reclaim their full channels every now and then. And when urbanization increases the frequency of flooding, building on floodplains becomes increasingly hazardous (see Figure 11-10).

So, in conclusion, we can see that the urban ecosystem is sensitive to any kind of alterations. Disruptions such as landslides, flooding, air pollution, temperature increases, and earthquakes are events that we must

FIGURE 11-10
Often urbanization disturbs the natural hydrology, so that both frequency and magnitude of flooding are increased. This flood resulted from an afternoon thundershower in Virginia.

expect as cities expand. We must develop skills and understanding that will lead to sensitive environmental planning—that is, planning capable of predicting disruptions in natural systems resulting from urban growth, and capable of promoting city expansion in ways that will make the least impact on the physical environment.

Cultural Integration and Models of the City

In our look at centralizing and decentralizing forces, we saw that many factors influence the location of an activity within a city. A logical follow-up question is: Does a predictable land-use pattern result from the interplay of these factors? One method of seeking an answer is to create models that describe and simplify the relationships among the different social, economic, and geographic factors. Various academic disciplines have long sought to isolate the most important processes at work in a city. The goal is to derive a model that describes the pattern of a city and explains how it evolved. Following a discussion of urban processes, the three most widely used models are described below.

There are a number of processes at work in a city, leading to different social and economic patterns. Seven are briefly discussed here. The first is *concentration*, which refers to the differential distribution of population and economic activities in a city and the manner in which they have focused on the center of the city. A related process, already described, is *centralization*. This refers not only to the focusing of activity in the central city, but also to its clustering around important activity points, such as transportation routes, factories, or major stores. *Decentralization*, defined earlier, refers to the location of activity away from the central city. *Segregation* is the sorting out of population groups due to conscious preferences for associating with one group or another through bias and prejudice. A somewhat similar process operates among economic activities; we call this *specialization*. The process through which a new activity or social group enters an area has traditionally been called *invasion*. And if that new use or social group gradually replaces the former occupants, this illustrates the process of *succession*. Both of these terms have been adopted from plant ecology and were originally used to describe changes in vegetation.

With these seven processes in mind, let us examine how they might influence urban patterns. We shall do so by looking at three models of city structure.

Concentric zone model

The **concentric zone model** was developed in 1925 by Ernest W. Burgess, a sociologist at the University of Chicago. Although his model closely resembles Chicago (if the east side were not cut off by Lake Michigan). his intent was simply to construct a theoretical model of urban growth.

Figure 11-11 shows the concentric zone model with its five zones. At first glance, you can see the effects of residential decentralization. There is a distinct pattern of income levels from the **CBD** (central business district) out to the commuter's zone. This shows that, even at the beginning of the auto age, American cities expressed a clear separation of social groups. The extension of trolley lines into the surrounding countryside had a lot to do with this pattern.

Zone 2, a transitional area between the CBD and residential Zone 3, was characterized by a mixed pattern of commercial and residential land use. Rooming houses, small apartments, and tenements attracted the lowest income segment of the urban population. Often this zone included slums and skid rows. Here also many ethnic ghettos began. Landowners, while waiting for the CBD to reach their land, erected shoddy tenements to house a massive influx of foreign workers. An aura of uncertainty was characteristics of life in Zone 2, because commercial activities rapidly displaced residents as the CBD expanded. Today, this area is often characterized by physical deterioration (see Figure 11-12).

Zone 3, the "workingmen's quarters," was a solid blue-collar arc, located close to the factories of Zones 1 and 2. Yet Zone 3 was more stable than the zone of transition around the CBD. It was often characterized by ethnic neighborhoods: blocks of immigrants who had broken free from the

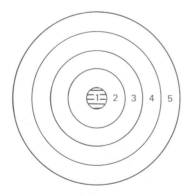

1   CBD (central business district)
2   Transition zone
3   Blue-collar residential
3   Blue-collar residential
4   Middle-income residential
5   Commuter residential

FIGURE 11-11
The concentric zone model is shown in this diagram. Each zone represents a different type of land use in the city. Can you identify examples of each zone in your community?

FIGURE 11-12
The transitional zone in the city contains vacant and deteriorated buildings. Broken windows and boarded storefronts are part of the landscape.

FIGURE 11-13
Residential areas of Chicago in 1920 were used as the basis for many studies and models of the city. (After Hoyt.)

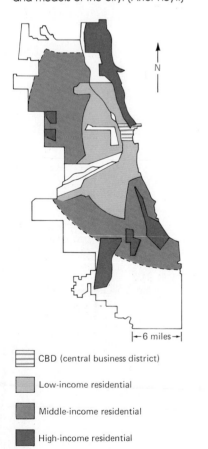

|←— 6 miles —→|

▤ CBD (central business district)

▨ Low-income residential

▨ Middle-income residential

■ High-income residential

ghettos in Zone 2 and moved outward into flats or single-family dwellings. Burgess suggested that this working-class area, like the CBD, was spreading outward, because of pressure from the zone of transition and because blue-collar workers demanded better housing.

Zone 4 was a middle-class area of "better housing." From here, established city dwellers, many of whom moved out of the central city with the first streetcar network, commuted to work in the CBD.

Zone 5, the commuter's zone, consisted of higher-income families clustered together in older suburbs, either on the farthest extension of the trolley or on commuter railroad lines. This zone of spacious lots and large houses was the growing edge of the city. From here, the rich pressed outward to avoid the increasing congestion and social heterogeneity brought to their area by an expansion of Zone 4.

Burgess's concentric zone theory represented the American city in a new stage of development. Before the 1870s, an American metropolis, such as New York, was a city of mixed neighborhoods where merchants' stores and sweatshop factories were intermingled with mansions and hovels. Rich and poor, immigrant and native-born rubbed shoulders in the same neighborhoods. However, in Chicago, Burgess's hometown, something new occurred. In 1871, the great Chicago Fire burned out the core of the city, leveling almost one-third of its buildings. The city was then rebuilt on a new concentric pattern that segregated classes. This segregated city started with a "core of poverty" and worked its way out in what one scholar has called "rings of rising affluence."

However, as you can see from Figure 11-13, the actual residential map of Chicago does not exactly match the simplicity of Burgess's concentric zones. For instance, it is evident that the wealthy continue to monopolize certain high-value sites within the other rings, especially Chicago's "Gold Coast" along Lake Michigan. According to the concentric zone theory, this area should have been part of the zone of transition. Burgess accounted for certain of these exceptions by noting how the rich tended to monopolize hills, lakes, and shorelines, whether they were close to or far from the CBD. Critics of Burgess's model also were quick to point out that, even though portions of each zone did exist in most cities, rarely were they linked in such a way as to totally surround the city. Burgess countered that there were distinct barriers, such as old industrial centers, that prevented the completion of the arc. Still other critics felt that Burgess, as a sociologist, overemphasized residential patterns and did not give proper credit to other land uses—such as industry, manufacturing, and warehouses—in describing the urban mosaic.

Despite these criticisms, concentric zone theory was fairly accurate in describing the cities of 1925. In fact, many of the zones can still be seen in contemporary cities, particularly the zone of transition around the central business district. It is still a jumbled mixture of land uses, neither totally residential nor totally commercial. Usually it is still the area of skid rows and slums. It is easily recognized by its pawnshops, rescue missions, large parking lots, rooming houses, transient hotels, old factories, and—since the 1950s—massive urban renewal projects, which seek to "upgrade" the land by replacing older residential buildings with convention centers, offices, and parking garages. Because these projects usually displace the transient population, they in effect expand the zone of transition. Skid rows are like bumps under the carpet: They can be moved by sweeping the surface, but they never completely disappear.

Sector model

Homer Hoyt, an economist who studied housing data for 142 American cities, presented his **sector model** of urban land use in 1939. He maintained that high-rent residential districts ("rent" meaning capital outlay for the occupancy of space, including purchase, lease, or "rent" in the popular sense) were instrumental in shaping the land-use structure of the city. Because these areas were reinforced by transportation routes, the pattern of their development was one of sectors or wedges (see Figure 11-14) rather than concentric zones.

Hoyt suggested that the high-rent sector would expand according to several factors. First, a high-rent sector moves from its point of origin near the CBD, along established routes of travel, toward another nucleus of high-rent buildings; that is, a high-rent area directly next to the CBD will naturally head in the direction of a high-rent suburb, eventually linking the two in a wedge-shaped sector. Second, a high-rent sector will progress

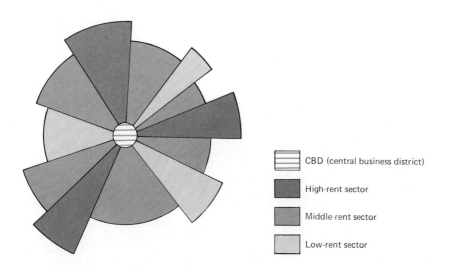

FIGURE 11-14
Another model of urban land use is the sector model. In this model zones are pie-shaped wedges radiating along main transportation routes.

CBD (central business district)

High-rent sector

Middle-rent sector

Low-rent sector

toward high ground or along waterfronts, when these areas are not used for industry. The rich have always preferred such environments for their residences. Third, a high-rent sector will move along the route of fastest transportation. Fourth, a high-rent sector will move toward open space. A high-income community rarely moves into an occupied lower-income neighborhood. Instead, the wealthy prefer to build new structures on vacant land where they can control the social environment.

As high-rent sectors develop, the areas between them are filled in. Middle-rent areas move directly next to them, drawing on their prestige. Low-rent areas fill in the remaining areas. Thus, moving away from major routes of travel, rents go from high to low.

There are distinct patterns in today's cities that echo Hoyt's model. He had the advantage over Burgess in that he wrote later in the automobile age and could see the tremendous impact that major thoroughfares were having on cities. However, when we look at today's major transportation arteries—which are generally freeways—we see that the areas surrounding them are often low-rent districts. According to Hoyt's theory, they should be high-rent districts. Freeways are rather recent additions to the city, coming only after World War II. In a sense, they were imposed on an existing urban pattern. To minimize the costs of construction, they were built as often as possible through low-rent areas, where the costs of land purchase for the rights of way were less. This is why so many freeways rip through ethnic ghettos and low-income areas. Economically speaking, this is the least expensive route. This will continue to be the case until low-income neighborhoods organize effective political resistance against such disturbances.

Multiple nuclei model

Both Burgess and Hoyt assumed that a strong central city affected patterns throughout the urban area. However, as the city increasingly decentralized, districts developed that were not directly linked to the CBD. In 1945, two geographers, Chauncey Harris and Edward Ullman, suggested a new model, the **multiple nuclei model.** They maintained that a city developed with equal intensity around various points, or "multiple nuclei" (see Figure 11-15). In their eyes, the CBD was not the sole generator of change. Equal weight must be given to an old community on the city outskirts around which new suburban developments clustered; to an industrial district that grew from an original waterfront location; or to a low-income area that developed because of some social stigma attached to

FIGURE 11-15
The multiple nuclei model is shown in this diagram. This model was devised to show that the CBD is not the sole force in creating land-use patterns within the city. Rather, land-use districts may evolve for specific reasons at specific points elsewhere in the city, hence the name *multiple nuclei.*

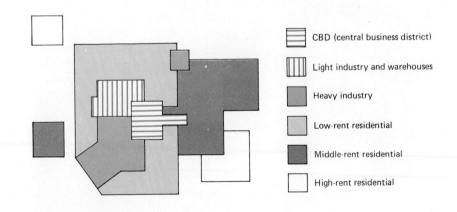

CBD (central business district)

Light industry and warehouses

Heavy industry

Low-rent residential

Middle-rent residential

High-rent residential

the site. In other words, the city grew from a number of unrelated points, not from a single center.

Harris and Ullman rooted their model in four geographic principles. First of all, certain activities require highly specialized facilities, such as accessible transportation for a factory or large areas of open land for a housing tract. The second principle is that certain activities cluster together because they profit from mutual association. One such cluster would be banks, used-car lots, and jewelry stores. Third, certain activities repel each other and will not be found in the same area. Examples would be high-rent residences and industrial areas, or slums and expensive retail stores. Fourth, certain activities could not make a profit if they paid the high rent of the most desirable locations. Therefore, they seek lower-rent areas. For example, new-car dealers may like to locate where pedestrian traffic is greatest in order to lure the most people into their showrooms. However, they need great amounts of space for showrooms, storage, service facilities, and used-car lots. Therefore, they cannot afford the high rents that the most accessible locations demand. They compromise by finding an area of lower rent that is still relatively accessible.

The multiple nuclei model, more than the other models, seems to take into account the varied factors of decentralization in the structure of the North American city. The concentric zone theory and the sector theory are rather deterministic. They emphasize one single factor (residential differentiation in the concentric zone theory or rent in the sector theory) to explain the city. But the multiple nuclei theory encompasses the whole spectrum of economic and social possibilities. Harris and Ullman could probably appreciate the variety of forces working on the city because they did not confine themselves to seeking one strict explanation. As geographers, they tried to integrate the disparate elements of culture into a workable model.

Urban Landscapes

Urban areas, like all places occupied by humans, have cultural landscapes. Indeed, the human-made landscape is nowhere more evident and overpowering than in the city. Here nature is quite subdued, and humans rule the landscape totally. These urban landscapes, or **townscapes,** differ greatly both within cities and from one urban culture to another.

Street plan

One major facet of any townscape is the street plan, or layout of routeways. Americans are perhaps so accustomed to the grid pattern, or "checkerboard" layout, of streets that they often assume that this form is dominant everywhere in the world. The American love affair with the grid pattern led to its application even in areas of rough terrain, such as San Francisco. The grid pattern for streets apparently originated several thousands of years before the Christian era in the prehistoric Indus Valley. Then it spread slowly westward through the Middle East, Greece, and the Roman Empire. Much later, this plan was revived in central and western Europe and diffused to the Americas.

By contrast, most European, Asian, and African cities have very irregular street plans. Streets meet at odd angles with no apparent planning, and square or rectangular blocks are rare. Thoroughfares are uncommon, and the flow of traffic is seriously hampered. Many cities of southwestern Asia are dominated by a mazelike pattern of narrow dead-end streets and walkways. To persons accustomed to grid-pattern towns, such irregular layouts can be frustrating.

Types of structures

Cities also differ greatly in the types of buildings they contain. The American city typically is dominated by skyscrapers, single-family residences surrounded by private yards, and glass and plastic shopping centers amid seas of asphalt. Most buildings are new. In Europe, however, skyscrapers are rather uncommon, and the skyline is dominated by church spires. The large majority of people live in multistory apartments, and stores are not concentrated in shopping centers. The line between residential area and shopping district is blurred, because many proprietors live above their shops. Typically, the European city boasts structures of considerable age—perhaps the remnants of a town wall, an old cathedral, a medieval town hall, or an ancient fortress.

Perception of the urban landscape

A city consists of physical objects, such as streets, buildings, parks and fountains. We call these objects, which exist in space, the landscape. But there is also a psychological city in each person's mind. On the basis of this city of the mind, we find our way around the "real" city, make decisions about where to live or shop, and decide whether to approve or oppose changes in the city.

Our urban images result from a process of selection called "perception." As you probably know, living itself is a process of selection. We do not see all that we "see"; that is, our brains do not choose to take in all the information that lands on the retinas of our eyes. The same can be said for the other senses. We do not hear all that we hear, nor feel all that we touch, nor smell all that we smell.

If we were not selective, our brains would be overwhelmed by useless information. A hungry person driving down a street will quickly note the hamburger stand on the far corner but will probably not take in the row of old brownstone houses or the gas station or the variety store, even though all of them are closer than the hamburger stand. In other words, what we choose to perceive is a function of our purpose. We take in only bits of information from the overwhelming range of possibilities in the "real world" and interpret them on the basis of our past experiences, our values, and our desires. In other words, we base our decisions to a large extent on images created by our brain.

Differing images of the city. As an example of how individuals each of us perceives the city, imagine a couple who are visiting San Francisco for the first time. On a stroll, with no other purpose than to "see" the city, they approach Union Square. The plaza is surrounded by large downtown hotels and department stores; the sidewalks are crowded with pedestrians; the streets are jammed with cable cars, buses, and cars. In the square itself, benches are filled with office workers taking in the noon sun. Street musicians beat on bongo drums, and a few derelicts move among the crowd asking for spare change.

Our two tourists form completely different images of this scene on the basis of their different experiences and value systems. The woman, who was raised in New York City, enjoys the scene tremendously. She associates busy street life with pleasant memories of her youth. The crowd is friendly, the sun is enjoyable, and the music is strangely stimulating. She wants to stay. But her companion, raised in a small Montana town, does not like cities. In fact, the derelicts remind him of the time in Chicago when a drunk pursued him for blocks insisting that he hand over his spare change. He has never quite forgotten the embarrassment and anxiety of that moment. The office workers sitting on the benches remind him of his job at home and all the work that awaits his return. The traffic is noisy, the bongo drummers are irritating, and the derelicts are somehow threatening. Different perceptions result in different decisions. He wants to leave. She insists on staying.

This probably happens hundreds of times every day. In a city of a million inhabitants, there are a million different images. But people with similar experiences, similar values, and similar desires are likely to share images—that is, there will be great areas of overlap between the mental cities each of them carries.

However, one group's images may be drastically different from another group's images. Black teen-agers in New York City will undoubtedly hold mental images of that city quite different from those of a group of Wall Street stockbrokers. For one thing, the way they travel around the city is likely to be different. Thus they will be exposed to a different set of visual clues. The teenagers, traveling mostly by subway, may well have a far-reaching "underground" map of New York but aboveground know little beyond their own ghetto area. The brokers, traveling in their own cars or perhaps by taxi, make their way around the surface of the city with ease, yet have to ask directions as soon as they step through a subway turnstile. For each of these groups, the other's "turf" is probably unfamiliar territory. To the broker, Harlem is a virtual blank on the map; and to the black teenager, the fashionable areas of the city are places of danger where he or she may be considered with suspicion or stopped by a police officer. In short, the experiences and values of the stockbrokers and black teenagers are so different that the same visual clues will be interpreted in completely different ways (see box, "The Handwriting on the Wall").

Measuring perceptions of the city. During the last twenty years, social scientists have been concerned with measuring people's perceptions of the urban landscape. They assume that if we really know what people see and react to in the city, we can ask architects and urban planners to design and create a more humane urban environment, one that we would respond to in a positive manner.

Kevin Lynch, an urban designer, pioneered a method for recording people's images of the city. He assumed that all people have a mental map. After all, they must find their way about their cities in the course of daily life. Lynch then figured out ways that people could convey their mental maps to others. With this information, he could discover which parts of the urban landscape are being used as visual clues by which people. What do people react favorably to or negatively to? What do they block out?

On the basis of interviews conducted in Boston, Jersey City, and Los Angeles, Lynch suggested five important elements in mental maps of cities: (1) *Pathways* are the routes of frequent travel, such as streets, freeways, and transit corridors. We experience the city from the pathways.

THE HANDWRITING ON THE WALL

Graffiti have always been part of the urban landscape, from ancient Rome to modern-day New York, from the bathroom wall to war-torn Belfast. Furthermore, due mostly to the aerosol spray can and the felt-tip pen, wall-writing is on the increase, adding still another financial burden to city budgets. New York City spends $1.5 million a year to erase graffiti, while the Philadelphia Transit Authority spends over $1 million each year to repaint its rolling stock and cover the markings of the graffiti artists.

Why do people do it? Some are frustrated individuals seeking to make their mark on an alienating society. The more brazen the mark, the greater the status. In Philadelphia, the master graffitist is "Cornbread," whose spray-can markings cover the city, even to the point of welcoming new arrivals to the airport and reportedly defacing a TWA jet with "Cornbread" just as it left the terminal.

Political upheaval has always nurtured graffiti. The walls of Berkeley are mute indicators of the turbulent decade from the Free Speech Movement of 1964 to antiwar protests into the 1970s. Walls became people's bulletin boards as messages were passed about protests, meetings, and boycotts. Written graffiti gave rise to posters, which can be mass-produced, yet have the same essential purpose as wall markings.

Probably the category of graffiti that most interests the geographer is that which speaks to territorial claims or the definition and protection of "turf." Street gangs in New York and Philadelphia have long used graffiti to delimit their territory, posting warnings at the borders against incursion by outsiders, or using wall space deep within their territory to list members or spread the gang's reputation. Ethnic neighborhoods are commonly defended through graffiti, as in Belfast, where Catholics and Protestants are involved in a bloody civil rights struggle. Protestant neighborhoods are easily detected by their pro-British, anti-Catholic graffiti, whereas the Catholic neighborhoods are bounded with anti-Protestant and anti-British slogans. Residents have no difficulty telling one group's territory from another: therefore they know which is safe and which hostile.

Similar use of graffiti is seen in cities where neighborhoods are experiencing change, such as when blacks are moving in. Often walls will be covered with racist markings, open threats, and slogans of ethnic pride. The recent court-ordered busing of blacks into the Irish area of South Boston gave rise to an explosion of pro-Irish, anti-black graffiti.

As crude and offensive as such wall messages may be, they are nevertheless an expression of neighborhood defense and the protection of territory. Perhaps because such graffiti flourish when groups are in conflict and probably recognize the inevitable loss of territory, the expression "the handwriting is on the wall" has become a common part of our vocabulary.

Therefore, they become the threads that hold our maps together. (2) *Edges* are boundaries between areas, or the outer limits of our image. Mountains, rivers, shorelines, and even major streets and freeways are commonly used as edges. They tend to define the extremes of our urban vision; then we fill in the details. (3) *Nodes* are strategic junction points, such as breaks in transportation, traffic circles, or any place where important pathways come together. (4) *Districts* are small areas with a common identity, such as ethnic areas and functional zones (for instance, the CBD or a row of car dealers). (5) *Landmarks* are reference points that stand out because of shape, height, color, or historic importance. The city hall in Los Angeles, the Washington Monument in Washington, D.C., or the golden arches of a McDonald's hamburger stand are all landmarks.

Using these concepts, Lynch saw that some parts of the cities were more **legible** than others. Overall, Lynch discovered, legibility comes when the urban landscape offers clear pathways, nodes, districts, edges, and landmarks. The less legible parts of the city do not offer such a precise landscape. Thus it is more difficult for a person to form a mental map of that area. And further, some cities—such as Boston—are more legible than other cities. For example, Lynch found that Jersey City is a city of low legibility. Wedged between New York City and Newark, Jersey City is fragmented by railroads and highways. Residents' mental maps of Jersey City have large blank areas in them. When questioned, they can think of few local landmarks. Instead, they tend to point to the New York City skyline just across the river.

In 1970, the planning department of the City of Los Angeles undertook a comprehensive study to see what images different residents held of Los Angeles. Figure 11-16b shows the composite mental map of hundreds of residents. Note the important role of the mountains as visual edges. When visible, they set limits to the image of the Los Angeles basin. However, the mountains often are hidden by smog, which deprives Angelenos of an important point of reference.

In Los Angeles, freeways obviously serve as the major pathways. Note that, in areas without freeways, there are large voids in the mental maps. This demonstrates the important role that pathways play in our image of a place. Some people seem to know how to get to a certain point only by the freeway, even though it may be faster and shorter to cut across town. However, rarely is a person's mental map changed with updated information.

Figure 11-17 illustrates how different social groups have vastly different images of the same city. Residents of the upper-income communities of Westwood and Northridge are highly mobile, traveling throughout Los Angeles for work, recreation, and services. As a result, their mental maps are rather comprehensive. In contrast, Avalon and Boyle Heights are low-income communities where social discrimination and economic hardship inhibit physical mobility. Boyle Heights is largely Mexican-American, so a language barrier further aggravates the situation. As you can see, the mental maps held by residents of these two communities are far less comprehensive than the images held by Westwood and Northridge residents. It is important to recognize that a limited mental map reinforces social isolation, which in turn furthers the plight of these communities. People rarely venture into unfamiliar areas; thus they miss potential job opportunities or other activities that might better their situation. Therefore, the mental map is both a product of isolation and a cause of it. People rarely have images of places where they haven't been, and they don't go into areas where they lack psychological reference points in the form of an urban image.

Other studies of urban perceptions focus on other topics. Researchers investigate the boundaries of neighborhoods, knowledge of shopping facilities, attitudes toward the downtown area, and the way children learn about the city and form mental maps. Geographers—as well as psychologists, anthropologists, sociologists, and urban planners—are constantly developing new ways to study the cities in the minds of urban dwellers.

Freeways

▨ Recreation and open space

▨ Commercial and industrial

0   3   6   9
Miles

FIGURE 11-16
Compare the map of physical form and land use in Los Angeles to the images of the city. The image is a map compiled from many mental maps described by residents. How do you think this exercise would turn out in your city?

Conclusion

The internal structure of a city expresses great variety. People and activities spread themselves across the city in an intricate urban mosaic. But we see that there is order to the pattern. The concept of culture region is useful in examining social areas and activity areas within a city.

We also see that two major forces are at work in the cities: one that

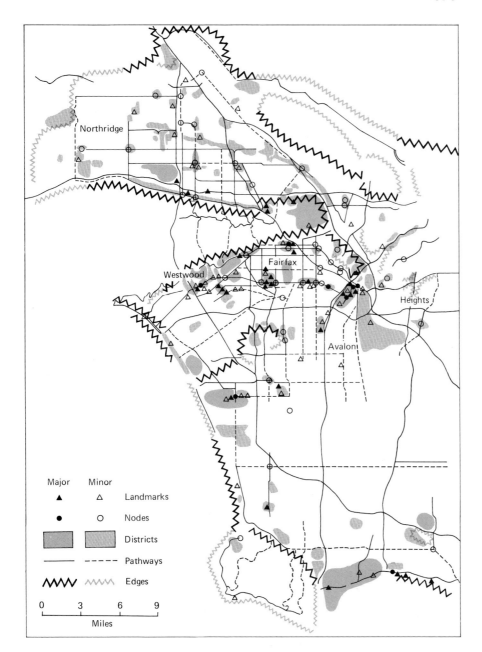

Major   Minor

▲   △   Landmarks

●   ○   Nodes

[shaded] [shaded] Districts

———   - - -   Pathways

ʌʌʌʌ ᴧᴧᴧᴧ Edges

0   3   6   9

Miles

works to centralize activities in the inner cities; the other, decentralization, working to locate activities in the suburbs. The latter is the dominant
process currently at work in North American cities. But the costs of
decentralization run high—not just to the suburbs, where growth causes
problems, but also to the inner cities, where decay and deterioration take a
high economic and social toll.

The cultural ecology of a city is a complicated pattern, for urbanization
has substantially altered many aspects of the physical environment. In

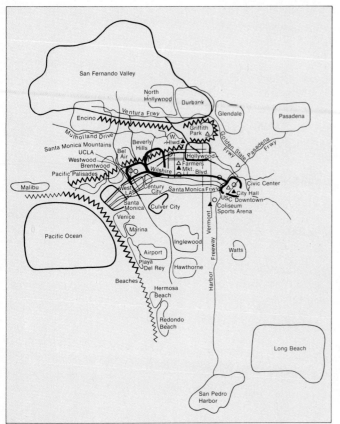

(a) Westwood

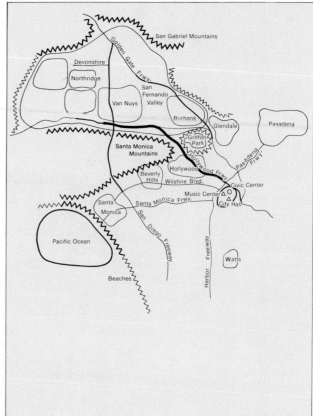

(b) Northridge

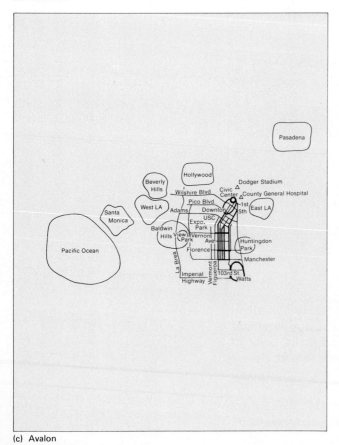

(c) Avalon

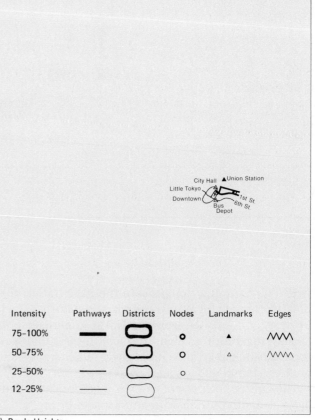

(d) Boyle Heights

Intensity	Pathways	Districts	Nodes	Landmarks	Edges
75-100%			◦	▲	∿∿∿
50-75%			◦	△	∿∿∿
25-50%				◦	
12-25%					

◄─FIGURE 11-17
Compare these four mental maps of Los Angeles. Those for Westwood and Northridge illustrate the comprehensive mental images carried by upper middle-income people who have high mobility and move freely around the urban region. In contrast, the mental maps for two low-income groups, Avalon and Boyle Heights, show less knowledge of the city, which is a function of limited mobility. What causes a group to have reduced mobility? Both are minority areas. (From *The Visual Environment of Los Angeles*, Los Angeles Department of City Planning, 1971.)

many cases, this alteration has reached the point where feedback from the environment—in the form of landslides, air pollution, or floods—damages the cities. Increasing care will have to be taken to assure that natural systems are not turned against urban dwellers.

But not all patterns and processes within the cities are explained by economic or physical theories. Each individual carries around a unique mental image of his or her city. This perception of the urban landscape forms a mental map that is the basis for decisions. There are similarities between the images held by people of similar experiences. But images held by groups with different backgrounds and experiences may differ dramatically. It is not enough to simply describe and explain a city; we also need to know how it is perceived by people, since this is the basis for action.

Glossary

CBD the central business district of a city.

Census tracts small districts used by the United States Census Bureau to survey the population.

Centralizing forces diffusion forces that encourage people or businesses to locate in the central city.

Concentric zone model a social model that depicts a city as five areas bounded by concentric rings.

Decentralizing forces diffusion forces that encourage people or businesses to locate outside the central city.

Dust dome a pollution layer over a city that is thickest at the center of the city.

Ecological fallacy an invalid statement about individuals drawn from statistical material on groups.

Ecosystem a unit through which the flow of matter or energy is traced.

Ethnic culture region an area shared by people of similar ethnic background, who share race or language.

Feedback repercussions on a system when an element is returned in modified form.

Heat island an area of warmer temperature at the center of a city, caused by the urban concentration of heat-retaining concrete, brick, and asphalt.

Input a resource, such as water, flowing into an ecosystem.

Lateral commuting traveling from one suburb to another in going from home to work.

Legible city a city that is easy to decipher, with clear pathways, edges, nodes, districts, and landmarks.

Multiple nuclei model a model that depicts a city growing from several separate focal points.

Neighborhood a small social area within a city where residents share values and concerns and interact with one another on a daily basis.

Output elements produced by and flowing out of an ecosystem; for example, water may leave a system in many forms—as sewage, as a component of food or drinks for export, as vapor produced by industry.

Particulate matter bits of matter spewed into the air by incinerators, car exhausts, tire wear, industrial combustion, and so forth.

Sector model an economic model that depicts a city as a series of pie-shaped wedges.

Social culture region an area in a city where many of the residents share social traits such as income, education, and stage of life.

Townscape the urban landscape, including the layout of streets and the characteristic structure of buildings.

Suggested Readings

John S. Adams (ed.) *Contemporary Metropolitan American.* Cambridge, Mass.: Ballinger, 1976.

John S. Adams. "The Geography of Riots and Civil Disorders in the 1960's," *Economic Geography,* 67 (January 1972), 24–42.

Martin Anderson. *The Federal Bulldozer.* Cambridge, Mass.: M.I.T. Press, 1964.

Wilfrid Bach and Thomas Hagedorn. "Atmospheric Pollution: Its Spatial Distribution over an Urban Area," *Proceedings of the Association of American Geographers,* 3 (1971), 22.

Brian J. Berry. *The Human Consequences of Urbanisation.* New York: St. Martin's Press, 1973.

T. J. Chandler. "The Changing Form of London's Heat Island," *Geography,* 46 (1961).

City of Los Angeles. *The Visual Environment of Los Angeles.* Los Angeles: Department of City Planning, 1971.

Thomas Detwyler and Melvin Marcus (eds.). *Urbanization and Environment: The Physical Geography of the City.* Belmont, Cal.: Duxbury Press, 1972.

Joe Feagin (ed.) *The Urban Scene.* New York: Random House, 1973.

John Fried. *Life Along the San Andreas Fault.* New York: Saturday Review Press, 1973.

Homer Hoyt (ed.) *Structure and Growth of Residential Neighborhoods in American Cities.* Washington, D.C.: Federal Housing Administration, 1939.

James H. Johnson (ed.). *Suburban Growth: Geographical Processes at the Edge of the City.* New York: Wiley, 1974.

R. J. Johnson and D. T. Herbert. *Social Areas in Cities.* 2 vols. New York: Wiley, 1976.

Kevin Lynch. *The Image of the City.* Cambridge, Mass.: M.I.T. Press, 1960.

Peter A. Morrison. "Urban Growth and Decline: San Jose and St. Louis in the 1960's," *Science,* 185 (August 1974), 757–762.

Lewis Mumford. *The City in History.* New York: Harcourt Brace Jovanovich, 1960.

Howard Nelson. "The Form and Structure of Cities: Urban Growth Patterns," *Journal of Geography,* 68 (1969), 198–207.

John Palen. *The Urban World.* New York: McGraw-Hill, 1975.

Robert Putnam, Frank Taylor, and Philip Kettle. *A Geography of Urban Places.* Toronto: Methuen, 1970.

Gerald Suttles. *The Social Construction of Communities.* Chicago: University of Chicago Press, 1972.

Yi-fu Tuan. *Topophilia: A Study of Environmental Perception, Attitudes and Values.* Englewood Cliffs, N. J.: Prentice-Hall, 1974.

James E. Vance, Jr. *This Scene of Man: The Role and Structure of the City in the Geography of Western Civilization.* New York: Harper & Row, 1977.

David Ward. *Cities and Immigrants.* New York: Oxford University Press, 1971.

Sam Bass Warner, Jr. *The Urban Wilderness: A History of the American City.* New York: Harper & Row, 1972.

Chapter-opening photo: In the port of ➤ New York.

Industry and the Web of Transportation

12

There have been two great economic "revolutions" in human development. The first of these was the domestication of plants and animals, which occurred in our dim prehistory. This agricultural revolution, discussed in Chapter 3, ultimately resulted in a huge increase in human population, a greatly accelerated modification of the physical environment, and major cultural readjustments. The second of these upheavals, the **industrial revolution**, is still taking place. We live today at a pivotal point in the destiny of our species, for we are witnesses to this second revolution.

The industrial revolution, which began in the eighteenth century, released for the second time in history undreamed-of human productive powers. Suddenly, whole societies were able to engage in the seemingly limitless multiplication of goods and services. Rapid bursts of human inventiveness followed, as did gigantic population increases, and a massive, often unsettling remodeling of the environment. Today, the industrial revolution, with its churning up of whole populations and its restructuring of ancient cultural traditions, is still running its course. There are lands still largely untouched by its machines, factories, transportation devices, and communication techniques. Western nations, where this revolution has been underway the longest, are still feeling its sometimes painful, sometimes invigorating effects.

This chapter concentrates on the industrial revolution as the cultural geographer sees it. Industry, of course, is a livelihood, and livelihood is a facet of culture. In Western culture, the majority of the population owe their livelihood either directly or indirectly to industry and its related products and services. Add to this the uneven spatial distribution of industrial and transport facilities, and you can understand the cultural geographer's interest in this topic.

On an individual level, there is scarcely a facet of American life that has not been affected in a major way by the industrial revolution. A Friday night out might involve a drive in a car to a single outlet in a nationwide chain of restaurants, where you can order fried chicken raised several states away on special enriched grain, brought by refrigerated truck to a deep freeze, and cooked in an electric oven. Later, at a movie, you might buy a candy bar manufactured halfway across the country and have a soft drink delivered to you by a machine that has its own ice. Then you would enjoy a series of machine-produced pictures passing in front of your eyes so fast that they seem to be moving. You could just as easily pick almost any other moment in your life, from sleep, with its permanent-press contoured sheets and its mass-manufactured alarm clocks, to your pet cat, with its chemical flea collar, canned food, and distemper shots. What you discover is that just about every object and every event in your life is affected, if not actually created, by the industrial revolution.

The cultural geographer distinguishes three types of industrial livelihood. **Primary industries** are those involved in extracting natural resources from the earth. Fishing, lumbering, and mining are examples of primary industries (Figure 12-1). Agriculture is also a primary industry, but it was treated in Chapter 3.

Secondary industry is the processing stage, commonly called manufacturing. It lies at the very heart of industrial activity. Secondary industries process the raw materials extracted by primary industries, transforming them into more usable forms. Ore is converted into steel; logs are milled into lumber; fish are processed and canned. As a rule, several steps are involved in manufacturing. In this secondary stage, many factories turn

out products that serve as raw materials for other secondary industries. Thus, steel mills provide steel for automobile factories, and lumber mills provide building materials for the construction industry.

Tertiary economic activity does not involve either the extraction of resources or the manufacture of goods, but instead the distribution of goods and services. Tertiary institutions include wholesale and retail outlets, banking and other financial services, governmental and educational services, medical facilities, and the many other business and service functions upon which we depend daily. A filling station, a department store, a post office, a hospital, and a university are all tertiary activities. Part and parcel of this tertiary stage is the system of transportation and communication. Highways, railroads, airlines, pipelines, telephones, radios, and television are all vital to the distribution of goods and services.

Primary, secondary, and tertiary industries should not, however, be thought of as totally separate operations that can be dealt with separately from one another. The worker in Detroit who gets laid off because her plant is moved to Singapore, the Argentinian who drinks a cola bottled in Argentina while watching "Love Boat" on his American-made TV, and the lumberman who buys a Japanese table made with wood he cut in Oregon are all involved in an interconnected economic system of global proportions. Single corporate entities called conglomerates may own scores of industries of all three types in a variety of fields. As a result, corporate planning, whether in the United States, Japan, Germany, or elsewhere, goes on at all three levels at once. Scholars, for instance, have pointed out that labor costs and other factors have increasingly led United

FIGURE 12-1
An example of a primary industry, this lumber mill is in Gabon, a nation of equatorial Africa. The oil industry has become one of the most controversial primary activities in recent years. Shortages and repeated price increases have made every citizen of the industrialized world aware of our dependence on this primary industry. The oil wells shown here are in Lake Maracaibo, Venezuela. Why has the industrial revolution become so dependent on oil?

States corporations to send secondary industries overseas and export their products back to the United States. In turn, tertiary or service activities, rather than actual factory production, make up the employment of a larger and larger proportion of America's work force.

Because industrialization is closely interwoven with the physical environment and with other facets of culture, because industry is unevenly distributed, because the industrial revolution is a series of ideas spreading by means of cultural diffusion, and because entire landscapes have been remolded and often deformed by industrialization, we can profitably apply the five themes of cultural geography to the study of industry. Thus, we will discuss industrial regions, the diffusion of industrial innovations, industrial ecology, the place of industry in cultural integration, and the industrial landscape.

Industrial Regions

Each type of industrial activity—primary, secondary, and tertiary—displays unique spatial patterns. Geographers, applying the theme of culture region, refer to these as industrial regions, and Figure 12-2 reveals some of these patterns.

Primary industry

Primary industries extract both renewable and nonrenewable resources. **Renewable resources** are those that can be used without being permanently depleted, such as forests, water, fishing grounds, and agricultural land. **Nonrenewable resources** are those that are depleted when they are used, such as minerals.

Many primary industries, especially those engaged in mining, are spread widely across the earth. In fact, many regions that lack significant manufacturing activity have major primary industries. Figure 12-2 shows the main areas of primary and secondary industry. As a rule, however, primary industries are more likely to develop in conjunction with manufacturing districts. Zones of primary industry distant from manufacturing centers are likely to spring up only if the resource is very valuable and rare, and thus worth enough to withstand the cost of transporting it long distances. On the other hand, almost every major area of secondary industry is surrounded by a "halo" of primary activity.

Secondary industry

Most of the world's industrial activity is found in the midlatitudes of the northern hemisphere, especially in parts of the United States, Europe, the Soviet Union, and Japan. This is particularly true of manufacturing. In the United States, many secondary industries are clustered in the northeastern part of the country, a region often referred to as the American Manufacturing Belt (see Figure 12-3). On the opposite Atlantic shore, manufacturing is concentrated in the central core of Europe, surrounded by a less industrialized periphery (see Figure 12-4). Most Soviet manufacturing is in the western third of the Soviet Union, while Japan's industrial complex is concentrated around the shore of the Inland Sea and throughout the southern part of the country (see Figures 12-5 and 12-6).

Many different types of manufacturing are found within the world's

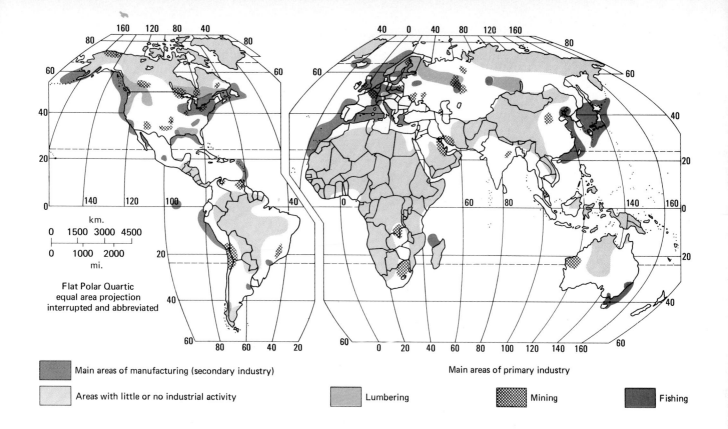

Main areas of manufacturing (secondary industry)

Areas with little or no industrial activity

Main areas of primary industry

Lumbering

Mining

Fishing

FIGURE 12-2

Industrial areas appear on all continents. Manufacturing is concentrated in relatively small areas, and large regions support little or no industry.

FIGURE 12-3

Major manufacturing regions of Anglo-America. The largest and most important region is still the American Manufacturing Belt, the traditional industrial core of the United States. Dispersal of manufacturing to other regions has occurred mainly since World War II. What factors might explain the location of these regions?

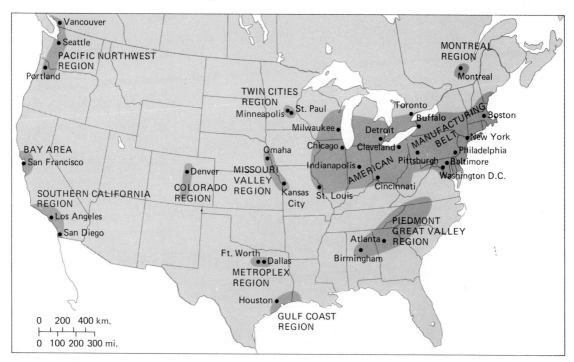

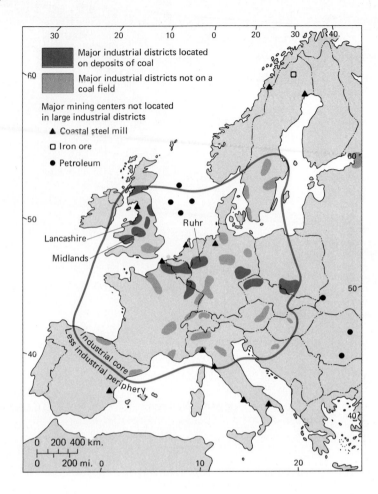

FIGURE 12-4
Industrial areas of Europe are plotted on this map. An industrialized core is surrounded by a less industrialized area. How does this compare to the pattern in North America?

FIGURE 12-5
The Soviet manufacturing belt developed close to Europe. In spite of Soviet attempts to disperse their industry, it remains concentrated in the western third of the country. What political and economic problems does this cause for the nation? (In part, after R. E. Lonsdale and J. H. Thompson, "A Map of the U.S.S.R.'s Manufacturing," Economic Geography, 36 (1960), 36–52.)

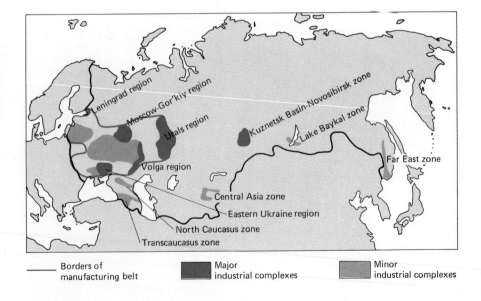

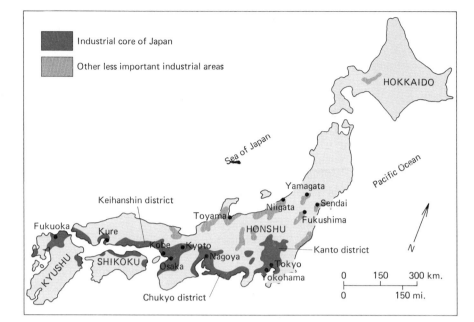

FIGURE 12-6
Japanese industrial areas manufacture products for the entire world. (In part, after John H. Thompson and Michihiro Miyazaki, "A Map of Japan's Manufacturing," Geographical Review, 49 (1959), 1–17.)

major regions. These often display considerable spatial segregation, so that a single industrial district might be composed of several zones, each dominated by a particular kind of industry. Figure 12-7 shows this segregation in the Ruhr district of West Germany. Iron and steel manufacture might be concentrated in one of these zones, chemical factories in another, textiles in a third, and automobile manufacture in a fourth.

Beyond the major manufacturing areas of the world are numerous countries in which secondary industries have been established but are still not fully developed. Many, if not most, of these nations received their industrial beginnings as producers of raw materials for manufacturing countries. Now they are attempting to develop the manufacturing capability to process their own raw materials, rather than simply exporting them and buying the finished products from other countries. Brazil and Mexico are such nations. Oil-rich nations such as Iran and Saudi Arabia are also moving toward a manufacturing capability, accomplishing this by investing some of the wealth they are accumulating through petroleum sales. Success in such industrial development will depend in part on whether the nation in question has good access to the major shipping lanes of the world. Landlocked countries are handicapped in this respect.

Finally, there are many nations that have little industrial development and very few prospects of acquiring it. In ex-colonies, commercial plantation agriculture is often the only type of economic activity that even approaches the description of "industry." Some nations lack even that. Many of the newly independent nations of Africa fall into this category, particularly those in the interior of the continent. Typically, they are hampered by a lack of natural resources as well as poor transportation connections, both internally and with the rest of the world.

Tertiary industry

The distribution of transportation facilities, key to tertiary activity, closely parallels the spatial pattern of primary and secondary industry. Modern

FIGURE 12-7
The Ruhr industrial district in West Germany is the single most important industrial area in all of Europe. Note the spatial segregation of different types of industry and the relatively small size of this particular district.

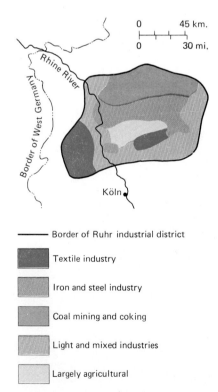

— Border of Ruhr industrial district

Textile industry

Iron and steel industry

Coal mining and coking

Light and mixed industries

Largely agricultural

industries require well-developed transport systems, and every industrial district is served by a network of such facilities. Figure 12-8 maps the number of persons per motor vehicle by country. However, there are major regional differences in the relative importance of the various modes of transport. In the Soviet Union, for example, highways are of very little significance; railroads, and to a lesser extent waterways, carry most of the transport load. In the United States, on the other hand, highways are very important, while the railroad system is in decline. Many western European nations rely heavily on inland waterways. However, regional contrasts can be seen even within an area as small as Europe: The Netherlands moves 86 percent of all goods by river and canal; France has traditionally emphasized railroads at the expense of highway construction; and Italy uses highways far more than either railways or waterways.

Beyond the industrialized regions, transport systems are much less developed. In most of Africa, interior Asia, and other nonindustrial regions, motorable highways and railroads are rare. One notable exception to this generalization is India. In spite of a relatively low level of industrialization, India has a good network of railroads, largely a legacy of British colonial rule.

Some culture regions, then, are highly industrial and well served by transport facilities, while others are little touched by the manufacturing and transport technology of the industrial world. How did such spatial patterns evolve? Why are industry and transportation so unevenly distributed? Perhaps the best device for beginning the explanation of this phenomenon is the theme of cultural diffusion, and the best approach, the cultural-historical method.

FIGURE 12-8
The number of persons per motor vehicle (cars and trucks) about 1975 is mapped here. The most highly industrialized nations have the largest numbers of cars and trucks per unit of population. (United Nations, *Statistical Yearbook, 1978.* 545–551.)

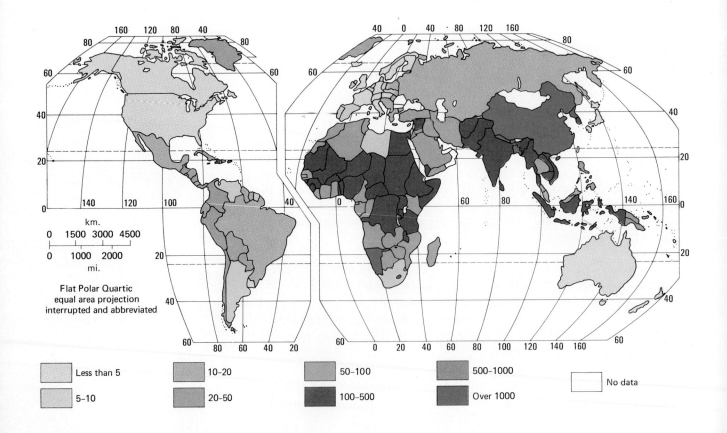

Less than 5   5–10   10–20   20–50   50–100   100–500   500–1000   Over 1000   No data

km.
0   1500   3000   4500

0   1000   2000
mi.

Flat Polar Quartic equal area projection interrupted and abbreviated

Origin and Diffusion of the Industrial Revolution

The world map of industrialized and nonindustrialized regions is a good measure of how far the industrial revolution has spread, how far the cultural diffusion of this revolution's technological ideas has proceeded. Until the industrial revolution, the large majority of people were concerned with the most basic of primary economic activities—acquiring from the land the necessities of survival. Society and culture were overwhelmingly rural and agricultural. To be sure, industry existed in this setting, since humans are by nature makers of things. For as long as our biological species has existed, we have fashioned tools, weapons, utensils, clothing, and other objects. But traditionally these items were made by hand, laboriously and slowly. Before about A.D. 1700, virtually all such manufacture was carried on in two rather distinct systems: **cottage (household) industry** and **guild industry**.

Cottage industry, by far the most common, was practiced in farm homes and rural villages, usually as a sideline to agriculture. Objects for family use were made in each household, and most villages had a cobbler, miller, weaver, and smith who worked part-time at these trades in their homes. Skills were passed from parents to children with little formality.

By contrast, the guild system consisted of professional organizations of highly skilled, specialized artisans engaged full-time in their trades and living in towns and cities. Membership in a guild was attained through a long apprenticeship, during which the master craftsman taught the apprentice the secrets of the profession. The guild was a fraternal organization of artisans skilled in a particular craft, so that there were guilds for weavers, glassblowers, silversmiths, potters, and so on.

Origins of the industrial revolution

While the cottage and guild systems were different in many respects, they did share one trait. Both depended on hand labor and human power. Because they shared this characteristic, both were changed radically by the coming of the industrial revolution. These changes were so basic as to render the traditional systems largely obsolete.

First, human hands were replaced by machines in the fashioning of finished products, rendering the word *manufacturing* ("made by hand") technically obsolete. No longer would the weaver sit at a hand loom and painstakingly produce each piece of cloth. Instead, large mechanical looms were invented to do the job faster and more economically (though not necessarily better). Second, human power was replaced by various forms of **inanimate power**. The machines were driven by water power, the burning of fossil fuels, and later by hydroelectricity and the energy of the atom. Men and women, once the proud producers of fine handmade goods, became tenders of machines.

We know a lot more about the origins and diffusion of the industrial revolution than we do about the beginnings of agriculture. The industrial revolution is a matter of recorded history and has been studied in great detail. We can pinpoint its origin. The industrial revolution began in England in the early 1700s, though it is possible to trace its antecedents back even earlier. Within a century and a half of its beginnings, this economic revolution had greatly altered all three levels of industrial activity.

FIGURE 12-9
The first major industry of the industrial revolution was the production of cotton cloth. This etching, dated 1835, shows cotton being spun into thread. The textile industry was characteristic of manufacturing in the United Kingdom.

Textiles. The initial breakthrough came in the secondary or manufacturing stage. More exactly, it occurred in the British textile industry, centered at that time in the district of Lancashire in western England. At first the changes were modest and on a small scale. Mechanical looms were invented, and flowing water, long used as a source of power by grain millers, was harnessed to drive the looms. During this stage, manufacturing industries remained largely rural, scattered about at the sites where rushing streams could be found, especially waterfalls and rapids. Later in the eighteenth century, the invention of the steam engine provided a better source of power, and a shift away from water-powered machines was made.

In the beginning, the industrial revolution was really a cotton revolution. In England, until about 1830, "factories" or "industry" meant the production of cotton cloth (Figure 12-9). No other industry even remotely approached the million and a half people directly or indirectly involved in Britain's textile production. This cloth trade had grown with the British Empire. In 1850, for instance, one-quarter of all Lancashire cloth exports went to colonial India. Furthermore, the explosion of the British textile industry proceeded hand in hand with the preservation of the slave-fueled plantation economy of the American South. American raw cotton was fed continuously into the seemingly insatiable Lancashire textile mills. In the United States, too, the first factories were textile plants.

"Manufactured" metals. Traditionally, metal industries had been small-scale, rural enterprises. They were carried on in small forges situated near ore deposits and relied on forests to provide charcoal for the smelting process. The chemical changes that occurred in the making of steel were not understood even by the guildsmen who used them, and much ritual, superstition, and ceremony were associated with steelmaking. Techniques had changed little since the beginning of the Iron Age, two thousand years before.

The industrial revolution radically altered all this. In the eighteenth century, a series of inventions by master ironmakers living in the valley of the Severn River in Shropshire, south of Lancashire in the English Midlands, allowed the old traditions, techniques, and rituals of steelmaking to be swept away and replaced with a scientific, large-scale industry. Coke, which is nearly pure carbon and is derived from high-grade coal, replaced charcoal in the smelting process. Large blast furnaces were invented to replace the forge, and efficient rolling mills took the place of hammer and anvil. Mass production of steel was the result, and the new industrial order was built of steel. Other manufacturing industries made similar transitions, and entirely new types of manufacturing arose, such as machine-making.

Mining. Primary industries were also revolutionized. The first to feel the effects of the new technology was coal mining. The adoption of the steam engine necessitated huge amounts of coal to fire the boilers, and the conversion to coke in the smelting process further increased the demand for coal. Fortunately, Britain had large coal deposits. New mining techniques and tools were invented, so that coal mining became a large-scale, mechanized industry. Because coal was heavy and bulky, it was difficult to transport. As a result, manufacturing industries began flocking to the coalfields in order to be near the supply. Similar modernization occurred in the mining of iron ore, copper, and other metals needed by rapidly growing industries.

Railroads. The industrial revolution also affected the tertiary sector, most notably in the form of rapid bulk transportation. The traditional wooden sailing ships gave way to steel vessels driven by steam engines, canals were built, and the British-invented railroad came on the scene (Figure 12-10). The principal stimulus that led to these transportation breakthroughs was the need to move raw materials and finished products from one place to another, both cheaply and quickly. The impact of the industrial revolution would have been minimized had not the distribution of goods and services also been improved (see box, "Distance in the Preindustrial Age"). It is no accident that the British, creators of the industrial revolution, also invented the railroad and initiated the first large-scale canal construction.

It should be realized, however, that the development of all three sectors of industry was closely intertwined. The English railroad was the creation

FIGURE 12-10
The invention of the railroad played a vital role in the development of the industrial revolution. This old print depicts the Phoenix locomotive and carriage.

DISTANCE IN THE PREINDUSTRIAL AGE

Our lives are a constant adventure in shrinking space. With a car, we're just minutes from a friend miles away. The airplane has put us within jet-lag distance of Paris, Moscow, or Calcutta. Rockets are bringing the solar system into our distance calculations. In such an age, it is hard to imagine what an obstacle distance often proved to be before the industrial revolution.

A record of 10,000 letters sent to Venice, Italy, in the early sixteenth century shows clearly what a factor distance was in the preindustrial world. Letters from nearby Genoa took an average of 6 days to arrive; London, 27; Constantinople, 37; Lisbon, 46; Damascus, 80. But these average figures hardly tell the whole tale. Changing human and climatic conditions lent a striking elasticity to mail delivery. Deliveries from Paris ranged from a maximum of 34 days to a minimum of 7 days; Barcelona, 77 to 8; and Florence, 13 to 1, to pick three places at random. Zara, which was separated from Venice by only a short stretch of the Adriatic Sea, hold the record. Its letters, depending upon sailing conditions, took from a maximim of 25 to a minimum of 1 day to arrive. Compared to other goods, however, letters moved briskly across the map. Sixteenth-century Italian businessmen normally assumed that it took even their privileged goods three months to reach London.

In fact, before the eighteenth century, distance had been a relatively constant factor for centuries. In terms of travel, the Mediterranean was about the same "size" in the sixteenth century as it had been in Roman times over 1000 years earlier. Traveling times did not change much until the nineteenth century.

Source: Fernand Braudel, The Mediterranean and the Mediterranean World in the Age of Philip II *(New York: Harper & Row, 1972), vol. 1 p. 356.*

of the coal mines. The first modern railway ran from the inland coalfield of Durham to the English coast. The earliest locomotive drivers were all hired out of coal areas. In turn, the iron and steel industries, the basic core of the industrial system, were mainly the creation of the railroad. It was the burst of railroad building that provided Britain's tiny iron industry with a demand large enough to justify investment in its expansion. For a single mile of rail, 300 tons of steel were needed for track alone. As a result, the first two decades of railroad building, 1830-1850, saw iron and steel production increase from 680,000 to 2,250,000 tons. In the same period, the output of coal, which first fostered the development of the railroad, soared from 15 million to 49 million tons, in part to stoke the growing steel industry.

Diffusion from Britain

For a century, Britain maintained a virtual monopoly on its industrial innovations. Indeed, the British government actively tried to prevent the diffusion of the various inventions and innovations that made up the industrial revolution, because they gave Britain an enormous economic advantage and contributed greatly to the growth and strength of the British Empire. Nevertheless, this technology finally diffused beyond the bounds of the British Isles (see Figure 12-11). Continental Europe was the first to receive its impact. In the last half of the nineteenth century, the industrial revolution took firm root in Germany, Belgium, and other nations of northwestern and central Europe. The diffusion of railroads in Europe provides a good index to the spread of the industrial revolution there (Figure 12-12). The United States began rapid adoption of this new technology about 1850, followed a half century later by Japan, the only major non-Western nation to undergo full industrialization (Figure 12-13). In the first third of the present century, the diffusion of industry and modern transport spilled over into the Soviet Union.

In the United States, the spread of the railroad affected both the

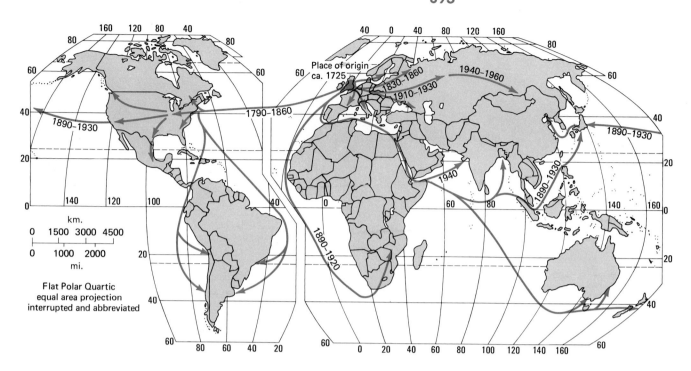

FIGURE 12-11
The diffusion of the industrial revolution has changed cultures in much of the world.

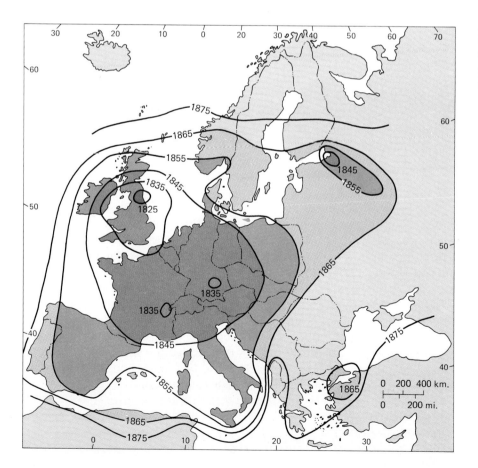

FIGURE 12-12
The diffusion of the railroad in Europe. The industrial revolution and the railroad spread together across much of the continent.

FIGURE 12-13
This Japanese steel mill is typical of many heavy industrial plants. Because the manufacturing techniques of secondary industry have diffused to many parts of the world, factories in many nations look similar.

distribution of industries within cities and within regions. Steel mills, refineries, meat-packing plants, and other industrial complexes sprang up at major rail terminals. Wherever it went, the railroad concentrated industry; yet, at the same time, its presence allowed for a greater regional diversification of industrial tasks. Small cities began to specialize in the production of specific industrial goods based on local skills and resources, as parts of large, railroad-linked industrial clusters. By 1916, the American rail network had reached its height with 254,000 miles of track, carrying 77 percent of all intercity freight tonnage, and 98 percent of intercity passengers.

Few cultures exposed to industrial innovations have proved resistant to them. However, the spread of the industrial revolution could be halted or even reversed by determined political administrators. A striking example was Britain's deliberate deindustrialization of its Indian colony to create a market for its cotton products. India's textile industry had traditionally exported cotton goods to all parts of the world. As late as 1815, India exported to England cotton goods worth fifty times the British cotton goods it imported. However, imperial Britain, which had used high tariffs to protect its own cotton production, opened India to "free trade." Using its imperial power, it caused India's old industrial centers to die. Dacca, for instance, became partly overgrown with jungle, and skilled Indian workers were forced into the countryside to take up agricultural pursuits. In the end, India, once a great cotton textile producer, exported only raw cotton to Britain, where it was turned into textile goods and sent back to India to be bought.

Britain's political and military pressure helped it to conquer a world market for its exploding industrial plant. In a sense, then, it "spread" the industrial revolution across the planet. However, in practical terms, it turned its colonies into giant plantations or mines for the production of raw materials to be processed in Britain. India's actual industrialization was set back at least half a century. Perhaps only the independence of the United States, through its revolutionary war against Britain, saved it from a similar fate. The United States government's imposition of a high protective tariff barrier helped its weak businesses survive the nineteenth-century onslaught of cheap British industrial goods.

Results of industrial diffusion

As early as 1870, the spread of industrialization had produced the gap between the "developed" and the "undeveloped" countries that is so familiar to us today. In the following century, only Japan, the Soviet Union, and perhaps China really succeeded in bridging that gap. Present-day industrial expansion in the age of corporate globalism seems to be intensifying this gap, in many cases increasing the dependence of less industrialized on more industrialized nations. The modern-day equivalent of Britain's deindustrialization of India is the siphoning off of corporate profits from the nonindustrialized world. Between 1960 and 1968, for instance, American-based corporations took, on the average, 79 percent of their net profits out of Latin America. As a result, the industrialization of "undeveloped" countries is actually increasing the power of the world's leading industrial nations. In fact, today we face a world in which, while industrial technology has spread everywhere, the basic industrial power of the planet is more centralized than ever. It has been suggested that if present trends continue, by 1985 about 300 global corporations will control most of the nonsocialist world's productive assets. These corporations have their headquarters mainly in those areas where the industrial revolution took root earliest—the midlatitude countries of the northern hemisphere. A more modest prediction by economist Judd Polk is that by the year 2000, a few hundred companies will produce goods and services equaling $4.2 billion, or approximately 54 percent of the value of all goods and services in the world.

Within cultures, actual barriers to industrial diffusion have usually been economic or physical in nature, based on remoteness or shortage of necessary natural resources. As a result, we are well advised to look into the themes of cultural ecology and cultural integration for a better understanding of the spatial distribution of industries and the causal interaction of industry and environment, industry and culture.

Industrial Ecology

The diffusion of the industrial revolution has occurred only at enormous environmental expense. By its very nature, the technology of modern industry consumes nonrenewable resources and destroys the natural environment. Massive pollution of the air and water seems to be an unavoidable by-product of mechanized industrial processes, at least in our present state of knowledge. While pollution and environmental alteration could be significantly reduced, can they ever be totally eliminated if mechanized culture is to maintain its industrial base? Perhaps in the final analysis we will find that industrialization, which has become so integral a part of our culture in the past two centuries, is simply ecologically untenable and cannot be maintained.

Our experience with industrialization has been too short and shallow to permit an adequate perspective on the problem. In the United States, we have lived with the industrial revolution for a little over one century. What would the ecological impact of this system be after two centuries, ten centuries, twenty centuries? We can only guess, but many experts are not optimistic. What we do know is that the technology of the industrial revolution has demanded that we modify our habitat on a previously undreamed-of scale, and at the same time it has provided us with the tools and techniques to carry out that massive modification.

Almost every year, it seems, we learn of some new, previously unsuspected impact of our industrial economy on the environment. A case in point is "acid rain" (Figure 12-14, and box, "Acid Rain"). Various chemicals released into the air as a consequence of the burning of fossil fuels are cleansed from the atmosphere by precipitation. The resultant rainfall has a much higher than normal acidity and is capable of poisoning fish, damaging plants, and diminishing the fertility of soil. Ninety lakes in the seemingly pristine Adirondack Mountains of New York state are now "dead," devoid of fish life, and 50,000 lakes in Canada are in danger of suffering a similar fate. Pine trees, soybeans, and other plants can be killed or retarded by acid rain, and even automobile paint finishes are adversely affected. The rain is often as acidic as vinegar.

But if the industrial revolution has brought accelerated environmental change, it has also been governed in part by the same environment. The

FIGURE 12-14
The geography of acid rain in the upper Midwest and Ontario, 1979. The problem of acid rain, only recently detected, now threatens plant and animal life across much of the eastern United States and Canada. (Source: International Joint Commission on the Great Lakes.)

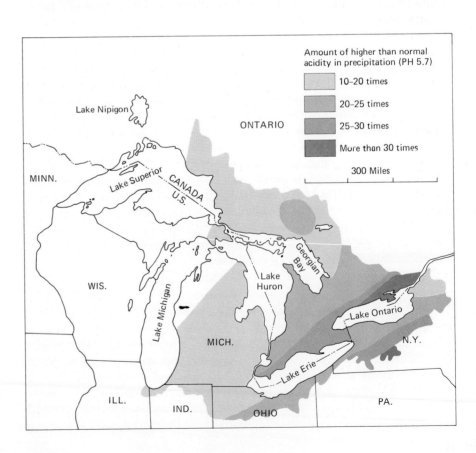

ACID RAIN

People don't see it, feel it, or smell it, but when it rains or snows east of the Mississippi, sulfuric acid falls on their heads. And into the water they drink, wash in, swim in, and fish in, and onto the food they eat.

Sulfuric acid is highly corrosive. It sails in from the West with the wind, born as sulphur oxides in the belching smokestacks of power plants in the great industrial river valleys, landing on earth as "acid rain."

There is nitric acid rain too. It is born mostly as nitrogen oxides in automobile exhaust pipes. Nitric acid is also corrosive and is used to make bombs.

Pennsylvania, a state rich in forest, field, and stream, is particularly threatened, researchers say. Tests show it is being soaked by the most acidic rain anywhere in the country, possibly in the world. Take the shower that fell on the town of Kane, located along the state's northern tier, on September 19, 1978. It had a pH reading of 2.32, according to the Pennsylvania Forestry Association. That's like being doused with vinegar.

"What we see is frightening a lot of scientists," says Dr. George Hendrey, a researcher at the Brookhaven National Laboratory in New York, which serves as a research arm for ten large Eastern universities. "It's a lot worse than we thought."

Source: An Associated Press release, March, 1980.

spatial distribution of industry in particular has been influenced by environmental considerations. To be sure, many factors are involved in industrial location, but some of these are environmental.

Raw materials

In the early stages of the industrial revolution, industries grew where the raw materials were. The reason was simple. The development of efficient means of mass transportation only came about a century after the beginning of the revolution. Before about 1830 or 1840, it was impossible to move bulky, heavy raw materials very far. In the last century and a half, the attraction of industry to raw materials has steadily decreased because of improved transportation facilities, yet it has not been eliminated altogether.

As a rule, we can say that manufacturers will locate near their raw materials if there is a great loss of weight or bulk in the manufacturing process, or if the finished product is less perishable than the raw materials from which it is made (Figure 12-15). The refining of minerals, the manufacture of iron, steel, and paper, and the canning of fish are examples of industries attracted for these reasons to the source of raw materials.

In industrial location, we should also recognize the phenomenon called **industrial inertia**. This refers to the tendency of industries to remain in their initial location, even after the forces that attracted them there cease to act. Thus, some industries that were drawn to the sources of raw materials in the 1700s or early 1800s, before the advent of modern modes of transportation, remain in the same location. This inertia occurs because capital investment in the form of land and structures would have to be sacrificed if the industry were relocated. In addition, the present labor force would be difficult to relocate with the industry. It is not uncommon to find industries that remained in the same place even after the nonrenewable raw materials that originally attracted them were completely exhausted.

Energy supply

The quantity of energy consumed by industries, measured either as a total amount or per unit of goods produced, has increased greatly since the

FIGURE 12-15
The location of industry is influenced by the location of raw materials and energy supply, among other factors. This steel plant benefits by locating close to sources of coal in Pennsylvania. Enormous quantities wait nearby for use in the manufacturing process.

beginning of the industrial revolution. In a proper sense, energy was not "consumed" at all when water power was used, because water is a renewable power source. Rather, the rapid increase of power use began with the shift from water power to the steam engine and accelerated with the subsequent adoption of other power sources, in particular, electricity.

During the early part of the industrial revolution, long-distance shipment of fossil fuels, from which inanimate power was derived, was too costly to be economically feasible. As a result, industrial plants requiring large amounts of energy were forced to locate where water power or coal was available. Later inventions, such as the railroad, pipeline, motorized barges, and sea-going tankers, have largely removed this restriction on location. The harnessing of electricity and development of high-tension power lines further reduced the locational pull of power supplies.

A few types of manufacturing are still strongly attracted to the sites of energy production. One of these is the aluminum industry, which consumes huge amounts of electricity in the process of converting the raw material bauxite into aluminum. Hydroelectric sites are preferred, since the electricity generated by falling water is renewable and hence cheaper than electricity generated by burning coal or petroleum products. Since electricity cannot be transmitted great distances without considerable loss of power from the transmission lines, location near the hydroelectric facility is best. Hydroelectric sites have attracted aluminum industries to relatively remote places such as Soviet Siberia and the Pacific coastal mountains of Canada. So great are the needs for electric power in this industry that such remote places, hundreds or even thousands of miles removed from the sources of bauxite and the markets for aluminum, are economically practical.

The world entered a new phase of energy consumption when many of the leading oil-producing nations banded together to form OPEC, the Organization of Petroleum Exporting Countries. Because of OPEC actions, the price of petroleum soared, reaching more nearly its valid market value. The "problem" in this case, however, is not one of industrial location as related to energy source and not one of energy transport, but rather the cost of energy at the wellhead. It seems unlikely, therefore, that rapidly increasing energy costs will cause any significant relocation of manufacturing industries, because transportation expenses constitute a smaller than ever proportion of total energy costs.

Restrictions of terrain and climate

Few industries are excluded from an area because of the nature of the terrain, the surface of the land. Only in cases where very large amounts of land are required, or where special characteristics such as the ability to support heavy loads are required, does terrain become a major factor in industrial location. Since suitable terrain can generally be found within a region, terrain becomes an important factor only when specific terrain characteristics must be paired with other site characteristics. One example would be an industry that requires both level land and a port, which is true of some steel mills relying on imported ore.

The role of climate in industrial location is hardly more significant than that of terrain. Our increasing ability to control indoor atmospheric conditions has greatly reduced the impact of climate and weather in choosing location. We can now heat, cool, humidify, or dehumidify any structure. However, modifications of natural atmospheric conditions can be achieved only through the application of energy and the use of machinery, each of which adds to the cost of operations. For this reason, the location of a factory in an area where substantial air conditioning is required will be practical only if there are compensating advantages. For example, the cost of humidifying cotton textile mills in dry climates, necessary to prevent fibers from breaking in the cloth-making process, can be justified only if the needed cotton is grown nearby.

Thus, industry both shapes the environment and is influenced by it. But even more pronounced relationships exist between industry and the other facets of culture. With that in mind, let us turn now from cultural ecology to the theme of cultural integration.

The Industrial Component in Cultural Integration

The list of factors influencing industrial location includes far more than the considerations of raw materials, energy, terrain, and climate. In a very broad sense, literally every aspect of culture is involved in the analysis of industrial location. Among the most important are economic and political factors. Industry has a broader role in culture as well—creating cultural changes.

The economic element in industrial location

In capitalist systems, most of the dominant factors affecting the location of an industry are economic. We will now turn our attention to these.

Labor supply. Labor availability and costs are a factor in choosing an industrial location, but they are seldom the decisive factor. Most affected are **labor-intensive industries**, for which labor costs form a large part of total production costs (Figure 12-16). Examples are industries depending on highly skilled workers producing small objects of high value, such as transistors, cameras, and watches.

Manufacturers consider several characteristics of labor in deciding where to locate factories: availability of workers, average wages, necessary skills, and worker productivity. Traditionally, workers with certain skills tended to live and work in a small number of places, partly as a result of the need for person-to-person training in handing down such skills. Consequently, manufacturers often sought locations where these skilled workers lived.

In recent decades, the increasing mobility of labor throughout the Western world has lessened the locational influence of labor. Migration of labor has accelerated since World War II, especially in Europe and the United States. Large numbers of workers in Europe have migrated from south to north, leaving homes in Spain, southern Italy, Greece, and Yugoslavia to find employment in the main European manufacturing belt.

Factory "migration" itself is an increasingly powerful force on the labor market. For those industries dependent on largely unskilled labor, or labor that can be trained quickly and cheaply, relocation to economically depressed rural areas can result in higher profits. The main attraction of such areas is the large supply of cheap labor, a contrast to the high wages typical in established industrial districts. Much industry has been attracted to the American South for this reason. However, in the United States,

FIGURE 12-16
Some industries depend on a supply of skilled workers. One example is this transistor factory near Tokyo. The women in the assembly line are working on printed circuits.

the wage disparities between existing industrial districts and rural or small-town areas are gradually decreasing due to the imposition of uniform regional or national wage scales, thus eliminating the availability of cheap labor.

Nonetheless, this pattern is now being repeated on an international scale, and a new global division of labor seems to be in the works. Behind these changes in the international labor market lies the strategic thinking by directors of the global corporations. According to a recent Department of Commerce study, for instance, 298 American-based global corporations employ 25 percent of their workers outside the United States. A typical example is General Electric, which ships component parts to Singapore. There they are assembled into products to be exported back to the United States by workers who are paid 30 cents an hour. If the same products were assembled in GE's Ashland, Massachusetts, plant, the cost would be $3.40 an hour. Between 1959 and 1969, GE constructed no less than sixty-one plants abroad. Other major corporations, like Fairchild Camera, Bulova, RCA, and Zenith, are moving their plants to Hong Kong, Taiwan, and other Asian cheap-labor areas, where the labor pool includes children as well as adults who work up to seven days a week.

Such factories, despite relocation costs, quickly drive up corporate profit margins. In addition, the ability of these corporations to plan on such an international scale and to shift the production of a given product thousands of miles away is having a strong effect on the organized labor movements inside the United States.

Markets. A market is the area in which a product may be sold in a volume and at a price profitable to the manufacturer. The size and distribution of markets are generally the most important factors in determining the spatial distribution of industries. Many experts who have studied industrial location consider the market attraction so great that they regard locating an industry near its market as the norm.

Certain industries, in an economic sense, must locate at the market. That is, some manufacturers must situate their factories among their consumers if they are to minimize costs and maximize profits. Such industries include those manufacturing a **weight-gaining** finished product, such as bottled beverages, or a **bulk-gaining** finished product, such as metal containers or bottles. In other words, if weight or bulk is added to the raw materials in the manufacturing process, location near the market is economically desirable due to the transport cost factor. Similarly, if the finished product is more perishable than the raw materials, which is the case with bakery goods and local newspapers, a location near market is also required. In addition, if the product is more fragile than the raw materials that go into its manufacture, as in the making of glass, the industry will be attracted to its market. In each of these cases—gain in weight, bulk, perishability, or fragility—transportation costs on the finished product are much higher than on the raw materials.

Obviously, the degree of importance of market as an attractive force increases with the degree of clustering of population. If population is relatively evenly distributed across a country, no single location can be said to be nearest to the market. But the clustering in cities so typical of modern industrial societies pulls manufacturers to the urban centers.

Similarly, the type of market being served can affect the location of industries. Some manufacturers supply highly clustered urban markets, while others, such as the makers of farm machinery, cater to a more dispersed body of consumers. Industries selling goods to dispersed markets have greater freedom in their choice of location.

As a rule, though, we can say that in Western industrial cultures, the greatest market potential exists where the largest numbers of people are found. This is the result of what is sometimes called the **multiplier effect**. Once an industry locates in a particular place, it provides additional jobs, attracting laborers into the area. This additional population in turn enlarges the local market, thereby attracting other industries. In the same way, the industries arriving later attract still more people and still more industries. This is how industrial districts develop, through a snowballing increase in people and industries. It is a process that is very difficult to control in free-enterprise systems, and if it is allowed to run its course, the multiplier effect will produce serious overcrowding and excessively clustered population. This intense concentration of industries and population is characteristic of most industrialized nations. Consequently, most such countries suffer from associated problems such as congestion, inadequate housing and recreational facilities, and extreme local pollution of the environment.

Global corporations. It must be kept in mind that, increasingly, we can no longer think of decisions on market location, labor supply, or other aspects of industrial planning within the framework of a single plant controlled by a single owner. Instead, we are dealing with a highly complex international corporate structure that plans on a gargantuan scale. As George Ball, former government official and now partner in an international investment banking firm, commented: "Working through great corporations that straddle the earth, men are able for the first time to utilize world resources with an efficiency dictated by the objective logic of profit."

Today, the size of corporate conglomeration is breathtaking. The total sales of global corporations are greater than the gross national product of every country except the United States and Russia. In 1971, for instance, General Motors' gross annual sales of $28 billion were greater than Switzerland's gross national product of $26 billion. Some of these giant firms have more power to plan where people will live and work than many governments have. On a world scale, the effect of corporate planning is to internationalize production. This is not surprising. In the 1970s, the top 298 United States-based corporations earned approximately one-third of their net profits abroad.

These corporate giants based in the United States, Europe, and Japan have such sweeping control over international communications networks, the latest advances in modern technology, and large amounts of investment capital that they have effectively penetrated and often control the economic structures of underdeveloped nations. To suggest the extent of this penetration, two scholars, Richard Barnett and Ronald Miller, quote the following figures: "In Mexico, as of 1970, sixty-seven percent of the metal-products industry, eighty-four percent of the tobacco industry, and a hundred percent of the rubber, electrical-machinery, and automobile industries were under foreign control. In Argentina, global corporations control more than fifty percent of each company in the top fifty." Since the decision-making mechanisms of these locally based companies are geared toward the profit structure of the parent corporation and not toward the local economies in which they exist, their decisions, some scholars have argued, may well result in the further impoverishment of already poor countries. Certainly, the global corporation has done little to reverse the widening gap between rich and poor nations.

The political element in industrial location

Political influence on the spatial distribution of industrialization is common. Governments often intervene directly in decisions concerning industrial location. Such intervention typically results from a desire to establish strategic, militarily important industries that would otherwise not develop; to decrease vulnerability to attack by artificially scattering industry to many parts of the country; to create national self-sufficiency by diversifying industries; to bring industrial development and a higher standard of living to poverty-striken provinces; to place vital strategic industries in remote locations, far removed from possible war zones; or to halt the multiplier effect in existing industrial areas. Such governmental influence is most pronounced in highly planned economic systems, particularly in Communist or socialist countries such as the Soviet Union and China, but it can be seen to some extent in almost every industrial nation (Figure 12-17).

The existence of armaments factories in the Republic of South Africa, a country that fears a possible United Nations arms embargo is a good example of the artificial development of government-encouraged strategic industries. The scattering of industry in the Soviet Union, motivated partly by a desire to lessen the catastrophic effect of a military attack, is another. The development of a major industrial complex in the Soviet Ural Mountains, deep in the interior of the country, was partially in response to the German military advance in 1941. For similar strategic reasons, the United States government during World War II encouraged the development of an iron and steel industry in Utah, an economically

"inefficient" location that would not have attracted such industry without government intervention. The American aircraft industry was similarly dispersed as a result of government policy. The peacetime Italian government has deliberately caused industries to be established in the impoverished southern part of the country in an effort to improve the standard of living there. Similarly, the American government has encouraged new industrial development in economically depressed Appalachia. The United Kingdom, with some limited success, has attempted to retard further industrial development in existing population centers, causing many new factories to be situated in rural or small-town areas.

A problem common to attempted industrialization of poverty regions is **multiplier leakage**. Capital is invested in the economically depressed areas, but most of the profits tends to flow back to the dominant industrial areas, with the result that the "prosperity gap" between the two areas actually increases rather than decreases.

Local and state governments are often directly involved in efforts to influence industrial locations. Action by such governments sometimes takes the form of tax concessions, such as those granted by a number of states, counties, and cities in the United States. These concessions commonly last for a specified period of time, frequently ten years or less, and are designed to persuade industries to locate in areas under their jurisdiction. Conversely, governments can act to prevent the establishment of industries viewed as undesirable. A beer brewery, for example, could be kept out of an area where influential local church leaders had prohibitionist views and brought their influence to bear on government officials. Oil refineries and "superport" facilities for large tankers are presently being blocked from New England by state action, and some American municipalities have refused to allow development of particularly pollution-prone industries such as copper smelters and paper mills.

Another type of government influence comes in the form of tariffs, import-export quotas, political obstacles to the free movement of labor

TARIFFS AND TOYOTAS

In the summer of 1980, the impact of tariffs on industrial location found expression in a dispute between the United States and Japan. According to U.S. tariff law, motor vehicles imported fully assembled are subject to a 25 percent tariff, while importers pay only a 4 percent tariff on vehicle parts. The Japanese Toyota firm had for years imported vehicles that were almost fully assembled, lacking only superficial work to be ready for sale. Toyota paid the 4 percent "parts" tariff on these vehi-

cles. The "final touch" assembly took place at a Long Beach, California, plant which, owing to the large volume of imports, employed a sizable labor force. When the United States acted to reclassify the vehicles as "fully assembled," thereby raising the tariff to 25 percent, Toyota countered by threatening to close the Long Beach plant on the grounds that it would no longer be economically profitable.

and capital, and various types of hindrance to transportation across borders (see box, "Tariffs and Toyotas"). Tariffs, in effect, reduce the size of a market area proportional to the amount of tariff imposed (see Figure 12-18). A similar effect is produced when the number of border crossing points is restricted. In some parts of the world, especially Europe, the impact of tariffs and borders on industrial location has been greatly reduced by the establishment of free-trade blocs, groups of nations that have banded together economically and abolished most tariffs. Of these associations, the European Common Market is perhaps the most famous. Composed of ten nations of non-Communist Europe, the Common Market has succeeded in abolishing most tariffs within its area.

Industrialization as an agent of cultural change

In all of these ways, then, different aspects of culture influence industrial location. But equally pronounced are the effects of industry on culture. Indeed, industrialization is the most potent and effective agent of cultural change ever to operate. Entire cultures have been reshaped as a consequence of the industrial revolution. Traditions thousands of years old

FIGURE 12-18
The impact of political borders on market area is illustrated in this diagram. The presence of a political border reduces the market area of a factory if a tariff is imposed or if the number of border-crossing points is restricted. As a result, factories tend not to be located in border zones. (After Herbert Giersch, "Economic Union Between Nations and the Location of Industries," *Review of Economic Studies,* 17 (1949–50), 87–97.)

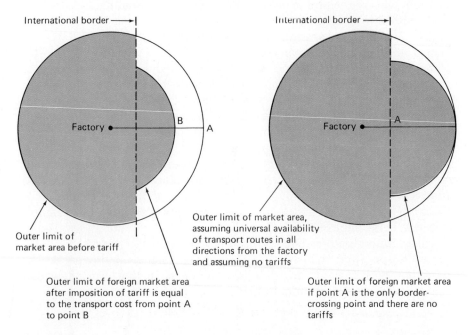

Outer limit of market area before tariff

Outer limit of foreign market area after imposition of tariff is equal to the transport cost from point A to point B

Outer limit of market area, assuming universal availability of transport routes in all directions from the factory and assuming no tariffs

Outer limit of foreign market area if point A is the only border-crossing point and there are no tariffs

have been discarded almost overnight. Much of the replacement of folk culture by popular culture can be attributed at least indirectly to the industrial revolution, (Figure 12-19). With spreading industrialization went the most concentrated burst of invention in history. From the steamship and the simple tack to the revolver and the ballistic missile, from the typewriter and the rotary printing press to the computer and the atom bomb, the list of innovations is almost endless.

Some of the more important and far-reaching changes brought by industrialization include increased interregional trade and intercultural contact, basic alterations in employment patterns, a shift from rural to urban residence for vast numbers of people, the release of women from the home, the ultimate disappearance of child labor, an initial increase in the rate of population growth followed by a drop to unprecedented low birth rates, greatly increased individual mobility and mass migrations of people, a decline in the role of organized religion, the decline of the multigeneration family, greatly increased educational opportunities for the nonwealthy, and an increase of government influence and functions.

Perhaps the most basic change, however, is in the way people make their living. Industrial development in a region typically produces a restructuring of employment. A market increase occurs in the proportion of the labor force employed in secondary and tertiary activities, as well as in such primary activities as lumbering and mining. There is a resultant decline in agricultural employment. Worker productivity increases greatly, both in industry and agriculture, mainly due to the adoption of machinery in the production process. This increased productivity allows the number of children and elderly persons in the labor force to decline substantially, but the number of women working outside the home increases.

The large-scale expansion of interregional trade is largely due to industrialization, for no industrial region is self-sufficient. Each must rely on other regions for raw materials, foodstuffs, laborers, and markets. Such

FIGURE 12-19
Industrialization brings culture change. Today we see men in Senegal, Africa, pouring molten metal in a factory, but their clothes remind us that only a few years ago their lives and occupations were very different.

trade contacts, often between peoples with very different cultural heritages and social patterns, naturally accelerate the processes of cultural diffusion. While intercultural contacts can serve to reduce prejudice and suspicion, too great a dependence upon an unfamiliar people for basic necessities can result in feelings of hostility if one or both trading partners feel taken advantage of. The rise of anti-Arab sentiment in the United States since 1973 is in part the result of greatly increased oil prices.

Before the industrial revolution, education was a luxury available only to the wealthy. In an industrial society, however, worker productivity is closely related to the educational level of the labor force. This recognition has led all industrial countries to devote large portions of their financial resources to the support of education. This has been facilitated by release of children from the labor force.

As a rule, people strongly resist substantial changes in their basic cultural patterns unless some immediate and great personal benefit is perceived. It is some measure of the appeal and promise of the industrial revolution that so many people in such a great variety of cultures have been willing to discard tradition in order to adopt this new way of life.

Industrial Landscapes

The industrial landscape is part of our daily life, for industry is a prominent and often disturbing visible feature of our surroundings. It is a landscape not normally designed for beauty, charm, or aesthetic appeal, but rather for utility. Often it is, by almost anyone's standards, ugly. As a rule, industrial landscapes are poor places for humans to have to spend their lives (Figure 12-20).

Each level of industrial activity produces its own distinctive landscape. Primary industries have perhaps the most drastic impact on the land. The resultant landscapes contain slag heaps, strip-cut commercial forests, massive strip-mining scars, gaping open-pit mines, and "forests" of oil derricks. But primary industrial landscapes can also be pleasing, as in the comfortable fishing villages of New England and Portugal.

The manufacturing landscapes of secondary industry are most notable in the form of factory buildings. Some of these are imaginatively designed and well landscaped, others are less appealing and surrounded by grey seas of parking lots. They range from the futuristic, harsh, solid geometry of chemical refineries and formless, stark "brick-pile" factories to award-winning structures designed by famous architects.

Manufacturing landscapes first appeared in Britain, since that island was the first area touched by the industrial revolution. It is interesting to observe how British poets and artists of the eighteenth and nineteenth centuries reacted to the emerging manufacturing landscape. Poets and artists are widely acknowledged to be aesthetically sensitive and more perceptive than the average person, so their reactions should interest us. Geographers Gary Peters and Burton Anderson studied the works of such writers and painters. They found that after an early period of optimism about industrialization, some poets and artists quickly sensed that something was amiss in the landscape. Their warnings, in the form of paintings and poems, began appearing in the 1775-1800 period. Typical is the

FIGURE 12-20
Industry shapes the landscape in many ways. The vast copper mine in Arizona is a mark of primary industry. The architects, Walter Gropius and Adolf Meyer, designed the German factory above, part of the landscape of secondary industry. This Belgian landscape includes many elements of tertiary activity: roads, highways, a bridge, and river transportation.

description of an iron foundry written by the poet Robert Burns in his native Scottish dialect:

> We cam na here to view your warks,
> In hopes to be mair wise,
> But only, lest we gang to Hell,
> It may be nae surprise.

Some artists of the period left us paintings that convey a sinister, foreboding, unpleasant landscape. By the time ordinary people began to see with the eyes of poets and artists, the manufacturing landscape was seemingly out of control, and much of the British industrial region was already known, appropriately, as the "Black Country" (see box, "How Green Was My Valley").

The tertiary landscape is quite varied. Its visual content includes elements as diverse as high-rise bank buildings, hamburger stands, and the concrete and steel webs of highways and railroads. Some highway interchanges can only be described as a modern art form. But perhaps the aesthetic high point of the tertiary landscape is found in bridges, often graceful and beautiful structures. There are few sights of the industrial age that can match a well-designed rail or highway bridge.

Industrialization has even changed the way we view the landscape. As the geographer Yi-Fu Tuan has commented, "it was only in the early decades of the twentieth century that vehicles began to displace walking as the prevalent form of locomotion, and street scenes were perceived increasingly from the interior of automobiles moving staccato-fashion through regularly paced traffic lights." Los Angeles, the ultimate automobile city, is perhaps the best example of the new viewpoints provided by the industrial age. Its freeway system allows individual motorists to observe their surroundings at nonstop speeds up to fifty-five miles per hour. It also allows the driver to look *down* on the world. The pedestrian, on the other hand, is slighted. The view from the street is not encouraged. In some areas of Los Angeles, streets actually have no sidewalks at all, so

---

"HOW GREEN WAS MY VALLEY"

Richard Llewellyn, a Welshman, wrote a beautiful novel about growing up in the coal mining district of Wales in the late nineteenth century. He saw the industrial landscape expand across his native valley, and he lamented it:

". . . Bright shone the sun, but brighter shown the Valley's green, for each blade of grass gave back the light and made the meadows full of golds and greens, and yellows and pinks and blues were poking from the hedges where the flowers were hard at work for the bees. May and almond were coming, and further down, early apple was doing splendid in four tidy rows behind Meirddyn Jones' farm. His herd of black cows were all down in the river up to their bellies in the cool quiet water, with their tails making white splashes as they dropped after slapping flies, and up nearer to us, sheep were busy with their noses at the sweet green. When the wind took breath you could hear the crunching of their jaws.

"Beautiful was the Valley this afternoon, until you turned your head to the right. Then you saw the two slag heaps. . . .

"Below us, the river ran sweet as ever, happy in the sun, but as soon as it met the darkness between the sloping walls of slag it seemed to take fright and go spiritless, smooth, black, without movement. And on the other side it came forth grey, and began to hurry again, as though anxious to get away. But its banks were stained, and the reeds and grasses that dressed it were hanging, and black, and sickly, ashamed of their dirtiness, ready to die of shame, they seemed, and of sorrow for their dear friend, the river. . . .

"Big it had grown, and long, and black, without life or sign, lying along the bottom of the Valley on both sides of the river. The green grass, and the reeds and the flowers, all had gone, crushed beneath it. And every minute the burden grew, as cage after cage screeched along the cables from the pit, bumped to a stop at the tipping pier, and emptied dusty loads on to the ridged, black, dirty back.

"On our side of the Valley the heap reached to the front garden walls of the bottom row of houses, and children from them were playing up and down the black slopes, screaming and shouting, laughing in fun. On the other side of the river the chimney-pots of the first row of houses could only just be seen above the sharp curving back of the far heap, and all the time I was watching, the cable screeched and the cages tipped. . . ."

From Richard Llewellyn, How Green Was My Valley (London: Michael Joseph; New York: Macmillan, 1940), pp. 103, 104, 116. Copyright © 1939 by Richard D. V. Llewellyn Lloyd, renewed 1967 by Harry J. McIntyre. With permission of Michael Joseph and Macmillan.

that the nonautomobile viewpoint is functionally impossible. In other areas, the layout of the main avenues has been planned with the car in mind, and the pedestrian is likely to feel ill at ease amid the nonhuman surroundings—noise, traffic jams, drive-in banks, and parking lots. Often the shopping street is no longer scaled to the pedestrian—Los Angeles's Ventura Boulevard extends for fifteen miles.

There are areas where such industrial landscapes are overwhelmingly dominant. But the imprint remains rather local, reflecting the highly centralized nature of industrial activity. It is possible, even in industrial districts such as the Ruhr region of West Germany, to find rural scenes and functioning farms.

Conclusion

One of the most significant events of our age is the spread of industrialization. This has brought a host of far-reaching cultural changes. Already the industrial revolution has modified the cultures and landscapes of some lands so greatly that people who lived there a century ago would be completely bewildered by the modern setting.

We discussed the three types of industry—primary, secondary, and tertiary. Primary industries extract renewable and nonrenewable resources from the earth. Secondary industry is the heart of industrial activity—manufacturing. Tertiary industry includes the distribution of goods and the provision of services.

We traced the spread of the innovations that made up the industrial revolution, following the routes of diffusion from Britain to the rest of the world. The spatial result of this diffusion can be graphically portrayed using industrial regions.

The impact of industrial activity on the environment becomes apparent through the study of cultural ecology. In some places, the ravages of industry have reached an alarming state. But the relationship between industry and the land is not one-sided. The environment influences industrial location.

Through the approach of cultural integration, we found that industry is related in countless ways to other elements of culture. In particular, industrial location is often governed by economic and political factors.

The characteristics of industrial landscapes are familiar to us. Primary, secondary, and tertiary industries have different visual imprints. The transportation network of freeways, railways, and bridges is the connecting web in the industrial landscape.

Glossary

Bulk-gaining product a product in which volume is added to the raw materials in the manufacturing process.

Cottage (household) industry a traditional type of manufacturing in the preindustrial revolution era, practiced on a small scale in individual rural households as a part-time occupation and designed to produce handmade goods for local consumption.

Guild industry a traditional type of manufacturing in the preindustrial revolution era, involving handmade goods of high quality manufactured by highly skilled artisans who resided in towns and cities.

Inanimate power   power derived from sources other than humans and work animals; in particular, the use of water or wind power, steam, and electricity. Today it is generated through the burning of fossil fuels such as coal or oil or by means of nuclear fusion.

Industrial inertia   the tendency of industries to remain in their original location, even after the forces that originally attracted them there have disappeared.

Industrial revolution   a series of inventions and innovations, arising in England in the 1700s, which led to the use of machines and inanimate power in the manufacturing process.

Labor-intensive industry   an industry for which labor costs represent a large proportion of total production costs.

Multiplier effect   the process by which industries attract people, thereby enlarging markets and attracting still other industries; a snowballing growth process responsible for the development of industrial districts.

Multiplier leakage   the process by which industrial profits "drain" back to major industrial districts from factories established in outlying provinces.

Nonrenewable resources   resources that must be depleted in order to be used, such as minerals.

Primary industries   industries engaged in the extraction of natural resources, such as agriculture, lumbering, and mining.

Renewable resources   resources that are not depleted if wisely used, such as forests, water, fishing grounds, and agricultural land.

Secondary industries   industries engaged in processing raw materials into finished products; manufacturing.

Tertiary activity   the distribution of manufactured goods to consumers; the provision of a variety of wholesale, retail, educational, governmental, and medical services, along with transportation and communications.

Weight-gaining product   a product in which weight is added to the raw materials in the manufacturing process.

Suggested Readings

Gunnar Alexandersson. *Geography of Manufacturing.* Englewood Cliffs, N.J.: Prentice-Hall, 1967.

Brian J. L. Berry. *The Geography of Economic Systems.* Englewood Cliffs, N.J.: Prentice-Hall, 1975.

Brian J. L. Berry. *Geography of Market Centers and Retail Distribution.* Englewood Cliffs, N.J.: Prentice-Hall, 1967.

R. C. Estall and R. Ogilvie Buchanan. *Industrial Activity and Economic Geography: A Study of the Forces Behind the Geographical Location of Productive Activity in Manufacturing Industry.* 2nd ed. London: Hutchinson, 1966.

Andreas Grotewold. "The Growth of Industrial Core Areas and Patterns of World Trade," *Annals, Association of American Geographers,* 61 (1971), 361–370.

Nathaniel B. Guyol. *Energy in the Perspective of Geography.* Englewood Cliffs, N.J.: Prentice-Hall, 1971.

A. M. Hay. "Transport Geography," *Progress in Human Geography,* 1 (1977), 313–318.

Walter Isard. *Location and Space-Economy: A General Theory Relating to Industrial Location, Market Areas, Land Use, Trade and Urban Structure.* New York: Wiley, 1956.

H. R. Jarrett. *A Geography of Manufacturing.* Plymouth, England: Macdonald and Evans. 2nd ed. 1977.

Gerald J. Karaska and David F. Bramhall. *Locational Analysis for Manufacturing: A Selection of Readings.* Cambridge, Mass.: M.I.T. Press, 1969.

David Keeble. "Industrial Geography," *Progress in Human Geography,* 1 (1977), 304–312.

Gary L. Peters and Burton L. Anderson. "Industrial Landscapes: Past Views and Stages of Recognition," *Professional Geographer,* 28 (1976), 341–348.

Norman J. G. Pounds. *The Ruhr: A Study in Historical and Economic Geography.* London: Faber, 1952.

Kenneth R. Sealy. *The Geography of Air Transport.* London: Hutchinson, 1957.

David M. Smith. *Industrial Location: An Economic Geographical Analysis.* New York: Wiley, 1971.

Wilfred Smith. *Geography and the Location of Industry.* Liverpool: University Press, 1952.

Edward J. Taaffe and Howard L. Gauthier, Jr. *Geography of Transportation.* Englewood Cliffs, N.J.: Prentice-Hall, 1973.

Richard S. Thoman and Edgar C. Conkling. *Geography of International Trade.* Englewood Cliffs, N.J.: Prentice-Hall, 1967.

Alfred Weber. *Theory of the Location of Industries.* Edited by Carl J. Friedrich. Chicago: University of Chicago Press, 1929.

Leonard C. Yaseen. *Plant Location.* New York: American Research Council, 1956.

Cultural Geography and Global Problems: A Case Study Approach

13

As you've read through this text, you have seen that not all is well with the world. Population pressures stress resources, the physical environment is damaged by unwise uses in ways that threaten humankind, and cultures are in conflict throughout the world. Newspapers and television bombard us daily with still more news of our global crises: war in Africa, poverty at home, food shortages in India. Some scientists see a new Ice Age coming due to climatic changes, while others argue that industry-caused air pollution is causing a warming of global climates. Drought plagues one part of the earth, floods devastate another. We might seriously ask whether people can survive much longer on this earth. Many experts see only increased political, economic, social, and environmental turmoil in the next decades, leading to a breakdown of the world system, widespread warfare, and possible extinction of the species.

Yet others, including many cultural geographers, believe that humanity can survive if we direct our efforts toward problem-solving on a world-wide scale. A new generation of scholars is tackling global problems in a holistic way, integrating solutions into the total world picture rather than adopting a short-sighted, nationalistic approach. As this new global science takes shape, it becomes apparent that several components are necessary to achieve a worldwide view: (1) an understanding of culture, so that problems can be viewed within the context of social systems: (2) an understanding of the physical environment, since so many of our global problems are concerned with environmental backlash; and (3) an appreciation of world resource patterns, since many problems boil down to questions of wise use of scarce natural resources.

Since cultural geography has long been concerned with the interaction between cultures and environment and the way people use resources and occupy the land, our field has much to offer global problem-solving. This is not to suggest that geography is an intellectual panacea; it is only to say that geographers have been interested in world problems for decades, and that we are actively involved in examining topics of importance to the future of humanity.

The specific goal in this chapter is to share four case studies with you that exemplify recent research done by geographers on world problems. By presenting these case studies, we will illustrate how the five themes of cultural geography presented in this book are being put to work in the "real world."

Geographers and the Global Population Crisis

The world's population explosion was discussed in Chapter 2 of this text. Never before have so many people lived on the earth and demanded so much from world resources (see Figure 13-1). It took all of human history until the year 1850 to reach 1 billion people; yet only 80 years later, in 1930, there were 2 billion, and in 1975, just 45 years later, this had doubled to 4 billion. Most estimates agree that by the year 2000 the world will have a population of 6 billion. At that time, China and India will exceed 1 billion each, and there will be 11 countries with populations between 100 million and 1 billion; in 1950, there were only 4. And where will this lead? Will the world's population continue to grow until disaster—such as war or famine—limits growth as Malthus predicted, or

Chapter-opening photo: One of the world's challenges is housing our urban population. This picture from San José, Costa Rica, shows squatter settlements and new apartments.

FIGURE 13-1
Population pressure puts great demands on both natural and human resources. Even as population growth slows in industrialized countries, certain facilities, such as the New York transit system, experience problems of overcrowding.

will people begin regulating their numbers as they see resources becoming ever more scarce?

No one knows for sure, but understanding world population patterns necessitates insight into the relationship between health care and population growth. On the one hand, improved health care leads to higher population growth by decreasing mortality, but, on the other, it seems that improved health conditions are a precondition for a lowered birthrate. A poor family in India, for example, has to have six or seven children to be 95 percent certain of having one healthy son: We must remember that surviving children are an economic necessity in much of the world.

The following case study examines the health of a small population resettled on a land development in Malaysia and helps us understand the complicated relationship between settlement pattern, health care, and population. This study sheds light on a process repeated in thousands of different areas of the world.

Land development and health in West Malaysia

Geographer Melinda Meade examined the relationship between human health and land development in Malaysia to determine whether modification of the natural landscape resulting from agricultural expansion might aggravate health problems. This question is raised by evidence in other parts of the world that agricultural expansion often changes natural systems in such a way as to offer disease-bearing organisms an expanded habitat, resulting in increased sickness for the human population. Probably the best example involves the snail-dependent *schistosomiasis*, which is now one of humankind's greatest plagues because the snail's habitat is enlarged through irrigation schemes. Professor Meade points out that land development planners rarely consider the potential health problems that might result from disruption of the natural environment. Instead, they automatically assume that health will improve if the people's standard of living is improved. But this is not always the case.

To test her ideas, Meade analyzed a major land development scheme in Malaysia to see if human health had actually improved as a result of rainforest clearance, expansion of rubber plantations, and resettlement of the native population into a new plantation village. This plan, called Project Gedangsa after the name of the plantation on which it was carried out, was executed in 1962 and is typical of development now taking place in Malaysia. Some 200,000 people have been recently relocated onto plantation villages; over one million acres of rain forest have been replaced with rubber or palm oil crops (Figure 13-2).

The first part of Meade's study documents the modification of the natural environment by the land development plan. Her approach is an excellent example of how the cultural ecology theme can be used to guide research. As she examines changes in the natural landscape, Meade is particularly interested in whether rain-forest clearance has enlarged the habitat of the malaria-bearing mosquito. She notes that in its natural condition the Malyasian rain forest supports hundreds of different mosquito species because the environmental niches are so varied and numerous that no single species can attain great numbers. But when the rain forest is cleared and burned, one niche is expanded as others are wiped out. If a malarial mosquito occupies that expanded niche, its population will explode and a higher incidence of malaria in the nearby human population will result. In the past, the history of plantation expansion in Malaysia has been the history of malaria epidemics. Today there is almost total dependence on insecticides to control mosquitos in the new plantations, but the last few years have seen mosquito species emerge that are resistant to several types of pesticides.

Meade finds that because the Gedangsa plantation is more than 15 years old, trees are now mature enough to shade many of the streams and ponds where malaria mosquitos might breed. The mosquito prefers waters exposed to sunlight, so it is mainly in the early years of land development, before trees grow up, that the mosquito's habitat is expanded. At this later stage the main danger has passed.

In a second phase of Meade's study, she examines the plantation settlement pattern to see if it promotes or inhibits sickness and disease. This question touches upon another of the themes introduced in this

FIGURE 13-2
Some argue that rain-forest lands offer great potential for the expansion of agriculture and human settlement. Others maintain that tampering with this fragile ecosystem will have far-reaching negative consequences.

book, cultural landscape. House types, road patterns, and settlement location are all components of the cultural landscape. As Meade analyzes the plantation's settlement landscape, she finds problems. Settlers are provided with simple three-room, iron-roof houses, oriented to the road network rather than to prevailing winds. Houses are poorly ventilated and debilitatingly hot, which could have an adverse effect on health. But there are some improvements over native villages: Most importantly, latrines and piped water are provided. The latrines deprive infectious worms of a habitat in soiled earth; piped water means that women no longer are exposed to mosquitos as they spend long hours doing laundry in streams. Both of these features have reduced the usual health problems.

So when all factors are considered, Meade finds that the health advantages of this particular land development scheme outweigh the disadvantages. As a result, the plantation's population is expanding due to a lowered mortality rate. Malaria is momentarily under control due to spraying and other precautionary measures. The incidence of worm-carried infections in small children (who normally crawl about in contaminated soil) is down, mainly because of the latrine system.

The broader demographic implications coming from Malaysian land development schemes are varied and could affect the country's population in several ways. First, new plantation schemes might trigger malaria epidemics as rain-forest clearing takes place unless precautionary measures are taken; there is also some danger that population mobility—travel and migration—might introduce new strains of malaria and other diseases into previously resistant populations. But the most important effect is that improved health facilities generally reduce mortality rates; therefore the country's population will express this growth.

Since similar development programs are found in many other emerging countries, Meade's study serves as an excellent model for evaluating the health problems and advantages accompanying development and for calculating potential population growth resulting from improved health conditions. Furthermore, as an illustration of how cultural geography can be put to work on world problems, Meade's study underscores the vitality of both the cultural ecology and the cultural landscape themes as guideposts for research.

As mortality rates decline, populations continue to increase at high rates, straining world resource systems. Food is a major problem, so let us now look at some aspects of the global food crisis.

The Global Food Crisis

One of the most serious resource problems now confronting the world is the production of food. There are more hungry people on earth than at any time in previous history; 15 million people die from starvation yearly, and another half billion suffer from malnutrition. Yet, paradoxically, while some areas suffer from famine, other parts of the world reap bumper crops, store enormous surpluses, and even destroy foodstuffs to keep prices artificially high.

One component of the food crisis is the ratio between food production and population growth. In the 1950s, food production increased faster on a global scale than did population, but this relationship was reversed during most of the following decade. A number of good years in the late 1960s once again put food production ahead of population, but then drought in India, Pakistan, and the Sahel (the southern fringe of the Sahara) limited production so that world population increased at a faster rate. Bumper crops in the mid-70s gave food experts cause for optimism; yet the possibilities of world climatic change, war, and other forms of social disruption cast a shadow of concern.

Solving the food crisis is not simply a matter of slowing population growth. Due to the large numbers of young in the developing countries, food requirements will increase steadily even if population increases are checked. Food demand is *twice* as high in 1980 as it was in 1960 for the emerging nations. And even if we accept the most optimistic population projections—which assume decreased growth rates—the food demand will still increase because as a population matures, food demand increases even if no new children are born. This suggests that population control may be only one aspect of the food crisis; major breakthroughs must be made by increasing food production. During the 1960s, the "Green Revolution" led to increased yields in many parts of the world. New hybrid seeds that doubled and tripled yields of wheat and rice were planted, and at first glance the results were amazing: In two years, the wheat harvest increased 60 percent in Pakistan and was up 30 percent in India. The Philippines changed from a rice importer to a rice exporter. Similar results were recorded in other parts of the globe.

But the Green Revolution has brought mixed blessings to some areas. Although there is little doubt that the Green Revolution has been important in alleviating some food problems, it cannot be thought of as a panacea, for there are distinct limitations. Green Revolution crops need four to seven times more water per square kilometer; therefore, new irrigation schemes usually must accompany changes in seed varieties. More fertilizer is also needed for the new hybrid strains, and some experts predict that developing countries must increase their fertilizer output sevenfold to keep up with the new demands created by the Green Revolution. But fertilizer is expensive to produce and purchase. A dangerous side effect of the Green Revolution is the loss of genetic variability by replacing indigenous crops with a few crossbred strains. Furthermore, the new monoculture stands of Green Revolution strains are particularly vulnerable to pests; consequently, heavy dosages of pesticides are necessary.

The following case study by the Canadian geographer, A. K. Chakravarti, pinpoints many of the problems of the Green Revolution in India, and concludes that it has actually aggravated the differences between rich and poor areas.

The Green Revolution in India

In analyzing the results of the Green Revolution in India, Chakravarti used the theme of cultural diffusion as a major research tool: He traced the spread of high-yield hybrid seeds across India, then examined the results on a region-by-region basis.

Some background material is necessary to fully appreciate the impact of high-yield seeds on India's agriculture. First, most of the country's farming is subsistence cultivation of food grains for family use; there is little commercial, export-oriented agriculture. Secondly, there are many regions that must draw on grains from other parts of India, and one goal of agricultural planning is to make all regions self-sufficient. Lastly, since there is no land available for farm expansion, increased food production must come only from improved yields.

Chakravarti points out that earlier attempts to raise production through fertilization and irrigation of native grain seeds were not encouraging. Local plant strains evolved over centuries and are suited to the specific conditions of low soil fertility and periodic drought. They did not respond well to fertilizers and supplemental watering, so new hybrid seeds were developed that would benefit from improved conditions. The new seeds first appeared in 1966 and at first glance led to major progress. Total food-grain production in 1970 was twice that of 1950.

But the benefits have not been shared equally. As Chakravarti examined the diffusion of the new grain seeds, it became apparent to him that major improvements in production came to those areas best able to bear the higher costs of cultivating the new seeds. Poorer, backward people, who could not afford expensive changes in production techniques saw their relative position in the country's agricultural spectrum actually worsen. What are the reasons behind this differential response? The problem is capital.

The new hybrid seeds are highly responsive to fertilization, but many farmers cannot afford chemical fertilizers and the banks are unwilling to lend money to marginal farmers. Even the agriculturists themselves are reluctant to borrow, knowing that they will lose their land if payments are not met. Most farmers would rather struggle on, secure with their traditional seeds and poor crops, than face the risk of becoming landless. Consequently, yields remain low even with the new seeds, since many farmers cannot afford commercial fertilizers.

A similar problem keeps many poorer farmers from using pesticides and developing irrigation systems that are necessary to bring the best yields from the new seeds. Chakravarti notes that high-yield seeds are more susceptible to disease and pests than traditional seed varieties, since the former have adapted over thousands of years to local conditions. Because the new seeds are more vulnerable, they need more protection in the form of expensive chemical pesticides. Once again, the author finds that in the richer agricultural regions pesticides are implemented, while in the poor areas the crops do without. Damage from insects and disease takes a very high toll.

Irrigation is also necessary to gain full benefits from the new seeds, while native grains are adapted to the normal Indian pattern of drought and monsoon. But irrigation—like fertilizer and pesticides—costs money; so once again the richer farmers who can afford these changes reap the benefits and the poor do without.

In summation, Chakravarti finds that the new hybrid wheat seeds are about 155 percent more expensive to farm than native seed varieties. However, this higher cost is compensated for by yields that are twice as high and a net income that is 190 percent greater than that of native seeds. So, looking at the higher costs—and higher returns—it is easy to see how a vicious cycle is perpetuated. The richer farmers can afford the additional expense of the new seeds, while those in poor regions cannot. The prosperous areas gain the benefits, the poor ones do not. Furthermore, poor farmers suffer additionally because the demand for new hybrid wheat is higher than for the traditional wheat causing prices for native grain to drop in the last few years.

This disparity between rich and poor is not quite so apparent in the rice-growing regions. The author points out that new hybrid rice strains have not been as successful as wheat because of several problems. First, the new rice crops are extremely susceptible to disease, and because the cash return is not high, even well-to-do farmers cannot afford pesticides to protect their crops. Also, returns are low because market demand is low. Buyers prefer the taste of traditional rice for food purposes, and the native rice has longer stems that can be used for cattle feed. Consequently, prices paid for the new hybrid rice are lower than for traditional crops and few farmers are interested in converting to the new rice seeds.

In conclusion, Chakravarti's study shows that the Green Revolution has actually aggravated long-standing economic and social disparities in India; the rich have become richer, while the plight of the poor has worsened (Figure 13-3). Although the author does not mention it in his study, recent evidence suggests that tenant farmers are being evicted from rented lands, now that landlords see the possibility of increased profits by growing new high-yield wheat strains. In the past, the poor had the security of their own land, even though it may have been rented, and the knowledge that some sort of crop could be harvested. But now, a whole new class of displaced poor may plague India, placing additional burdens on the country's food supplies and adding complications to the Green Revolution.

The global food crisis has also led to the farming of marginal lands, where the potential for environmental damage is very great. For example, some suggest that massive clearing of tropical rain forests would offer millions of acres of potentially arable land. But others argue that clearing away the rain forest might change tropical climatic patterns so as to disrupt global moisture and heat exchanges, which would be disastrous for midlatitude agriculture.

Other global scientists are concerned about the farming of semiarid

FIGURE 13-3
One strategy for solving the global food crisis is to make subsistence farming more efficient. Yet that approach often aggravates some social problems. This is a scene from southern India.

lands, where rainfall is marginal and soils easily exhausted. Some suggest that the world's climate is warming just enough that these semiarid areas will suffer from increased drought, so that to farm these areas would be to court disaster. A phenomenon known as *desertification,* or the slow expansion of desert areas due to both natural and human-caused activities, has been the topic of recent United Nations conferences and has focused attention on the topic of semiarid land agriculture. Cultural geographers are among the scholars concerned about desertification.

Desertification of the Great Plains: Will it happen?

Martyn Bowden, a geographer at Clark University, looks at the cultural ecology of North America's Great Plains agricultural region to determine whether the area is vulnerable to desertification (Figure 13-4). Using the cultural-historical method common to cultural geography, Bowden examines three issues central to continued agricultural viability: (1) Will the Great Plains climate change? (2) Will the region's soil and water resources be depleted by current livelihood systems? And (3) will people continue to farm the Great Plains?

The topic of climatic change is clouded by controversy and contradiction. Some scientists see us entering a new Ice Age resulting from human-caused industrial pollution modifying our atmosphere so that gradual cooling is taking place. Even if this is true, Bowden concludes that global cooling will not affect Great Plains productivity— except possibly in the Canadian wheat belt, where the growing season could be critically shortened.

Other climatologists argue that pollution is actually causing a warming of the world's climate. This might increase the possibility of drought in semiarid regions like the Great Plains. Still others argue that droughts occur on faily regular cycles and that these are totally removed from whether the earth is warming or cooling. Bowden reviews each of the theories concerning drought periodicity and concludes that the Great Plains will not experience another period of extreme warmth and dryness until the early twenty-second century.

Bowden next examines human demands on soil and water resources, asking whether these essential components of agriculture will remain intact to meet the needs of future Great Plains farming. The author treats the soil resource question by critically evaluating claims made during the 1930s Dust Bowl period that the region suffered irreparable damage from misuse, drought, and wind. At that time, experts estimated that 75 percent of the soil surface in western Kansas was lost and ruined for crop production. Yet, Bowden finds that in 1945 this same area produced some of the highest yields in the state. Obviously, the extent of soil damage was overestimated. Indeed, some areas abandoned in the 1930s are still out of production, but the author calculates that this acreage totals only one-fifth of 1 percent of the entire arable land in the Great Plains.

Bowden concludes that further abandonment is unlikely for several reasons. First of all, there is slight prospect that conditions of the 1930s will be repeated, since farmers are now much more familiar with sound soil conservation practices such as summer fallowing and contour plowing. Furthermore, farms are now larger, so there is less pressure for unrealistically high yields from small parcels.

Even if soil conditions are not a problem, water for irrigated agriculture might be. Bowden examines the contemporary pattern of water usage in

FIGURE 13-4
The Great Plains of North America provide foodstuff for many countries, but are they being managed correctly in terms of climatic fluctuations, domestic needs, and world food problems?

the Great Plains, finding that consumption is higher than natural replenishment, and that irrigated farming will suffer serious shortages in the future, particularly in the Texas and Oklahoma panhandles, where subsurface waters are being "mined" at a rapid rate. At present rates of usage, shortages will force drastic reductions of irrigated acreage in those areas by the year 2015. Even in areas dependent on surface runoff, such as the Platte regions of Colorado and Nebraska, shortages have already been experienced.

One major reason for scarce water supplies is that Great Plains urban areas have grown rapidly and now use water that was formerly available for irrigated agriculture. The trade-off between urban and rural use is taking its toll.

The last topic examined by Bowden is the possibility of farm abandonment during periods of resource stress. Have people left the Great Plains in the past during hard times, and might they desert their farms in the future? The author begins by taking a historical look at periods of stress in the region. Droughts in the 1870s and 1890s caused widespread food shortages among new settlers. In fact, evidence suggests that people got by only because military garrisons shared food supplies. Still, there were numerous drought-caused deaths from starvation, and hundreds of new farms were abandoned. Bowden suggests that Americans were then still novices in coping with dry lands and periodic drought. Farmers lacked experience in how to adapt to stressful times.

Again in 1916, the region was hit by drought, particularly the Dakotas and Montana, where farmers had just settled the land. Droughts take a particularly high toll when farms have just been settled, since farmers will not have any savings or capital to fall back on when crops fail. Bowden notes that in this 1916 drought, government aid was slow in coming because Washington blamed the problem on careless farming. As a result, thousands of farmers pulled up stakes and headed north to Canada, where the government played a more active supporting role in helping new settlers.

The next period of stress was during the 1930s. Our stereotype is of thousands of farmers abandoning the Dust Bowl and heading west to seek their fortune in California. Steinbeck's Joad family in *The Grapes of Wrath* did much to further the myth of the Dust Bowl farmer. But as Bowden points out, these people were not all from the Great Plains; most of them were southern tenant farmers who had been displaced by banks foreclosing on loans in order to consolidate small parcels into larger holdings. Consolidation of parcels also took place in the Great Plains, and many farmers were indeed dislocated because of this process (Figure 13-5). But the end result was larger holdings better suited to periodic drought. Larger farms have more cushion to fall back on during hard times.

Bowden argues that the time was ripe for farm consolidation, both because large farms are better suited to the environmental conditions and also because mechanization was beginning to play a major role in Great Plains agriculture. Large parcels are better suited for machines. So the dislocations that resulted were not totally a product of drought; social and technological change was equally responsible. Bowden is not attempting to minimize the Dust Bowl tragedy. He is interested only in setting the record straight by explaining various causes behind the disruptions of the 1930s. However painful this period of adjustment might have been, Bowden sees it as having had positive consequences. Today, because parcels are larger, because banks understand the needs of Great Plains farmers, and because the government is more supportive of agriculture in the region, future droughts will not be as disruptive as in the past. A wealth of experience has built up in the Great Plains concerning the optimum use of the resource base, so the future, in Bowden's opinion,

FIGURE 13-5
Numerous factors converged to create the Dust Bowl in the 1930s. Here, dust clouds roll over Lamar, Colorado.

appears fairly secure. The Great Plains will continue to serve the needs of the country and, to a smaller degree, the food needs of the world. Problems experienced in the past will not be repeated.

Bowden's research is an outstanding example of how the cultural-historical method can be used to analyze past adjustments and modifications of the environment in order to better predict the future. A systematic examination of human adaptation to resource stress tells us much about how problems were met in the past. This gives us strong footing for making statements about how problems will be met in the future and illustrates the valuable contributions that cultural-historical ecology can make to understanding current-day resource problems.

The expansion of agricultural production is contingent on the amount of energy available to a country or a region, for where energy supplies are scarce, the possibilities of producing fertilizers, fuel for farm machinery, and even fuel for the manufacture of farm implements will be reduced. The world's energy problems will affect world food supplies, so let us now turn our attention to energy.

The Global Energy Crisis

Human welfare is obviously dependent on wise use of world energy resources, both for efficient agricultural production and for industrial development. Furthermore, the materialistic standard of living achieved by many Western countries—and sought after by many others—demands an incredibly high amount of energy. Up to now, cheap energy has been available, but the end of the fossil fuel age is in sight.

Let us look briefly at world energy consumption patterns. As expected, there is a clear relationship between high industrial activity and energy consumption. For example, the United States, containing only 6 percent of the world's population, uses fully 35 percent of the world's energy. India, on the other hand, consumes only 2 percent of the earth's energy while containing 15 percent of the world's population. But India uses more energy as its industry expands, as do scores of other countries. This means that world energy consumption is increasing rapidly.

Energy consumption rates can be measured in terms of doubling rates, or the period of time that it takes to double energy consumption. During its period of early industrialization (1850-1915), the United States doubled its energy consumption in forty years. But since 1960, the doubling rate has dropped to fifteen years, mainly because of massive changes in transportation technology, expansion of industrial activity, and, of course, increases in home consumption. Currently in the United States, industry uses about 53 percent of all energy, households 14 percent, transportation 23 percent.

On a global scale, we see that energy consumption has increased to where world doubling time is now ten years (Figure 13-6). Remembering that each doubling involves increasingly large amounts of energy, it is possible to say that in the last ten years, humankind used as much energy as in our whole previous history!

Obviously, this consumption pattern cannot go on. Oil supplies will be 90 percent gone by 2020, coal by 2300. In the United States, natural gas will be 90 percent depleted by 2015. (The 90 percent figure is used in measuring exhaustion because extraction and processing of energy resources itself involves an expenditure of energy; when fuel supplies are 91 percent depleted they are useless, since there is no energy left to process them.)

There are some alternatives to fossil fuel energy production. Solar power offers much promise, but at the current rate of funding and experimentation, it may take several decades to develop the sophisticated methods of capture, storage, and transmission that the world needs.

FIGURE 13-6
Mainly due to increased industrial needs, the world's energy consumption is now doubling every ten years.

Nuclear power also offers some hope, but the topic remains clouded by issues of safe waste material storage, limited fuel (unless breeder or fusion reactors are perfected), and the actual cost of the energy produced. Geothermal, wind, and tidal power can fulfill only limited energy demands in restricted parts of the world.

The conservation of energy is obviously one topic that the world will have to confront right away. Homes must use less energy, industry must find ways to consume less, as must transportation. But what about agriculture? Can it continue to produce food for the world in a time of scarce, expensive energy? Are there traditional farming methods that can produce satisfactory yields while at the same time using less energy than the highly fertilized, mechanized farming of the world's major agricultural regions?

Our next case study looks at this important question by comparing the energy conservation agriculture of Amish farmers with yields of non-Amish farmers. The study was done by Warren Johnson, Victor Stolzfus, and Peter Craumer.

Energy conservation in Amish agriculture

Although most people look upon the Amish as remnants of traditional America, the authors suggest that, because of their energy conservation, the Amish might offer insights into how the world could get along with less energy. The Amish use less energy than typical American communities and farms because the sect generally avoids modern mechanized technology (Figure 13-7). Many of them do not use public electricity or natural gas, for their literal interpretation of the biblical passage "Be ye not unequally yoked together with unbelievers" prevents them from drawing on secular society's utilities. Instead, the most conservative Amish generate their own power with a central engine, then transmit it to outlying buildings with a complicated system of belts and pulleys. This system has obvious limitations for running machinery, so little mechanization is apparent in Amish homes or farms. However, other Amish are more open to machinery and do use small engines for power milkers, mechanical hay balers, and feed grinders. Nevertheless, even among the less conservative Amish, their level of mechanization is still far lower than their non-Amish neighbors (Figure 13-8).

The authors designed their study with two goals in mind: First, they wished to calculate just how much less energy Amish use than non-Amish farmers; second, they then determined whether Amish farmers pay a penalty for low energy use through reduced yields. The first step was to calculate the energy ration or caloric gain for both Amish and non-Amish farms. Caloric gain is a rather complicated term—and we refer you to the study for details on how it is actually calculated—but, stated most simply, it measures the amount of food energy produced per unit of enery spent to produce food. An energy ratio greater than 1.0 indicates that the farming process produces more food energy than total energy used; less than 1.0 indicates that the farm consumes more energy than it produces in food form.

Three different groups of Amish were studied; in central Pennsylvania, eastern Illinois, and southwestern Wisconsin. This was done to obtain results from different environments, ranging from ridge and valley dairy country to the Midwestern corn belt. A small number of non-Amish farmers were studied in each of the three areas for the sake of comparison.

FIGURE 13-7
Since the Amish do not use mechanized agriculture, they use considerably less energy than their "modern" neighbors.

The resulting energy ratios and yields are present in Table 13-1.

In central Pennsylvania, the Amish sample consisted of two groups: an extremely conservative group (the Nebraska Amish) and less conservative Amish (Old Order Amish). Both groups of Amish, along with the non-Amish, are primarily dairy farmers.

The results show that the less conservative Old Order Amish produce milk rather efficiently. Their yield is actually higher than that of the non-Amish, who use 83 percent more energy to produce a gallon of milk. In this case, Old Order Amish pay no penalty in the form of reduced yields. But the more conservative Nebraska Amish, who use less machinery, do pay a penalty: yields are much lower, mainly because they use less fertilizer and can only milk up to twenty cows without milking machines. Without refrigeration, their milk must be sold as Grade B, cooled only by spring water. Their farms are smaller than those among the Old Order Amish, and they have fewer cows, in large part because they do not use milking machines. All milking is done by hand.

The eastern Illinois study was done in an area of corn growing and hog raising. Because the Amish are not highly mechanized, their farms are considerably smaller than those of the non-Amish (495-acre average for non-Amish, 96 acres for the Amish). The Amish energy ratio of 0.9 suggests that their farms actually consume more energy than is produced in food form; whereas the non-Amish, with an energy ratio of 2.0, are relatively efficient. However, it is important to realize the two types of farming are not directly comparable, since the Amish concentrate on pigs, the non-Amish on corn. Looking at this sample area, the authors suggest

TABLE 13-1

	Energy ratio	Yield*
Pennsylvania		
Old Order Amish	1.0	3,151
Nebraska Amish	1.5	1,710
non-Amish	0.5	3,071
Illinois		
Amish	0.9	3,165
non-Amish	2.0	11,444
Wisconsin		
Amish	1.6	1,305
non-Amish	0.2	1,668

*The yield figure is in the number of 1,000 kilocalories, abbreviated Mcal. per hectare. A hectare is an area measurement in the metric system. One acre equals 0.405 hectare.
(Adapted from Johnson, Stolzfus, and Craumer, *Science,* 198 (October 28, 1977), p. 376.)

that scarce energy would drastically limit yields from intensive farming, while Pennsylvania-type dairy farming could better adjust to lower energy consumption without paying high penalties. Illinois farming is ideally suited to mechanization, with its large parcels, needs for heavy applications of fertilizers and pesticides, and efficient food processing machinery. Dairy farming, on the other hand, might be able to adjust more readily by using more manual labor.

The southwestern Wisconsin study was done in dairy country similar to Pennsylvania and demonstrates once again that Amish dairy farming is highly efficient. Although Amish yields are slightly lower than those of

FIGURE 13-8
Corn-belt farms, such as this one in Iowa, are highly mechanized and, as a result, use great amounts of energy. As energy costs increase, so must food prices.

their non-Amish neighbors, the energy ratio of 1.6 shows that they are net producers of food energy, whereas the non-Amish are energy consumers. Note also that the Wisconsin yields—for both Amish and non-Amish—are considerably lower than those in Pennsylvania. This can be attributed to poorer soils, and modest herd size. Also, the Wisconsin Amish are almost as conservative as the Nebraska Amish in Pennsylvania, so little machinery is used on their farms.

The authors are cautious in drawing conclusions from their study. Based on the data collected, they are not optimistic about all types of agriculture adjusting to conditions of scarce energy. Certain kinds of farm production will suffer more than others. The penalty paid by intensive crop cultivation might be extremely high in the form of reduced yields, whereas other kinds of agriculture, where human labor can more easily replace mechanization, might be able to adapt without paying penalties. And if workers are displaced from industry as energy becomes scarce and factories close down, perhaps farm employment can profit by absorbing former industrial workers.

Energy analysis has long been a research tool in cultural ecology, for work, done by both mechanical and animal or human means, can be transformed into units of energy. Similarly, household activities, animal fodder, fertilizers, and other agricultural needs like pesticides and fuel can be measured. In fact, most human activities can be examined through energy analysis, just as energy flow through a biological ecosystem—such as a marsh—can be measured. This research method will become increasingly important in an age of scarce resources as we seek the most efficient ways of producing goods and effecting their distribution.

Conclusion

In this chapter, we have seen how the themes of cultural geography are being put to work on world problems. Each case study illustrates how cultural geography synthesizes diverse information about cultural systems, the physical environment, and space.

The five themes of cultural geography used throughout this text also appear in the case studies (Figure 13-9). Melinda Meade, examining the problems of health in plantation populations in Malaysia, used the themes of cultural ecology and landscape; A. K. Chakravarti applied the cultural diffusion theme to his study of the Green Revolution in India; Martyn Bowden's research on the Great Plains illustrated the value of the cultural-historical method in analyzing contemporary resource problems; and lastly, Warren Johnson and his co-authors used an aspect of cultural ecology—energy analysis—to investigate food production penalties of low-energy agriculture.

These case studies give the reader a hint of the different ways that cultural geography is working on world problems. By bringing together various views on uses—and abuses—of world resources, we can better predict future problems and suggest strategies for minimizing the detrimental effects of human activities. The end result, we hope, will be not simply a better understanding of the human mosaic, but also information to assure the survival of the species.

FIGURE 13-9
Humans have taken varied paths to
solve resource problems, and the five
themes of cultural geography offer
tools for the study of this human mosaic.

Suggested Readings

Russell Ackoff. *Redesigning the Future.* New York: Wiley, 1974.

Ronald Alves and Charles Milligan, *Living with Energy: Alternative Sources in Your Home.* New York: Penguin, 1978.

Bradley Askin. *How Energy Affects the Economy.* Lexington, Mass.: Heath, 1978.

Martyn Bowden. "Desertification of the Great Plains: Will it Happen?" *Economic Geography,* 53 (1977), 397– 406.

Lester Brown. *The Twenty-ninth Day: Accommodating Human Needs and Numbers to the Earth.* New York: Norton, 1974.

Reid Bryson and Thomas Murray. *Climates of Hunger: Mankind and tbe World's Changing Weather.* Madison: University of Wisconsin Press, 1977.

A. K. Chakravarti. "Green Revolution in India," *Annals, Association of American Geographers, 63 (1973), 319–330.*

Earl Cook. *Man, Energy, Society.* San Francisco: Freeman, 1976.

Pierre Crosson and Kenneth Frederick. *The World Food Situation.* Washington, D.C.: Resources for the Future, 1977.

James Echols. "Population vs. Environment: A Crisis of Too Many People," *American Scientist,* (1977) 165–173.

Warren Johnson, Victor Stolzfus, and Peter Craumer. "Energy Conservation in Amish Agriculture," *Science,* 198 (October 28, 1977), 373–378.

Eliot Marshall. "Energy Forecasts: Sinking to New Lows," *Science,* (1980) 1353–1356.

Melinda Meade. "Land Development and Human Health in West Malaysia," *Annals, Association of American Geographers,* 66 (1976), 428–439.

G. Tyler Miller, Jr. *Living in the Environment.* 2nd ed. Belmont, Cal.: Wadsworth, 1979.

Stephen Schneider. *The Genesis Strategy: Climate and Global Survival.* New York: Plenum, 1976.

Index